ABOUT FACE:

The China Decision
and Its Consequences

ABOUT FACE:

The China Decision and Its Consequences

edited by

John Tierney, Jr.

$\boxed{A}$RLINGTON HOUSE·PUBLISHERS
NEW ROCHELLE, NEW YORK

Library of Congress Cataloging in Publication Data

About face: the China decision and its consequences.

    1. United States—Foreign relations—Taiwan—Addresses, essays, lectures. 2. Taiwan—Foreign relations—United States—Addresses, essays, lectures. 3. United States—Foreign relations—China—Addresses, essays, lectures. 4. China—Foreign relations—United States—Addresses, essays, lectures. I. Tierney, John Joseph, 1940-
E183.8.T3A26   327.73′051′249   79-4545
ISBN 0-87000-438-7

Contents

327.73051
T444a

To
the memory of
Dr. James E. Dornan, Jr.
colleague and friend

Foreword

John J. Tierney, Jr.

This book is being published in direct response to the decision by President Carter, on December 15, 1978, to unilaterally terminate America's historic commitment to the Republic of China. This alliance, which spanned more than two decades and was honored by both Republican and Democratic administrations, came to a rude and abrupt end by the President's announcement. His decision has sent shock waves throughout the American body politic. The collection of articles assembled in this volume represents a sampling of the U.S. opinion on the value of our association with Taiwan. The intent of this book is *not* to argue against U.S. relations with the Peking regime, but, rather, to challenge the wisdom and tactics of ending our historic and valuable relationship with the Republic, and to question the price that we as a country have been made to pay for Mr. Carter's action.

Herein are contained a series of statements, of varying length and range of interest, on the President's decision. Some of the articles have been written since his action, others have been published elsewhere in various books and journals of opinion. Together, they represent an assembled collection of expert viewpoints on the importance of Taiwan in U.S. foreign policy and human rights and on the necessity for America to uphold a firm and definitive geopolitical position in the western Pacific.

We have been fortunate to obtain Introductions by four distinguished U.S. Senators and closing statements by several Congressmen from both parties. Opinions on the President's decision go beyond political loyalties. The remainder of the book is divided into sections dealing with the issue of human rights and the nature of the two Chinese societies, the normalization process and background issues to the decision and, finally, articles analyzing the President's move and reactions thereto.

A concerted effort has been made to draw from a host of political and academic experts whose credentials span years of expertise on the Chinese question. It is hoped that this book will be of value to the general reader as well as to the professional, and that it may play some role in reminding Americans of the historic and political magnitude of Mr. Carter's action as well as serving as a guide to the various implications of ending relations with Taiwan.

The editor is indebted to the many authors and editors of this book who have graciously consented to permit publication of their material: Dr. James E. Dornan, Jr., Chairman of the Politics Department of Catholic University was instrumental in the formation and presentation of the idea. In particular, the editor would also like to thank Mr. Edwin J. Feulner Jr., President of The Heritage Foundation in Washington, D.C. and Mr. Robert L. Schuettinger, Editor of Policy Review, for their cooperation and encouragement in its preparation. Without the assistance of these individials and their respective institutions such a publication would have been impossible. A special note of appreciation goes to Dr. Richard Bishivjian, Senior Editor of Arlington House Publishers for his unstinting patience and support throughout, and to Miss Beatrice Puglisi who typed portions of the manuscript and served as an "associate editor" during the book's final preparation.

Part I
Introduction

The Abandonment of Taiwan

Senator Robert Dole (R-Kansas)

Much effort has been made by the Carter administration in the past few weeks to downplay the suddenness with which our agreement to normalize relations with mainland China evolved. The administration has consistently tried to link Carter's abrupt decision with the Nixon and Ford initiatives, highlighted by the Shanghai Communiqué, as part of an inevitable evolution leading to the Friday night bombshell. But the fact that there were no lengthy or well-handled negotiations with Peking is borne out by this point: the United States did not gain a single advantage in the exchange.

Presidents Nixon and Ford could have made this same agreement long ago in the negotiating process, but they were not willing to cave in to the Communist bargaining demands. The chief obstacle was always the status of our long-time ally and friend, the Republic of China on Taiwan. But Mr. Carter found it expedient to abandon Taiwan without a warning to its government or consultation with our own.

The resultant public criticism of the president's action makes it easy to misunderstand the position of those who oppose the abrogation of military and political ties with Taiwan in order to gain this recognition with Peking. There are tremendous potential benefits for the American people in a closer relationship with the one billion Chinese on the continent. As a representative of a midwestern state with large farming interests, I am keenly aware of the economic advantages increased trade might bring, as well as the cultural and strategic benefits that would accrue to the United States. It is already apparent that the administration plans to use these potential "carrots" to beat down the opposition and confuse the real issue. This issue is not the diplomatic recognition of Peking. It is the manner in which the negotiations were consummated and the price that was demanded in payment.

The United States cannot afford to abandon good allies and friends for short-term political expediency. The international perception of our own country as an honorable, reliable nation, willing to abide by its agreements and to stand firm for its principles, is bound to suffer. This is especially true with the perceived reduction in strength of the United States vis-á-vis the Soviet Union, and the withdrawal of U.S. forces from Vietnam, the Philippines, Korea, and the Panama Canal.

Jimmy Carter had pledged to conduct important foreign policy negotiations openly, "with the participation of Congress from the outset." While it is true that sometimes the delicate nature of negotiating prohibits immediate public disclosure, in this case the president has made only token efforts to consult with Congress, even after the passage of the Dole-Stone Amendment by a vote of 94-0 in the Senate. This amendment specifically expressed the sense of the Senate, and later the sense of the Congress, that any new relationship with Peking and Taiwan should be first discussed with Congress, precisely because so many members of Congress were deeply concerned about the safety of Taiwan and our economic and strategic interests in Asia.

During the Carter-Ford debates, Mr. Carter said he "would never let that friendship [with Peking] stand in the way of preservation of the independence and freedom of the people of Taiwan." Yet the president received absolutely no commitment from Peking in this latest agreement that the safety of Taiwan would be assured. In fact, Mr. Carter agreed with the mainland position that Taiwan was a part of China and that its future would therefore become an internal matter for the Chinese to decide themselves. Naturally, the president would not be so foolish as to enter into this agreement if he believed an invasion of the island republic was imminent. For the moment it better suits the purpose of the current ruling elite in Peking to let matters stand as they are.

Over the next five years, China, by its enhanced world prestige and position after U.S. recognition, can further isolate Taiwan. With the inevitably reduced flow of modern weapons to Taipei, and the concomitantly increased gains in technology on the mainland, China will then be able to virtually dictate terms to the island they outnumber 45 to 1.

To take one small example: when Red China entered the worldwide satellite communications system, they demanded that all matters regarding Taiwan be cleared by Peking. This would have meant that the Republic of China would be barred from modern, international communications and would have seriously hampered the island's business economy. Only strong U.S. action prevented this from becoming true. We can expect this same ploy to occur over and over again in every conceivable international organization or group. Yet when the United States no longer officially recognizes Taiwan, can we expect to be able to prevent it? The future of Taiwan looks bleak indeed.

In the meantime, Peking has adroitly played its "U.S. card" in its dealings with the Soviet Union, and delayed indefinitely the previously certain SALT II rapprochement between Carter and Brezhnev. Only the Red Chinese have received any benefits in this latest example of Carter diplomacy. They had much to gain and lost nothing. Why shouldn't they agree to our recognition.

As it stands now, not only did we not receive any concessions from Peking, we did not even make sure the United States would be in a position

16

to take advantage of the potential benefits of normalization. Under the proper circumstances I am very much in favor of normalizing our relationship with the People's Republic of China. The possible cultural and trade benefits are enormous, but we must first make certain the Communists are going to deal on equal terms with us. Other nations that have established relations with Peking have learned that trade with China is usually a one-way street. The Chinese have far to come to reach Western standards of living, and analysts say they are two generations away from being able to buy consumer goods in any significant quantities.

Nevertheless, I believe opportunities for economic exchange are possible. I would first like to see Peking agree to accept credits from foreign trading partners. I would like to see that American buying and selling offices are allowed to open on the continent. I would like to make certain that U.S. financial institutions have the chance to handle trade transactions between our two countries. There are many details such as these that must be carefully worked out.

China should carry some of the responsibilities of expanded world participation if it is to stand in the forefront of the world political scene. It is my intention to require China to join with other nuclear nations in banning atmospheric tests, which are frequently made in China, to the peril of the health of the citizens throughout the world. Expanded travel and communication with the Chinese people should broaden their knowledge of Western culture. This open-door policy may lead to some alleviation of China's extremely repressive human rights activities. In the area of financial responsibility, the Carter administration has failed to get a commitment from Peking to settle more than two hundred million dollars in U.S. claims against the Chinese Communist government. This point must be resolved.

The most significant failure of our negotiating team, however, was in not ensuring that our strategic interests in the Pacific and the future of the people of Taiwan will continue to be secure. It will be the job for us, during the 96th Congress, to rectify these mistakes and omissions in order to ensure our strategic interests, while at the same time realizing the full potential of closer relations with a billion Chinese.

In the final analysis, President Carter's decision to unilaterally abrogate our 25-year-old Mutual Defense Treaty with Taiwan may have more significance for the fate of Taiwan, the security of the North Pacific region, and the strategic interests of the United States than the simple act of normalizing diplomatic relations with Peking. I have urged the president not to follow through with his announced intention to sever our security accord with Taiwan, effective January 1, 1980. That could be the one saving grace of this entire episode.

Diplomatic "normalization" itself erupts unexpectedly as an impulsive move by this administration, perhaps to distract attention from its recent policy shortcomings in the Middle East and South Africa. Certainly there is every reason to suspect that Peking's latest mood of "sweetness and light"

17

may be only another in the long series of political quirks that have come to characterize the unstable domestic situation on the mainland. Undercurrents of instability still pervade the scene in the People's Republic, and the next group of communist leaders might find it equally expedient to slam the door in our face.

There can be no particular pride attached to our resolution of this long-standing China question. Clearly, the Carter administration caved in to the Communist Chinese insistence on three pre-conditions in return for normalization: the president agreed to break off political relations with Taiwan; the president agreed to sever our security agreement with the Republic of China; the president agreed to pull the remaining U.S. defense forces out of Taiwan—all in perfect accord with the mainland government's demands.

And we, in turn, received no *quid pro quo* for our concessions. We received no public guarantee against communist attacks on Taiwan either now or in the future. We received no commitment to resolve the outstanding U.S. financial claims against the Chinese Communist government—some two hundred million dollars. We received no assurances that the People's Republic of China is ready to join with other nations in banning atmospheric tests of nuclear weapons—a Chinese activity which still imperils the health and safety of citizens throughout the world. And, perhaps most ironic, President Carter received no assurance that Peking will alter its repressive human rights conditions—among the most restrictive in the world—which harbor no responsible system of justice and which levy heavy penalties for unorthodox words and deeds.

In view of the irreversible series of events which has been set in motion, there is one thing we, as public representatives in Congress, must now insist upon: no cancellation of our nation's formal commitment to Taiwan's future security. Public opinion on this point is absolutely clear—surveys show far more than fifty percent of the American people oppose severing our military ties with Taiwan regardless of our diplomatic policy on the China question. Mr. Carter himself, during the 1976 presidential campaign, pledged: "We are bound by a treaty to guarantee the freedom of Formosa, Taiwan, the Republic of China. . . . I wouldn't go back on a commitment that we have had to assure that Taiwan is protected from military takeover." What became of that commitment?

The essential security interests of the U.S., as well as those of Japan, the Philippines, and South Korea, are inherently tied to the future of the Taiwan defense treaty. Termination of this accord, together with the withdrawal of U.S. troops from South Korea and the phase-out of U.S. bases in the Philippines, will demonstrate continued erosion of American strength in the region. It will yank one important leg out of the "security triad" we maintain through mutual defense treaties with Japan, South Korea, and Taiwan. Our allies will inevitably reassess their traditional reliance on our commitments and look toward new measures to guarantee their security. There is no doubt that tension will increase, and aggression and instability will be encouraged, once our defense ties to Taiwan are unilaterally broken.

In the end, the American people are left with the impression that we have "shot down" another friend, another faithful ally, and that perhaps this administration will continue to find it easiest to press its foreign policy demands on those, like Israel and the Republic of China, who are most dependent on our continued friendship and support.

In Defense of Taiwan

Senator Jake Garn (R-Utah)

President Carter's decision to extend diplomatic recognition to mainland China, and to abrogate the United States' Mutual Defense Treaty with Taiwan, is constitutionally and morally objectionable. The Republic of China, a staunch and faithful ally, has been treated in a shabby manner—one that flies in the face of this administration's professed commitment to human rights. The abrogation of a defense treaty with a loyal ally is unprecedented in our history, and an ignominious act undeserving of a great nation.

The 1954 Mutual Defense Treaty between the United States and the Republic of China has played a key role in ensuring the security of the Taiwanese people from communist aggression. During the past thirty years, Taiwan has emerged as a productive and prosperous country with close economic ties to the United States. American investment in Taiwan continues to grow, and Taiwan is the twelfth largest trading partner of the U.S.

On the other hand, the People's Republic of China is a totalitarian society with which the United States shares few, if any, cultural, economic, political, or security ties. Under the leadership of Mao Tse-tung, millions of Chinese were put to death while millions more were enslaved. And a recent editorial in the *New Republic* correctly points out that "despite the much-heralded thaw in the latest version of the new China, a tyranny is exactly what China still is and is likely to remain."

A great deal of speculation and debate has surrounded the issue of normalization of relations with mainland China, particularly since President Nixon's visit to Peking in 1972. Until now, however, efforts to improve U.S.-Chinese relations have always faltered over the question of Taiwan. Peking established three pre-conditions for establishment of diplomatic relations with the United States: (1) recognition of the People's Republic as the sole legal government of China; (2) withdrawal of United States' military forces from Taiwan; (3) Termination of the mutual defense treaty.

Since Mao's death, however, China has undergone serious political turmoil, and the new leaders have attempted to step up their contacts with the outside world. Normalization of relations with the United States became a key objective for which Peking seemed willing to make significant concessions. In August 1978 the People's Republic revealed a shift in its attitude toward Taiwan when both countries were represented at an international

20

conference for the first time in three decades. This was a major conciliatory move by Peking which carried with it the implicit acceptance of Taiwan's independent existence, and which further dampens any enthusiasm one might have for the so-called concessions this administration claims to have gained in return for its betrayal of Taipei.

The leaders in Peking are anxious about the increasing military prowess of the Soviet Union, and are deeply interested in the industrial development of their country. They desire to gain greater access to technology and investment capital available from the West. But are we to believe that these concerns and objectives will not be present in the future—with or without full diplomatic relations with the United States? Certainly not. The simple fact of the matter is that Peking has a great deal to gain from relations with the United States, and is well aware of this.

From the perspective of our national interest, there was simply no reason to act in haste as we did. The situation did not warrant such precipitate action. Our interests were not threatened by a preservation of the status quo. In fact, the status quo was at least as conducive to world and regional peace and stability as the present situation we have now created. In the end, we accepted all three of the Chinese pre-conditions and received nothing in return but assurances that "as for the way of bringing Taiwan back to the *embrace* of the motherland and reunifying the country, it is entirely China's internal affair" (emphasis added).

I am afraid that this administration's infatuation with playing the "China card" may backfire. We are sadly mistaken if we think that mainland China can provide a military counterweight to the Soviet Union. In addition, the Soviets may be tempted to stir up trouble in Korea or the western province of Sinkiang, for example, in order to demonstrate just how fragile these new-found fraternal feelings between the Communist Chinese and the Americans really are. A strong and vigorous United States defense posture, not a hollow and propped-up China, is the best means to counter any aggressive moves by the Soviet Union in Asia or elsewhere.

It is in my opinion a mistake to think that mainland China will somehow constitute a trade bonanza for American business. China never has been, nor is it likely to be, a significant trading partner of the United States. Its economy is still vastly underdeveloped and it lacks the foreign reserves necessary to conduct trade. As for the question of oil, the extent of China's oil reserves is still a subject of debate, and are we to mortgage the credibility of our word as a nation for one more barrel of oil?

President Carter claims that his decision to establish relations with mainland China is a simple recognition of political and international reality. I disagree. I have received hundreds of letters from individuals in Taiwan who raise the question, "Are not the seventeen million people of Taiwan a reality?" The only policy compatible with political reality is a two-China policy, not the creation of a myth that the leaders in Peking are the legitimate rulers of Taiwan. Moreover, it is a serious misconception to view the conflict between Peking and Taipei as merely a domestic, internal problem. As one individual wrote in the *New York Times,* "It is a struggle between the Chinese on Taiwan who wish to remain free and independent and the Communists who wish to dominate a free people under the cloud of communism."

Time and time again public opinion polls have shown that the American people support the goal of normalized relations with mainland China, but *not* at the price of abandoning Taiwan and ending our Mutual Defense Treaty. I think that the good sense of the American people is clearly reflected in these polls, and has helped shape congressional attitudes toward this contentious issue.

In early 1978, the Senate passed the Dole-Stone resolution, requiring the president to consult with Congress before any action is taken regarding the recognition of the People's Republic of China. A telephone call one hour prior to his announcement on national television informing us of his decision is not what I consider adequate consultation.

While the Constitution gives the president the power to extend formal recognition to foreign governments, it also clearly states that ratification of any treaty requires the advice and consent of the Senate. In 1954, the Taiwan treaty was ratified through this procedure. It is my firm conviction that the same process must be followed to end a treaty. After all, a treaty is a law, and the president cannot repeal a law by himself. To do so would violate the Constitution. Article X does allow for termination of the treaty one year following notification by either party involved. However, the president alone cannot qualify as a party.

In addition, this provision for termination is included in the NATO treaty, the nuclear non-proliferation treaty, and the test ban treaty, as well as virtually every treaty the United States has with a foreign government. Yet, no one is claiming that the president has the constitutional authority to end these treaties without congressional approval.

Regardless of this legal question, I believe that the president's action was morally unconscionable given our country's long-standing commitment to the security of the people of Taiwan. The fate of these people is now uncertain. Peking still insists that the future of Taiwan is an internal question, and we have only recently been informed that the United States commitment to sell arms to Taiwan is less than conclusive. It seems the administration inadvertently failed to state explicitly that we will impose a moratorium on new arms sales for a full year, beginning January 1, 1979. Can we now fault Israel for its caution in accepting America's assurances regarding its security?

In the final analysis, one must agree with John B. Oakes who recently wrote in the *New York Times* that "President Carter has seriously undermined America's pretensions to be the moral leader of the world and an exemplar of constancy and faithfulness to our friends." The abrogation of our Mutual Defense Treaty with Taiwan is not an act of diplomacy—it is rather a shameful act of weakness and capitulation.

22

The Betrayal of Taiwan by President Carter

Senator Barry Goldwater (R-Arizona)

On the evening of December 15, President Carter delivered a short speech to the nation which history may well record as ten minutes that lived in infamy.

In that address, the President—without prior consultation with the Congress—recognized a communist regime on the mainland of China which has one of the worst records on human rights in the history of the world. In that address, the president downgraded, humiliated, and victimized the Republic of China on Taiwan, one of this nation's most faithful and valuable allies.

In that address the president called into question this nation's treaty credibility throughout the world.

And in that address, President Carter committed the United States of America to what may be the costliest building project in the history of the world. Chinese officials are already talking in terms of *several tens of billions* of U.S. dollars in foreign credit for modernization of the mainland.

Much of this financing would come from, or be backed by, U.S. government institutions. That is you, the American taxpayer, who would pay for it or whose assets would be at risk in case of a communist default in payment.

And what did we receive in return for these outrageous concessions? Nothing. We did not gain a single thing that we did not already have before the sell-out of Taiwan.

President Carter's supporters make a great point of stating that the Red Chinese—and mark this well—*allowed* the United States to assert, without formal challenge, an interest in the peaceful resolution of the Taiwan issue.

Now let me ask you, is that not a great concession—that we be *allowed* to state that we do not want to see a faithful ally clobbered by the military might of a new diplomatic partner? If I were a Taiwanese I would take absolutely no solace from such a so-called concession.

It took a few days, but on December 19 we got the full answer from State Department officials, who acknowledged that China gave the United States *no* explicit assurances, open *or* secret, about Taiwan's security when the Carter administration agreed to normalize relations with Peking.

Aside from its immediate effect upon a friend and ally which has never opposed American interests in any way, the treatment of Taiwan calls into question the honor—the very soul—of America's word in the field of foreign relations. Over the years, our word has been our bond in dealing with the family of nations.

For years, we made much of how worthless were treaties and agreements entered into by the Soviet Union. We told the world that our commitments were matters of honor, while commitments made by the Soviets were matters of expediency. Now, in this crucial era, we have come down on the side of expediency and thrown honor to the wind.

I don't believe I have to stress the importance of this question. Put yourself in the place of the Israelis, or South Koreans, or our partners in NATO, and ask yourself whether American commitments can be trusted— whether our promises to come to the defense of freedom throughout the world can any longer be held with any assurance and credibility.

President Carter, in making his announcement, described his action as a confirmation of simple reality. I say it is a confirmation of expediency over honor—a confirmation of the doctrine of might and size make right.

I submit that there is nothing either simple or realistic in what the president has done in the name of peace. In the joint communiqué which he signed, the president said: "The government of the United States of America acknowledges the Chinese position that there is but one China and Taiwan is part of China."

In other words, he is saying that Taiwan has no right to exist in a two-China world. He is saying Taiwan is merely a rebel province of the mainland.

One wonders whether if, on some future date, he will tell us that West Germany has no right to exist outside of Communist Germany, or whether South Korea has no right to exist outside of Communist Korea. The idea that there can be no such concept as two Chinas flies in the face of realities, such as exist in Germany and Korea.

I say this agreement was a contrivance to curry favor with totalitarian regime whose only interest is to *use* the United States. Let me point out what the true reality is.

The truth is that the communist dictators on the mainland depart in every way from the principles of human rights for which Americans have fought throughout history. The Chinese Communists are known to have executed several millions of landowners during the so-called "agrarian reform" of 1949 to 1952. They are known to have conducted mass public spectacles, which they called trials, at which more than two million political prisoners were executed.

The Chinese Communists have, by all knowledgeable accounts, exterminated a minimum of fifty million people during their first quarter century of rule. Even today, the Red Chinese arbitrarily imprison over thirty million innocent people in what they call labor reform camps, where they are subjected to the harshest of hard labor.

Moreover, there is no independent judiciary in Red China. There is no freedom of travel. There are no free elections, no freedom of the press, no free expression, no free trade unions.

Freedom of religious worship has also been brutally suppressed by the Chinese Communists. Millions of religious believers have been imprisoned, beaten, and murdered. Churches have been destroyed or converted into warehouses and stables. For the first time in centuries, there is no open practice of any religion in the most populated area of the globe.

This is the reality of the situation and it is not pretty to look at. We are rewarding a lawless system of government which has suppressed the most basic rights of its population. It is not such a simple concept as the president would like us to believe.

Also important was the manner and timing of the president's announcement. It came as a complete surprise not only to our friends on Taiwan, but also to the Congress of the United States which had specifically asked, through a public law, to be consulted before the president took any step to break the defense treaty with Taiwan.

It came at a convenient time for the administration's image-makers who were struggling with the problem created by having President Carter's highly vulnerable Camp David breakthrough in the Middle East fall apart for all the world to see. It came at a convenient time for administration officials who were worried that a Congress in session would make a great deal of noise in opposition to a move which traded American honor for something defined as simple reality.

If the American people had been allowed to speak through the voice of their elected representatives in the Congress, I know a wave of outrage would have swept the country. But President Carter acted when Congress was not in session. He did not listen to the voice of the American people as he promised during his presidential campaign.

Moreover, I believe the president has abused the Constitution. He has usurped powers that belong to the Congress and to the people.

It is clear that the Constitution prevents any president from unilaterally terminating a treaty without legislative authority.

There is no such thing as absolute power in any department of the government. The checks and balances doctrine, which is known to every American school child, bars unilateral action of the kind the president has taken.

The Constitution says a treaty is part of the supreme law of the land. Since the president alone cannot repeal a law, he cannot repeal a treaty. He must first ask Congress, or at least the Senate, which was a partner with him in ratifying the treaty, for approval to cancel it.

Together with several of my colleagues in Congress, I am challenging the president's attempt to cancel the defense treaty in the courts. We will pursue the case all the way to the Supreme Court, if necessary.

The Future Credibility
of the United States

Senator Richard Stone (D-Florida)

The Carter administration's decision to reopen full diplomatic relations with the People's Republic of China (PRC) and terminate formal relations with the Republic of China (ROC) on Taiwan raises questions about the credibility of the U.S. as an ally and our future relationship with Taiwan as a commercial and military partner.

The Republic of China has long been an important military ally of the U.S. and has assured us a reliable military base in the Far East.

As a condition of recognizing the PRC, the president announced the termination of the Mutual Defense Treaty signed by the U.S. and Taiwan in 1954. As a result, we gave up a strategic military location and left the Republic of China, a long-time friend and ally, with no assurance of protection. Although the administration has stated that there will be continuing U.S. arms sales to the Republic of China, no details have been released.

Conspicuously missing from the joint communiqué issued by the U.S. and Peking governments is a pledge by the PRC not to use force against Taiwan. Statements by PRC officials reported since then have specifically reserved the military option. President Carter has stated that the PRC knows of our firm expectations that the differences between China and Taiwan be settled peacefully. One must question, however, whether this unilateral declaration of our expectations represents an adequate security guarantee to Taiwan.

I visited both the Republic of China on Taiwan and the People's Republic of China in 1978 as a member of the Senate Foreign Relations Committee. When I returned from the PRC my clear impression was that there was no sense of urgency on their part to "normalize" relations. There were already working level contacts—business and government—that boded well for possible future rapprochement between the PRC and the United States.

In terms of our own government, the U.S. may have sacrificed a reliable ally and military base in the Far East on the assumption that the pragmatic policies of Teng Hsiao-ping will remain the cornerstone of China's emerging foreign policy. What the U.S. has left unresolved is what will happen if Teng's policy is changed or the leadership of the PRC is changed.

More importantly, we must ask what the impact of our treatment of the Republic of China will be on our other allies, especially those in Asia. What nation will stay our ally if we are so willing to desert our allies? Our will power, our firmness in support of our own stated alliances and goals, and our trustworthiness are called into question.

We must now consider what action can be taken to strengthen our commitments and to improve our credibility as an ally. There may be enough support in Congress to accomplish this. Hopefully, with executive branch cooperation, we can repair the damage to the ROC on Taiwan and look for constructive ways to rebuild our relationship. The U.S. has many commercial and cultural agreements with the Republic of China in addition to the mutual defense treaty of 1954, and they must be reviewed by Congress. Congress also can insure that Taiwan is able to adequately defend its independence.

In the opening days of Congress, I submitted a bill that would extend full diplomatic privileges and immunities to all representatives of the Republic of China in the United States. In view of the ROC's long relationship with our nation, it is only fair that at least the same rules which applied to the liaison office for the PRC before diplomatic recognition now apply to the Republic of China. The authorized representatives of that government working in the U.S. were entitled to full diplomatic privileges and immunities.

In another effort to strengthen our commitment to the ROC, I have co-sponsored a resolution, submitted by Sen. John C. Danforth (R.—Mo.), expressing the sense of the Senate that in the event of military aggression by the PRC against the ROC, the U.S. will terminate diplomatic and commercial relationships with the PRC, provide military assistance to the ROC on an urgent basis, bring the matter to the attention of the U.N. Security Council, and take other actions necessary to bring the aggression to an end and secure a peaceful future for the people of Taiwan.

Even now, there are appropriate means for the U.S. to reassure the independence, well-being, and security of the Republic of China, even though recognizing the People's Republic of China.

Part II
The Two Societies

Allies, Human Rights, and Diplomacy: An Overview*

*Ernest W. Lefever***

Human rights are what politics is all about. Fifteen centuries ago Saint Augustine said that were it not for government, men would devour one another as fishes. He was, of course, referring to good government, but governments often become corrupt, cruel, or tyrannical. When this happens, they are the most monstrous fish of all. Depending on its character, government can be the most effective protector of human rights or the most vicious violator of them. Hence, the struggle for viable and humane government is the heart of politics.

It is important to distinguish between two frequently confused concepts of human rights.[1] One has more immediate universal application because it is rooted in the religion and ethics of virtually all cultures and calls for sanctions against political authorities and others guilty of genocide, brutalizing innocent people, and similar atrocities. The second and more precise concept of human rights is the fruit of the recent Western democratic experience and embraces a variety of substantive and procedural rights and safeguards that are enforced in perhaps fewer than a score of states. These rights include freedom of speech, assembly, press, and religion; equality before the law; periodic elections; the concept of being innocent until proved guilty; a judicial system independent from executive authority; and a range of safeguards for accused persons. Many of these Western democratic rights are unknown and unattainable in large parts of the world where both history and culture preclude the development of full-fledged democratic institutions. Nevertheless, there are significant differences in the extent to which human rights, more generally defined, are honored in undemocratic states. And some of these states have introduced a few of the specific Western safeguards.

The never-ending battle to maintain and enlarge the areas of proximate

*Copyright 1978, The Heritage Foundation. Reprinted by permission.
**Ernest W. Lefever is the Director of the Ethics and Public Policy Center of Georgetown University.

liberty and justice must be fought against external and internal forces which seek to impose authority without freedom, often by brutal means. Human rights as we know them in the United States and other democratic countries can be eroded or even obliterated from within by acquiescing to willful men who seek to capture the reins of power for their own narrow ends or from without by totalitarian regimes determined to extend their dominion.

Our Founding Fathers wrestled with the problem of creating a free and independent country ruled by a government with sufficient authority to overcome domestic and alien threats and with sufficient openness to respond to the will of the people. Their formula was the judicious balance between authority and freedom embraced in the Declaration of Independence and elaborated in the Constitution. The former asserted that "governments are instituted among men, deriving their just powers from the consent of the governed" to secure certain fundamental rights, among them "life, liberty, and the pursuit of happiness." The Constitution was promulgated to "establish justice, insure domestic tranquility, provide for the common defense, promote the general welfare, and secure the blessings of liberty."

This audacious experiment prospered in an inauspicious world. In the face of new challenges, the American system provided for increasingly broader political participation and other specific rights spelled out or implied in the Constitution and its amendments. Our history is not without blemish, but compared to other political communities past and present, the American record is a beacon of freedom and justice in a world bedeviled by chaos, authoritarian rule, and messianic tyranny.

I

THE CURRENT HUMAN RIGHTS CAMPAIGN

The current wave of concern for human rights around the world was foreshadowed by several developments, notably Woodrow Wilson's crusade for "self-determination" and the Universal Declaration of Human Rights adopted by the United Nations in 1948. The U.S. campaign to make the advancement of human rights abroad an objective of foreign policy is more recent, but it did not start with President Jimmy Carter. He simply built on the lively interest developed in Congress during the past several years which has been expressed largely in foreign aid legislation designed to prohibit or restrict economic or military assistance to any government "which engages in a consistent pattern of gross violations of internationally recognized human rights, including torture or cruel, inhumane, or degrading treatment or punishment, prolonged detention without charges, or other flagrant denial of the right to life, liberty, and the security of person" (Foreign Assistance Act, Section 502B, adopted in 1974). Most of the congressional human rights activists have limited their advocacy of punitive measures to Chile, South Korea, and Iran. In practice, the restrictions have had little effect on limiting aid, loans, or military sales, even to these countries.

Human rights was a natural cause for President Carter. As a born-again Baptist and a latter-day Wilsonian, he repeatedly stated his intention to restore integrity and compassion to American domestic and foreign policy. In his address at Notre Dame University on March 22, 1977, Mr. Carter looked back to the immediate past and deplored our "intellectual and moral poverty," illustrated by our Vietnam policy, and our "inordinate fear of communism which once led us to embrace any dictator who joined us in that fear." He called for a "new" American foreign policy, "based on constant decency in its values and an optimism in its historical vision." The most conspicuous manifestation of his new policy is the effort to promote human rights in other countries by means of U.S. statecraft, including private diplomacy, public preaching, and measures to deny or threaten to deny economics, military, or nuclear assistance. Mr. Carter's campaign has been given bureaucratic visibility by establishing a new post, Assistant Secretary of State for Human Rights and Humanitarian Affairs, currently filled by Patricia Derian, who sometimes discusses her assignment in moralistic rhetoric alien to traditional diplomatic discourse.

The human rights campaign has received mixed reviews at home and abroad. Last July in a *New Yorker* article friendly to the effort, Elizabeth Drew reported that Mr. Carter's people "are pleased, and some even a bit awestruck, at the impact that the human rights campaign has had thus far. 'I think,' says one, 'that the mulish world has noticed the two-by-four.' "

There is no doubt that the threatening plank has been noticed, and probably in isolated cases it has accomplished some good. But it should be recorded that some unmulish elements in the world, including friendly and allied governments, have also seen the two-by-four and are not convinced that its whack, however well-intended, has always been redemptive. There is no doubt that it has harmed relations with some allies and has both irritated and comforted adversaries.

It is by no means clear that the campaign has resulted in any significant relaxation of Soviet restrictions against emigration or political dissent. There is evidence that the opposite may be the case. On December 30, 1977, a *New York Times* front page story reported: "The small Soviet human rights movement . . . is at its lowest point in years after a campaign of arrests, threats, and forced exile."

It is clear, however, that a score of allies have been unhappy with a policy they regard as arrogant and unfairly applied. Brazil, Argentina, Uruguay, and Guatemala have been alienated to the point where they have refused military assistance from Washington. And Brazil has served notice that it wishes to withdraw from its security assistance agreement of twenty-five years' standing. This alienation of allies gives aid and comfort to Moscow which more than offsets the minor embarrassment it suffers from Mr. Carter's conspicuous "intervention" on behalf of Soviet dissidents.

SIX FLAWS IN THE HUMAN RIGHTS POLICY

⸤ Far more serious, however, the Carter campaign has confused our foreign policy goals and trivialized the concept of human rights. It both reflects and reinforces serious conceptual flaws in the world-view of its most articulate spokesmen. These flaws, if permitted to instruct foreign policy, or even influence it unduly, could have catastrophic consequences for the security of the United States and the cause of freedom in the world. Six interrelated flaws deserve brief mention:

1. Underestimating the Totalitarian Threat

Human dignity and freedom are under siege around the world. It has been ever so. The islands of community protected by humane law have been contracting ever since post-war decolonization began. The citizens of most of the newly independent states in Asia and Africa now experience less freedom and fewer guaranteed rights than they did under Western colonial rule.

But the greatest threat to human rights comes from messianic totalitarian regimes whose brutal grip brooks no opposition. Their self-anointed and self-perpetuating elites have become the arbiters of orthodoxy in every sphere—politics, economics, education, the arts, and family life. The ruling party even usurps the place of God. In totalitarian states like the USSR, Cuba, Cambodia, and Vietnam, there are no countervailing forces to challenge the power, will, or policies of the entrenched elite.

In spite of notable exceptions, the general political situation in the third world is characterized by chaos and authoritarian regimes. Democratic and anti-democratic ideas and institutions are competing for acceptance. In this struggle, we should not underestimate the attraction of the totalitarian temptation to leaders who are grappling with the perplexing problems of moving traditional societies into modern welfare states.

The human rights activists tend to underestimate the totalitarian threat to the West and the totalitarian temptation in the third world. Hence, they neglect or trivialize the fundamental political and moral struggle of our time—the protracted conflict between forces of total government based on coercion and the proponents of limited government based on popular consent of humane law. In their preoccupation with the minor abridgment of certain rights in authoritarian states, they often overlook the massive threat to the liberty of millions. They attack the limitation of civil rights in South Korea and at the same time call for the United States to withdraw its ground forces, an act that may invite aggression from North Korea. It would be a great irony if Washington in the name of human rights were to adopt a policy that would deliver thirty-five million largely free South Koreans into virtual slavery.

2. Confusing Totalitarianism with Authoritarianism

In terms of political rights, moral freedom, and cultural vitality, there is a profound difference between authoritarian and totalitarian regimes. Most Asian, African, and Latin American countries are ruled by small elites supported by varying degrees of popular consent. Some are run by brutal tyrants like General Idi Amin of Uganda, others by one-party cliques, military juntas, or civilian-military committees. Almost all authoritarian regimes permit a significantly greater degree of freedom and diversity than the totalitarian ones in all spheres—political, cultural, economic, and religious. Authoritarian rulers often allow opposition parties to operate and a restrained press to publish. Foreign correspondents usually can move about freely and send out uncensored dispatches. These rulers often permit and sometimes encourage relatively free economic activity and freedom of movement for their citizens. The quality of life possible under such rule, of course, depends not only on the character of central control, but on the cultural and economic level of the population as well.

There is, for example, far more freedom of choice, diversity of opinion and activity, and respect for human rights in authoritarian South Korea than in totalitarian North Korea. There is also far more freedom and cultural vitality in Chile—even under its present state of siege—than in Cuba. There have been political prisoners in Chile and there may be a handful now, but there are an estimated 15,000 to 60,000 political detainees in Cuba. These facts are noted, not to priase Chile or condemn Cuba, but to emphasize the consequential difference of human rights in the two kinds of regimes.

Another crucial difference is the capacity of authoritarian rule to evolve into democratic rule. This has happened recently in Spain, Portugal, Greece, and India. In sharp contrast, a communist dictatorship has never made a peaceful transition to more representative and responsive rule.

3. Overestimating America's Influence Abroad

If the human rights zealots do not indulge in what Denis Brogan once called "the illusion of American omnipotence," they tend to overestimate our capacity, or the capacity of our government, to influence the external world, particularly domestic developments in other countries. America is powerful, but it is not all-powerful. Our considerable leverage of the 1950s and even our diminished leverage of the 1960s has been seriously eroded by OPEC, the great leap forward in Soviet military might, and our abandonment of Vietnam.

Quite apart from our limited capacity to influence intractable realities abroad, there is and should be a profound moral constraint on efforts designed to alter domestic practices, institutions, and policies within other states. Neo-Wilsonian attempts to make the world safe for human rights seem to be rooted in what Professor Ronald Berman has called "a planned

35

confusion between domestic and foreign policy. The rest of the world is depicted as if it were an American constituency, driven by our own motives, vulnerable to our own rhetoric."[2] To be sure, the extravagant rhetoric of a Carter or a Wilson, with its crusading and paternalistic overtones, draws upon a persistent idealistic stream in the American character. But there is another and quieter stream equally honorable, but less pushy and perhaps more persuasive, symbolized by the biblical parable of a candle upon a candlestick or a city set upon a hill, an example to the "lesser breeds without the law," as it was put in a more candid era.

John Quincy Adams expressed this more modest understanding of America's external responsibility: "We are the friends of liberty everywhere, but the custodians only of our own." Thirty years later, Abraham Lincoln spoke of "liberty as the heritage of all men, in all lands everywhere," but he did not claim that the United States was the chosen instrument for fulfilling this heritage.

4. Confusing Domestic and Foreign Policy

Elaborating on Professor Bergman's point, many human rights crusaders confuse the fundamental distinctions between domestic and foreign policy which are rooted in age-old practice, international law, the UN charter, and common sense. They do not take seriously the distinctions in authority and responsibility that flow from the concept of sovereignty which underlies the modern state system. Our president and all other heads of state have authority to act only in their own states, within the territory of their legal jurisdiction. They are responsible only for the security and welfare of their own people, including their citizens living or traveling abroad.

There are, of course, multiple modes of interaction and cooperation between states based on mutual interest, ranging from trade, investment, and cultural exchange to military assistance and alliance ties. These activities are consistent with the concept of sovereign equality and non-interference in internal affairs. But short of a victorious war, no government has a right to impose its preference on another sovereign state. The mode and quality of life and the character and structure of institutions within a state should be determined by its own people, not by outsiders, however well-intentioned. The same is true for the pace and direction of social, political, or economic change.

U.S. foreign policy toward another state should be determined largely by the foreign policy of that state. Domestic factors and forces are significant determinants only if they bear on external realities. Washington is allied with Iran, Taiwan, Thailand, and South Korea, not because their governments are authoritarian, but because they are regarded as vital in the struggle against the expansion of Soviet or Chinese power. It is, therefore, appropriate to provide economic or military assistance to them, even if they do not hold regular elections. In sum, U.S. aid can properly be given to encourage a friend or ally to pursue constructive external policies, but not to promote internal reforms opposed by the assisted government. This leads to the next point.

5. *Ignoring the Perils of Reform Intervention*

The impulse to impose our standards or practices on other societies, supported by policies of reward and punishment, leads inevitably to a kind of reform intervention. We Americans have no moral mandate to transform other societies, and we rightly resent such efforts on the part of the totalitarians. There is more than a touch of arrogance in our efforts to alter the domestic behavior of allies, or even of adversaries.

As noted above, the Foreign Assistance Act states that a principal goal of U.S. policy is to promote internationally recognized human rights abroad. Further, Title IX of the Act says that U.S. aid should be used to encourage "democratic private and local government institutions" within the recipient states. The implications of this seemingly innocent phrase are disquieting. Should U.S. assistance be used to alter domestic institutions? Should we insist on an ideological or reform test before providing economic or military aid? Is this not a form of uninvited interference in domestic matters? If we take sovereign equality seriously, we will recognize that the people of every state should determine their own system of justice and how they want to defend themselves against domestic and foreign dangers.

Other states may request assistance from friendly governments on mutually agreed terms. But external forces, however nobly motivated, cannot impose justice, human rights, or freedom on other states without resorting to conquest. It may be possible to "export revolution"—as the phrase goes—but we cannot export human rights or respect for the rule of law. Freedom and justice are the fruit of long organic growth nurtured by religious values, personal courage, social restraint, and respect for law. The majesty of law is little understood in traditional societies where ethnic identity tends to supersede all other claims on loyalty and obedience.

6. *Distorting Foreign Policy Objectives*

A consistent and single-minded invocation of a human rights standard in making U.S. foreign policy decisions would subordinate, blur, or distort other essential considerations. After all, our foreign policy has vital but limited goals—national security and international peace—both of which have a great impact on human rights. Aggressive war and tyranny are the two chief enemies of freedom and justice. Our efforts to deter nuclear war and nuclear blackmail are calculated to protect the culture and free institutions of Western Europe and North America. In the third world we seek to maintain a regional stability conducive to responsible political development and mutually beneficial economic intercourse among states. Economic productivity alleviates stark poverty and thus broadens the range of cultural and political choice.

Therefore, our policies of nuclear deterrence should be determined by our understanding of the Soviet nuclear threat and our trade policies toward Moscow should be determined by our economic and security interests. Neither should be influenced, much less determined, by the extent of human rights violations in the Soviet Union. Likewise, in dealing with third world countries, their foreign policy behavior should be the determining factor, not their domestic practices. Even though South Korea has an authoritarian government, we should continue our security support because it is a faithful ally under siege from a totalitarian neighbor and because its independence is vital to the defense of Japan and Japan's independence is vital to the U.S. position in the Western Pacific and the world.

III

The Pitfalls of Selective Application

These six conceptual flaws which underlie the human rights crusade have already led to unwise policies and, if carried to their logical conclusion, could end in disaster. Perhaps the most widely criticized and resented aspect of the campaign thus far has been its capricious and selective application to both communist states and American allies.

During his visit to Poland last December, President Carter raised the human rights issue several times in public. On the one hand, he criticized his hosts for not permitting a handful of dissident journalists to attend his press conference. On the other, he praised Poland's rights record (compared to that of other Eastern European states) and said: "Our concept of human rights is preserved in Poland," to which a Polish writer replied: "The words are the same," but they "mean different things in the United States." The impropriety, not to say irony, of raising the sensitive rights issue in a communist state whose fragile and problematic autonomy is precariously maintained at the sufferance of a totalitarian superpower did not seem to concern Mr. Carter. Nor did the fact that Poland is forced to imitate many of the repressive measures of its master. By focusing on the absence of a handful of dissenting journalists at his press conference when the entire Polish people are held in bondage by the Soviet Union, President Carter distorted and trivialized the real meaning of human rights.

The policy of the administration and the Congress toward the Soviet Union has also been vacillating and confused, seemingly more intent on scoring merchandisable victories than on grappling with the fundamental problem. Were it not for the Jewish emigration issue, Moscow would probably be receiving less critical attention than it is. How else can one explain the almost complete neglect of the massive violation of civil and political rights in Communist China, North Korea, Vietnam, and Cambodia?

Cambodia provides a particularly poignant example of this double standard toward totalitarian countries. Since the Communists took over on April 17, 1975, reliable studies estimate that 800,000 to 1,500,000 Cambodians have died by execution or from starvation and disease caused by the forced evacuations from cities. This means that one in every six or seven has perished in the ruthless communist bloodbath. Yet, where is the outcry from the advocates of human rights? Why this strange silence about what may well be the most brutal atrocity of our century? Measured by relative population, the communist purge in Cambodia has destroyed more lives than Hitler's concentration camps or Stalin's Gulag Archipelago.

The great silence can be explained in part by racial and ideological factors. To certain rights advocates it somehow seems more reprehensible if violations or brutality is directed toward members of a different race. A white South African regime denying blacks the vote seems more morally repugnant than black regimes denying all citizens the vote (which is the case in most other African states). Filtered through a racist lens, it does not seem as bad for Cambodian communists to murder thousands of innocent Cambodians—men, women, and children—as for a much smaller number of Cambodian soldiers to die in a war in which the United States was involved.

This suggests that an ideological factor is also present. A recent *Wall Street Journal* editorial pointed to the frequent alliance between liberal moral outrage and revolutionary causes; the "crimes of the Khmer Rouge, even though they dwarf some other state crimes of our times . . . have attracted less attention because they are inflicted in the name of revolution." One can only wonder what the reaction would be if the new government had employed "conservative" rhetoric and announced that it was going to cleanse the country of all socialist or Marxist influences.

Turning to American allies, some of the most articulate rights advocates concentrate their outrage on the very regimes that are under the most severe pressure from the totalitarians—South Korea, Taiwan, Iran, and Chile. The first three are geographically and militarily exposed to communist power. Chile under Allende was the target of a massive internal and external assault by Marxist forces seeking to transform it into a Cuban-style dictatorship. All four of these states have authoritarian regimes, primarily in response to their present or recently endangered position, but in each the range of rights permitted or guaranteed by the regime is far greater than that of the communist governments that seek to subvert or replace them. This suggests that the human rights standard is sometimes used, not to advance freedom, but as a cloak to attack anti-totalitarian allies.

Some rights advocates have simultaneously urged punitive policies against Chile and measures to normalize relations with Cuba. This is a double irony. Human rights are more honored in Chile than in Cuba, and

Chile is pursuing a more peaceful foreign policy than Cuba. Havana is a mischief-maker on a grand scale, acting as a cat's-paw for Moscow. Castro, in addition to shoring up a minority regime in Angola with 19,000 Cuban troops, has sent Cuban soldiers to support the Marxist military junta in Ethiopia and to assist "revolutionary" regimes and other groups in a dozen other African states.

This double standard is often promoted by the media. According to a tabulation of news stories, editorials, and signed opinion for 1976, the prestige media's big five—*New York Times, Washington Post,* and the TV evening news shows of ABC, CBS, and NBC—carried 227 items about rights violations in two allied countries, Chile and South Korea, in contrast to only 24 stories about violations in three Communist countries, North Korea, Cuba, and Cambodia. The tabulation drawn up by Accuracy in Media follows:

	Chile	South Korea	North Korea	Cuba	Cambodia
New York Times	66	61	0	3	4
Washington Post	58	24	1	4	9
ABC - TV	5	2	0	0	1
CBS - TV	5	3	0	0	2
NBC - TV	3	0	0	0	0
Totals:	137	90	1	7	16

The content of the items was not examined, but the bias was clearly revealed by the inordinate attention given the small human rights sins of two loyal allies compared to the massive sins of three totalitarian adversaries—a ratio of almost ten to one.

Admittedly, it is far easier to get reliable information about the imperfections of authoritarian societies than those of closed, totalitarian states, but this is hardly an excuse for the media which pride themselves on vigorous investigative reporting. Certainly a little effort could have yielded considerably more data on violations in Cambodia, North Korea, and Cuba, to say nothing of China, where both blunt and subtle forms of repression have been developed into an exquisite craft.

The lopsided application of human rights criteria is justified by White House and State Department spokesmen on pragmatic grounds. They frankly admit that they give more critical attention to allies than to adversaries because they have more leverage over the former—we can withhold or threaten to withhold aid from our friends, so why not strike a blow for freedom where we can, or, if one prefers, why not administer the two-by-four to a mulish friend?

IV
What Is America's Responsibility?

In a formal and legal sense, the U.S. government has no responsibility—and certainly no authority—to promote human rights in other sovereign states. But this is hardly the whole story. Because of our heritage, our dedication to humane government, our power, and our wealth, we Americans have a moral responsibility, albeit ill-defined, in the larger world consistent with our primary obligations at home and commensurate with our capacity to influence external events. We are almost universally regarded as a humanitarian power and as the champion of freedom and decency. We should be proud of our humane occupation policies in Germany and Japan. But we enjoy no occupation rights now, and the role of our government abroad is less clear. Saying this, the American people and their government can make two major contributions to the cause of human rights in other countries.

First, in the spirit of John Quincy Adams and Lincoln, we can be worthy custodians of the freedom bequeathed us by the Founding Fathers and thus continue to give heart to the aspirations of peoples everywhere. We can give hope to those in bondage by illustrating what the late Reinhold Neibuhr has called "the relevance of the impossible ideal." We can never fully realize our own ideals. And in most other cultural settings, full respect for human rights cannot be expected in the foreseeable future. A quick change in government will not enshrine liberty or justice. The message of our example is subdued, but not without hope—the struggle for a bit more freedom of choice or a better chance for justice is a never-ending one, and after small gains have been made, eternal vigilance is vital to avoid sliding back into bondage. Serving as an example of decency, then, is our most effective way to nudge forward the cause of human dignity.

Second, our government can advance human rights by strengthening our resolve and our resources to defend our allies who are threatened by totalitarian aggression or subversion. This requires security guarantees, military assistance, and in some cases the presence of U.S. troops on foreign soil. Our combined effort to maintain a favorable balance of power has succeeded in preserving the independence of Western Europe, Japan, and South Korea. But because of our half-hearted commitment, we failed in Vietnam, Cambodia, and Laos, and, in a different sense, in Angola.

We have a domestic consensus for continued support of our North Atlantic allies and Japan, but some of our commitments elsewhere have been eroded by confusion over the nature of the threat. We are being severely tested in Taiwan, South Korea, and southern Africa. In each case, the totalitarians are pressing relentlessly by military, economic, political, and subversive means to destroy and replace Western influence. The struggle in these areas is hardly one of pure freedom against totalitarianism, but human rights (as well as peace) are clearly at stake. Any regime installed or

41

sponsored by Moscow or Peking in Seoul, Taipei, or Pretoria will certainly provide less justice and freedom than the imperfect regime it displaced.

Beyond serving as a good example and maintaining our security commitments, there is little the U.S. government can or should do to advance human rights, other than using quiet diplomatic channels at appropriate times and places. Moscow and other governments should be reminded of their pledges in the United Nations Charter and the Helsinki Agreement. Public preaching to friend or foe has limited utility. As we have already seen, it is both embarrassing and counter-productive to threaten punitive measures against friendly, but less than democratic, regimes which are attempting to achieve a reasonable balance between authority and freedom at home, often under severely trying circumstances, and are pursuing constructive policies abroad.

V

THE IRONY OF VIRTUE

The Carter administration is not of one mind on the significance, purpose, or effects of the human rights crusade. The administration is even less united in the implementation of the program in specific cases. During his visit to Iran last December, President Carter gave his final approval for the sale of six to eight nuclear reactors to that country whose government has been the target of human rights activists as well as of Marxist groups. Alleged rights violations by the Shah's government have apparently had little effect on U.S. arms sales there. The same appears to be true of South Korea. In fact, some observers believe that the entire campaign so far has been more rhetoric than reality, and some suggest that it was launched more to satisfy the impulses of U.S. domestic groups than to effect real changes in the external world.

In any event, there appears to be a growing recognition of the moral and political limitations of a foreign policy crusade which, to repeat Mr. Carter, is based on "constant decency" and "optimism." While defending the campaign in principle, Secretary of State Cyrus Vance notes some of the reservations and flaws developed above. In a Law Day address, April 30, 1977, Mr. Vance warned against a "self-righteous and strident" posture and said: "We must always keep in mind the limits of our power and of our wisdom." He added that "a doctrinaire plan of action" to advance human rights "would be as damaging as indifference."

The tone of Mr. Vance's address stands in sharp contrast to President Carter's Notre Dame speech, which has been criticized as arrogant, self-righteous, and naive by Senator Daniel Moynihan and eight other foreign policy observers in a monograph published last December.[3] Among other things, these critics took exception to Mr. Carter's view that there have been "dramatic worldwide advances in the protection of the individual from the arbitrary power of the state." In his pragmatic response to the security and other political realities, however, the president is far closer to Mr. Vance's words than to his own rhetoric. In the interests of reasonable consistency, the president has two choices—he can alter his rhetoric or alter his actual policies. Politically and morally, reality is more compelling than rhetoric.

The canons of prudence, statesmanship, and accountability all suggest that the president tone down his rhetoric. He should quietly recognize the political and moral limits of promoting particular reforms in other societies. He should recognize that a policy rooted in a presumption of American righteousness and in our capacity to sponsor virtue in other states often leads to the opposite effect. In some circumstances, the invocation of a rigid standard could undercut our security ties and invite a disaster in which millions of persons would move from partial freedom to tyranny.

Mr. Carter's policy is full of irony, precisely because his good intentions may lead to dire consequences. Irony is not the result of evil intention or malice, but rather of a hidden defect in virtue. In Mr. Carter's case, at least in rhetoric, the defect is a kind of vague, romantic optimism with an excessive confidence in the power of reason and good will. This comforting view of human nature, the child of the Enlightenment and social Darwinism, differs sharply from the more sober biblical understanding of the nature and destiny of man. Be that as it may, the president should not be judged on his philosophical consistency, but rather by the actual policies he pursues. Since there is some relation between how one thinks and feels and what one does, it is not inappropriate to recall the words of columnist Michael Novak: "One of the best ways to create an immoral foreign policy is to try too hard for a moral one."

NOTES

1. This distinction is elaborated in Peter L. Berger's "Are Human Rights Universal?" *Commentary*, September 1977.

2. See note 3.

3. See *Morality and Foreign Policy: A Symposium on President Carter's Stance*, ed. Ernest W. Lefever, published by Ethics and Public Policy Center, Georgetown University, December 1977. The other critics are Robert L. Bartley, Ronald L. Berman, Jeane Kirkpatrick, Charles Burton Marshall, Michael Novak, John P. Roche, Eugene V. Rostow, and Roger L. Shinn.

Are Some More Equal
Than Others in the
New China?*

*Robert L. Schuettinger***

Since at least the time of Plato, human beings have hungered after an ideal society—one in which everyone lived together in peace and harmony and where everyone was both virtuous and equal. From time to time people like Sir Thomas More would write about "Utopia" or a Rousseau would "discover" the "noble savage" in the New World who was unspoiled by the corruption of materialistic civilization.

After 1917, Western intellectuals flocked to the Soviet Union to report that they had "seen the future and it works." The great socialist experiment was praised in countless books and articles by uncritical not to say naive observers of first Lenin's and then Stalin's version of "equality."

Even the slowest of pupils will learn a lesson, however, provided it is repeated often enough. By the middle 1950s, therefore, only the diehard members of Western communist parties would any longer maintain that the Soviet Union was a model of democracy, liberty, or equality. It was clear to even the casual traveler that a well-defined hierarchy existed in the USSR in which leading members of the party formed a recognizable elite with special privileges of all sorts. The small percentage of the Soviet population who are party members are allowed to purchase scarce foreign goods at special shops; the higher members of the party have vacation retreats; higher salaries and foreign travel are rewards for loyalty to the leadership.[1] There is even a special school in the Kremlin to educate the small children of party leaders, rather like the school set up by President Kennedy for his two children and their "peer-group"—offspring of high White House and Cabinet officials.

As idealistic and leftist intellectuals around the world became more and more disillusioned with the all too obvious human weaknesses of the so-called "socialist" regime in the USSR they began to look elsewhere for an exemplary society. Some turned to the democratic socialist governments in

---

*Copyright 1976, Council on American Affairs, Washington, D.C. Reprinted by permission.
**Robert L. Schuettinger is the Editor of *Policy Review,* Washington, D.C.

Sweden or Great Britain. They soon found, however, that Sweden was hopelessly bureaucratic with all the usual petty corruption and favoritism associated with a political elite. Anyone reading the British press could not fail to be unaware of the blatant hypocrisy of the leaders of the Labour Party. They regularly demanded, and received, private rooms and extra privileges for themselves whenever they used a National Health Service hospital, while in their public lives they waged fierce warfare against those who paid, under private health insurance, for a private room. Many of the Labour Cabinet sent their own children to private schools while voting to require other parents to transfer their children from state academic high schools to comprehensive schools, in the name of equality.[2]

Upon examination, the same sort of sordid selfishness went on in Yugoslavia.[3] Even Cuba, it turned out, was not immune from the persistent human desire to further the interests of oneself and one's family and friends at the expense of the common welfare.[4]

Where on this earth was there a nation the pure in heart could honestly admire and hold up as an example to their children? Surely at least one part of the world must have conquered greed, selfishness, and inequality?

China—People's China—was the answer. Here was a nation free of all the old sins of humanity. Travelers in recent years have positively *gushed* over the glories of the new China. We are told constantly by returning observers that "there are no flies or dogs in China today, that beggars are gone, the streets clean, the fields tilled, the peasants well-fed, and the children looked-after."[5] Mrs. Marion Javits could not wait to rush home and inform *Women's Wear Daily* that homosexuality had been abolished in a nation of 900 million.

Even so experienced and able a man as the Senate Majority Leader, Mike Mansfield, could barely restrain himself as he reported: "There is no unemployment or inflation. Officials report that there are no social problems or drug addiction, alcoholism, prostitution, or juvenile delinquency. The streets are safe. . . . Everyone appears to be busy at productive and purposeful work. . . . There is a discernible community spirit from one end of China to another. The spirit is perhaps a key to China's effective management. . . . It is the antithesis of 'dog eat dog'."[6]

Most of the recent visitors have emphasized their *impression* (it could hardly be more than that) that Communist China is the most egalitarian country in the world. Again and again we are told that in China almost everyone has the same sparse but adequate standard of living, that everyone is dedicated to "serving the people," that competition and personal ambition are dying relics of a feudal past, and so forth.

What are the facts? Just how equal a society is the new China?

Communist Chinese hosts consider the matter of wage-differentials to be a delicate one and they are not eager to discuss this subject with foreigners. Allan Brownfield, in his column for December 2, 1975 *(Phoenix Gazette),* recounts the experience of President William Bowen of Princeton

University who recently visited the mainland: "He encountered only evasiveness when he inquired about salary differentials between ordinary workers and those who had received technical training at a factory-run university in Shanghai. 'You could just feel the tension in the room rise,' he said. 'The answer I got was that people did not go to the universities in order to earn money. I said that I had not suggested that they do, but I was interested as a point of fact in what the salary relationships were before and after. I was then told that the policy is not to have salary differentials based on whether one did manual work or mental. I said I understood that, but I was still interested in the actual salary levels there. We went on in this vein for about fifteen minutes, and that was it.' Later, he was told that 'there are differentials, but they are not very large.' "

Senator Humphrey, however, after his visit in September 1974, was able to obtain figures. He informs us that the average urban wage is about 50 to 60 yuan per month (roughly equivalent to $25 to $30). Agricultural workers earn much less. Skilled workers, however, receive about twice that amount, $50 a month, and professionals and managers earn from $100 to $150 a month.[7]

Another source maintains that in the mid-1960s the lowest level civil servants were paid about one-tenth the salaries of heads of ministries (this scale was comparable to the U.S. where cabinet members are paid $60,000 and the beginning civil service pay now rarely goes below $6000 a year).[8]

Senator Robert Byrd of West Virginia, the Assistant Majority Leader, after his visit in August 1975, stated that the salaries of most surgeons in a hospital he visited were about $40 a month. The highest paid surgeon-professor in the hospital, however, received a salary of $180 a month, more than four times that of most of his colleagues. This would seem to indicate that while many professionals have official salaries similar to those of skilled workers (Senator Byrd does not mention any extra perquisites which the surgeons may have received), senior professionals and managers receive differentials higher than would be normal in most Western nations.[9]

A Canadian journalist who visited the mainland in 1975 confirms these general wage figures. He states that there are eight monthly grade levels for most non-agricultural workers ranging from $14 a month for apprentices to $285 a month for the most senior officials, a differential of 1-20. The American minimum wage is now about $4,000 a year and very few government officials are paid more than $60,000 a year; we can conclude from these figures that the new China is at least somewhat less egalitarian than the leading capitalist nation in the world.[10]

According to an American sociologist, many of the ordinary Chinese citizens she spoke to were enthusiastic in discussing their improved material conditions. "Self-interest," she notes, "was evident as people gleefully listed household acquisitions (sewing machine, bicycle, etc.), spoke of new opportunities for higher education for themselves or their children, and even waved savings-account deposit slips to show how big a nest-egg they were accumulating. Political consciousness was raised, but selfishness and competitiveness," she concludes, "were not eradicated by the Cultural Revolution."[11]

The *Asia 1976 Yearbook* published by the liberal-leaning *Far Eastern Economic Review* generally confirms this view of Chinese social attitudes. In this past year, the *Yearbook* notes, "Corrupt and arrogant officials still flourished. . . . Both peasants and workers were still mainly motivated by personal interests. *Red Flag* referred to the existence of prostitution and pornography. Juvenile delinquency had emerged in some areas. Young people were not always enthusiastic about being conscripted from the towns for agricultural work. . . . The response to calls for unpaid, voluntary overtime was far from enthusiastic."[12]

It seems fair to say that the charges of personal corruption and luxurious living do not apply to Mao himself or to his late deputy Chou En-lai who was reported to live fairly simply. However, there seems a strong likelihood that special privileges of various sorts have been commandeered by Chinese leaders quite high up the hierarchy; that is, the feathering of one's nest is not confined to a minority of local bureaucrats. The *New York Times* of July 26, 1976, published a dispatch from a Canadian newsman who described how many party members have alleged that former Deputy Prime Minister Teng Hsiao-ping was building a $1 million home for himself on the outskirts of Peking—fairly lavish in a nation where the average annual urban income is about $360 a year![13]

There is evidence from some recent visitors to China that many of the bureaucratic elite live on a far more expensive scale than does the average skilled worker. Many such up-and-coming members of the new class have accounts with substantial savings. A department store in Nanking, a city of two million people, is reported to sell yearly about 100 Omega watches costing about $365 (more than the average annual wage of a city worker). The same store sold about 500 television sets in 1973 at a price of $260 each (the monthly wage of a very high official). The fact that so many of the elite have such large amounts in "discretionary income" would indicate that their official salaries, high as they are in comparison to the general population, must be only a part of their total or real compensation.

There are other privileges enjoyed by the new elite. On trains, for instance, officials have first preference, after distinguished foreigners, on the limited soft-seat compartments, while the ordinary comrades sit on hard boards. On airlines, persons with influence are seated in what would be called the first-class section in the capitalist nations; in China, of course, there are no first-class sections, but officials who need "room to work" are regularly given more space and better service.

There is even a private "gentlemen's club" in Peking set aside for the exclusive use of members of the Peking Revolutionary Committee. It is the building which formerly housed the foreigners' International Club and has a swimming pool, gymnasium, dining room, and tables for snooker.[14]

The privileged elite are distinguished from the ordinary people not so much for their greater talent or productivity but above all for their political reliability. Most of the members of party cadres who wield the most influence in People's China are veterans of the pre-1949 days or, in the case of younger people, party members directly and closely connected (often by family ties) to these tried and proven leaders of the movement.

"Judging by the scanty information available," asserts one group of scholars, "politics is already the chief source of social prestige, in the sense that persons well connected to politically powerful persons at the supravillage level are respected and are influential in their home communities."[15]

The higher levels of the elite system are incredibly in-bred by Western standards; the Oxford-Cambridge or Grande Ecoles "old boy networks" in Britain and France pale by comparison. A study of the leaders of the PRC in 1971 revealed that the Politburo and Central Committee have been dominated since the late 1960s by veterans of two army units that had served together almost without interruption for forty years.[16]

There seems little doubt that except for a small number of essential professionals (engineers, scientists, etc.) the road to higher status in China today is almost exclusively through the party hierarchy (which includes the People's Liberation Army). The skills or attributes needed to excel under these conditions are largely political: the ability to get along with different factions, to appear to have always been loyal to whatever group is on top at the moment, and the judicious manipulation of political connections. Friendships outside the party structure are of little help, and in fact are frowned upon.

As in the Kremlin and the Kennedy White House there have recently been schools reserved for the children of elite cadres, and some of these schools probably still exist in various cities of China. A Red Guard publication exposed one such school in Peking in an article entitled "The August First School System for Children of High Ranking Cadres."[17] Urban dwellers in general, however, have great advantages in educational opportunities over the eighty percent of the population who live in rural areas—despite the continuous Maoist rhetoric of a revolution based on the peasantry. Approximately sixty percent of rural school age children attend primary school (this is in sharp contrast to the Republic of China, by the way, where education is universal) but only a small minority go on to the middle schools (grades 7 to 12). Even these middle schools offer only agriculture training; college preparation is reserved for the urban schools. This means that the chances of a farmer's son attending a university in the new China are very slight indeed.[18] For the great mass of China's population, therefore, equality of opportunity is almost non-existent.

The urban workers, throughout the history of the People's Republic of China, have formed a relatively elite class, earning usually two to three times the incomes of agricultural workers. In addition, industrial workers have received many benefits (health, pensions, social services, education) paid for by the state not available to the peasantry.[19] (Again this sharp differential contrasts with the relative equality of farm and urban workers in the Republic of China and the Republic of Korea, for example.)

The Peking government, in what amounts to an essentially cosmetic operation, has been attempting to ameliorate this gross inequality between the two large classes of the people through a kind of urban-rural exchange program. Selected peasants are brought to work in factories, and urban workers, including students and professionals, are periodically sent to the farms "to renew their contact with the masses." There has been, however, widespread dissatisfaction, to say the least, with this very limited venture into egalitarianism.

According to one scholar of the Cultural Revolution, "resistance and opposition to the rustication program has persisted, judging from press reports in China. For example, according to a May 4, 1975 article in the *People's Daily* written by Hsing Yen-tsu, a model rusticated girl who is now a member of the CCP Center Committee, many youths have found ways to evade rustication or to cut short their tour of duty, and they are admired by others as 'resourceful.' "[20]

Senior members of the party have not hesitated to use their political influence to keep their own children from being sent to the farms (or, if this is not possible, at least to shorten their tours of duty). It is also fairly common to find the higher levels of the government pulling strings to have their children admitted to universities.[21]

Repeated press reports have told of strikes, demonstrations, unrest in units of the army, and other indications that all is not as well in the "People's China" as the more naive observers might wish to believe.[22]

The democratic socialist quarterly *Dissent* recently published an article by an Australian authority on Chinese culture and politics, Simon Leys, who summed up in two paragraphs an insightful analysis of how a new class has arisen on the mainland which is determined to preserve and extend all the privileges it has gathered to itself, under the name of socialist equality. Mr. Leys uses as one of his sources a *samizdat*, circulated within the "People's Republic" by critics of the regime; their typology of the new China is, not surprisingly, remarkably similar to Yugoslavia's Djilas.

This is because, as Mr. Leys notes, "Like causes produce like effects, and in the framework of bureaucratic totalitarianism, variations are necessarily limited. Within the limits of a socialist economy, the new ruling class has managed to privately appropriate and embezzle the wealth of the community. This is achieved by inflating and expanding its special status by increasing its various political, economic, and social privileges, by making these privileges quasi-hereditary, and by consolidating and protecting them through a system of sectarian oligarchical cliques able to suppress whatever criticism might arise from among the masses."[23]

An impartial student of the facts can have little doubt that Communist China is by no means a just or equal society, much less a worker's paradise.

The fundamental reason for this is not hard to understand; there are two main classes in China, the governing class of party members which the *New Republic* refers to as the "25 million or so who lead the country,"[24] and everyone else. Were it not for the mystique of "equality" which, incredibly enough, has been accepted by many Western vistiors and commentators, the People's Republic of China would simply be described as a nation where three percent of the population have, at a minimum, much more political power, and far greater social, economic, and educational advantages than the other ninety-seven percent. No doubt in another twenty years or so the liberal intellectuals will finally conclude, as they have so many times in the past, that Orwell's prediction has come true once again and that in the new China, as elsewhere in the "socialist" world, "all animals are equal, but some are more equal than others."

NOTES

1. Among many sources, see, for instance, Eugene Lyons, *Worker's Paradise Lost*, New York, 1967 and Warren Nutter, *The Strange World of Ivan Ivanov*, New York, 1969.

2. Philip Vander Elst exposes the private vs public stance of the "socialist" leaders in Britain in his chapter on this subject in *1985: An Escape From Orwell's 1984*, edited by Dr. Rhodes Boyson, MP, London, 1975. He tells how Mrs. Barbara Castle, MP, while Minister of Health and campaigning for an end to private beds for privately insured patients in NHS hospitals, demanded and received a private room when she was recently hospitalized, claiming that she needed room to work. The far-left Anthony Wedgwood Benn, who renounced his title to stay in the House of Commons, registered his children when they were ill in a private hospital under his wife's maiden name (his wife is a wealthy American). Many other examples could be cited.

3. The classic work on bureaucratic privilege in the New Yugoslavia, is, of course, *The New Class*, by former Vice President Milovan Djilas. He received a rather harsh review from the Tito government for this book— seven years in prison.

4. See Rene Dumont, *Cuba est-il socialiste?* Paris, 1970.

5. Sheila K. Johnson, "To China, With Love," *Commentary*, June 1973, p. 3. the author lists a number of such books and articles, most of which restrain from much critical commentary on what they were told by their hosts. These include: Joseph Alsop in *The New York Times Magazine*, March 11 and 18, 1973; John K. Galbraith, *A China Passage;* Arthur Galston in *Natural History*, October/November 1972; Wassily Leontief in the *Atlantic*, March 1973; Neville Maxwell in the *American Scholar*, Autumn 1972; Jonathan Mirsky in *Saturday Review of the Society*, July 1, 1972; *The New York Times Report from Red China; The President's Trip to China;* Harrison E. Salisbury, *To Peking—And Beyond;* Ross Terrill, *800,000,000: The Real China;* Jan C. Ting, *An American in China*, and Barbara W. Tuchman, *Notes from China*.

6. Quoted in Allan Brownfeld's column in *The Anaheim Bulletin*, October 16, 1975. Sheila Johnson in her *Commentary* article (p. 9) quotes several similar impressions by recent visitors. For instance, Joseph Alsop: " [Chou en-lai] moves like a young man, and the years have failed to blur the remarkable bold, yet fine-cut, lines of his face. It is a face, too, with more expression than most Chinese permit them-

selves. By turns, he is genial or stern, wryly amused or deeply serious. Overall, he conveys a memorable impression of inner strength combined with lucid intelligence." Or Harrison Salisbury: "I was fortunate enough to spend evenings with two of this remarkable company [of Chinese leaders], Premier Chou En-lai and Mme. Soong, and I concluded that if all of China's leadership was as vigorous, as sparkling and sharp-witted, China was not ill-served by relying on age rather than youth. . . . As each course was served, Mme. Soong rose in her chair . . . and insisted on serving me, as is the Chinese custom. . . . Soon we were eating enormous prawns, and then a Peking fish. . . . The dinner went on and on, from one delight to another." Or Audrey Topping: "Dinner with Premier Chou En-lai is a gourmet delight. Even the table talk, centered on hard political issues, couldn't detract from the joy of eating numerous superbly prepared and served exotic dishes. . . . The hors d'oeuvres included a sumptuous array of cold chicken slices with paprika, stuffed crab meat, tomatoes and cucumbers, ham, sliced pork, bean curd, and cold string beans. There were untold side dishes of buns, stuffed dumplings, and boiled rice." (One is also tempted to conclude, from these recitals, that one of China's great secret weapons is its cuisine. John K. Galbraith's travel dairy consists almost exclusively of descriptions of palaces visited and banquets consumed.)" In the 1930s many visitors from democratic countries were equally sycophantic and uncritical in telling of their hospitality received from the Nazi leaders, especially from Hermann Goering, who could be quite charming—when it suited his purposes.

7. *Congressional Record,* January 28, 1975, p. S1101. Senator Humphrey offers some prices for comparison purposes. A bicycle costs from $60 to $70, and a watch about the same amount. On the other hand, rent and food are very inexpensive. According to John Burns in his article "The Chinese Elite," *Washington Post,* April 13, 1975, a worker's apartment costs about $1 to $2 a month, but a leading party member may pay about $28 a month for a large house. A tailor-made suit costs about $85 but a worker can buy denims for $14.

8. Donald P. Whitaker and Rinn-Sup-shinn (and others), *Area Handbook for the People's Republic of China,* Washington, D.C., 1972, p. 128.

9. Senator Robert C. Byrd, "Report on Trip to People's Republic of China," *Ninth Congressional Delegation to the People's Republic of China, August 17-30, 1975,* House Document no. 94-521, US Government Printing Office, Washington, D.C., 1976, p. 18.

10. John Burns of the *Toronto Globe and Mail,* reprinted in the *Washington Post, op. cit.* in footnote 7.

11. Susan Shirk, "Assessing the Cultural Revolution," *Current,* May 1973, p. 63.

12. *Asia 1976 Yearbook,* published by the Far Eastern Economic Review, Hong Kong, 1976, pp. 141-42.

13. Ross H. Monro (of the *Toronto Globe and Mail),* "Hints of Unease and Indiscipline Appear in China," The *New York Times,* July 26, 1976, p. 1.

14. John Burns (*op. cit.,* footnote 7). Philip Vander Elst (*op. cit.* footnote 2) recounts how the Rt. Hon. Richard Crossman, MP, author of many books on democratic socialism and left-Labour member of the British Cabinet would regularly take over an entire first-class compartment (six seats) for himself (having bought one ticket) because he needed privacy. He stopped this practice after it was called to his attention in the House of Commons.

15. Whitaker, *op. cit.* (footnote 8), p. 135.

16. *Ibid.,* p. 128.

17. *Ibid.,* p. 139.

18. *Ibid.*

19. *Ibid.*, p. 131.

20. Parris H. Chang, "China's Rustication Movement," *Current History,* September 1975, p. 89.

21. *Ibid.;* see also *Time,* February 3, 1975, pp. 30-32.

22. See Chan Lien (ed.), *Proceedings of the Third Sino-American Conference on Mainland China,* Taipei, 1974, especially the chapters by Yuan Chiu Kung on "The Current Problems of Mainland China" and by Chu-Yuang cheng on "Economic Fluctuations on the Chinese Mainland."

23. Simon Leys, "Turmoil in China," *Dissent,* Summer 1976, p. 237.

24. *The New Republic,* March 1, 1975, p. 6.

Political Imprisonment in the People's Republic of China*

Amnesty International

Since 1977 the Chinese official press has publicized a number of cases where violations of human rights committed in the People's Republic of China (PRC) during the past ten years have been redressed. Amnesty International welcomes these measures; it also welcomes a decision reported to have been adopted in the spring of 1978 by the Chinese People's Political Consultative Conference on the release of, or restoration of rights to, thousands of people who had been classified as "rightists" since 1957. However, Amnesty International is concerned by the fact that arrests on political grounds are continuing and that the legislation permitting imprisonment on such grounds is still operative.

An article in the Chinese newspaper the *People's Daily* of July 13, 1978 indicated that changes in the legislation are being considered. The article stated that the country needed a "criminal code," "civil code" and a set of "rules of legal procedure" on the basis of which the "masses of the people" could "institute legal proceedings under the law so as to protect their legitimate interests." Amnesty International welcomes these proposals and would also welcome positive measures which the government might take toward an overall review of the laws and procedures affecting political offenders.

During the past few years, Amnesty International has addressed appeals and inquiries to the authorities in the PRC about cases or prisoners of conscience, arrests and death penalties—including reported executions of political offenders—in the country. On several occasions Amnesty International stressed its wish to discuss these cases and other matters of concern with representatives of the government of the People's Republic of China. However, all appeals and inquiries, as well as requests to meet representatives of the government, have met with no response.

In May 1978, the Chairman of the International Executive Committee of Amnesty International, Thomas Hammarberg, wrote to the Ambassador of the PRC in Sweden, His Excellency Chin Li-chen, informing him that Amnesty International had prepared a report on aspects of the legislation and penal practice in the PRC which were of particular concern. The letter indicated that Amnesty International wished to submit this report to the government and proposed an interview with the ambassador.

On June 13, 1978 the typescript of Amnesty International's "Report on Political Imprisonment in the People's Republic of China" was transmitted to the embassy of the PRC in Stockholm for submission to the government. In a covering letter, Amnesty International said that it would welcome comments on the report, as well as an opportunity of discussing the matters raised in it with representatives of the government of the People's Republic of China.

By mid-August 1978 no comments or replies had been received from the authorities of the PRC. On August 18, 1978 the International Executive Committee of Amnesty International decided to publish this report, which reflects the organization's concern at imprisonment for political reasons in the PRC. The International Executive Committee emphasized that it would still welcome any corrections to, or comments on, the facts presented in the report from the government of the People's Republic of China.

The report describes the major aspects of political imprisonment in the People's Republic of China (PRC)—the laws providing for imprisonment on political grounds, the judicial process and prison conditions.

Amnesty International is particularly concerned about the following issues:

• The existence of a legislation providing for political imprisonment. The report notes that the legal provisions defining political offenses are loosely worded and have been interpreted broadly, permitting large-scale imprisonment on political grounds; and that the Constitution and other official documents also provide that certain categories of people—defined as "class enemies"—are deprived of their political and civil rights on the basis of their "class origin" or political background.

• Arrests on political grounds carried out during "mass mobilization campaigns." These campaigns have been continuous since the 1950s, and have been used as a means both of mass education and of identifying offenders, including people dissenting from official policy. They have contributed to broadening the range of political offenses to the extent that each of them has defined new types of offenders according to the political necessities of the period.

• The practice of detaining political offenders for long periods before trial and the lack of formal guarantees of their right to defense. According to the law, pre-trial detention may be unlimited once an "arrest warrant" has been issued by the police (Public Security), and is often used to compel offenders to write confessions before they are brought to trial. Political defendants are usually tried in camera or, in some cases, through "mass public trials" where no defense is possible. The right to defense is generally limited by the fact that non-admission of guilt is officially regarded as an aggravating circumstance when judgment is passed.

• The imposition of certain punishments on political offenders without judicial investigation. Apart from "formal" penalties, ranging from a term of imprisonment to the death penalty, there are also "informal" or "administrative" sanctions which do not require judicial investigation or other legal process. The offenders affected by these "non-criminal" sanctions are not brought before a court of justice, but they are assigned, as convicted prisoners are, to compulsory labor under special control either in society or in penal establishments.

• Some aspects of detention conditions which fall below the national standards prescribed by Chinese law for the maintenance of prisoners, and do not conform to the United Nations Standard Minimum Rules for the Treatment of Prisoners regarding the rights and treatment of individual prisoners.

• The fact that some political prisoners are "retained" or placed against their will to work in penal establishments at the end of their term of imprisonment.

It must be emphasized, however, that due to the lack of detailed information on political imprisonment in the People's Republic of China, the report is not meant to present a picture of the conditions of detention prevailing in the whole of the country at any particular moment. Scarcity of such information is due to various factors, including the lack of free circulation of information inside the country.

Nevertheless, official documents alone present sufficient evidence that the treatment of political offenders results from a consistent policy of denying to individuals the right to deviate from standards of behavior defined by official policy.

I

THE LAW AND THE CONCEPT OF POLITICAL OFFENSES

In the People's Republic of China, political offenders are usually called "counter-revolutionaries"—a term which refers to people charged with a broad range of political offenses, including offenses of opinion.

1. Political Offenses in Legal Documents

A revised text of the Constitution of the PRC was adopted on March 5, 1978 by the Fifth National People's Congress of the PRC. Like the Constitutions of 1954 and 1975, it guarantees a number of basic rights, such as "freedom of speech, correspondence, the press, assembly, association, procession, demonstration and the freedom to strike" (Article 45). However, it also includes provisions limiting these fundamental rights. In particular Article 18 provides for punishment of political offenders and for deprivation of rights for certain categories of people:

> The state safeguards the socialist system, suppresses all treasonable and counter-revolutionaries, and punishes newborn bourgeois elements and other bad elements.

> The state deprives of political rights, as prescribed by law, those landlords, rich peasants and reactionary capitalists who have not yet been reformed, and at the same time it provides them with the opportunity to earn a living so that they may be reformed through labor and become law-abiding citizens supporting themselves by their own labor.

The first law affecting political offenders which was drawn up after the establishment in 1949 of the People's Republic of China is the Act of the PRC for Punishment of Counter-Revolution (1951). The Act is still in force.

Article 10 of the Act stipulates that people who "with a counter-revolutionary purpose" provoke "dissension among the various nationalities, democratic classes, democratic parties and groups, people's organizations or between the people and the government" (paragraph 2), or who conduct "counter-revolutionary propaganda and agitation" and create and spread rumors (paragraph 3), shall be punished by no less than three years' imprisonment, or by death or life imprisonment when the "circumstances of their cases are major."

2. The Policy Principles and the Importance of Class Background

The principle underlying the policy of "suppression of counter-revolutionaries" are outlined in several official texts written by Mao Tse-tung on the "class struggle." According to Mao's analysis, classes still exist in a socialist society after the victory of the revolution and, therefore, "class struggle" must continue throughout the period of "socialist construction." Class struggle means "to enforce the people's dictatorship" over the "enemies" of the "people."

The categories traditionally singled out as the "class enemies" in the PRC are: the "landlords," "rich peasants," "counter-revolutionaries," "bad elements" and "rightists." These categories are called the "five categories of elements" or more commonly the "five bad elements." Whereas the "rightists" are no longer officially counted among the "class enemies," the 1978 Constitution has introduced a new category: the "new-born bourgeois elements." They are defined as "those newly emerged elements who resist socialist revolution . . . or violate the criminal law."

The importance of the "class struggle" and of the differentiation of classes is still stressed daily in China nowadays. Everyone in China has both a "class origin" and a "class status." Family or (class) background constitutes the "class origin" of an individual; "class status" is determined by a person's work.

Class background becomes particularly important during the "mass mobilization" campaigns which are launched periodically in China. These campaigns can have various purposes, including the search for people who dissent from official policy. Those who have a "bad" class status or origin are usually the first to be scrutinized in this process (see Appendix, Deng Qingshan).

3. The Range of Political Offenses and the Scope of Political Imprisonment

The distinction between criminal and political offenses is not clearly drawn by law in China, as all cases are treated in the light of political considerations. However, on the basis of official accusations against people arrested on political grounds, political offenders can be divided into three main categories:

a. "Historical counter-revolutionaries" *(lishi fangeming),* which generally designates people punished for their activities or position before 1949.

b. "Active counter-revolutionaries" *(xianxing fangeming);* this term is used to designate people accused of involvement in "current" opposition activities. In fact it covers a wide range of offenses, from simple expression of dissent to politically motivated criminal offenses.

c. The third category might be called simply dissenters. It is composed of people who occasionally voiced opinions critical of official policy: for instance, the "rightists," people accused of "spreading reactionary propaganda," etc.

According to documents collected and circulated by Red Guards during the Cultural Revolution (1966-68), Mao Tse-tung said in April 1956 at an enlarged meeting of the Politburo of the Chinese Communist Party (CCP) that "two to three million counter-revolutionaries had been executed, imprisoned or placed under control in the past."[1]

In 1957 an "anti-rightist" campaign was launched in mid-June, putting an abrupt end to the "Hundred Flowers" liberalization movement during which many intellectuals had strongly criticized the Party's bureaucratic practices. The most outspoken critics were then labeled as "rightists" and subsequently detained. Among them were Ding Ling, a well-known woman writer; Lin Xiling, a twenty-year-old (girl) student who is reported to have been sentenced to twenty years imprisonment, and many others. More than 300,000 people are said to have been labeled as "rightists" during that campaign. In April 1978, foreign correspondents in Peking reported that the Chinese authorities had decided to "rehabilitate" the "rightists"—i.e., to lift their "rightist" label and to release those who were still detained. However, no information is as yet available on the implementation of this decision.

Other campaigns led to political arrests before and after the Cultural Revolution. The Cultural Revolution itself (1966-68) was accompanied by another wave of repression, but in a totally different context as it occurred at a period of violence and chaos. Many people were arbitrarily arrested on political grounds, maltreated or even killed by *ad hoc* groups or rival factions operating on their own. At the same time, in 1967 the CCP Central Committee and the State Council issued internal regulations to guide the work of the Public Security (police). The regulations stipulated that the following acts were "counter-revolutionary" and should be punished according to law:

- sending counter-revolutionary anonymous letters;
- posting or distributing secretly or openly counter-revolutionary handbills;
- writing or shouting reactionary slogans;
- attacking or vilifying Chairman Mao and Vice-Chairman Lin Biao.

A considerable number of people are said to have been either temporarily detained or sentenced from the end of the Cultural Revolution until the early 1970s. Many were political offenders. A wall poster displayed in the streets of Canton in 1974 stated: "In Guangdong province alone nearly 40,000 revolutionary masses and cadres were massacred and more than a million revolutionary cadres and masses were imprisoned, put under control and struggled against."[2]

After the CCP Vice-Chairman, Lin Biao, disappeared in September 1971 (allegedly after an attempted coup), several political campaigns succeeded each other without interruption until 1976. They reflected increasing conflict among the leadership, which resulted, shortly after Mao's death in September 1976, in the purge and arrest of the four "radical" leaders now stigmatized in the official press as the "gang of four." The four are Jiang Qing (Chiang Ching—Mao's widow) and Wang Hungwen, Zhang Chunqiao and Yao Wenyuan (three party leaders from Shanghai).

A national campaign to criticize the "gang of four" was launched at the end of 1976 and is still going on. During this campaign, the official press has revealed many cases of people who were imprisoned or harassed for political reasons since the Cultural Revolution and who have now been released or have had their reputation and rights restored. However, official accounts of this campaign also show that a large number of people are being investigated or arrested as alleged "followers" of the "gang of four." Whereas some of them are accused of having used violence against other people out of political ambition, others are reported to be detained simply for their alleged connections or sympathies with the policies of the "gang of four." It is reported, for instance, that several young officials from Canton have been purged in 1977 and detained for their alleged connections with Wang Hungwen (one member of the "gang of four"). One of them, Liu Junyi, is a former Red Guard who became a member of the Guangdong provincial Revolutionary Committee in 1968 and had been appointed a full member of the Tenth CCP Central Committee in 1973. Liu Junyi has been missing since early 1977; his present whereabouts are unknown.

Unrelated to the campaign against the "gang of four," other cases of people arrested or sentenced on political grounds have also been reported in the past two years. Among them were the three authors of a wall poster displayed in Canton in 1974, who were put "under surveillance" in 1975 after their poster was criticized, and who were later reported to have been labeled "counter-revolutionaries" and sent to labor camps (see Appendix, Li Zhengtian).

II
THE JUDICIAL PROCESS

According to the Constitution adopted in March 1978, the cases of offenders are now, as before the Cultural Revolution, handled by three institutions, which are officially referred to in China as "dictatorship organizations":

- the Public Security (police) agencies, in charge of the detention and the investigation of suspects and offenders;
- the Procuratorates, which deal with reinvestigation and review of cases;
- the Courts, which deal with trials.

These three institutions, however, were practically paralyzed during the Cultural Revolution, and "mass organizations" partly assumed the maintenance of public order during the following years. In some places the Courts did not function until 1972-73, and the Procuratorates themselves were officially abolished when the Constitution was amended for the first time in 1975. Their functions were then given to the Public Security agencies who were therefore empowered both to make and to sanction arrest.

1. Arrest and Detention

In the past ten years, formal legal procedures were seldom followed and numerous arbitrary arrests were carried out on political grounds.

According to the Arrest and Detention Act of the PRC (1954), there are two types of warrants allowing the Public Security agencies to detain a suspect:

- a "detention warrant," which permits a suspect to be detained from 24 to 48 hours for preliminary investigation, in order to establish whether there is enough evidence to warrant "arrest";
- an "arrest warrant," which is usually issued when enough *prima facie* evidence is found; it permits the *unlimited* detention of the suspect in order to establish whether there is sufficient evidence against him or her to justify prosecution.

According to the testimonies of former prisoners, this procedure is seldom followed. The Public Security personnel who make arrests can apparently ask their superiors for a renewal of the "detention warrant," and it happens that people are detained for months without an "arrest warrant" being issued. It must be emphasized that, even then the proper procedures are followed, the "arrest warrant" permits unlimited detention before trial.

Yang Rong is an example of someone arrested at the end of the Cultural Revolution by a "mass organization"—in this instance a group of Red Guards. His case was reported to Amnesty International by a former prisoner who became acquainted with it while in detention himself. Part of his account is summarized here:

Yang Rong, in his forties and a resident of Canton, was detained in 1968 on vague charges of being "anti-socialist." Until the Cultural Revolution Yang had been a secretary in the Cultural and Historical Department of Guangdong Province Museum. He was married, had a young daughter and a good political record since he had participated in the Revolution, and had the class background of office worker. He had also occasionally published poems and short articles in the *Yangcheng* evening paper.

During the Cultural Revolution, Yang joined one of the Red Guard factions of Canton and once participated in an armed fight toward the end of 1967. This experience shocked him and he decided not to involve himself in any more fighting. As this was not possible if he remained in Canton, he went to his native village for a time. Soon, however, he became worried about his work at the museum, and decided to return to Canton to see what was happening.

At that time, members of the faction to which he had belonged were reviewing a number of internal problems. As Yang had been away without giving any reason, they suspected him of "betrayal" and arrested him after his return to Canton. Yang was locked up in a room in the museum for questioning. The reason for his detention was suspicion of betrayal, but his accusers tried to find something from his past that could be held against him. They closely examined his articles and poems, and pressed him in various ways to confess that he had "spoken" against Chairman Mao and against socialism. He was told that his wife was also detained in the museum and that she had already admitted this. At night Yang could hear a woman's cries. He thought that his wife was indeed detained and had confessed under pressure. . . . Although he was detained for only ten days, as a result of his distress and of the pressure, he confessed that he had once "spoken against socialism" when he was alone with his wife, and signed a confession on which his fingerprint was marked.

Yang was then taken by some Red Guards to Canton's Public Security Department where his confession was presented. Because of lack of evidence, the Public Security officers at first did not want to detain him. However, after several hours of discussion with the Red Guards, they agreed to keep him for questioning and signed a detention warrant (juliuzheng) against him. His family was told to bring him clothes, blankets and articles for daily use. Yang was then sent to Hemulang detention center, west of Canton City, and put in a cell with two other prisoners.

Yang Rong was arrested in 1968. Amnesty International has been told that by 1975 he had not yet returned to his family.

Interrogation during detention is particularly important in the case of political offenders, as various means are used to lead them to "confess their crimes." For instance, it is a common practice to ask detainees to write lengthy reports on their past thinking, relations and activities. This—in addition to information collected during sessions of interrogation—may provide useful details for the interrogators, and will be followed up by more questions and more requests for written reports. The accused cannot refuse to write such reports because this is officially considered a "lack of cooperation with the government" and is practically treated as an offense in itself. The use of coercion to extract "forced" confessions is officially prohibited, but not the practice of obliging detainees to write autobiographies and reports about their past activities. As pre-trial detention is unlimited, the accused is easily led to include self-incriminating evidence in such reports before being brought to trial.

2. Trials

The revised text of the Constitution adopted in March 1978 does not restore the guarantee of judicial independence laid down in Article 78 of the 1954 Constitution. This guarantee had been removed from the Constitution when it was first amended in 1975.

The party leadership in judicial work is an established practice. Chinese judges and officials have stressed on many occasions since the

1950s that the courts' work is supervised by the Chinese Communist Party (CCP). In political cases, investigators and party officials cooperate closely until prosecution starts and make recommendations for punishment; the judges seldom reject their recommendations, generally because they share the same viewpoint but also because they are responsible to political authorities. In any case, they cannot resist on the grounds of procedure because, when a case is brought to court, the dossiers prepared by the Public Security would normally include "sufficient evidence."

The judgment is therefore decided in advance after consultations between the judges, the investigators and party officials involved in the case, and trials are a mere formality.

The accused's right to defense, which was removed from the Constitution when it was first amended in 1975, was re-established in the 1978 Constitution. However, the function of defense lawyers, which existed in the mid-1950s in the PRC, has now disappeared. Besides, the right to defense is, in practice, very limited because non-admission of guilt is usually considered an aggravating circumstance (see below, penalties).

Trials can be divided into three main categories:

a. Closed trials: It is reported that the majority of political offenders have closed trials. Generally the defendant is taken to the court, but may also be called to a room in the place of detention. One or several judges and investigators may be present. The judge gives a summary of the case and asks the accused whether he agrees, or has anything to add. Then the sentence is announced and the defendant signs the judgment. After judgment, the sentence will sometimes be announced publicly through an official court notice posted in a public place.

b. Open trials (kaiting): During these the defendant can summon relatives, friends or neighbors to speak in his or her defense. To the extent that this procedure is used, however, it applies mainly in criminal cases and cases of minor importance, and has been rarely resorted to in the decade from 1966 to 1976. These "trials" in any case take place after the sentence has been decided, in the form of small-scale public meetings held in the defendant's work unit.

c. "Mass public trials": these trials take two forms: *xuanpan dahui,* "big meeting to announce the sentence," and *gongsheng,* "mass trial." Both involve a very large number of participants—up to tens of thousands of people—and are organized to mobilize the population and educate it through "negative examples." The *xuanpan dahui* is generally used for a group (sometimes large) of offenders belonging to various categories who are tried simultaneously. The *gongsheng,* on the other hand, involves fewer offenders; the purpose behind it, too, is to criticize harshly and "struggle against" the defendants. The *gongsheng* is a severe ordeal for the accused. The *gongsheng* occurs mainly during political campaigns, but may be held at other times also for cases involving the death penalty or long-term imprisonment.

3. Penalties

There are various types of informal penalties in China for those who make political "mistakes," such as "criticism" and "struggle" sessions (described later in this article). They apply to people who are considered to have simply committed "minor mistakes."

For more serious "mistakes" or offenses, China has both "administrative" and "criminal" penalties. The first category applies to offenders who are not officially regarded as "criminals." These "administrative" penalties can be inflicted by simple police order or by decision of a work/neighborhood/party unit, without a court decision. The "criminal" penalties apply to offenses officially defined as "crimes" and are imposed by the courts on police recommendation. The administrative and criminal penalties affecting political offenders are the following:

a. Administrative penalties (xingzheng chufen)

- "Supervised labor" or work "under supervision of the masses" (pei junzhong kanguan), which means that offenders may remain in society but are under surveillance: they have to engage in productive work, attend political sessions and report regularly to the cadres.
- "Rehabilitation through labor" (laodong jiaoyang), for which the offenders are sent to special camps (or farms) to labor and "re-educate" themselves. This is quite similar to "reform through labor" (see below), although it often involves slightly better detention conditions and is regarded as a milder punishment.

b. Criminal penalties (xingshi chufen)

- "Control" which is, in practice, similar to "supervised labor" since the offender usually remains in society, but which is imposed by a court on people convicted of an offense. It is often applied to offenders who have previously been given an informal or administrative punishment, and whose behavior has not improved.
- A term of imprisonment, generally carried out in a "reform through labor" (laodong gaizao) institution (camp, prison or farm).
- Life imprisonment, generally served in a prison.
- Death penalty suspended for two years, during which time the offender's attitude is observed to see whether commutation may be warranted. The sentence is generally carried out in a prison.
- Death penalty followed by immediate execution.

The decision as to which of these punishments to inflict is determined by the general characteristics of a case rather than by the nature of the specific offense. The main factors determining the punishment are the following ones:

- Whether the accused has "confessed" (i.e., pleads guilty or not).

Chinese officials have often stated that the main principles of the "party's policy" in judicial work is that "leniency is given to those who confess their crimes and severe punishment is given to those who refuse to do so."

- The determination of whether the accused belongs to the "people" or is an "enemy of the people." For this, class status is taken into account, and past history is examined in detail. Class origin is particularly important for political offenders since a "bad" family background makes them automatically potential "enemies of the people."

- The "seriousness" of the "crime" itself. It is weighed according to two sets of criteria: first, the official policy at the time (which defines as "criminal" certain attitudes or acts) and the importance of this type of "crime" in the local context; second, the accused's background and attitude (class status, past history, willingness to confess and repent) and in some cases the "opinions of the masses."

Thus, depending on the "circumstances of a case," the same offense may be treated either as a "mistake" or as a "crime," and punished either by an "administrative" or by a "criminal" punishment. However, there are no strict legal standards to help in making that distinction, and judges, police and party officials have wide discretion as regards judgment, especially in political cases.

4. Appeal and Reviews

Chinese law allows the defendant to make one appeal against conviction to a court higher than the one that passed the sentence. Political defendants seldom appeal. Just as a refusal to confess is considered an aggravating factor when sentence is decided upon, so may an appeal be similarly regarded and result in an increased sentence.

As well as the appeal permitted by law, a process of review can be undertaken while the offender is serving sentence. Political prisoners, however, seek redress through this procedure even more rarely than through appeal. Usually, they venture to ask for review only if strong evidence that the charges were unfounded has been discovered, or in special circumstances, such as those described below.

Apart from the judicial reviews, special "reviews of verdicts" have been undertaken at the national level since 1949. These special "reviews" are initiated by the central authorities. They are usually due to changes of policy. For instance, after the purge of the "gang of four" in October 1976, efforts were made to correct transgressions which they or their "followers" are alleged to have committed. Many examples of "reversal of the wrong verdicts" passed while the "gang of four" was in power were given by official sources in 1977 and early 1978. The total number of those rehabilitated or released in this process has not been disclosed, but partial figures have been given. On March 13, 1978, for instance, the official press reported that since

1976 more than 10,000 "victims of the gang of four" had been rehabilitated in Shanghai, some posthumously.

5. *The Death Penalty*

The main offenses liable to be punished by the death penalty in China are "major counter-revolutionary" acts, serious cases of corruption or of counterfeiting bank-notes, murder, sexual assault and other crimes involving violence.

The official policy regarding the death penalty has been recently reiterated by Professor Han Yu-tung, the Deputy Director of the Law Institute of the Chinese Academy of Social Sciences. In an interview with the New China News Agency in February 1978, he stated: "It is not yet possible to abolish capital punishment in China. But, our policy also stipulates that . . . in cases where it is marginal whether to execute, under no circumstances should there be an execution."

Between 1966 and 1976, a large number of executions were reportedly carried out during the political campaigns which marked the end of the Cultural Revolution.

Since the purge of the "gang of four" in October 1976, the international press has reported the appearance of many official notices announcing executions and death sentences. This suggests that a large number of executions have been carried out since the end of 1976, not only for crimes such as murder, rape, robbery and other common-law offenses but also sometimes for political offenses. For instance, the execution of a political offender named He Chunshu was announced in February 1978 in Canton by means of a public notice from Guangdong province High People's Court. The notice was dated February 18, 1978 and said that He Chunshu had been sentenced to death with immediate execution for printing and distributing a "counter-revolutionary" leaflet. The notice was remarkable in that, unlike most official announcements of convictions, it specified that He Chunshu had been sentenced to death according to Article 10, paragraph 3, of the "Act of the PRC for Punishment of Counter-Revolution," and that the sentence had been approved by the Supreme People's Court.

The notice stated that, after his arrest, he "persistently refused to admit his crime" and that "the people's anger" was "very great." Thus, the court sentenced him to immediate execution.

III
CORRECTIVE LABOR AND PENAL POLICY

The penal policy of the People's Republic of China places emphasis on the "reform" of offenders. Such reform is carried out by compelling both criminal and political offenders to engage in productive labor while undergoing political re-education. This policy is based on the principle that offenders can be and should be "transformed into new people" through work—that is, that their consciousness should be changed to conform to the political and economic standards of society. The prisoners' compulsory labor also serves the purpose of making penal institutions economically self-sufficient and of contributing to the economic development of the country.

Convicted or unconvicted political offenders are sent to a variety of places of detention. Various categories of offenders are often held in the same place of detention, but each category has its own regime. The penal institutions are officially defined as "instruments of the people's democratic dictatorship." They are run by the Public Security. The different categories (or places) of imprisonment are the following:

1. Detention Centers

The law provides that detention centers are to be used mainly for offenders who have not yet been tried, but that they may also hold convicted offenders sentenced to two years' imprisonment or less when it is "inconvenient" to send them to "labor-reform brigades."

Convicted offenders and those not yet convicted have different regimes in detention centers. According to the law, they must be kept separate, and whereas convicted offenders are compelled to work, those whose cases have not yet been judged may do so only if this does not hinder the investigation or trial. Furthermore, the law specifies that offenders not yet convicted whose cases are "major" must be kept in solitary confinement.

Whatever the seriousness of their case, political offenders appear to be often held in solitary confinement for varying periods at the beginning of their detention. Detainees as yet unconvicted reportedly receive only two meals a day, with insufficient food. Another frequent complaint made by former detainees concerns the overcrowding of cells in detention centers, especially during political campaigns.

2. Rehabilitation Through Labor Groups

The Chinese term *laodong jiaoyang*—more commonly used in its abbreviated form *laojiao*—can be translated as "rehabilitation through labor," "re-education through labor," or, more briefly, "labor re-education."

Those who are given this "administrative" punishment (without being convicted or tried) are sent either to farms holding only labor-rehabilitation offenders or to penal institutions (prison-factories, camps, farms) holding other categories of offenders, in which case they work and live separately from the latter.

3. Reform Through Labor Brigades

Reform through labor in Chinese is *laodong gaizao,* abbreviated to *laogai* (labor-reform).

The majority of sentenced prisoners serve their terms of imprisonment in "reform through labor corrective brigades" (abbreviated henceforth to "labor-reform brigades"). These penal brigades may constitute a part or the whole of a prison-factory, farm or camp; they may also constitute a temporary (or mobile) camp set up to build factories, railways, bridges, etc.

Labor-reform prisoners are often transferred from one camp to another according to the states' "economic needs." Those who receive long sentences (generally ten years or more) are particularly liable to be sent to do pioneer work in sparsely populated areas, often very far from their own homes. There is evidence that even when they remain in their home provinces, labor-reform prisoners are given the hardest work to do for the sake of the country's economy and are used as a mobile, unpaid labor force.

The prisons, farms and camps which hold various categories of offenders have separate "brigades" for labor-reform (convicted) prisoners, labor-rehabilitation offenders and "free-workers," but in the "labor-reform brigades" criminal and political prisoners usually live and work together.

4. Prisons

Prisons are generally in cities and provincial capitals. According to the law, they are intended to hold mainly major offenders sentenced to long-term imprisonment, over whom a strict control can be better maintained in prison than in labor-reform brigades. In fact, most prisons are factories and therefore include other types of offenders—labor-reform or labor-rehabilitation offenders, as well as "free-workers."

Major convicted offenders are separated from other offenders in prison and subjected to a different regime. They are in general not allowed to work until they are considered to have progressed in "ideological reform." The prohibition on work is regarded both as a punishment and a security measure to prevent contacts with other prisoners and the circulation of information about their cases.

IV
TREATMENT AND CONDITIONS

Conditions for prisoners in Chinese penal institutions have varied greatly at different periods according to changes in the country's economic or political situation. There are also, at any given time, important regional variations in the treatment of prisoners, and each type of imprisonment has its own particular regime. The conditions described in the report, therefore, are not meant to give an overall picture of the situation of prisoners in the whole of the country at any given moment.

However, several aspects of detention conditions have, over the years, been the subject of constant complaints by prisoners, in particular the system of punishment, the inadequacy of food, and the lack of proper medical care, which make it difficult for prisoners to comply with the requirements of corrective labor. Prisoners are expected to accept hard work and suffering without complaint as an indication that they are trying to make up for their past crimes or mistakes. If, on the other hand, they complain, are slow at work or are judged to have a "bad" attitude, they are classified as "resisting reform" and are punished in various ways, the ultimate punishment being an increase of sentence.

1. Work

Prisoners' testimonies and interviews with officials indicate that the "normal" working day in prison-factories and penal farms varies from eight to twelve hours depending on production needs, and the prisoners normally have one day of rest either every week or every fortnight.

The hardship caused by forced labor is officially regarded as an integral part of the prisoner's reform and is generally made more acute by other aspects of the treatment of prisoners, in particular:

• The close examination of everyone's attitude at work. On a routine basis, this is done during the evening's "study sessions." Insufficient work is considered an indication of a "bad" attitude and leads to punishment.

• The inadequacy of food. The energy needed for an average of eight to twelve hours' manual work a day, plus one or two hours of "study" in the evening, could only come from a high food ration, enabling prisoners to remain in good health and still do the work expected of them. However, the majority of prisoners receive insufficient food.

2. Food

In considering prisoners' diet, it should be noted that dairy products are rarely used in China, and that fruit and sweets are usually taken between meals. Oil and pork fat is used for cooking and sugar is included in some meat or fish dishes.

Prisoners receive a basic diet of cereals, vegetables, oil, and only occasionally fish or meat. The lack of protein is not compensated for by quantity.

A man between 30 and 40 undertaking eight to twelve hours' manual labor a day generally needs between fifty to sixty *catties* of cereals a month

(1 catty = 500 grams). The majority of prisoners have almost always received less than this amount and hunger is a feature of their lives.

Food is rationed according to the category of imprisonment; for instance, typical rations in labor-reform brigades seem to have been about forty *catties* a month in the early 1970s. Offenders not yet convicted and held for investigation in detention centers generally do not work and are fed only twice a day. For instance, the diet in the detention center of Huiyang county (Guangdong province) in 1970-72 consisted of:

- 25 or 26 *catties* of rice a month.
- 150 grams of oil a month.
- vegetables (amount depending on what the detainees grew). Four different kinds were served, but they were badly cooked, being boiled until they turned black.
- 100-150 grams of meat only four times a year during the annual festivals. As the meat was fatty, and a rare dish for the prisoners, it caused diarrhea.

Offenders undergoing "rehabilitation through labor" have slightly better food than convicted prisoners. However, in general, their treatment is not substantially different from that of "labor-reform" prisoners. Although they receive wages and have some additional privileges, their work conditions and the discipline to which they are submitted are similar to those of convicted prisoners.

3. Medical Care

Amnesty International does not know what is at present the prevailing situation regarding prisoners' medical treatment. However, over the years, prisoners have often complained that proper medical care is not given to them until they are seriously ill, and some cases have been reported of prisoners who have died of illnesses which were not treated in time. Although responsibility in such cases usually lies with local officials, there is no doubt that their attitude stems from official policy vis-à-vis offenders. Self-sacrifice is constantly demanded of prisoners as a proof of reform, and so they are expected to work to the limit of their strength. Often they are not considered worthy of being treated as citizens, and adequate medical attention is granted as a privilege rather than a right.

Some recent reports continue to mention the inadequacy of medical care. In Guandong province, the *Lianping* camp, which was opened in 1971 and held more than 2,000 prisoners in 1974, had no medical establishment and no doctor among the official staff of the camp throughout that period. One of the prisoners was a doctor and was probably able to examine prisoners occasionally. However, it is said that sick prisoners were not treated until they became very seriously ill, in which case the doctor from a nearby people's commune was sometimes called in to examine them, and if they were in a desperate state, they were sent to a hospital in the district.

4. Discipline and Treatment

The Act for Reform Through Labor includes a system of rewards and punishments.

For prisoners who are considered to behave "well," the rewards in order of importance are to receive a commendation, a material reward, a "merit," a reduction of sentence or conditional release. The last two are granted only after the camp or prison officials' recommendation has been submitted to the Public Security agency in charge of review and approved by the appropriate people's court.

Prisoners whose conduct is not judged satisfactory can be punished in various ways. One can distinguish between "ordinary" punishments and "formal" ones.

"Ordinary" punishments are those which can be inflicted at any time for minor "misconduct," such as breaches of discipline in the daily routine. They include: reduction of food ration for a short period; temporary loss of the right to receive visits, correspondence or parcels; subjection to criticism meetings or, in more serious cases, to a "struggle" session.

"Formal" punishments are usually announced during special meetings held once or twice a year, depending on the place. These meetings are preceded by a period of intense ideological mobilization, during which each prisoner's attitude during the previous year or six months is closely examined. At the end of this period, all prisoners are assembled for an "award/punishment meeting" to hear the result of this special "training."

"Formal" punishments are generally imposed on prisoners who have been noted for bad behavior during the preceding months—that is, who are likely to have already been given ordinary punishments. The mildest "formal" punishments are "warnings" and "demerits." Both are simple records of bad behavior, but an accumulation of several warnings or demerits results in a harsher punishment. The most severe punishments include solitary confinement and increase of sentence.

A former prisoner has described to Amnesty International the conditions in which he was held twice in solitary confinement:

The cell was very small, just about large enough to lie down in. There was only straw on the floor and a small window in one wall. The cell was guarded day and night by "activists" (zealous or highly regarded prisoners). The food received in solitary confinement is about one-third less than the normal rations. Once a day a bucket is passed in to the punished prisoner to evacuate the excrement. During the seasonal production [period of intensive work] prisoners in solitary confine-

70

ment may be allowed to go out to work. They are escorted to the place of work by activists and have to work harder than other prisoners. During work they are forbidden to talk to other prisoners. In any case, other prisoners would run away if a punished prisoner tried to do so. In case of illness, a prisoner in solitary confinement may be treated. The length of the punishment depends on how thoroughly the prisoner recognizes his "mistakes," and guarantees that he will labor actively, reform his thoughts, side actively with the government and struggle against the "bad things" and "bad elements." The maximum length of solitary confinement would normally be half a year.

The duration of solitary confinement apparently varies from camp to camp, but conditions are generally similar to those described above. In other words, solitary confinement is not only a period of physical isolation, but a punishment involving confinement in a tiny cell and a significant reduction in food rations.

Officials in penal institutions occasionally use handcuffs and fetters to break the resistance of an offender. This method is said to be used both in labor-reform institutions and in detention centers.

In detention centers, detainees have been handcuffed or fettered either as a disciplinary measure (for a breach of regulations) or to hasten confession. The report gives several examples of such cases.

In the case of convicted offenders in prison-factories, labor-reform farms or camps, prisoners put in solitary confinement or to work under special discipline are sometimes chained during part or all of the period of punishment.

The suffering caused by such practices, even if their use is "limited," is apparently not regarded by officials who employ them as a contravention of Article 5 of the law on reform through labor, which strictly prohibits cruel treatment and corporal punishment (torture).

The maltreatment of detainees and arbitrary arrests carried out since the Cultural Revolution are now officially attributed to the influence of the purged leaders. However, some of the forms of harassment described by victims of the "gang of four" were used long before the Cultural Revolution. Intimidation and humiliation have always been part of interrogation techniques, and "struggle" sessions are still used nowadays against political offenders.

Physical torture is prohibited by law and is generally not inflicted on prisoners. Quite often, however, people brought to "struggle" sessions are subjected to intense psychological pressure, molested and sometimes even beaten up. A former prisoner, *Bao Ruowang,* has given the following description of the "struggle" session:

It is a peculiarly Chinese invention, combining intimidation, humiliation and sheer exhaustion. Briefly described, it is an intellectual gang-beating of one man by many, sometimes even thousands, in which the victim has no defense, even the truth. . . .

There is a system and a rationale behind it all. . . . A man must be made to confess before he is punished, even if his punishment has been decided beforehand. . . .

At the beginning, even if the victim tells the truth or grovelingly admits to any accusation hurled at him, his every word will be greeted with insults and shrieks of contradiction. He is ringed by jeering, hating faces, screaming in his ear, spitting; fists swipe menacingly close to him and everything he says is branded a lie. At the end of the day he is led to a room, locked up, given some food and left with the promise that the next day will be even worse. . . .

After three or four days the victim begins inventing sins he has never committed, hoping that an admission monstrous enough might win him a reprieve. After a week of struggling he is prepared to go to any lengths.[3]

V

REFORM, RELEASES AND AMNESTIES

1. Reform

In addition to compulsory labor, offenders are subjected to compulsory "political education." The Chinese penal system does not simply make such education compulsory: it also requires that all prisoners demonstrate that they "voluntarily" accept their reform and that they participate actively in their own program of reform.

The reform program includes both political education and ideological or "thought" reform. This is carried out by daily "study sessions" (held in the evening by groups of ten to fifteen prisoners) and by periodical "examinations" of the prisoners' behavior. These include routine sessions of "self-examination" and "self-criticism," "criticism" and "struggle" meetings for misconduct, as well as periodical campaigns of "mutual denunciations" and "admission of guilt" during which each prisoner's behavior is examined in depth.

In spite of official requirements that offenders should "voluntarily" acknowledge their need for reform, they are, in fact, left with no free choice. As non-conformity with the rigid standards of behavior imposed by official policy may lead to severe punishment and ultimately to an increase of sentence, the majority of offenders generally feel obliged to comply with them.

A former prisoner, who had been held in 1968 in the prison of Sechen Ho *(Shiquanhe,* Autonomous Region of Tibet), reported that during the five months he was there, seven prisoners were punished by solitary confinement, either because they had complained about their treatment or because they did not express "proper thoughts" during the political education sessions. He also said that all of them were kept in solitary confinement for at least the five months that he himself spent in prison. The daily study sessions were held from 8:30 p.m. to 9:00 p.m. by groups *(xiaozu)* of about twelve prisoners. Prisoners had to submit their views on the subject in hand to the two officials conducting the sessions. Those who refused to do so, under the pretext of ignorance, were, according to this report, branded "enemies of socialism" and threatened with solitary confinement.

2. Releases

According to Chinese law, the reform through labor bodies can "retain," place and find employment for offenders due for release in any one of the following circumstances:

1. when they themselves want to stay in the labor-reform brigade and get employment, and are needed for reform through labor production;

2. if they have no home to return to and no chance of employment;

3. if they are criminals who have undergone reform through labor in sparsely populated districts and, at the end of their term of imprisonment, are needed to join settlers, found a family, and stay where they are.

"Retained" ex-prisoners are called by various names: *liuchang renyuan,* "stay longer" or "retained" personnel; *xinsheng renyuan,* "new life" or "reborn" personnel; *nongchang nongong,* "state farm agricultural worker;" *zhigong,* "hired worker." The term "free-workers" has been used frequently outside China for "retained" ex-convicts and, for convenience, is used in this report.

Amnesty International does not know what proportion of prisoners is released (unconditionally) and what portion is "retained," but it has received information about "free-workers" retained in penal institutions against their will. Ex-prisoners have reported that the practice of "retaining" offenders at the end of their sentences is widespread and affects equally those sentenced to labor-reform and those "assigned" to labor-rehabilitation. The discipline to which they are subjected and the fact that they are often treated as second-class citizens makes their life very much like that of prisoners. In one such case, a carpenter from Canton named Hu, who became a "free-worker" in 1970, is said to have committed suicide after despairing of ever being allowed to return to normal life.

3. Amnesties

There has been only one general amnesty in the People's Republic of China since 1949. It was declared by presidential order on September 17, 1959 to commemorate the tenth anniversary of the founding of the PRC. The amnesty was to apply to the following categories of prisoners; "war criminals," "counter-revolutionary criminals" and "ordinary" (common-law) criminals. In all cases there was a condition: the prisoners concerned were to be those who had "really reformed from evil to good."

Special amnesties for war criminals were also decreed in 1960, 1961 and 1963 by presidential orders, and there were reportedly two others up to 1966. According to a former Nationalist official, Duan Kewen, who was imprisoned in Fushun until 1975, between fifty and sixty "war criminals" were released from Fushun under the amnesties declared between 1959 and 1966. More recently, several groups of high-ranking officials from the former Guomindang administration, most of whom were arrested about 1950, were released by special amnesty in 1974 and 1975.

VI

APPENDIX

The report gives in appendices detailed information about five prisoners, which is summarized below.

1. Lin Xiling

In 1957, the year of her arrest, Lin Xiling was a fourth-year law student at China People's University in Peking and a party member.

Lin Xiling came from a poor family and had received only an elementary education before she entered university. When she was fifteen, she joined a People's Liberation Army art group, leaving it in 1953 with the qualification of "cultural teacher." She was then allowed to enter university on the recommendation of the party and was admitted to China People's University in 1953.

In the spring of 1957, she took an active part in the "Hundred Flowers" movement, criticizing the lack of democracy in Chinese society. Like many others, she was consequently labeled a "rightist" and arrested. According to information received by Amnesty International, Lin Xiling was sentenced to twenty years' imprisonment with deprivation of civil rights for life, and was still detained in the mid-1970s. Her present whereabouts are unknown.

2. Wang Mingdao

Wang Mingdao is a Chinese Protestant pastor who has been imprisoned since 1957 because of his religious beliefs. If alive, he will now be 78 years old.

Wang Mingdao was first arrested and detained for a few months in 1955 for refusing to join a pro-governmental religious movement—the "Three Self-Reform Movement"—which advocated severance of relations between Chinese churches and churches abroad. He was released after he signed a confession, but later reportedly informed the authorities that his

74

confession had been made under duress and did not represent his true opinions. Probably because of this, he was rearrested in 1957 during the "anti-rightist" campaign. It is reported that he was first sentenced to fifteen years' imprisonment and that this sentence was increased to life imprisonment when he was retried in 1963. Wang Mingdao was last reported to be still alive and detained in 1974.

3. Chamba Lobsang

Prior to his arrest in 1959, Chamba Lobsang, about 26, was a monk in the Shekar Chode Monastery in Shekar District (Autonomous Region of Tibet).

According to the testimony of a Tibetan refugee who witnessed the events, Chamba Lobsang was arrested in October 1959 together with thirty-seven other people from the district, after the area was surrounded by Chinese troops. At a public meeting organized in April 1960 in Shekar, he was accused of "exploiting the masses in the name of religion" and sentenced to life imprisonment.

Chamba Lobsang and others sentenced at that meeting were last reported to have been detained in Ngari prison (jurisdiction of Karkang) in 1964. Their present fate is unknown.

4. Deng Qingshan

Deng Qingshan, a young man of 26, was arrested in 1970 in a rural production brigade during the "one-strike three-anti" campaign and accused of having spread stories "slandering Chairman Mao" between 1967 and 1969.

According to information published in *Huang He* (No 1, 1976), a Chinese language Hong Kong review, Deng Qingshan was made the object of investigation during this campaign because of his "bad" background. The charges against Deng were reportedly based on the statements of "witnesses" who had been intimidated to testify against him. In November 1970, an official notice announced that Deng Qingshan had been sentenced to fifteen years' imprisonment, plus three years' deprivation of civil rights after release, on this charge of slander.

5. Li Zhengtian

Li Zhengtian is one of the three authors of a wall poster displayed publicly in Canton in November 1974. The poster—which was signed by the pseudonym "Li Yizhe"—criticized the repression that had taken place when Lin Biao was in power and demanded that the "rights of the people" be protected.

Shortly after it was publicized, the poster was officially criticized as "reactionary," and in the spring of 1975 its three authors— Li Zhengtian,

Chen Yiyang and Wang Xizhe—were sent to work "under supervision" outside Canton. Li Zhengtian was sent to a mine in Shaoguan district, north of Guandong province, and was said to be still there in 1976.

In early 1977, it was reported that the three young men had been labeled "counter-revolutionary." Another report in July 1977 alleged that Li Zhengtian had been sentenced to life imprisonment. This has not been confirmed, but other reports have mentioned that Li, Chen and Wang had been sent to labor camps. Their present fate and whereabouts are unknown.

NOTES

1. *Mao Zedong Sixiang Wansui* (Long Life Mao Tse-tung Thought), 1969, pp. 38-39.

2. "On Socialist Democracy and Legal System" by Li Yizhe; translated in *"Chinois Si Vous Savez . . . ,"* Paris 1976; *"Issues and Studies,"* January 1976; *"China: Wer Gegen Wen?"* Berlin, 1977.

3. Extracts from Bao Ruowang (Jean Pasqualini) and Rudolph Chelminsky, *Prisoner of Mao,* New York, 1973, pp. 58-61.

Chiang Ching-Kuo
and Taiwan: A Profile*

*Tillman Durdin***

I

One of Asia's least known national leaders, Chiang Ching-kuo is an affable but steely Chinese who some day may determine what the United States can, or will, do about one of the most intractable problems it now faces—the ultimate fate of Taiwan. Strongly influenced by a communist education and the adoption of a Russian life-style during twelve years as a young man in the Soviet Union, Chiang brings a strangely mixed, some feel an enigmatic, personality and background to an area sure to be a major Asian trouble spot in the years ahead. Today, at sixty-six, he is the new power-holder on the strategic island of Taiwan, having three years ago moved into leadership of the Chinese Nationalist government long dominated by his famous father, Chiang Kai-shek.

Protected by the United States, Taiwan is claimed by the rulers of Communist China, and they are determined some day to control it. Adamantly, Chiang Ching-kuo vows to the contrary. Since establishment of de facto relations between Washington and Peking in 1972, the Chinese Communists have talked less belligerently than before about "liberating" Taiwan. But more recently, as neither the United States nor the Nationalist regime has shown any signs of giving up their claim to the island, they have begun to display increasing impatience and irritation.

Save for fifty years of rule as a Japanese colony (1895-1945), Taiwan has been officially a part of China for at least three centuries, and its return to China from Japan was one of the pledges made by Allied leaders during World War II. The Chinese Communists plainly do not intend to see it indefinitely continue as a presumptuous, rival, separate entity. As Peking leaders push their demands and tempers mount, Chiang Ching-kuo's position will be pivotal. Were he to remain intransigent, not even U.S. pressure could nudge Taiwan, just one hundred miles off the China coast, into Pe-

*Copyright 1975, Foreign Policy Research Institute. Reprinted by permission.
**Tillman Durdin is the former *New York Times* correspondent for Asia.

king's orbit. Thus, in the making or avoidance of a Peking-Washington-Taipei crisis over Taiwan, Chiang's cards may turn out to be as strong as those of Henry Kissinger or Chou En-lai.

The cult of concealment that surrounds the personal life of this shy and wary man—the press is restricted to reporting only his public acts and image; few anecdotes circulate; and he reveals his inner self only to a few intimates, who decline to talk about him—makes him something of an unknown quantity to the world at large. But his public record indicates that as a decision-maker he measures up to the company of Kissinger and Chou.

Sons who succeed to the positions of forceful fathers often turn out to be weak and disappointing. Chiang Ching-kuo does not fit this pattern. He has already shown himself to be strong-willed, decisive and effective. These characteristics largely account for the fact that the subtropical island of Taiwan is today stable and remarkably relaxed in spite of pressure from the communist-controlled mainland and the snubs and buffeting its government has received in international affairs over the past few years. The island's economy grew in 1974 despite the world energy crisis, its per capita income reached $700, and its foreign trade rose in value to more than $12 billion.

A short, rather stout, amiable-looking man, Chiang Ching-kuo wields authority from his position as president of the Executive Yuan—premier of the cabinet, in Western terminology—reinforced by his rank in the top leadership of the Kuomintang, the authoritarian party that prescribes policy for the government. In this position, he has combined toughness and efficiency with the outward geniality suited to his rotund appearance.

In a fashion far different from his lean, aloof, austere father's, Chiang Ching-kuo, or CCK, as he is often familiarly called, tempers sternness with a man-of-the-masses approach to the sixteen million people of Taiwan. Because he believes it good statecraft and also enjoys it, he mingles freely in crowds, attends many public affairs, makes impromptu, often emotional speeches, and several times a month deserts his work-laden Taipei office for non-protocol forays into down-country Taiwan to visit casually with farmers, factory hands, youth groups and soldiers. His father was incapable of this kind of informality.

The premier enjoys venturing, unheralded and unguarded, with a companion or two, into small country restaurants, and sitting down to chat with other patrons while having a bowl of thick soup with steamed bread. Recently, lunch time came when he and several officials were visiting a fisherman's family in southern Taiwan. The fisherman urged them to share his family's food. Ching-kuo insisted, however, that they must be no expense to their host, whereupon he and his companions pulled out packets of instant noodles and produced their own meal. On such occasions he cracks jokes with a boyish grin and looks half his age. "Some people may think this is a sham," a Taipei official close to him says, "but the fact is that he really is interested in ordinary people, and would much rather be with them than attending a reception with a head of state."

He can also be amiable in relaxed official situations. But Taiwan today is beset with manifold domestic and international problems and unrelenting political and military pressure from the colossus of mainland China. Its governance demands almost unremitting attention to state duties little conductive to pleasantries. Chiang Ching-kuo directs a regime that, under his father, lost a bloody, twenty-year struggle with the Chinese Communists for control of China. In failure, it retreated in 1949 from the mainland to the small, beautiful island of Taiwan. There, on 13,885 square miles of territory, it still calls itself the government of the Republic of China—all China—and still contests world status and the loyalty of the 800 million Chinese people ruled by Mao Tse-tung in Peking. Seasoned by long and earnest tutelage under his father, decades of experience in war-torn China, and twelve formative years in the alien environment of Stalinist Russia, CCK has taken over this legacy.

II

He was born in the ancestral town of Chikow, in the coastal province of Chekiang, the child of an arranged union between his father at the age of twenty and an unschooled village girl named Mao Chieh-ju. As a child, he rarely saw his father, who was away from home most of the time engrossed in revolutionary and military activities. Sent to elementary and high school in Shanghai and Peking, he himself was soon caught up in the revolutionary ferment sweeping China at the time, and became a leader of student demonstrations against foreign control of Chinese affairs and against local Chinese despots. In warlord-ruled Peking, he was arrested during one riotous demonstration and held for two weeks.

As nationalist and revolutionary sentiment increased, the newborn Chinese Communist movement had begun to cooperate with the Nationalist Kuomintang Party, of which Chiang Kai-shek was then the military chieftain and Sun Yat-sen the titular and ideological leader. The USSR, the new home base of revolution, promoted and assisted this alliance, whose aim was overthrow of the old order of social oppression, poverty, disunity, warlordism, and foreign imperialist exploitation. Soviet military and political advisors came to work with the elder Chiang, and he left his revolutionary base in Canton briefly for an orientation visit to Moscow.

In Peking, Ching-kuo fell under the influence of Chinese and Russian communists who inspired him with the idea, then popular among Chinese youth, of going for study and training to the Soviet Union—where, Russians had told him, "neither an emperor nor a god" was in control, but "the workers and peasants themselves." Years later, Ching-kuo was to say that he "became a victim of the psychological atmosphere" of the times. One of his last acts before leaving China, at the age of sixteen, was to join his father's Kuomintang Party.

In Moscow, he was an apt pupil at Sun Yat-sen University, a training center the Russians had set up under Karl Radek for Chinese revolutionary cadres. With considerable frankness and detail, he has recounted his experiences there and during his subsequent life in the USSR in a book written after returning to China called *My Days in Soviet Russia.* Impressed by the frugality and discipline shown by Chinese Communist students at the university, in contrast to the loose behavior of some Kuomintang students, he joined the Chinese Communist Youth Corps and seemed well on the road to becoming a good communist. "The Chinese Communist Party had a branch office in Moscow," Ching-kuo recalled in his book, "and its organization and methods of training were well arranged."

He rapidly conquered Russian, wrote revolutionary articles for student publications, and found he could rouse Moscow workers to applause with speeches in Russian on revolutionary subjects. But his developing communist orthodoxy was shaken by news from China in 1927 that his father had turned violently against the Chinese Communists, and by his own growing tendency, under the influence of Radek, to agree with Leon Trotsky's opposition to Stalin, whose views were being slavishly followed by the Chinese Communist leadership in Moscow. Ching-kuo became the leader of a secret Trotskyite student underground, arguing that Stalinist ideas on revolutionary tactics were unsound, and that Stalinist-type communism was not applicable to China. He met Stalin for the first time during this period, when Stalin came to the university to lecture on "The Mistakes of the Trotsky Clique" in an attempt to counteract Trotskyite influence at the school. Ching-kuo says that he "was not impressed" and "stuck to my activities against the Stalin regime."

When he finished the university in 1927 he wanted to return to China. But the Chinese and Russian communists thought it against their interests to allow him to rejoin his now violently anti-communist father. He was at loose ends for a time before deciding to enlist in the Soviet Red Army, a not uncommon practice for Asians drawn to and kept in the USSR during those turbulent years. Some became permanent members of the Soviet Communist Party. The Soviets were quite prepared to take individuals like Chiang Ching-kuo into their armed forces in anticipation of the possibility that, after years of indoctrination and service, they would serve Moscow's purposes in some way. One such, the Korean Kim Il Sung, was installed in power by the Soviets in North Korea after World War II.

Ching-kuo was accepted, and made such a good record as an enlisted man that he was among five top trainees selected in 1928 for advanced studies at the Central Tolmatchev Military and Political Institute in Leningrad. "I began to be interested very much in my new life," he wrote in his book. His instructor in strategy was Marshal Tukashevsky, one of the top

Soviet generals later executed by Stalin in his bloody political purges. He did well in both political and military studies, and in his second year (under pressure of the Chinese Communist delegation in Moscow, and after renouncing his Trotskyite leanings in a public statement), Ching-kuo became an alternate member of the CPSU. By the time he had completed his three years at the Institute, he had been promoted to be chief of staff of a division. He had also made a special study of guerrilla fighting, and in addition to numerous other articles on political and military subjects, he wrote a paper on the "Tactics of Guerrilla Warfare."

But because he was his father's son, the Chinese Communist delegation continued to view him with suspicion and to urge a similar caution on the Russians. Just before his graduation in May 1930, the Moscow delegation charged him (he says falsely) with intriguing with Chinese students in the USSR against the Stalin regime. This seems to account for the fact that his request either to be allowed to return to China or to be assigned to duty in the Soviet army was turned down. Seeking a new career, he began to work as a common laborer in a Moscow electrical plant, while studying engineering at night. He did so well at the plant that he was recommended for the post of assistant engineer. But again the Chinese Communist delegation used its influence with the Soviet authorities, and the appointment was never made.

Embittered by such experiences, Ching-kuo became implicated in political disturbances at Lenin University (the new name of Sun Yat-sen University), where he was living in a student dormitory, and publicly denounced Chen Shao-yu, the head of the Chinese Communist delegation. Chen engineered a harsh punishment. The Soviets assigned Ching-kuo to forced labor, first on a collective farm near Moscow and then in a Siberian gold mine. After three years of this grim existence, during which (he says) he developed an "invincible attachment in my heart" for the professors, students, aristocrats, engineers, thieves and kulaks who worked and suffered alongside him, he was evidently judged to have done his penance and was transferred in 1933 to be a technician at the Ural Heavy Machinery Plant in Sverdlovsk. Here he abjured politics, resumed his studies, applied himself diligently to his job, and soon became assistant director of the plant and editor of the local *Heavy Industry Daily*.

Late the following year, he again became the object of political harassment. In his book, Ching-kuo says: "Despite my own inactivity on the political scene, I became again a pawn in the hands of the Chinese Communists and, for some reason unclear to me, under tighter control by the Russian Communists." From his account of what happened, it appears that both the Chinese and Russians wanted to imbue him with a sense of apprehension preparatory to using him for a propaganda coup. He was regularly shadowed by NKVD agents, and once was called to Moscow by his old nemesis, Chen Shao-yu, to answer vague charges of anti-Soviet and anti-communist views and activities. When he was summoned to Moscow once more in January 1935, it became clear that Chen and the Soviets wanted a statement from him to counteract stories circulating in China about his mistreatment in the USSR, and to answer what an NKVD official told him was a request from his father's government that he be sent back to China. Chen told him: "It is rumored in China that you have been arrested in Russia. You should write a letter to your mother saying that you are working and are completely free here."

Under pressure by Chen during four days of interrogation, vague threats of death and equally vague promises that he might some day be able to realize his frequently voiced desire to return to China if he cooperated, he signed a letter to his mother written by Chen. In recounting the episode in his book, Chiang does not say what the letter contained. But this appears to have been the missive published at the time in the Leningrad *Pravda*, in which he denounced his father (who by now had divorced Ching-kuo's mother so that he could marry Soong Mei-ling, the present Madame Chiang) as a "traitor to our country," and rejected an appeal from his mother that he return home.

The harassment continued. Almost his only solace during this period was the understanding and solicitude of an attractive young Russian woman who worked in his factory. They were married in 1935, shortly before official hostility toward him increased in concert with the 1936 Moscow purge trials. Chiang was dropped as a party candidate and dismissed from his factory and from his job as newspaper editor. He seemed headed for another period of forced labor.

III

Then, almost miraculously for him, came the Soviet-approved rapprochement between the Chinese Communists and the Kuomintang—the united front against the threatened Japanese invasion of China. Now all smiles, the Russians suddenly told him he could return to China. He left in April 1936, with his wife Faina and their two children.

Neither Ching-kuo nor his father has ever revealed his inner thoughts as they had their first rendezvous in the lake city of Hangchow. They must have regarded each other warily. Ching-kuo must surely have had qualms about the prospect of adjusting himself to a father he scarcely knew, and to a society so vastly different from the one in which he had lived for so long. But the bitterness of his experiences in the USSR and the critical views he had come to hold about Soviet communism eased the path to reconciliation. He agreed to subject himself to a period of retraining, study and self-examination; his father held out the prospect that after this remolding, he would be named to an official post. To signal their rapprochement, inspired articles appeared in the Shanghai press branding reports of their estrangement as "Russian inventions."

Thus, both his reactions to his life in the Soviet Union and the attractions of a "crown prince" role in the Nationalist regime motivated Ching-kuo in his reintegration into the Chinese scene. His book—the outcome of this period of self-examination—is testimony to the political conclusions reached from his Russian experience. He calls his twelve years there a "nightmare," and brands the communists as "red bandits" who depended chiefly upon "violence and heretical doctrine" to ensnare young people—who, "once caught, can hardly struggle free without considerable courage, determination, and peril."

Much of his twelve years as a communist cadre inevitably remained with him, including a predilection for a strong centrally-controlled system of government, his wariness, his affinity for socializing with the ordinary man—his "proletarian outlook," as his friends put it—and a first-hand knowledge of how communist regimes think and act. But upon returning home, his initial undertaking was a program of resinification under his father's guidance, and during the following years Ching-kuo's Chinese heritage and loyalties have clearly gained dominance over the legacy of his Soviet years. He has repeatedly proved his fealty to his native land and to his father, and also his ability to adjust to a Chinese life-style. In the quietness of the old family residence in Chikow, he refurbished his knowledge of the Chinese national language and embarked on an intensive study of Chinese history, philosophy and culture. Significantly, the language spoken between his wife and himself today is not the Russian he learned so well in the Soviet Union, but the Ningpo dialect of his ancestral district, a difficult idiom Faina, in deference to him, has learned to speak with easy fluency.

With the outbreak of the Sino-Japanese war in August 1937, the Generalissimo put Ching-kuo in charge of a major area in South Kiangsi that remained outside the control of invading Japanese armies. (Left behind in Chikow, his mother was killed in a Japanese air raid.) He ran an efficient, if authoritarian, administration. He and Faina gave boisterous, hard-drinking parties in the Russian manner for Americans stationed at his Kanhsien headquarters after the United States entered the war against Japan. A favorite stunt was to strip to the waist and challenge his guests to a wrestling match, or to lie flat on his back and invite anyone to jump on his hard-muscled stomach.

Frequently called to the wartime capital at Chungking, Ching-kuo increasingly became the trusted confidant of his father in the latter's tortured dealings with the Americans and with intriguing Chinese political factions. As a member of an official mission to Moscow in 1945, he helped to negotiate the Sino-Soviet treaty whereby China recognized the independence of Soviet-dominated Outer Mongolia—once Chinese territory—in fulfillment of a pledge Roosevelt had given to Stalin at Yalta. During a personal meeting with Stalin, he failed to soften Soviet terms.

He flew to see Stalin again in 1946 as Foreign Affairs Commissioner for Manchuria, then occupied by Soviet troops, in an effort to reach an agreement with the Soviets in view of the looming Communist-Kuomintang civil war. The Generalissimo had nourished some slender hope that yielding on Outer Mongolia might be reciprocated by Soviet support for his government as against the Communists. Stalin's terms were too stiff. He demanded a Kuomintang-Communist coalition that would turn away from the United States and move within the Soviet orbit. Ching-kuo relayed his father's decision to reject the proposition. On either of these trips to Moscow, he could easily have defected if his communist training had so inclined him. The fact that he did not was evidence that he had firmly reoriented his loyalties to China and to his father. He was to demonstrate this repeatedly by his actions in the years ahead.

IV

The agonizing years of Kuomintang defeat by the Communists followed. During this time Ching-kuo served as a troubleshooter for his father. His duties ranged from helping to organize Taiwan (which had reverted from Japanese to Chinese rule in 1945) as a base of retreat, to serving briefly as an economic czar in Shanghai in a stern but futile effort to check runaway inflation and official corruption at the point of a gun.

The embittering fallback to Taiwan in late 1949 found government personnel and the beaten Kuomintang forces that managed to reach the island confused, demoralized, and riddled by Communist agents. A revolt by the Taiwanese—the local-born people of Chinese ancestry—against the harsh rule of Kuomintang administrators, who had preceded the Chiangs, had been suppressed only after thousands had been killed. The mass of the population was hostile and sullen toward a regime run by mainland Chinese. The Nationalist leadership decided that survival and an eventual return to the mainland were possible only through rigorous ideological reindoctrination and the elimination of dissidents.

Turning to one he knew he could trust, the Generalissimo put Ching-kuo in charge of a massive crackdown in both the military and civilian sectors. An all-pervasive secret police system was employed to root out individuals and groups regarded as subversive and to expose conspiracies. The regime executed hundreds and imprisoned thousands more. Named head of a General Political Department in the Ministry of Defense, CCK organized a communist-style political commissar system that checked on loyalty and indoctrinated the armed forces in anti-communist, Kuomintang precepts and fealty to the Generalissimo. He formed a China Youth Anti-Communist National Salvation Corps to spearhead political action among the young. Taiwanese who found rule by the mainlanders intolerable and supported independence for the island were rigorously suppressed. Operating in the shadows, CCK became one of the most feared men in the leadership. He had no apologies for the repression that went on well into the 1970s. Arguing that the Communists had won the mainland with smaller but thoroughly indoctrinated and disciplined forces because the huge Nationalist army was corruptly led, poorly indoctrinated, and without discipline, he told Allen Whiting, an American Sinologist, in 1955: "This is the only way to fight communism. Our principles commit us to democracy; but so long as we let communism exist, we can never implement our principles and can never have democracy."[1]

In any case, Taiwan survived outside the communist orbit. With American aid and protection, it has stabilized and developed into a flourishing, prosperous island state. In contrast to the first desperate years on Taiwan, the regime has softened. A measure of elected representative government has been instituted at local and provincial levels, and more and more Taiwanese have been appointed to important posts in the national government. Ching-kuo's National Salvation Corps has evolved into a welfare and recreational organization only secondarily concerned with political surveillance. Repression is less than it used to be, and in fact is less necessary. Economic growth, rising living standards and full employment have combined with government reforms to make the regime more acceptable to the island's population. The Taiwanese majority has particularly benefited from the general prosperity.

To be sure, the system is still authoritarian. The Kuomintang continues to use the guided democracy principles of Sun Yat-sen as the ideology for one-party rule. Under martial law and the emergency regulations in effect since the retreat from the mainland, the president has arbitrary powers and the regime retains the underpinnings of clandestine police controls, secret arrests and arbitrary imprisonment. Nevertheless, society is certainly much freer than on the communist-ruled mainland.

The father-son collaboration of the initial years on Taiwan further consolidated the elder Chiang's confidence in Ching-kuo. As the Generalissimo became more feeble with age, he made clear his intention of handing over the Nationalist leadership to his son by naming him to a succession of progressively more important posts that completed Ching-kuo's apprenticeship. He was put in charge of demobilizing and developing a job program for 100,000 aging war veterans, as well as resettling 15,000 Chinese Communist soldiers—prisoners of the Korean War—who elected to come to Taiwan rather than go back to mainland China. Given the rank of general by his father and appointed secretary general of the National Defense Council, he moved into military policy formulation. In 1958 he was named minister without portfolio, and, in 1960, vice minister of defense. In this post, he was put in charge of an upsurge of Nationalist guerrilla activity on the mainland launched in the hope that the disarray of the communist regime following the failure of the Great Leap Forward might lead to its collapse. The hope proved illusory and the guerrilla effort subsided after a few years.

With the rank of three-star general, Ching-kuo was made Minister of Defense in 1965. In this role he improved the effectiveness of the armed forces by instituting new administrative techniques, weeding out hundreds of inefficient and overage senior officers and non-coms, and developing the manufacture of military equipment on Taiwan. In a further move to broaden his outlook and experience, he was shifted from the Defense Ministry in 1969 and put in charge of overall economic policy, with the title of Vice Premier.

Then, in 1972, the Generalissimo (who has in his later years preferred his elected title of president), ill and in failing health at eighty-four, ended all speculation about the succession and how it was to be accomplished by appointing his son premier. The modest and competent C. K. Yen stepped aside as premier, while retaining the vice presidency. Obviously, the president's intent was that, when he died, Yen would move up to the presidency, while CCK wielded the real power as premier. Thus, a dynastic-like succession has apparently been accomplished without a disturbance. Nationalist officials like to contrast the smooth transfer achieved on Taiwan with Mao Tse-tung's failure to relinquish power to two designated successors, Liu Shao-ch'i and Lin Piao. Both antagonized their sponsor and were destroyed.

Within months after he had taken over, Premier Chiang appointed able new men to positions in both the government and the ruling Kuomintang Party. He pleased the Taiwanese by naming a Taiwanese deputy premier, a Taiwanese provincial governor, and other Taiwanese to important government and Kuomintang posts. In the economic sphere he kept in office, with some reshuffling, the veterans who had engineered Taiwan's remarkable economic growth—men such as Finance Minister K. T. Li, Economics Minister Y. S. Sun, and Governor of the Central Bank K. H. Yu. This has ensured continuation of the island's successful mixed state-private enterprise system, under which key industries—public utilities, railways, steel, petroleum, fertilizer, sugar, and certain others—are state-operated, while private enterprise occupies the remainder of the economic sector and incentives are provided for foreign investment, particularly advanced technology ventures.

Broadening the intellectual quality of the regime, CCK has enlarged the role of university-trained men in policy-making. Periodic "seminars" bring specialists—mostly Chinese-Americans—to Taipei to meet with local government and non-government specialists for the purpose of exchanging views, discussing the latest advances in technology, and critically examining policies being pursued in scientific, economic, cultural, engineering and other fields. At recent economics, engineering and technology seminars, for example, Dr. L. W. Lu (Professor of Civil Engineering at Lehigh University), Dr. Liu Ta-chung (Professor of Economics at Cornell University), Paul Thayer (Chairman, LTV Corporation of Dallas), Dr. Anthony Koo (Professor of Economics at Michigan State University) and Edwin H. Gott (Chief Executive Officer, United States Steel Corporation) were among the scores of prominent outside experts who gave papers and participated in intensive discussions in Taipei.

Among numerous government shifts, Y. S. Tsiang, a graduate of the University of Minnesota and a noted economist and agricultural specialist, was advanced from a subordinate position and made Minister of Education to push improvements in training youth for national development. The government planning agency was reorganized and fresh talent brought in. Its Secretary General, Walter Fei, a Harvard graduate in engineering, became the premier's closest adviser and was made secretary general of the cabinet, a move that improved liaison with other government agencies dealing with the economy and with private entrepreneurs.

Perhaps most remarkable was Ching-kuo's crackdown on corruption, long a flagrant weakness of the Nationalist regime. His Ministry of Justice investigators caught up with hundreds of bribe-takers, embezzlers and tax evaders inside and outside the government, and the courts sent them to prison in large numbers. High rank and official connections provided no safeguard. The mayor of Kaohsiung, Taiwan's biggest industrial city, was among those convicted of corruption. "All those guilty must be punished," declared the premier in public statements. When investigators produced proof of bribe-taking by Wang Cheng-yi, a distant relative and onetime secretary to President Chiang, his case went to court like many others, and he received a life term in prison. The signal was clear. Past connections provided no immunity from punishment for misdeeds.

The premier has also tried to promote wider knowledge and acceptance of government actions by regularly explaining policies in public speeches and well-publicized reports to the Legislative Yuan. A reorganized Government Information Office increased the flow of information on government activities to press, radio and television, and officials were encouraged to expound and justify government measures in public appearances and statements for the news media. Intellectuals and the media have found that they are a shade freer, though still subject to police-state supervision, in their commentaries on local and world affairs, including developments in mainland China. CCK's approach is to try to build up a consensus and to bring public opinion along with whatever he is trying to do.

V

Despite an outward charm and gregariousness, Ching-kuo by temperament and experience always seems "on guard," says one close associate. A certain aura of mystery surrounds him, even though he is said to maintain warm and friendly relationships with a limited number of intimates. Within this circle—the nucleus of which is made up of individuals like Li Huan, chief of the Organization Department of the Kuomintang and CCK's successor as head of the Youth Corps, who served with Ching-kuo in South

Kiangsi during the Japanese war—he likes to relax at informal evenings in his home, shoes off and shirt collar unbuttoned, for rambling talk about anything and everything.

Those who know him well say he has become more and more Chinese in life-style and attitude as the years have passed. Since taking over as premier, he is also said to have gained poise and confidence. He can still be rough with subordinates who displease him, but they report that he has curbed the temper that was frequently on display when he was younger. He gets along extremely well with Americans and keeps well briefed on U.S. affairs. "Dealing with him couldn't be more pleasant," one U.S. embassy official has said. "He grasps a problem quickly, gets your view, and then comes straight to the point in discussion without emotional bias." During a visit to the United States in 1970, the most recent of five, he was shot at in New York City by a Taiwanese nationalist. As security men grabbed his assailant, Ching-kuo looked coolly about and asked, "Is anyone hurt?"

Years of working with a tutor have made him fluent in English, but he prefers using an interpreter for serious official talks or press interviews with foreigners. He has an un-Chinese liking for directness and brevity in official dealings; but where his own decisions on major questions are involved, he has a more Chinese way of listening to the opinions of others while reserving his and waiting to reach a conclusion in private. Since he became premier, Cabinet meetings have changed markedly from the relaxed, discursive sessions presided over by his predecessor, C. K. Yen. Ching-kuo told his ministers that he wanted brief, concise reports, and that hereafter all official documents were to be written in plain, everyday language rather than in the semi-literary bureaucratese used up to that time.

His work load is enormous. He is up at 6:30, and at his desk in the solid, old, Japanese-built, four-story Executive Yuan building on Chung-shan Road by 7:30. He regularly schedules breakfast meetings with officials to get the work day going, an idea he picked up from officials he met during one of his visits to Washington. A painting of him standing with his father in a rural setting dominates his big, neatly-furnished office, where his days are a crowded succession of visitors, conferences and decisions. He tries to get home to his modest, two-story brick house in suburban Taipei for dinner but takes papers with him for evening study. Security around his home and office is strict but discreet. When he moves by automobile, there are no motorcycle outriders, only a car ahead and one behind carrying escorts.

Ching-kuo and his wife have three sons and a daughter, all married and all except the youngest son with children of their own. None of the sons have shown any disposition to climb the official ladder, and it thus appears unlikely that another Chiang could succeed Ching-kuo as Nationalist leader. Ching-kuo and Faina do only a minimum of official entertaining, and go out little. To combat the diabetes he has had for years, Ching-kuo follows a strict routine of proper diet, exercise and regular habits that keeps him in excellent physical condition. An unassuming, warm-hearted woman, Mrs.

Chiang is well liked among both Chinese and foreigners in Taipei. Her chief recreation is golf. She speaks both the Chinese national language and the Ningpo dialect well, but with a heavy Russian accent.

President and Madame Chiang, both faithful Methodists, drew Ching-kuo and Faina to Christianity years ago, and the two became intermittent churchgoers. But their interest has lapsed. A person close to Ching-kuo said recently: "I do not know whether he is a Christian now or not."

Ching-kuo's recreations consist of trips to the countryside, hikes in the hills behind his house, and reading. He particularly likes going to Quemoy, the Nationalist island fortress off the Fukien coast. There, security is good and he can stroll alone down narrow, winding village streets and visit pleasurably with shopkeepers and artisans. He has read Heming-way novels in English, and recently publicly recommended *Jonathan Livingston Seagull* to civil servants for its lesson of persistence. His favorite foods are a smelly kind of bean-curd and seafood in the Ningpo style. Faina calls him Ko, from Nicolai, the name he used in the USSR. Under the unwritten press code that prevails on Taiwan, no unauthorized details of his private life or that of his family are ever publicized. Thus, his personal life is veiled; most of the people of Taiwan know him only as a public figure.

VI

His government, though essentially authoritarian, has been less repressive and more responsive to democratic processes and influences than some similar non-communist but authoritarian Asian regimes. By opposing certain basic themes—the return to the mainland, anti-commu-nism, the top leadership's right to rule— or voicing support for an inde-pendent Taiwan, a person still risks a warning and blacklisting by the secret police at a minimum, and at worst arrest, secret military trial and imprison-ment. Outside the range of these key subjects, however, freedom of expres-sion is considerable, and criticism in the press and other public forums is quite freewheeling.

Chiang Ching-kuo's importance at the present stage of world history does not stem from any impact his personality or the character of his government may have outside Taiwan. His own influence has been severely restricted, not least because his government's curtailed diplomatic relation-ships have curbed his freedom for travel. His importance lies in the fact that he is the man on the spot in control of a territory, the final disposition of which involves a tangle of international interests that could easily provoke a major crisis.

With respect to the great issues that concern his government and Taiwan, CCK adheres faithfully to fundamentals established by his father. He holds that Taiwan is but a province of the Republic of China, of which his is the national, legitimate government. He flatly rejects any compromise, even any negotiations about a compromise, that would bring Taiwan under any sort of communist control exercised from the mainland. He scorns reports that he or anyone representing him has talked about such a possibility with the Peking authorities. "We will never negotiate with the Chinese Communists. We would not be so stuipd as to do that," he told this writer in a recent interview. "They would only use any contacts for propaganda purposes." The vast majority of the people of Taiwan, mainlanders and Taiwanese, have no desire to be part of Communist China and thus go along with his views.

He argues that the Chinese Communist regime is faction-ridden, impermanent, and disliked by the Chinese people, and that a breakup of the Peking government and/or revolt against it will some day give the Nationalists their chance to return to the mainland. Meanwhile, Taiwan is to be built up as an economic and government model for all China. "The Chinese Communist regime cannot last," he said in the interview. "The 800 million Chinese will not long suffer communist control. And when disruption occurs, the people will turn to us because our way of life and political system suits the needs of the people of the mainland. It may not be a military solution, but our government will return."

He deplores the worldwide shift in the last few years, including the U.S. change of policy, toward dealing with Peking—a trend that has cost his government its UN membership and loss of recognition by all major powers except the United States and by all but some thirty small countries. He believes time and the inevitable problems with mainland China flowing from this shift will eventually prove him right. "I do not believe that the United States has benefited from relations with Peking," he said, "and any further step toward normalizing relations could be a tragedy for all mankind."

He shows special irritation with the idea that he might some day favor some sort of entente with Moscow as a counter to Peking. He told the writer: "We do not now and never will make any deal with the Soviets. We are anti-communists, and what Western observers should realize is that we stick to our principles."

Despite its many problems and uncertainties, Taiwan under Chiang Ching-kuo is coping thus far with considerable success. Its now widely industrialized economy is producing increasingly for export. In 1974, notwithstanding the shattering effects on Taiwan—as elsewhere—of the world energy crisis, the island's foreign trade soared over the $12 billion level, larger than that of the China mainland and an increase of about $4 billion over 1973. The Gross National Product rose to approximately $14 billion, and per capita income reached $700. In recent years, the average annual economic growth rate has exceeded ten percent, despite the burden of a swollen defense budget. However, the drastic increase in the cost of oil and other raw materials in 1974 produced sharp inflation, a billion dollar trade deficit, and a GNP growth rate of only slightly more than one percent in real terms. A $400 million leap in oil import costs was the main cause of the trade deficit.

CCK's determination not to allow circumstances to deter a huge program of infrastructure building now under way (a new international airport, two new seaports, a petrochemical complex, an integrated steel mill, an island-long superhighway, an electrified double-tracked west coast railway system, and an east coast line linking Taipei with Hualien) is putting a severe strain on available resources. He says this program will give Taiwan a really modern, developed economic base that should enable the island to weather any future economic storms. The recent discovery of major gas and promising but not yet large-scale oil deposits in the Taiwan Strait off Kaohsiung has created exciting prospects of eventual self-sufficiency in energy resources, prospects heightened by the huge program of atomic power plant construction the Taipei regime is undertaking.

The island is secure as long as the U.S. defense commitment, based on a mutual defense treaty, remains valid. American investments total almost $500 million, mostly in sophisticated electronics and other light industries, and liberal credits extended by the Export-Import Bank and other financial institutions bolster the economy. Economic aid ceased almost ten years ago, and military aid was recently terminated.

VII

But the future will undoubtedly be full of problems. Chinese Communist leaders have made it clear, through their own statements and in conversations with visiting statesmen such as Senators Henry Jackson and Mike Mansfield, that they want the United States to move soon toward withdrawing recognition from the Nationalists and establishing full diplomatic relations with Peking. The long-range trend of U.S. policy seems to be in this direction. Peking's temper about Taiwan these days is shown in regular denunciations of the Nationalist regime by the mainland media. A recent broadcast from Fukien, just across the Formosa Strait from Taiwan, charged "the Chiang Kai-shek clique" with arresting and killing people "at will," and with "ruthless economic exploitation and political suppression." The developing situation was called "very favorable to the struggle for liberation of Taiwan and unification of the motherland."

The U.S. government has acknowledged that Chinese in Taiwan and mainland China both regard the island as a part of China, and has informally expressed the hope that the Taipei and Peking regimes can get together on a solution to their problems. But there is little realistic prospect of this. Hence, Washington faces a dilemma. To withdraw recognition from the Nationalists, and to terminate our defense commitment, would be a gross abandonment of oft-repeated undertakings, and would leave Taiwan virtually at Peking's mercy. Not to go this route means to perpetuate our erratic, touchy, unfulfilled relationship with the major power on the mainland.

Premier Chiang is trying hard to keep U.S. good will and forestall any further shift toward Peking. Even if a future shift did not entail a break in Washington-Taipei diplomatic relations, it might trigger for him serious domestic unrest, possibly Taiwanese agitation for independence, certainly a flight of capital and economic recession. Transfer of U.S. recognition from Taipei to Peking would produce on Taiwan a grim sense of political isolation and economic deterioration.

The Chinese Communists are not at this stage threatening a military attack, but are pursuing a strategy of political blandishments and subversion designed to attract Taiwan toward the Communist regime. Radio broadcasts denounce the Chiang government and depict the favorable conditions said to prevail on the mainland. Continuous efforts are made to recruit and infiltrate underground agents. Peking propaganda promises lenient treatment, an easy period of transition, and an unspecified degree of autonomy if and when Taiwan comes under mainland rule. Intensive efforts are made to convert Chinese in Hong Kong, the United States and elsewhere to support reunification with the mainland, and to influence the Nationalist government and the Taiwan people in this direction.

This approach appears to be having little effect on the Taipei regime thus far. But if Peking moved into the economic sphere with pressures on Taiwan's trading partners to cut or reduce their ties with the island, real damage could be done. The termination in 1974 of services to Taiwan by Japan Airlines in response to a complex of Chinese Communist demands made in connection with granting permission for flights to the China mainland, indicated graphically the kind of economic sanctions that could be resorted to. Even more ominous—though rejected so far by the Japanese— was a Peking demand, as a condition for the conclusion of a Peking-Tokyo shipping agreement, that Japan bar Nationalist-flag vessels from Japanese ports. The Nationalists have a large and growing merchant fleet, and Japanese acceptance of this demand would be quite harmful to Taiwan.

Premier Chiang's capacity to influence events is mainly defensive. His military forces (a small but highly trained air corps, a moderately well equipped army of 350,000 with more than a million trained reservists, a small navy, and an elite contingent of marines) total altogether about 600,000 combat-ready regulars. While too few in numbers and appropriate equipment for an assault on the mainland, they are capable of a rugged defense of Taiwan. In the same manner, Ching-kuo's administrative control of the island gives him politically strong defensive leverage but little political impact on the mainland or the outside world in general. He can be expected to be tough and astute in using what tools he has, including the U.S. sense of obligation to an old ally and the usefulness of keeping Taiwan as a friendly territory of potential military importance to the United States off the China coast.

Over the long term, however, his prospects will depend to a great extent on whether he—rather than Mao Tse-tung or Mao's successors—gets history's breaks. The Chinese Communist regime has built-in instabilities reflected in the sharp factionalism of recent years and the difficulties of preparing for a smooth transition of power when the eighty-one-year-old Mao and his seventy-five-year-old lieutenant, Chou En-lai, pass from the scene. If serious disruptions result, they would not only weaken Peking's pressure on Taiwan, but might even provide the Chiang regime with an opening for leverage in mainland affairs.

NOTES

1. *Saturday Evening Post,* March 12, 1955.

China after Mao*

*Franz Michael***

At the outset I want to stress one factor which nowadays is sometimes neglected: the importance of ideology in world politics, particularly in dealing with the communist world, but by no means the communist world alone.

What has happened to the People's Republic of China can perhaps best be expressed in one short phrase: the end of Maoism. Chairman Mao Tsetung died on September 9, 1976 in the early morning hours. In the official picture of the lineup of the mourners at Mao's bier all the leading figures of the government and party, including Madame Mao, were standing in line, paying their respects. Those who had predicted that there would be a collective leadership felt justified, and many proceeded—here in America—with their extraordinary eulogies to the dead Chinese leader. This proved to be premature. On October 6—less than a month later—there occurred a major coup. The East Germans call it, with a rather unexpected sense of humor, "The Chinese October Revolution." The group of four, the closest followers of Mao in the Maoist tradition, were arrested (apparently with some resistance), and have since become branded as the gang of four, accused of all these incredible crimes that any loser in the Chinese political game is always accused of—being right-wingers, traitors, spies of the Kuomintang who had sabotaged Mao's policies and were responsible for all the failures of China that now came to light, the economic decline, the fall in production, and even the earthquake that destroyed the city of Tangshan and did other tremendous damage that could have been alleviated if the gang of four had not sabotaged the warnings.

If you look at the same picture of the mourners at Mao's bier as published now by Peking, Madame and her "ilk" are no longer there—now you see them, now you don't. They have simply disappeared from this as from many other photo-documents. They have become non-persons in the official history—but not altogether. They are still useful; they have become the

*This essay was presented as a lecture at the Cosmos Club in December 1978.
**Franz Michael is Emeritus Professor of History and International Affairs at George Washington University.

scapegoats for everything that went wrong in the last decade or more, since the Cultural Revolution that began in 1966. They are used to protect Mao's image.

In fact though there has been a de-Maoization, parallel to the de-Staliniization that Khrushchev initiated at the 20th Soviet Party Congress, three years after the death of the Vozhd, yet there is a basic distinction between de-Maoization and de-Stalinization, a distinction that helps to shed some light on the internal problems of the Chinese political and ideological power struggle that is still going on today. When Stalin was de-Stalinized, the attack was directed against Stalin's personality cult and his methods of terror used to destroy his comrades in the party. Stalin's political course was maintained. In the case of Mao there was a 180-degree change of course while the attempt was made to keep Mao's image intact, indeed to protect him by blaming all his blunders and his cruelties on the gang of four. Stalin was thrown out of Lenin's mausoleum, while Mao's successor, the victor in the coup against the gang of four, built in a great hurry a mausoleum for Mao sixty times the size of that of Lenin, and there rests Mao's body today in a crystal sarcophagus, paid homage to by a steady stream of organized mourners. Mao can no longer speak or act but his image can be used and is still an issue.

In the meantime the Chinese policy has totally changed from the line established by Mao in the early 1950s and brought to its culmination in the so-called Great Proletarian Cultural Revolution (1966-1969). Mao's ideas of ideological purity, of political priority over technical know-how, of self-reliance, of pulling China up by her own bootstraps, and of having China shaped in his image have been totally discarded and replaced by new emphasis on economic realities, on production, on incentives, on real education, and on the so-called four modernizations once proclaimed by Chou En-lai—the modernization of industry, of agriculture, of defense, and of science and technology.

In the power struggle in Peking today which is even now becoming more obvious, the lines are incredulously still leading back to the past. The problem with Mao was that he was a revolutionary, not interested in the routine of government and particularly of phased economic development as carried out in the planned economy of the Soviet Union and other communist countries. To Mao, revolution was to continue as a perpetual series of upheavals that would bring about the goal of communist man as a result of will power, organization and the willingness to sacrifice for a faith which Mao himself would provide. It was a faith in which Mao mixed his simplistic interpretations of Marxism with a belief in perpetual struggle and the survival of the fittest which he had derived from Darwinism. To create his following Mao had introduced the most extraordinary cult witnessed in our time. We remember the little Red Book of Chairman Mao's sayings memorized and quoted aloud by millions of youngsters in China and even abroad. At the time during the Cultural Revolution, anything accomplished in China, from any scientific discovery, to a successful sale of cucumbers, to medical miracles or inventions, was made possible "thanks to the thought of Chairman Mao." To prove his physical stamina when he was rumored to have had a stroke, Chairman Mao allegedly took the famous swim in the Yangtze River. Not only did he beat all Olympic records, as could be expected, but he performed a number of miracles, all straightfacedly reported in the Chinese newspapers. The one that impressed me most was the story that while swimming at record speed, Chairman Mao explained problems of Marxism-Leninism to a fellow swimmer, a feat that must impress any teacher. (Economist headline: "Did he try to walk on it?") That cult is now dramatically ignored, but even though the gang of four has been purged— along with hundreds and probably thousands of secondary Maoist leaders, many of whom have been executed—there is still a mass following of Mao left over from the Cultural Revolution. It is of some interest to note the figures. In August 1975 the Chinese Communist Party had thirty-five million members. Of these one-half had been admitted since 1966, the beginning of the Cultural Revolution, and seven million had been brought in since 1973, co-opted by what is today called the gang of four. Though the Maoists at the top have been purged, the problem of rebuilding the party still remains.

The Cultural Revolution is also still the measuring rod for judging the factions of the power struggle today. Essentially we may discern three factions. The first includes those who profited from the Cultural Revolution and rose to power as a result of it, and are still at the helm—Hua Kuo-feng and his supporters. In the second group are those who suffered, the victims of the Cultural Revolution—Teng and the many rehabilitated leaders (two-thirds of the Central Committee). In the third group are those who were not victimized, but who by playing along with Mao's policies retained their positions and survived—Yeh Chien-ying is one example.

The new leadership can be conveniently classified along this division. To the first group, the beneficiaries of the Cultural Revolution, belongs Hua Kuo-feng, the new party chairman and prime minister, Mao's successor. As district head in Mao's home district, in Hunan province, Hua had built a shrine for Mao at Mao's birthplace and thus endeared himself to Mao who brought him to Peking and eventually placed him in charge of the security agency after Mao's former and long-standing security chief died. Hua claims to have been selected by Mao for the successorship with the words: "With you in charge, I am at ease" (big billboards all over). Whether, if he wrote it, Mao meant to place Hua in charge not only of security but of the party and government is impossible to say. But with Mao's anointment, later confirmed by the reorganized Party Committee, as his major claim to his new leadership position, Hua was in a great hurry to build the mausoleum for Mao and place him there, from where it is obviously much more difficult to remove Mao than it would have been to denigrate him if he had not been placed in this exalted place.

96

Why then did Hua turn against the Maoists and lead in the arrest of Madame Mao and her three companions, whom Mao in my view had meant to succeed him. I believe that Hua switched from Maoism to the opposition when he saw the handwriting on the wall. The clearest sign that the majority of the party, government and army leadership as well as ordinary Chinese had had enough of Mao's policies and cruelties came on April 5, 1976—the Chinese All Souls Day—in the first ever large anti-Mao demonstrations at Tienanmen Square in Peking and in other cities. Starting out as demonstrations in memory of the late leader Chou En-lai who had been under Maoist attack when he died, the demonstrators (over 100,000 people) shouted slogans and distributed poems against Mao and Madame Mao and attacked police stations and cars while the army stood by. Suppressed eventually by Mao's militia at a loss of allegedly several thousand lives, the demonstration was denounced at the time as anti-revolutionary and led to the dismissal of Teng Hsiao-p'ing as acting prime minister and the elevation of Hua Kuo-feng to the prime minister position from which he later stepped to the number one position. Today the Tienanmen Square demonstration has been reclassified as revolutionary while Teng has become the strong man in the new leadership. Hua is in a dilemma. He knows of the underground current against Mao, but needs Mao's prestige for his own safety. With Hua stands Wang Tung-hsing, the head of Mao's former bodyguard and security police, Unit 8341, who is believed to have actually carried out the arrest of the gang of four and as a reward received one of the five deputy chairman positions of the new regime.

When Hua and Wang came to power at the end of 1976, it was with the support of the PLA. Yeh Chien-ying, over 84, the dean of the PLA leaders, seems to have provided the military backing for the two policemen, Hua and Wang, in their coup. Yeh may even have initiated or at least shared in the planning of the coup and became second in command after Hua. One of those who survived the Cultural Revolution without reduction in his position, Yeh can be regarded as the senior leader of that group.

The PLA provided more than backing. In Shanghai, the PLA surrounded and disarmed Mao's militia, and the senior commander, Hsu Shih-yu, is believed to have shot personally a regional commander unwilling to abandon the gang of four.

After the Hua faction with the support of Yeh and some of the PLA had taken over, the pressure was on to bring Teng Hsiao-ping back into the party and government leadership. Teng was known as an extremely able administrator and an outspoken, somewhat abrasive person. Purged during the Cultural Revolution and rehabilitated by Chou En-lai, Teng was purged for a second time after the Tienanmen Square demonstration but had taken refuge with military commanders in Canton. Now the military and the cadres pressed for Teng's reinstatement. Hua resisted accepting his obvious competitor whom he and his supporters had in fact continued to attack. But Hua had to yield to strong pressure in a compromise arranged by Yeh. In July 1977 Teng was reinstated to all his former positions.

In the present troika of Hua, Yeh and Teng, there is a representative of each group—the Cultural Revolution profiteers, the victims and the survivors. It was clear that with Teng's return, policy decisions and government management would be in Teng's hands. The question was: Would every party be satisfied with its slice of the pie or would the winner take all? For Teng it was not so much a vendetta as the need for elbow room against opposition by profiteers of the Cultural Revolution trying to stay under Mao's more and more leaking umbrella.

The latest spectacle of wall posters attacking Mao as a fascist demanding democracy and a constitution, attacking Hua and Wang, and pointing to the example of Taiwan's extraordinary successful economic development and the prosperity of the United States after only two hundred years of history, is all the more extraordinary since Teng declared his support of such free expression of the "masses" and their right to use such wall posters. But then Teng proceeded to defend Hua and also Mao—though with faint praise—and declared that high-level meetings now in progress would not lead to a change or shuffling of leadership.

The very fact that Teng made these statements demonstrates, of course, that he is in full control. At the very least he may have wanted to impress his colleagues of the Cultural Revolution faction with the realization that he had the power to remove them if they opposed his policies. Whether he will eventually try to remove them remains to be seen. As of now Teng can be regarded as the architect of Peking's new policy.

In the meantime the Chinese policy has totally changed from the line established by Mao in the early 1950s and brought to its culmination in the so-called Great Proletarian Cultural Revolution (1966-1969). Mao's ideas of ideological purity, of political priority over technical know-how, of self-reliance, of pulling China up by her own bootstraps, and of having China shaped in his image have been totally discarded and replaced by a new emphasis on economic realities, on production, on incentives, on real education, and on the so-called four modernizations once proclaimed by Chou En-lai—the modernizations of industry, of agriculture, of defense, and of science and technology.

When taking account of the heritage left by Mao, the new leadership appeared to have more and more realized the urgency for a dramatic change. The celebrated Cultural Revolution is today regarded more and more as a disaster. In part that may be because all those purged in the Cultural Revolution and now rehabilitated—over a million of them—naturally do not have the kindest feelings regarding this great venture of Mao. First, the Cultural Revolution was characterized as having been seventy percent good, thirty percent bad. But by now in an article in the Army paper the percentages have switched to 70 percent bad and thirty percent good. And the only policies of Mao which appear to be still in favor with the military are the introductions of the so-called barefoot doctors (neither barefoot nor doctors but a type of medical orderlies who brought medical services into the villages) and the Hsia fang movement (down to the countryside) by which the Red guards and other youngsters were sent to the villages to work with the peasants and carry on Mao's revolution there, a measure regarded by the PLA perhaps as a just retribution for the trouble they had caused.

The tragic results of Mao's policies could be sensed by any visitor during the last couple of years who knew enough about China to see beyond the official story. In the last months it seems that the officials themselves have bcome more and more honest in the admission of the terrible backwardness of the country, as seen in the clear failure of the four modernizations:

1. Industrialization

Under the old Banyan tree near the beautiful city of Kweilin I met in October 1977 three British economists—editors and writers of the well-known British journal *The Economist* of London—who tried desperately to make some sense of the confusing data they had been given by the authorities in Peking, the provinces and the factories. Their conclusions coincided with mine (I am not an economist) that industrial production was in bad shape. In the factories we and they visited, about half the half the machines stood idle and there were many idle hands around. The evasive answers given to our questions did not really explain the reason. Whether there was a basic lack of skilled workers, a decline of work discipline and morale, a shortage of raw material, a breakdown of transport, or all these and other factors combined, was for us a matter of speculation. The result was obvious—an admitted decline in production.

This was the time when the government promised a raise in wages as an incentive to improve performance. It was a very limited raise of ten percent, and only for the lowest wage level of those who had been at this level since 1972 without a raise. Forty-seven percent of the higher paid grades were also given a raise of an indefinite amount. How this would affect the problem of availability of consumer goods and of funds remained uncertain. Since then, the government has gone further, in the interest of efficiency. It abolished the groups that ran the factories, and re-established instead the authority of directors and managers whose expertise will no longer be hampered by political bosses. In time these measures are hoped to lead to a revamping of industrial production, which, however, will depend not only on a reliable work force and expert management, but also on an overhauling and modernization of the industrial equipment that can only be and is already being obtained from the West.

2. Agriculture

One of the main myths about Maoist China has been provided by the belief that Mao may have been ruthless as a leader, as indeed he was, but that he improved the livelihood and life-style of the ordinary people in villages and towns of China. My greatest surprise when I visited China again in 1977 after forty years of absence was that I found not only no improvement, but indeed a decline in living standards both in the city of Hangchow and in the countryside of Chekiang province, which I had known so well during my nearly five years of residence there as a professor at a national university.

When the communists compare conditions today with the time "before liberation" they take as their starting point the year 1949, the year they came to power. This is roughly comparable to comparing the United States of today with the years of the great Depression. In 1949, China had been through eight years of a most devastating war with Japan and four years of an equally destructive civil war. There were large armies all over the country, uncontrolled inflation, a breakdown of communications, and vast nationwide destruction. Development could go nowhere but up. But if you take as your point of comparison the last good years before the war and the region that was then under direct control of the national government, the story differs. When I walked on my own for a couple of hours through Hangchow's side streets, including the street where I had lived, I noticed with sadness the decline from a better past—the new slums, the trash, the overcrowdedness, the patched clothing, the drabness and grimness of the people, and the whole disappearance of the more colorful, outgoing and lively atmosphere of the past. When I went through the villages through which I had walked in years past, the weathered houses and mud walls and the cobbled footpaths were still the same. Only most of the temples and shrines had been destroyed in the city and the countryside. But there appeared to be more people both in town and in the villages. And village life too appeared to have deteriorated. I knew of course of the rationing of staple food and clothing and of the belief that as of now the food was adequate. That goes for the staple food. But there is a grave shortage of fats and protein, and also of vegetables and fruit. It could be worse, were it not for the private plots, ingeniously and intensely cultivated, that cover supposedly four percent of the land and produce thirty percent of whatever crops. They are easily recognizable in the landscape.

For a first-rate account of the reality of Chinese agriculture behind outward appearance, I recommend highly a report of 1978 in the American University's Field Staff series by Albert Ravenholt, entitled: "Whose Good Earth? Health, Diet, and Food Production in the People's Republic of China." Ravenholt, who is an agricultural economist with long experience in China in the past, went this year with a group of American horticulturists and fruit growers for a fifteen-day visit to several agricultural areas of China. He gives high credit to the improved health conditions of today, which have, however, led to population increase and aggravation of the food problem. In essence his judgment, based on observation and an expert study of whatever direct and indirect data are usable, is that food is adequate in calories but bastly inferior in protein to what it was before. (Ravenholt's starting year is not even 1936 or 1937 as in my case, but 1941, during the war, but before inflation and destruction had taken their toll. He also lived then in less favored areas than I did before the war, and yet his comparison is as negative for the present, as has been mine.)

The reason for this imbalance is, according to Ravenholt, to be chiefly seen in the agricultural policy of today. Because of the pressure to produce the necessary amount of staple crops (rice, wheat, potatoes) to pay their allotments to the authorities and still have enough for seed and to fill their own stomachs, peasants or cadres of the teams and brigades found it less advantageous to grow more soybeans, rapeseed and other protein vegetables than they needed or could afford. Instead of raising soybeans as a single crop which was the practice formerly in the main growing areas, soybeans became an interplanted crop. The same holds true for rapeseed and other vegetable oils. The result has been a drastic decline in the production of these crops to about half of what it had been in the early 1950s or before the war. From a large exporter of soybeans China has become a net importer. And Chinese abroad have been increasingly asked by relatives in China to send liquid protein or other similar nutrients. Even with the emphasis on staple crops, however, China has also become a net importer of wheat to the tune of about five million tons a year ever since the catastrophe of Mao's Great Leap Forward. To become reasonably self-sufficient in food China would need at least six times more chemical fertilizer than she can produce at present, and the several new plants being built by foreign companies are only a limited beginning. Most of all there is a need of rebuilding the morale of the rural population, suffering under a lethargy resulting from the heavy political hand of the state.

3. Defense

In defense, the wisdom of Mao was the theory of a people's war in which the ground would be contested to the enemy village by village. China would need no technical know-how from the outside world and would be self-sufficient in the weapons she would need. People's morale was more important than weapons, and both the Soviet Union and the United States were paper tigers. However, a great effort was still made to allocate enough of the limited resources in material production and trained manpower to the development of a nuclear deterrent large enough to keep the Soviet—or for that matter, the United States—nuclear threat at bay. Whether with the rapid development of modern nuclear technique that is still the case is a matter of argument.

In any case there is today in China a complete change of the strategic conception. Chinese military missions in Japan and Europe and a number of foreign military missions in the People's Republic have dealt with the upgrading of the Chinese military potential. Few have gone so far as the British chief of staff, who toasted in Peking the unity against the common Soviet danger, but the British Rolls-Royce engine for the Chinese air force, the French-German anti-tank weapon for the Chinese army, and the U.S. sophisticated computer equipment for the Chinese air force have been some examples of outside support. Strategically and in the intelligence area, Chinese contact with NATO has led General Haig to speak of China as the sixteenth NATO power, and China has been regarded in the West as a key factor in the military balance against the Soviet Union. Even assuming that the Sino-Soviet conflict will continue for a long time—a dangerous assumption in my view—the weakness of the Chinese military forces is such that the forty-seven Soviet divisions on the Chinese border could easily be substantially reduced without risk for the Soviet Union. It is, I believe, very dangerous to discount these divisions in the European balance. They are at the Chinese border as a leverage of pressure against Peking, not out of fear of an attack against Soviet territory.

It has been calculated that all the existing equipment of the United States army and marine divisions would not be enough to bring half the Chinese military force to a level that would qualify them to withstand a Soviet onslaught. So much for China's military deficiency. Having realized how far behind they are in military preparedness thanks to Mao's policy, the new leaders are making obvious efforts to begin a modernization of their forces—but, as in all other fields, they have a long way to go.

4. Science and Technology

The greatest gap between China and the rest of the world as a result of Mao's policy of seclusion has become apparent in the field of science and technology. What you hear in China now is that they have lost a generation—and indeed they have. Mao's policy of replacing knowledge and accomplishment with political fanaticism and loyalty, of abolishing examinations and selecting students instead on the basis of proper class parentage, has created a nation of ignoramuses whose ignorance even of Chinese history, let alone world affairs, often astonishes the visitor. The new leadership's most important decision was to reintroduce in December 1977 qualifications and examinations for admission to colleges. Of twenty million candidates who applied to enter the examinations, five million were found admissible to the examinations and 277,000 passed—and that in a country of over 900 million people! The most telling proof of this problem was perhaps the recent Chinese decision to send thousands of students to Europe and the United States to learn what they could no longer learn in China. It soon became apparent, however, that the People's Republic could not provide such numbers of youngsters qualified to enter and profit from undergraduate college work in the free world of thought and knowledge. As a result there will be only few such students, even in the sciences and engineering, and mostly of the age of forty and above, who will be able to go abroad and make up their deficiencies on the basis of the educational foundation they had obtained before Mao's utopianism ruined Chinese education. To improve the situation in China, the new leadership appears to be going back to the so-called imperialist period with its Western missionary schools, if one wants to be sarcastic. The first example is the invitation to Japan to establish in Harbin in Manchuria a Japanese university of science and technology with Japanese professors teaching in the Japanese language. The American contribution to this teaching in China appears to be mainly in the field of English language, where a number of American university professors have been invited to China for a year or more to establish English language programs and teach at several universities throughout the country. It is almost as if we were back in the nineteenth century, starting all over again. And while today technological developments can be telescoped, to build a new educational generation takes a generation, and in the meantime the generation of the Red Guards that was misled and then abandoned will remain bitter and troublesome.

In essence, with the four modernizations, Communist China has a long way to go. And the fundamental question still remains: to go where? There we are back at ideology.

The end of Maoism should logically mean a return to regular communism, so-called Marxism-Leninism. The most critical question is still that of the future of Sino-Soviet relations. Will the conflict continue? Will it get worse? Will Moscow and Peking follow parallel or competitive policies? In 1977 there have been feelers between Moscow and Peking, but then there has been revived and increased hostility.

This "no peace, no war" situation appeared to continue through 1978 with Moscow having offered Peking a greatly improved bilateral relationship if Peking chose to move in that direction. At the same time, however, Soviet military pressures along the border and in Asia increased. The Chinese remained intransigent while upping the ante through big power diplomacy, wooing the United States, Japan and the countries of Europe for a "united front" against the Soviet Union.

Since the summer of this year though, the confrontation between Moscow and Peking has entered a new phase globally as well as in Asia where Vietnam and Japan became the new focuses of conflict. The Soviet success in Africa, Afghanistan, the Indian Ocean, Vietnam and Laos obviously began to arouse "grave concern" in Peking where the leaders regarded these moves as an intensification of the Soviet encirclement drive.

But then there has been an important Chinese success in international politics. The peace and friendship treaty with Japan, negotiated for eight years, has finally been concluded and ratified. How important this event was for China could be seen from the fact that Teng Hsiao-ping himself went to Japan for the occasion. It was a strange spectacle indeed, to see

Teng hugging a very surprised Prime Minister Takeo Fukuda and bowing respectfully to the Japanese emperor. The event and the picture have been exploited by Peking in a great propaganda effort and with some glee for having stolen a march on the Soviet Union by finally getting the Japanese to include the controversial hegemony clause into the treaty. The article which states that the treaty is not directed against any other country is quietly ignored by Peking. One can sense the Chinese hope that Japan's capital and technical know-how combined with Chinese manpower and resources will provide the basis for the rapid development of China to that great power goal which Chou En-lai envisioned. Following the $20 billion, eight-year economic agreement concluded with Japan earlier, the figures are now mushrooming. Teng spoke first of $40 billion, then $100 billion as the tag of future Sino-Japanese cooperation. (Recall also the Chinese proposal to the Japanese education mission for Japan to build in Harbin a science and technology University teaching with Japanese staff in Japanese language).

The United States State Department totally discards this possibility, arguing that it would forever preclude Sino-Soviet reconciliation. Even that, I feel, is not necessarily so—and I could describe a number of scenarios for this eventuality.

Let us engage in no rash action, keep our powder dry, and maintain our position in Japan, in Korea, and on Taiwan. "Normalization" yes, but on our conditions, without giving up Taiwan. This is a matter of security for us, for Japan and for northeast Asia, whatever the future of events in China and in Sino-Soviet relations. If worst comes to worst, it is essential to have Taiwan as a vital fall-back position—without forgetting the importance of standing by our commitments for the sake of our credibility and those moral principles on which our policy in the last resort must be based.

There is, in my view, not even any need for sacrificing so much—and for what? We have already the political contact with Peking, the economic openings and the beginning cultural exchanges with the People's Republic on which they depend much more than we do. We can wait and follow closely these extraordinary events in the People's Republic. In all these tumultuous events we should remain cool and firm and use our political, military, economic, and moral strength to preserve that stability in northeast Asia that we have successfully maintained over the last quarter of a century.

Current Conditions on the Mainland: An Analysis*

Tsai Wei-ping**

The extensive exchange of information between experts of the Republic of China, the United States, Japan and Europe on mainland China affairs in recent years has led to a growing consensus on the future of the Chinese Communist regime. Conferences on mainland China, held in Tokyo and in Saarlandes, West Germany last May, and in Taipei last June, have further strengthened the consensus. The delegates generally foresaw continuing political instability on the mainland, with the possibility of local conflicts sparking widespread unrest. A summary of their views is presented below.

I

As an outcome of the enlarged politburo conference at Tsunyi in 1935, Mao Tse-tung assumed the chairmanship of the Military Affairs Commission of the CCP Central Committee, a position from which he was to wield control over the communist military apparatus for forty-two years. Having established control over the military, Mao purged the international faction of the party during a rectification movement on Yenan in 1942. The purge paved the way for his assumption of the party chairmanship in 1945, a post which he was to retain until his death thirty-one years later, in 1976. Mao maintained his position as "state chairman" from 1949-1959 when, following the Three Red Banners debacle, he was compelled to relinquish control of the post to Liu Shao-ch'i. Liu was swept from power at the start of the Cultural Revolution in 1966 and, although the state chairmanship had by then been abolished, Mao maintained an iron grip on the levers of power until his death in 1976.

The death of a dictator almost invariably involves a certain degree of contention over the question of succession. This reaction was particularly

**Tsai Wei-ping is Director of the Institute of International Relations.

severe in the case of Mao, because he had held sway over the party, government and military for so long without ever really coming to grips with the problem of finding a successor. Mao's death thus gave rise to a succession crisis which promises to threaten the stability of the regime for some time to come.

There is little historical precedent for the iron-handed manner in which Mao controlled the party, government and military. He frequently pitted the party against the government and the army, or used one military faction as a counterbalance against another. He might lash out at one influential faction while promoting the interests of a weaker one, in an attempt to attain a better balance of power among potential rivals. All the while Mao took care never completely to annihilate a faction that had fallen from favor. Such policies fanned the flames of hatred among rival cliques contending for power in Peiping, and led to the present situation in which no one group of leaders can exercise complete control over the others.

Also unique is the manner in which Mao incriminated those he saw as his enemies. Cadres he intended to purge were vilified in nationwide smear campaigns in which the people were obliged to join. A victim was always presumed guilty, even before the nature of his alleged crime had been determined. As a result of these tactics, Chinese Communist cadres lived in constant terror. Realizing that Mao's successor, once he managed to consolidate control, might wield the same life-and-death power over them as had the late "chairman," they had no desire to see the development of a strong central authority and the emergence of another strong man. As for the average man in the street, he realized that many of those purged had been convicted on trumped-up charges. As the expression goes, however, might makes right, and no one dared show disapproval of whatever criticism or struggle campaign might be in progress. Nevertheless, in the anti-Teng criticism campaign that occurred shortly before Mao's death, quite a few people seemed to be merely going through the motions half-heartedly, with little enthusiasm for the party line. Perhaps Teng Hsiao-ping himself best expressed this weariness with constant political turmoil when he told a foreign visitor shortly after his second comeback, "No more national struggle and criticism campaigns! From now on we've got to get down to work!" Teng may very well realize that even if the regime wished to resurrect the struggle campaigns of the past, passive resistance by the overwhelming majority of the mainland population would doom the campaigns to failure.

Under Mao's tyrannical hand the regime in Peiping never developed the system of laws and institution that characterizes democratic forms of government. Order and discipline were thrown out the window and "struggle" became the order of the day. Mao's successor Hua Kuo-feng himself displayed contempt for the process of law when he seized power in a military coup less than a month after Mao's death, imprisoning Chiang Ch'ing and other members of the gang of four who had been his allies during the days of the Cultural Revolution. The decision of the CCP Central Committee to restore twice-purged Teng Hsiao-ping to all his former posts in the party, government and army was in direct contradiction to an earlier resolution calling for the censure and criticism of Teng. With disregard for the legal process so deeply embedded in the regime, the prospects of achieving political stability in Peiping remain dim indeed.

Over the past years Peiping constantly called for a tightening of party discipline. The regime also openly admitted that while individual acts of disobedience had been know to occur in the past, today entire units were refusing to comply with directives from above. As Teng's lieutenants in the provinces called for the purge of the gang's remnants and struggle against those who had previously participated in the anti-Teng campaigns, the common man, emotionally drained by the constant political turmoil of the past, remained apathetic and unresponsive. Aware that today's purge victim may be tomorrow's leader, the people of the mainland are extremely reluctant to participate in any new struggle and criticism campaign drummed up by the current regime.

II

The present situation in Peiping is one of standoff between the supporters of Hua Kuo-feng and Teng Hsiao-ping, with Yeh Chien-ying and the party elders attempting to maintain a precarious balance of power between the two.

The Third Plenary Session of the Tenth CCP Central Committee in July 1977 restored Teng Hsiao-ping to his former prominence. The present troika (Hua, Teng and Yeh) was officially endorsed later the same year by the Eleventh CCP Congress and the Fifth National People's Congress. Despite the superficial appearance of unity, however, Hua and Teng remain sharply divided over the following questions of policy and ideology.

1. Affirming or Rejecting the Value of the Cultural Revolution

Both Hua and Teng originally took a favorable view of the Cultural Revolution, evaluating it in terms of "seventy percent for accomplishments and thirty percent for mistakes." (The accomplishments, of course, were credited to Mao, the mistakes to the gang of four.) But following the arrest of the gang and the release of a large number of party cadres who had been imprisoned during earlier purges, the party began to modify many of the measures advocated by Mao during the Cultural Revolution. New policies adopted by the party on such diverse questions as education, the treatment of intellectuals, science and technology, remuneration according to labor and material incentives constitute at least a tacit rejection of the cultural revolutionary line. As a result, Hua was compelled to downplay the earlier thirty-to seventy-percent assessment. At the Eleventh CCP Congress we

107

find him declaring that the Cultural Revolution had come to a victorious conclusion with the arrest of the gang of four.

2. Criticizing and Struggling Against
Remnant Supporters of the Gang of Four

Although Hua Kuo-feng has called for the waging of four campaigns against the gang of four,[1] he has emphasized the educational value of such movements over their punitive functions. At the same time Hua has generally advocated leniency in dealing with one-time followers of the gang. Teng Hsiao-ping, meanwhile, has pointed to the existence of secret underground networks organized by the gang and demanded their complete eradication. Teng has also called for a thorough investigation of all persons and incidents in any way connected with the gang and for the launching of a nationwide movement to redress the grievances of those who had been framed, unjustly accused or imprisoned on trumped-up charges during the period when the gang held sway. According to Chinese Communist radio broadcasts, 10,000 such miscarriages of justice were redressed in the city of Shanghai alone. While "old debts" were settled with Liu Kuang-tao in Heilungkiang, Wang Huai-hsiang in Kirin, and Hsieh Hsueh-kung in Tientsin, the "One Criticism and Two Blows" movement (criticize and struggle against the gang of four, smash the sabotage plots of the class enemy, beat back the advance of capitalist influence) reached new heights in Anhwei, Chekiang, Szechwan, Kweichow, Yunnan, Inner Mongolia, Sinkiang and Tsinghai. The *Liberation Army Daily* poured oil on the flames with its exposé on the activities of "those who follow the wind," "slip-away factions," "Quakers," and "those who keep the lid on the campaign against the gang of four," as the struggle against the gang's former adherents spread from the grass-roots level to provincial party organs and even as high as the Central Committee.

3. The Future of Science and Technology

Hua and Teng split sharply over the question of science and technology during a national science and technology conference held last March. Teng called science and technology a form of productive power, rejecting the Marxist-Leninist concept by which they are considered part of the political superstructure of a state. He further asserted that mental efforts is a form of labor, and that intellectuals should be regarded in the same light as laborers. Equating scientific-technological expertise with "redness," Teng urged scientists and technicians to spend five-sixths or even all of their time working in their fields of specialization, and to reduce to a minimum participation in politics and social activities. Hua Kuo-feng took an entirely different approach to the question when he addressed the conference several days later. Emphasizing the importance of uninterrupted revolution and the

108

three great movements (class struggle, production struggle and scientific experimentation), Hua declared that science and technology must follow a mass line, that all people must take part in the raising of scientific-technological standards and that science and technology must not be allowed to become the province of a small, select group of individuals or organizations.

4. Mao Tse-tung's Thought

During a forty-day conference on political work in the armed forces from late April to early June of this year, Hua Kuo-feng delivered an address on Mao's philosophy regarding the founding of the Red Army. Later in the conference, Teng Hsiao-ping, in remarks that seemed almost a rebuttal of Hua's earlier speech, said: "There are those who, day in and day out, talk of nothing but Mao Tse-tung's thought while failing to grasp even its most fundamental elements—practical experience, the empirical method and the combination of theory with practice. In their opinion one needs only to incessantly repeat the sayings of Marx, Lenin and Mao; consideration of the actual situation, study of objective conditions and other practical matters may then be dispensed with." During the conference a number of newspapers came out with articles that paralleled Teng's speech and criticized certain members of the Peiping hierarchy for their hollow, bombastic, impractical statements. These developments underscore the widening rift between Teng and Hua on policy line questions and foreshadow a gradual sharpening of the regime's internal power struggle.

III

Scholars attending the Sino-Japanese and Sino-American conferences on mainland China generally agreed that industrial and agricultural development on the mainland have slowed, with natural and man-made disasters leading to stagnation and even the loss of previous gains in certain areas. They concurred that the man-made disasters had had much more deleterious effects on economic development than those brought about by nature. The organization of people's communes during the Great Leap Forward, the scholars contended, had resulted in a shrinkage of production and widespread famine. They noted that the attack on monetary incentives and private land plots during the Cultural Revolution had set back the mainland's development program by a good many years. The campaign to criticize Lin Piao and Confucius, the scholars concurred, had caused a great waste of time and manpower and had adversely affected industrial and agricultural production.

Participants in the Seventh Sino-American Conference on Mainland China, held in June, not only saw constant political turmoil as a block to economic progress; they also agreed that after each episode of political unrest subsided, a substantial amount of time was required to allow the economy to regain its original momentum. Scholars cited political stability and a protracted period of economic growth as pre-conditions for steady, long-term economic development. Equally important, they declared, is a positive work attitude on the part of farmers, laborers and other members of the work force.

American scholars at the Seventh Sino-American Conference on Mainland China made the following assessment of agricultural development on the mainland over the last twenty years: "The efforts and resources Peiping expended in the agricultural sector in the 1960s and 1970s have not spurred a dramatic increase in agricultural production; in fact, the growth of agricultural productivity has remained just barely ahead of the population growth rate. Prior to 1972 all of Peiping's agricultural development plans concentrated on improvements in earlier cultivation techniques. The results of each succeeding plan became progressively smaller, and such improvements will not bring a period of protracted growth in the agricultural sector. The 'Learning from Tachai' movement cannot, within the next fifteen years, bring about the modernization of the mainland's agriculture, although progress may be made in certain areas which have sufficient water and other natural resources and which have received foreign assistance." In short, the scholars concluded, sluggish agricultural growth will continue to hinder the mainland's overall economic development, precluding any substantial rise in the living standards of its people.[2]

Scholars attending the Sino-American Conference also attempted to assess the role played by foreign trade in the mainland's overall economic development. Their conclusion: "Foreign trade in 1977 recovered to the point where it approximated that of 1975, registering a growth of twelve percent over the amount of trade conducted during the preceding year. The twelve percent growth rate is deceptive, however, because it is based on trade performance in 1976, a particularly poor year for Peiping's foreign trade. In effect, then, 1977's twelve percent trade growth was much farther below the twenty-one percent annual average for the years 1970-1976 than it would seem."

American scholars agreed that to carry out its four modernizations, Peiping would have to vastly step up its imports, which would have to be paid for by an equivalent increase in sales of such major export items as textiles, agricultural produce and oil. At the same time, they noted that a number of obstacles stood in the way of increased export sales.[3] First of all, the regime can expand exports only by slighting consumer and military needs, a move likely to result in political unrest and a loss of productivity. Thus the Chinese Communists at present face a serious resource allocation dilemma. Domestic problems are not the sole impediment to increased exports. Japan, the chief importer of mainland petroleum, is unable to make unlimited purchases of Peiping's oil. This is largely because the high wax

110

content of the crude produced by major oilfields at Taching and Shengli makes it less than ideal for industrial use, and because of the serious technical difficulties encountered in extracting the oil from these wells. As a result, the Tokyo-Peiping trade agreement stipulates that Japan will purchase up to fifteen million tons of oil from the Chinese mainland by 1982, far below the fifty million ton annual amount that Peiping had hoped for. Moreover, the agreement provides no guarantee that Japan will actually purchase fifteen million tons of petroleum by then; the figure is merely a quota limit and Japan could conceivably purchase much less. Textiles, another of the regime's major export items, are increasingly subject to a rising tide of protectionism in Japan, the United States and other countries. Since 1973 Tokyo has vastly reduced its import of raw silk from the Chinese mainland. In 1975 Australia followed suit by placing stiff quotas on textiles from the mainland. Such developments do not augur well for any extensive increase in export sales of mainland textiles.

The foregoing data represent an attempt to forecast future economic development on the mainland from current trends in agricultural production and foreign trade. In preparing for the Sino-Japanese and Sino-American conferences on mainland China, the Institute of International Relations invited a number of China experts to submit papers on Peiping's four modernizations program. Not one, however, accepted the challenge. The scholars mentioned the unrealistically high targets set by the Chinese Communists for agricultural and industrial production and the regime's unwillingness to make public details of its production plans as reasons for their reluctance to undertake the assignment.

Both Japanese and Chinese delegates to the Sino-Japanese Conference on Mainland China pointed out that Peiping once claimed that its four modernizations are a part of "socialist modernization," in which politics is just as important as economics. Those attending the conference further noted that in addition to political unrest and a negative work attitude on the part of peasants and laborers, shortages of capital, equipment and technical know-how also stood in the way of the program's success. In view of the numerous factors which militate against the modernization effort, the scholars concluded that "modernization" is basically political in nature, with other considerations taking a back seat to politics.

According to foreign reporters, the negativism of farmers and workers on the mainland has reached the point where it seriously threatens economic production. The correspondents tell of workers sitting down on the job immediately after supervisors turn their backs, and conclude that the work ethic of traditional China is all but dead. Visitors returning from tours of the mainland claim that work stoppages and slowdowns have become endemic. They claim to have observed five-man work groups on people's communes in which one member works while the four others remain idle. This negative attitude toward work has had its most serious effects in the countryside, where wide dispersion of work crews makes supervision more difficult.

111

Such problems exist under all dictatorial regimes, but they are particularly serious in technologically backward rural societies. It is no surprise, then, that disorganization, shirking and low productivity plague the mainland regime even more severely than they do the Soviet Union and the communist satellites of Eastern Europe.

IV

The communist regime on the mainland is presently facing three major problems in the field of education.

1. The Intellectual Caliber of Students

During the Cultural Revolution, Peiping abolished the college entrance examinations and stipulated that having received a junior high school education would be the only prerequisite to enter a university. As a result, academic standards in higher education nosedived. The situation led former Tsinghua University president Chiang Nan-hsiang to describe Tsinghua as "a university in name, with a junior high school curriculum and students of primary school caliber."

The science and technology section of the Shanghai Municipal Revolutionary Committee last year conducted a test to measure the ability of recent college graduates who had been assigned to the Shanghai area as technicians. Although the difficulty of the test questions was on a par with that of material taught in high school, rates of failure among examinees in the mathematics, physics and chemistry portions of the test were as follows: mathematics—sixty-eight percent; physics—seventy percent; chemistry —seventy-six percent. Most surprising was that a number of those taking the examination were unable to answer even a single question in their own fields of specialization, and had no recourse but to turn in blank answer sheets. This dismal performance was repeated in the college entrance examinations which were reinstated last year. Out of twenty million applicants, 5.7 million were qualified to take the test; of these only 278,000 passed.

In October 1977, the Chinese Communist Ministry of Education and China Academic of Sciences decided to re-establish the graduate studies program scrapped twelve years before and began to recruit new students for the mainland's graduate schools. At present, nearly two hundred graduate institutions on the mainland are accepting candidates for their programs. Programs of instruction are generally three years long, with the first year devoted to the study of Marxism-Leninism and other basic courses. In view of such practices, prospects for enhancing the intellectual caliber of the mainland's graduate students appear none too bright.

2. Quantity and Quality of Teachers

The so-called "teacher problem" is another way of referring to the regime's problem with intellectuals. An irreconcilable antagonism has long existed between the CCP and mainland China's intelligentsia. This chasm grew deeper during the Cultural Revolution when teachers from educational institutions at all levels were subject to intense struggle, criticism and abuse. Not only were mainland China's more renowned educators condemned as "black elements;" even relatively unknown teachers were hard put to escape the torrent of criticism and invective directed at them. Many of the latter were deprived of work for long periods, assigned to the May 7 Cadre School for re-education, or sent down to the countryside for labor reform.

Although a large number of teachers who were targets of abuse during the Cultural Revolution have since been reinstated, most educators on the mainland remain wary of doing anything that might result in their once again being singled out for retribution. A recent request by Education Minister Liu Hsi-yao for new lesson plans and teaching materials, for example, drew not a single response from the mainland's educators. When Liu called a meeting of university professors in Peiping to discuss the problem, the professors recommended that the central authorities themselves issue the new material. This is but one instance of the passive resistance Peiping is presently encountering from the mainland's intellectuals. Deprivations suffered by educators during the Cultural Revolution have discouraged many of the younger generation from entering the teaching profession. As a result, secondary and primary schools of the future may very well find themselves confronted with a serious teacher shortage. The implications of such a situation for the four modernization programs are obvious. In a recent attempt to bolster its teaching force, Peiping decided to recruit two hundred visiting professors from abroad as instructors in science and technology at mainland universities. The recruiting effort has fallen flat, however, with no more than a handful of the foreign professors accepting the offer.

3. Teaching Materials

The Chinese Communist Education Ministry last November issued a directive to begin the compilation of basic physics and engineering texts for use at the college level. More recently it ordered the translation of foreign science and technology texts into Chinese. No work whatever has been done on the preparation of teaching materials for courses in the humanities and liberal arts. Realizing the ease with which ideological errors may be committed in these areas, professors have avoided such tasks like the plague. A short time ago Lao She's *Lo-t'ou hsiang-tzu (Ricksha Boy)* and *Ssu-tai tung-tang (Four Generations Under One Roof)* and Pa Chin's *Chia (Family)* were chosen for literature courses at Futan University. Educational authorities gave the books a "progressive" rating for their generally positive attitude toward national revolution. Nevertheless, the authorities noted, certain portions of the novels were tinged with anarchist sentiment, and the books should, on that basis, have been subjected to criticism. The incident provided an object lesson to Futan and other universities on the mainland, which are discovering that it is much easier to proscribe old books than to come up with new ones to take their place.

4. The Rustication of Youth

In 1955 Mao engineered and launched the movement to send educated youths "up to the mountains and down to the countryside" to solve the problems of large concentrations of population in urban areas, the joblessness of educated young people who were prone to discontent, and labor shortages in rural and border areas. Current estimates put the number of youths who have been rusticated since then at sixty million. A large number of these young people, unwilling to "spend their best years buried in mud," found release in the glamorous Red Guard movement and armed struggle during the Cultural Revolution. Some have stolen back to the cities where they have become "black persons" in "black households," unable to obtain employment or to obtain ration coupons to buy food and other daily necessities. Not a few have even joined guerrilla bands to carry on direct resistance against the regime.

The reinstatement of college entrance exams last year came as a slight ray of hope to mainland China's rusticated youths. Nevertheless, the number of students selected for college entrance has been so small as to cause the party to admit: "We accept several hundred thousand and alienate tens of millions!" It thus appears that the regime's new educational policies will have little effect in alleviating the pent-up frustration and resentment of young people compelled to spend the prime of their lives in rural exile.

Li I-che's wall poster and the steady stream of refugees from the mainland underscore youth's disenchantment with the heavy-handed policies of the regime. After his second return to power, Teng Hsiao-ping promised to curb some of the excesses of rustication. But "sending down" continues, although on a smaller scale than in Mao's day. And the sixty million youths who have suffered under this policy have become a powder keg of social unrest for a regime in which they have lost all trust and confidence.

V

The Chinese Communist military services are the descendants of armed guerrilla bands of the 1920s and 1930s. In the beginning, each of these

114

units had its own leaders and chain of command. For example, in the days before the War of Resistance against Japan, Mao Tse-tung and Chu Teh headed the First Red Front Army, Ho Lung was in charge of the Second and Chang Kuo-t'ao and Hsü Hsiang-ch'ien led the Fourth. During the insurgency which followed the war, the Chinese Communists reorganized their forces, yet the semi-autonomy of army commanders continued. The leadership lineup at the time was as follows: P'eng Teh-huai—First Field Army; Liu Po-cheng—Second Field Army; Chen I—Third Field Army; Lin Piao—Fourth Field Army. Nieh Jung-chen, meanwhile, commanded a special force directly under the control of the Central Committee. In 1954 the armed forces were once more reorganized, but by that time military factions, with their conflicting loyalties and interests, had taken deep root. Historical conditions were largely responsible for the development of such factionalism, yet Mao Tse-tung's particular brand of leadership hardly inhibited the process.

In a speech at Chengchow in 1959, Mao admitted the existence of "mountaintops" (Chinese Communist jargon for factions) in the Second and Fourth Red Front Armies and among local communist partisans in northern Shensi during the Red Army era. Over the years, Mao became a past master at turning disputes between military factions to his own advantage. In 1959, for example, Mao obtained Lin Piao's help in purging Defense Minister Peng Teh-huai, Huang Ke-cheng and their supporters after Peng publicly criticized Mao during a party conference at Lushan. He next prevailed upon former elements of the Fourth Red Front Army to dispose of Lin Piao's supporters following Lin's abortive coup attempt in 1971.

Some Western analysts who attach great importance to the role of the military in the mainland power equation believe that all the regime in Peiping needs to do to achieve stability is to obtain the backing of the armed forces. They fail to perceive that the Chinese Communist military is far from monolithic, and that no one military faction or leader is capable of riding herd on all the others. Mao's efforts at counter-balancing the various military cliques were successful, largely because of the undisputed sway he held over the party, government and armed forces. No communist leader in Peiping today can even dream of exercising the type of power Mao had at his disposal during his long career.

American analysts believe that Peiping must rapidly develop a strong defense deterrent if it is to counter the formidable Soviet military might arrayed against it. But today the regime remains a third-rate military power, its armed forces hamstrung by poor and insufficient equipment and outmoded forms of training. To pose a credible deterrent to Soviet military power, the Chinese Communists will have to develop their anti-armor, air defense and coastal forces to the point where they are on a quantitative and qualitative par with those of the United States.[4] Such an ambitious military buildup would require extensive purchases of weaponry and equipment from abroad, something that the regime's meager foreign currency reserves do not permit.

VI

In foreign affairs the Chinese Communists have always been guided by Mao Tse-tung's three world theory: unite with the third world, and win over the second world in order to surround and overwhelm the hegemonistic superpowers of the first world. When the Soviet socialist imperialists became its number one enemy, however, Peiping was forced to temporarily modify this plan. The regime's most immediate foreign policy objective today is to obtain sufficient military and technological assistance from Japan, the United States and other Western countries, to place itself in a better position to resist Soviet pressure and launch an attack against the Republic of China. This interim objective will in no way deter Peiping from pursuing its ultimate goal—world revolution.

According to Japanese political commentator Shigenobu Inoue, Peiping's current world strategy calls for "getting as much mileage as possible out of its new relationship with Japan, the United States and the countries of Western Europe. Once these countries have been fully made use of and are no longer useful, Peiping will then attempt to defeat them one after another,"[5] Inoue claims that Peiping's insistence on the inclusion of an anti-hegemony clause in the Peiping-Tokyo Treaty of Peace and Friendship is a ploy to draw Japan into a united front against Soviet hegemony. Should Japan sign the treaty without demanding a revision of its language, says Inoue, it will be the first time a free world nation has been party to an international agreement containing an antihegemony clause. Citing Japan as a precedent, Peiping will attempt to impose similar agreements upon the second and the third world nations in an effort to expand the worldwide movement against Soviet hegemony. It is with this goal in mind that Peiping has so insistently called for the conclusion of the treaty of peace and friendship with Tokyo.

The growing Soviet military threat on its northern border and worsening relations with its former Vietnamese ally to the south have stirred old fears of encirclement in Peiping. Such fears have prompted a number of diplomatic forays by Hua Kuo-feng, Teng Hsiao-ping and others, during which the Chinese Communist leaders expressed eagerness to cooperate with the West in stemming Soviet expansion. The objective of the diplomatic junkets is twofold: (1) to win political support from other countries; (2) to obtain urgently needed military and technological assistance. Peiping, however, has failed to score any notable successes from its diplomatic offensive. Most discouraging of all, Western nations have proved unwilling to sell the regime the advanced weaponry it so desperately needs.

Scholars at the Sino-American and Sino-Japanese Conferences on Mainland China shared the view that Peiping and Moscow would, in the foreseeable future, neither advance down the road to all-out war nor return to the close comradeship that marked their relations in the 1950s.[6] While scenarios ranging from limited rapprochement to small-scale non-nuclear military clashes were not ruled out, most scholars saw a continuation of the current state of cold war between the two communist giants as the most likely prospect for the immediate future. Analysts agreed that Peiping might negotiate the border dispute and other matters with Moscow, should the Soviets prove willing to withdraw their troops from its northern frontier. Should a massive infusion of Western aid enable Peiping to significantly enhance its status internationally, the scholars contended, it might choose to moderate its anti-Soviet stance and once more turn against the West.

There has been much controversy in Washington lately over "playing the Chinese Communists off against the Soviets." In actuality, however, Peiping has been attempting to do the same thing with the United States for quite some time. The Chinese Communists decided to adopt the tactic during the 1960s when worsening relations with the Soviet Union and the growing chaos of the Cultural Revolution caused Peiping's leaders to harbor second thoughts about their collision course with the United States.

Former U.S. President Nixon's trip to the mainland in 1972 was the high water mark of the Washington-Peiping rapprochement. But as early as 1973 America's "China fever" began to cool, after certain Americans, anxious for new trade and investment opportunities on the mainland, returned from their first look at actual conditions under the Chinese Communist regime.

The Carter administration did not consider normalization of relations with Peiping a top diplomatic priority when it assumed office. At that time President Carter declared a strategic arms limitation agreement with the Soviets and a Middle East peace as his administration's most overriding foreign policy concerns. When questioned whether he would speed up the normalization process with Peiping, Carter merely answered that Secretary of State Cyrus Vance would be traveling to Peiping that November. (The implication of Carter's statement was that any new initiatives toward Peiping would not take place before November 1977, approximately ten months away.) But by May, the president's advisors, pointing to his diminishing popularity and the end of his honeymoon with the Congress, saw the need for a dramatic foreign policy coup. All in all it seemed an opportune moment to pursue full normalization of relations with Peiping, especially since the president's party was in full control of both houses of Congress. As for public opinion, it could be "educated." During his presidential campaign, however, Carter had frequently criticized former Secretary of State Kissinger's secret diplomacy and insisted that the government should rally public support for its foreign policy initiatives before, and not after, such initiatives had taken place. This may very well have been the reason for Secretary Vance's address before the Asia Society shortly before his departure for the mainland.

In the fifty days before Vance's departure the American government and people hotly debated the advantages and disadvantages of normalization on Peiping's terms. An absolute majority in both houses of Congress unequivocally expressed their opposition to any move that might weaken the traditional friendship and military ties between the United States and the Republic of China. The response of thirty-one state legislatures and the American public was basically the same. It was pressure like this that caused President Carter to revise the designation of Vance's mission from "negotiatory" to "exploratory." Following Secretary Vance's visit to Peiping, the question of normalization was placed well on the back burner of the administration's foreign policy agenda.

Nevertheless, certain influential Americans, dismayed over the loss of momentum toward normalization, presented arguments as to the inevitability and even necessity of establishing full diplomatic relations with the Chinese Communists. Not long ago they asserted that normalization would be the next order of business to be taken up by the Congress following passage of the Panama Canal treaty. Now they are saying that to avoid passing up another excellent opportunity, Congress must act on normalization immediately after the 1978 congressional elections. But this argument too has become increasingly less convincing.

A short time ago American advocates of normalization argued that normalization was essential not because of any benefit the United States might gain through expanded commercial activity or cultural exchange, but because only by establishing full relations with Peiping could the U.S. hope to employ the regime as a counter-weight against Soviet expansionism. Following National Security Advisor Brzezinski's return from the mainland, however, talk of "playing the China card" aroused widespread criticism from those who realized the dangers inherent in such a policy ploy. Even liberal Democratic Senator George McGovern lent his voice to the growing chorus of opposition. Finally, President Carter's recent statement that the United States has no intention of playing the "China card" took a good deal of wind out the sails of those who advocate normalization at any price.

The U.S. Trilateral Commission recently considered three counter-proposals as a response to Peiping's three conditions for normalization of relations with the United States: (1) not to use force to "unite Taiwan"; (2) to continue U.S. trade and aid, including military assistance, to Taiwan; (3) to establish a U.S. economic mission in Taiwan. Although foreign wire service reports described the counter-proposals as "recommendations made in secret," in my opinion they were most likely leaked by the Carter administration to test the reaction of all parties involved in the normalization prospect. Nevertheless, such recommendations have been debated before, and they are not likely to win the approval of the American Congress and people now.

In attempting to read the future of Washington-Peiping relations, we should give serious consideration to the following:

1. The sticking point in normalization is that there is no normalization formula mutually acceptable to both sides. Even former Secretary of State Kissinger, referring to Peiping's three conditions, admitted: "Peking has never made it easy for us to solve this problem." Meanwhile, the U.S. Congress and the overwhelming majority of the American public—according to a recent poll, ninety-two percent—firmly oppose a unilateral abrogation of the Sino-American Defense Treaty of 1954.[7]

2. The Chinese Communists ever since the Geneva Conference have refused to accept a peaceful solution of the "Taiwan problem." They also remain adamantly opposed to the continued sale of weapons to the Republic of China by the United States. Meanwhile, Peiping should know that the price of a military invasion of Taiwan would be prohibitively high.

As for the United States, having insisted on a non-military solution of the "Taiwan question" for some thirty years, it is unwilling to accept a written statement, oral commitment or tacit understanding as the basis of an agreement with Peiping or Taiwan. The United States realizes that if it forecloses its option to supply the Republic of China with military equipment, it can no longer exercise any leverage over what happens in the Taiwan Straits. By allowing such a situation to develop, President Carter would be acting against the wishes of the American people and violating his oft-repeated pledge to do nothing that might compromise the security and well being of the people of Taiwan.

3. Reportedly under consideration by the Trilateral Commission is a joint declaration that would contain the conditions and counter-proposals set forth by both sides. By supporting the declaration, Peiping would ostensibly be indicating tacit acceptance of the American conditions for normalization. The potential for mis-adventure inherent in such an agreement is so large, however, that it can hardly be expected to win broad support in the United States.

At a press conference in Shanghai one day after the signing of the Shanghai Communiqué, former Secretary of State Kissinger remarked that U.S. defense commitments to the Republic of China had been outlined in President Nixon's recent state-of-the-world address. In his speech, made twenty days before the signing of the communiqué, Nixon asserted: "We shall maintain our friendship and diplomatic relations with the Republic of China and continue to honor our defense commitments to that country." The Chinese Communists refrained from commenting on Kissinger's remarks, a reaction which could be interpreted as tacit acceptance. Nevertheless, by its future statements and actions, Peiping clearly demonstrated that there had never been any "understanding," and that it was in no way obliged to observe whatever President Nixon had enumerated in his address.

4. At present the United States and Peiping are unable to produce a formula for normalization that would satisfy the conditions set by both sides and not create serious problems for them at home and abroad. The prospects for discovery of such a formula remain bleak. At a time when no workable solution is in sight, temporizing may be the least of a number of evils. On the other hand there are those who, insisting on the inevitability of normalization, have counseled us to do our best to prepare for the day when it comes. I myself regard this as a form of psychological warfare designed to induce concessions on our part which might be used by the United States as a bargaining chip in its next round of normalization talks with Peiping.

5. Much more than just U.S. relations with the Peiping regime is at stake in America's China policy. The spectacle of the United States unilaterally abrogating a treaty with a long-standing ally to court the favor of an erstwhile enemy could well blow American credibility right out of the Pacific and seriously damage it in other parts of the world as well. Such a scenario seems even more incredible when we recall the key role the Sino-American Defense Treaty has played in preserving peace in northeast Asia these last twenty-odd years and in fostering economic prosperity in the region. By renouncing the treaty the United States would so shake the confidence and trust of its Asian allies that it would be left standing along to shoulder the crushing burden of providing for the defense and security of the entire region.

Last March 17 President Carter declared: "Our ability to defend the Pacific has been enhanced by mutual defense agreements with allies in the region." He further remarked, "The continued stability of northeast Asia is of the utmost importance." Last February 21 Secretary of State Vance, testifying before a House Committee on the 1979 foreign aid budget, declared: "The United States will continue to supply arms to its allies in East Asia, including the Republic of Korea, the Republic of China, the Philippines and Indonesia." These statements by American leaders have not only helped restore American credibility in Asia; they have also demonstrated the U.S. government's recognition that the best guarantee for the success of its Asian policy lies in strengthening currently existing collective security agreements with its Asian allies. In the final analysis, bolstering time-tested alliances with trusted allies promises to be much more conducive to regional stability than attempting to court one communist regime as a check against another. Or, to put it another way, the United States should not view "normalization" as the only road to peace and stability in Asia.

NOTES

1. Exposing the gang's plot to seize power, exposing and criticizing its anti-revolutionary background, criticizing its policy errors and conducting an ideological struggle with it in such areas as philosophy and social science.

2. Robert F. Dernberger, "The Program for Agricultural Transformation in the People's Republic of China," a paper presented at the Seventh Sino-American Conference on Mainland China, Taipei, June 6-9, 1978.

3. Yeh Kung-chia, "Foreign Trade under the Hua Regime: Policy, Performance, and Prospects," a paper presented at the Seventh Sino-American Conference on Mainland China.

4. Edward N. Luttwak, "Problems of Military Modernization for Mainland China," a paper presented at the Seventh Sino-American Conference on Mainland China.

5. Shigenobu Inoue, "Communist China's Diplomatic Strategy and Japan's Security," a paper presented at the Sixth Sino-Japanese Conference on Mainland China.

6. Harold C. Hinton, "The Outlook of Sino-Soviet Relations," a paper presented at the Seventh Sino-American Conference on Mainland China.

7. Senator Richard Stone and fifteen other members of the Senate voiced opposition to abrogation of the treaty in an amendment attached to a foreign security assistance authorization bill passed by the Senate last July. The amendment requires the president to consult with Congress before undertaking any new moves to resolve the China question.

Part III
Background to Betrayal:
The Normalization Process

Free China in U.S. History: A Brief Synopsis

John J. Tierney, Jr.

If values have any meaning in foreign policy, they have most clearly been manifested in the history of America's relations with a free China. Americans have always prided themselves on their commitment to friendship with the Chinese nation and with a consistent support for the ideals of economic and political liberty that have emerged from twentieth-century China.

Practically alone among the great powers of this era, the United States has a profound record as the singular champion of the Chinese people. This policy has brought us into conflict with other states, both European and Asian, which have sought to carve China among themselves or to otherwise compromise China's integrity and freedom of action. It brought us into war with Japan, and, during the height of the Cold War, it saw the United States remain firm as the consistent defender of a non-communist, non-totalitarian Asia.

The American record as the defender of the values of free men in China is one to be proud of. It symbolizes the very core of the American ideal in foreign policy and stretches back to the mid-nineteenth century, marked by the famous "Open Door" policy in the 1900s, resistance to European colonialism and Japanese imperialism and, until recently, by our deep feelings for the preservation of the free Chinese ideal as represented by the independence of Taiwan.

That independence was mortgaged on the altar of relations with Peking by President Carter on December 15, 1978. That day may yet "live in infamy"—as another historic occasion has—in U.S. relations with free Asia. The values of American associations with non-communist Asian countries has now been definitively cut short by the president's profound about-face. What will emerge from the ashes of this decision only history will record. One central fact, however, is already clear: by abandoning Taiwan for Communist China the long and consistent U.S. goal of a free society in China has come to a shameful end. By compromising Taiwan we have compromised ourselves, and by replacing ideals with expediency we are left with a bankrupt and empty foreign policy. Perhaps it was inevitable, as some will say, but it was certainly not always the case.

Sailing along the coast in search of trade, the first American vessel to visit China stopped at the port of Canton in 1748. The first treaty between the United States and China was signed in 1844. This agreement—the Wangsha—reflected the equality of opportunity in trade that, from the beginning, marked the nature of U.S.-Chinese economic relations. Unlike many other countries which sought wealth from China, the Americans did not demand extra-territoriality or partition of the Middle Kingdom. Other trade agreements in the nineteenth century, the treaty of Tientsin in 1858 and the Burlingame Treaty of 1868, contained the most-favored nation clauses.

The first American minister to the empire of China was Anson Burlingame, appointed by President Abraham Lincoln in 1861. He negotiated China's first bilateral agreement with a Western power, thus making America the first Occidental nation to recognize China as an equal—an important precedent in international law. Burlingame also protested the lucrative "spheres of influence" which had been ruthlessly carved out by the European powers. Alone among Western diplomats, Burlingame often left the U.S. enclave to meet with the Chinese workers and officials. His sincere effort to understand the complexities of Chinese society gained him an unusual confidence in the imperial court. His influence on America's China policy left its mark thirty years later when Secretary of State John Hay enunciated the Open Door policy in an attempt to keep European states and Japan from a final dismemberment of the crumbling Ch'ing dynasty. Although most of the replies were evasive, Hay announced the Open Door Policy in open defiance of China's enemies.

Decades before Pearl Harbor brought the United States into World War II at China's side, Americans had sought to prevent Japanese expansion. The Root-Takahira Agreement of 1908 included Japan's agreement to uphold the Open Door and to support China's independence and integrity. During World War I, in violation of this treaty, Japan made the infamous Twenty-One Demands which, had they been enforced, would have transformed China into a Japanese vassal-state. The United States intervened and the demands were moderated. During the 1920s, when Chiang Kai-shek was leading the Nationalists northward through the Yangtze Valley in the unification of China, Secretary of State Frank B. Kellogg reasserted the traditional policy of non-interference in China's domestic affairs. Once China had received internal unity under the Kuomintang, the U.S. government extended diplomatic recognition to the Nationalist government, and in 1928 the United States became the first nation to conclude a treaty restoring China's tariff autonomy.

In 1931 the Republic of China was again the object of aggression from Japan. The takeover of Manchuria began a series of Japanese attacks that were destined to continue until the end of World War II. This time, however, diplomacy from Washington would not suffice to curb Japan's appetite. In effect, the United States waged the Pacific war against Japan almost wholly in support of the principles of its China policy that had roots going back to the mid-nineteenth century.

For ten years the United States tried measures short of war. In answer to the forcible seizure of Manchuria, Secretary of State Henry L. Stimson announced the long-standing U.S. policy of not recognizing territorial changes made by force. The declaration of this policy—known since as the Stimson Doctrine—had an important moral effect against Japan's action, but failed whatsoever to deter the new Asian imperialists. When Japan began a full-scale invasion of China in 1937, Secretary of State Cordell Hull urged restraint on Tokyo, but again to no avail.

Between 1937 and 1941, the United States took many steps short of war to support the Republic of China in its resistance against Japan. President Roosevelt publicly condemned the Japanese and called for a global "quarantine" against aggression. After Washington terminated its 1911 trade treaty with Japan, shipments of oil, iron, machinery, and other implements of war were restricted. By May 1941, China was declared eligible for lend-lease. An American military mission was sent to China, and U.S. army airmen were allowed to enter the reserves and join the Chinese armed forces. In July, President Roosevelt froze all Japanese assets in the United States. By November the Burma Road was paved, and the tonnage distributed to Chiang Kai-shek's forces from Burma more than tripled within a few months. The famous American volunteer air group popularly known as the "Flying Tigers" was established in August 1941. Commanded by Major General Claire L. Chennault, they provided air defense in southwest China and supported land operations in Burma.

During World War II the existence of the China theater was significant in the defeat of Japan. Some two million Japanese troops were tied down on the mainland, unable to defend their home islands against the approaching American forces. V-J Day was a major triumph of Sino-American friendship and alliance.

Eight years of war with Japan had exacted a heavy toll of economic and military resources, and a heavy toll of life, on the Nationalist government. True to their word, the Chinese Communists devoted seventy percent of their own war effort to expansion, twenty percent against the government, and only ten percent of their fighting against the Japanese invader. Aided and backed by the Soviets, the Chinese Communists expanded their internal war after the Japanese had been defeated. With the United States preoccupied with the Russian threat to Western Europe, and with the official attempt by Washington to exact a negotiated compromise doomed to failure, the government of the Republic of China withdrew to Taiwan in 1949.

For a brief interlude, the situation remained transitory. The United States, seemingly uncertain as to what to do, stood aloof from China. Assistance to the National government ceased, but, at the same time, the

Communists were not recognized. In the meantime, Mao Tse-tung visited Stalin and a treaty of alliance and friendship between the two totalitarian giants was concluded. But it was the Korean War, more than any other single event, that determined the future course of American relations with both Taiwan and the mainland. With an armed Communist attack from North Korea, the United States government ended its "hands-off" policy toward China, a policy which had now been outweighed by considerations of the necessity of meeting the immediate military threat. One month later, in July 1950, the Joint Chiefs of Staff affirmed that Taiwan was of strategic value for the U.S. war effort. By bringing the United States and Communist China into direct hostilities, the Korean War increased American distaste for the communist government and, conversely, strengthened American sentiments for the Nationalist government on Taiwan and for the historic and political values which it represented.

The administration reacted promptly to the North Korean attack. Two days after it occurred, President Truman announced that the status of Taiwan in international law was still undetermined and that Taiwan was not, by any necessity or definition, to be considered as part of the mainland.[1] In addition to this announcement, the president ordered the Seventh Fleet to the Taiwan Straits to prevent the mainland and Taiwan from attacking each other. This, at least, was the official motive, although historians have since suggested that political pressure to protect the Nationalists was a major factor in the decision.[2] Military strategy, however, certainly influenced the move, since a communist takeover of Taiwan would have freed a number of Chinese troops stationed across from the island and allowed them to assist the effort in Korea.[3] The movement of the Seventh Fleet has also been interpreted as a temporary measure to stabilize the existing situation in the Taiwan Straits, since it was felt that American pressure in the area was necessary to avoid Taiwan's involvement in the war.[4] Truman's statement to this effect was quoted in the United Nations in response to Russian charges of U.S. aggression against mainland China.

Russia was, of course, not the only nation to respond to the action by the United States. Upon the movement of the Seventh Fleet to Taiwan, the Chinese Communists intervened with troops in an attempt to stop American involvement. This had a decisive impact upon the situation. As one authority puts it:

After China intervened, Taiwan assumed an infinitely greater importance to Americans, especially to the American military who were charged with the responsibility for meeting American commitments to Japan and the Philippines. The defenses of the island were built up, large-scale aid poured in, and American bases developed.[5]

Hence, the movement of the Seventh Fleet placed Taiwan squarely under the American protective wing. Despite General MacArthur's in-

128

sistence on using Chiang-Kai-shek's troops to fight in the Korean War, however, the administration, acting on the advice of Secretary of State Acheson and the Joint Chiefs, refused Chiang's offer.[6] The rationale for this decision was, first, the contradiction of defending Taiwan with the Seventh Fleet while allowing Nationalist troops to leave the island, and, second, the inconvenience of supplying the necessary support for the Nationalist forces. Although Washington refused Chiang's generous offer of support, the overall policy resulting from the Korean War continued to show overwhelming support of Taiwan and a deepening national opposition toward recognition of Peking.

A major influence on the fast-evolving policy was criticism from Congress. This criticism was heightened when the firing of General MacArthur led to an outpouring of sentiment and support not only for MacArthur, but for the Chinese Nationalist government which he supported. Congress reflected this national attitude, and leaders from both parties criticized the administration's handling of the Taiwan problem. In addition, pressure for an anti-Communist policy had been developing largely in response to American frustrations in the aftermath of the Chinese Communist victory and the Korean stalemate. According to one authority, "the total impact of criticisms of American policy was to deprive the administration of any degree of diplomatic freedom and maneuverability."[7] MacArthur's strong stand against Communist China was crucial. After consultation with Chiang and an explanation of the American refusal to use Nationalist troops, MacArthur issued a statement in which he emphasized that arrangements had been completed for the effective coordination of Chinese and American troops in case of attack upon Taiwan. If President Truman harbored any designs to recognize Peking, they were largely undercut by MacArthur's initiatives. Hence, the nation was already committed to a pro-Nationalist policy by the time the Eisenhower administration took office.

President Eisenhower continued and strengthened the pro-Taiwan policy he inherited. Both the president and Secretary of State Dulles were guided by a firm commitment against world communism and by a manifest necessity to preserve Taiwan as a vital strategic link in the Pacific theater. In addition to the strategic and political considerations that influenced President Truman, Eisenhower was motivated by favorable reactions that came from his own administration. Republicans blamed the Democrats for the loss of China to communism, for the near-disaster in Korea, and for what they defined as a defensive and reactive Asian policy. Like West Berlin in Europe, Taiwan in Asia came to represent a symbol clash of two worlds, one free and open, one totalitarian and closed. Most of the U.S. media, furthermore, were in full support of Taiwan.[8]

Despite Secretary Dulles' belief in Chiang's legal authority over the mainland, the U.S. did, in fact, acknowledge the existence of two Chinas in some of its displomatic actions. The administration conducted several private negotiations with the communists over Taiwan between 1953 and 1955. The basic pro-Taiwan policy asserted itself, however, when the first shots from the mainland hit Quemoy in 1954.

Quemoy is an island off the coast of the mainland and within firing distance of it. By 1954, Chiang Kai-shek had positioned troops on Quemoy and other nearby islands. The United States, while not officially committed to Chiang's military buildup, nevertheless decided that the situation demanded a major effort to defend his position. As Washington understood it, the protection of the offshore islands was vital to the morale of Taiwan which, in turn, was vital to the American defense chain throughout Asia. Yet, this defense could result in an attack on the mainland if Chiang ever decided to push too far. President Eisenhower's desire to defend Taiwan's offshore islands without committing the United States to an attack on the mainland led him, in January 1955, to request Congress to pass the "Formosa Resolution" which authorized the president to employ American forces to defend Taiwan, the Pescadores, and related positions and territories of that area now in friendly hands (i.e., the offshore islands).

The Formosa Resolution signaled U.S. intentions to defend Taiwan but did not provide a permament solution. In September 1958, the communists again began shelling Quemoy. In response, President Chiang further strengthened his military position on the islands. The United States, however, believed that this move was "unwise" and represented an attempt to put undue pressure on Washington to support an offensive move against the mainland. Nevertheless, using similar logic as before, the administration still supported Taiwan. During 1958, the United States outlined a formal statement which explained the administration's position on the new crisis. This statement reflected the strategic importance which the U.S. had come to place on Taiwan and the offshore islands, while deliberately avoiding any U.S. commitment to "unleash" Chiang. In part, this statement read as follows:

If the foregoing [a Communist takeover of Quemoy] occurred, it would seriously jeopardize the anti-Communist barrier consisting of the insular and penisular positions in the Western Pacific. U.S. positions in this area, would probably become untenable, or unusable, and Japan with its great industrial potential would probably fall within the Sino-Soviet orbit.[9]

This document reflected a number of assumptions rooted in the historic association of the United States with the free Chinese and in the prevailing political atmosphere of the Republican Party and the 1950s. It assumed that Russia and China, however much they may differ in perspective and approach, shared an ideological goal implacably hostile to liberty as understood by Americans and as supported by American foreign policy. Over the past twenty years these assumptions have steadily eroded in the minds of U.S. leaders from both parties. As the assumptions changed, so did policy.

During the era of the Vietnam War, American military support of Taiwan changed very little. One reason for the basic continuation of policy, according to one expert, was:

By 1960 the commitment to the GRC [Government of the Republic of China] had become one of the firmest and most widely accepted commitments in American foreign policy, and no change was possible without a fundamental reordering of American priorities in the Far East.[10]

No such "reordering" took place as long as the U.S. was involved in the Vietnam fighting. President Kennedy publicly accepted the idea that the Republic of China represented an alternative to Peking and that the defense of Taiwan should continue as a vital national interest. The pressure of the Indochina War, furthermore, resulted in Kennedy's lack of preoccupation with the Taiwan question.

The Kennedy administration did, however, inaugurate a slightly different diplomatic tone by announcing that it had altered the old assumption that communism in China was a "passing phase." Another break with established policy occurred when, in response in 1962 to the strengthening of communist forces opposite Quemoy, Mr. Kennedy, influenced by Secretary of Defense Robert McNamara, noted that the buildup was a response to Chiang's moves. These subtleties reflected Kennedy's personal discomfiture with the situation which he had inherited but which, at the same time, he found himself helpless to change.

Kennedy's decision to oppose Communist China's admission to the United Nations was largely a result of two factors. First was the loss of global prestige that the United States would suffer if its long-standing policy was reversed. Previous attempts to open the question of admission for Communist China had met with flat rejection from the United States. The General Assembly for several years had voted to sustain the U.S. position and to reject the admission of Communist China. However, in each year that the question was raised, the United States was faced with diminished support in the world body. Second was the election-year impact of a diplomatic defeat. With the increasing likelihood of defeat, therefore, the United States began searching for a possible compromise solution. A blatant retreat on this issue would have had negative political repercussions in the United States, where popular support for the Republic of China was—and still is—overwhelming.

Despite disapproval from some members of Congress, the administration supported a plan to introduce the idea of Red Chinese admission as an "important question" requiring two-thirds approval of the General Assembly. The way was opened, therefore, for the eventual removal of the Republic of China from its seat without the appearance of American approval. In retrospect, the Kennedy administration, while strategically committed to Taiwan as a necessary link in American strategy for the western Pacific, began a series of subtle diplomatic choices which had the effect of loosening the bonds between the United States and the Republic of China. The first cracks in the alliance came during these years.

The Johnson administration's policy on Taiwan was basically the same as that of Kennedy's. President Johnson's lack of personal interest in the situation and the concerns of the Vietnam War obviously contributed to this continuation. The Vietnam War, in particular, made a change in policy practically impossible. Indeed, as long as the war went on, America's China policy remained frozen. Ironically enough, it was Richard Nixon, as Vice President implacably hostile to Peking, who would be responsible for the first major diplomatic changes in America's historic commitment to the Republic of China. Conventional wisdom now has it that only a Republican President, and, indeed, only Nixon, could have so reversed previous policies. Assuming this to be true, it indicates the depth of feeling that all Americans had developed for the Republic of China in a close relationship that spanned the course of four major wars of the twentieth century.

The general political atmosphere of 1968-1972 no doubt did its part in developing improved relations with the mainland. The winding down of the Vietnam War, the announcement of the "Nixon Doctrine" and the general policy of détente with the Communist powers contributed greatly to the new atmosphere.

The Nixon administration wasted little time. Within two weeks of its inauguration, initial contacts were made with the Chinese Communists in secret negotiations held in Warsaw, Poland. In the fall of 1969 during the UN debates on Red China, the U.S. took the position that Peking's aggressive policies disqualified it for membership in the United Nations. In the following year, however, the administration shifted position and based its stand solely on the unwillingness to see the Republic of China expelled from the UN as the price tag for Peking's admittance. However, certain diplomatic actions of administration officials weakened the official American position of recognition for the Republic of China. Secretary of State Kissinger's visit to Peking during the UN vote undoubtedly caused Taiwan to lose support. The State Department's public reminder that the question of Taiwan was still unsettled since the end of World War II, and Secretary Kissinger's implication that this should be a matter of negotiation between the two Chinas, also eroded support for Taiwan.

The Nixon administration's official policy was probably designed for public consumption. The failure of the United States to make a strong fight for Taiwan in the United Nations certainly reflected an underground change in official governmental circles, while the conduct of U.S. policy—from secret talks to the flamboyant Nixon trip to China—began a process of slow erosion for support and protection of free China.

The effect of such changes on America's Asian policies had many allies worried. In conjunction with the withdrawal from Vietnam, the Nixon visit to the mainland had been most disturbing for the countries of east and southeast Asia, many of which were deeply apprehensive about China and had entrusted their own security to the power and integrity of the American alliance. For the first time, the U.S. commitment in Asia was being openly questioned and was visibly being reduced.[11]

The Nixon administration's major policy statement on U.S.-Republic of China relations was the Shanghai Communiqué, issued in 1972, which, in part, stated:

> The United States acknowledges that there is but one China and that Taiwan is a part of China. . . . It [the U.S.] reaffirms its interest in a peaceful settlement of the Taiwan question by the Chinese themselves. With this prospect in mind, it affirms the ultimate objective of the withdrawal of all U.S. forces and military installations from Taiwan. In the meantime, it will progressively reduce its forces and military installations on Taiwan as the tension in the area diminishes.[12]

This was an important document, which represented a profound break with America's historic association with the Republic of China. Since that time, however, neither the Nixon nor the Ford administration was willing to abandon Taiwan altogether in the face of Peking's unrelenting demand to abrogate the security treaty. President Carter's decision to take the final step will be judged by historians, however, as the irrevocable break with the past, a past which has been—until December 1978—a near-unbroken commitment to the values of free economic and political ideals in the Far East.

The China decision will be a landmark in other areas as well. Essentially an accommodation with a philosophical enemy, it will go no further than any other accommodation can be expected to. The Peking government will be no more inclined to change its ideological views toward the United States than, for example, the Soviets have been, even though we have recognized them since 1933. Détente with Russia, therefore, has been complemented by détente with Red China. The overall effect will be to dilute any remaining anti-Communist spirit in U.S. foreign relations. If we can accommodate to communism in China, therefore, we can accommodate to it elsewhere. The net result augers for a near 180-degree reversal in U.S. foreign policy since the end of World War II. The abandonment of Taiwan, in effect, symbolizes the abandonment—unilaterally—of "containment" of communist influence as an American strategic goal in Asia. Like the Shanghai Communiqué, the Nixon Doctrine has come full circle under Jimmy Carter.

In a larger sense, the abandonment of Taiwan, coming as it does on the heels of defeat in Vietnam and withdrawal from Korea, may signal the end of America as an Asian superpower. Guided by a shallow and crude raison d'être and with an alliance system crumbling under our very eyes, we will have little motivation to act as a decisive balancer in the East Asian and Pacific theater. In effect, we will again become isolated from the crucial strategic moves that will shape the future Asian balance of power. Taiwan was an important link in the Pacific chain-of-command, as defined and supported by six post-World War II U.S. administrations. With that link now officially abandoned, the United States has no other strategic direction than eastward—toward a historic continental neo-isolationism that promises to leave the future of Asia to the totalitarian giants of that continent.

NOTES

1. Joseph W. Ballantine, *Formosa: A Problem for United States Foreign Policy.* Washington, D.C.: The Brookings Institution, 1952, p. 130.

2. Warren I. Cohen, *America's Response to China: An Interpretative History of Sino-American Relations.* New York: John Wiley & Sons, Inc., 1971, p. 202.

3. William M. Bueler, *U.S.-China Policy and the Problem of Taiwan.* Boulder: Colorado Associated University Press, 1971, p. 11.

4. Carl Berger, *The Korea Knot: A Military-Political History.* Philadelphia: University of Pennsylvania Press, 1957, p. 117.

5. Cohen, *op. cit.,* p. 216.

6. Jerome Alan Cohen, *Taiwan and American Policy: Dilemma in U.S.-China Relations.* New York: Praeger, 1971, pp. 41-42.

7. John W. Spanier, *The Truman-MacArthur Controversy.* Cambridge: Harvard University Press, 1959, pp. 68-69.

8. Bueler, *op. cit.,* p. 40.

9. *Ibid.,* p. 32.

10. *Ibid.,* p. 42.

11. Richard Moorsteen and Morton Abramowitz, *Problems of U.S.-China Relations and Governmental Decisionmaking.* Santa Monica: The Rand Corp., 1971, p. 21.

12. *The New China Policy: Its Impact on the U.S. and Asia Committee on Foreign Affairs.* House of Representatives, 92nd Congress, Washington, D.C., 1972, p. 15.

Principles
over Pragmatism

*Anthony Kubek**

In the closing year of the last century the eminent American diplomat John Hay uttered one of the truly prophetic statements of modern history. "The storm center of the world," he said in 1899, "has gradually shifted to China." No phenomenon of the twentieth century has been more striking than the fulfillment of this remarkable prediction. World War I may have been strictly European in origin, but certainly one of the most significant results of that "Crusade for Democracy" centered on the inclusive question of the fate of China and the future of free Asia. World War II was at least one-half Asian in origin, and the fate of China was the question which finally brought the United States into that crusade as freedom's heavyweight champion. What befell that hard-won freedom in the years immediately following V-J Day was nowhere more pointedly illustrated, and nowhere more tragic in its implications for so many millions, than on the Asian mainland. The smashing of freedom in China, at the very moment when the fulfillment of freedom in that most populous country on earth seemed at last possible, provides the classic example of communist ascendency in the cold war. But the part played by Americans in that unparalleled tragedy is still only slightly understood today.

China's loss to communism has indeed witnessed the fulfillment of John Hay's prophetic remark of 1899. No American can rightly doubt this when recalling Korea or while reading, hearing, and talking daily of Vietnam. Many Americans have come to see clearly, moreover, that the theaters of war in Korea and Vietnam are, like fingers of a giant hand, mere extensions of the great conflict between human freedom and bondage that has characterized the recent history of China. So far, of course, freedom has been the loser; the contagion of Chinese communism has infected and debilitated not only the Asian mainland but much of the rest of the Far East. But the communist victory was not one of, by, or for the communist ideology. It was achieved by the skillful use of well-equipped armies and by the marvelous

*Anthony Kubek is Professor of Political Science at Troy State University, Troy, Alabama.

propaganda of big lies and bigger promises. In 1945 the communists were the "outs" capitalizing on conditions of distress which, after the Japanese, they themselves had helped create—and which the Nationalist "ins" were unable, as the communists have since been unable, to alleviate. The communists broadcast to the Chinese people that these conditions were all the fault of the Nationalists; they would replace the "corrupt" and "incompetent" National government, would set up a system of and by and for the people, and would make China prosperous and strong. And many of the Chinese people and many of the Nationalists soldiers—impoverished and frustrated by two decades of warfare, yearning for peace, discouraged, and demoralized by the discontinuance of American moral and material support of the National government, and noting the success of the Soviet-supported communist armies—were totally taken in by that line. Many good folk elsewhere, with no such pre-conditioning, also believed what the communists told them in those days.

As the American frontier humorist Will Rogers used to say, "Communism is like Prohibition. It may be a nice idea, but it won't work." Over two decades ago, as his cadres assumed control of the cities and villages of mainland China, Chairman Mao Tse-tung was parading before the Chinese people as a kind of magical master chef who was supposed to have in his hat or somewhere in his apron the best recipes for the intellectual, political, and economic diet of the whole country. If the proof of the pudding is in the eating, as the English say, then Chairman Mao has proven himself a poor chef indeed. After more than twenty years in control of the kitchen, he still cannot cook for the people of China. His menu may still be attractive on paper, but the meal is always bad. Mao's siren song to the intellectuals may be as seductive as ever as it echoes around the radicalized world today, and the outpouring of party-line propaganda from Peking may be as steady and abundant as ever. But inside China, where Mao has been free to experiment with his recipes for almost a generation, his promises to the people are still nothing more than pie-in-the-sky. As early as 1957, it will be remembered, some of his own cadres were beginning to complain about the thin diet, and Mao responded to that early disillusionment with the deceptive and devastating "Let One Hundred Flowers Bloom" campaign. Then in rapid succession came his backyard furnaces, his people's communes, his co-called "Great Leap Forward," his destruction of the family unit, his distribution of the land to the peasants, and then the repossession of that land by the regime. Each program failed in turn, the disillusionment spread and deepened, and the Chinese people reacted with the only protest possible under Mao's system of political enslavement. This was the silent protest of peasants refusing to work, and it brought on three years which caused great suffering among the voiceless masses but also shocked the regime to its bottom.

In desperation, Chairman Mao went again to his cupboard of political strategy and tactics—and came up this time with a new recipe which he grandiosely labeled the "Great Proletarian Cultural Revolution." Launched in 1966 under Mao's personal guidance, it was entrusted to the one group left in China still naive enough and immature enough to swallow Mao's paper recipes: that new generation of student radicals calling themselves the "Red Guards." Born and bred under Maoism, these deluded boys and girls knew nothing better and in fact nothing else, for they had been schooled to follow the leader with a blind faith reminiscent of the Hitler Youth of Germany in the 1930s. The ostensible purpose of the Red Guard movement was to declare unremitting ideological war on Western imperialism in all its forms, on Soviet revisionism of the original teachings of Marx and Lenin, and on the four so-called "olds" of Chinese life—Old Thought, Old Culture, Old Customs, and Old Habits. The actual purpose, of course, was chiefly diversionary; it was to turn the attention of China's urban and rural masses away from their daily misery and away from the insurmountable practical problems of economic survival under Mao's oppressive and unproductive system. That, put simply, is the record to date of what the Chinese Communists have done, or tried to do, since their usurpation of the mainland in 1949. It has been all recipe and no repast, all kitchen blundering and no banquet. By their deeds, not their words, we now know them. "Communist China," writes the globe-trotting James Michener, "is the most frozen-faced society I have ever seen. I met no one who greeted me voluntarily with a smile and only a few who would smile back if I tried to break the ice."

The best tool of the Chinese Communists has always been their real mastery of the art of disguise. By carefully concealing their aggressive tendencies on their way up to power, they succeeded in deluding not only many leading Chinese intellectuals but some important Americans as well. Once in power, however, they soon dropped the facade and consolidated their gains by the mere expedient of establishing a police state.

But the Chinese masses were not long deceived. Traditionally conservative and wise in the teachings of Confucius, they could not reconcile Mao's atheistic materialism with their own ancient cultural concepts of filial piety, parental love, and individual morality and dignity. They have endured the communist regime for these two decades only because they have had no means of confronting the Red Army, which upholds the regime with its millions of rifles—the first of which, it is important to remember and to repeat, were Japanese weapons obtained through Russian generosity in 1945 when the U.S. government made the incredible mistake of permitting the Soviet Union to accept the surrender of Hirohito's armies in Manchuria.

Without those guns to back up their rhetoric, the Chinese Communist leaders would soon be talking to themselves in the fraudulently named "Great Hall of the People" at Peiping. Fear fills the Communist halls today, as it has for a long time, but no form of intimidation can force the humble Chinese masses finally to forget Confucius and open their ears instead to the godless arrogance of Mao's cadres. If history has any meaning at all, the cultural heritage of Confucianism will never be destroyed in China. On the

137

contrary, that which confronts these traditions head-on—as Chinese Communism is doing today in the programs of Chairman Mao's heralded cultural revolution—will eventually destroy itself.

The fact that the so-called "People's Republic" of Chairman Mao was somehow very un-Chinese, as well as anti-Christian and anti-Western, was seen quite clearly by many informed Americans in 1949. While few Americans at that time were as yet deeply suspicious of the Chinese Communists as possible aggressors on an international scale, most of the thinking citizens of the United States had a feeling that the Old Confucianism was dovetailing pretty well with Western and Christian concepts in the emerging Republic of China founded by Sun Yat-sen and led since his death by Chiang Kai-shek.

For almost a quarter of a century it had been Chiang Kai-shek who represented China to the world. When one thought of freedom in the Far East, one thought of the Generalissimo's troops valiantly fighting back the Japanese invaders of the Asian mainland. His armies contributed more to the final victory in the Pacific than did the Soviet Union; but because of the supposed necessity of placating wartime ally "Uncle Joe" Stalin, President Roosevelt yielded at Yalta to Soviet demands in the Far East and we ended up by rewarding the Communists more than we did the Free Chinese. The retreat of President Chiang's Nationalist government to the island province of Taiwan in the Formosa Straits was viewed generally with dismay, therefore, even by those Americans to whom the name of Mao Tse-tung then meant nothing at all.

Some American diplomats predicted in 1949 that Taiwan would be lost to the communists within six months at the most. Now, twenty-three years later and despite the recent diplomatic setbacks and others that are threatening, Taiwan is still on a solid footing, still undaunted, still looking to an ever brighter future. The foreign trade of the Republic of China will pass the $5 billion mark this year and move out ahead of the Chinese Communists' volume of commerce. An island of less than 14,000 square miles and 15.5 million people will be out-trading a subcontinent of 3.7 million square miles and over 725 million people. No less an authority than Walter McConaughy, the American ambassador to the Republic of China, has predicted that Taiwan's trade advantage over the mainland will reach $1 billion within the next two years and yet more by 1975.

Moreover, Taiwan is no longer dependent on American aid. The fact is that all economic assistance to the Republic of China was phased out in 1965, making it one of the first countries in the world to become independent of American economic aid. The Republic of China now finances ninety-six percent of its annual military expenditure. Some American help is still needed to upgrade the defense system in order to keep it an effective deterrent against Communist China's aggressions, but there has been a steady decline in direct grants-in-aid. And, of course, the Republic of China has done more than any other free Asian nation to shoulder the responsiblities of security in that part of the world.

The miracle of Taiwan has not been wrought in a day. It has been in the making since those dark days of 1949 when the communists usurped the mainland and the Free Chinese began transforming their island province into a bastion for its recovery. What Taiwan has over the mainland is the single element of freedom. The island is not rich in natural resources. It has, for example, scarcely any discovered and exploited petroleum, while the mainland now claims self-sufficiency in crude oil. Taiwan's coal seams are running out and the potential for additions to hydroelectric power is small. What Taiwan has, however, in plenty is free enterprise encouraged by a democratic government. Entrepreneurs are motivated by the expectation of a fair and legitimate profit. Workers are motivated by a rising standard of living and, in many cases, by the attainable hope of becoming entrepreneurs.

Estimating national income on the mainland as based on data reported by the Chinese Communists, growth for the last twelve years has amounted to only 13.4 percent, or an annual rate of just 1.12 percent. Taiwan's annual growth rate of 9.32 percent has been eight times larger. According to the experts, the per capita income of mainland China during this period could have been only a little more than $90 at the highest, which was less than a third that of Taiwan—and may have been as low as $60, which is not even comparable with the Taiwan level. When we contrast the living standard on the mainland today against the Chinese people of Taiwan in terms of food, clothing, housing, travel, education and entertainment, the figures become ludicrous. For example, according to the research of experts, the average daily calorie intake in Taiwan is 2,680 and protein consumption 69.2 grams while respective figures for the mainland are 1,780 calories and 30 grams. Taiwan's annual per capita consumption of cottom fabrics is about 7.8 pounds, synthetic fibres 10 pounds, and woolen fabrics 1.2 pounds; on the mainland the figure for cotton fabrics in only 1.7 pounds. Annual per capita electricity consumption in Taiwan is 216 KWH; that on the mainland is a mere 13 KWH. For every thousand persons Taiwan has 139 bicycles, 49 motorcycles and 9 automobiles; for every thousand on the mainland there are 20 bicycles, 0.3 motorcycles and 0.8 autos. In Taiwan 98.5 percent of school-aged children are receiving a primary education, and of these about 80 percent are continuing into high school and 72 percent are going on to universities and colleges; on the mainland corresponding percentages are 78, 50, and 20. In terms of medical care and facilities, Taiwan has a hospital or clinic for every 13,000 persons compared with one for every 110,000 on the mainland. In Taiwan there are 210 radio and 53 TV sets for every thousand persons. On the mainland, the figure for radios is only 0.5 sets, and there is no TV at all except at designated public locations.

From such statistics we can readily judge the wide gap between the people's living conditions in the free Taiwan cities and countryside, under the blessings of Dr. Sun Yat-sen's Three Principles of the People, and those under the communist tyranny on the mainland. This is a record of which all Americans, once they understand it adequately, may be tremendously proud, for their nation alone has had the wisdom and courage to distinguish consistently between freedom and slavery in the Far East. The Chinese mainland is a closed economy. The open economies of the free nations cannot sell goods in a closed market except upon the humiliating terms of Mao Tse-tung's go-between. There can be no hope of reasonable profits when the regime is able to rig every economic operation to its own narrow advantage and gain. American businessmen who are now expecting early, easy profits from the anticipated "thaw" in Washington-Peiping relations should heed the words of C. W. Robinson, president of the Marcona Corporation, who has had long experience in Far Eastern ventures. "In new trade with the Peiping Regime," he says, "we may have to learn to crawl before we can walk—and we may have to do a lot of crawling."

Testifying recently before the joint congressional committee on economic affairs chaired by Senator Proxmire, Professor Liu Ta-chung of Cornell University has declared the Chinese mainland to be "practically the slowest growing region in Asia" between 1957 and 1970 in terms of per capita Gross National Product. He cast doubt on the existence of "a viable economic base" on the mainland. The only economic achievement of Communist China, he said, was the "technical and industrial capability of producing nuclear devices for the war machine"—and this, of course, at a terrible cost in terms of the standard of living. The per capita food situation on the mainland has deteriorated steadily from 1957 to 1970, Professor Lui said. The reason why 1957 was chosen as a watershed year for comparative study is that Chinese Communist statistics reached in that year a degree of respectability which has since been destroyed by the "Great Leap Forward," he explained. Despite glowing reports on the abundance of food and clothing on the mainland, Liu suggests that a careful reading of the Proxmire committee's own study would reveal that the Chinese people on the mainland were fed less well in 1970 than in 1957; and it is not at all certain that they were better clothed in 1970 than in 1957.

Meanwhile the indomitable people on the island of Taiwan have attained a standard of living second in the Far East only to Japan. Taiwan has indeed become the economic showcase of Asia, but this development was scarcely anticipated in 1949 by the "China experts" of the U.S. Department of State. The State Department at that time was openly advocating full diplomatic recognition of Mao's regime, and our government would have done so had it not been for the humiliation suffered by American officials at the hands of the Chinese Communists.

The intrusion of Red soldiers into Ambassador John Leighton Stuart's bedroom in the American Embassy at Nanking, the physical violence inflicted upon William Olive in the consular office at Shanghai, the arrest and maltreatment of Consul-General Angus Ward of Mukden, and

140

the seizure of consular offices at Peiping early in 1949 produced such waves of popular resentment in America that official action "affirmatively favorable" to the Chinese Communists was "precluded."

On January 14, 1949, the day following the seizure of Peiping offices, Secretary of State Dean Acheson had to recall all American consular personnel from the Chinese mainland. But even though he could not then propose an outright recognition of Mao's rebel forces, the Secretary of State was clearly determined to abandon the Chinese Nationalists to their own fate.

William D. Pawley, a former ambassador to Peru and State Department advisor, credits General George C. Marshall with dissuading President Truman from outright recognition. Pawley was on friendly terms with both Acheson and Marshall at the time. Testifying before the Senate Internal Security Subcommittee in 1960, Pawley recalled his own urgent efforts to block the recognition of Red China in late 1949. These included a direct and impassioned appeal to the President in which he warned of disasters ahead. Pawley testified as follows:

General Marshall has been criticized greatly for the China episode, but he . . . stopped Phil Jessup, representing Dean Acheson, from bringing back from the Far East a recommendation to recognize Red China. It was general knowledge in the Department of State that we were about to recommend recognition of Red China, and the way it was planned was for Jessup to represent Acheson at a meeting of United States ambassadors in the Far East and get from that meeting a recommendation to recognize Red China and bring them into the UN.

Taiwan now became a paramount issue in American foreign policy. On December 22, 1949 the Joint Chiefs of Staff, under the chairmanship of General Omar N. Bradley, decided to help the Chinese Nationalists to defend against a possible communist invasion and advised the dispatch of a military mission there. At a meeting of the National Security Council a week later President Truman, after hearing the opposite views of Secretary Acheson, overruled the Joint Chiefs and upheld the hands-off policy. The day following the decision made by the Joint Chiefs, Secretary Acheson sent a direct directive, which later leaked out from Tokyo, to American diplomatic and consular representatives throughout the Far East telling them of the abandonment of Taiwan by the United States. This message read in part: "Formosa (Taiwan) has no military significance. . . . We should occasionally make clear that seeking United States bases in Formosa, sending troops, supplying arms, dispatching naval units, or taking similar action would (a) accomplish no material good for China or its Nationalist regime; (b) involve the United States in a long-term venture, producing at best a new era of bristling stalemate and at worst possible involvement in open warfare."

In his famous speech at the Washington Press Club on January 12, 1950, Secretary Acheson declared that henceforth neither South Korea nor Taiwan would be considered as within the U.S. defensive perimeter. This remark invited the aggression of the North Korean communists. With the coming of the Korean crisis, of course, the United States government once more altered its official attitude toward China. The American effort to repel communist aggression in Korea would be in jeopardy if a communist attack on Formosa should occur concurrently. In his statement of June 27, 1950 President Truman, after announcing that he had ordered American air and sea forces to "give the Korean government troops cover and support," went on to say: "The attack upon Korea makes it plain beyond all doubt that communism has passed beyond the use of subversion to conquer independent nations and will now use armed invasion and war. . . . In these circumstances the occupation of Formosa by communist forces would be a direct threat to the security of the Pacific area and to United States forces performing their lawful and necessary functions in that area. Accordingly, I have ordered the Seventh Fleet to prevent an attack on Formosa. As a corollary of this action I am calling upon the Chinese government on Formosa to cease all air and sea operations against the mainland." The commander of the Seventh U.S. Fleet was also instructed to "see that this is done."

Adversaries of Red China interpreted President Truman's order as the "leashing" of Chiang Kai-shek. Truman's decision was indeed an advantage to the communists. Relieved of the necessity of guarding against a sea attack from Formosa, Mao was able to transfer troops from coastal Fukien province to the Korean frontier in preparation for the autumn crossing of the Yalu. By his order the president had committed American forces to the two-fold task of preventing an invasion of Formosa by the Chinese Communists and of preventing any attack by Chiang Kai-shek against the shaky communist regime on the mainland. The United States was committed primarily, of course, to the objective of keeping Formosa out of communist hands, and that objective naturally coincided with the main objective of the Chinese Nationalists. This leads us quickly to the central question: Did the Truman administration really intend to cooperate with, and accept the help of, the Chinese on Formosa? Or did we intend, as soon as convenient, to overlook the fact that there was indeed a common interest and common objective? The American government soon came to the conclusion that long-term cooperation with the Chinese Nationalists was desirable.

In the opening weeks of the war, the North Koreans quickly overran most of the South. The United States rushed in with air, naval, and ground forces under General Douglas MacArthur, and various other members of the United Nations sent manpower or equipment and supplies. During the summer General MacArthur's counterattack drove the invaders northward across the 38th parallel and, in full flight, almost to the border of China at the Yalu River.

Then came the incredible November "swarm" of Mao's Red Chinese hordes across the Yalu to the aid of the North Koreans. Soon the defenders of South Korea were falling back, and enemy forces were coming south of the 38th parallel. By this time some sixteen of the United Nations were represented on the battlefront, and at New York the U.N. General Assembly unequivocally branded Red China as an aggressor. By June 1951, a second United Nations counter-attack had pushed the fronts to a line approximately on the 38th parallel. At that point diplomatic efforts led to a ceasefire, which was followed by more than a year of inconclusive negotiations and a second year of inconclusive fighting.

Next to the United States, the Republic of China made the earliest offer of military assistance to South Korea. The Chinese Nationalists notified the State Department that they were ready to send three divisions, 33,000 men, but this offer was rejected with the explanation that these forces were needed more urgently in the defense of Taiwan against a possible invasion. The chief reason, however, was probably that U.S. officials feared that Chiang's participation in Korea would invite Mao Tse-tung also to intervene.

As it happened, Mao intervened anyway—and General MacArthur was tragically relieved of his command by President Truman. MacArthur had committed the diplomatic mistake of going to Taiwan to confer with the Generalissimo concerning not only the defense of the island but also the possible use of Nationalist troops in Korea.

During this critical period the American government generously supplied Taiwan with economic assistance to establish a stable currency and to improve production in agriculture and industry. In addition, a U.S. Military Assistance Advisory Group (MAAG) was assigned there to strengthen the island, maintain internal security, and provide small arms. Some heavier arms began to flow after President Eisenhower assumed office in 1953, since his advisors considered Taiwan a most important factor in deterring the mainland communists from moving into Southeast Asia.

The new administration immediately lifted President Truman's restriction against a possible move by Chiang Kai-shek's forces toward the mainland while American troops were engaged with Chinese Communist forces in Korea. In his first State of the Union message, President Eisenhower indicated that the Seventh Fleet would no longer be employed to "shield" Communist China.

American support of the Nationalist government on Taiwan grew stronger. Late in 1954 the Sino-American Mutual Defense Treaty was signed in Washington. It gave the United States the right to "dispose such land, air and sea forces" in and about Formosa and the Pescadores Islands "as may be required for their defense as determined by a mutual agreement." Since the treaty was to remain in force indefinitely, Secretary of State Dulles confidently hoped that it would "put to rest once and for all" the recurring rumor that the United States was about to abandon what the pro-communist "China expert" Owen Lattimore liked to call "that driftwood government on the beaches of Formosa."

Secretary Dulles was warmly congratulated by President Chiang for forging the necessary link in the chain of a perimeter of freedom in Asia. Newspapers in both countries lauded the treaty, including the *New York Times* which conceded in an editorial that the pact expressed "a position that most Americans strongly support."

Since the Mutual Defense Treaty did not cover the several offshore islands also held by the Free Chinese, Mao Tse-tung saw a fine chance to put American policy to a test. He chose the tiny Tachen Islands, about 250 miles northwest of Taiwan, where no outside aid could easily be brought in and a heavy communist bombardment could quickly make the Nationalist position there untenable.

Generalissimo Chiang was stubbornly determined to defend the Tachens until he was persuaded, and wisely so, by his American military advisors to evacuate with the help of the U.S. Seventh Fleet. At the same time, however, Foreign Minister Yeh received assurances from Secretary Dulles that the United States would defend the remaining offshore islands. President Eisenhower, angered by Mao's naked action against the Tachens, vowed that Formosa and the Pescadores would not be allowed to fall into the hands of "aggressive communist forces" and asked Congress for a resolution authorizing him to prevent any such attack.

Responding to this urgent request, Congress spoke almost unanimously: the affirmative vote in the House was 409-8, and three days later the Senate concurred by a vote of 85-9. The famous Formosa Resolution of 1955 authorized the president to "employ the armed forces of the United States as he deems necessary" to protect Formosa, the Pescadores and related territories.

As the resolution did not mention by name the offshore islands of Quemoy and Matsu, the question arose of what to do if the communists attacked these atolls. Secretary Dulles clarified the matter somewhat at a press conference by expressing that the president would use American air and sea forces if he should deem an attack on these two islands as part of a "larger assault" on Taiwan.

The question of admitting the Peiping regime to the United Nations became a perennial issue before the American people as early as 1949. Mao Tse-tung's crude invasion of Korea necessarily caused a shift of attitude in the State Department and forfeited the hopes of some for early endorsement of admission by the U.S. government. The British applied some pressure for the quick seating of a Chinese Communist delegation, but President Truman now declared the Red Chinese to be merely "Russian satellites." Secretary Acheson's view was reflected in his remark that we could not "buy" the friendship of the Chinese Communists, but General Marshall more realistically declared: "We cannot afford to let Formosa go." The Senate felt called upon, therefore, to adopt the first of eight unanimous resolutions against the admission of Red China into what its critics already were calling the East River Debating Society. On January 23, 1951, acting on a resolution introduced by John L. McClellan of Arkansas, the Senate voted 91-0 that "the Communist Chinese government should not be admitted to membership in the United Nations as the representative of China." By the following September, the various pressures for UN admission and, as well, formal U.S. diplomatic recognition again so alarmed the Senate that a majority of 56 members of both parties addressed a letter to President Truman opposing "the recognition of Communist China by the government of the United States, or its admission into the United Nations." Among the senatorial signers were the liberal Paul Douglas of Illinois, the conservative Robert A. Taft of Ohio, and Richard M. Nixon. Again in 1953 both houses adopted unopposed expressions against admission. The Senate, acting on an amendment to an appropriations bill offered by Senator Styles Bridges of New Hampshire, resolved 76-0 that "the Communist Chinese government should not be admitted to the United Nations as the representative of China." The House, on a motion by Congressman Robert B. Cheperfield of Illinois, concurred by vote of 379-0.

Robert J. Donovan, Eisenhower's biographer, has suggested that the president was basically unconvinced that "the vital interest of the United States" was actually best served by "prolonged non-recognition" of Red China. Nevertheless President Eisenhower and Secretary Dulles on many occasions made it quite clear that they did strongly oppose both UN admission and U.S. recognition of the Peiping regime. The President expressed himself with considerable emphasis as follows:

I am completely and unalterably opposed, under the present situation, to the admission of Red China to the UN. I personally think that 95 percent of the population of the United States would take the same stand.

There is a moral question first of all. . . . The UN was not established primarily as a super-government, clothed with all the authority of a super-government. . . . On top of that, Red China is today at war with the UN. They were declared an aggressor by the UN. . . . That situation has never been changed.

To disapprobate admission, Secretary Dulles relied heavily on the inhibition in the United Nations charter against admitting any state answering to Red China's description. At the San Francisco founding conference, Dulles recalled, the proposition that the United Nations should be unselective and universal was "strongly argued," but "the proponents of selectivity" won out. Furthermore, said the Secretary, the objection to Red China as less than "peace-loving" was strengthened by the charter provision that "any nation against which enforcement action was taken [as in Korea] should be liable to suspension from membership in the UN."

Among the influential private citizens in those days who urged the unacceptability of Red China, Adolf A. Berle, Jr., the former Assistant Secretary of State, was conspicuous. A profound student of international affairs, Berle summarized his views:

> The United Nations charter names the Republic of China as a permanent member of the Security Council. It is absurd to suggest bringing into the peace-keeping machinery of the United Nations a country which has made war against Korea and signed an armistice there but which has refused to make peace. . . . It is one thing to admit a member to an organization, being convinced that the member will join in and forward its work. It is another to admit a tough, or a gangster, who hammers at the door with a gun butt.

Meanwhile, organized expressions of public concern underscored such personal anxieties. The American Federation of Labor, the United States Chamber of Commerce, the American Federation of Women's Clubs, and other national organizations stood solidly opposed to admission. A poll conducted in 1954 by the Council of Foreign Relations among 800 selected "leaders of American thought and action," including businessmen, lawyers, educators, and newspaper editors, showed that eighty percent were opposed to the admission of the Chinese Communists to the UN while seventy-six percent were generally satisfied with the administration's posture in Far Eastern affairs.

In a speech late that year President Eisenhower was explicit. Reviewing the spasmodic aggressions of Red China from Korea in 1950, through the 1953-54 incursions into Indochina, to the current bombardments of the offshore islands, the President adverted to the disastrous attempts by the Atlantic Powers to appease the Japanese warlords in Manchuria, Mussolini in Ethiopia, and Hitler in the Rhineland, Austria, and Czechoslovakia. He said:

> Let us suppose that the Chinese Communists conquer Quemoy. Would that be the end of the story? We know that it would not be the end of the story. History teaches that, when powerful despots can gain something through aggression, they try, by the same methods, to gain more and more. . . . The shooting which the Chinese Communists started on August 23 . . . is part of . . . an ambitious plan of armed conquest . . . [which] would liquidate all the free world positions in the Western Pacific area and bring them under captive governments . . . hostile to the United States. . . . Thus the Chinese and Russian Com-

munists would come to dominate at least the western half of the now friendly Pacific Ocean.

In 1956 Congress again spoke with a united voice (391-0 in the House, 86-0 in the Senate) to re-emphasize previous interventions against the seating of Red China. Congress expressed the conviction that such admission would "gravely injure the United Nations and impair its effective functioning in accordance with the provisions of the United Nations charter." Visiting Taipei in July of that year, Vice President Nixon delivered a personal message from President Eisenhower to President Chiang Kai-shek which, besides paying lavish tribute to the Generalissimo's leadership and courage, asserted: "Let there be no misapprehension about our own steadfastness in continuing to support the Republic of China." The next month, at the Democratic and Republican national conventions in Chicago and San Francisco, both parties inserted planks in their platforms pledging continued opposition to the seating of the Peiping regime in the United Nations. On that occasion President Eisenhower remarked with deadly seriousness:

I must say to you very frankly and soberly [that] the United States cannot accept the result that the communists seek. Neither can we show . . . a weakness of purpose, a timidity, which would surely lead them to move more aggressively against us and our friends in the Western Pacific. . . . A Western Pacific Munich would not buy us peace or security.

Congress has made clear its recognition that the security of the Western Pacific is vital to the security of the United States and that we should be firm. The Senate has ratified, by overwhelming vote, security treaties with the Republic of China covering Formosa and the Pescadores, and also the Republic of China. We have a mutual security treaty with the Republic of the Philippines, which could be next in line for conquest if Formosa fell into hostile hands. . . . In addition, there is a joint resolution which the Congress passed in January 1955 dealing specifically with Formosa and the offshore islands of Free China in the Formosa Straits.

If the present bombardment and harassment of Quemoy should be converted into a major assault, with which the local defenders could not cope, we would be compelled to face precisely the situation that Congress visualized in 1955.

President Eisenhower was re-elected in 1956 by a landslide plurality of nearly ten million votes. He ran on a platform that tersely declared: "We shall continue to oppose the seating of Communist China in the United

Nations." The authorship of that plank was attributed to Secretary Dulles.

As long as he was on the job, Secretary Dulles held firmly against any softening of the official American attitude toward the Peiping regime. In the lower echelons of government, however, there remained a persistent interest in the idea that some basic revisions were desirable. When ill health forced the retirement of Dulles, the rumbles from below became more audible. In the presidential contest of 1960 the China question was hotly debated, particularly the issue of the offshore islands, in the famous televised confrontations of candidates Nixon and Kennedy. The position of Vice President Nixon on this issue was predetermined; he was obligated to uphold the actions and attitudes of the past eight years. Senator Kennedy, on the other hand, was under no such wraps. With nothing to lose, the charismatic senator gave expression to his current view that the defense of the offshore islands was not "worth" American blood. The larger question of the defense of Taiwan, if that became necessary, was left in the air.

Senator Kennedy's hairbreadth victory brought to Washington a new group of officials and advisors whose commitment to Free China was somewhat less enthusiastic than that of the outgoing Republican administration. But the American people were clearly unready for any drastic shift of policy. The brutal record of Mao's regime, as evidenced perhaps most graphically by the recent reports of atrocities in Tibet, was still too fresh in the public consciousness. Moreover, the president was perhaps still aware of what he had once said on the subject of the loss of mainland China to communism.

Early in 1949 young Congressman John F. Kennedy had spoken boldly and plainly on what had gone wrong in the Pacific at the end of World War II: "A sick Roosevelt . . . gave the Kurile Islands, as well as the control of various strategic ports . . . to the Soviet Union. . . . The responsibility for the failure of our foreign policy in the Far East rests squarely with the White House and Department of State. . . . What our young men had saved, our diplomats and our president have frittered away." Ten years later, however, Senator John F. Kennedy had changed his mind on some related issues. While President Eisenhower was standing firm against further appeasement of the Chinese Communists in their attempt to seize Quemoy and Matsu, Senator Kennedy was declaring in his speeches that these atols were "not essential" to the defense of Formosa. After JFK's inauguration in 1961, therefore, the China policy of the past decade was certain to be subjected to an agonizing reappraisal.

What the new president's advisors on foreign policy finally advanced was the outworn and improbable "Two China" solution. Under the chairmanship of J. William Fulbright the Senate Foreign Relations Committee quietly commissioned a study, prepared by the private research firm of Conlon Associates, Ltd., of San Francisco, recommending a gradual shift in policy. The suggested shift would lead ultimately to U.S. recognition of

Communist China and support for the seating of Mao's agents in the UN Security Council, on the one hand, and U.S. recognition of Taiwan as a "new" republic and its seating in the UN General Assembly on the other. But the current behavior of the Chinese Communists was such that no immediate plans for this basic change in the official American attitude in policy could be advertised. The president told newsmen in June 1962, for instance, that he would certainly "take the action necessary" to assure the defense of Taiwan and the Pescadores, as provided for in the 1955 Formosa Resolution, if Communist China were to take any "aggressive action" against Quemoy or Matsu. "Any threat to the offshore islands," he now said, "must be judged in relation to its wider meaning for the safety of Formosa and the peace of the area."

The assassination of President Kennedy and the succession of Lyndon B. Johnson resulted in no official alteration of policy. Deepening troubles in Indochina, together with Mao's flat rejection of a proposal to permit American scholars, doctors, and other interested persons to visit the mainland, prevented much sympathetic attention to the business of easing tensions with the Communist regime. While Senator Goldwater's candidacy in 1964 did raise many questions regarding future American military involvement in Asia, the challenger and the incumbent did not disagree publicly on the basic matter of the American commitment to the Republic of China.

During the next four years American policy remained essentially unchanged. The highly visible role of the Chinese Communists in the Vietnam War was the obvious reason why it could not then be changed. It was too glaringly evident that Mao Tse-tung was deeply involved in the war by proxy, sending his military advisors and engineers to bolster Hanoi against the increasing numbers of American troops sent to Indochina by the Johnson administration. Because of Mao's sustained support of North Vietnam, any alteration in American policy on the China question had to be held in abeyance until after the 1968 election.

Little was said about it in the campaign, and with Richard M. Nixon coming to the White House any prospect of change seemed more remote than ever. Yet just a few weeks after he assumed office, President Nixon requested his national security advisor, the ubiquitous Henry A. Kissinger, to prepare a policy paper on the China question. It was during President Nixon's first months in office, therefore, that the machinery was actually put into motion for the most momentous shift of U.S. foreign policy within a generation. The steps designed by Dr. Kissinger were gradual, almost imperceptible. First, travel restrictions were lifted; then there was a slight easing of trade restrictions; next, the mission of the Seventh Fleet in the Formosa Strait was brought to a virtual end; and then the Warsaw "talks" at the ambassadorial level, broken off during the Johnson years, were quietly resumed.

The decade of the 1970s will very likely be decisive in the history of modern Asia. The fickle winds of change are sweeping over the Eastern world. Choices that are made in the next few years promise to shape irrevocably the future of thousands of millions of people in that half of the globe. These choices may also determine, perhaps irrevocably, the American posture in the whole Pacific area.

No single issue in U.S. foreign relations in the last generation has stirred such frenzied interest as the China question today. Since the disastrous developments on the Asian mainland immediately following World War II, four presidential administrations have affirmed our stance to be one of strength in dealing with the malicious masters of Peiping.

Until now, official policy has reflected the negative sentiments of the preponderant majority of Americans toward that atheistic, collectivist regime which has grown more arrogant, aggressive, and imperialistic each year. But now, early in the decade of the 1970s, our official policy seems certainly to be shifting. But this is all that is certain. Such a shift may or may not prove permanent, and the sentiments of the American people may or may not shift with it.

It is therefore vital for Americans today to grasp the fact that Peiping's enmity toward the United States has deep ideological, geopolitical, and practical roots. Among the most important of these is the messianic complex of Chairman Mao. Since the death of his mentor Marshall Stalin two decades ago, Mao Tse-tung has regarded himself as the torchbearer of global revolution. He believes himself to be the only true successor of Marx and Lenin, the orthodox leader of the world communist movement, and hence the arch-foe of "capitalistic imperialism."

The United States is necessarily his primary target, his bull's eye, because this nation just happens—not so much by choice as by force of circumstances—to be the pacesetter of the free world. Not only is it the ideological incompatibility of systems which separates Peiping from us, but the American presence in Asia is correctly seen by Mao as the insurmountable—and therefore intolerable—obstacle to his geopolitical ambitions. In the two decades of its existence, every move by the shaky Peiping monolith to subvert its neighbors has been checkmated or challenged by American action or influence.

Whatever flaws the Chinese Communist system may possess, historical nearsightedness of leadership is not one of them. Mao Tse-tung and his cohorts clearly recognize the tendency in America toward isolationism—a tendency inherited from the American frontier past and nourished in recent years by our futilities in Korea and Vietnam—a tendency that is stronger right now than at any time in the last three decades.

The Red Chinese mandarins, together with their counterparts in the Soviet Politboro, desire to exploit that old weakness in the American stance. There is presently much evidence of neo-isolationism and defeatism in the thinking of many Americans in and out of public life. Those who argue for a completely isolationist course—no more military alliances, no more foreign commitments of any sort, no more overseas "adventures"—are not only badly dated but also evidently blind to all the lessons of the recent past.

The principal objective of United States foreign policy, in this century as in the last, has always been to keep war as far away as possible from our shores. Yet some Americans seem to have completely forgotten the error of those in yesterday's England who thought of Czechoslovakia as a faraway place and cheered Chamberlain's fatuous slogan of "Peace in Our Time" in 1938, who did not want to "die for Danzig" in 1939, but who died instead in 1940 and 1941 for a Britain herself beleaguered and beset.

An isolationist "Fortress America" was not a very sound concept in the first half of the twentieth century; it is simply not a pragmatic possibility in the latter half. As President Lyndon B. Johnson warned: "We have to recognize that there is no safety in a sudden turning away from Europe or Asia, from the Middle East or Latin America. If we fall into isolationism, we will find that we are the ones who are isolated." The machinery of the United Nations is presently tooled to produce just such an isolated condition for the United States.

There is much more to be said about the recent seating of the Red Chinese delegation in the UN than the tired, simplistic parroting of the misconceived line that this finally provides "representation" for 800 million people previously "ignored." A diplomatic offensive is well under way in the UN to oust American influence not only from Indochina but from all of Asia.

The Chinese sense that this is the moment to capitalize on the dejected, frustrated mood of many Americans regarding the mess in Vietnam. They realize how weary the people at large, and even some patriots, have become of that "crazy Asian war." Unable to intimidate four American presidential administrations with center plunges, the Chinese Communists now are trying an end run with their ping-pong matches, acupuncture and "smiling diplomacy." The first objective of this new offensive is to diminish the international status of the Republic of China so as to eradicate the symbolic influence of the Free Chinese upon the restless mainland population.

Many Americans are still confused as to how Nationalist China, a cofounder and charter-abiding member of the United Nations, could be "expelled"—and how Communist China, a declared aggressor, could be "admitted." It may be appropriate here to quote the eloquent European statesman who said: "The people have a right to know, for only through knowledge can wisdom come—and only through wisdom, justice."

What actually did happen in the UN on that day, October 25, 1971, branded as another "moment of infamy" in modern history by U.S. Ambassador George Bush? Technically speaking, Communist China was not "admitted" to the UN under the charter rules because that would have been impossible. If it had been a simple question of the "admission" of Red

China, either of two Security Council members—the United States or the Republic of China—could have exercised the single-vote veto to prevent it. The Soviet Union has so acted on an average of twice annually—fifty-one times in twenty-six years—to block the admission of an applying state not sufficiently socialistic to pass muster in Moscow.

If "explusion" of Nationalist China were the issue, then Ambassador Bush, professing to deplore such a suggestion, could simply cast his veto on behalf of President Nixon's administration. The charter is clear on both of these points. Article 9 provides that admission "will be effected by a decision of the General Assembly upon the recommendation of the Security Council," but any such proposed recommendation of the Security Council could be vetoed by a single vote. Moreover, in all questions of either admission or expulsion, the will of the General Assembly must be by a two-thirds vote.

What actually happened, of course, was that the UN Secretariat decided to make "representation" or "credentials" the issue. Which of the two claimants—the Republic of China on the island province of Taiwan with fifteen million people, or the People's Republic of China on the mainland with a population fifty times larger—deserved to be accredited to the UN? In this way the whole matter could be kept securely in the General Assembly. "Representation," unlike admission or expulsion, did not carry a mandatory two-thirds vote in the Assembly; it must be expressly made so by a preliminary majority vote. That procedural vote failed, but this point has not yet been thoroughly explained to the American people. There was no other way except through the issue of "credentials" that Red China could obtain a seat in the UN. It was much like a bandit squeezing his way into the back door of that glass house on the bank of the East River in New York City.

Every American should try to take a close look at the possible implications of the monstrous decision of the United Nations to remove a respectable member like the Republic of China. The retiring Secretary-General, U-Thant of Burma, declared the action to be "a tremendous step forward." Many of the members hailed the China vote as the opening of a new page in history. Just what will be written on that page remains to be seen, but the real losers in the gargantuan diplomatic mockery of October 25, 1971 were the American people and the United Nations itself.

Over the past two decades, beginning with the Korean War, the American people have become increasingly disillusioned by the ineffectiveness of the UN as a peace-keeping force. The international organization has very definite utility, particularly in the economic and public service activities of such agencies as UNESCO and UNICEF, but it has proven virtually useless in great-power confrontations, and has been able to apply only tangential pressure in conflicts involving smaller nations.

Neither Biafra nor Vietnam, Israel nor the Arab states depend upon it for security. No international body which forsakes honesty and morality, as did the UN in the China vote of 1971, can long retain the respect of freedom-loving peoples. Many rational Americans, therefore, may well wonder why we should continue to foot the bill for an organization which staggers between ineffectiveness at best and, at the worst, outright betrayal of the free world.

Almost since its inception the United Nations has been faced with serious financial problems. Since the population of the United States is only six percent of the total UN membership, the individual American taxpayer who contributes thirty-six percent of the annual budget needed to save the UN from bankruptcy is now questioning whether he has been making a wise investment.

There is some serious soul-searching in America today as to the future role of the United Nations. This is reflected in critical remarks by such early UN supporters as former Secretary of State Dean Acheson, who has recently said that the best thing to do now is to treat the United Nations with "intelligent neglect." Whatever this may mean, others may feel that simple neglect should be enough. After having been insulted so grossly in the General Assembly vote on the China question, the United States does appear a little ridiculous continuing to bet so heavily on the good faith and efficacy of the United Nations.

Many Americans are also seeking answers to the big questions concerning the future role of the United States in the Far East. Should we now take the big gamble and withdraw our influence completely from east Asia, as the Chinese Communists have repeatedly demanded? If we do this, what will be the fate of the Republic of China on the island of Taiwan? Will Taiwan become another Tibet? Or, if the Red Chinese behave themselves, should we move gradually toward full diplomatic recognition of the Peiping regime? What are we to do about Japan, the Philippines, Malaysia, and Australia and New Zealand? Since the close of World War II, America has contributed greatly to the security and independence of Asian peoples. We have engaged directly in two Asian wars, and through our mutual security programs we have met the pervasive threat of communism by helping to build up the military, political, and economic strength of our Far Eastern allies and friends. But every one of the small, free nations of Asia continues to have a gnawing fear of the propaganda machinery and military potential of Peiping. Red China is seen as the major threat to their free institutions, which are still young and developing. In view of this, can the United States now coldly abandon these nations to their own defense?

In the days and years ahead there is bound to be a great deal of speculation as to how the American president, whoever he may be at the time, will react to pressure from Peiping for the annexation of Taiwan and withdrawal of all American commitments to that island. Certainly President Nixon was vague in his report to the Congress on what he and Dr. Kissinger obtained from the "Journey for Peace." He has asked those who are reacting negatively to his new initiative to trust him. Pointing to his long record as a realistic student of communism, he tried to reassure the American people that he knows what he is doing and that he has no intention of selling America's allies down the river in Asia. But if President Nixon's initiative fails to achieve its advertised purpose of lessening tension in Asia, what will it do instead? It could do exactly the opposite by encouraging the aggressive ambitions of the communists—and that, of course, could spell global tragedy in the 1970s.

As has often been said, the U.S. security position in the Far East depends on the continued integrity of the island chain running from Japan in the north down through Okinawa, Taiwan, and the Philippines to Australia and New Zealand in the south. This position is maintained militarily by the forward deployment of American ground, naval, and air forces in the western Pacific. It is supported politically by a series of bilateral and multilateral defense treaties with the nations concerned. And it is reinforced psychologically by generous aid programs designed to help our Asian allies to build stable societies capable eventually of providing for their welfare and security. But the Chinese Communists now are making it very plain that they expect the United States quickly to withdraw all such commitments from the island of Taiwan, the base of the Republic of China, so as to permit the Peiping regime a perfectly free hand in determining the future of that island. Premier Chou En-lai specifically reiterated this position in an interview with James Reston of the *New York Times* and in other recent interviews.

Why are the Red Chinese so urgently demanding that the anti-Communist redoubt in Taiwan be turned over to them? It is because they know, as they have always known, that they will never be completely secure in their grip on the mainland provinces until the voice of freedom in Taiwan has been silenced. After twenty-three years of totalitarian suppression on the mainland, after an extended reign of terror in which about a million people a year have been tortured and murdered or have otherwise lost their lives, there still exists a great underground of silent opposition to Maoism. This underground has been kept alive by heroic anti-communists from Taiwan who risk their own lives to operate on the mainland. Over the years, more than 20,000 brave men and women from Taiwan have died on such missions. They have been willing to give everything in the cause of freedom for their compatriots on the mainland.

The United States has nothing to gain by the wooing of Red China except perhaps a little trade, but we certainly have a great deal to lose. We could easily lose our credibility and our national honor. We could lose forever the loyalty and trust of the free nations of the East, and the free nations of the Western world would not be long in getting the message. Paul Scott, one of the best informed columnists in the United States, suggested in an article late in 1971 that President Nixon's chief military advisors believe the president's hope for easing tensions could turn out to be "one of the great illusions of our time." Many Asian leaders feel the same way, and wiser heads throughout the Western world are nodding also.

When President Marcos of the Philippines, an unfailing friend of the United States whose nation suffers from a large militant Maoist underground, learned of the American switch in China policy, he cried out: "If this can happen to Nationalist China, there is no assurance that it won't happen to us." Premier Lee Kuan Yew of Singapore, who has backed the United States consistently in many crises, said sadly: "Some countries may now be allowed to go neutral. Some will become pro-communist." One of the sharpest revelations on the Far Eastern outlook was made by Senator Adlai E. Stevenson III of Illinois after a trip to the western Pacific late in 1971. "I found Asians everywhere," he said, "deeply concerned, bewildered. Nobody knows what is going to become of it. But they are concerned that the American president is going to Peiping to pay homage." Many Asians apparently feel there is real danger that the United States is not going to stay the course. They fear that the hegemony which Mao Tse-tung has not been able to achieve by his own resources may now be handed to him by a war-weary Uncle Sam.

The rush to "reduce tensions" in an election year has suggested to some that President Nixon's new policy may have arisen largely from the exigencies of domestic politics. It is just as easy to assign other motives for the president's timing of the Peiping and Moscow summits, and just as fruitless. What is really important to ponder is that this American president seems inexplicably to be turning his back on an old and loyal ally, a government which has proven itself by making a bombed-out island into a self-sustaining, relatively free country by Asian standards. The island of Taiwan under the Republic of China has, moreover, been recognized as vital to the perimeter of freedom in Asia. When asked by a congressional committee for his assessment of the strategic importance of Formosa, General Douglas MacArthur answered: "I have known every naval commander that has operated in the Pacific in the last ten years intimately, and most of those which have operated in the last thirty years, and there isn't a single exception to it. . . . If you lose Formosa, you have lost your littoral line of defense."

A chain, of course, is no stronger than its weakest link, and any break in the island chain weakens materially the entire system. Taiwan under the Chinese Communists would mean a break in the island chain; it would immediately threaten the Japanese islands to the north and the Philippines to the south. Its loss would have a profound political influence over the rest of Asia because Taiwan represents, psychologically, a deadly potential peril both to the regime at Peiping and to the facade of Maoism everywhere that it exists.

If the Chinese Nationalists are to retain their strategic viability in a strong flanking position on their island opposite the very heart of mainland China, it is essential that the new military aid program that has been recommended by the Joint Chiefs of Staff be initiated at once to bolster the air, anti-aircraft, and naval forces of the Republic of China. Taiwan must be retained as a bastion of free world strength. Chinese Communist possession of Taiwan is intolerable, indeed unthinkable, to any American whose respect for freedom goes beyond his own back yard.

A majority of the American people believe that President Nixon's visit to Peiping was a sincere effort on his part to reduce tensions in Asia and elsewhere. The people have generally approved President Nixon's desire to develop a "dialogue" with the leaders of Communist China, but they do not expect this president or any other to deal away the material advantages of the free world posture in exchange for Maoist slogans and sayings. They may have seen no great harm in the president responding to Chou En-lai's invitation to pay a visit to Peiping, but they have plenty of reason to question the exact meaning of the five nebulous principles of the Shanghai Communiqué which are supposed to govern relations henceforth: mutual respect for sovereignty and territorial integrity, mutual non-aggression, non-interference, equality and mutual benefits, and peaceful co-existence.

By his pilgrimage to Peiping—and that is the appropriate description—President Nixon has launched us into uncharted waters. He has loosened the moorings and set us adrift in treacherous channels. In the Shanghai Communiqué he agreed to "territorial integrity," and to the Chinese Communists this has meant one thing—that the "Taiwan question" is to be solved by them alone. Any hope that Mao Tse-tung would ease his stance on this issue was as uninformed as it was vain. The United States may eventually realize some benefits from the president's journey, but if such benefits do materialize, the price paid for them in Taiwan must always be weighed.

There is psychological danger in the fact that some Americans have come away from their television sets with the impression that the so-called People's Republic is a land of work and progress inhabited by happy millions, however indoctrinated and mechanical they may seem to Western eyes. The TV viewers watched the president and Mrs. Nixon smiling, toasting, and shaking hands in Peiping, Hangchow, and Shanghai. The president's party did not visit Tibet, not did it speak freely with the people.

Perhaps, as some insiders have said, the president's trip to the mainland was really a device to drive a wedge between Moscow and Peiping. The reasoning goes that today the only immediate military threat to China comes from Soviet forces arrayed on her borders. As seen from Peiping, this is indeed a cause for concern. With such a threat before them, it makes sense for the Red Chinese to seek better relations with the United States, particularly if the American president will come in the role of the humble supplicant and is prepared to make large concessions in order to achieve better relations. This, of course, is one possible explanation for the president's visit. Playing Peiping against Moscow may appear to be good strategy, but it rests on the mistaken idea that communism is basically nationalistic. Precisely the opposite is the case, as has been proven endlessly but is still hard for many to accept.

The lead players in the global drama are not really three separate nations with the traditional goals and objectives of great powers, but rather two systems which are still fundamentally in conflict with each other. Moreover, such an effort as driving a wedge between Peiping and Moscow will hardly be time well spent if we also succeed in driving a wedge between ourselves and our Asian allies. It is the latter possibility that appears, just now at least, far more likely to result. There is one long-term objective on which the Red Chinese and the Red Russians consistently achieve full cooperation—the eventual destruction of the United States. It is highly improbable that either communist power would ever fight with us against the other. William E. Griffith, professor of political science at the Massachusetts Institute of Technology Center for International Studies, has defined the realities cogently and correctly: "Russia remains our immediate concern. The Kremlin is not suddenly going to be friendly with us simply because of the Chinese threat. Rather the Soviet Union, like China, is an expansionist, imperialist power basically hostile to the United States."

The notion that the seating of the Red Chinese at the UN, and ultimate U.S. recognition of their regime, will somehow exacerbate communist frictions is absolutely schizophrenic. We Americans are often the world's most gullible people. After a generation of cold war we are tired of bearing international burdens and, moreover, are presently preoccupied with unique and complex domestic problems. We like to imagine, therefore, that the president's journeys to Peiping and Moscow will somehow bring us out of the cold war and into a new era of low global tension.

The assumption is that the dragon and the bear will fall happily to sleep once they are fed. When this is finally seen not to be the case, it may be too late to avoid a diplomatic disaster. Some Americans are already saying that it is more important for our president to keep our alliances together than to undertake a series of Machiavellian maneuvers—with no assurance whatever of success—that may encourage the two communist beasts to leap at each other's throats. The Sino-Soviet "split," as their family quarrel has incorrectly been called, developed rather fully a decade ago without any encouragement on America's part.

The Japanese ambassador to the United States under the Sato government recently expressed the fears verbalized by many non-communist Asian leaders. If the United States persists in projecting the idea that it is determined to thin out its security commitments, the ambassador anticipates an adverse effect. "In Asia as a whole," he observes, "psychological measures are sometimes more important than actual military protection." A simplistic but prevalent misconception in some quarters in the United States is that Peiping, plagued by border clashes with the Soviets externally and by factional disputes and economic weakness internally, is actually powerless to "take" southeast Asia. But Chairman Mao is like Stalin, not like Hitler. He would rather talk than fight—if someone else is willing to do the actual fighting.

For Mao Tse-tung, nothing is more desirable than to stir up fresh armed conflicts in which his political agents, military advisors, and engineers may play a pivotal part. He depends on such conflicts to prove the correctness of his line of millitancy, with which he can silence his opponents at home and compete with the Kremlin for ideological leadership of communism. A Red Chinese thrust of this sort into southeast Asia is a double-edged knife with which Mao can cut away the opposition of both Soviet and domestic rivals. And it costs very little. Merely an indirect form of aggression, it is fought with other lives and in other lands.

As a matter of fact, Peiping has been behind the insurrections in southeast Asian countries all along, and Mao now needs only the smallest excuse to give these a fresh impetus. This drive dates back to the Bandung Conference of 1955 when Chou En-lai began to woo the developing nations of Asia and Africa. Their basic idea is that while the United States heads a "first world" which is capitalistic and white, and while the Soivet Union heads a "second world" which is communist but also white, only Communist China and Chairman Mao are qualified to lead the "third world" which is generally socialistic but, more importantly, colored.

In this new struggle of the basically rural areas of the world against the basically urban areas that are Europe and North America, an important battlefield is the United Nations. Mao Tse-tung is now ready to use his platform in the UN to win over all the "underdeveloped" countries. This intent was manifested in a recent speech by Chou En-lai, whose stock seems to have risen lately in the Red Chinese hierarchy since the purge of Mao's designated successor Lin Piao. Praising the decision to seat his regime, Chou En-lai called it a clear sign of "strong opposition to imperialist control and plunder and racial discrimination" on the part of the many smaller nations represented in the General Assembly. He spelled out for them what the Chinese Communists would do in the world body for "all the oppressed nations and peoples of the world and all the medium and small countries bullied and injured by the superpowers." By uniting under the Chinese leadership, he promised, they would "surely win greater victories."

Mao Tse-tung and Chou En-lai are at this moment conducting insurgency schools for revolutionaries from many southeast Asian countries, including Malaysia, Burma, and Thailand. What is more, the Red Chinese for the last few years have been busy trying to stir up domestic trouble in the United States. According to Justice Department intelligence reports, as many as 4,200 aliens from Communist China have been sneaking into the United States every year in the guise of seamen from Hong Kong and elsewhere. Only one out of ten are caught, and many go directly into subversive work or the narcotics traffic. In one of his last articles, F.B.I. Director J. Edgar Hoover warned that Red China's new place in the United Nations has now given Mao a "legal base" from which to accelerate his espionage activities.

There is ample proof that Mao has lent financial support to the Black Panther Party and other revolutionary groups, including the notorious Progressive Labor Party. The columnist Joseph Alsop has commented on the strange mentality of some American intellectuals, college professors, and students, who have been anxious for some time to come out openly in their adoration of the person and "thought" of Mao Tse-tung. Mao's "Little Red Book" of revolutionary philosophy and slogans proliferates on college campuses, and in anti-war demonstrations all over the country his roundish, benign face has smiled out of thousands of pin-on buttons. "This is the state of intellectual corruption," Alsop writes, "that has been very widely reached by America's left-wing intellectuals and the young people who follow them."

What can we derive from an awarness of these documented communist activities? One may find it helpful from time to time to dust off a remarkable little book entitled *Why Don't We Learn from History?* by the late British scholar, B. H. Liddell Hart, who was purported to be the world's greatest military historian. This extract is timely: "The longer I watch current events, the more I have come to see how many of our troubles arise from the habit, on all sides, of suppressing or distorting what we know quite well is the truth, out of devotion to a cause, an ambition, or an institution."

We might take to heart the two inscriptions engraved on the National Archives building in Washington: "What Is Past Is Prologue" and "Study the Past." We ought also to ponder the wise words of George Santayana: "Those who refuse to learn from history are condemned to repeat it." But, sad to say, the worst mistakes of the past are not even being reviewed today. The past, to be sure, should teach us not to be discouraged; we should try again and again where we have failed before.

But why repeat the old mistakes? Why dally with aggressors when recent history informs us unmistakably that the threats of an international bully must be met head-on with resolution. But what are our diplomats, and some of our legislators, talking about today? Their favorite word is "accommodation"—by which they can mean nothing other, really, than the discredited and disastrous Munich philosophy of appeasement.

Too often in our own times we have seen the tendency on the part of some national leaders to believe that they could purchase security for their own nations by trafficking in freedom of other nations. How many catastrophes does it take to prove that softness in the face of aggression fosters further aggression?

Today in America there are some misguided publicists, some muddle-minded professors, and some unthinking businessmen who pooh-pooh the menace of communism. They raise smoke-screens about the "need for trade" or try to defend communist activity as a constitutional right. Newspapers are filled with stories giving the minutest details of the travels of American correspondents and others in Red China. But we can find little about the continuing influx of refugees from the Chinese mainland into Hong Kong. This is a matter that has been neglected by our press, our "experts" on China, and our decision-makers alike. The fact is that there are more Chinese escaping across Deep Bay to Hong Kong than East Germans scaling or tunneling under the Berlin Wall. The size of the influx from the mainland into the tiny British crown colony in fact reflects the degree of political instability in China. In the last twenty-three years, at least two million refugees have fled to Hong Kong, accounting for more than forty percent of the island's total population. The largest exodus occurred ten years ago, in April and May 1962, when a total of 142,000 escapees swarmed into Hong Kong, roughly over 70,000 a month, but two out of every three were turned back by the British authorities. Each year since, many thousands have fled from that regime which now proposes to wear the credentials of the Chinese people in the United Nations.

It is time to look squarely at the record of communism in China. In his book, *Out of Red China,* Liu Shaw-tong observes: "If the rains of communism flood the world, humanity will drown. Would you understand me, dear friend, if I told you I saw an old woman weep because the sun had died in China?" Many millions of Chinese have died of communism in China. The immensity of the crimes against his own people by Mao Tse-tung, his long-time lieutenant Chou En-lai, and their entourage is thoroughly documented in a recent study entitled *The Human Cost of Communism in China* by Professor Richard L. Walker of the University of South Carolina and released by the U.S. Senate Committee on the Judiciary. Professor Walker estimates that no less than thirty-four million, and perhaps as many as sixty million, have been victims of communism in China—and ninety percent of these were killed *after* Mao seized power in 1949.

It takes no courage to become so flexible as to desert moral principles in international life. Secretary of State John Foster Dulles was maligned as "inflexible" because he would not compromise with communism. He was denounced as "too rigid" because he refused to bow to the deceptive wiles of an unscrupulous adversary. But Dulles tried every resource of argument, and every formula of honorable adjustment, to achieve acceptance of the simple truth that peoples must be left free to work out their own destinies and that military force must be renounced as the sole means of settling international disputes. The essence of the Dulles philosophy in foreign policy was that morality must triumph over immorality, that a surrender to expediency can only lead to eventual disaster. He was mindful of how the path of appeasement had led to a world war in 1939. He saw no merit in cringing before the enemy or in taking any step that could be construed as weak or irresolute. To avoid war, he believed that it was necessary to risk war. On this he never deviated, though the cynics ridiculed his willingness to take risks as "brinksmanship." Dulles knew, as we should have learned by now, that we cannot advance freedom while accommodating those dedicated to the elimination of freedom; nor can we advance justice by placating those who despise justice.

To avert a third world war, Americans must maintain an uncompromising idealism. Appeasement can never pay. Irresolution has often been the precursor of war. The free world is being threatened today in every continent. The conditions we face are unique. Many people today are questioning, and often denying, the objective distinction between good and evil and the ability of human reason to know with certainty what is right or wrong. Ignorance of moral principles and rejection of the very notion of international morality are on the rise, and this threatens to undermine the most sacred traditions of all of mankind. But the eternal will to freedom is something that no dictator has ever succeeded in suppressing. That is why the rulers in Peiping must, after two decades, still maintain themselves in power by means of naked power itself.

The recent action of the United Nations in replacing the Republic of China with the so-called People's Republic of Chairman Mao will be set down in history as a classic denial of international justice. The United States now has an obligation to help find a way to guarantee preservation of the legitimate rights and aspirations of the Free Chinese government on Taiwan. This is a challenge of the very first priority in our diplomacy in the years ahead. The Free Chinese have stood steadfast as our friends for many years, a fact which Americans cannot in good conscience forget. The United States is bound by treaty to defend the Republic of China. Yet a subtle campaign has already begun in the American media to scrap our relationship with the Chinese Nationalists on Taiwan. The president and various high officials have stated repeatedly that the United States government is not going to abruptly abandon Taiwan, but at the same time it is dead certain that in the months ahead the American people are in for a major propaganda drive from the left to try to get us to do exactly that.

Winston Churchill, the actual father of the cold war strategy, was once asked if he thought the United States could continue to hold the position of world leadership inherited from Great Britain in World War II. He answered, out of his deep wisdom: "It can do so, if it will stay in course." What Churchill said can certainly be made applicable today. Despite some recent pooh-poohing by left-leaning American intellectuals, there is still such a thing as an identifiable "free world." What America needs now is staying power to carry on with the leadership of the free world. This is what the communists seem to have over us— they are dedicated to "stay the course" regardless of the defeats they may experience.

This, above all other reasons, is why they have been winning. In his book, *War and Peace,* John Foster Dulles explained the basic problem: "What we lack today are not material things. Our material production has broken world records time and again. What we are truly short of is the commitment of justice and motive power. Without such a conviction all other things will have little value. Our material power is enormous, but our moral power is growing increasingly weaker." A ranking statesman of the Republic of China has likewise cogently observed that the greatness of the United States does not lie in its wealth, higher living standard, or arsenal of nuclear weapons, but rather in its dedication to the ideas of global freedom and democracy. We ought to pray that he is right.

The time has come for Americans to look long and hard at the historical record, to compute the current score in the complex continuing game of international affairs, and to reach some correct conclusions. Freedom has been steadily losing, and totalitarianism gaining, since V-E Day and V-J Day marked the grand victory of the democracies a quarter of a century ago. The largest single loss has been the Chinese mainland.

The decline of freedom since 1945 is understandable only when the realities of the cold war are themselves understood. The foremost of these realities, and the most significant single historical fact of the century in which we live, is that communism is an international rather than a national phenomenon. Mao's China is "Chinese" only in a technical and geographical sense.

In a cultural and historical sense the real China exists today only on the island province of Taiwan where a small republic, still imperfect in some aspects but developing impressively under a wise and tolerant government, stands as a bastion of freedom and as a beacon of hope for hundreds of millions of less fortunate Chinese. Americans of the 1970s must recognize what Taiwan really means to China, and act accordingly, for the fate of that island will serve to prophesy the fate of the Far East and perhaps of the world.

The U.S. and China in Another Era: The Farewell Address*

General Douglas MacArthur

Mr. President, Mr. Speaker, and distinguished Members of the Congress, I stand on this rostrum with a sense of deep humility and great pride—humility in the wake of those great American architects of our history who have stood here before me, pride in the reflection that this forum of legislative debate represents human liberty in the purest form yet devised. [Applause.] Here are centered the hopes, and aspirations, and faith of the entire human race.

I do not stand here as advocate for any partisan cause, for the issues are fundamental and reach quite beyond the realm of partisan consideration. They must be resolved on the highest plane of national interest if our course is to prove sound and our future protected. I trust, therefore, that you will do me the justice of receiving that which I have to say as solely expressing the considered viewpoint of a fellow American. I address you with neither rancor nor bitterness in the fading twilight of life with but one purpose in mind—to serve my country. [Applause.]

The issues are global and so interlocked that to consider the problems of one sector, oblivious to those of another, is but to court disaster for the whole.

While Asia is commonly referred to as the gateway to Europe, it is no less true that Europe is the gateway to Asia, and the broad influence of the one cannot fail to have its impact upon the other.

There are those who claim our strength is inadequate to protect on both fronts—that we cannot divide our effort. I can think of no greater expression of defeatism. [Applause.] If a potential enemy can divide his strength on two fronts, it is for us to counter his effort.

The communist threat is a global one. Its successful advance in one sector threatens the destruction of every other sector. You cannot appease or otherwise surrender to communism in Asia without simultaneously undermining our efforts to halt its advance in Europe. [Applause.]

*From *Congressional Record,* April 19, 1951.

Beyond pointing out these general truisms, I shall confine any discussion to the general areas of Asia. Before one may objectively assess the situation now existing there, he must comprehend something of Asia's past and the revolutionary changes which have marked her course up to the present. Long exploited by the so-called colonial powers, with little opportunity to achieve any degree of social justice, individual dignity, or a higher standard of life such as guided our own noble administration of the Philippines, the peoples of Asia found their opportunity in the war just past to throw off the shackles of colonialism, and now see the dawn of new opportunity, a heretofore unfelt dignity and the self-respect of political freedom.

Mustering half of the earth's population and sixty percent of its natural resources, these peoples are rapidly consolidating a new force, both moral and material, with which to raise the living standard and erect adaptations of the design of modern progress to their own distinct cultural environments. Whether one adheres to the concept of colonization or not, this is the direction of Asian progress and it may not be stopped. It is a corollary to the shift of the world economic frontiers, as the whole epicenter of world affairs rotates back toward the area whence it started. In this situation it becomes vital that our own country orient its policies in consonance with this basic evolutionary condition rather than pursue a course blind to the reality that the colonial era is now past and the Asian peoples covet the right to shape their own free destiny. What they seek now is friendly guidance, understanding, and support, not imperious direction [applause]; the dignity of equality, not the shame of subjugation. Their pre-war standard of life, pitifully low, is infinitely lower now in the devastation left in war's wake. World ideologies play little part in Asian thinking and are little understood. What the peoples strive for is the opportunity for a little more food in their stomachs, a little better clothing on their backs, a little firmer roof over their heads, and the realization of the normal nationalist urge for political freedom. These political-social conditions have but an indirect bearing upon our own national security, but do form a backdrop to contemporary planning which must be thoughtfully considered if we are to avoid the pitfalls of unrealism.

Of more direct and immediate bearing upon our national security are the changes wrought in the strategic potential of the Pacific Ocean in the course of the past war. Prior thereto, the western strategic frontier of the United States lay on the littoral line of the Americas with an exposed island salient extending out through Hawaii, Midway, and Guam to the Philippines. That salient proved not an outpost of strength but an avenue of weakness along which the enemy could and did attack. The Pacific was a potential area of advance for any predatory force intent upon striking at the bordering land areas.

All this was changed by our Pacific victory. Our strategic frontier then shifted to embrace the entire Pacific Ocean which became a vast moat to protect us as long as we hold it. Indeed, it acts as a protective shield for all of the

Americas and all free lands of the Pacific Ocean area. We control it to the shores of Asia by a chain of islands extending in an arc from the Aleutians to the Mariannas held by us and our free allies.

From this island chain we can dominate with sea and air power every Asiatic port from Vladivostok to Singapore and prevent any hostile movement into the Pacific. Any predatory attack from Asia must be an amphibious effort. No amphibious force can be successful without control of the sea lanes and the air over those lanes in its avenue of advance. With naval and air supremacy and modest ground elements to defend bases, any major attack from continental Asia toward us or our friends of the Pacific would be doomed to failure. Under such conditions the Pacific no longer represents menacing avenues of approach for a prospective invader—it assumes instead the friendly aspect of a peaceful lake. Our line of defense is a natural one and can be maintained with a minimum of military effort and expense. It envisions no attack against anyone nor does it provide the bastions essential for offensive operations, but properly maintained would be an invincible defense against aggression.

The holding of this littoral defense line in the western Pacific is entirely dependent upon holding all segments thereof, for any major breach of that line by an unfriendly power would render vulnerable to determined attack every other major segment. This is a military estimate as to which I have yet to find a military leader who will take exception. [Applause.]

For that reason I have strongly recommended in the past as a matter of military urgency that under no circumstances must Formosa fall under communist control. [Applause.] Such an eventuality would at once threaten the freedom of the Philippines and the loss of Japan, and might well force our western frontier back to the coasts of California, Oregon, and Washington.

To understand the changes which now appear upon the Chinese mainland, one must understand the changes in Chinese character and culture over the past fifty years. China up to fifty years ago was completely non-homogeneous, being compartmented into groups divided against each other. The war-making tendency was almost non-existent, as they still followed the tenets of the Confucian ideal of pacifist culture. At the turn of the century, under the regime of Chan So-lin, efforts toward greater homogeneity produced the start of a nationalist urge. This was further and more successfully developed under the leadership of Chiang Kai-shek, but has been brought to its greatest fruition under the present regime, to the point that it has now taken on the character of a united nationalism of increasingly dominant aggressive tendencies. Through these past fifty years, the Chinese people have thus become militarized in their concepts and in their ideals. They now constitute excellent soldiers with competent staffs and commanders. This has produced a new and dominant power in Asia which for its own purposes is allied with Soviet Russia, but which in its own concepts and methods has become aggressively imperialistic with a lust for expansion and increased power normal to this type of imperialism. There is little of the ideological concept either one way or another in the Chinese make-up. The standard of living is so low and the capital accumulation has been so thoroughly dissipated by war that the masses are desperate and avid to follow any leadership which seems to promise the alleviation of local stringencies. I have from the beginning believed that the Chinese Communists' support of the North Koreans was the dominant one. Their interests are at present parallel to those of the Soviet, but I believe that the aggressiveness recently displayed not only in Korea, but also in Indochina and Tibet and pointing potentially toward the south, reflects predominantly the same lust for the expansion of power which has animated every would-be conqueror since the beginning of time. [Applause.]

The Japanese people since the war have undergone the greatest reformation recorded in modern history. With a commendable will, eagerness to learn, and marked capacity to understand, they have, from the ashes left in war's wake, erected in Japan an edifice dedicated to the primacy of individual liberty and personal dignity, and in the ensuing process there has been created a truly representative government committed to the advance of political morality, freedom of economic enterprise and social justice. [Applause.] Politically, economically and socially Japan is now abreast of many free nations of the earth and will not again fail the universal trust. That it may be counted upon to wield a profoundly beneficial influence over the course of events in Asia is attested by the magnificent manner in which the Japanese people have met the recent challenge of war, unrest, and confusion surrounding them from the outside, and checked communism within their own frontiers without the slightest slackening in their forward progress. I sent all four of our occupation divisions to the Korean battle front without the slightest qualms as to the effect of the resulting power vacuum upon Japan. The results fully justified my faith. [Applause.] I know of no nation more serene, orderly, and industrious—nor in which higher hopes can be entertained for future constructive service in the advance of the human race. [Applause.]

Of our former wards, the Philippines, we can look forward in confidence that the existing unrest will be corrected and a strong and healthy nation will grow in the longer aftermath of war's terrible destructiveness. We must be patient and understanding and never fail them, as in our hour of need they did not fail us. [Applause.] A Christian nation, the Philippines stand as a mighty bulwark of Christianity in the Far East, and its capacity for high moral leadership in Asia is unlimited.

On Formosa, the government of the Republic of China has had the opportunity to refute by action much of the malicious gossip which so undermined the strength of its leadership on the Chinese mainland. [Applause.] The Formosan people are receiving a just and enlightened administration with majority representation in the organs of government; and politically, economically, and socially they appear to be advancing along sound and constructive lines.

With this brief insight into the surrounding areas I now turn to the Korean conflict. While I was not consulted prior to the president's decision to intervene in support of the Republic of Korea, that decision, from a military standpoint, proved a sound one [applause] as we hurled back the invader and decimated his forces. Our victory was complete and our objectives within reach when Red China intervened with numerically superior ground forces. This created a new war and an entirely new situation—a situation not contemplated when our forces were committed against the North Korean invaders—a situation which called for new decisions in the diplomatic sphere to permit the realistic adjustment of military strategy. Such decisions have not been forthcoming. [Applause.]

While no man in his right mind would advocate sending our ground forces into continental China and such was never given a thought, the new situation did urgently demand a drastic revision of strategic planning if our political aim was to defeat this new enemy as we had defeated the old. [Applause.]

Apart from the military need as I saw it to neutralize the sanctuary protection given the enemy north of the Yalu, I felt that military necessity in the conduct of the war made mandatory:

1. The intensification of our economic blockade against China;

2. The imposition of a naval blockade against the China coast;

3. Removal of restrictions on air reconnaissance of China's coast areas and of Manchuria [Applause];

4. Removal of restrictions on the forces of the Republic of China on Formosa with logistical support to contribute to their effective operations against the common enemy. [Applause.]

For entertaining these views, all professionally designed to support our forces committed to Korea and bring hostilities to an end with the least possible delay and at a saving of countless American and Allied lives, I have been severely criticized in lay circles, principally abroad, despite my understanding that from a military standpoint the above views have been fully shared in the past by practically every military leader concerned with the Korean campaign, including our own Joint Chiefs of Staff. [Applause, the Members rising.]

I called for reinforcements, but was informed that reinforcements were not available. I made clear that if not permitted to destroy the build-up bases north of the Yalu; if not permitted to utilize the friendly Chinese force of some 600,000 men on Formosa; if not permitted to blockade the China coast to prevent the Chinese Reds from getting succor from without; and if there were to be no hope of major reinforcements, the position of the command from the military standpoint forbade victory. We could hold in Korea by constant maneuver and at an approximate area where our supply line advantage were in balance with the supply line disadvantages of the enemy, but we could hope at best for only an indecisive campaign, with its terrible and constant attrition upon our forces if the enemy utilized his full military potential. I have constantly called for the new political decisions essential to a solution. Efforts have been made to distort my position. It has been said, in effect, that I am a warmonger. Nothing could be further from the truth. I know war as few other men now living know it, and nothing to me is more revolting. I have long advocated its complete abolition as its very destructiveness on both friend and foe has rendered it useless as a means of settling international disputes. Indeed, on the 2nd of September 1945, just following the surrender of the Japanese Nation on the battleship *Missouri*, I formally cautioned as follows:

"Men since the beginning of time have sought peace. Various methods through the ages have been attempted to devise an international process to prevent or settle disputes between nations. From the very start, workable methods were found insofar as individual citizens were concerned, but the mechanics of an instrumentality or larger international scope have never been successful. Military alliances, balances of power, leagues of nations, all in turn failed, leaving the only path to be by way of the crucible of war. The utter destructiveness of war now blots out this alternative. We have had our last chance. If we will not devise some greater and more equitable system, Armageddon will be at our door. The problem basically is theological and involves a spiritual recrudescence and improvement of human character that will synchronize with our almost matchless advances in science, art, literature, and all material and cultural developments of the past 2,000 years. It must be of the spirit if we are to save the flesh." [Applause.]

But once war is forced upon us, there is no other alternative than to apply every available means to bring it to a swift end. War's very object is victory—not prolonged indecision. [Applause.] In war, indeed, there can be no substitute for victory. [Applause.]

There are some who for varying reasons would appease Red China. They are blind to history's clear lesson. For history teaches with unmistakable emphasis that appeasement but begets new and bloodier war. It points to no single instance where the end has justified the means—where appeasement has led to more than a sham peace. Like blackmail, it lays the basis for new and successively greater demands, until, as in blackmail, violence becomes the only other alternative. Why, my soliders asked of me, surrender military advantages to an enemy in the field? I could not answer. [Applause.] Some may say to avoid spread of the conflict into an all-out war with China; others, to avoid Soviet intervention. Neither explanation seems valid. For China is already engaging with the maximum power it can commit and the Soviet will not necessarily mesh its actions with our moves. Like a cobra, any new enemy will more likely strike whenever it feels that the relatively in military or other potential is in its favor on a world-wide basis.

The tragedy of Korea is further heightened by the fact that as military action is confined to its territorial limits, it condemns that nation, which it is our purpose to save, to suffer the devastating impact of full naval and air bombardment, while the enemy's sanctuaries are fully protected from such attack and devastation. Of the nations of the world, Korea alone, up to now, is the sole one which has risked its all against communism. The magnificence of the courage and fortitude of the Korean people defies description. [Applause.] They have chosen to risk death rather than slavery. Their last words to me were "Don't scuttle the Pacific." [Applause.]

I have just left your fighting sons in Korea. They have met all tests there and I can report to you without reservation they are splendid in every way. [Applause.] It was my constant effort to preserve them and end this savage conflict honorably and with the least loss of time and a minimum sacrifice of life. Its growing bloodshed has caused me the deepest anguish and anxiety. Those gallant men will remain often in my thoughts and in my prayers always. [Applause.]

I am closing my fifty-two years of military service. [Applause.] When I joined the army even before the turn of the century, it was the fulfillment of all my boyish hopes and dreams. The world has turned over many times since I took the oath on the plain at West Point, and the hopes and dreams have long since vanished. But I still remember the refrain of one of the most popular barrack ballads of that day which proclaimed most proudly that—

"Old soldiers never die; they just fade away."

And like the old soldier of that ballad, I now close my military career and just fade away—an old soldier who tried to do his duty as God gave him the light to see that duty.

Good-bye.

The Crisis of the
Republic of China*

John H. Esterline**

Within the past five years two American presidents—Richard Nixon and Gerald Ford—have flown halfway around the world to confer with Chinese Communist leaders in Peking. Henry Kissinger, first as Assistant to the President for National Security Affairs, then as his Assistant for Foreign Affairs, and from 1973 to 1977 as Secretary of State, has made nine visits to the capital of the People's Republic of China (PRC). Since acceptance by Canada in 1970 of the so-called "Canadian formula," namely, agreement to terminate diplomatic relations with the Republic of China (ROC) on Taiwan as a condition for establishing them with the PRC, all major Western nations which still recognized the ROC in 1970—except the United States—have switched recognition from the ROC to the PRC. Only twenty-three nations, most of them—except the United States—inconsequential in world politics, have maintained diplomatic relations with the ROC in 1977.

The Republic of China was ousted from the United Nations in 1971 in favor of the PRC. Its membership in substantive international agencies (e.g., the International Monetary Fund) as distinguished from procedural organizations (e.g., the Universal Postal Union) has dwindled to four because it has been forced out of the others by pressure from the PRC. A new low point was reached in 1976 when Canada refused to permit the ROC to participate as such at the Twenty-First Olympiad in Montreal; Prime Minister Trudeau asserted that the ROC team was "masquerading" as Chinese. Following President Ford's 1975 visit to Peking, the United States reiterated its intention to normalize relations with the PRC in accordance with the 1972 Shanghai Communiqué of President Nixon and Premier Chou En-lai. President Carter also appears determined to pursue vigorously the goal of normalization. He announced that Secretary of State Cyrus R. Vance would visit Peking in August 1977.

Despite this series of adversities the ROC has managed to survive

*Copyright 1977, *Journal of International Relations*. Reprinted by permission.
**John H. Esterline is currently Chairman of the Department of Political Science at the California State Polytechnic University in Pomona, California.

in the international political system and to prosper economically. When the impact of the "Canadian formula" ended juridical relations with most of the world's governments, the ROC countered by developing private bilateral expediential arrangements with many countries. Republic of China friendship, cultural and economic associations were formed, especially in East Asian countries, to facilitate visa-issuance and trade. Similarly, some nations which have broken diplomatic relations with the ROC maintain unofficial organizations in Taipei which fulfill some diplomatic or consular functions, notably the Japan Interchange Association manned by Japanese citizens. Despite the avowed intention of the United States and the PRC to complete "normalization" of relations, Taipei, not Peking, is where the American embassy remained in 1977. Vigorous promotion has produced record volumes of trade for the ROC with the United States and Japan, its principal trading partners. Even the Canadian refusal to allow athletes from Taiwan to participate in the 1976 Olympics under the name of the Republic of China was not an unmitigated defeat. The resulting, wide, popular criticism of the Canadian action, especially in the United States, produced more favorable publicity for the ROC than it has achieved in years.

It seems certain, however, that the ROC will arrive at the crisis point in its political history during 1978. Its survival in its present form appears almost entirely dependent upon the interacting triangle of the United States, the PRC and the ROC. Policies of the Carter administration in the United States and the direction of PRC post-Mao politics have added new dimensions to the impending crisis. It is the purpose of this paper to examine the ROC crisis and to suggest possible outcomes.

The Republic of China: A New Model

The government of the ROC on Taiwan realizes that the survival of its political system is dependent upon a strong economy to meet the rising expectations of its citizens, continuing progress toward an open society to enhance its legitimacy, and maintenance of its military strength and alliance with the United States in the face of the physical threat posed by the PRC.

During the past ten years the ROC has become one of the principal industrial and trading nations of the world, ranking currently among the first ten. Its major exports are garments, textiles, electrical machinery, electronic equipment, metal products, plywood, food products, unprocessed agricultural products and fishery products. Its major imports are agricultural products (wheat, corn, soybeans and cotton), machinery and raw materials. The United States is the leading trading partner of the ROC, followed by Japan. The ROC's two-way foreign trade during January-June 1976 amounted to $7.142 billion, thirty-eight percent more than for the same period of 1975. Its trade with the United States alone amounted to $3.5 billion. During that same period it enjoyed a trade surplus of over $125 million.[1]

The ROC population of over sixteen million enjoys one of the highest standards of living in Asia, and the spread between the rich and the poor is narrower than in any other developing country. In Taipei, a city of 2.5 million, some ninety percent of the households have television sets. The government devotes a great deal of attention to the rural sector and hopes to eliminate the last vestige (ten percent) of tenant farming within the decade.

Under the leadership of Premier Chiang Ching-kuo, eldest son of the late Generalissimo Chiang Kai-shek, the ROC is approaching the status of what political scientists call "tutelary democracy." Tutelary democracies are characterized by Edward Shils, Gabriel Almond and James Coleman as developing nations where rule-making and rule application tend to be concentrated in the executive and the bureaucracy, and where the formal democratic norms of universal suffrage, freedom of association and speech, as well as the structural forms of democracy—legislatures and elections—have been adopted. These scholars also identify what they term "dominant non-authoritarian party systems" as political systems where the party which led the independence movement "continues as the greatly dominant party, opposed in elections by relatively small left wing or traditionalist and particularist movements."[2] With remarkably few qualifications the ROC appears to meet both of these criteria.

While few will dispute the concentration of decision-making authority within the ROC's Executive Yuan and bureaucracy, it is increasingly evident that the ruling party, the Kuomintang, is willing to share power with other political groups in the Legislative Yuan. Prior to the election of December 20, 1975, to fill thirty-seven seats allocated to the province of Taiwan and the special municipality of Taipei, the government party pledged to "observe scrupulously the principle of impartiality and openness" in the election.[3] Representatives of minor parties were invited to work at election offices and the government pledged no restriction on campaign activities. Although no minority party candidates were elected in 1975, minority parties are represented in the Legislative Yuan.

The earlier conflict between the Taiwanese (overwhelmingly Chinese who settled Taiwan over the centuries, usually from Fukien province[4]) and the mainlanders (Chinese who arrived with Chiang Kai-shek in 1949) has in effect disappeared on the island, in part because the Taiwanese own most of the land and dominate the economy. Eighty percent of Kuomintang membership currently is Taiwanese and Taiwanese hold a similar percentage of civil service appointments. Six Taiwanese hold cabinet level positions.

Foreign observers note also that "within clearly defined limits, there is a remarkable degree of freedom in Taiwan."[5] Newspapers and other publications thrive. University libraries include well-known works containing critical passages about the earlier history of the Nationalist regime. Taipei is increasingly a center for exchange of news and is considered by many scholars as the single best source of information about developments on the Chinese mainland. Freedom of discussion takes place at various levels of the society as this author can attest from experience and observation throughout the academic year 1975-76.

In these contexts the ROC, whose party system approximates the dominant non-authoritarian pattern, emerges as a near example of the model for a tutelary democracy. The term "authoritarian," so easily—and at the time deservedly—applied to ROC leadership in former years, is less and less appropriate, particularly when the ROC political system is compared to those of its neighbors, North and South Korea, the People's Republic of China, and even the Philippines. Advances in personal freedom in the ROC have been achieved even though the country remains under martial law which, given Taiwan's exposed physical position vis-à-vis the mainland, is perhaps justifiable. Certainly, except for democratic Japan, no other east Asian country is moving in democratic directions at the pace of the ROC; indeed, many are moving in the opposite direction.

The ROC has also fundamentally transformed society on Taiwan. The nation is more than the modernized island of Taiwan. It does not merely reflect the incorporation of Taiwanese and Mandarin culture with the political values of 1949-vintage Chiang Kai-shek nationalism. Rather, a genuine fusion of values has occurred—of a traditional society and a modern one, of centralized control and democratic procedures, of Taiwanese and mainlanders, of state socialism and private enterprise. A new dynamic is the result.

In only one aspect is the ROC unchanging, namely in its unremitting ideological opposition to communism. If in the United States the word détente is suspect, in the ROC both the word and the concept are anathema. The government, the military establishment, the media, the educational system and ethical teaching in the ROC emphasize the evils of communism and the futility of compromising with it. As a result no national leadership, including the Maoist ideologues who have managed the PRC, exceeds it in ideological fervor.

It is ideology which motivates ROC youth and galvanizes 650,000 of them into one of the world's strongest military establishments. It is also ideology carried to an extreme which produces the spectacle of the ROC and the PRC shouting over loudspeakers at each other across 2,500 meters of water between ROC-held Quemoy Island and PRC-held Amoy on the mainland. However, expectation of regaining the mainland is voiced less today; rather, emphasis is on ROC ability to repel attack by the PRC.

While the precise amount of the ROC defense budget is a secret, 43.4 percent of the total national budget for fiscal year 1977 is devoted to "national defense and foreign affairs."[6] Observers estimate that approximately forty percent is spent for defense. The offshore islands of Quemoy and Matsu are bristling fortresses, prepared both to defend and to attack. In a direct military confrontation with the PRC, the ROC could hardly survive a frontal assault by millions of mainlanders, but the ROC would almost certainly exact an unacceptable toll of the attackers. Presumably the ROC does not possess nuclear capability since this would directly counter United

States non-proliferation policy and could hardly be concealed from the United States. ROC fear of loss of United States support, however, might alter ROC perceptions of what is necessary for its security. The popularly accepted view in the ROC is that, although the PRC possesses nuclear weapons, it will not use nuclear force against a Chinese brother.

The continuing role of the ROC in the international system, however, is dependent as much on the perceptions and responses of the United States and the PRC as it is upon the ROC's strong economy, internal political stability, and military strength. The questions must be asked: How vital to the PRC will the absorption of Taiwan appear to post-Mao leadership, and what direction regarding the ROC will United States leadership take?

People's Republic of China: Emergent Power

In 1949 the armies of the People's Republic forced the withdrawal of the Nationalist government to what both sides recognize as "the island province of Taiwan." Since then a proclaimed goal of the PRC has been to force the reintegration of Taiwan with the mainland, or, in the terminology of the communists, to "liberate Taiwan."

The position of the United States in the conflict between the PRC, pledged to "liberate Taiwan," and the ROC, pledged to "return to the mainland," was originally one of non-involvement. The Korean War drastically altered American perceptions. In 1950 the United States announced that it would act to prevent either party from launching an attack across the Taiwan Strait, in effect guaranteeing the defense of Taiwan. PRC involvement in the Korean War further alienated the United States and the PRC. In 1954 a formal mutual security treaty was signed by the United States and the ROC. Since 1956, when the PRC unsuccessfully tried to persuade the Nationalists to return to the mainland "peacefully" and promised an "autonomous status" for Taiwan, the efforts of the PRC to "liberate Taiwan" have concentrated more on dislodging U.S. support for the ROC than in attempting to influence the ROC directly.[7]

The year 1971 was a watershed for the People's Republic of China. On October 25 the PRC was admitted to membership in the United Nations by a decisive vote and assumed the permanent seat on the Security Council previously held by the ROC. The stage was set for a precipitous decline in the international political fortunes of the ROC and for acceleration of the influence of the PRC in the international community of nations. The increasing willingness of the members of the international community to grant diplomatic recognition to the PRC and to admit it to international organizations was the consequence of several developments discussed below.

First, the PRC reversed its diplomatic posture. During the tortured years from 1965-1970 of the Cultural Revolution the PRC had deliberately isolated itself. It had withdrawn some of its embassies from abroad, it did not actively seek admission to the UN, and it sought, as one aspect of the revolution, to expunge any lingering Western, especially U.S., influences in the communist society.

The Cultural Revolution was primarily an attempt by Mao Tse-tung to revive revolutionary fervor, to reinforce his leadership, and to widen the influence of the ideologues. The record shows that the revolution was difficult to generate and quickly became uncontrollable when it did take hold, with consequences that fragmented the very leadership that inspired it. In 1967, Mao engaged in a major effort to capture the party apparatus with the help of the Red Guards. They and he failed, and the Guards proved unamenable to controls. Of necessity the army assumed a stronger role, and by 1970 the army and the pragmatists under Chou En-lai were able to regroup and achieve a degree of stabilization. Stabilization tended to produce a less frenetic PRC foreign policy, and the two became mutually reinforcing. In a diplomatic offensive begun as early as 1970, PRC ambassadors were returned to countries from which they had been withdrawn during the Cultural Revolution. Subsequently, new ambassadorial posts were created as the PRC expanded its diplomatic relations at the expense of the ROC.

The second factor which affected third nation perceptions of the PRC was the reduction in intensity of the Sino-Soviet quarrel. The quarrel, which began in the late 1950s, was precipitated on the part of the Chinese by their reaction to perceived Soviet expansionism, resentment over withdrawal of Soviet economic assistance, and Mao's need to draw attention away from the effects of his disasterous economic policies. As the Cultural Revolution wound down, and the militancy of the Maoists lessened, the armed clashes that characterized the year 1969 ended. A reasonable case can be made that the quarrel was deliberately managed by each side to influence favorably third nations' perceptions of it. By 1971 an announced Soviet objective was détente with the United States, and a PRC objective was to obtain greater acceptability within the international political system. Interests of the two powers in a better "image" prevailed; ergo, the antagonisms were muted.

The third factor which made 1971 a decisive year in PRC-third nation relations was that by then it was clear that U.S. withdrawal from Vietnam— without achieving its objectives—had become a political imperative. Between 1964, when Hanoi had for the first time moved its main forces into South Vietnam, and 1971, when U.S. withdrawal was assured, the United States had first won and then lost international support for its intervention. The impact upon the international community's perceptions of the actors in the Pacific region was profound: the United States was perceived to be weak; the PRC and the Soviets were perceived to be strong. Moreover, with the winding down of the Vietnam War and the resultant reduction of American influence in the area, Sino-Soviet competition gravitated to southeast Asia. PRC interest in good relations with its southeast Asian neighbors increased.

From the visit by President Nixon in 1972, when the Shanghai Communiqué spelled out to the world a new PRC-United States relationship, until 1975, when Thailand and the Philippines renounced the ROC for the PRC, the PRC made dramatic progress in international politics. The nine Kissinger visits to Peking, the two state visits by American presidents, increasing trade with other major powers, quantum advances in diplomatic representation, and a new euphoria about the PRC on the part of the international community gave the PRC leverage it needed to press its claims against the ROC with almost a guaranteed acquiescence within the international system.

The international community increasingly relegated the Taiwan issue to that of a strictly Chinese affair, and PRC "sovereignty" over the island, was, in effect, taken for granted. Diplomatic representation on Taiwan fell away rapidly to less than thirty foreign accreditations by July 1975. The continued downward course of ROC international political fortunes seemed inevitable—until another PRC leadership upheaval in 1976 complicated the scenario.

In January 1975, during Premier Chou En-lai's increasing incapacitation due to terminal illness, Teng Hsiao-ping, who had been publicly humiliated and purged during the cultural revolution, was elected to membership on the Politburo Standing Committee and later named first vice-premier. Teng used the time until Chou's death in January 1977 to advantage. Appointments for his supporters increased rapidly. As Richard Thornton says, "As long as Chou was alive although incapacitated Teng was premier in fact if not in name."[8] Teng, a pragmatist, set out to modernize the PRC's industrial and military underpinnings—and to press the PRC claim to Taiwan. His statements on that issue were the clearest expression thus far of PRC intentions.

Teng told American newspaper editors who visited the PRC in June 1975 that the PRC "will probably have to use force" to regain Taiwan. Repeating his point, he said the PRC would attempt peaceful means but would probably have to use force. He also emphasized that there could not be normal relations between the PRC and the United States until the United States cut all diplomatic and military ties with the ROC and that downgrading the U.S. embassy in Taipei to a "liaison office" would not be acceptable. He reiterated the PRC pre-conditions for establishment of diplomatic relations: (1) withdrawal of American troops in Taiwan; (2) abrogation of the U.S.-ROC mutual security treaty; and (3) termination of diplomatic ties between the U.S. and Taiwan.[9]

When Teng agreed, following Chou's death, to the selection of Hua Kua-feng as "temporary and acting" premier, observers believed he was gambling on his ability to block permanent appointment of Hua in the full Politburo or in the ratifying Central Committee, or that he expected to induce Hua to embrace his pragmatic policies. If so, the gamble failed. As Thornton notes, "Hua moved firmly into Mao's camp—if indeed he ever left it."[10] and on April 7, 1976, the government announced Hua's formal appointment as premier of the State Council, and first vice chairman of the Central Committee. Simultaneously, Teng was stripped of all his posts, both inside and outside the party.

After Hua's accession to the premiership and Teng's expulsion from office and party positions, a new ideological and leadership struggle ensued, centering on the person and policies of Teng. "Radical" Chiang Ching, Mao's wife, led the attack as a "capitalist roader." Preoccupied with ideological attacks on Teng, the ruling clique appeared to devote less attention to the external problems. Upon Mao's death, on September 9, 1976, the struggle assumed new and contradictory dimensions. Hua was formally appointed party chairman to succeed Mao in an announcement October 21; simultaneously, Chiang Ching and three other "radicals" already under arrest were themselves denounced as "unrepentent capitalist roaders" who had been thwarted in their attempt to "usurp party and state power." With Hua Mau-Mauing* the "radical" Maoists, the direction of internal policies again swerved in July 1977 as wall posters in Peking announced Teng's reinstatement to all of his previous positions.

Some Sinologists suggest that the tough pragmatist approach to foreign policy associated in the past with Teng Hsiao-ping—devoted to modernizing industry and the armed forces and to achieving an expanded power base for the PRC—would pose a more immediate threat to ROC fortunes than continuation of Maoist policies. Maoists are more apt to stress ideology at the expense of development and to keep alive the "revisionist" controversy with the Soviet Union. Rapprochement with the Soviets, which the pragmatist might embrace, would, on the other hand, leave the PRC freer to deal with Taiwan and to get tougher with its protector, the United States.

Early U.S.-ROC Relations

The overthrow of the Manchu dynasty in 1911 by revolutionary national forces in China marked also the beginning of a long and intimate relationship between China and the United States. Sun Yat-sen, principal ideologue of the 1911 revolution, and Chiang Kai-shek, its principal military figure in ensuing years, were both subject to American ideas through early education or through their American-educated wives. In 1913 President Woodrow Wilson recognized the new Republic of China despite opposition from the consortium of great powers—Britain, France, Germany, Japan and Russia—which largely controlled investment and economic development in China. It was the United States which almost alone among the great powers opposed Japan's notorious Twenty-One Demands on China in 1915. The United States opposed Japanese expansion into Manchuria in 1931 as well as its subsequent partial conquest of China proper. In waging the Pacific war from 1942 to 1945 the United States embraced the Republic of China as a full ally, and at the Cairo Conference of 1943 President Roosevelt and Prime Minister Churchill promised Chiang Kai-shek that the allies would restore China to the Nationalist government at the conclusion of the war.

The intimate relationship between the two countries lessened in the late 1940s over U.S. disillusionment at Chiang's inability to stop Chinese Communist advances despite massive American economic and military aid. The relationship reached a low point in 1949 and with the flight of the Nationalist government to Taiwan and the subsequent explicit declaration of Secretary of State Acheson that the island lay outside the U.S. defense perimeter in east Asia. The United States, however, continued to underwrite the economic development of tht Taiwan-based ROC through a Joint Commission on Rural Reconstruction, possibly the most successful bilateral developmental project ever entered into by the United States.

The Korean War of 1950 reinvigorated the U.S.-ROC relationship. The U.S. decision to intervene militarily in Korea automatically extended the concept of a U.S. security umbrella to northeast Asia, and the American commitment became complete with the decision of the United States to defend the island as enunciated in the Sino-U.S. mutual security treaty of 1954. Although subsequent U.S. interpretations of the treaty have narrowed its scope in terms of which ROC-held islands it covers in addition to Taiwan itself, nonetheless the treaty remained in full force in 1977.

U.S.-PRC Relationships

Years of sporadic "ambassadorial" contacts between American officials and officials of the PRC began in Warsaw as early as 1955. The talks produced no tangible results and were suspended in 1970, but the United States continued to seek limited accommodation with the PRC. U.S. initiatives increased significantly with the accession of Richard Nixon to the American presidency. For example, U.S. import restrictions on mainland products and trade were eased. The Department of State repeatedly sought to bring American scientific scholars in contact with mainland Chinese scientsts at international meetings in third countries. In late 1969 Nixon withdrew the U.S. Seventh Fleet from patrol of the Taiwan Strait, and in 1970 an American president for the first time publicly used the term "People's Republic of China."

The PRC responded privately to the American gestures during 1970. Rumanian President Ceausescu was used as a message-carrying intermediary between Peking and Washington regarding a possible visit by President Nixon to the mainland. By 1971 the mainland regime had embarked upon an overt program of "people's diplomacy" under which an American table tennis team and news media representatives, academic figures, scientists and selected Chinese-Americans were invited to the PRC. The improved atmosphere resulted in the secret visit to Peking in July

1971 by Henry Kissinger, which was followed by the formal invitation from Premier Chou En-lai to President Nixon to visit the PRC.

Nixon announced his acceptance of the invitation on July 15, 1971, stating that the purpose of his visit in 1972 would be to seek normalization of relations between the two countries and to exchange views on questions of mutual concern. Mao Tse-tung received Nixon on February 22, 1972. Subsequently, the American president and Premier Chou En-lai agreed in the Shanghai Communiqué of February 28, 1972 that "progress toward normalization of relations between China and the United States is in the interests of all countries." The communiqué did not specifically define normalization, although without exception scholarly and media opinion interpreted it to mean the establishment of diplomatic relations between the two countries.

The question of U.S.-ROC relations is faced head-on by the PRC in the communiqué with its declaration that the "Taiwan question" is the crucial problem obstructing normalization. A U.S. statement in the document merely says that the United States favors a peaceful settlement of the Taiwan question by the Chinese themselves.

Having set in motion a normalization process which, by PRC definition, requires a resolution of the status of the ROC for its completion, the United States subsequently tried to clarify its position. In August 1972 the Department of State said, "We have, however, made it clear that such normalization cannot be made at the expense of old friends; our defense commitment and ties of friendship to the Republic of China remain intact."[11] However, in conformity with the terms of the Shanghai Communiqué, the U.S. troop presence on Taiwan was reduced, lending credibility to the idea that American withdrawal from the island would be forthcoming. Henry Kissinger's February 1973 visit to Peking, his fifth, achieved agreement to the establishment of liaison offices in Peking and Washington.[12] His sixth visit in November 1973 produced a communiqué in which the United States reiterated its acknowledgment "that all Chinese on either side of the Taiwan Strait maintain that there is but one China and that Taiwan is a part of China, a position the U.S. does not challenge."[13] In the same document the PRC reiterated that the "normalization of relations can be realized only on the basis of confirming the principle of one China."[14] In early 1974 the president announced the appointment of a senior ambassador, Leonard Unger, to the Taipei embassy, an action which confounded many. It had been widely assumed that retiring Ambassador Walter P. McConaughy, a fervent admirer of the ROC who had headed the mission since 1966, would not be replaced.

It was against this backdrop of events, guidelines, and declarations that President Ford's state visit took place in December 1975. PRC diplomacy effectively exploited the Ford visit—as it had the Nixon visit and the numerous trips of Kissinger. In return for supplying meager information to Ford and Kissinger about seven American servicemen who were missing in action, the PRC used the occasion to impress upon the United States the unwisdom of détente, to state that the PRC wants the United States to follow the "Japanese model" regarding normalization of relations, and to reaffirm that its leaders do not intend to accept the standing invitation to visit the United States until full normalization has been achieved.[15]

The "Japanese model" differs from the "Canadian formula" in that Japan maintains quasi-governmental relationships with the ROC, an outcome which was unintended by the PRC but which it has tolerated. The Japan-ROC relationship is rationalized as being *unofficial*. Thus Japan Airlines, flag carrier of Japan, becomes Japan Asia Airways for its flights to Taiwan, while China Airlines flies to Tokyo displaying the ROC national flag but under the fiction that the flag is merely the logo of the airline rather than the national flag. "Liaison offices" on the other hand, as currently operating in Washington and Peking, are *official*, not diplomatic, missions, but whose individual officers enjoy diplomatic status and personal immunity. The PRC has already rejected the possibility of official liaison offices in Washington and Taipei as a follow-up to United States derecognition of the ROC.[16] Immediately following the Ford visit the United States felt obliged to point out: "We have certain treaty obligations with Taiwan which Japan did not have,"[17] suggesting that the United States does not perceive the Japan-ROC arrangement as an applicable model, presumably either with or without residual unofficial relationships. In effect, each new contact between the People's Republic and the United States has narrowed the options for both sides and placed constraints on American policy alternatives.

Equally apparent, the limit of U.S. concessions was being approached. A communiqué was conspicuous by its absence at the conclusion of President Ford's visit. Inevitably, rumor arose that Ford had tried and been unsuccessful in persuading Peking to renounce force with respect to the resolution of the Taiwan issue, the PRC, according to the rumor, holding that the United States had already, through its earlier one-China statement, acknowledged the issue to be an internal one. Another theory to explain the absence of a communiqué was that the PRC declined to participate in a multi-power conference to help resolve the issue of a divided Korea.

As though to counteract such speculation, as well as the flood of editorial expression questioning whether further "progress" had been achieved and whether the trip was "worthwhile," the president, on his way home from mainland China, Indonesia, and the Philippines, enunciated a new Pacific Doctrine.

President Ford proclaimed his new Pacific Doctrine at the East-West Center on December 7. The premises of the doctrine are that "American strength is basic to any stable balance of power in the Pacific," "partnership with Japan is a pillar of our strategy," and the U.S. goal is "normalization of relations with the People's Republic of China."[18] Although President Carter has not specifically addressed himself to the question of the balance of power, the question arises: If the third premise is achieved, can the first two premises be maintained, or, if not, will the restructuring of the power balance that will result from normalization of relations with the PRC be in the interests of the United States?

Balance of Power in the Northwest Pacific

If, however, a balance among the powers bordering the Pacific Ocean is basic to American interests, and "American strength is basic to any stable balance of power," a stable power balance in northeast Asia is critical to U.S. interests. U.S. withdrawal from southeast Asia—specifically from Vietnam and Thailand—has reduced the U.S. Asian defense perimeter to the northeast where it has clear security commitments. The United States is obligated by formal bilateral security treaties to defend Japan, the Republic of Korea (ROK), and the Republic of China. The United States maintains major military forces in Japan and South Korea, and a residual force of some 1,300 in Taiwan, engaged mainly in electronic surveillance of the mainland.

In the balance-of-power equation the position of Japan must be set forth first. Japan has not rearmed since World War II and is protected by the security umbrella provided by the U.S.-Japan mutual security treaty. Japan and the USSR maintain full diplomatic relations although they have not concluded a formal peace treaty to end the state of war. In 1972 Japan inaugurated full diplomatic relations with the PRC, dropping diplomatic relations with the ROC with whom, technically, it never made peace after World War II. Thus Japan finds itself involved in a fragile balance with both the PRC and the USSR. Trade and diplomacy proceed apace with both communist giants but the unresolved legal and political situation constantly threatens to disturb the ad hoc structure of interrelationship. Japan is reluctant to sign a peace treaty with the USSR while the latter holds four of Japan's northern islands seized at the end of the war. It is also hesitant to enter into a peace treaty with the PRC which insists upon an "antihegemony" clause, since the USSR claims such a clause would amount to an alliance against the Soviet Union. Japan's pillar relationship, its security treaty with the United States, is dependent on the ability of the Liberal Democratic Party to maintain control of the coalition government. The LDP is the only Japanese political party which unreservedly supports the treaty with the United States. Japan's relationship with Taiwan is close even though the two nations do not have diplomatic relations. Japan is Taiwan's second largest trading partner. Japanese tourism is a substantial component of Taiwan's economy, and Japanese investment in and trade with Taiwan produce a substantial balance of trade in favor of Japan.

Although the political variables are in precarious balance, nonetheless the present balance is preferable to Japan than any likely changes. In July 1976 when U.S. Senator Mike Mansfield asked then Japanese Foreign Minister Kiichi Miyazawa his personal feelings about normalization of relations between the United States and the PRC, Miyazawa replied: "Any sudden movement which would disturb the existing stable situation in Asia would be undesirable."[19]

The politico-military position of Korea is equally delicate. In 1977, some twenty-four years following the Korean War armistice and after almost four hundred largely fruitless meetings of the Korean Military Armistice Commission, diplomatic settlment of the Korean question which the armistice anticipated remains unachieved. Nor has Korea been admitted to the United Nations. The communist and non-aligned nations propose annually that the UN General Assembly call for the dissolution of the United Nations Command (UNC) in Korea, or demand withdrawal of foreign troops in Korea under the UN flag. The latter proposal is aimed directly at the United States which maintains some 42,000 combat troops in South Korea to enforce the armistice. In 1975 the UN General Assembly adopted two resolutions concerning Korea which were mutually contradictory and therefore have not been acted upon. Following an abortive effort in 1972 to bring the two Koreas into dialogue through the Red Cross, the two sides have become ever more hostile. U.S. congressional support for maintenance of U.S. troops in Korea has weakened and President Carter has announced his intention to withdraw U.S. ground forces. Nevertheless, the ROK is politically stable, its economy continues to expand at a notable rate, and the ROK and the ROC are mutually supportive ideologically and psychologically.

The balance of power in northeast Asia is reinforced by a strong ROC. The Republic of China has a superb military establishment, including an air force ranked among the best in the world. The ROC's ideologically homogenous society has produced a strong nationalistic political system. Ideology also undergirds the maintenance of a strong military posture since the youth—who discharge their military obligations under a compulsory system—appear to accept the system and perceive the national need for self-sacrifice.

The strong economic position of the ROC depends to a major extent upon its favorable political relationship with the United States. The ROC's most-favored-nation status, a status dependent upon diplomatic recognition, enables the ROC to qualify for a preferential list of tariffs in trade with the United States, and the ROC is the second largest customer of the U.S.-sponsored Export-Import Bank, with loans and investment guarantees of some $1.7 billion. The ROC-U.S. Treaty of Friendship, Navigation and Commerce, in force since 1948, sets forth mutually agreed upon terms regarding the almost one-half billion dollars of American investment in the ROC. Finally, the close political relationship with the United States assures the ROC a nuclear fuel supply from the United States to power the six nuclear plants which eventually are expected to provide half of Taiwan's power.

The ROC's political, military and economic relationships with the United States have been mutually advantageous. They contribute to the balance of power, and the Americans have been loath to dismantle them. In mid-1977 a senior American ambassador continues to head the U.S. diplomatic mission in Taipei. But, ominously, the U.S. refuses to accept a replacement for the ROC's ambassador to Washington. The U.S. Congress continues to lend the ROC about $80 million annually for purchase of U.S. military equipment, and the United States Military Assistance Advisory Group, although significantly reduced in size, continues to operate. The Taiwan Defense Command of the United States remains intact.

However, President Carter appears determined to pursue the goal of normalization with the PRC. In early April 1977 Secretary of State Vance briefed Huang Chen, chief of the PRC Liaison Office in Washington, on U.S. arms talks the previous month in Moscow, and affirmed the Carter administration's desire for normalization and trade expansion. Later in April when Peking complained that "while [Carter and Vance] are talking about normalizing relations, they are talking about how they will not discount their old friends, and of course they are talking about a small handful of people like Chiang Ching-kuo (the ROC premier)," the American response was immediate: The United States announced that Vance would visit Peking in August 1977. Finally, on June 30, President Carter told a news conference that he hopes to establish full diplomatic relations with the PRC, and that formal relations with the ROC would be severed although the U.S. would maintain trade, cultural, and social exchanges with the ROC. What effect such moves would have on the security treaty was not addressed, nor the effect on the balance of power in northeast Asia.

Prospects

What, then, might be expected if the United States alters the political and strategic balance of northeast Asia by recognition of the PRC, derecognition of the ROC, and abrogation of the security treaty?

If the ROC is cast adrift by the United States, the PRC will be free of current restraints upon its policy imposed by present U.S. insistence, through the medium of its diplomatic relations with the ROC, that the latter is indeed a sovereign state. A PRC assurance not to use physical force against Taiwan as a *quid pro quo*, for recognition seems unlikely since the United States has already acknowledged that Taiwan is a part of China. U.S. severance of diplomatic relations with the ROC would repudiate the concept of ROC sovereignty. Thus, as a matter of internal policy toward a recalcitrant province, Peking could invoke far stronger sanctions than the ones it has already employed. Thus far, direct PRC pressures have forced the ROC out of most international organizations, and indirect pressures, such as denying United States firms with heavy investment in Taiwan access to the mainland market, are apparently being applied.

The ROC would be confronted with very limited options. Any sort of "residual American defense commitment," such as envisaged by Thomas W. Robinson,[20] would hardly be taken seriously by the ROC if the formal security treaty is abrogated by the United States. Taiwan could struggle on despite attempts by the PRC to strangle it, relying upon the stand-off among the United States, the Soviet Union, and the PRC to prevent an actual PRC seizure. But, subject to direct and more intense PRC pressure, it would surely suffer economically and would eventually wither. Since capitulation is a word not found in the ROC vocabulary, it is not inconceivable that the ROC might precipitate its own Armageddon by engaging in a physical conflict with the PRC, a move which could possibly ignite a general war in Asia. The United States could become involved by reason of its bilateral security treaties with Japan and Korea, as well as by reason of its worldwide security interests.

Japan could find itself surrounded by communist powers if the U.S. presence is removed from Taiwan, and it would undoubtedly be forced to reappraise its policies in consequence of its exposed position. It would need to decide whether to trust the United States to honor its treaty commitments to Japan in light of its unilateral abrogation of similar arrangements with the ROC. Japan would have to decide whether to develop a military capability for its own defense—with nuclear weapons since it would be facing two nuclear-armed powers—or whether to demand a U.S. commitment to defend it unequivocally. The NATO concept might serve as a model: an attack on a NATO power is an attack on the United States, and the U.S. military response is automatic rather than subject to debate. Would the United States accept such a commitment, or, conversely, would the leftist parties of Japan permit nuclear rearmament?

South Korea, given the Carter policy of U.S. ground troop withdrawal, would be left in an even more exposed position. It would have to decide among several alternatives: to press for even grater amounts of U.S. military hardware, including nuclear weapons, to provoke a war with North Korea to keep the United States involved, or, conceivably, to make accommodation with one or another communist power. Incrased external instability would have an unsettling effect on the internal politics of a government already facing opposition over its abridgment of civil rights.

If, on the contrary, President Carter should decide on a longer timetable for full normalization of relations with the PRC—i.e., takes no action in the foreseeable future but continues to recognize the ROC and continues relations with the PRC through the already established liaison offices in Washington and Peking—the balance of power in northeast Asia likely remains unchanged. The deaths within 18 months of each other of the three old men of the ROC-PRC struggle—Mao, Chou, and Chiang—may bring changes in leadership to both countries that can, within the next decade, resolve the dilemma without resort to force, either military or economic. The answer may be pragmatic accommodation based upon legal fictions yet to be devised as John K. Fairbank proposes, for "Taiwan has become less assimilable to the new continental society, in fact almost indigestible, by reason of being more highly capitalized and export-oriented." And, as he concludes, "we have no moral obligation to destroy Taiwan's separateness but on the other hand a considerable moral responsibility after our long association to see it continue."[21]

NOTES

1. *Data Asia* (Manila: Press Foundation of Asia, 1976), p. 3911.
2. Abriel A. Almond and James S. Coleman, eds., *The Politics of the Developing Areas* (Princeton: Princeton University Press, 1960), p. 41.
3. *The China News,* Taipei, Taiwan, ROC, December 4, 1975, p. 4.
4. Taiwanese is basically Amoyese, a northern Fukienese dialect.
5. Keyes Beech, "Taiwan Thriving as a Political Outcast," *Los Angeles Times,* August 15, 1976, part IX, p. 4.
6. *The China News,* February 26, 1976.
7. See Harold C. Hinton, *An Introduction to Chinese Politics,* (New York: Praeger, 1973), pp. 298-299.
8. Richard C. Thornton, paper delivered at the Fifth Sino-American Conference on Mainland China at Taipei, June 1976, entitled "Teng Hsiao-p'ing and Peking's Current Political Crisis: a Structural Interpretation," pp. 9-34.
9. *Data for Decision* (Manila: Press Foundation of Asia, 1975), p. 2953.
10. Thornton, *op. cit.,* pp. 9-36.
11. *Gist #6* (Washington: Department of State, 1972), revision 5, August 1972.
12. PRC presence in the United States is buttressed by its United Nations mission in New York and by the U.S.-China People's Friendship Association with 79 chapters throughout the country and 30 more in process of organization as of October 1976.
13. *Gist #6,* revision 6, February 1974.
14. *Ibid.*
15. "Secretary Kissinger's December 4 Peking News Conference," U.S. Information Service, Taipei, December 8, 1975, p. 7.
16. See Vice Premier Teng's remarks *supra.*
17. Assistant Secretary of State for East Asian and Pacific Affairs, Philip C. Habib, as quoted in "'Japanese Formula' Not Applicable to ROC-U.S. Ties," *The China News,* December 18, 1975, p. 4.
18. "President Ford Outlines U.S. Policy in Pacific," U.S. Information Service Taipei, December 10, 1975.
19. Extract from a press conference by Kensuke Yanagiya, Director General of the Public Information Bureau, Japan, July 16, 1976, released by the Consulate General of Japan, Los Angeles, Calif.
20. Thomas W. Robinson, "Some Possible Developments in Sino-American Relations After the American Presidential Elections of 1976," paper delivered at the Fifth Sino-American Conference on Mainland China, Taipei, June 1976.
21. John K. Fairbank, "East Asia: Our One-China Problem," *The Atlantic,* September 1976, p. 8.

The China Question:
Some Observations

*Richard L. Walker**

Since the issuance of a unique and vague document, "The Shanghai Communiqué" of February 28, 1972, almost seven years ago, the question of China policy has been debated from every conceivable angle. But events have tended to push aside some of the arguments which were advanced with most convincing force during that period. As so often happens in history, problems are beginning to sort themselves out and priorities get rearranged.

Much of the problem for the United States, as we have confronted the changing scene in the western Pacific, has been with ourselves. Americans are impatient; we want solutions and results; we are not very good servants of the goddess of time. That great observer of American democracy Alexis de Tocqueville noted: "Democracy appears . . . better adapted for the conduct of society in times of peace, or for a sudden effort of remarkable vigor, than for the prolonged endurance of the great storms that beset the political existence of nations." And throughout most of our twentieth-century China policy debates, this has been the case. Further, debates have tended to be conducted in terms of simplistic words and the slogans of the moment rather than in terms of the complexities and subtleties which must of necessity come to involve our dealings with China. In particular, with reference to our relations with the People's Republic of China (PRC), American democracy has seemed singularly unprepared for the many levels of relations and the many ramifications of policies.

The Chinese are fond of separating surface from reality. Surface appearances are maintained for the sake of "face" and to insure harmony. The reality is frequently quite different. It was for this reason that the recent master of the Chinese dialectic Chou En-lai tried to urge Westerners to judge China by what she did, not by what was said officially. Even in dynastic times, the policies followed by the court were frequently the opposite of what was proclaimed with such force in official proclamations. Thus even those who have studied the Chinese tradition are frequently misled by the

*Dr. Richard L. Walker is Director of the Institute of International Studies, University of South Carolina.

Peking opera-style official pronunciamentos and confuse what Peking has to say with what Peking will do.

A good example of this is when visiting delegations go to the PRC and raise the question of Taiwan. Usually this is bypassed by the particular Chinese leader at the time. Unable to see that the Chinese hosts would just as soon not explore the issue, the U.S. delegates usually pursue the question in which case they get back with full explosive rhetorical vigor the official surface position of Peking's three conditions for "normalization" of relations. This frequently gives the impression that the Chinese were just being polite and avoiding an unpleasant topic and were willing to "unload" if pushed, which is not at all the case. Chinese leaders would prefer not to have to express what are sometimes overly uncompromising positions which might subsequently make them look silly in future moments. This was especially true during the visits of former Senator Hugh Scott and his colleague, now Ambassador Mike Mansfield, to China. The Chinese did everything possible to push aside the Taiwan issue, but the two gentlemen insisted on pursuing it and were given back a full load. A December 3, 1978 UPI dispatch noted that Senator Dick Stone of Florida recently returned from China:

Stone said Peking is still insisting the United States break diplomatic ties with Taiwan, abrogate the U.S.-Taiwan defense treaty and remove its remaining forces from the Nationalist island as conditions for diplomatic relations. But he noted the Chinese are saying there's no urgency about resolving the Taiwan problem. And they are reportedly suggesting China and Taiwan could cooperate in some undefined way.

Despite the fact that the Chinese Communist leaders have been themselves soft-pedaling the Taiwan issue, it seems to have become one of urgency in the United States. There are several reasons for this, and they lie, as I have already suggested, more with ourselves than with Peking and the PRC.

First there is the *American romance with China*. This has affected our relations with Taiwan which are often played up in overly emotional terms with such slogans as "bastion of democracy" or "faithful ally," etc. Though we have a unique relationship with the personnel of the government on Taiwan, and though we can legitimately take some pride in the success of joint ventures which we have undertaken with them in the past three decades, the top officials in Taiwan preside over a government which has its own priorities and interests, and when those conflict with the positions of the United States, state interest and not friendship counts. In the same manner, we must understand that our own policies must be dictated by what serves best the long-run interest of the United States.

Our tendency toward China romance, however, has also led us toward very unrealistic positions about mainland China. We have a full stable of academics and other well-wishers who are not only willing, but anxious, to believe all the best about that society with which we have what they perceive to be a special relationship. They go for a guided-tour of the PRC and come back singing praises, more than faintly reminiscent of the early euphoria about the Soviet Union in the days of Lincoln Steffens. One wonders today where the professors are who talked and wrote about the human rights and the achievements of the PRC in the mid-1970s. Within the past six months it has been revealed that in China there has been repression, political persecution, forced labor, torture, and even widespread malnutrition and starvation. Just recently it has been revealed that another 110,000 "good Communists" had been released after unjustified persecution and oppression, naturally at the instigation of the "gang of four." But where was the analysis and detachment which could have provided American observers with the investigative questions to ferret out the realities of the Chinese scene which led to such oppression at the very moment when the American romantics were assuring us that China was the society on the way to perfection without oppression of man by man?

We have tended to accept the briefings, take meticulous notes, and report back to the United States what those in charge at a particular moment wish us to report back. And what we report back is the form, the surface, not the reality or the substance. Thus, while we can rejoice that there is a loosening up in China and that there is currently more interchange with the West and with the United States, it is still necessary to distinguish form from substance. In the current power struggles and settling of old scores which is taking place in China now, it becomes necessary to consider the fate of those who were once leaders during the Cultural Revolution and are now the object of repression by the resurgent group around Teng Hsiao-ping.

Our China romance leads the Americans to believe that somehow they must solve, and solve *now*, the "China Question." Those who are currently still enthused about the great experiment in the PRC are pushing hard for an immediate action.

This leads us to a second reason for the urgency which seems to attach to a change in the status quo, the *American tendency toward activism.* The conditions of our relations with the two Chinas are not entirely satisfactory. The normal American reaction to this situation is "Something must be done" or "Nothing could be worse." Both are rather questionable propositions. The past decade has witnessed most of the arguments adduced in support of these propositions negated by events. Let us look at a few of them.

1. *The Argument:* The United States should accede to Peking's demands before Mao and Chou die; otherwise their successors may turn back to an alliance with the USSR.

   The Facts: With most of the Maoist generation gone, including the great Chairman himself, relations with the Soviet continue to be bad or even worse. The national interests of the Chinese state have remained unchanged.

2. *The Argument:* The United States will lose out on the fabled China market unless we accede to Peking's "three conditions."

   The Facts: Prospects for U.S. trade and for U.S. businessmen look bright, but the China market fable has always been overplayed, and the PRC will trade with whom it wishes in the manner which best suits its national interests. If trade with the U.S. is now picking up, the major factor is because Peking finds our advanced technology to its liking.

3. *The Argument:* Unless we have full diplomatic relations with China, the Chinese will shut us off from intellectual and cultural exchange, including student exchanges.

   The Facts: Peking is now searching to send possibly as many as one thousand students and researchers to the United States for training—it may prove to be somewhat a drain on our own facilities if it increases too rapidly—and soon American tourists and visitors to the PRC will outnumber all except the Japanese.

A third factor behind the American push for action lies possibly in our tendency to accept slogans and short-phrase advertising-style gimmicks in place of solid (if sometimes subtle) and carefully reasoned analysis. In fact, much of the problem with the China policy question seems to derive from the term "normalization" itself. If there is a drive for normalization, then it would seem that by definition our relations with Peking are abnormal. Abnormal is bad; therefore, some drastic action seems needed now. Never mind the fact that no nation today has relations with the PRC which could be deemed "normal" by any sense of the word, for something needs to be done, or so the argument goes. Americans therefore seek *the answer.* And the answer is right at hand in terms of Peking's three conditions and the fact that the leaders there advocate a "Japan formula." The idea of a "formula" fits right into the simplistic framework. Or, again, there is the current tendency—derived in large measure from the elementary geometry classes of Drs. Kissinger and Brzezinski with their trilateral, triangular, quadrilateral, pentagonal and other balances—to approach the China question in terms of a game—a simple game, it is to be noted, in which we play a "China card" or a "Japan card" or Peking plays its "Soviet card." The problem here is that American semantics are interfering with sound foreign policy. A sound foreign policy is not a game but a process, not a formula (Japanese, German, or other) but an approach.

The reason the Japanese were able to adjust their foreign policy processes to the demands of Peking and still have the benefits of that vital economic relationship with Taiwan lay in the very fact that the United States did have a security treaty with the Republic of China on Taiwan. And the duly ratified treaty which the United States still has with the government on

Taiwan remains a major interest not alone for the U.S. but for all of those countries which still have close relations with Taiwan. Thus, when there is talk of the "Japan formula" as a way out for the United States in its fretsome China question, it usually reflects not the complex problem itself, but rather the fact that "games" which are played in the public media frequently demand slogans and oversimplification. And China policy has been one of the items most reflective of this American tendency.

All this is by way of introduction to a set of propositions about the China question and U.S. policies in the months ahead. I believe much of the evidence to support these propositions is already in, and there is no need to belabor them. But these are factors which need to be taken into account as Peking's proxies in the United States such as the more than 140 chapters of the U.S.-China People's Friendship Association, the China romantics, and the academics with vested interests in their own infallibility begin to crank up in 1979.

1. The only ones *really* pushing hard for acceptance of Peking's three conditions for "normalization" today are lobbyists in the United States and some PRC representatives with deep feelings—especially if pushed by their American friends on the issue. The Chinese have advised again and again that they can wait.

2. The U.S. relationship with the PRC is bound up in the whole range of United States relationships in the western Pacific, and it is not therefore a simple bilateral question. Japanese statesmen have spoken eloquently on this issue before Congress and to the Department of State; Koreans have been especially concerned, and leaders from southeast Asia have advised Washington to be cautious and not risk precipitate action.

3. The PRC does not want "normalization" on its own terms now if that means the undermining of America's credible presence in the western Pacific where the force which they refer to as "The Polar Bear" is becoming so clearly a threatening one. They would like to have their three conditions met with some sort of process which would keep the United States presence, but they are sufficiently sensitive to the psychological dimensions of the politics in their region that they are not pushing for any destabilizing action.

4. What the United States does or does not do will not likely have a major impact on Peking's overall goals or middle-range policies. These are dictated more by their own internal politics and by their perceptions of their national interests and, above all, by the approach of the top leadership at any given moment.

5. The Chinese leaders are, however, sensitive about the United States. They are aware of the great power of America, and as the past years have already demonstrated, they will be willing to make necessary adjustments over time as long as we do not disrupt the surface smoothness of the face which they must maintain. They will not be excessively upset if the

United States were to adopt the old Chinese formula of *wu-wei*—"action through inaction"—on the Taiwan question.

6. We have, in effect, two Chinese embassies in Washington today, and the United States has two legations staffed by State Department specialists in Taipei and Peking. It is only if we insist on pushing through the surface smoothness of this situation and disturbing it that problems of formulas and definitions and slogans interfere with the reality and substance of what has been accomplished. Of course, for the sake of face and ideological credibility it is necessary for the PRC occasionally to tug at Uncle Sam's whiskers, but the current situation, which has been described by the scholar Robert A. Scalapino with the phrase HOC BEIT (having one's cake, but eating it too), does not demand drastic action. Already many issues have been negotiated out with satisfactory results between Washington and Peking.

7. Finally, it seems time that the United States begin to survey some of the conditions which it wishes to seek in its relations with Peking when the time comes for the actual adjustment toward diplomatic full status—and it must be assumed that this will involve maintenance of a credible commitment to Taiwan. Most of the debate to date has centered on Peking's three demands. But Peking's foreign relations with other countries have already given us clues as to what the United States should be preparing in response. For example, PRC representatives in France have full run of the country, but French diplomats are severely restricted in their movement in China. Or Japanese newsmen have been played off against each other in such a manner as to enable Peking to exercise the equivalent of censorship of news over the Japanese press. Thus the United States, as the last major power which will be negotiating terms for full diplomatic relations with Peking, needs to develop a full shopping list that will help in encouraging the kind of openness with the Western world which is currently in vogue in the PRC. We must understand that relations with a communist dictatorship can *not* always be on the basis of *reciprocity* (after all, a member of the National People's Congress in Peking is hardly the equivalent of a member of our Congress, nor are their elections contested in the same manner as ours, nor do they regard the press as serving the same functions which we attribute to it), *but* we can insist on *equivalency*. The following would be some of the conditions which we should begin to assert as necessary before we can work out with Peking its "normalization" of relations with us:

1. Reciprocity in access of scholars and news media to officials and sources of information.
2. Immunity from harassment or expulsion for any reporting deemed by the host country to be critical.
3. Access to private individuals and scholars.
4. Equivalent rights in organizing, supporting, and developing information programs about our country in the host country.
5. Equivalency in freedom to travel within the country.

6. Agreement to tone down official statements of the two countries about each other. (Some of the official statements of the ideologue of Foreign Minister Huang Hua exceed any of the standards on which normal relations can be fostered.)

There are many other economic, social, and communications problems to be worked out with Peking, but this short list should indicate that there are far more conditions for "normalization" than just Peking's three.

If the only real urgency for altering our HOC BEIT situation with the PRC lies in the United States, then it is all the more necessary that the process be approached slowly, coolly, and rationally. Much more is at stake than is generally understood. What is at the heart of the matter is the integrity of the United States. Presidents and secretaries of state, including the present ones, have stated that we shall honor our defense obligations to Taiwan. Other similar defense obligations lie in the balance—NATO, ANZUS, Japan, Korea, the Philippines. Obviously there are complex interrelations involved.

In 1979 we are in the position to proceed with our developing relations with the PRC without major or dramatic changes which would destabilize the network of positive faith that the United States constructed in the noncommunist world, beginning at the time of the presidency of Harry Truman. An approach which uses an old Chinese method of declaring a "moratorium" on the final decision about mainland China and Taiwan but gets on with the business of the modernizations which the PRC needs and the security which Taiwan needs seems a process which the Chinese would understand, even if it does not rest well with the small cabal in the Department of State, determined to "normalize" no matter what the cost, with the members of academe who have a long vested interest in eliminating a Kuomintang-run Taiwan in favor of their PRC vision of the future, or with the large number of Sinophile American romantics who still want to believe only glowing reports emanating from the land where Mao was once infallible.

The American answer to "The China Question"? Time and patience.

U.S.-China Relations

Ray S. Cline*

Some serious misunderstandings have grown up in the United States, especially in the minds of senior officials in the Carter administration, around the issue of normalizing relations with the People's Republic of China (PRC) on the mainland, and, at the same time, dealing realistically and honorably with the fact of the existence of a second Chinese political entity of considerable consequence, the Republic of China (ROC) on the island of Taiwan in the west Pacific.

These misunderstandings stem from unthinking acceptance of the doctrine that there is only *one* China. Many people say that there is only *one* China, but what they really mean is that there is one Chinese civilization or culture, about four thousand years old and richly fascinating to sociologists, cultural anthropologists, and historians. Actually, in terms of present-day political organization, there are plainly *two* Chinas if we mean large groups of people of Chinese ethnic origin living in territory controlled by their own governments. One has its capital in Peking, the other in Taipei.

Each of these governments claims to be by right *(de jure)* the government of both Chinas, but actually *(de facto)* neither has been able to translate its claim into control of the population or territory of the other since the communist People's Republic of China seized control of mainland China in 1949. For its part, the PRC has never controlled the island of Taiwan.

The reality as distinct from political fantasy and propaganda is that the Republic of China has *de facto* control of Taiwan and the offshore islands of Kinmen, Matsu, and Penghu (the Pescadores), an area of nearly 14,000 square miles. The Republic of China very effectively governs about seventeen million ethnic Chinese, and this puts it among the forty largest populations of the 159 independent countries in the world today. By all the normal legal, political, and cultural definitions of the attributes of statehood, the Republic of China is an independent self-governing nation, with an inherent right of self-defense.

Even the distinguished scholar from Harvard, John Fairbank, who has often strongly urged the United States to "legitimate" the communist regime

---

*Ray S. Cline is Executive Director of The Center for Strategic and International Studies, Georgetown University.

in Peking, reluctantly concluded in *The Atlantic* of September 1976 that one China is "not a workable fact." He observed, accurately: "The one China doctrine is one of those hoary Chinese devices for manipulating the unsophisticated barbarian."

The Carter administration has naively adopted the one China doctrine as a basic element of its Asian policy, and keeps pronouncing that it will raise the existing liaison offices in Peking and Washington to full embassy status. This policy presages one of those self-destructive moves in defense and foreign policy that the Carter administration has so often proposed without counting the costs.

To achieve the modest, mainly symbolic, changes proposed in the Washington-Peking diplomatic relations, President Jimmy Carter, Assistant for National Security Zbigniew Brzezinski, and Secretary of State Cyrus Vance all imply they plan to capitulate to Peking's rigid, oft reiterated, demands for the United States to break off diplomatic relations with the Republic of China. Worse, and this is the heart of the strategic error, they also suggest they will accept the additional Peking demand that the United States unilaterally abrogate the U.S.-Republic of China mutual defense treaty. This treaty has protected the pro-American Chinese in Taiwan from a communist takeover since 1954 and maintained a strong and friendly island redoubt on the seaward southern flank of South Korea and Japan.

President Carter has repeatedly said he intends to protect the security of the Chinese people of Taiwan, but neither he nor any of his policy spokesmen have explained how this can in reality be done once Washington accepts Peking's view that it rightfully rules all of China and that Taiwan is not a country but merely a province of *one* China. In these circumstances, abrogation of the mutual defense treaty clearly eliminates any international right or opportunity for the United States to defend the island, regardless of any pious American rhetoric that might accompany the deed.

In abrogating the mutual defense treaty, the United States simply ignores Peking's aim to "liberate" Taiwan by military force if necessary and to absorb its people in its totalitarian embrace whenever feasible. This act of appeasement that would be implicit in unilateral abrogation of the treaty could only result, after a "decent interval," in the destruction of the Republic of China. It is wishful thinking to claim, as President Carter's senior advisors do, that appeasement of Peking would not damage the Chinese people on Taiwan and the adjacent islands.

The Republic of China—which we are in danger of consigning to "nonbeing" in an almost Orwellian "1984" manner—operates under a constitutional government established in 1947 on the mainland, at a time when its legitimacy as the government of all China was not in question. It transferred to Taiwan when its president, Chiang Kai-shek, took up his duties in its capital there in 1949. Under the ROC constitution, the county and city electorates of Taiwan enjoy full self-government, choosing local and provincial

194

officials by secret ballot. At all levels, the ROC is moving steadily toward democratic electoral procedures and representative government. The leaders of the Republic of China during the last twenty-five years or more have formed a politically cohesive nation, stable, tranquil, and friendly toward the United States. They have created a comparatively open society and, in the eyes of much of the world, have earned the title "Free China."

Ever since 1971 when President Richard Nixon acquiesced in the expulsion of the Republic of China from the United Nations, not for cause, but to meet Peking's requirements for entry, the Taipei government has become increasingly dependent on American good will and support. Before that event more than one hundred nations had diplomatic relations with Taipei; now only twenty do. Because of the American security umbrella, Taiwan has become an island of hope in Asia. In this Chinese society the best of Asian and American philosophies and technologies have been blended to show how to modernize China without giving up political freedom to totalitarian controls.

Political accommodation between the two Chinas may come, but not soon, and not until there is a major shift away from totalitarianism on the mainland. It will not come as a result of capitulation by this generation of American-oriented Chinese leaders on Taiwan who have no intention of succumbing to communist rule if they can in any way prevent it. President Chiang Ching-kuo has many times declared, "We shall never change our clearly defined stand of opposing communism adamantly nor change our determination to remain in the democratic camp."

Since 1949 the Republic of China has developed its economy in a very rapid way with extraordinary success in both agriculture and industry. The "land-to-the-tiller" program is a model recognized for its social justice and its agricultural productivity throughout Asia. The labor force is well disciplined and highly educated, increasingly concentrating on production where skill and technology are required, as in the case of the flourishing electronics industry. Overall, unemployment is only 1.5 percent of the labor force. The government absorbed the economic blow of the worldwide energy price rises in 1974 and quickly brought the inflation rate down to less than two percent annually, an unparalleled achievement.

The gross national product (GNP) has steadily expanded, and in 1977 it was at the level of $19.5 billion, with a per capita income of $1,079, between three and four times that of the Chinese mainland. The Republic of China has substantial commercial ties with 140 countries, and is among the top thirty trading nations of the world. For 1977, foreign trade, including exports and imports, was $17.8 billion, an increase of 13.1 percent over 1976; approximately one-quarter is with the United States. This ROC trade with the United States is, incidentally, about ten times the U.S. trade with the PRC.

The Republic of China continues to make a major contribution to the military security of the whole long east Asian island chain stretching from Japan to Indonesia, as well as to the security of the vital shipping lanes along the periphery of all of Asia. In this way, of course, Taiwan contributres directly to the strategic defenses of the west Pacific, a matter of prime importance to the United States, Japan, and their trading partners in the Pacific Basin.

Nobody in east Asia believes this eminently successful experiment in Oriental nation-building on the island of Taiwan can long withstand the psychological shock that will result from American removal of Taipei's security unbrella. If the United States capitulates to Peking's demands, east Asians predict that the People's Republic of China will begin an economic strangulation of the island to force this flourishing society into political captivity. It is one thing, they feel, for America to flatter the leaders of the PRC in order to encourage them in their anti-Soviet stance; it is quite another to destabilize the whole region in the process.

For President Carter to pretend, in subscribing to the *one* China doctrine, that the Taipei government does *not* exist, that it does not have a right to exist, or to treat it simply as a subordinate province of Communist China is a ridiculous and destabilizing reading of the real situation in Asia.

The irony of the Carter administration's willingness to risk the sacrifice of Taiwan in order to curry favor in Peking is that there is no evidence that PRC top officials are or claim to be basically friendly toward the United States. In fact, the formal constitution of the Chinese Communist Party contains a platform that is not only anti-Soviet but also flatly anti-American. This constitutional position was most recently approved, unanimously, on August 18, 1977, four days before Secretary of State Vance's arrival in China. It states that the Communist Party "unites with the proletariat, the oppressed people and nations of the whole world and fights shoulder to shoulder with them to oppose the hegemony of the two superpowers, the Soviet Union and the United States, to overthrow imperialism, modern revisionism and all reaction. . . ."

Prior to the adoption of this constitution, Premier Hua Kuo-feng candidly explained that the United States is the less dangerous of the PRC's two enemies: "The Soviet Union and the United States are the source of a new world war, and Soviet social-imperialism, in particular, presents the greater danger." Quoting Lenin, he continued, "The more powerful enemy can be vanquished . . . by taking advantage of every, even the smallest, opportunity of gaining a mass ally, even though this ally be temporary, vacillating, unstable, unreliable and conditional." This, plainly, is where the United States comes in—temporarily. The PRC does not consider itself a true or in any way reliable ally of the United States; it simply fears the USSR more at this point in history.

Yet Carter, Brzezinski, and State Department officials are putting their reliance on the political fortunes of the newly-formed communist coalition of Hua Kuo-feng and Teng Hsiao-ping. They seem to have given no thought to the fact that they are counting very heavily on two communist leaders who, as yet, have not firmly established themselves in Peking. Hua became premier soon after the death of Mao Tse-tung in September 1976. To secure his position he almost immediatlely arrested the group of rival political leaders whom he stigmatized as "the gang of four" and put them in jail. This eliminated Mao's ambitious widow, Chiang Ching, originally one of Hua's strong supporters, and her principal followers in the Politbureau. They were accused of sabotaging the Communist Party bureaucracy and seizing power at national and local levels during the "Great Proletarian Cultural Revolution" (1966-1976). Hua was able to purge Madame Mao's clique because he formed an alliance with the strongest element of the Chinese military leadership.

In a reluctant payoff for this support, in July 1977 Hua acquiesced in the move by the Central Committee of the Chinese Communist Party to name as Vice Premier Teng Hsiao-ping, twice disgraced and removed from high office during Mao's lifetime, but always a favorite of the most influential generals. Of the two Teng is in the better political position, receiving his support from the ubiquitous, all-powerful Chinese army. On the other hand, Hua (age 57) gets his immediate strength from the security police and the younger Communist Party bureaucrats who, like him, came into prominence during the upheavals of the Cultural Revolution, long after the veterans loyal to the much older Teng (age 74).

These two leaders seek unity in order to recover from the ravages of the ten-year reign of the gang of four. Their task, as Premier Hua stated in March 1978, is to "transform China into a great, powerful socialist country with modern agriculture, industry, national defense, and science and technology by the end of the century."

Modernization has always been the goal of China, but success has been limited. Today Hua and Teng have the handicap of starting from a very low economic base. The margin of food supplies, despite much improvement in the techniques of cultivation, is very slim for a population of one billion people, with no allowance for short-falls in either rice or wheat crops. From 1970 to 1975 agricultural growth averaged only one-half percent annually, whereas the population increased on the average of two percent. Sources of investment funds are scant. Per capita income for 1977 was on the order of $320, not a high level even for the less developed countries. The educational system ground to a complete halt during the turbulent decade of the Cultural Revolution, and the progress sought in science and technology hence will be hard to achieve. Modernization across the board will not be easy for a nation that still keeps eighty percent of its population in agriculture and has trained only one person in four to read and write.

The Chinese Communists, with their third-rate armies and fifth-rate economy, are clearly trying to use the United States to fight their war with the USSR, literally in the military sense, if they can manipulate Washington into direct confrontation with Moscow. They are more likely to succeed in this aim of "playing the American card" against Moscow than Carter is in "playing the China card" against the Soviet Union. Nobody knows what the China card really is, what the rules of the game are, or what points the United States can score by irritating Soviet leaders on the issue they are most emotional about—China. Certainly Moscow is annoyed with our Asian policy, and hostile Soviet behavior can hurt us much more than Peking can help us.

On the other hand, this game-playing is immediately damaging to American interests in east Asia. The political stability, the economic strength, and the international economic contribution to the whole American alliance system is enormously benefited by the friendly relations now existing with Japan, the Republic of Korea, and the Republic of China. Together these three nations, each fearful of domination by either the People's Republic of China or Soviet Union, are more powerful in every sense, except in sheer mass of manpower, than all of the PRC. Yet the thrust of American foreign policy appears to be to sacrifice the vital interests of the U.S. alliance system in pursuit of placating Peking and annoying Moscow.

The robust, dynamic, American-oriented societies of northeast Asia (Japan, South Korea, and Taiwan) are stable and optimistic except for one thing: they worry over the possibility that the Carter administration will, perhaps unknowingly but most irresponsibly, pull the rug out from under them even though much investment of American effort has built them up over the past thirty years.

Most Asians still think the United States is a great nation whose friendship and support are worth having, and they believe great nations do not take such shabby actions. American allies, worldwide, are visibly uneasy at the picture of U.S. cooperation with the monumentally anti-human rights regime of the PRC at the cost of confrontation with the Soviet Union and simultaneous destabilization of South Korea and Taiwan. Weakening these outposts flanking the Japanese islands profoundly affects Japanese confidence in America's reliablity as an ally and defense guarantor.

It is incumbent on thoughtful Americans to raise questions about the rationale involved in the Carter administration's China policy. The Shanghai Communiqué, drawn up on February 27, 1972, did not commit the United States to a full diplomatic relationship with Peking based on the *one* China concept, as is frequently alleged. Nor did it abrogate America's treaty commitment with the Republic of China for the defense of Taiwan. At a press conference held in Shanghai as soon as the communiqué had been issued, Henry Kissinger, the President's Assistant for National Security, clarified the ambiguity of the text on these issues by explaining that the U.S. position, as described in the president's world report, had not been changed. The world report, which had come out about twenty days earlier, on

February 9, states explicitly, under the president's signature, "With the Republic of China, we shall maintain our friendship, our diplomatic ties, and our defense commitment." This statement has never been officially repudiated or altered. It poses no moral obligation for the United States to endorse the PRC's *one* China interpretation of that communiqué.

What then ought to be the main principles of American policy toward the People's Republic of China? They can be simply stated.

1. Base U.S. foreign policy on facts, on fair dealing with all nations, not geopolitical maneuvering, and on straightforward protection of U.S. strategic interests, not hope or fantasy about wooing concessions from the dictators at the helm of either the USSR or the PRC.

2. Very bluntly, do not try to buy off adversaries at the expense of allies and friends.

3. With respect to the U.S.-China policy, specifically, the right position is not a Peking formula or a Japanese formula, but a formula of willingness to extend *de facto* recognition to and conduct normal international business with the two Chinese states so long as they are demonstrably able to govern their territory and their people.

It is a position proposing fair treatment for both the Republic of China and the People's Republic of China. It calls for accepting the reality that the PRC has *de facto* control of the mainland territory of China, and offering to extend full diplomatic recognition to Peking on this basis without subscribing to its *de jure* claim to be the rightful ruler of all territory that is called Chinese. This is a substantial gesture toward Peking in view of the fact that the PRC's political and economic system is one of which Americans thoroughly disapprove.

At the same time, to be fair, American policy-makers should also announce coolly but firmly that the United States does not permit any other government, certainly not the government of the PRC, to dictate their decisions on U.S. diplomatic and security relations with other states. They should say flatly that the United States will maintain full diplomatic relations and honor its mutual defense treaty with the Republic of China. If Peking rejects closer ties with Washington, it is the PRC's loss.

Taiwan's Strategy and America's China Policy*

John F. Copper**

I

In 1971 the United States made an about-face in its China policy. The causes for this were myriad. One was the Vietnam War and Peking's influence over its protégé, North Vietnam. Another was the fear in Washington that an escalation of Sino-Soviet hostilities might lead to nuclear war and involve United States. A third was that America's attitude toward China was the subject of criticism in many third world countries, and so it seemed clear that Washington could not keep Peking out of the United Nations much longer. Finally, many scholars and statesmen in the United States argued that the international system was evolving away from bipolarity; thus, improving relations with China would help dispel one of the rigidities that characterized the old style of international relations. In any event, the reasons for a rapprochement with China were compelling

Inasmuch as Taiwan was considered a major obstacle to closer relations with Peking, President Nixon signed a joint communiqué with the Chinese government in early 1972—the Shanghai Communiqué—acknowledging that Taiwan is a part of China. Nixon also committed the United States to withdraw its 8,500 troops from Taiwan. Subsequently, an across-the-board cut was made that left about 3,000 American troops on the island. United States warplanes also were relocated and Washington cut Taiwan's military aid. Finally, Congress invalidated the resolution under which President Eisenhower promised U.S. help in the defense of the Nationalist-held offshore islands of Quemoy and Matsu.

In spite of leadership changes in both the United States and China, détente remained a major foreign policy tenet on both sides. In 1975 President Ford reaffirmed the provisions of the Shanghai Communiqué during his visit to China. En route back to the United States after the trip, in a public speech in Hawaii, he asserted that U.S. friendship with the People's

*Copyright 1977, Orbis, Foreign Policy Research Institute. Reprinted by permission.
**John F. Copper is a Research Fellow at the Hoover Institution, Stanford University.

Republic of China "is becoming a permanent feature of the international landscape." Shortly after, in early 1976, he sent a letter to China's new premier, Hua Kuo-feng, reiterating his commitment to continue better relations, after which Thomas Gates became head of the liaison office in Peking—with ambassadorial status. Meanwhile Henry Kissinger conferred with Chinese officials on the topic of formal diplomatic ties. Both sides seemed to agree that diplomatic relations should be established without much delay. But because of Mao's illness and death and the U.S. election, a final decision was held in abeyance.

President Carter promised improved relations with China during his campaign, and it was a plank in the Democratic Party's platform. Since taking office, he has pledged closer relations with China, leading to formal diplomatic relations. In an apparent effort to fulfill this promise, Carter has sent a number of his advisors to Peking, including many who are influential in foreign policy-making. Most analyses predict that an exchange of embassies is not far off.

In Taipei, U.S. officials hint that they will start phasing out or closing down operations soon. The U.S. ambassador to the Republic of China, Leonard Unger—a man who some have speculated was sent to Taipei for that purpose—said recently that the "nature of U.S.-Republic of China relations will change." When the United States closes its embassy, Taipei will be recognized by no important nation, and probably most of the fewer than twenty-five countries that retain ambassadorial ties will depart. Other corollary difficulties will no doubt arise. American investment in Taiwan will decline because such investment is now guaranteed by the U.S. government, and that provision is tied to diplomatic relations. Other sources of foreign investment may be difficult to find. Trade with the Untied States will suffer—America took thirty-seven percent of Taiwan's exports last year. Either the U.S.-Republic of China defense pact will be automatically nullified, or Washington will give a year's notice to cancel it. United States military aid will cease.

Many observers feel that when this happens Taipei will be forced to seek some sort of accommodation with Peking, leading to an eventual reversion of the island to Peking's jurisdiction. They argue that the situation has been all downhill in the past six years for Taiwan and that Taipei has few, if any, options—none of them promising. Without the United States, they say, Peking can employ economic and military pressures to force the Nationalist Chinese government to bargain or capitulate.

Others, however, contend that the United States will not abandon Taiwan, which has been its historical ally and a showcase of American aid. They also note that Taiwan has considerable support if it makes a bid for independence, including public opinion in the United States. In addition, Taipei has options in regard to ties with the United States. Finally, Peking has more critical problems, the most important of which is the continuing Soviet threat.

Clearly, Taiwan is at a crossroads. Moreover, its leaders are charting a future course for Taiwan. Past policies will not suffice. An examination of Taiwan's policies shows that Nationalist Chinese leaders have designed a strategy to deal with the shock of America's move to Peking, which they now perceive as inevitable. Their policies are not announced openly for several reasons: Nationalist leaders have to worry about Taiwanese demands for an independent Taiwan for Taiwanese. Peking could veto Taiwan's admission to the United Nations, and it might win on a vote concerning whether or not the Taiwan question is a domestic matter. Chinese leaders in Taiwan hope that if they can survive the impact of the loss of U.S. recognition, time will be on their side in terms of maintaining their autonomy.

An assessment of Taipei's strategy is made in the following pages. The political, military, and economic dimensions of the plan are analyzed separately in the next three sections. The last section contains conclusions concerning the possibility for success of Taipei's policies and the importance of the issue to the world

II

In the political realm, Taipei's strategy is to delay Washington's move to Peking for as long as possible. In the meantime, it is abandoning the claim to represent China and seeking support in the United States on the Taiwan question. Chinese leaders in Taiwan realize that Washington will eventually establish formal diplomatic ties with Peking and that they cannot prevent this. But they also know that the United States is Taiwan's only important friend and ally at present and that America might not abandon Taiwan when it makes the move to Peking. They also feel that they can alter Washington's policy concerning Taiwan's future status.

In order to influence America's decision on Taiwan's future, Taipei has made special efforts to present its side of the problem to influential leaders in the United States. (Nationalist Chinese leaders argue that the Shanghai Communiqué is intentionally vague on the question of Taiwan and that Washington has made no final decision on the question.) Taipei has invited a number of congressmen, congressional staff personnel, journalists, and scholars to visit Taiwan in the last two or three years. All have been treated royally in the hope that they might return to the United States with a favorable impression of Taiwan. The list of invitees is quite different from former ones; it is bigger and includes both liberals and conservatives.

Taipei has also pulled out all stops to encourage tourism. In contrast to past policies, which limited travel to Taiwan, the government is now doing all it can to increase the number of foreign guests. Furthermore, tourists are not hampered by restrictions while in Taiwan. This more liberal policy toward foreign visitors also applies to students and retired or vacationing U.S. military personnel. Taipei espouses the doctrine of "see what you want to see, good or bad"—while noting that freedom of travel is not allowed on the mainland and that very few foreign tourists are given entry visas. They also flaunt progress in individual liberties, democracy, and social and economic development in Taiwan in contrast to the mainland. Observers contend that Taipei wants to attract more foreigners, especially Americans, because their "advertising" for Taiwan might eventually influence public opinion. It also allays criticism of Taiwan as a less-than-free country, especially in comparison to the mainland.

Taiwan has also expended considerable energy and money in the United States to increase cultural and other less official contacts. Three new consulates have been opened in the United States since the Shanghai Communiqué, and various athletic, entertainment and cultural groups have been sent to tour U.S. cities. Special efforts have likewise been made to preserve contacts with and win the support of Chinese living in the United States. Taipei would hardly make these efforts if it did not think that it could influence the American people and that this in turn might affect decision-makers in Washington.

In marked contrast to its past policy, Taipei now cites the principle of self-determination when discussing Taiwan's future. Its representatives in the United States have purchased advertising space in several large newspapers to present its case to the public. In addition, friends of Nationalist China have written numerous letters to editors of American newspapers and magazines, specifically suggesting that a United Nations-sponsored plebiscite be employed relative to the Taiwan question. They present the argument that ignoring the wishes of the people of Taiwan would be undemocratic and contrary to the principles on which world institutions are based.

Taipei's position in various international organizations is also telling. With the exception of the United Nations, Taipei has not withdrawn from world organizations when Peking has been admitted unless it has been forced to do so. Instead, Taiwan maintains an active membership. Likewise, it endeavors to play a part in international forums. economic summits, athletic meets, and so on. Since it cannot represent China, it must have in mind representing an autonomous Taiwan. This suggests, along with evidence already presented, that Nationalist Chinese leaders have adopted a "two Chinas" policy or a "one China, one Taiwan" policy. Certainly it reflects their desire to remain self-governing.

Despite this new and probably far-sighted policy toward the United States and the world community, at home Taipei still espouses a doctrine of retaking the mainland. At first glance this appears to be inconsistent and unrealistic. However, considering all of the variables, it may not be unwise. The anti-communist posture justifies the continuance of the minority government of Chinese that went to Taiwan when Chiang Kai-shek left the mainland, as well as the postponement of constitutional civil rights. The call for self-determination, which the Nationalists have made in the United States and elsewhere, increases the danger of demands for proportional representation and "full democracy" by the native-born Taiwanese. This in turn threatens political stability in Taiwan at a critical juncture. Likewise, increasing political freedom and flaunting human rights as Taipei has been doing carries with it the peril of encouraging dissent. The return-to-the-mainland policy helps keep this within bounds and justifies periodic harsh reactions against protesters in the name of national security.

Taipei's refusal to negotiate with the communists is a policy line taken for similar reasons. There is fear on the part of the Taiwanese that the main-landers, who hold political power, will sell them out and make a deal with Peking; and though some say that the government in Peking has intention-ally planted such rumors, it is also a natural apprehension. This might ex-plain why Taipei refused Peking's offer in 1976 to repatriate Nationalist prisoners, which ended in a propaganda victory for Mao.

Meanwhile, more Taiwanese are encouraged to participate in the government by joining the Nationalist Party or seeking government employ-ment. At the Nationalist Party Congress held in November 1976, for the first time the majority of representatives were Taiwan-born. Also, more Taiwanese have applied for government jobs in the last two or three years than they represent proportionally in the population. Efforts have even been made toward reconciliation with the Taiwanese Independence Movement leaders in Japan and the United States. Nationalist Chinese leaders under-score the realities: the Shanghai Communiqué undermined the cause of Taiwanese independence, and now Taiwanese and mainlanders are in the same predicament regarding the threat of incorporation.

On the other hand, Nationalist Chinese leaders do not want to declare their independence or officially disclaim ties to the mainland. This would carry the same dangers that more democracy carries; according to global trends, an independent Taiwan should be ruled by Taiwanese. It might also unnecessarily provoke Peking. Chinese officials in Taipei doubtless hope that Taiwan can maintain an ambiguous status in the near future, and that someday Taiwan will become simply another representative of the Chinese people, like Singapore.

Taiwan's political policy for coping with the problem of U.S. recogni-tion of Peking may be regarded as a good will campaign, acknowledging that public opinion in the United States favors recognition of China while not abandoning Taiwan, but also realizing that Taiwan's traditional support in the United States (in the form of the China Lobby) is inadequate. National-ist Chinese leaders also perceive that Washington may defer the Taiwan question to the United Nations or that world opinion may in some other way have a bearing on their future. They know that the people on Taiwan, Taiwanese and mainlanders alike, do not want to be incorporated by China.

If they are allowed to choose their destiny, there is no question that their choice will be for independence; thus, Taipei can rally for self-determination. Nationalist Chinese leaders know their cause is furthered by at least paying lip service to democratic principles; so Chiang Ching-kuo and other leaders make trips to rural areas in Taiwan and speak to the farmers, the poor, and the young. Concern for human rights is publicized, but almost always in comparsion to mainland China. More leniency has been shown toward political crime, but most notably in those cases that gain attention abroad. Taiwanese are invited to participate in politics and are given some positions of real importance. Even though much of this may be facade, it does represent a definite change from the past, and it has resulted in good press for Taiwan in the United States and elswhere.

III

Taipei's military policies follow and complement its political strategy in regard to the U.S. recognition of China. Nationalist Chinese leaders seek to delay the complete withdrawal of American troops, knowing that Peking will not use military force against Taiwan as long as they are there. Taipei hopes to keep the troops at least until Washington recognizes Peking and, if possible, for at least a year thereafter—during what will be a critical period for Taiwan. In the meantime, Taiwan is making a concerted effort to attract American weapons-builders to Taiwan and is purchasing U.S. military technology and sophisticated weapons to build up its own defenses.

Applying this policy, Taiwan has issued a number of warnings to U.S. military leaders, and to the American public as well, that Taiwan should be maintained as a U.S. fortress in the wake of the loss of Indochina. They also present the case that the Sino-Soviet dispute is spurious and may be a trick to get the United States to relax its guard (even though other evidence suggests that Taipei knows that the dispute is real). The Nationalist Chinese military, however, has made no effort to activate hostilities with Peking to force Washington's hand, knowing that it would be counterproductive to preserving temporary defense ties with the United States. Meanwhile, Taipei continues to grant U.S. military advisors in Taiwan a high protocol status and invites other American military decision-makers to Taiwan for inspection tours and visits. Nationalist Chinese leaders want to preserve their good relations with the U.S. military, knowing that the Pentagon has a major influence in U.S. policy-making and that it favors an independent Taiwan. It is said that there is no U.S. general or admiral who favors a total U.S. troop evacuation from Taiwan. Furthermore, the Joint Chiefs of Staff have recommended a residual U.S. presence on Taiwan as a means of guaranteeing its security once the United States leaves.

Regarding the U.S.-Republic of China mutual defense treaty, Nationalist Chinese leaders consider the treaty valid and contend that it is legal for at least twelve months (since a year's advance notice is required by either side to abrogate the pact). While some argue that the treaty would be automatically invalidated if the United States switched its embassy to Peking, Taipei does not agree with this interpretation. Moreover, it seems prepared to make an issue of the validity of the treaty when Washington makes the move to Peking. Taipei might win in such an effort; in fact, it may have already succeeded inasmuch as the United States has not officially stated that the treaty would be nullified by derecognition.

Another important facet of Taipei's military strategy is to attract U.S. arms manufacturers to Taiwan to set up subsidiary companies or to aid Taiwan's growing arms industry. Taiwan is investing heavily in its own weapons-building and it needs foreign technology and aid. The United States is the best source. To date, Taipei has been successful in attracting several American companies to Taiwan. Northrop Corporation, for example, is building F-5E fighter planes in Taiwan, which are now being purveyed to the Nationalist Chinese air force. Huey helicopters, U.S.-designed tanks and artillery, and M-14 rifles are also locally built. Among its purchases from U.S. companies is a $34-million air defense system from Hughes Aircraft. This was one of the largest single contracts for military equipment a U.S. company has signed with a foreign country. The purpose of all this is to defend Taiwan against an attack from the mainland. But the publicity given to increased military preparedness is also aimed at the populace of Taiwan, to give them assurance that their government can and will defend the island, and at the international community, which wonders whether Peking can invade Taiwan without destabilizing international politics.

Concurrent with its efforts to build a local arms industry, Taipei has implemented a policy which clearly reflects that defense rather than offense (retaking the mainland) is now paramount. The size of its air force and navy, as well as its reserves, has been increased, while the strength of the army has declined. This gives military planners a single objective, making their tactics simpler and more credible. Just as important, it is a move that makes Taiwan's overall foreign policy appear that of a non-belligerent nation seeking to develop on its own and wanting merely to control its own destiny.

Meanwhile, Taipei appears to be trying to tie its security to Japan's, thereby indirectly keeping Taiwan under the protective wing of the United States. Nationalist Chinese leaders are aware that the United States regards Japan as the cornerstone of its Asian defense policy and so will continue to defend Japanese interests. Furthermore, the U.S.-Japanese defense treaty contains provisions for evoking cooperation in the event of overt hostile acts against Taiwan. Thus, Taipei did not object in 1969 when Japanese Prime Minister Sato stated that Taiwan is "within Japan's defense zone"— even though this may have been construed as a violation of sovereignty.

Since then, it has been trying to encourage the continuation of this policy. Over the past few years, moreover, Nationalist Chinese leaders have held frequent meetings with conservative Japanese leaders, particularly those with ties to the Japanese military, to discuss the future of east Asia. Taipei has used these talks to point out the problems Japan will experience if Taiwan is incorporated by China: Japan's oil life line is vulnerable; its trade might be disrupted; its influence in south and southeast Asia would be reduced.

Nationalist China also maintains contacts with the Soviet Union to use as leverage against Peking. Soviet representatives have gone to Taiwan periodically in recent years, and Taipei has sent both official and unofficial spokesmen to Moscow. "Unofficial" spokesmen in Taipei have stated publicly on several occasions that Taiwan may grant the Soviet Union base facilities on Taiwan or on the Pescadores Islands if the United States withdraws its military forces and recognizes Peking. Several points of mutual interest stand out if one speculates about cooperation between Taipei and Moscow. Nationalist Chinese forces tie down a large number of troops in adjacent provinces on the mainland that might otherwise be sent north to the Sino-Soviet border. Moscow's growing naval presence in the Pacific and its interests in south and southeast Asia dictate a desire to keep the Taiwan Strait open and limit China's naval expansion. Neither Taipei nor Moscow wants Peking to be able to pressure Japan militarily.

Taipei wants the Soviet Union as a friend and ally in reserve, and it seeks to convey the message to Peking that if the United States evacuates its forces, Taipei has alternatives. Although switching defense ties from Washington to Moscow would be problematical for Taipei, and would involve political and economic bonds that would doubtless be less advantageous, its "Russian connection" serves as a big bargaining card vis-à-vis Peking. Some even suggest that Taipei's return to the mainland policy is maintained partly at the Kremlin's request and that, as a *quid pro quo,* Moscow will initiate hostilities on the Sino-Soviet border should Peking prepare to launch an invasion against Taiwan. On the other hand, it is possible that Taipei hopes to achieve an agreement with Peking that there will be no Soviet bases on Taiwan in return for no Chinese military build-up in Fukien province across the Taiwan Strait.

Another "hole card" that Taipei holds is its nuclear program and potential to build atomic bombs. Nationalist Chinese decision-makers have given a high priority to the development of nuclear energy—even though other forms of energy are more economical. This is a purposeful effort to create speculation concerning Taiwan's potential as a nuclear power. Its efforts to train nuclear scientists in the United States in areas that go beyond the use of nuclear energy for peaceful purposes is further confirmation. Taipei ostensibly sees its progress in this area as a means to counter a military threat from the mainland. Furthermore, it makes any conflict between the

Nationalist and Communist Chinese—explicitly, an invasion of Taiwan—a matter of international concern.

IV

In assessing Taiwan's economic policies, there are also discernible facets of planning that reflect anticipated problems connected with the U.S. departure. Most apparent is the stimulation given to short-range growth without concern for future down-trends and inflation. Taipei is deliberately planning an economic boom in anticipation of less readily available capital and probably a decline in trade when the United States recognizes Peking. Nationalist Chinese leaders also foresee the possibility of Peking employing economic warfare tactics to force Taiwan to negotiate incorporation. Rapid growth prevents defeatism, which is injurious to the morale of the government and the resistance of the people to a communist overture. Likewise, economic expansion is good for Taiwan's image abroad and bolsters economic contacts with other countries, helping to supplant the loss of political ties.

Most obvious in Taiwan's accelerated economic growth plans are the "ten projects." These are massive public-sector projects that require huge investment and government supervision and support. They include two seaports, an international airport, a shipyard, a steel mill, a petrochemical complex, a superhighway, a new rail line, and the electrification of several existing rail lines. Nuclear power plants are also included. The projects will be completed by the end of the decade at a cost of five billion dollars, or one-half of Taiwan's current annual gross national product. Half of the investment will come from abroad.

Notwithstanding the fact that economic growth will be influenced in a positive way, various liabilities involved with these projects have become apparent. First, it has become necessary to import construction materials and machines at a high cost and to the detriment of Taiwan's balance of payments. Second, the projects are taxing present port facilities as well as internal transport facilities. Third, a labor shortage is being created in many areas, putting a strain on the private sector of the economy and on social stability. Clearly, the simultaneous construction of so many large public works is questionable economics: not only will they compete with each other for skilled labor and technicians, but they are highly inflationary. These projects were originally designed to stimulate economic growth in order to compensate for political defeats resulting from the flight of embassies from Taiwan (after President Nixon announced his trip to China and Peking was voted into the United Nations). The projects, however, are still accorded a high priority and have short-term completion dates. The continuation of rapid-growth economic policies clearly involves much more than the loss of embassies, which is now in the past.

First, expansionary growth was needed to bring the country out of a serious recession caused by the oil crisis of 1973. In 1974, Taiwan's gross national product increased by less than one percent, while per capita income dropped slightly. In 1975, economic growth returned to a reasonable five to six percent. In 1976, it was over twelve percent. The return to rapid growth probably deterred the development of a recession mentality, which might have contributed to pessimism and weakened the nation's resistance to Peking's enticements and intimidation. A continuation of a high rate of growth will be salutary in terms of coping with the ordeal of a U.S. evacuation.

Second, rapid economic growth insures rising per capita income and reduces the likelihood of rebellion or opposition to the government. Since the government will face a legitimacy problem when the United States withdraws, this may prove to be crucial. Nationalist Chinese leaders are no doubt aware of the fact that political unrest is not usually prevalent in an environment of economic growth. They are also aware that this is particularly relevant to Taiwan, since the Taiwanese constitute both the business sector and a major portion of the poor and dissatisfied.

Third, rapid growth is good for Taiwan's image abroad, and it contributes to increasing commercial contacts with foreign countries. These ties are valuable in that they supplant political relationships and establish an interdependency, which may sway the decisions of nations that otherwise might not care whether or not Taiwan remains self-governing. Taiwan's future may well become an international question, and vested interests will help Taipei's cause. The same is true of attracting foreign investment. A high growth rate makes possible larger investment input and foreign borrowing, which evokes a greater concern abroad for Taiwan's future independence.

Fourth, while Taiwan's rapid economic growth has the disadvantage of forcing infrastructural changes and financial crises for businessmen in sectors of the economy that rely on low labor costs, it prompts innovation and the constructon of new industries. It also induces greater specialization and technology input. This is an advantage in that it reduces the worry about economic pressures from Peking through the dumping of similar products on the market at low or below-cost prices. China does not produce in sufficient quantity many of the products now being developed in Taiwan and probably will not be able to do so in the future. It would also make incorporation less beneficial for Peking, because China would have to maintain Taiwan's ties with the world economy—meaning the acceptance of capitalism—or engineer the destruction of Taiwan's economic progress and relocate a sizable portion of the population. Finally, rapid economic growth, particularly in high technology and specialized industry, promotes cultural changes that will make the integration of Taiwan with the mainland difficult.

In its endeavors to generate business ties and foreign investment, Taiwan has specifically aimed first at the United States and then at Japan—nations that will play paramount roles in determining Taiwan's future. Last year, foreign investment in Taiwan totaled over $1.3 billion; nearly half of this came from the United States. Japan followed a close second. In the case of U.S. investment, Taipei has sought to attract large U.S. companies, especially those that are known to have political influence in Washington. With Japan, on the other hand, Taiwan has invited small investors so as to avoid competition between U.S. and Japanese companies and to involve Japanese businessmen in Taiwan in such a way that they cannot recover their investments should Taiwan lose its autonomy. Considering Taiwan's size and economic situation, its debt is clearly bigger than it need be, and its arrears to the United States and Japan are inordinately large.

Taiwan's efforts to maintain a high level of trade with the United States and Japan similarly fit into its strategic planning. One could argue that Taiwan is dangerously dependent on the United States, where protectionist sentiment is strong, and on Japan, where economic pressure from Peking is portentous, and that it should therefore diversify its trade. Taiwan's planners, however, want to increase commercial ties with the two countries that will have the greatest influence on Taiwan's future. Taipei has also adjusted the balance of payments to maintain influence with its important friends. Specifically, Taipei has made moves to correct its overly favorable balance of trade with the United States over the past three to four years, and it has publicized this in the United States. It is now buying American products even though in many cases they are more expensive than goods of comparable quality elsewhere. Besides allowing an unfavorable balance of trade with Japan, Taiwan is permitting Japanese companies on the island to make large profits.

This strategy makes sense for two reasons. First, China is now giving high priority to economic development, based in large part on increased trade with the West. Japan and the United States are China's most important trading partners, and Peking cannot afford to alienate business leaders in these two countries. Second, Taipei is seeking to alter many of the U.S. regulations and laws governing America's trade and investment abroad, particularly rules that would discriminate against Taiwan once it loses recognition. Taipei, however, in the aftermath of Korean attempts to influence Congress, is using more indirect means.

V

Taiwan's strategy vis-à-vis U.S. recognition of Peking is fraught with contradictions. Nationalist Chinese leaders must maintain a policy of return-to-the-mainland in order to placate the old hands in the Kuomintang and alleviate Taiwanese fears that they will make a deal with Peking. They have to oppose negotiations for the same reason. They do not want to bargain with Peking on Taiwan's future; they want to remain free of ties to China. Yet they have to convince Washington that they are reasonable. They want American military support, but they cannot force a crisis situation to keep it, as this would be counter-productive. They must persuade America that they are concerned for democracy and human rights, yet in Chinese eyes America has overdone both. Also, they must preserve political stability and must worry about an escalation of demands for political rights; since the Nationalists are a minority government, political rights are dangerous.

For these reasons, Taipei is following a low-key policy. This gives the impression that Taiwan has no policy and is perhaps fatalistic about the future. Likewise, it gives the impression that Peking will win on the issue of the Taiwan question. The alternative would be for Taipei to openly declare its independence as the Republic of Taiwan—which for reasons already mentioned has serious disadvantages. Nevertheless, Taipei can make this move later if it perceives a need. At present, Taipei appears to have a number of assets it can exploit, and it has some options. Thus its policy, though not dramatic, seems to be astute. And, with what little evidence there is to offer, it appears to be working.

Taiwan has considerable support in U.S. government circles on the issue of its independence. There is less support, however, on U.S. non-recognition of Peking and almost none on a return-to-the-mainland policy. Taiwan's retreat from the latter two issues will probably augment U.S. support on the former. Public opinion in the United States favors Taiwan's autonomy by a large margin. In fact, Taipei provided the impetus for at least one public opinion poll on the subject and has done all it can to publicize the results. Since U.S. decision-makers seem equivocal on the issue of the Taiwan question, public opinion may play a significant role. Washington's stance at present seems to be that it is a "Chinese question." Clearly, this is not true. Taiwan's future is in the hands of the United States. There is little hope that Taipei and Peking can negotiate a lasting, peaceful solution.

It would not be in Japan's interest for Taiwan to be incorporated by China—another point that Taipei is underscoring. This would allow China to close the Taiwan Strait and prevent Japanese passage (which China could easily do if it opted to employ naval force). It would also give China a stronger bargaining position with Tokyo regarding the settlement of territorial issues in the vicinity of Okinawa and, more important, the ownership of vast undersea oil reserves in that area. The same applies to the Soviet Union. The Kremlin is locked into a serious conflict with China, and presumably when Peking resolves the Taiwan issue, it will make a stronger claim to "lost territories" in the Soviety Union. Both Tokyo and Moscow would prefer to see Taiwan self-governing and independent. Taipei has thus maintained good relations with both countries—better than events would seem to justify.

The Taiwanese Independence Movement is now weak and factionalized. Thus, Nationalist leaders have conveyed to the Taiwanese the message that they will continue to rule Taiwan, but their exclusive hold on political power will be relinquished in the near future and assimilation will eventually resolve all differences. That the two groups have almost identical interests in avoiding incorporation is a picture drawn vividly by the government—and it is being understood. The differences separating Taiwanese and mainland Chinese are being buried by time and official policies. Nationalist Chinese leaders must still worry about die-hards in their party who oppose Taiwanese participation in the government and also about radical Taiwanese who want independence on the basis of expelling the mainland Chinese or reducing their status to that of a persecuted minority group. However, no perceivable polarization has occurred in spite of the fact that more Taiwanese are in the government and that encouragement has been given to the Taiwanese Independence Movement by the granting of more political freedoms.

Optimistically, Taipei hopes that Washington will recognize two Chinas, following the Soviet precedent of recognizing two Germanys. Considering China's need for American support (to cope with the Soviet military threat) and the fact that China's economic development plans are now founded on increased trade with the West, as well as the acquisition of technology and investment funds, this may not be out of the question. Another potentially auspicious solution for Taiwan would be for the United States to follow the "Japan formula"—recognize Peking and retain a "liaison office" in Taipei—but keep a U.S. military presence in Taiwan and extract a non-aggression pledge from Peking. These solutions are certainly preferable to relying on Japan, which is militarily weak compared to China, or using the Soviet option, which would certainly imperil Taiwan's commercial relations with the West and hurt its economic development.

Taipei can also make a good case for independence. Taiwan has been *de facto* a separate nation for twenty-eight years. It has had ties with the mainland for only four years in this century. More remote historical connections are likewise weak. Taiwan is clearly a viable nation. Its size, population, and economy are all larger than at least a third of the member states in the United Nations. Nevertheless, Taipei does not want to anger Peking. Nationalist Chinese leaders perceive that the case for independence can best be made gradually.

Taipei can even present the Taiwan question as an international issue. If China were to invade Taiwan it would probably result in casualties upward of one million, and it might take months before Peking would succeed. Taiwan's military forces are equipped with modern weapons and in terms of strategy are totally programmed to the defense of Taiwan. Peking might choose the nuclear option, but Taiwan might have its own to use in return. In any case, this could not go unnoticed by the rest of the world. Meanwhile, Taiwan is gradually garnering friends and commitments from the international community. Certainly Peking's claim that Taiwan is a domestic issue has less and less support as time passes.

Taiwan's foreign policy today manifests a great deal of realism and flexibility. One of Taipei's principal tactics is to keep the world guessing; moralism is being played down. Taipei's actions clearly reflect the realization that Taiwan's hope does not lie in China. Hence, Nationalist Chinese leaders seek to maintain Taiwan's autonomy as a *sine qua non*. Moreover, Taipei's stance reveals an understanding of Taiwan's place in the world and a comprehension of the influence of world politics on Taiwan's future; it shows an ability to adapt to the world situation. This policy may well succeed.

The U.S. and Taiwan: Is This Divorce Necessary?*

*James D. Hessman***

Why is it so important to normalize relations with China? *"Because it is there. Because you can't ignore 900 million people. Because, without full ties, the United States might stumble into war with China—over Korean reunification, perhaps. Because China is a counterweight to the Soviet Union."*

That was the rhetorical question—and the multi-faceted answer—which the *Washington Star* featured in its lead editorial on Feb. 11, 1978.

The question appeared in the text of the editorial, however, and the "answer" just quoted was not the *Star's* own, but rather its short (and accurate) summary of the reasons many others have given for breaking U.S. ties with Taiwan and "normalizing" U.S. relations with Communist China.

The *Star's* own sentiments, it should be noted, were reflected in the editorial's headline: "What's the Hurry on China?"

A lot of other people are asking the same question these days—but not many of those people, it seems, carry much weight with the Carter administration.

On raw statistics alone, those who advocate formal diplomatic recognition with the mainland, even at the cost of breaking relations with a long-time and loyal ally, would seem to have all the better of the argument.

Mainland China or the People's Republic of China—the terms "Red China" and "Communist China," both considered somewhat pejorative, have been dropped from the U.S. diplomatic lexicon since President Nixon's 1972 visit to Peking—is the world's most populous nation as well as the third largest geographically (3,691,000 square miles). Its Gross National Product, an estimated $223 billion in 1974, is fifth largest in the world—almost equal to the collective $241 billion of all the countries of Latin America combined.

**James D. Hessman is editor-in-chief of *Seapower* magazine, the official publication of The Navy League of the United States.

There are other arguments. Throughout the 1950s the possibility of mainland China uniting with the Soviet Union in a massive onslaught against the free world (as it was then quaintly called) helped focus and, to a certain extent, transfix U.S. defense policy into a position of worldwide "containment." The post-Stalin PRC/USSR tension which in the early 1960s escalated to an open and acrimonious split between the two Communist giants evolved in turn to the present status of armed truce, with an estimated one million Soviet troops poised just north of the Ussuri River ready to defend Mother Russia (the Soviet view) or to launch unprovoked new attacks against their erstwhile allies (the PRC view).

Whatever the merits of the various ideological arguments which still divide the Soviet Union and the People's Republic of China, the practical fact remains: not only are one million Russian troops tied up in the USSR's far eastern provinces, but the very possibility of having to fight a major two-front war must give the Kremlin pause and might, just perhaps, deter Soviet adventurism in Europe if not elsewhere.

U.S. Playing "The Chinese Card"?

For both selfish and altruistic reasons, the United States does not want, and will do nothing to instigate, armed conflict between the USSR and the PRC. Neither, however, does it desire a complete reconciliation between the two—not, at least, until one or both shift from their posture of evangelical militance (old-fashioned imperialism, in other words) in the cause of communism to a more amicable *modus vivendi* toward the West. Fearful in any case, therefore, of a renewed ideological—and, worse, military—Sino-Soviet partnership, the new wave of PRC partisans suggests what amounts to a preemptive U.S./PRC friendship. They sometimes add, not altogether convincingly, that by thus playing "the Chinese card" the United States will somehow force the Kremlin to be more cooperative in the Strategic Arms Limitation Talks (SALT) negotiations.

There is also, as there has been for decades if not centuries, the rather hypothetical economic argument that the 900 million citizens of mainland China are, from a purely business point of view, "900 million potential customers." Compared to that huge untapped market, Taiwan's seventeen million pale into shadowy insignificance. Adding economic credence and political visibility to the "trading partner" rationale, which thus far has been stronger in promise than in performance, Commerce Secretary Juanita Kreps said on June 14 that she expects U.S. trade with mainland China to almost double this year to a level of over $700 million. (Most of the projected increase is based on the $115 million PRC purchase in April of a million metric tons of U.S. wheat. Commerce Department officials say the PRC may purchase as much as two million more tons this year, but not necessarily all or any of it from U.S. farmers.)

Finally, there is a burning political desire, sometimes barely distinguishable from missionary zeal, in the Carter administration to conclude an accord with the PRC which would at long last guarantee "peace in our time" between the world's most populous nation and its greatest economic power. Administration spokesmen always insist, of course—with what sometimes seems more hope than conviction—that attainment of that laudable objective will not be at Taiwan's expense; that, in other words, the United States will not formally recognize the People's Republic of China unless the latter "pledges" not to use force against Taiwan and "guarantees" the continued freedom of that island nation. The nature and extent of such pledges and guarantees are never spelled out, though.

President Carter's own convictions about the desirability of a comprehensive long-term relationship with the People's Republic are clear. His intentions toward Taiwan are somewhat less so. At an April 11 press conference, Bud Smyser of the *Honolulu Star-Bulletin* noted: "The present Peking government says that it will not use force in the near term to settle the Taiwan question but it will not rule out the use of force for the indefinite future. Does this reservation by Peking pose an insurmountable obstacle to our full diplomatic recognition of Peking?"

The President's answer (with emphasis added): "I would not acknowledge any insurmountable obstacle in reaching the goals expressed in *the Shanghai Communiqué, which is binding on us*—and which I fully support—and binding on the People's Republic of China leaders. We recognize the concept that is shared in Taiwan and on the mainland that there's only one China. We recognize that it's for the best interests of our own nation to have full diplomatic relationships with China. And my hope is that *over a period of months*—we are not in any big hurry; neither are the People's Republic of China leaders—that we will completely realize the hopes expressed in the Shanghai Communiqué."

It will be recalled that the Shanghai Communiqué, issued on February 27, 1972 by President Nixon and Premier Chou En-lai, recognized what was never disputed: "that all Chinese on either side of the Taiwan Strait maintain there is but one China and that Taiwan is a part of China."

"The United States does not challenge that position," the communiqué continued. "It reaffirms its interest in a peaceful settlement of the Taiwan question by the Chinese themselves."

So far, nothing which either the PRC or Taiwan, or the supporters of either, would find objectionable. But there was more: "With this prospect in mind, it [the United States] affirms the ultimate objective of the withdrawal of all U.S. forces and military installations from Taiwan. In the meantime, it will progressively reduce its forces and military installations on Taiwan as the tension in the area diminishes."

A few observations are pertinent.

First, the communiqué, which President Carter says "is binding on us," has in fact no legal validity. It is not a formal treaty ratified by the U.S. Senate. Its well-intentioned but necessarily vague provisions have never been tested in a court of law—nor could they be, considering the reality. It was, and is, nothing more nor less than the personal political views of its human signatories. (Parenthetically, it might also be noted that the Communiqué is a most selective example of the Carter administration's willingness to accept any such extra-legal Nixon precedent or initiative as binding on President Carter himself.)

Second, despite Mr. Carter's protestation that "we are not in any big hurry," his immediately prior reference to "a matter of months" as the time frame in which he wants to "completely realize the hopes expressed in the Shanghai Communiqué" raises again the *Star*'s question: "What's the hurry on China?" Mao Tse-tung and Chou En-lai both died in 1976. Since then, Liu Shao-chi, Mao's personally designated successor, was purged by his peers, as was Lin Piao—whose name once was written into the PRC constitution as Mao's successor. Meanwhile, public recriminations continue on the Mainland against the so-called "gang of four," a sure sign, according to long-time China watchers, that the present PRC regime (headed by Premier Hua Kuo-feng and Vice Premier Teng Hsiao-ping) is not yet in full control. Unless and until the turbulence subsides, hasty U.S. acceptance of any change in the current U.S./PRC/Taiwan relationships could prove in the long run to be disastrously premature.

Third, intentionally or otherwise, President Carter did not specifically answer the question asked by Bud Smyser: whether Peking's refusal to "rule out the use of force for the indefinite future" poses an "insurmountable obstacle" to full diplomatic recognition of Peking by the United States. The President's reply that he would not "acknowledge" any insurmountable obstacle begs the point. He could very simply have said, but didn't, that if the PRC does not formally forswear the future use of force against Taiwan, then the United States would have no honorable course open to it but to continue the status quo, unsatisfactory as that might be in some other respects.

If the President was ambiguous on the conditions, Secretary of State Cyrus Vance left no doubt that "full diplomatic recognition"—and soon—is still a very high priority goal. Vance said April 30—on "Face the Nation" (CBS)—that "normalization of relations with China is one of the fundamental goals [of the administration]. I would hope that during the first term we would be able to normalize relations."

Underscoring that oft-expressed determination, the administration shortly thereafter added insult to injury by dispatching Zbigniew Brzezinski, President Carter's security advisor, to Peking—to arrive on the same day, May 20, that Taiwan Premier Chiang Ching-kuo was inaugurated as that country's new president. Incredibly, State Department and White House officials maintain there was no insult intended, that the remarkable coincidence in timing was "not realized" when the Brzezinski trip was scheduled. If so, that is an admission that the administration's already much-criticized staff work may have retrogressed from the appalling to the abysmal.

Still, what's done is done, and cannot be undone. Besides, such past hurts and humiliations are unimportant to Taiwan compared to what could be, for it, a cataclysmic future.

The Question of Taiwan's Future

What about that future? Is Taiwan's position now untenable, given the apparent predilections and publicly stated positions of the Carter administration?

Not necessarily. But before going into specifics it might be relevant to recall what John F. Kennedy once said in another context: "I hear it said that West Berlin is militarily untenable. And so was Bastogne. And so, in fact, was Stalingrad. Any dangerous spot is tenable if men—brave men— will make it so."

That the brave men of Taiwan have already made their position, their "dangerous spot," highly tenable, and would fight to the death to keep it so, is indisputable. On the small island of Quemoy, just over one mile from Communist-held Chiao Yu, there have been six major battles since the PRC took over the mainland on October 1, 1949. In the first of those, the battle of Ku Ning T'ou (October 25-27, 1949), some 13,000 communist troops, two-thirds of the entire invasion force, were killed in battle; 7,000 more PRC soldiers were captured. Not one man escaped. (For comparison: in the entire Vietnam War, 1961-75, the United States suffered 46,752 "battle deaths," 10,390 "other deaths.") How many deaths would occur in a battle for Taiwan itself is unimaginable, but the total could easily be in the millions.

Taiwan, the Republic of China or ROC—sometimes called Formosa, Free China, or Nationalist China—does not have to depend solely on the uncommon valor of its troops, however. Despite the political reverses and public humiliations of recent years, it still has many strengths—and many friends.

Among those friends, it seems obvious, are the majority of the American people—who, ironically, are more consistent in their espousal of human rights than is the president who made the term his political battle cry. Numerous surveys have shown that the American public: (1) favors establishing formal diplomatic relationships with mainland China; but (2) is

218

adamantly against severing relations with Taiwan if that is the price required.

Opinions from the Media

The U.S. media, although far from unanimous on the subject, has also been holding the administration's feet to the fire, and in less-than-complimentary language. A few examples:

• An editorial in the February 19, 1978 *Detroit News* telegraphed its punch with the straightforward headline "Only Moral Bankrupts Sell Out Their Friends," and then commented: "Especially after its performance in Vietnam, the United States would be wise to husband the moral capital it has left. Without doubt, deserting Taiwan would just about deplete the supply."

• The *Salem* (Oregon) *Statesman* echoed the same theme in a February 28 editorial: "The world has seen, in Vietnam, what can happen to people who put their trust in the United States. The grievous miscalculation there has left uncounted numbers in prison camps and 'retaining' centers, plus hundreds of thousands of refugees. . . . Are we willing to spawn another horde of 'boat people,' this time from Taiwan?" The *Statesman* answered its own rhetorical question: "While we curry China's favor to counter Russian strength, we should not violate our own integrity in so doing. There is no reason we should sacrifice the sixteen million people of Taiwan in a futile effort to gain friendship with China."

• Rutgers professor Peter Berger, in a February 14 column in the *New York Times*, also discussed the "boat people," as follows (his emphasis throughout): "These boats bear a message. It is a simple and ugly message: *Here is what happens to those who put their trust in the United States of America.* . . . All of this is terrible enough in itself. But it now appears that the abandonment of those who trust us is becoming a habit. *We are getting ready to do it again—this time in Taiwan.* . . . If there is one universal, indeed primeval, principle of morality, it is that one must not deliver one's friends to their enemies. And if there is one maxim in which morality coincides with politics, it is that a nation that breaks its solemn word twice will never be trusted again."

If the several moral arguments just cited are not persuasive to an administration which has so often staked its reputation on its own morality and rectitude, there are some practical considerations also worth noting.

Practical Considerations

First, the gossamer allure of "900 million potential customers" on the mainland has to be balanced against a hard economic fact: Taiwan's two-way trade with the United States last year totaled $5.7 billion, or about sixteen times the PRC's two-way trade with the United States. What is more, Taiwan is proving itself just as loyal a trading partner as it has been a military ally. At a time when the United States is suffering unprecedented balance of payments deficits, the government of Taiwan has pledged to substantially increase its imports from the United States—an ROC trade mission left Taipei in mid-June on a $731 million shopping trip for American-made goods, and two other missions are scheduled to visit the United States later in the year to make similarly large purchases.

Second, Taiwan is, whether the current administration approves or not, the current leader among the developing countries of the world. Thanks in about equal shares to earlier U.S. economic aid and to the native genius and industry of its own people, Taiwan is now leagues ahead of the mainland in virtually every measurable category of economic (and human) progress. A few examples (from the 1978 CBS News Almanac—the PRC statistics are estimates): the PRC's per capita income in 1975 was $320, the ROC's $809; life expectancy on the mainland is sixty-two years; on Taiwan, seventy-one years; forty-five percent of mainland China's population is still illiterate, only eleven percent of Taiwan's population; the PRC's death rate is 10.3 per thousand population, the ROC's death rate 5.2 per thousand.

Third, if the United States were to play its "Chinese card" against Russia, Taiwan might be forced, against its own wishes, to play its "Russian card." ROC officials are insistent that Taiwan would never ally itself with the Soviet Union, which it ideologically despises as much as do the mainland Chinese. But desperate situations sometimes require desperate measures. Niu Sien-chong points out (in the February/March issue of NATO's *Fifteen Nations*) that "naval and air base rights on the island [which the United States now has, incidentally, under its mutual defense treaty], could easily enable the Soviet Union to dominate the South China coast, effectively close the ring around the Chinese mainland, and, as a bonus, put Japan in a Soviet vise. . . . It is not out of the question that the ROC might seek an alliance with the USSR if the Taipei government felt itself abandoned or betrayed. . . . For the PRC [and for the United States, it seems fair to add], Soviet naval access to port facilities in Taiwan would be the worst of all possible worlds."

Fourth, Taiwan has yet another odious option: development and deployment of nuclear weapons—indeed, political analyst Ranan R. Lurie reported in the *Chicago Sun Times* (October 26, 1977) that the ROC already has developed "tactical nuclear bombs designed to annihilate an invading armada or prevent a Chinese sea blockade." That report is denied by ROC officials; U.S. intelligence officers will "neither confirm nor deny"—but they concede that Taiwan has for several years had the capability to manufacture nuclear weapons. It would be both ironic and tragic if Jimmy Carter, who has waged a sincere and zealous campaign against the proliferation of nuclear weapons, were—because of his own foreign policy decisions—to force smaller unprotected nations such as Taiwan to stockpile nuclear arsenals. (It seems reasonable to conjecture that an abandonment of Taiwan might well force other erstwhile U.S. allies to re-examine their own defense requirements.)

For all of the foregoing and other reasons both theoretical and practical which could be cited, many analysts believe any unilaterally-pursued U.S./ROC divorce would be neither necessary nor beneficial.

Fortunately (in the view of those who favor a continuation of the status quo), the Carter administration may have no choice in the matter. Senator Barry Goldwater (R-Ariz.) argues—in a Heritage Foundation monograph ("China and the Abrogation of Treaties") released on May 17—that "it would be unconstitutional for the president to abrogate the mutual defense treaty with Taiwan without obtaining the approval of two thirds of the Senate or both houses of the Congress."

Goldwater contends—and musters an impressive phalanx of constitutional arguments to back him up—that "it is the clear instruction of history that the president cannot give valid notion of an intention to withdraw from a treaty, let alone void a treaty in violation of the formalities required by any provision it may contain regarding duration. . . .

"Although the constitutional question arises in connection with the defense treaty between the Republic of China and the United States," Goldwater adds, "it is also important to explore the principle involved because it touches every one of our nation's treaty commitments. If the president can break the treaty with Taiwan on his own authority, then he can withdraw from NATO or pull out of any other treaty without consulting Congress or getting its consent. . . .

"The truth is that, were the shoe reversed," the Arizona Republican also points out, "many Americans who are falling all over themselves to give in to every demand by Communist China would be the first to condemn unilateral presidential action of a kind they do not like."

Goldwater also says: (1) it is the view of "several subordinate officers" at the State Department that the President could indeed terminate the U.S./ROC Mutual Defense Treaty "at his own discretion;" and (2) that "the Legal Advisor's Office in the Department of State" already has been "studying this contingency."

Senator Goldwater tactfully sidesteps the point, but if President Carter and/or his spokesmen and legal advisors do seriously defend the thesis that a president could unilaterally and "at his own discretion" terminate treaties, they would necessarily be promoting a principle which could make an *ex post facto* shambles of the Carter administration's own foreign policy goals and achievements.

They would be saying, in effect, that the next president could at *his* discretion terminate the Panama Canal treaties.

One doubts that the administration really wants to set a precedent which could lead to that result. For then one risks having a set of formal and sacred agreements with friends and allies little different than the "live-in" arrangements so common today among those whose real commitment is suspect.

Taking all factors into account, and much as it is to U.S. national interests to maintain friendly relations with the PRC, it is still prudent to ask, "U.S. and Taiwan: is this divorce necessary?"

The Sino-Soviet Relationship: Reflections Upon Its Past and Future*

Robert A. Scalapino**

Rarely in history have two neighboring societies, each possessing substantial power, been able to consummate and sustain intimate ties of a strategic nature. When such an alliance has occurred, moreover, it has almost invariably been directed against a common foe, and fallen into dissolution when one or both parties came to regard the primary threat as having ended.

In these terms, the course of Sino-Soviet relations over the past three decades cannot be considered abnormal. Unquestionably, the alliance formed between these two giant communist societies in 1949-1950 constituted one of the major events of the time. Some three-quarters of a billion people living in two highly organized societies were brought into unity by their respective elites and dedicated to a common set of causes. Had the alliance endured for any length of time, all parts of the Eurasian continent would have felt its impact in the most intensive fashion.

The Raison d'Etre of the Sino-Soviet Alliance

As is well known, however, the alliance lasted less than a decade and broke up under circumstances of the utmost acrimony. What caused this dramatic turn of events? Let us first recapitulate the essential reasons for the creation of the alliance. As in the case of most political events, a number of causative factors were involved. From the Chinese standpoint, a substantial legacy of loyalty to international communism existed. Notwithstanding the complexities involved in a movement forced by circumstances

*Copyright 1977, Strategic Review, United States Strategic Institute. Reprinted by permission.
**Robert A. Scalapino is Robson Professor of Political Science at the University of California at Berkeley.

to become more self-reliant and further propelled in this direction by that highly indigenous communist, Mao Tse-tung, it is a great mistake to view either Mao or the Chinese Communist Party as committed to a course of ideological and political independence at the outset of their advent to power. On the contrary for economic and strategic as well as ideological reasons, the People's Republic of China (PRC) sought and initially cherished its ties with the Soviet Union. Mao was sincere when he denounced neutralism and proudly averred China's commitment to the socialist camp: "We lean to one side, led by the Great Soviet Union."

Despite Stalin's doubts that the Chinese Communists could win the civil war, the Soviets had given significant support to the cause in Manchuria—a region which proved to be crucial to the military contest. In the aftermath of victory, moreover, who was better suited than the USSR to assist a new socialist nation in its quest for economic modernization? At the time, any basic model other than that of the Soviets was inconceivable to China's revolutionary modernizers. The thesis that the new Chinese leaders ever seriously contemplated military and economic aid from the United States, either in the course of their quest for victory in the civil war or in its aftermath, is untenable.

If these considerations were dominant factors in the Chinese commitment to alliance, this new relationship was equally logical from a Soviet perspective. Stalin, it should be remembered, had been prepared to work with any Chinese government in the period after World War II, providing Russian interests were safeguarded. These interests, consistent from czar to commissar, had been granted by the Allies at Yalta, and translated into reality via the Sino-Soviet treaty of August 1945. One of the great historic Russian goals has been to be an Asian as well as a European power. The advent of a communist government in China, from Moscow's standpoint as of 1949-1950, could only abet that objective. In more general terms, the advent of China to the international communist union provided both political and psychological stimulus to the communist cause everywhere. Nor were its strategic consequences lost upon the Soviet leaders. A dramatic shift in the balance of power, especially in Asia, had taken place—one upsetting American calculations and weakening the American position. Suddenly, the communist cause had been provided with unexpected leverage in one of the world's vital regions. It was even possible for the Soviets to contemplate some division of labor, allowing the Chinese a priority of interest and responsibility within the Asian sphere.

Thus, in the case of both parties, one consideration underwrote all others in nurturing the alliance, namely, the common antagonism toward and fear of the United States. In the eyes of both Moscow and Peking, the United States represented the richest, most influential nation in the world, a formidable military power and one with a long lead in nuclear weapons, and "the leader of the imperialist camp," expansionist in intent. Thus, the new alliance provided an in-depth defense against the United States by securing the Eurasian heartland. In doing so, moreover, it provided an enhanced capacity for offensive activities as well, rendering the peripheries of both Europe and Asia more vulnerable, and permitting client states or affiliated movements to undertake "liberation" campaigns with less risk and greater hope of success. This era, it must be emphasized, can only be understood against this background of combined defensive-offensive strategy on the part of the communist leaders. It should not be forgotten that Sino-Soviet ties were officially inaugurated at the precise time when a hot ingredient— Korea—was being planned as an addition to the cold war.

The Dissolution of the Alliance

The essence of the Sino-Soviet cleavage after 1956 can be summarized as follows. Two societies sharing a common ideology, and thus certain common values and institutions, nevertheless had different cultural heritages, different timings of revolution, different stages of development and different degrees of power. Hence, their respective elites perceived their national interests differently, a fact that soon affected both policies and attitudes.

As these trends developed, two factors abetted the movement from difference to antagonism. A personal factor lay in the very dissimilar political styles of two forceful men, Nikita Khrushchev and Mao Tse-tung, and underlying this seemingly idiosyncratic element were those profound differences in culture that had long been translated into racial prejudices. An impersonal factor was contained in the fact that in both countries nationalist feelings were being intensely cultivated. And, paradoxically, allegiance to a common ideology served to exacerbate rather than alleviate the conflict, since in a fashion reminiscent of medieval Christianity both parties struggled to claim orthodoxy while finding heresy in the other. In this manner, error and evil became interchangeable.

It is commonly and correctly assumed that the first serious issue of a specific nature to come between the Soviet Union and China involved de-Stalinization. Presumably, the Chinese understood the pressing domestic reasons for Khrushchev's unprecedented assault upon a man so revered by orthodox communists everywhere. But this did little to mitigate the pain and anger felt in Peking—pain at the embarrassment caused after so many eulogies to Stalin had come from the pen of Mao and others, anger at not having been consulted or even forewarned.

This issue alone, however, could have been handled. A more complex problem was emerging. To what extent was the Soviet model of economic development applicable to China? While the opening years of the communist era could generally be adjudged a striking success in economic terms, certain basic problems soon became apparent. Foremost among them was the increasing gap between urban and rural growth. Soviet assistance in the heavy industrial field had resulted in major gains, although it was difficult to alleviate unemployment and underemployment in China's densely packed cities, and the need to push handicraft-type production remained acute. But more importantly, could the rural sector be allowed to lag, with the prospect of hundreds of millions of peasants pressing against the urban areas, seeking economic opportunities? To put the matter simply, China, given its extremely low economic base-line and its heavily rural population, could not afford the same degree of neglect toward the agrarian sector that had characterized the Soviet drive for modernization. Hence, the commune experiment—an experiment that was regarded by the Soviets as an unsound deviation from correct developmental principles. In this setting, tension increased over many aspects of the Soviet aid program, with both sides harboring grievances.

Even these problems, however, might have been contained had not another issue emerged that challenged the very foundations of the alliance. The controversy which produced the first great crisis in Sino-Soviet relations and led to the irreparable breach centered upon how to handle the United States. Mao and his colleagues had been greatly pleased at the rapid progress made by the Soviet Union in acquiring a nuclear arsenal. With a credible nuclear deterrent, the Soviet Union would no longer need to treat "American imperialism" with great caution. The Chinese also placed a very high value on the Soviet treaty commitment to aid in the development of the Chinese nuclear program. At an early point, Mao was dedicated to China's rapid acquisition of nuclear weapons. Then came the second Taiwan Straits crisis of 1958. In the events surrounding this crisis, it became clear that Khrushchev's policies would not be those of confrontation, but of caution. Indeed, in Chinese eyes, the new Soviet leadership seemed less inclined than previously to take the risks of war with the United States. Instead, the Kremlin was opting for a policy of détente.

In vain, the Soviets sought to persuade the Chinese that a conflict over the offshore islands and Taiwan would be unwise. In vain, they sought to convince Peking's leaders that, in the long term, détente could bring major victories to the communist camp, and without the risk of the type of massive destruction that would surely come with nuclear war. Suddenly the Russians lost credibility in Chinese eyes, and with this the principal *raison d'être* of the Sino-Soviet alliance was gone.

The fact that events took a very ugly turn at this point, with the Soviets withdrawing their technicians and taking home their blueprints in 1959, in effect casting the Chinese adrift, unquestionably contributed to the bitterness which was to surface in the years ahead. But the primary cause for the crisis was not Soviet behavior in China. Rather, it was Soviet behavior toward the United States, a behavior which the Chinese leaders felt they had thoroughly tested in 1958. Further demonstrations were to follow, notably the Cuban missile crisis and, to add insult to injury, Soviet attitudes toward the Sino-Indian border clash. In Peking's eyes, the specter of Munich, the stench of appeasement, now hung over the communist camp.

None of the three parties to the Sino-Soviet-American triangle was prepared for the climactic events of 1958-1961. The Chinese were plunged into the most serious domestic crisis they had faced since communist ascension to power. Not only did this period represent a time of serious economic reverses and severe hardships for the Chinese people; it also produced fissures among the political elite that have not yet been closed.

Primary attention had to be focused on domestic problems. Moreover, the dispute with the Soviet Union had not yet become a public affair, and, recognizing the gravity of trends, both sides made various unsuccessful efforts to solve or contain the controversy. In this period, the two primary parties used substitute targets in the open arena—Yugoslavia in the case of China, Albania in the case of the Soviet Union. Partly camouflaged, the public debate was laden with elaborate argument over the true tenets of Marxism-Leninism.

Despite its preoccupation with domestic matters, however, China now sought to create a global foreign policy, one that would concentrate on "the emerging world," but that would not neglect targets of opportunity elsewhere. In this, a dual purpose could be discerned. On the one hand, such a policy represented an effort to build a united front against Soviet "big nation chauvinism," with solicitations to various communist parties and movements, as well as to a wide range of non-communist governments in power. On the other hand, it was also a potential answer to the U.S. policy of seeking Chinese containment through isolation. But if the current trends were to continue, China would clearly have to review periodically its basic policies toward the USSR and the United States to determine whether its own interests were best served by a "plague on both your houses" approach or a new policy of tilting toward the West.

The Soviet Union was also caught unprepared by the extraordinary events of the late 1950s. Khrushchev and his colleagues had not anticipated either the intensity or the rapidity with which Soviet hegemony over the international communist movement would be challenged. Suddenly, the Soviet Union found itself on the defensive within that very political circle which it had considered indisputably its own. Moreover, no effective countermeasures to stem the erosion of its authority could be discovered. The force of nationalism was now overrunning the communist barricades, rendering the old order in this world obsolete.

Moreover, problems implicit in Soviet resources, and in a broader sense in Russian culture, served to accelerate the new trends. The Soviet Union was not equipped to pursue "benevolent internationalism" on a scale that might have mitigated the rising storm. On the contrary, Khrushchev seemed to epitomize that tactless, harsh approach that turned opponents into enemies, and made Soviet diplomacy appear so heavy-handed and foreign to other peoples.

At the same time, however, many factors on the domestic front prompted the Soviet leadership to continue its quest of an alternative to the policies of intensive confrontation with the United States. The new policies were by no means fully sustained or wholly consistent, but they placed the Kremlin in opposition to those elements within the international communist movement which wanted to see the status quo abruptly overturned. A growing involvement in aid to the Vietnamese communists provided partial compensation, but not sufficiently so to assuage Peking, P'yongyang, or a number of other centers.

The escalating Vietnam War had two opposing effects. On the one hand, it temporarily raised the ideological component on all sides and appeared to increase hostility between the United States and the two major communist states. In these senses, it contributed to a continuation of the older patterns of behavior. On the other hand, the Vietnam conflict served to sharply delineate each nation's perceptions of its own fundamental interests and to identify behavior patterns based on these interests in a manner sufficiently clear for all to discern. In the end, the latter developments proved to be more significant than the former.

Contrary to the fears of many Americans, the extensive U.S. involvement in Indochina during the 1960s neither brought the Soviets and Chinese together, nor did it lead to a direct confrontation between the major powers supporting the communist and non-communist causes. Indeed, quite the opposite trends developed. Indochina proved to be another abrasive issue between the USSR and China, with a number of other communist parties implicated. For example, Mao severely alienated the Japanese communist leaders by refusing to agree to any joint action with the Soviets on behalf of Hanoi. The shipment of supplies to the Vietnamese communists proved to be a most complex matter, with Peking insisting that the Soviets could neither accompany such supplies overland across China nor have airfield landing rights. Far from bringing the big communists together, the Vietnam War witnessed a steady escalation in acrimony.

Conflict between the United States and either of the two major communist nations was avoided, but, necessary or not, Washington paid a heavy price for insurance on this score. At an early point in the course of the expanding American involvement, U.S. officials communicated two important themes to Peking: first, the United States had no desire to see the war expanded, and wanted to avoid a conflict with the PRC; second, if the PRC did become heavily involved, in the manner of Korea, there would be no privileged sanctuaries. Since Mao was prepared to launch the Cultural Revolution shortly thereafter, this combined assurance-warning must have had an effect.

Nevertheless, the possibility of full-scale Chinese participation preyed on the minds of U.S. decision-makers and deeply influenced military policies. A land invasion of the Inchon-landing type that broke the back of the

North Korean offensive was ruled out. It was determined, moreover, that the bombing of the North should be incremental and sharply restricted in its initial phases, despite the argument that such a policy would permit communist adjustment. In sum, the perceived threat of China contributed mightily to a military approach that guaranteed a protracted, limited war, raising profound problems for U.S. policy, given the nature of American society.

Nor were the self-imposed U.S. limitations met by strictly limited Chinese commitments. The Chinese avoided a direct confrontation with the United States, to be sure, with the memories of Korea and the possibilities of homeland damage in mind. But in addition to extensive supplies (although Soviet military aid was paramount), some fifty to sixty thousand Chinese were sent to North Vietnam to repair communications and perform other services. Contrary to common belief, moreover, Chinese aid was significantly increased in the final stages of the war.

Both the Soviet Union and the People's Republic of China, however, signaled in various ways that they did not wish the Indochina conflict to interfere with their respective relations with the United States. Possibly this was a policy easier consummated in the context of an American defeat than would have been the case in the event of an American victory, but there is no evidence to suggest that either Moscow or Peking would have been devastated by the prospect of separate communist and non-communist states in Indochina.

The U.S.-Chinese Rapprochement

Signals that a new era was at hand in the complex relations among China, the Soviet Union and the United States came in 1968-1969, and they had little to do with Indochina. The Soviet invasion of Czechoslovakia and Brezhnev's edict that no nation was free to leave socialism were coupled with a major rise in the decibel level of the polemics between Moscow and Peking, and, more seriously, by a series of border clashes, with the Ussuri River incident representing a climax. Responsibility for that incident remains unclear, but there can be little doubt that the events of this period were sufficiently threatened from Peking's perspective to warrant dramatic new approaches. It should be remembered that as a result of the Cultural Revolution, Peking found itself in an unprecedented degree of isolation. Chinese foreign policy in the 1967-1968 period had even alienated most of China's friends, causing some to ask, "Has the PRC gone mad?" Thus, Peking was in no position to negotiate from strength, not to mention the possibility of having to fight.

It should not be assumed that the foreign policy of the PRC was a product of unanimity among China's ruling elite. On the contrary, there is considerable evidence that foreign policy, while a less potent issue than domestic concerns, had evoked considerable controversy in the 1950s. Some within the PRC policy-making cycle (presumably elements from both the technocratic and military groups) felt that the conflict with the Soviet Union was being carried too far, causing China to pay a prohibitive price in both security and developmental terms. Similarly, in the 1960s, there were differing evaluations of the threat from the United States, or, conversely, of the possible benefits of a limited rapprochement.

One could assert, therefore, that by the end of the 1960s, three general positions existed in China regarding the all-important question of relations with the superpowers: a "pro-Soviet" remnant, an emerging "pro-American" contingent, and a "plague on both your houses" group. To pose the issue in this form and to use this terminology, however, is to risk serious distortion. Few if any Chinese leaders of recent times can be considered either "pro-Soviet" or "pro-American." A resurgent nationalism combined with an historic xenophobia made all Chinese "pro-China." Earlier ties with the Russians, to be sure, may have inclined some individuals toward the Soviet Union, but the charges against Mao's opponents to the effect that they were lackeys of Moscow and traitors were either exaggerated or false in the overwhelming number of cases. Far less likely was any genuine "pro-Americanism" among the top communist elite.

The opening to the United States which took concrete form in the early 1970s was not the product of either ideological or political convergence. On China's part at least, it was a cool and deliberate decision based upon an assessment of national interests. If the Soviet threat were to be countered and China were to break out of its isolation, Peking needed U.S. help, or, at a minimum, American acquiescence. Only in this manner could it enter the United Nations and its auxiliary bodies. Only thus could it hope for rapid normalization of relations with Japan and certain other American allies. And only then could China's international visibility—together with its access to economic and military aid—improve. In addition to strengthening its position vis-à-vis the Soviet Union, such developments would also provide ascendancy over Taiwan.

From the American standpoint, the advantages were less tangible. It was hoped, to be sure, that a China connection could help in bringing the United States "peace with honor" in Indochina. That hope was scarcely realized. A more general consideration, however, did materialize, namely, the ability of Washington to achieve a centrist position in the all-important triangle. It could communicate with both Moscow and Peking at a time when communications between the latter two were minimal and hostile. The strategic and political advantages of such a position would be difficult to overestimate.

The dramatic aura surrounding the first Kissinger and Nixon visits to Peking and the Shanghai Communiqué of August 1972 resulted in a flood of romanticism pouring forth from the American scene. Admiration for Chi-

230

nese culture intermingled with endless eulogies to Mao, Chou and the new order. As in the early days of the Soviet Union, a number of American pilgrims came back from China asserting that they had seen the future and it worked. Close-up negotiations brought a few policy-makers nearer to reality and produced divisions in U.S. official circles. Hence, it was necessary to leave some issues, notably Taiwan, in an ambiguous status. Peking accepted this despite its earlier assertions that any concessions on this issue would be intolerable. Now, however, the Soviet threat was a far more urgent concern.

Recent Soviet Policy Toward China

The USSR could only observe these developments with a resigned, if grim, countenance. Peking's tilt toward Washington had been anticipated in Moscow, but not with relish. From the Soviet perspective, as long as Mao lived and dominated PRC politics, no improvement in Sino-Soviet relations could be expected. The Chinese approach to the border issues was indicative of Peking's toughness. The Soviet threat that, in the event of war, it would not shrink from using nuclear weapons may have brought the Chinese to the bargaining table. Once there, however, they demanded that the Soviets first acknowledge the illegal seizure of vast tracts of territory in Czarist times; then, with China magnanimously forgiving the new Tsars for these old transgressions, serious negotiations relating to current disputes could get under way. Since it was not likely that any Soviet government would make such admissions, the initiative presumably lay with Peking in determining when it wanted to remove or modify this condition, enabling the settlement of the dispute over relatively minor tracts of land.

As was indicated earlier, however, the boundary issue is a symbol, not the cause, of the Sino-Soviet split. Indeed, reflecting the intensely hostile confrontation of two neighbors and posing as it does the most immediate security issues, it represents the culmination rather than the beginnings of the dispute, and brings it to the brink of open conflict.

Yet conflict of a major type has not come, despite the predictions of some observers. Probably there were a few Soviet advocates of a preemptive strike against China's embryonic nuclear installations, just as such advocates had existed in the West in the first stages of Soviet nuclear development. From a Soviet standpoint, however, consider the risks of war against its possible gains. If the strike were to be a surgical one, with no follow-up operations, the damage could ultimately be repaired. In the meantime the USSR would have to face a China unified in its seething rage against Soviet actions. Occupy China? Or expect to find in the context of war a new and acceptable Wang Ching-wei? Given both the experiences of the Japanese and the subsequent evolution of China, such a path seems most unpromising. Set up "independent" buffer states in areas like Manchuria or

Sinkiang? Once again, the commitment would have to be to long-term hostilities, and at a point when Russia's first concerns are still with Europe.

Thus, Soviet policy toward China to date has involved a more logical, if less than fully successful, course. On the one hand, in its global propaganda, including that directed against China, the Soviets initially sought to focus the attack upon Mao himself, seeking to separate Mao from the "legitimate" Chinese revolution. On the other hand, a containment policy akin to the earlier U.S. program was pursued: alliances were forged, a complex struggle was waged both within the international communist movement and in third world circles, and a military presence was maintained or increased. Since in considerable measure these remain the China policies of the Soviet Union at present, they warrant further consideration.

Until now, Soviet leaders have been greatly disappointed by trends in post-Maoist China. Their prognosis of internal developments in China, incidentally, was not too wide of the mark. Analyzing Mao as increasingly paranoiac (was Stalin the model?), many Soviet specialists predicted that he would lend his support to his wife, Chiang Ching, and her Shanghai associates. Thus, in the final, climactic period, the left would move into the ascendancy. While this would carry over into the immediate post-Mao era, the left would ultimately be toppled by the moderates, and with China returned to the control of "true Marxist-Leninists," the prospects for improvement in Sino-Soviet relations would become much brighter. The quasi-official Soviet position was that no one anticipated a return of the conditions of 1950, but that it should be possible to establish the type of relations that currently exist between the Soviet Union and Yugoslavia.

Thus, a conspicuous effort was made immediately after Mao's death to initiate a new atmosphere. Condolences were proffered, anti-Chinese propaganda was halted, and other signals were given, including the expressed desire to resume border negotiations. One seemingly discordant and mysterious note was sounded in the form of an article by the well-known Soviet journalist, Victor Louis, suggesting that the Chinese had only a brief time in which to respond to Soviet overtures, or other policies would prevail. In any case, all Soviet efforts, as we shall soon note, met with a sharply negative response from Peking.

Meanwhile, a containment policy continues to be enforced on the international front. In the north, the Soviet Union makes it emphatically clear that it intends to develop Central Asia and Siberia both economically and strategically. Its relations with (and control over) Outer Mongolia remain all-pervasive. On the Korean and Japanese fronts, however, the present situation is far from optimal from a Soviet viewpoint.

Moscow, P'yongyang and Tokyo

North Korean-Soviet relations have ranged from cool to hostile for many years, with ideology, policies and personalities all in some degree of conflict. Until recently at least, Kim Il-song has consciously tilted toward Peking, partly because of his strong dislike of post-Stalin Soviet policies and his personal experiences with the Russians as head of one of their client states. Yet dependence on Soviet production, both in the military and economic realms, has not been completely removed. In recent times, moreover, a crisis in the North Korean economy, combined with the political and economic uncertainties surrounding China have caused P'yongyang to revise some of its attitudes and policies.

Thus, in January 1977, the North Korean Premier, Pak Song-chol, traveled to Moscow to discuss economic and technical relations with Kosygin and others, thereby making a trip which Kim Il-song had conspicuously not undertaken in 1975 in the course of his visits to the PRC, Rumania, Bulgaria, Albania and Algeria. While Pak obtained public expressions of full Soviet support for North Korean efforts toward the peaceful reunification of Korea and the removal of all foreign (American) troops from South Korea, a note of reserve in the various reports and speeches connected with the Pak visit suggests that various issues have not been resolved. Nor is it clear that the North Koreans have now obtained the type of economic assistance currently needed, reference being made only to a few specific projects, most of them already underway. In truth, the Soviets neither like nor trust Kim Il-song, and they have been resentful over the relatively close P'yongyang-Peking ties of recent years. Necessity is the progenitor of change in foreign relations as in other matters, but it will take far more than one North Korean mission to Moscow to establish mutual trust or cordiality on this front.

Soviet relations with Japan have also been troubled and uneven in recent times. Actually, Soviet policies toward Japan since World War II have been difficult to understand in terms of the USSR's own interests. Generally speaking, those policies have contained an unremitting harshness. The Soviet violation of their non-aggression pact with Japan at the close of the war naturally rankled many Japanese, but more important were policies toward Japanese prisoners of war, the tough stance on reparations, and a judgment that Japan's status should be that of a weak, dependent nation. Nor have recent policies been less stringent. A refusal to consider return of the four northern islands to Japan, increased military activities, including overflights, in the area, continuous problems over fishing rights, and the dispute over the anti-hegemony clause in the Sino-Japanese treaty have combined to keep relations difficult. Japanese public opinion polls reflect this fact, all of them indicating a strong distaste for the Soviet Union.

At one point, it seemed both logical and likely that the Soviet desire to develop Siberia rapidly, together with the considerable capacity of Japan to provide assistance in this task, augured well for a new Soviet-Japanese relationship based upon mutual economic interests. This prospect certainly cannot be ruled out for the future, but up to date, only a few Siberian ventures of this nature have been consummated, none of them of the magnitude earlier envisaged. Both economic and strategic considerations have inter-fered. From a Japanese viewpoint, many of the Siberian projects have not yet been made economically attractive. Beyond that, Japan has wanted the insurance of U.S. participation, given the delicate strategic questions re-volving around such programs as expanding Siberian communications and harbor facilities.

Before considering Japanese options in the international arena, it is appropriate to note here that since the Sino-Soviet split, Japan, like a num-ber of other countries, has generally seen its interests best served by seek-ing a position of rough equidistance between the two major communist states, careful not to become too greatly identified with either, and in some degree seeking to play one side off against the other. In theory, it is difficult to take exception to such a policy. In practice, it has been exceedingly diffi-cult to achieve and maintain. The Japanese government has found itself con-fronted by diverse internal as well as external pressures to pursue specific policies, including pressures from Peking and Moscow. Thus, the Japa-nese position has frequently been most uncomfortable, with acceptable compromises not readily available and both external powers playing upon internal Japanese politics, the Chinese usually with greater effect.

The Soviet Union and Southeast Asia

On balance, the Soviet position in northeast Asia is thus a mixed one. Is the picture in southeast Asia significantly different? In this region, the most substantial Soviet connection is that with Vietnam and, by extension, with Laos—a connection forged in war, continued in the "reconstruction" era, and carrying implicit Chinese containment overtones. It is currently off-set by the ties Peking has established with the new Cambodian government. Thus, historic rivalries in the area are currently matched by the differing commitments of the two big communist states.

Yet the situation is inherently unstable. Soviet-Vietnamese ties are those of mutual convenience, not of close affinity. While such ties can sur-vive for a considerable period under certain circumstances, the record for Soviet alliances with states not in a close geographical relationship to the USSR is inauspicious. Moreover, this particular tie will be subject to heavy Chinese pressure. During the Vietnam War, the Chinese went to consider-able pains to demonstrate to Hanoi that the Soviet Union was a distant power whereas Chinese power was close at hand. If Peking becomes suffi-ciently exercised and finds the times propitious, that lesson can and will be repeated.

Over a period of time, it is Sino-Vietnamese relations that are likely to be most significant to this region, as we shall later indicate. Meanwhile, the precarious nature of relations among the Indochina states and the even more troublesome character of internal and external relations throughout southeast Asia suggest that this region is due for periodic crises, with supranational relations of all types susceptible to rapid, unexpected changes. In the global sense, for the Soviet Union, southeast Asia is a region of secondary importance compared to a number of other areas. While the support rendered Vietnam and Laos has both ideological-political and strategic significance at present, it is doubtful whether the Soviets are prepared to pay a heavy price to make their primary stand there.

Moscow has viewed south Asia as considerably more important in broad strategic terms and as an instrument of containment against China. Recent trends in India, therefore, must be regarded by the Soviets as alarming. The Soviet-Indian alliance, so instrumental in influencing Indian domestic and foreign policies earlier, now appears threatened. The chief momentum for change has come from internal Indian conditions, but New Delhi's grievances against Moscow and its desire to achieve a somewhat more independent stance in the international arena have been manifest for some time. Now, with Congress-Communist (CPI) relations at a low ebb and with economic policies being revised in a direction not likely to please the Soviets, the prevailing tides are running against Moscow.

There is no evidence at present that Soviet-Indian relations will erupt in the type of bitterness and recrimination that characterized Moscow's break with Peking and later with Cairo. Moreover, Indian dependence upon the Soviet Union remains substantial, particularly in view of its present relations with China and the United States. While these latter relations may and probably will undergo changes, it is by no means clear that the changes will provide an adequate substitute for the old Soviet ties. But once again the fragility of all alliances in this era has been signaled, along with the vulnerability of Soviet policies in Asia.

In sum, Soviet efforts to contain China in Asia hinge today primarily upon Soviet military power. Moscow is getting scant support from Asian allies, and, indeed, the Soviet political-economic position throughout east and south Asia is probably weaker at present than it has been at any time since World War II. This extends to Soviet influence over the communist parties of the region. With the exception of the Communist Party of India and the Mongolian People's Revolutionary Party, these parties either hew to the Chinese line or take an independent stance. Nor have the attempts to interest Asian governments in an Asian collective security arrangement borne fruit. This scheme, deliberately kept vague but modeled after the European concept that received its major hearing at Helsinki, has not struck a responsive chord in Asia. Generally, it is seen as part of the strategy to contain China, with participants required to align themselves against Peking.

Peking and the Three-Part World

Given these various Soviet setbacks, one is tempted to advance the thesis that the augmentation of Soviet military power in Asia is in part an attempt to compensate for serious weaknesses on the political and economic fronts. Is the position of the People's Republic of China stronger at this point? The answer is probably in the negative, although the mix of factors differs. Today, China's international standing and capacities are both affected adversely by the successive political crises that have marked its recent history. These crises have also taken a stern economic cost, at least in the short run, as Chinese authorities themselves admit. The military, moreover, are deeply involved in the domestic political scene, with much of their commitments and energies directed inward. Thus, China's capacity to project its military power externally at present is strictly limited, even should it wish to do so.

Yet the combined defensive-offensive strategy which motivated the Sino-Soviet alliance initially is still conceptually valid for Peking. Once again, the PRC leans to one side, but at this point that side is, first, the third world, and second—when the matter involves Soviet-American issues—the United States. Utilizing the tactics they employed after the Seventh Comintern Congress and the onset of the anti-Japanese war, the Chinese leaders seek to build a united front against the primary opponent, the Soviet Union. As they once aligned themselves with the Kuomintang, so they are now prepared to align themselves with the United States, representative of the big bourgeoisie. Similarly, the national bourgeoisie, now symbolized by Western Europe and Japan, are important, particularly since an appeal can be made to their nationalist sentiments cutting against the United States as well as the USSR when that seems desirable. Finally, there is the global peasantry and proletariat, represented by the third world. Here are the true masses, awaiting the guidance and leadership of a vanguard force.

Via this tactic, it is possible to take the political offensive even while hewing to great caution on the military front. Underlying the tactic is the concept of a world divided into three parts: the superpowers, the second intermediate zone, and the third world. Toward each of these sectors, Chinese foreign policy has firm guiding principles, although it cannot avoid substantial elements of ambiguity and contradiction in actual practice.

The approach to the superpowers combines sharp attacks directed against both parties, with a clear differentiation made between the two targets to the benefit of the United States. When the audience is the third world, the key themes are that imperialism (the United States) and social-imperialism (the USSR) continue to engage in aggression, plunder and exploitation everywhere, and, in their contention for global hegemony, pose the chief threat to the peace and security of all nations. Indeed, according to Peking, World War III is inevitable, and will come in the form of a conflict between the United States and the Soviet Union, with its main theater in Europe.

The distinctions made between the two superpowers are most sharply delineated when the reference point is to the West or Japan. Peking is openly supportive of the NATO alliance, including the American commitment, although it warns the West Europeans that they must strengthen their own unity and defense structure, since they may not be able to count on the

United States. It is equally clear that China now views the American-Japanese mutual security treaty as temporarily desirable, and it no longer worries about a militarist Japan. Indeed, it is helping to cultivate a new Japanese nationalism with the intent of seeing this directed against the Soviet Union.

Naturally, there are contradictions in these policies. On the one hand, the United States along with the Soviet Union is berated for global imperialism and aggression; yet, on the other hand, since China is pursuing a foreign policy based fundamentally upon balance of power principles, it requires the United States to play the countervailing role to that of the USSR on the global scene, particularly in those areas beyond the strategic-political reach of China. Its open support for the American advocates of more extensive defense preparations and the critics of détente stems from this need. It applies to Asia as well as Europe, although one should be clear about its limitations: Peking does not want the United States *everywhere* in Asia. Despite some American wishful thinking, there is no reason to doubt PRC spokesmen when they assert that all U.S. forces should be removed from South Korea, and obviously they do not want such forces in Taiwan. Their views with respect to continental southeast Asia are murky, although they clearly do not object to the general presence of the U.S. Seventh Fleet in east Asia at this point, nor to base agreements with the Philippines. And in every instance the Chinese warning to third world leaders is the same, namely: "While ousting the wolf through the front gate, beware of the tiger slipping in the back door."

Since a socialist camp no longer exists—its erstwhile leader having deserted to the "fascist" cause—China now proclaims its primary allegiance to and affiliation with the third world. Naturally, it prefers to treat this world as an undifferentiated whole, refusing to become involved in certain instances when the controversy is within this arena. On a range of North-South issues, such as the "new economic order" and on white-related colonialism and racism, however, the Chinese position is a clear and vocal one.

Yet in this policy realm, also, contradictions abound. Even when political rhetoric within China was at its most radical point, Chinese leaders were not inhibited from playing host to some of the most conservative figures of the non-communist world and speaking to them of common interests. Moreover, in the areas peripheral to it, particularly in southeast Asia, China, despite its claim of being a poor, developing, non-hegemonic state, is regarded as a major—sometimes threatening—power.

The key factor in China's Asian policies is, of course, Japan. It would be difficult to find two more dissimilar societies today than China and Japan. Will this situation result in cooperation, competition or some combination of both? To date, a combination of sorts has prevailed. To the extent that China has turned outward economically in recent years, Japan has served as the chief source of goods and technology. From both an economic and a political standpoint, moreover, Japan may be the most logical long-term external source of support for the Chinese industrial-agricultural revolution. As has been indicated, Peking has gradually ceased its earlier attacks on Japanese militarism and other once popular issues directed against the conservatives, encouraging Japan instead to develop its various weapons against Soviet encroachment. From such a trend had come the thought that a Sino-Japanese-American united front against the USSR could easily be consummated.

At the same time, the Chinese have taken risks in advancing statements and positions that can be—and on occasion have been—interpreted as interference in internal Japanese affairs. Indeed, Peking has not hesitated to manupulate Japanese organizations and individuals extensively to its own ends, thereby producing or widening various fissures in that nation. There are other factors that promote competition or conflict. To the extent that Asia moves into the Chinese orbit or even achieves an independent communist status, Japanese opportunities for investment, plant relocation and resource acquisition will be restricted, whatever the trade prospects. Even here, communist propensities for autarchy raise questions. A China growing in economic and military power, moreover, would almost certainly advance some conflicting claims in Asia affecting Japanese interests; the Senkaku Island issue is but one obvious example. If Chinese control were to reach new areas such as Taiwan, strategic and economic jurisdiction in the western Pacific would be profoundly affected. It is not surprising, therefore, that the Japanese government is apprehensive about American policies toward both Korea and Taiwan.

In sum, Chinese advantages in Asia relate to geographic position and cultural ties. In these terms, China is a part of Asia in a manner which the Soviet and Americans can never hope to duplicate. But there is another side to that coin. A great many Asians will always regard the Chinese with suspicion and fear, as small nations frequently regard powerful neighbors. The current weaknesses of China serve as a check on those sentiments, but even now they are not absent.

In the broader reaches of the third world, China is in no position to influence outcomes in any decisive manner, either economically or militarily. China today is a regional power, not a global power—much in the manner of the Soviet Union immediately after World War II. As such, it can take advantage of the unpopular actions of, or the disappointments engendered by, the superpowers, but every actor on the political stage knows the practical limitations that accompany Chinese rhetoric.

When the essential elements in Chinese foreign policy have been analyzed, however, the key to the future lies in the American variable. Peking sees the United States as a declining power, the Soviet Union as a rising power. Hence, its exhortations directed westward are once again filled with references to Munich and warnings against appeasement, as was the case vis-à-vis Moscow after 1958. The credibility of the United States is as much in doubt in Peking as in Taipei—or Seoul, Jakarta and Tokyo. And if the United States were to prove to be increasingly impotent and non-credible, the very foundations of China's balance of power policies would be challenged, prompting the same basic reconsiderations as occurred when Peking decided that the Soviets were non-credible.

The Changing U.S. Variable

Thus it is logical to turn directly to the United States. The defeat in Indochina startled even the staunchest opponents of the United States and made American credibility a burning issue in a number of capitals. Military withdrawal from Thailand completed the American disengagement from continental southeast Asia, with the Thai and others trying to readjust their foreign policies to fit the new era.

New uncertainties mark the U.S. position. Its military presence in Asia has been reduced, and further reductions are in store in Korea, with the possibility of parallel actions in Europe at a later time. Yet the United States continues to insist that it will maintain its Asian treaty commitments under the terms of the Guam Doctrine and supports a strengthening of NATO. Moreover, U.S. economic involvement in both regions continues to grow, particularly in east Asia. Given the general projections concerning resources, the Pacific-Asian region actually is likely to be far more important to the United States in the future than has been the case in the past. Meanwhile, military bases are being retained in Korea, Japan and the Philippines, with a strategic fallback area now available on a long-term basis in the Mariana-Marshall complex.

American relations with the Soviet Union are clearly the most important adversary relations in the world today. On them hinge chances for nuclear weapons control and disarmament and a host of other issues that could determine the economic and political health of the world, possibly the question of peace or war. At the moment, these relations are in a fluid, somewhat troubled, state. At the same time, U.S. relations with China have been in a holding pattern, with some elements of coolness detectable. Peking's disappointment at the slow progress toward "normalization" is one factor, but uncertainty regarding American-Soviet relations, and the general capability of the United States to play the role designed for it by Peking, is at least equally important. As noted earlier, the pressures within the United States have mounted for a sustained tilt toward Peking, but as yet, U.S. policy remains that of maintaining flexibility, treating relations with the Soviet Union and China on an issue-by-issue basis, and eschewing alignment.

Meanwhile, a new emphasis in official American quarters is being placed on trilateralism—in Chinese terminology, an effort to draw closer to the second intermediate zone. Positive approaches to the problems of the advanced industrial world are regarded by Washington as being equally crucial to, and possibly a necessary pre-condition for, meaningful approaches to North-South issues. Progress on this front, however, has been slow, with evidence of a rising economic nationalism and the possibility of increased competition in the period ahead. This same uncertainty beclouds American-Japanese relations. Here, institutional mechanisms for consultation have steadily improved, but stubborn economic problems such as a massive Japanese trade surplus and sea resource issues remain. In addition, certain broader questions relating to Japanese security arise in conjunction with U.S. policies toward Korea and Taiwan. To adopt an enclave policy toward Japan, treating it as the sole security commitment in Asia, clearly will not suffice.

Thus, the United States continues to assert that, despite a phased withdrawal of ground troops, the commitments to South Korea stand, and President Carter has also pledged that, in the negotiations on normalization of relations with the PRC, "the independence and freedom" of Taiwan will be preserved. In the aftermath of Vietnam, however, and in the face of various domestic pressures for withdrawal, doubts persist concerning both American intentions and capacities.

In southeast Asia, American commitments currently center upon the offshore regions, notably the Philippines and Indonesia—with no formal security commitments to the latter nation. At this point, it seems highly unlikely that U.S. military forces will return to continental southeast Asia, but U.S. naval and air power remain in the vicinity. And a scenario for establishing diplomatic relations with Vietnam is now being prepared. Thus, various types of American presence in the region are guaranteed.

When the contemporary scene is surveyed, several facts of signal importance to Sino-Soviet-American relations can be discerned. First, almost all alliances today, including those to which these three nations are a party, are more porous, less exclusive, and thus less clearly an additive in the security realm, either for the major state or for the international system.

Second, bilateral relations within the Sino-Soviet-American triangle are currently either unstable or hostile, an unfavorable sign for effective problem-solving or a secure international order.

Third, both the scope and the implications of each set of bilateral relations differ markedly. American-Soviet relations pertain to global issues, with far-reaching and near-universal impact. Soviet-Chinese relations have a direct bearing upon the international capacities of the two states, and, in a broader sense, upon the Eurasian continent and the global revolutionary movement. American-Chinese relations must be complementary in some degree to Sino-Soviet relations at this point, affecting both Soviet and American capacities and the general order in the Pacific-Asian region. It must be emphasized, however, that China today is at most a regional, not a global, power.

Fourth, a paradox surrounds these and all other relations among states at present, namely, the simultaneous rise or revitalization of nation-

240

alism and the growing fact of interdependence. Contrary to conventional wisdom, nationalism is not the hallmark of the developing state alone. It is currently mounting in a variety of ways in the "advanced" societies as well. There are also indications that ideology, far from coming to an end, is being sustained or rehabilitated, partly out of the need for values, partly as an instrument of national interest. Thus, all efforts to reach international accord or build an international order must reckon with the forces of nationalism and ideology—factors that also lie close to the heart of Sino-Soviet-American relations.

Finally, while the traditional balance of power concept is the central operative principle in relations among the major states today, in reality we must contend with a balance of weakness. Each of these states has signal weaknesses in projecting its influence or power abroad, weaknesses deriving from a combination of internal and external conditions. This is the ultimate paradox—that in an era when material wealth and military power are advancing to new heights, the capacities of individual states or coalitions to engage in regional or global management are, with a few exceptions, declining.

Future Triangular Relations: The Soviet Perspective

Given the fluid state of current Sino-Soviet-American relations, and the extraordinary number of variables with which one must deal, it would be foolish to attempt an unqualified, single prediction as to the course of these relations over the next ten to twenty years. Here, we shall make an effort only slightly less hazardous, namely, to construct a series of graded probabilities and improbabilities, using these to explore various possible outcomes in the triangular relations.

If we commence with those developments most probable in the course of the next two decades, certain factors with respect to the Soviet Union head the list. We assume a sufficient degree of stability within the USSR to enable the present system—with evolutionary modifications soon to be noted—to continue. In this context, the Soviet Union will almost certainly be a much more formidable power in Asia two decades hence, both economically and militarily. The gap between the USSR and China in these respects will grow rather than decline, even if one grants a successful Chinese developmental program.

Two internal factors, however, will serve to modify this power insofar as its possible application in Asia is concerned. First, Soviet minority problems will not be solved and probably will not show any significant improvements during this period. Thus, despite Russification efforts, the central Asian portions of the Soviet empire will be politically vulnerable. More importantly, the factors most recently present in the Soviet Union, namely, public unhappiness over bureaucratic bungling, economic failures, and alternating liberalization and regressive policies, will combine with the rising consumer pressures that emanate from improving living standards and the uncertainties among a fourth and fifth generation of technocratic managers as to the handling of such problems to produce an increasingly pluralistic society—Soviet-style. Under these conditions, Soviet leadership must weigh carefully the costs and risks of adventurous foreign policies.

Under these conditions, also, the advantages—indeed, the urgent necessity—of foreign technology become apparent. This, together with the desire to keep military expenditures under some degree of control, constitutes the chief *raison d'être* for the Soviet interest in détente today, and it is difficult to see how they could diminish as desiderata in the years immediately ahead. On the contrary, upon their realization hinges the questions of whether the USSR is to become a modern society or continue to wallow in quasi-backwardness, with increasing costs to be paid at home and abroad.

It is at this point, however, that the countervailing factors must be assessed. Will the Soviet Union be satisfied with military parity with the United States, or will the course of events, including the difficulty of defining parity, the natural momentum of the race, and the influence of pressure groups within the USSR, lead to a quest for military superiority? A prediction on this score is made all the more difficult because of the signs that the Soviet Union intends to be a truly global power, considering this to be a part of parity after having occupied a positon inferior to that of the United States for so many years.

The judgment here is that the odds slightly favor the primacy of the first set of factors and, consequently, that the probability of agreements between the United States and the Soviet Union in the field of weapons control as well as in the economic and cultural realms is better than fifty-fifty. It should be noted that the very scope of their power and the diversity of their commitments provides a basis for some common interests between the United States and the USSR. Thus, juxtaposed against the temptation to take advantage of a situation to augment one's own power or prestige is the desire not to be used in the game of playing off one superpower against another, or being pressured into strongly disadvantageous new economic rules at the international level.

Having made this evaluation, however, we would quickly add that the second set of factors is sufficiently potent to induce periods of heightened tension in United States-USSR relations as well as times of stalemate in the course of the decades ahead. At best, it will be a combined cooperative-adversary relationship.

Several further projections pertaining to Soviet foreign policy are critical. Naturally, the USSR has been deeply concerned about a two-front threat since the advent of the Sino-Soviet dispute. At this point, however, the threat from Western Europe has been largely neutralized, at least in military terms. The post-war boundaries of Europe have now been officially accepted by all parties—at least on a *de facto* basis—and only an internal upheaval of major proportions in some nation would be likely to alter these.

242

The Soviet Union has, and will continue to have, a strong superiority in the conventional military arena. NATO is a dubious force, even in defensive terms, except for the American nuclear deterrent. In addition, significant parts of Western Europe betray a grave political instability. Indeed, it is probable that within the next two decades some of these societies will acquire left-coalition or communist-controlled governments.

Whatever the proclivities of such West European governments for independence from the Soviet Union and for finding their own road to socialism, such a development would be of benefit to Moscow since it would cast further doubt upon NATO and current defense plans. At the same time, however, it is equally probable that in the decades ahead the Soviet Union will have more rather than less trouble with Eastern Europe. As this region develops, parts of it at a more rapid rate than the Soviet Union, the inequities of the present economic and political order will rankle even more. Thus, the limits of permissible independence will be repeatedly tested, and in ways making direct Soviet intervention very difficult. While the odds are against the type of war in Europe that Peking envisages, trends do indicate a murky situation of clear advantage to neither the United States nor the Soviet Union, and over which their influence can be extensive, but not necessarily decisive.

Observations concerning Eastern Europe suggest that while we are approaching the end of that process of decolonization stemming from seventeenth- to nineteenth-century Western expansion, the next twenty years will witness a rising reaction to the types of colonialism spawned by World War II and to repressive minority policies within a number of societies. The latter problem may be contained in situations where authoritarian controls remain strong and where the minorities involved are numerically small (in these respects the People's Republic of China has significant advantages), but elsewhere it will constitute one of the chief sources of political instability. Thus, much of Africa—and not just the white enclaves—will be subject to periodic upheaval. The problem will also be acute in southeast Asia, and it will not be absent from Latin America. To distract attention from this problem, and from numerous other socio-economic difficulties, many of the governments of these states will pursue a militantly nationalist policy at the international level while they pursue idiosyncratic, highly authoritarian policies at home.

It remains to look at the Sino-Soviet relationship from a Soviet perspective in the period ahead. This is the other front. Here, the Soviets approach the problem with strong emotional feelings. Whatever the opinions of the elites, there can be no doubt that deeply buried in the psyche of the average Russian citizen is a combined contempt-fear of the masses of yellow peoples to the east. These feelings are exacerbated by the knowledge that within their own society the Russians are being outbred, with large-scale assimilation thus far a failure. Without an apprecation of this factor and the impossibility of its disappearance in the near future, one cannot encompass the full dimensions of the Sino-Soviet problem. Clearly, this factor did not preclude an official alliance in the past, and it would not prevent some form of détente in the future, but it will always color the relations of the ethnically dominant portions of these two societies.

Earlier we outlined the reasons why an act of overt war initiated by the Soviet Union against China would probably be considered only under conditions of extreme desperation. There is no need to repeat those reasons here, except to note that the passage of time will be more likely to lengthen rather than shorten the odds against success in any such venture, despite the disproportionate growth of Soviet power in sheer military terms. Thus, a full-fledged Soviet-Chinese war must be assigned a low probability. However, there are a few variables that could significantly raise the level of probability: a Chinese military force that was being rapidly modernized with extensive Western/Japanese assistance; increasing Chinese involvement with Asian peoples within Soviet boundaries or in the People's Republic of Mongolia; a position of total intransigence on all outstanding issues and complete hostility of the type manifested now, continued by successive Chinese elites.

Even under these conditions, it seems more likely that the Soviet response, at least initially, would be something less than a full-scale military attack. The most logical intermediate position would be to foment trouble in China's border regions and, if possible, to encourage and support the formation of separatist regimes. Currently, however, the odds against the success of any such venture seem relatively high.

The most logical and probable Soviet approach to China in the period ahead is a continuance—with some variations—of the stick and carrot policy. On the one hand, there is virtually no chance that Soviet military power will be significantly reduced on its eastern front, although tactical, limited border withdrawls can certainly be undertaken. On the contrary, as noted earlier, Soviet power in this region will be steadily increased, even if a limited détente with China were to be achieved. This includes increases in naval power in and around China's sea frontiers.

Is it possible that at some point, in the event of an American abandonment, Taiwan could get a favorable response by turning to the Soviet Union? Such a possibility seems remote, now or in the foreseeable future. Quite apart from whether Taiwan was prepared to undertake a policy that would fly in the face of its heavy economic dependence upon Japan and the United States, the Soviets—except in the event of actual war with the PRC—are much more likely to confine their involvement to the politics of the mainland.

As noted earlier, the Soviet Union has carefully monitored developments within the PRC, and despite the disappointments of the present, it hopes and expects Peking eventually to have a leadership that will be interested in some degree of détente. The Soviets will certainly continue to offer limited inducements for such a policy, including a willingness to compromise on the limited border issues immediately at stake, a staged withdrawal of forces from the border, and, ultimately, economic, cultural and other exchanges. Before estimating the prospects of a limited Sino-Soviet détente of this nature, we must first assess probabilities with respect to the PRC.

Future Triangular Relations: The Chinese Perspective

The probability of periodic political instability in China remains very high. Such instability, a product of the events of the past ten years, the multi-tiered generational divisions that now exist, and the potential for continuing differences over socio-economic, political and military policies, can find expression both at the center and within military regions and provinces. Under certain circumstances, as we have seen, political crises—particularly when they are closely spaced together—can adversely affect economic development. Apart from this, China's economic growth from this point forward becomes a highly complex matter, with decisions relating to internal priorities and external assistance of critical importance.

When the various factors are weighed, the odds would seem to favor a containable level of instability, with high military involvement in Chinese politics and an increasing control over social and economic policies by technicians—individuals pragmatically oriented, but prepared to make extensive use of ideology as a shield. Such a scenario does not preclude a considerable degree of disputation, and even violence at points. Nor does it mean that a high level of centralization—probably the ultimate goal of Peking's technicians—will be quickly or easily reached. Many of China's nuclear units—its villages and hamlets—will still have only the vaguest appreciation of Peking's politics in the decades immediately ahead.

What are the consequences of such developments, if we have correctly assessed them? First, instability will not lead to the collapse or fragmentation of the People's Republic of China. Second, economic development will take place at a satisfactory but not spectacular level, and PRC leaders will step up the process of turning outward for economic and technical support. They will turn to Japan and various advanced Western countries, moreover, for the same reasons as the Soviet Union. Thus, in economic terms, the PRC and the USSR will not find major grounds for cooperation and interaction. On the contrary, each communist state will develop its own independent and increasingly complex network of economic relations with non-communist societies.

Political conditions, on the other hand, may be conducive to a Soviet-Chinese interaction—but of an unfriendly nature. Despite the persistent Chinese call for the Russian people to rise up and overthrow their fascist government, the opportunities for effective Chinese intervention in Soviet politics would seem exceedingly slim, other than with some of the non-Russians of central Asia. Political conditions in China, however, may prove tempting to the Soviets. They will be alert to any centrifugal tendencies in the

PRC and will keep a close watch on regional leaders, particularly those in border areas. They will also monitor developments in Peking as carefully as possible, hoping for the emergence of individuals with whom they can work.

In the event of a grave crisis such as the Lin Piao incident, or an internal split leading to bloodshed, the opportunity for intervention might be posed. Should some Chinese faction ask for military and political support, under what conditions should it be given, and how far should Moscow be prepared to go? It is this form of Soviet intervention in China that has most deeply concerned Chinese leaders in the past, and correctly so. The potentialities for its occurrence in the future hinge upon internal events in China, but from the Soviet side a willingness to take some risks will surely be present if the odds look reasonably promising. In this respect, Sino-Soviet relations are far more complex, and far more susceptible to psychological-political strains, than Sino-American relations—since the potentialities of American involvement in Chinese politics are scant indeed.

Yet there is another side to this coin, namely the possibility of a limited détente initiated by Peking. From Peking's perspective, what would be the rationale for such a move? Its advocates would advance the following thesis: China's political, economic and geographic circumstances make the continuance of a high level of tension with the USSR both costly and dangerous. Under current circumstances, we must maintain a huge military force on the border, most of it unable to engage in any constructive developmental work. Our military expenditures, however extensive, cannot enable us to close the gap with the Soviets. At present, moreover, we are too dependent upon American foreign policy, particularly its willingness to balance Soviet power. Meanwhile, our own foreign policy is rendered less flexible because of our need to oppose the Soviets on every front. We do not have to love the Soviets, or even trust them. However, reducing the current level of tension by resolving the border issues and ending the polemic campaign will be of benefit to us.

The logic embedded in the argument outlined above seems almost irresistible. One would have to conclude, therefore, that at some point in the future an experiment in limited détente with the Soviet Union will be undertaken by Peking's leaders. In determining the timing and extent of such a move, the Chinese assessment of America's global capacities and role, particularly the U.S. will to counter Soviet activities, will be a crucial factor. As noted earlier, China's balance of power foreign policy is based upon a United States-USSR equilibrium.

Having indicated the probability of an experiment in limited Sino-Soviet détente at some point, however, we should also enter several caveats. Emotions do not always yield to abstract logic, particularly when elements of contempt, prejudice and fear are present. *Logically*—from the standpoint of China's own interests—the dispute should not have been carried to the extremes it reached, a point made by various PRC leaders. There is, of course, a certain advantage in having an external scapegoat at this juncture in the evolution of the PRC, both as an inducement to unity and a cause for sacrifice. The United States can no longer play that role; only the Soviet Union is available, and the inevitable build-up of Soviet power in Asia makes Chinese apprehensions justifiable. Nor can one count on great Soviet diplomatic skill in handling "the China problem," as past relations with the PRC and current relations with Japan so clearly show.

Thus, the odds in favor of limited détente are by no means overwhelming, and at the moment the tides are running in the opposite direction, with the Hua Kuo-feng government carrying on in the tradition of its predecessors. Even if limited détente is undertaken at a future point, moreover, it will not necessarily be deep or permanent. As we noted at the outset, unless these two dynamic and massive neighbors have a clearly perceived external threat to unite them, their relations will be those of rivalry far more than of cooperation.

In this connection, it should be noted that China's goals today are symbolized by Chou En-lai, not Mao Tse-tung. In the great struggle over whether to give priority to "revolution" or "development," Chou made clear his preference for development, urging that China be made a strong and prosperous nation by the end of the twentieth century. Rhetoric in the PRC will be Marx-Lenin-Maoist, but the goals will be those of the Japanese Meiji restoration; and thus China—if at least partly successful—will cast a lengthening shadow over the rest of Asia. This alone will make competition with the Soviet Union short of war difficult to avoid.

These prospects will shape Chinese attitudes and policies toward both the United States and Japan. In its condition, now and for the decades immediately ahead, the PRC cannot afford a pure "plague on both your houses" position toward the superpowers. And even if an experiment with limited Sino-Soviet détente is undertaken at some point, Peking will surely want a relationship with the United States that serves both as insurance against and stimulus to Moscow. Ideally, Peking would like to be in roughly the current position occupied by Washington in the triangle—as would Moscow—but if our projections are correct, neither of the communist states will be able to achieve that centrist stance. If the Soviet Union continues to represent China's foremost enemy, the need for the American connection becomes increasingly urgent. In sum, while both parties benefit from limited détente, the PRC needs the United States more than the United States needs the PRC, and that state of affairs is very likely to continue.

It is difficult, moreover, to see the United States posing the type of threat to the PRC in the decades ahead that would cause a reversal to the pattern of the 1950s. Whatever the disposition of the Taiwan issue, neither Taiwan alone nor Taiwan in conjunction with the Unites States represents a security threat to Peking, now or in the foreseeable future. Indeed, it could be cogently argued that the Taiwan-U.S. combination is less threatening than a

Taiwan with no external restraints. The critical variable is not Taiwan, but Peking's perceptions of the basic foreign policies—and capacities—of the United States.

With respect to Japan, somewhat similar considerations prevail in Peking and are likely to continue. The PRC will remain extremely sensitive to the growth of any meaningful Soviet-Japanese relationship, even in the economic sphere, and it will do whatever possible to prevent this. Détente here, as in the case of Soviet-American relations, is threatening. As suggested earlier, in this instance the Soviets have the initiatives, and should they be prepared to take a more magnanimous course in their policies toward Japan, the Chinese might have cause for concern. Siberia remains an attractive economic locus for Japanese energies—at least potentially. While there is nothing in the recent history of Russo-Japanese relations to suggest this turn of events, some increases in Japanese-Soviet economic interactions are inevitable. Only the scope is in question. Meanwhile, there is little doubt that the PRC will also utilize Japan for developmental purposes on an expanding scale, hoping at the same time that this will serve to shape Tokyo's policies.

Yet it must be emphasized that PRC relations with both the United States and Japan will fall far short of alliance. Themes like "self-reliance" will remain in vogue, even as there is some movement away from them in practice. Relations with capitalist states will be of a mixed cooperative-adversary type, similar to those characterizing Soviet-American relations. Moreover, in the long term, the potential for controversy between Peking and Tokyo is considerably greater than that between Peking and Washington. Jurisdictional issues, access to markets, and problems over such areas as Korea and Taiwan suggest the wide range of difficulties that could, and in some instances probably will, emerge.

Even if relations between Washington and Peking are "normalized" in the period ahead, they will not be entirely smooth. China, as we have noted, will continue to exhibit a commitment to revolutionary communism in the international arena, and particularly in Asia, taking advantage of such opportunities as may develop. Far more than the Soviet Union, it remains disposed to challenge the status quo in its region. At the same time, China will continue to hold a highly competitive, polemical position generally adverse to that of the United States on North-South issues, pushing the political offensive. Nor is it clear that compensating elements of mutual interest in the economic and security fields will be strong. United States-PRC trade is not likely to represent a major item for either society in the near future. And it is doubtful that the PRC will be prepared to negotiate meaningful agreements on nuclear or conventional weapon controls within the next decade or so. On the other hand, the sense of mutual threat that exists in American-Soviet relations will be much less, and that will provide a more relaxed atmosphere in which to talk and negotiate.

The Broader Context

In conclusion, let us consider a few broader trends that are likely to prevail over the next twenty years, providing a context for the triangular relations with which we have been primarily concerned. The movement toward international diversity and complexity will continue to reduce the capacity of any single state or coalition of states to operate effectively in global terms. Thus, the premium upon priorities will steadily grow.

A certain body of international law will emerge from the continuous flow of conferences and negotiatory sessions, but the most significant developments at the supranational level are likely to be regional in scope. Indeed, we may well witness a rising level of regional as well as national autarchy, although this will be precluded in certain regions because of the specific conditions prevailing.

Global wars or wars between the major states have an excellent chance of being prevented, Peking's prediction notwithstanding, but violence will be an omnipresent factor in the decades ahead, and its management will be high on the agenda of most nations' concerns.

Political instability and a decline in Western-style parliamentary democracy will continue, but relatively few states will make the transition either from non-communist to communist status, or vice versa. Moreover, at some point toward the latter part of the period being projected, the trend away from statism, which has recently manifested itself in parts of the West, may gain momentum, though it will be labeled differently from state to state. Whether such a campaign will succeed in any measure is unclear, given the rising population/resource pressures and similar problems.

Since the decades ahead promise to be a rapidly changing, troubled period, the premium will be on the capacity of elites to reshape policies and institutions to accord with societal requirements, preventing the former from ossifying in old molds no longer applicable or acceptable. With the type of concentration needed for such a task, it is possible that for a great many states, including the major ones, foreign policies will continue to be handled primarily on a crisis basis, despite the certainty that interdependence is going to grow rather than diminish. Thus, the tension between nationalism and internationalism will remain a constant element in the politics of the late twentieth century.

Moscow and Peking: Past, Present and Future of Sino-Soviet Relations*

*Franz Michael***

At the outset I want to stress one factor which nowadays is sometimes neglected: the importance of ideology in world politics, particularly in dealing with the communist world, but by no means the communist world alone.

If we think of the present Sino-Soviet conflict with its ominous overtones of threats of military confrontation that are taken seriously by the United States Department of State, it is useful to remember that this is not a conflict between nation states as conceived by us in the past and still represented today in the pluralist state system of what we like to call the free world, but rather a conflict between two communist powers, both sharing basically the same Marxist-Leninist ideology and the same domestic and international goals. Domestically they claim to work toward the "self-regulating collective," and internationally toward a socialist world order brought about by worldwide revolution. These are still the proclaimed goals both in Moscow and Peking. If they mutually accuse each other today of having become "capitalist roaders," "revisionists" and "social imperialists," or of not ever having fully understood the Marxist-Leninist doctrine because of "peasant mentality" or "petit bourgeois fanaticism," these accusations themselves demonstrate that it is not the goal but the defections from that goal about which each side accuses the other. For both, Marxism-Leninism is the professed framework of all policy. To follow this fraternal fight, let us for a moment go back to the origins of the family relations between the Soviet and Chinese Communists before the conflict started.

We know that the Soviets are the older brother. The Bolshevik revolution in 1917 preceded by four years the founding of the Chinese Communist party in 1921, and the Soviets provided the organization and the strategy for Chinese as well as all other early communism. Under Lenin the USSR was

*This essay was the Andrew W. Mellon lecture given in Pittsburgh, Pennsylvania in November 1978.

**Franz Michael is Emeritus Professor of History and International Affairs at George Washington University.

conceived as a world state. The argument over the name clearly showed this. And the USSR had to expand by concept, but also as a matter of survival. When the hoped-for communist revolution failed in Germany after World War I, Lenin turned east, using the Comintern as the instrument of organizing and directing communist parties. China became the focus of this eastern strategy. In Lenin's alleged words: "The way to Paris leads via Peking."

There are a number of widespread myths connected with the emergence of a communist strategy in China. One is that Lenin and Stalin knew only about urban "proletarian" uprising and that it was Mao Tse-tung in China who understood "agrarian revolution" and the role of the peasant in these pre-industrial societies of what we call today the developing countries and what Peking calls the third world. In fact it was Lenin who had previously used the peasant in the Bolshevik revolution—much to the surprise of some of his colleagues—and it was Lenin and Stalin who directed the Chinese rural-based military strategy. Mao was a practitioner who learned to apply this strategy directed from Moscow—after initial bungling, according to the Chinese comrades, who demoted Mao for "military putschism" instead of peasant organization, in the fiasco of the autumn harvest uprising of 1927.

The second myth, perhaps no longer so widespread, is the exaggeration of the role of these peasants who did in fact not rise to make the revolution. Lenin's communist strategy for the pre-industrial world, regarded as colonial or quasi-colonial, was the use of nationalism in the so-called "national liberation movements." I call it communist strategy barricades and rapid seizure of power in the cities. "National liberation movements" depended on prolonged warfare, "wars of national liberation" which required the organiziation of politically indoctrinated armies as the real force of the revolution. Stalin in a famous quote of 1925 spoke of the "revolutionary army" in China, and indeed in this strategy it was the army itself that became the revolutionary force. We call it a party-army or army-party, a structure very different from the Soviet Union where Trotsky founded the Red Army after the revolution as a tool of the party. In China the line between party and army was indistinct, and almost all the older generation of Chinese Communist leaders, including Mao and Chou, had been army commanders and political commissars as part of their political leadership. It was this situation which Mao characterized in sloganizing Stalin's statement in the famous often quoted saying: "Political power grows out of the barrel of the gun."

All this has to be said to stress the fact that the rural strategy in China's civil war and the role of the military, different from that in the Soviet Union, was not a deviation from Moscow's strategic intent nor an ideological heresy. No conflict can be detected there between Moscow and the Chinese Communists.

Nor was there any real conflict between Mao and Stalin. When Mao was sent by the party in 1927 to his province of Hunan to investigate the revolutionary potential of the peasantry, his Hunan Report, which by the

251

way vastly exaggerated the probabilities of peasant uprising, was very favorably reprinted in Moscow in the communist journal *Imprecor.*

At the outset, Mao did not control the rural strategy in the so-called Kiangsi Soviet, but after the communists were driven out of Kiangsi, Mao used the disappointment of the junior communist commanders to take over the military leadership from Chou En-lai at a conference at Tsunyi in January 1936 at the beginning of what became the Long March. Mao's first act after assuming power was to send a message to Stalin for his approval. During the years to come at Yenan before and during the war, Mao, though sometimes obstreperous, knew well when he had to follow the line laid down by Stalin, and did so. One well-known incident was Chiang Kai-shek's kidnaping in Sian by mutinous troops who had been in contact with the communists. Mao was jubilant about this opportunity to bring this opponent to trial and execution, but under Stalin's orders to spare the only possible leader in a Chinese United Front resistance against Japan and to let him go, Mao fulminated and stamped his foot, but obeyed. It was the suave diplomacy of Chou-En-lai that arranged the almost impossible deal in Sian.

The same attitude of Mao prevailed throughout the war with Japan. Mao dragged his feet on any full military cooperation with the Nationalists against Japan, but obeyed each time when the threatening international situation forced the Soviet Union, fearing a two-front war with Nazi Germany and Japan, to order stronger military and political support for Chiang Kai-shek. At one occasion in November 1938, Mao acclaimed "Generalissimo Chiang Kai-shek" as the "supreme leader" of the national resistance, to whom "unanimous support" was to be given, and he even went so far as to predict that the China of the future would not be communist or socialist but a democracy with universal suffrage and private ownership, and that the cooperation with the Nationalist government would continue after the war. Needless to say this speech is not included in Mao's selected works. On his side Stalin confirmed Mao's leadership of the Chinese Communist Party. Beginning at the end of 1937 Mao received not only this message, but also communications equipment and, less known, Soviet textbooks and articles on Marxism-Leninism. It is on the basis of this material, as has been shown by a Japanese scholar, that Mao wrote his major lectures and essays that, together with later directions, were to make up the so-called Thought of Mao Tse-tung. Even after the Chinese Communist victory, Mao asked for, and was sent, as the first Soviet ambassador a man well versed in Marxist-Leninist doctrine, Ambassador Yudin, to assist Mao in his assertion of doctrinal leadership.

This approval was given by Stalin, as was his way, with some precaution. Stalin's Chinese expert Wang Ming was sent to Moscow, where he had been the Chinese Communist representative at the Comintern, to Yenan, to check on Mao Tse-tung. At the time of heavy Soviet involvement on the European front, Mao succeeded in out-maneuvering Wang Ming who eventually returned to Moscow where he died two years ago.

Fundamentally the relationship between Stalin and Mao remained intact until Stalin's death when Mao wrote a famous eulogy to the glory of the Soviet leader, the "sun" in our hearts, which proved to be of some embarrassment later. Mao's admiration, though, seemed genuine enough, since he had a real appreciation for the man of power whose picture is still shown today in all public offices in China, together with Marx, Engels, and Lenin and the Chinese Chairman Mao and Hua Kuo-feng.

That does not mean that Mao like other communists did not have his difficulties with Stalin after the Communist victory in China. It took eight weeks of a visit in Moscow for Mao to get from Stalin a treaty of friendship and alliance and some not too generous economic support. As Mao stated later, Stalin's suspicion of a possible Chinese Titoism was only allayed when the Chinese saved the North Korean communists from total defeat in the Korean War. Mao was furthermore too much of a megalomaniac not to suffer under the necessary submission to Stalin's will. Psychologically it is quite amusing that in later days Mao complained that in the typical communist idolatry, when Mao was pictured together with Stalin, Mao's figure was always made smaller. That obviously vexed Mao's vanity.

In the final crucial battles of the civil war in Manchuria, it was Soviet help that, much more than Peking is willing to admit today, was decisive in bringing about the communist victory, and the cooperation between Moscow and Peking continued after the establishment of the People's Republic. The general Soviet support in modern education, in economic development and in military modernization during the Korean War led to a flood of Soviet experts, blueprints, industrial plants and equipment that was to transform China into a socialist society with the obvious goal of a power economy based on heavy industry. In the inter-party relations the Chinese received some special recognition within the socialist camp. At the Communist interparty conference leading to the Moscow declaration of 1957 and the Moscow statement of 1960, the People's Republic was listed first after the Soviet Union before the other communist governments and parties charged with a special role in promoting "wars of liberation" in the developing world as a recognition of China's experience and success in applying the communist strategy in this field.

This is not the place and there is not the time to recall in more detail these years of the Soviet connection, but this short reminder seems important in order to understand the poignancy of the Sino-Soviet conflict, and to deal with the questions of its cause and of its future.

To me the origins of the conflict are to be sought to a large degree, though certainly not exclusively, in the area of personalities. Already during Stalin's last years there had been some tendency of decentralization of communist power. The emergence after World War II of a number of new "fatherlands of communism" would eventually by itself have undermined the central power of Moscow. But it was crucial that at this time the death of Stalin removed from the scene the senior leader to whom all communists were beholden or of whom they had been afraid. It was clear that the Soviet successors, whoever they were, could not speak with the same unquestionable authority that Stalin had. That was especially so for Mao who regarded himself not only in China but in world communist terms as superior to the Soviet epigones, men like Malenkov and Khrushchev, in whose ability he had not the greatest confidence. It was, however, more than a personality conflict. At the time of Stalin's death, the great drives with their destruction of all possible opposition were over in China, and the Chinese Communists were ready to begin a phased economic development a la Moscow and with Soviet support. It was at this moment that Mao began what I would call a deviation from the regular communist program, a deviation that, I believe, only ended with his death and the purge of the gang of four.

The problem with Mao was that he was a revolutionary and not interested in the routine of government and particularly of phased economic development as carried out in the planned economy of the Soviet Union and other communist countries. To Mao, revolution was to continue as a perpetual series of upheavals that would bring about the goal of communist man as a result of will power, organization, and the willingness to sacrifice for a faith which Mao himself would provide. When, in 1954, Mao's comrades—Chou En-lai, Liu Shao-chi, Tung Pi-wu and others—declared that there would now be an end to political drives and that there would be an orderly system with the introduction of communist law, Mao refused. Mao wanted to maintain the revolutionary flexibility of the drives, which he believed could accomplish faster than a planned order the final goal of communism. The first issue was collectivization which according to Liu was to be carefully approached by stages, depending on the availability of agricultural machinery that was yet to be produced. Mao wanted instant collectivization and ridiculed the slowness of Liu who, like Chinese women of the imperial generation, hobbled on bound feet. Mao had his way. He controlled the police and the military commanders, knew how to manipulate his colleagues and had the strength of personality to have his will obeyed. It was the beginning of a course that was to deviate more and more from Leninism, mixing Mao's simplistic interpretations of Marxism with a belief in perpetual struggle and survival of the fittest, which he had derived from Darwinism.

This beginning division among Chinese leaders was suddenly aggravated by the news of Khrushchev's secret speech at the 20th Soviet Party Congress and the Soviet policy of de-Stalinization. De-Stalinization affected not only the Soviet Union but the communist leaders of all parties, many of whom lost their positions, and some their lives. Mao too, as a Chinese Stalinist, came under fire, and at the Chinese 8th Party Congress he lost much of his power to the comrades who were aiming now at introducing "collective leadership" and the regular communist policy condemned by Mao. Mao was on the defensive, but tried first to roll with the punches. Following the Soviet period of greater freedom under the so-called "thaw," Mao introduced the policy of the one hundred flowers that could all bloom under communism, and of the one hundred schools of thought that could be permitted to contend as long as they remained within the Marxist-Leninist framework. But when, instead of a controlled discussion, a massive political demonstration against communism occurred in China, Mao quickly placed the lid back on and destroyed the "poisonous weeks" which had come out in the open. Mao's confidence in Khrushchev's more lenient policy was not improved.

Mao's major attempt at overcoming the confrontation with Soviet policy was made when he went to Moscow, in the same year of 1957, for the first communist interparty conference. His five-hour speech at Moscow University where he claimed that the east wind had overcome the west wind did not impress his Soviet and East European audience, according to many accounts. But, more important, Mao demanded from Khrushchev "real, not only formal consultation." What Mao wanted was to be consulted on all major communist policy decisions, so as not to be surprised again as with Khrushchev's sudden de-Stalinization. Khrushchev refused and Mao went home to go it alone.

To do that, China had to become independent of Soviet economic aid, and in typical revolutionary fashion Mao, who had regained authority in the party, initiated the policy of the three red hammers, known as the Great Leap Forward. Under Mao's leadership "the masses," organized in military fashion, were, through fantastic overwork, to increase production in all fields to such a degree that China would have the affluence needed to move on instantly from socialism to communism. There was a special anti-Soviet theme in the program. Soviet leadership of the socialist camp, not depending on any institutional structure, was proclaimed to be based simply on the Soviets being ahead on the way to communism, a way all others had to follow. Now Mao claimed that China was "bypassing the Soviet Union on the way to communism," assuming thus for China the leadership of the socialist camp. Needless to say, Khrushchev did not take this challenge lightly.

But the Great Leap proved to be a great flop, creating starvation and economic disaster, and Mao was removed from the chairmanship of the republic, which was taken over by Liu Shao-chi, and Chou En-lai traveled to Moscow to get another, though limited, economic agreement. In the summer of 1959, Mao staved off the accusations of his minister of defense Peng Teh-huai, made with the presumed support of Khrushchev. The Chinese arguments against Moscow were resumed and became more bitter in an exchange of documents containing a full vocabulary of interpretation in quasi-theological terminology of communist disputes. This phase of the so-called ideological battle ended in 1965. It was the time of U.S. intervention in Vietnam to save the Saigon government from collapse under the onslaught of Hanoi's open and guerrilla warfare. When the Soviet Union offered Peking renewed cooperation in support of Hanoi, Liu and other leaders were willing to accept. Mao, again feeling threatened by this danger of Chinese reconciliation with his Soviet enemies, fought back. Since he had lost control of the party, whose leaders were ready to side with Moscow, Mao decided to destroy the party and establish his own new system of leadership. For this Mao started the so-called Great Proletarian Cultural Revolution (1966-1969). Mao used the Red Guards, composed of college and high school students backed by the army, to attack and destroy nationwide the party and administrative structure, seeking to replace them with his own direct control backed by the "masses," a system without a communist party. Mao's new structure was supposed to have been copied from an historical precedent, the Paris commune of 1871, which had been at the time described by Karl Marx as a proletarian revolution. In China this was now to be a system where the leader, Mao Tse-tung, was to derive his authority directly from the masses—Mao's college students—a system that would clearly have been a shift from Marxism-Leninism to a leadership system. At the same time, the Mao cult reached its zenith. This was the time of the Little Red Book of Chairman Mao's sayings, printed with Lin Piao's introduction in over nine hundred million copies and distributed abroad as well as in China. Anything accomplished—from any scientific discovery to a successful sale of cucumbers to medical miracles or inventions—was made possible by the Thought of Chairman Mao. To prove his physical stamina when he was rumored to have had a stroke, Chairman Mao allegedly took the famous swim in the Yangste River. Not only did he beat all Olympic records, as could be expected, but he performed a number of miracles all straightfacedly reported in the Chinese newspapers. The one that impressed me most was the story that while swimming at record speed Chairman Mao explained problems of Marxism-Leninism to a fellow swimmer, a feat that must impress any teacher.

More seriously for the Soviets was the effect of the cult abroad. The communist parties in the non-communist world were split into Soviet and Maoist factions, challenging each other and challenging the Soviet control of international communism. When the Paris commune system in China failed, Mao had to bring in the army and some party experts in newly formed revolutionary committees to help him rebuild a party.

This was the time when the turmoil in China, the international challenge, the attack against the Chinese party and the abandonment of the regular communist course led the Soviet Union to concentrate on the long Chinese border a force of over forty-seven fully equipped divisions, more than a quarter of the Soviet military strength, as a threat and leverage of power for any opportunity of intervening in the on-going Chinese struggle. This Soviet military build-up transformed the political-ideological confrontation between Moscow and China into a military power game that is still going on today.

Since this original confrontation the military moves have gone on. Over the last two years the Soviets have kept their forces on the Chinese frontiers equipped with the latest in advanced weaponry, and they have also moved further. The Soviet fleet has moved into the Pacific. Based in Vladivostok and the southernmost Kurile island, the Soviet naval force in the Pacific has grown to a size of about double that of the U.S. Seventh Fleet in tonnage and military aircraft. It includes missile firing submarines. In 1979 an eighty thousand ton dry dock, built by a Japanese firm, will service the largest Soviet carriers. Today Soviet ships are frequently observed in the Sea of Japan, along the Chinese coast and in the Taiwan Strait. A Soviet position at Cam Ranh Bay in North Vietnam completes the encirclement. It is linked with the growing Soviet strength in the Indian Ocean. This is a totally formidable array of military forces and, obviously, a major Chinese concern. The beginning of this Soviet military build-up during the Cultural Revolution became all the more serious when there occurred in March 1969 bloody border clashes between Soviet and Chinese troops on the Manchurian border. The fight resulted from the contention over an uninhabited island in the Ussuri River, Chen Pao or Damansky Island, claimed by both sides. A Chinese ambush, which may have been locally authorized, led to the death of a Soviet colonel and his men. The Soviets retaliated, inflicting heavy Chinese losses. It appeared that the incidents might lead to major military actions.

Mao's first reaction to the Soviet military threat was to cut short the Cultural Revolution and to call in March 1969 the 9th Party Congress, called the Congress of Unity, to reunite the divided Chinese leaders in the face of the Soviet danger. At this Congress Lin Piao, who had directed the Cultural Revolution for Mao, was proclaimed Mao's successor. A high percentage of military leaders were elected to all party positions, and the old party leadership was officially purged.

After the Congress, China's first priority was to strengthen herself internally. This was to be Chou En-lai's task. In his report to the 10th Party Congress two years later, Chou claimed that China was "a piece of meat, very tough . . . to bite into."

When the Soviets demanded negotiations to settle their differences, the Chinese first played hard to get. When the Soviets set a deadline in August 1969, the Chinese responded: "We will give you a reply. Please calm down a little and do not get excited." But together with a second deadline in September the Soviets took military action through a limited incursion into Chinese Twakestan combined with a strong hint that they would use nuclear weapons for a strike against Chinese nuclear facilities. As a result of this threat Kosygin met Chou En-lai at the Peking airport on September 3, 1969, two days before the deadline expired, and the negotiations started that have been off and on ever since.

During these negotiations the Soviets several times made a number of substantial offers that are still open today. The very fact of calling these talks "negotiations" implied a Soviet acceptance that there were possibly

Chinese grievances that could be discussed, and the Soviet offers went at least part of the way to overcome these assumed Chinese complaints. At the outset, however, the Chinese set conditions which, as they must have known, the Soviets could not accept. The Soviet demands as presented by Kosygin were for broad negotiations on normalization of Sino-Soviet relations, including border issues, the resumption of full diplomatic relations and the restoration of economic cooperation.

The Chinese demanded that before any substantive talks could begin the status quo along the border had to be restored and that there must be reductions of Soviet forces to the strength of sixteen divisions as before the build-up. This the Soviets were unwilling to accept. Later the Chinese added the demand that Moscow should admit that the territory taken by Czarist Russia beyond the line of the treaty of Nerchinsk (1689) was the result of imperialist aggression for which the Soviet successors of the czars should apologize. The Soviets regarded this as an insulting demand. To them any attempt to reopen "historical issues" could not be taken seriously.

The Soviet substantive proposals included over a period of time the following points:

1. Acceptance of the shift from "party to party" to "state to state" relations, and to base these on the five principles of peaceful coexistence, at one time also proposed by the Chinese.

2. Acceptance of the Thalweg principle for the border demarcation as a change from the original treaties of 1858-60 between the czars and the Manchu dynasty, which drew the border line on the Chinese shores of the border rivers, leaving the navigation control in the Russian hands. This Soviet concession has already been introduced in the new navigation agreement of 1977. The only remaining issue in this regard is the Soviet control over the triangular island between the confluence of the Amus and Ussuri Rivers and the Kazakevichego or Hei Hia Tzu Channel which lies opposite Khabarovsk and is of strategic importance.

3. Offering of a non-aggression treaty—an offer ignored by the Chinese.

4. Proposal of a new border treaty, dealing with Chinese local complaints, so far avoided by the Chinese.

5. A suggested summit meeting.

6. A restoration of economic relations with renewed Soviet support, including scientific and cultural relations.

7. A suggestion to settle the boundry issues in a piecemeal fashion.

To all these proposals, some basic, some specific, which would have opened the way to a settlement or settlements of this major border aspect of the conflict and allayed Chinese fears about the meaning of the Soviet direct military threat, the Chinese remained intransigent and insisted on their demand of a pullback of Soviet troops from the "disputed areas" and Soviet admission that the czarist treaties had been unequal.

During all these years only one Chinese concession was made, when on December 27, 1975, under the government authority then of Teng Hsiao-ping (before Teng's second purge), a Soviet helicopter and its crew of three captured by the Chinese eighteen months earlier on Chinese territory in Turkestan were suddenly released. This release and whatever signal it conveyed to Moscow is still a matter of argument among specialists.

While the negotiations were going on, the conflict broadened and led to a jockeying for position between Peking and Moscow on a global scene, combined with mutual vituperations in the phraseology of Marxist doctrine. As one Soviet scholar commented privately: "All the garbage we have thrown at the West comes back from the East." But a new term was added, first by Chou En-lai, when he called the Soviets "social imperialists," a term that soon became commonplace.

To distinguish them from the "imperialist" United States, the original primary enemy as leader of the capitalist world, the Soviets as "social imperialists" became enemy No. 2, as the other one of the two superpowers that were "colluding" as well as competing for control of the world. They would, so the Chinese proclaimed, bring about World War III. Eventually with the United States defeat in Vietnam and the perceived weakening of the U.S. will to be a dominant force in Asia, the Soviets became the No. 1 danger and enemy of China and were listed first. After the Cultural Revolution, Mao's attempt to challenge the Soviet leadership of the socialist camp and the communist parties outside the communist countries was, as we know now, a failure. Of the communist countries, only Albania in its fight with Moscow followed Peking's lead, and a few others, mainly North Korea and Rumania, tried to balance their relations, but in a crunch they would have to submit to Moscow. Eventually Mao abandoned the lost battle with the Soviet Union for leadership over the socialist camp and shifted to another theater of operations, the so-called third world. It was a retreat, but it had a history.

As the practitioner of so-called wars of national liberation the Chinese had been given, even before the conflict, a special responsibility in the promotion of this communist strategy. In the interparty conferences in Moscow, this special Chinese role had been acknowledged. What was more, the Chinese had shared with the Soviet Union the training of functionaries for guerrilla warfare in the formerly colonial world. In 1955 at the Bandung Conference of the Afro-Asian countries, Chou En-lai played a major part and eventually outmaneuvered the Indian leader, Nehru, who did not long survive the disappointment in his misplaced trust in Chou's presumed promises.

From the outset the Chinese had attempted to keep the Soviets out of this Afro-Asian solidarity organization, with arguments that were clearly racist. When the Soviet Union forced its way in, claiming to be an Asian as well as a European power, and sending Soviet Asian representatives to the

African conferences, the Chinese abandoned the whole project rather than share it with their Soviet competitor. Now when the Sino-Soviet conflict hardened, Mao turned to this third world as the new field for revolutionary advance, sponsored by Peking. The slogan "Countries want independence, nations want liberation, and the people want revolution—this is the irresistible trend of history" became a password of Chinese foreign policy. Instead of the old juxtaposition of the "socialist camp" led by the Soviet Union and the "imperialist world" led by the United States, Peking now developed the concept of the "three worlds"—the first world of the two superpowers, the imperialist United States and the social imperialist Soviet Union; the second world of the lesser capitalist countries in Europe and Japan, who were also oppressed by the superpowers and could therefore be supported; and the third world of the Afro-Asian and South American countries, the revolutionary forces of our time. In April 1974, Teng Hsiao-ping, then acting prime minister before his second purge, outlined this new interpretation of the world structure in a speech before the United Nations in New York. In one sentence Teng did away with the socialist camp whose leadership Mao had not been able to wrest from Moscow: "As a result of the emergence of social imperialism, the socialist camp which existed for a time after World War II is no longer in existence." Instead Teng described the new alignment of the three worlds and added: "China is a socialist country and a developing country as well. China belongs to the third world."

The political events of the new world politics did not follow this Chinese plan. In the reality of world politics, the Chinese resources, even though carefully husbanded and applied in specific countries, were too limited to compete successfully with the Soviet Union, let alone the United States. A major Chinese emphasis was therefore in the field of propaganda and of exhibitions, stressing the model of China, allegedly more suited for developing countries than either that of the West or the Soviet Union. In the end, the Soviets with their Cuban mercenaries and the growing logistic ability for military action far away from home gained almost everywhere the upper hand over the People's Republic which sometimes, because of its propaganda offensive, was ridiculed as the real "paper tiger" in the growing confrontation. The Soviet goal, however, of coming to terms with the People's Republic and bringing China back into the fold appeared not to have changed. That any such rapprochement was next to impossible as long as Chairman Mao was alive was more or less taken for granted. The real question was: What would happen after Mao's death?

This is the question of today and the future. The answer so far is that any hopes the Soviet leaders may have nurtured of a basic change in Peking's foreign policy have been bitterly disappointed. On the contrary the conflict seems to have widened in scope and deepened in bitterness.

The attitude of the new leadership in China was at first cautious. The new chairman of the party and the government, Hua Kuo-feng, refused to accept a Soviet party-to-party communication congratulating him for elevation to the Chinese party chairmanship. But soon there were feelers and contacts from both sides to test the waters. In Tokyo the Chinese and Soviet ambassadors met and had a lengthy conversation. In Washington D.C., the head of the Chinese mission came to a Soviet reception and appeared to have a long cordial talk (Kissinger was shunted aside). And there appear to have been other less obvious exchanges.

In the summer of 1977, when Teng Hsiao-ping came aboard in Peking, there was also no change. On June 16, Vice Chairman Li Hsieu-uien, one of the key figures in the new leadership, defined the new-old policy in a speech at a dinner for the visiting Sudan president. As an expression of the whole Chinese attitude it is worth quoting the relevant paragraph:

When our great leader and teacher Chairman Mao passed away, social-imperialism employed both soft and tough tactics against us. On the one hand, by deliberate gestures, it feigned willingness to improve relations with us; on the other hand, it made the slander that our foreign policy had been "greatly discredited" in the vain hope that we would change the revolutionary line and policies which Chairman Mao laid down for us. Exasperated at being rebuffed and disillusioned, it has now thrown away its mask and revealed its true colors by hurling vicious slanders and curses at China. Delivering a diplomatic note, making public speeches and publishing articles, it rapidly abuses China as so-called dangerous adventurism, and extends to state relations the differences on matters of principle between the two states. But whatever tactics social-imperialism uses will prove futile. Who does it think will be cowed by such tactics? The great Chinese people will neither be taken nor intimidated. Under the leadership of the party Central Committee headed by our wise leader Chairman Hua, the Chinese people are holding high the great banner of Chairman Mao and unswervingly implementing his revolutionary line and policies, determined to carry through to the end the struggle against superpower hegemonism.

But in the general opening up of Chinese foreign relations, there were some contacts that raised interesting questions, especially the visit of President Tito of Yugoslavia who, after a trip to Moscow, came to Peking where he was given an extraordinary cordial reception. Whether this was an attempt to enlist Yugoslavia in the struggle against Moscow or an indirect approach between Moscow and Peking remained a matter of argument. In any case, each side expressed its differing view of the world situation without antagonism. It was quite a step for Peking not only to welcome the former arch-revisionist Tito himself, but even to establish party-to-party relations with the Yugoslav Communist Party, at least as big a jump as would be necessary for the re-establishment of such party-to-party relations with the Soviet Communist Party.

In October 1977, at the time of the sixtieth anniversary of the October Revolution, there was a further relaxation of tension. Chinese Foreign Minister Kuang Hua attended a reception given by the Soviet embassy in Peking—the first time since 1966 that a high-level Chinese representative had appeared at this annual event. The Sino-Soviet friendship association in Peking gave a Soviet film reception at which the Soviet Ambassador made an appearance. (Twelve Soviet films were then shown in China.) More important; in October a border river navigation treaty was concluded on the basis of the Thalweg principle. And of course the Sino-Soviet Treaty of Alliance of 1950 remained on the books, neither side apparently being willing to abrogate it—although at the conclusion of the Japanese Treaty this year the Japanese reported an oral Chinese indication that this Sino-Soviet Treaty might be abrogated formally in 1979.

But the media accusations and hostile statements soon resumed. In essence little appeared to have changed. On November 7, a joint editorial of the leading Chinese papers called the Communist Party of the Soviet Union a "fascist party of the bureaucrat monopoly bourgeois" under the leadership of the "Soviet revisionist renegade clique." On February 25, 1978, Hua Kuo-feng in a report to the Party Congress repeated the Chinese accusations against the Soviet "social-imperialist policy" but reasserted the continuing Chinese willingness to maintain the state-to-state relations on the basis of the five principles of peaceful coexistence. He contrasted Moscow's words for improvement of relations with actual hostility in Soviet deeds. He repeated the Chinese conditions for an agreement: maintaining the status quo (before 1960), discouraging the armed forces of both sides in the disputed border area, and the withdrawal of Soviet armed forces from the People's Republic of Mongolia and the Sino-Soviet borders.

This request was rejected in a Pravda article, and Brezhnev underlined Soviet determination by an extended tour of the Soviet armed forces' maneuvers along the border.

In May 1978 another border incident occurred when Soviet troops and helicopters penetrated Chinese territory across the Ussuri in pursuit of what may have been an escaping armed agent. The Soviets apologized, and Peking, after an initial protest, let the incident pass.

This "no peace, no war" situation appeared to continue through 1978 with Moscow having offered Peking a greatly improved bilateral relationship if Peking chose to move in that direction. At the same time, however, Soviet military pressures along the border and in Asia increased. The Chinese remained intransigent while upping the ante through big power diplomacy, wooing the United States, Japan and the countries of Europe for a "united front" against the Soviet Union.

Since the summer of 1978, however, the confrontation between Moscow and Peking has entered a new phase globally as well as in Asia where

Vietnam and Japan became the new centers of conflict. The Soviet success in Africa, Afghanistan, the Indian Ocean, Vietnam and Laos obviously began to arouse "grave concern" in Peking where the leaders regarded these moves as an intensification of the Soviet encirclement drive. An editorial of September 18, 1978 attacked this Soviet "expansionism" and called for vigilance and defense preparations by the people of all countries against a war of aggression by the "two superpowers, Soviet social imperialism in particular." Since then, this theme has been repeated in many articles and statements. An article of October 11, entitled the "Anti-China Outburst Cannot Harm China," paints a grim picture of the threat, but the Chinese consolation is that "the forces against appeasement in Western Europe and North America have gained in strength." China claims it has not been harmed and will not be. "Let the wind blow and waves beat; it is better than idly strolling in the courtyard. No amount of abuse and vituperation from the Kremlin can hinder the advance of the Chinese people."

What caused the new alarm in Peking was China's growing conflict with Vietnam over the latter's attempt to gain control of all Indochina, including the Chinese client state Cambodia. In October 1978, Taiwan obtained and published a copy of a secret speech by Peking's deputy director of the Overseas Chinese Affairs Office (Lin Hsiu-teh) given in Canton in June of that year. The speech reveals the Chinese political reasoning for the concentration of Chinese troops on the Vietnam border and the border fighting that followed. As stated, the Chinese purpose was "to apply some pressure on Vietnam from the north, in order to reduce Vietnam's threat to Cambodia by attracting their main forces to our side of the border." But the speaker also surveyed the Soviet threat to China, "from north to south, from east to west, wherever possible and regardless of the price." The Soviet purpose is to deter China from developing her economy, retarding her modernization. Lin complains that no country—except Nepal—has clearly sided with China. The north Korean attitude remains unclear; Tanzania and Zambia have become difficult; the "socialist beacon" of Albania has become extinguished; the United States is sacrificing others in exchange for her own security. Still, Lin takes refuge in the belief that the global united front against Soviet hegemony is growing.

But then there has been an important Chinese success in international politics. The peace and friendship treaty with Japan, negotiated for eight years, has finally been concluded and ratified. How important this event was for China could be seen from the fact that Teng Hsiao-ping himself went to Japan for the occasion. One can sense the Chinese hope that Japan's capital and technical know-how combined with Chinese manpower and resources will provide the basis for the rapid development of China to that great power goal, which Chou En-lai envisioned.

For Japan there is a catch and some concern over this trend and its consequences. To the government of Fukuda there has been an alarm signal in the emotional shift of opinion shown in a Japanese public opinion poll conducted on October 12 and 13, 1978. Forty-nine percent of voters still regarded the United States security treaty as "useful," but only twenty percent believed that the United States would help Japan in case of emergency. And only twenty-six percent (formerly forty-five percent) felt that Japan's most friendly relations should be with the United States, while twenty-nine percent (formerly twenty percent) thought they should be with mainland China.

Japan has attempted to maintain "equidistance" from Peking and Moscow and was concerned what effect that anti-hegemony clause, which it tried to water down, would have on the Soviet Union. There was speculation about whether the Soviets would retaliate by interfering with Japanese fishing rights north of Hokkaido, but little else was expected.

Now it has come. The Soviet Union has interpreted the Sino-Japanese treaty as a quasi-alliance and has given its own answer by concluding a treaty of friendship and alliance with Vietnam. The Japanese would had hoped to negotiate a forty billion dollar trade agreement with Hanoi see now their southeastern plans endangered. Peking's Japan treaty and Moscow's Vietnam treaty may thus have brought a shift in the strategic situation of east Asia.

There is another Japanese concern, and that is the safety of Taiwan, after an assumed American acceptance of Peking's conditions for "normalization." From Japan's point of view there is not only the danger of Peking taking the island by whatever means, but of the establishment of Soviet naval units in the Pescadores or the harbors of Taiwan with or without the approval of the Nationalist government. The Nationalist government has to date declared its absolute opposition to dealing with the communists of either Peking or Moscow. But if we were able to deal with the devil as Churchill had it, i.e., Stalin, against the danger of Hitler, it may not be impossible to imagine that if pressed against the wall Taiwan might make a pact with the Soviets. After all, the Soviets would only use the harbors while Peking would take over the island and the people and establish its communist system.

What about the United States policy in this fluid and to me very dangerous situation? So much of course depends on the future of Sino-Soviet relations. First of all is there still a chance of Sino-Soviet reconciliation? At the moment, in my view, there is not a shred of evidence that there is any move on either side in that direction, unless the conflict should be viewed as a big charade which I cannot believe. Yet I would say that it would be very unwise to preclude that possibility from our calculations, as we seem to do.

But if one wants to consider the eventuality of such future realignment, what necessary steps would have to be taken to overcome the present hurdles?

1. The still ongoing power struggle in Peking would have to be resolved so as not to offer the Soviets any possibility to interfere or exploit. This could well soon occur.

2. Until the People's Republic has obtained from the West all the advantages of economic and political concessions it wants, there will not likely be any shift that would spoil the game. And that is especially true for the three conditions demanded by Peking for "normalization" with the United States. As long as we do not give away that card, we can therefore hold up their game. Once we have given in, we have lost whatever counterweight we may have now.

3. The Soviets would have to make real concessions in sharing, in equal partnership, the communist role in the so-called third world. They have the advantage, and are known to hate giving up anything they hold, but it is dangerous to rely on the stupidity of your adversary.

U.S. Policy, Taiwan, and Northeast Asia*

*Edward Neilan***

The quickening pace of change in northeast Asia, perhaps the most critical geopolitical region in the world, requires an enlightened American policy for the area.

The area's significance today and tomorrow is underscored by the convergence there of the interests, borders or territorial waters of Japan, the Soviet Union, the People's Republic of China, South Korea, North Korea, Taiwan and the United States (as a Pacific power).

East Asia, economically, is the world's fastest-growing region. With its large population, an expected steady and significant increase in per capita income over the next few years will result in a market surge which can only be described as staggering.

Not the least important of the economic and developmental factors is the presence of large deposits of oil, particularly in undersea beds which follow geological rather than political boundaries. For the future, the situation provides the potential for serious disputes.

There is a variety of short- and long-term security considerations. The potential for armed conflict is present in Korea. There is uncertainty over whether Peking intends to use force against Taiwan. Japan is expressing more concern over the growth of the Soviet Pacific fleet and about the credibility of the United States as a defense partner. A nuclear-armed South Korea would cause serious repercussions among the other nations, particularly Japan.

Despite the complexity of the crossing lines of interests, threats and goals, there is a workable balance of power in the area today. Policy decisions taken by the United States ought to be executed so as not to disrupt this complex balance. The Carter administration's fascination with playing the "China card" against the Soviet Union, its Korean withdrawal timetable (which is based on unsound premises), and its failure to deal effectively

*Copyright 1978, *The Heritage Foundation,* Washington, D.C. Reprinted by permission.
**Edward Neilan is the editor and publisher of *The Asia Mail.*

with the United States-Japan economic relationship are examples of moves which have had a jarring effect on the balance.

United States policy in northeast Asia since the emotional experience of the Vietnam War has been more drift than design. The specific initiatives of the Carter administration—when they have occurred at all—have resulted in a confusing image of the United States among both foreign diplomats and American citizens at home and abroad.

First and foremost, United States policy emphasis for the immediate future in northeast Asia should be focused on maintaining and improving relations with Japan. This should include both cooperation and competition in the economic sphere. For the rest of this century—and perhaps beyond—our relationship with Japan will be fundamental to our interests in the region and more significant than ties with China.

The administration has mismanaged the trade situation with Japan by failing to deal effectively with problems which it inherited, but which have since been enlarged. President Jimmy Carter and National Security Advisor Zbigniew Brzezinski raised high hopes for an imaginative policy toward Japan because of their closeness to the Trilateral Commission. But these hopes were not fulfilled and U.S. policy toward Japan today is highlighted by Special Trade Representative Robert Strauss' fire brigade activities.

Beyond placing emphasis on the relationship with Japan because of its overriding importance, the United States must deal with each of the nations in a positive, imaginative and even-handed manner. This would include attempting gradually to improve relations with communist nations in the area as well as those with whom the United States already has trade and diplomatic ties.

The Pacific Century and American Leadership

According to several analysts, we are not on the verge of a Pacific century—it has already begun. Many of the world's leaders have not fully recognized this fact nor are they intellectually ready to meet the promise of the Pacific.

A few years ago, Norman Macrae, associate editor of *The Economist,* commented on the evolution of civilization from an economic standpoint. He wrote that the British century from 1775 to 1875, based on the steam engine and steel-producing technology, was replaced by the American century from 1875 to 1975. The United States was the world industrial leader during this period because of its superiority in aircraft, automotive and computer technology and the productive capacity of its work force. In Mr. Macrae's opinion, the American century gave way to the Pacific century in the mid-1970s because of the remarkable economic growth of Japan, South Korea and other Asian nations, the growing importance of the west coast of the United States over that of the east coast, and improvements in transportation and communication.

Such attempts at drawing historical demarcation lines are rather abrupt and oversimplified, of course, but Macrae's analysis makes sense. The shift he described from the American to the Pacific century does not suggest an end to American power as much as it suggests a future interdependent relationship between the U.S. and the growing economies of the Asia-Pacific basin.

There is ample room for American leadership, so far not exercised in the post-Vietnam era, in the Pacific.

Jiro Tokuyama, managing director of Tokyo's Nomura Research Institute, wrote in the June 23, 1978, edition of the *Asian Wall Street Journal:*

At present, neither Americans nor Japanese are fully aware of the great promise of the Pacific zone. U.S. Presidents Richard Nixon and Gerald Ford personally stressed the importance of Asia-Pacific to the United States and stated the U.S., as a Pacific nation, would continue to play a vital role in the region. This basic policy has been reiterated by such high officials in the Carter administration as Secretary of State Cyrus Vance, U.S. Presidential National Security Advisor Zbigniew Brzezinski and U.S. Ambassador to Tokyo Mike Mansfield. But the president himself has yet to make public his own policy toward Asia-Pacific.

In Tokuyama's view, this situation leaves Japan to take the initiative in Pacific affairs. But he questions whether the Japanese government, preoccupied with domestic and international economic problems, has a strategy or vision for leadership of the Pacific community.

Prior to the seven-nation Bonn economic summit meeting in July, the head of Japan's Economic Planning Agency expressed his country's disappointment with American leadership. The planning chief, Kiichi Miyazawa, who is generally regarded as the man who runs the economy for Prime Minister Takeo Fukuda, added during an interview that he regretted the failure of Congress to enact energy legislation and that he was fearful of a protectionist trend in the United States after elections this fall.[1]

Comments on a lack of direction and leadership in the Carter administration's foreign policy have increased within the United States this year. The addition of foreign voices, such as Miyazawa's, to the chorus suggests that longer-term American interests may be harmed by a weak president. For example, there is the possibility that a beleaguered Carter might be convinced by his aides to travel to the People's Republic of China next year more as an "event" to boost his sagging image than as a carefully planned segment of a clearly enunciated Asia policy.

The same public opinion polls which reflect confusion over Mr. Carter's foreign policy state conclusively that Americans do not wish the Republic of China (Taiwan) to be sacrificed in the name of U.S. normalization with Peking. If the administration attempts to push through normaliza-

268

tion too soon—as part of some desperate "China card" maneuver against the Soviets or as part of a political visit by the president—there will be further reduction of American prestige.

Fear of just such a ploy from the Carter administration probably was a principal motivating force for Senators Robert Dole (R.-Kansas) and Richard Stone (D.-Florida) to propose an amendment to a security bill requiring that the White House consult with the Senate before the executive branch moves to alter the Sino-U.S. Mutual Defense Treaty. The amendment was adopted 94-0 and amounted to a strong message to Mr. Carter that he had better have a carefully prepared China policy drafted before deciding to fly off to Peking.

Mismanagement of the U.S. relationship with Peking—a tie that requires delicate orchestration with every move because of political complexities on both sides—would result in setting back rather than advancing a solution to the China problem.

The furor over Brzezinski's "China card" statements and the development of his "tough guy" image may have contributed to the confusing impression given by the Carter administration in the foreign affairs field generally and in Asia specifically. The spectacle of Brzezinski talking tough on one hand and Secretary Vance speaking in more moderate tones on the same issue added to this misinterpretation of U.S. policy by many foreign statesmen.

According to *Newsday*'s White House correspondent, Martin Schram, an attempt to resolve this problem was made by Mr. Carter who told his close aides on June 9 that henceforth he wanted Mr. Vance to be his chief foreign policy spokesman.[2]

That effort at clarity must have pleased many world leaders, but must have added to the confusion of others. In Peking, there were fresh stirrings of anticipation following Brzezinski's visit to China that moves toward normalization would occur soon. The Chinese applaud Brzezinski's tough line on the Soviet Union during the talks in the Chinese capital. In contrast, the Peking leadership had reacted cooly after discussions with Secretary Vance in China in the summer of 1977.

The Asia Policy Network

In some ways it is surprising that the Carter administration's policy for Asia has gone so far wrong so fast. The mechanics who shape its course at the working level are well versed in the area and in the art of dealing with Congress. They came mostly from a network or elite tied closely to the liberal Democratic Senate staffs, the Brookings Institution, the Carnegie Endowment for International Peace, *Foreign Policy* magazine, and the Foreign Service.[3]

The appointment of Richard C. Holbrooke, former managing editor of

Foreign Policy, as Assistant Secretary of State for East Asian and Pacific Affairs was greeted with skepticism among some senior State Department people, American businessmen long conversant with Asian affairs, and many Asian diplomats.

Unfortunately and perhaps unfairly, the negative impression has persisted. Holbrooke came into the job as an unabashed supporter of normalization of ties with the People's Republic of China, recognition of the Socialist Republic of Vietnam and withdrawal of U.S. troops from South Korea.

None of those goals has been achieved. But the Carter administration's main policy setback in east Asia has been caused by the public outcry over the pace of withdrawal of troops from South Korea. This timetable was a campaign pledge that Mr. Carter seemed intent on fulfilling despite intelligence reports confirming the policy as unwise. In the face of the unhappy "Koreagate" situation, it is testimony to the recovery of American self-confidence in Asia that the administration's too hasty and in part politically conceived plan for withdrawal from South Korea has been slowed by public and congressional arguments and opposition.

In a speech to the Western Governors' Conference in Honolulu, Hawaii, on June 16, 1978, Holbrooke astutely discussed the U.S. role in Asia, never mentioning the question of recognition of communist Vietnam. On the China question, he reviewed the progress made to date toward improved Washington-Peking relations:

Nevertheless, there is an incompleteness in the relationship which, over time, could render it vulnerable to extraneous factors, raising again the prospects of needless confrontation or misunderstanding between two major powers. This would deprive us of the opportunity to achieve greater cooperation with China on global and regional issues.

Normalization would not solve all our problems, but it would help consolidate our non-confrontational relationship. And it would help insure that the current balance in the entire region remains intact. We are therefore convinced that normalization is an essential objective for our new Asian policy.

In pursuing this objective, we are constantly mindful of the well-being of the people of Taiwan. Thus we are continuing to seek the framework which allows us to move ahead with our strategically and historically important relations with the People's Republic of China, while at the same time taking full account of our concerns regarding Taiwan. Our interest is that, whatever solution there may be to the Taiwan question, it will be a peaceful one. We are confident that in the future we still would be able to continue the many mutually beneficial relationships which link us to the people of Taiwan.

The problem with the administration's pursuit of those goals toward China is that so far the American public is being asked to buy the solution on Peking's terms. The realities of the situation suggest that unless Peking can publicly state a moderated view on Taiwan, it will be inappropriate in terms of both domestic American and domestic Chinese politics to take the normalization step at this time. The application of both patience and persistence in seeking a proper course is advisable.

One is always being asked to be "pro-Peking" or "pro-Taiwan" on this issue; the correct position for American statesmen is to be "pro-United States" in a very tough way and to make that viewpoint clear to the leaders in both Peking and Taipei.

A more successful appointment than Holbrooke's was that of former Senator Mike Mansfield to be the U.S. ambassador to Japan. Whereas an early criticism of Holbrooke was that he was too young (35 at the time of his appointment) and too inexperienced for the job's responsibilities, there could be no such criticism of the seventyish Mansfield, who first served in Asia as a young Marine. Mansfield was given the Tokyo envoy post after it was widely known around the State Department that talented and Asia-wise career officer Marshall Green was in line for that job, but Mansfield has been such a success that the slight to Green, who will be around to serve in important positions in the future, has been all but forgotten.

The problem is that, once appointed, Mansfield has been virtually ignored by Washington. It seems as if the White House felt that placing a prestigious ambassador in a foreign capital would suffice in lieu of a carefully articulated policy.

Future Policy Considerations

Given the rapid changes in northeast Asia and the region's importance in the world's future, what are the most important policies for the United States to pursue in the area?

At the outset, we must recognize that the power relationships for the future will be basically economic, although military capabilities will continue to play important roles in the overall security of the region. Efforts to maximize trade and other commercial interchange among all the parties will be mutually advantageous.

The United States must be thoroughly aware of the trends and developments within each of the nations and then fuse and adapt those to our own policies where appropriate. Japan, for example, has been very successful in shaping its own policies toward China while maintaining correct relations with the Soviet Union, in the face of Sino-Soviet strains. The Sino-Japanese

Pact (ostensibly not directed at the Soviet Union—at Japanese insistence) is a good example of this kind of diplomacy.

The inter-relationships and inter-dependence of the region are shown in the following country-by-country analysis of some of the considerations and questions which should be addressed in making American policy decisions in Asia.

Japan

United States relations with Japan have been remarkably close in the quarter century since the end of the American occupation. Japan has relied on the United States for its security, and the U.S. "nuclear umbrella" is important to Japanese strategic thinking. There is an on-going debate in Japan in reaction to American insistence that Tokyo develop "self-defense" capabilities more quickly. There is some Japanese concern over the build-up of the Soviet fleet, and this could lead to a Japanese willingness to develop more of an anti-submarine warfare (ASW) capability.

Even the communist powers acknowledge that a tranquil U.S.-Japan relationship is essential to stability in Asia. Japanese public opinion seems more tolerant now of the U.S. military presence and the mutual defense treaty. But the Japanese wonder how future swerves in U.S. policy will affect Japan. The Korea withdrawal plan was opposed by Japan because it introduced abrupt change into a satisfactory balance.

Other questions relating to Korea arise for the Japanese: (1) Without the American deterrent, would North Korea attack South Korea? (2) Would a communized Korea affect Japanese domestic politics? (3) Would South Korea, without the presence of a restraining hand from the United States, develop a nuclear weapons capability of its own? What would Peking and Moscow think of such a development? (4) Would a precarious military balance in Korea, with U.S. troops withdrawn, give rise to a new militarism in Japan?

Japan's economic strength may mark it as the first and only major power to feel no need for a large military force. Except for probes from the Soviet navy, there has been no direct threat to the home islands.

Another element of uncertainty in the future U.S.-Japan relationships is the changing configuration of Japanese politics. Reduced Liberal-Democratic Party control could have important implications for the Tokyo-Washington partnership.

Japan, demonstrating adaptiveness, now has relations of one kind or another with every nation in northeast Asia and is the only nation which can make that claim.

Japan's trade with the People's Republic of China is growing rapidly, and it is evident that Peking is depending on the Japanese to play a major role in China's modernization drive. There will be U.S.-Japanese competi-

272

tion in the China market, but the result will be a positive contribution to the overall economic well-being of the area.[4]

The Soviet Union

Moscow's relations with Asian nations range from "very good" in India to "cool and correct" in Japan to "poor" in China. Sino-Soviet relations can only improve because they are at such a low point today. Prospects are good for a significant improvement after China feels industrially and militarily more confident.

There are no indications that the Soviet Union is either encouraging or restraining North Korea's Kim Il Sung on the question of a military invasion of South Korea. Because there would be competition between China and the Soviet Union to support North Korea in a prolonged war, the belief is that the Soviet Union is satisfied with the status quo on the Korean peninsula for the present.

Soviet commercial activities have been increasing in southeast Asia but not in northeast Asia to the same degree. However, Moscow is probing for openings.

Continued U.S. naval and air force presence is necessary in Asia to balance the Soviet Union's growing capability.

The People's Republic of China

Improved relations and full diplomatic relations between the United States and the People's Republic of China are inevitable and desirable. It is one of the challenges facing American policy-makers to improve relations with Peking while at the same time doing nothing to cripple in any way the viable state and economy of Taiwan. There is a degree of moderation necessary on Peking's part in order for that to be achieved; if Peking is unwilling, then normalization should be postponed.

The U.S. position and image in Asia would be severely tarnished if we were to cast Taiwan aside abruptly. Peking must be more convincing and open in its pledges not to use force in settling the Taiwan issue.

At the same time, it must be recognized that China is a developing nation and that it is in our best interest to work with Peking in its plan for modernization and development of its enormous potential. There are strong signals indicating that China is more intent on improving its society, industry and agriculture than on causing any military trouble.

The present state of relations between Peking and Washington is marked by cordiality and steady progress. As Richard Holbrooke has said (quoted above) there is an "incompleteness in the relationship" which should be corrected. But this correction should take place at the appropriate time and under appropriate conditions.

The Republic of China (Taiwan)

There are some "liberal" analysts who would like to see the United States, in effect, hand over Taiwan and then South Korea to the communists and begin a new era in Asia on that basis.

Fortunately, the United States is not capable of "handing over" either nation, as both are strong and independent. Taiwan is a genuine, developmental success story and the U.S. can be justifiably proud of the part it has played in this dramatic accomplishment. Essentially, however, it was the talent and effort of the leadership and citizens of the Republic of China that was responsible for the advance.

The reason that the "Japanese formula" is not acceptable for the U.S. in dealing with the Taiwan question is that Japan, unlike the U.S., was not the critical element in the political equation when it opted to recognize Peking. Unless handled with more skill than the current U.S. administration appears capable of, imposition of a "Japanese formula" solution would severely harm Taiwan. Such a development would be unacceptable and, as shown in opinion polls, the American public senses this. From the U.S. viewpoint, the best outcome would be an "American formula" as suggested by Ray Cline, Parris Chang[5] and some others. This formula would seek to recognize formally the governments in both Taipei and Peking.

Peking must be convinced (and there are a number of American lawyers and businessmen who are trying to make this point with Chinese officials) that the same American corporations and banks which lent their know-how and capital to help develop Taiwan can be very effective in assisting China's modernization.

Meanwhile, American ties with Taiwan should be continued and expanded in financial, trade, educational, scientific and other areas. There should be no diminishing of any ties with Taiwan merely because Peking wants it that way.

The idea of Taipei seeking ties with the Soviet Union is intriguing, but so far the Republic of China has publicly denied any intention to do so.

South Korea

There are a number of American academic specialists who persist in discussing the Republic of Korea (South Korea) as if it were some tentative or transitory entity that will not be around very long. Most of these are Japanese specialists who see Korea primarily as an afterthought to the study of Japan.

The Republic of Korea has created one of the major economic accomplishments of this century under some very adverse conditions. The nation deserves continued U.S. support, including the presence of a deterrent force based in that country.

The presence of U.S. forces in South Korea helps to maintain the existing balance, but will be less and less of a requirement as the Korean econ-

274

omy progresses beyond even its admirable performance to date (last year South Korea achieved its long-sought goal of $10 billion in exports, moving it from 88th place sixteen years ago to 17th among the world's exporting nations).

It is argued that the U.S. military provides a psychological crutch for the Koreans and that with American troops in a tripwire position we are in danger of becoming involved in another war.

In a recent television interview with the editor of the Paris newspaper *Le Monde*, North Korean leader Kim Il Sung again stated that unification will be achieved as soon as the American troop withdrawal is completed. What does he mean by that? Intelligence reports indicate the North Korean military spends virtually all of its training time preparing to invade the South. U.S. withdrawal, under these circumstances, would invite war.

The United States should help defend Korea for its own sake, although there are also cogent reasons that it should be defended because of the implications for Japan.

North Korea

Kim Il Sung is frustrated by South Korea's surging economy, plagued by his inability to pay overseas debts, and apparently threatened by an internal political faction about which we know only the barest details.

Kim has been able to loosen ties to both Peking and Moscow in the sense that he runs his own show. Both communist giants have reason to be interested in a continuation of peace in Korea although there are sharp indications that neither power has as much influence in Pyongyang as has been generally believed.

It would be in the U.S. interest to make some diplomatic contact with North Korea. The concept of cross-recognition, whereby the U.S. and Japan would normalize relations with North Korea while China and the Soviet Union set up diplomatic ties with South Korea, has some merit.

But the North Koreans do not wish to talk to the South Koreans, because Pyongyang wants to undermine the legitimacy of the South Korean government and move into a position as spokesman for all Korea. This is the type of approach used by North Vietnam at the Paris peace talks, where American negotiators mistakenly gave North Vietnam too large a role in the talks.

There are strong cravings for national unification on both sides of the demilitarized zone. But under present circumstances, two Koreas are better than one torn by warfare and conflict between two sharply differing ideological positions.

The United States

If it can be more widely recognized that Asia is the major economic arena of the future, it should follow that everything within reason should be

275

done to increase rather than decrease American power and potential in the area.

The United States has troops in Europe, far more than in Asia. What is wrong with retaining the token, deterrent force in Korea and Japan? All available evidence indicates that the U.S. military presence does more to prevent war than to promote war.

Washington could also do much more in the way of "unleashing" American businessmen by easing some of the tax and other regulations that impede American business performance in the region. Japan is far ahead of us in sending well-equipped "economic soldiers" abroad to do business.

The People's Republic of China would like to see a strong American presence in Asia because Peking now accepts the fact that the United States is no threat to China's progress and independence.

In summation, American policy in northeast Asia should be fundamentally based on a strong partnership with Japan and even-handed relations with every other nation in the region.

NOTES

1. *New York Times,* July 9, 1978, p. 1.
2. *Washington Post,* August 6, 1978, p. 1.
3. See Robert L. Schuettinger, "The New Foreign Policy Network," *Policy Review,* Summer 1977, and Chalmers Johnson, "Carter in Asia: McGovernism without McGovern," *Commentary,* January 1978.
4. For a comprehensive review of problems and opportunities in the U.S.-Japan relationship see Frederick B. Weinstein, ed., *U.S.-Japan Relations and the Security of East Asia—The Next Decade* (Boulder, Colorado: Westview Press, 1978).
5. Ray Claine is Executive Director of Strategic Studies of the Center for Strategic and International Studies, Georgetown University, and a former State Department official. Parris Chang is a professor of political Science at Pennsylvania State University. For a discussion of the normalization problem, see Edwin J. Feulner, Jr., ed., *China—The Turning Point* (Washington, D.C.: Council on American Affairs, 1976).

China and the
Abrogation of Treaties*

Senator Barry Goldwater (R-Arizona)

I

INTRODUCTION

Little or no public debate has occurred on the role of Congress in the abrogation of treaties. Yet, this subject is at the forefront of one of the critical foreign policy issues of the 1970s, our government's China policy.

Before Secretary of State Cyrus Vance went to mainland China last August for talks with the new triumvirate ruling that territory, he was urged by Senator Edward M. Kennedy to simultaneously recognize the People's Republic of China (PRC) and consider our defense treaty with the Republic of China on Taiwan (ROC) as having lapsed. That President Carter could so terminate the treaty at his own discretion was assumed, the theory being that after the United States cuts diplomatic relations with Taiwan, we can consider the defense treaty at an end because there is no government to deal with.

This was not the first time I had heard of the concept under which the defense treaty would be considered as having died a quiet death upon diplomatic recognition of the communist regime. A high official has informed me that the Legal Advisor's Office in the Department of State was studying this contingency even before Senator Kennedy's trial balloon, and it is apparently a view held by several subordinate officers at the Department.[1]

Whether Secretary Vance or any of the officials accompanying him to Peking actually broached this contingency in talks with the Communist Chinese is unknown, but the subject requires careful scrutiny because it represents the latest turn in thinking of those persons who are bent upon granting recognition to the PRC on its own terms.

It is known for certain that one of the announced indispensable requirements for a so-called normalization of relations between the PRC and the United States is abrogation of the mutual defense treaty with Taiwan. PRC Vice Foreign Minister Yu Chan and Vice Premier Li Hsien-nien each made it

---

*Copyright 1978, *The Heritage Foundation*, Washington, D.C. Reprinted by permission.

clear to visiting editors of the *Wall Street Journal* in October 1977 that the communist government is "absolutely inflexible" on this principle. In view of the unyielding position among PRC leaders and the seeming willingness of some American officials to accept the demand, it is urgent that a public debate be initiated on the threshold question of whether or not the president has constitutional authority to do, on his own, what the PRC is demanding.

And, although the immediate question arises in connection with the defense treaty between the Republic of China and the United States, it is also important to explore the principle involved because it touches every one of our nation's treaty commitments. If the president can break the treaty with Taiwan on his own authority, then he can withdraw from NATO or pull out of any other treaty without consulting Congress or getting its consent.

At the outset, it should be clarified that my argument is not intended to cover executive agreements or international agreements other than formal treaties. My concern at this time is only with treaties in the constitutional sense of compacts between nations or other international entities which have been formally signed, submitted for advice and consent to the Senate and ratified after having received the necessary two-thirds approval by the Senate. Since the defense treaty with the ROC is exactly such a constitutional treaty my discussion of the treaty termination power will address only that species of international instrument.

Nor shall I make any brief for the Senate or Congress as possessing the power to compel the president to denounce or abrogate a treaty, although there is strong evidence that such a legislative power exists. Again, that proposition is extraneous to the matter at hand, which is not an effort by Congress to break the treaty with Taiwan, but a proposed assertion of power for the president to arbitrarily force a decision upon the Congress as a *fait accompli* about which it can do nothing.

Also, let me record my strong opposition to any policy of normalization with Communist China that calls for a break in our relations with the free Chinese on Taiwan and the repudiation of our defense treaty with them. I am convinced such a policy of kowtowing to the PRC would dishonor the United States, increase the risks of a world conflict and run counter to constitutional provisions demanding a role for Congress in the treaty process.

Today, Taiwan has almost seventeen million people, more than Ireland, Norway, and 120 other countries of the world. Its economy ranks second only to that of Japan in the Pacific. The ROC is currently America's thirteenth largest trading partner. Two-way trade between the United States and Taiwan totaled $5.5 billion in 1977, compared with $374 million between the United States and the PRC.[2]

Acceptance of the Communist Chinese demands would be unprecedented in American history. No president of the United States has ever unilaterally abrogated a treaty with any foreign government in violation of the provisions of that treaty. Actually, we have a remarkable record of morality in keeping our treaty promises. The motto that "our word is our bond" has been a matter of faith for the American people and for foreign nations with whom we have dealt. If President Carter were now to accept the proposal of advisors who recommend that we recognize the PRC and abrogate our defense treaty with Taiwan, it would leave a permanent stain on our history.[3]

II
OVERVIEW: INTENT OF FRAMERS

Admittedly, treaty abrogation is a rather novel subject. There are virtually no court cases and very few academic papers on the subject. What we do have to go on is our history as a republic, several statements by the Founding Fathers, and common sense.

From these, my own reading of the Constitution is as follows:

- No President can terminate a treaty unless he first obtains the consent of Congress.

- The Constitution demands a rule for Congress in the abrogation of treaties, either in the form of joint action by the president and two-thirds of the Senate, or by the president acting together with both houses of Congress.

- Any President who would violate the Constitution on such a major matter as breaking faith with the nation's treaty obligations would run the risk of impeachment.

In *Foreign Affairs and the Constitution,* one of the few works to consider the question, the noted authority Louis Henkin states:

In principle, one might argue, if the framers required the president to obtain the Senate's consent for making a treaty, its consent ought to be required also for terminating it, and there is eminent dictum to support that view.

Yet, Henkin adds:

In any event, since the president acts for the United States internationally he can effectively terminate or violate treaties, and the Senate has not established its authority to join or veto him.[4]

It is true that the president could, under his power of general control over foreign policy, effectively weaken the credibility of our national commitment under a defense treaty, such as NATO, by ordering a withdrawal of most American military forces from the foreign area involved, but he cannot unilaterally destroy the international legal obligations of our country under a formal treaty without the consent of the Senate or Congress. Indeed Henkin does not claim the president can *legally* terminate or violate treaties. He writes only that the president has the ability to "effectively" breach treaties. This distinction would be of critical importance in any impeachment proceedings instituted by a Congress which considered the president to have violated the limits of his constitutional discretion. It also would have overriding weight in any judicial action challenging the legal validity of the president's purported denunciation or abrogation of a treaty.

In observing that the Senate has not "established its authority" to join or veto the president, Henkin is no more than restating the fact that there has not yet been a definitive court decision squarely settling a conflict between the Executive and Senate in the Senate's favor.

Henkin would agree, I presume, that it is for the judicial branch to say what the law is, not for the president to create law by fiat until the courts speak. And, as we shall see, there is no basis in historical practice for claiming the president has established his authority to denounce or abrogate treaties without legislative participation in his decision. To the contrary, the overwhelming weight of precedents supports a role for the Senate or Congress in treaty abrogation.

The records of the Constitutional Convention and the state ratifying conventions contain little discussion of how a treaty is to be rescinded. But it is well known that the framers were concerned with restoring dependability to our treaties and were anxious to gain the respect and confidence of foreign nations. It would hardly instill confidence in other nations if a single officer of our government could abrogate a treaty at will without any check from another branch of government.

Also, it is beyond dispute that the framers were worried the treaty power could be exercised to damage sectional interests. Repeated flareups occurred at the Constitutional Convention in which various delegates expressed fears that their region might be harmed if treaties could be easily made.

In particular, treaties of commerce, peace and alliance were mentioned. Spokesmen for the western settlers were afraid navigation rights on the Mississippi would be given away by a treaty, and George Mason suggested the treaty-making power could "sell the whole country" by means of treaties.

Thus, the framers sought to give each section of the country an influence in deciding upon treaties because of their possible adverse effect upon strong economic or political interests of particular states or areas. It is logical to assume the framers were as interested in protecting these same regional interests by making it difficult to revoke useful treaties as they were in protecting those interests by guarding against harmful treaties.[5] George Mason alluded to this situation when he warned against allowing one treaty to abridge another by which the common rights of navigation had been recognized to the United States. Moreover, it is inconceivable the framers meant to make it easy for a treaty of peace to be repealed.

This is not to say that the framers would have been as excited about a defense treaty with a small republic 6,000 miles away as they were over treaties involving local fishing or boundary rights, but it is to indicate that the 1954 treaty and all other U.S. treaties are protected by the same procedural safeguard as those treaties about which the framers were especially sensitive. Since the text of the Constitution makes no distinction between different groups of treaties—it does not single out those commercial or boundary treaties, which the framers did not want to have discarded without the check of legislative deliberation, from treaties of all other kinds—the obvious conclusion is that treaties of whatever nature are covered by the same protective mantle before cancellation. If any one group of treaties is secured against repeal without legislative consent, then surely all other treaties enjoy the same security, absent any textual or historical evidence to the contrary. All treaties were to be dealt with in the same way.

Proof that the framers meant for treaties to be kept and not broken at pleasure is found in their emphasis on gaining respect for the new nation among other countries by being faithful to our treaties. James Madison, Alexander Hamilton, and James Wilson each recognized that the ease with which treaties could be and were being broken under the Articles of Confederation was a major defect causing injury both to our respectability and power abroad. Madison, in the preface to his notes on debates in the Constitutional Convention, specifically identifies this failing as being one of the deformities of the Articles which the Constitution was designed to correct. Hamilton pinpoints this disease in number 22 of *The Federalist Papers*. Wilson regarded violation of the "sacred faith of treaties" as "wicked" and contrary to our interests in gaining respect among other nations.[6] Thus, the framers wanted to make it more difficult to violate treaties, not easier. Surely they would not have attempted to remedy the fault by substituting for the previous system one that was equally susceptible to abuse by a single official as the earlier one had been to the whims of individual states.

Another sign of the purpose of the framers is in their creation of a system of checks and balances. In this age of concern about what is described as the Imperial Presidency, it is remarkable that anyone would contend the president is unchecked and unaccountable in a matter of such grave importance as breaking our treaties with other countries. We have seen that they wanted the nation to keep its treaties. Therefore, it is difficult to believe that the framers, who created the presidency and Senate as checks upon each other in completing a treaty, did not intend a similar check in the reverse situation, the revoking of a treaty.

As the scholar-jurist Supreme Court Justice Joseph Story wrote in his *Commentaries on the Constitution of the United States* in 1833:

It is too much to expect that a free people would confide to a single magistrate, however respectable, the sole authority to act conclusively, as well as exclusively, upon the subject of treaties. . . . There is no American statesman but must feel that such a prerogative in an American president would be inexpedient and dangerous.

Story adds:

The check, which acts upon the mind from the consideration that what is done is but preliminary, and requires the assent of other independent minds to give it a legal conclusiveness, is a restraint which awakens caution, and compels to deliberation.[7]

The same fundamental principle that guided the framers in providing that the president can make treaties only with the added deliberation called for when a branch of the legislature must jointly decide the question applies with equal force to the power of annulling treaties. To use Story's words about treaties: "This joint possession of the power affords a greater security for its just exercise than the separate possession of it by either [the president or Senate]."[8]

In my opinion, the framers *assumed* the president would not attempt to break a treaty on his own, since Article II of the Constitution clearly requires that the president "shall take care that the laws be faithfully executed." In other words, the president must uphold the laws because the Constitution tells him to do so.

As we all know, Article IV of the Constitution spells out the fact that a treaty is every bit as much a part of "the supreme law of the land" as a statute is. Therefore, the framers undoubtedly expected future presidents to carry out treaties in good faith and not to break them at their pleasure.

It is true that the president is "the sole organ of the nation in its external relations, and its sole representative with foreign nations." So said John Marshall in 1800 as a member of the House of Representatives. Marshall's quote has been recited by federal courts on many occasions. At most, however, in the context of unmaking treaties this means that it is the president who must communicate the message notifying another country that a treaty is void, and, as we shall see, even this much was denied by the Fifth Congress which enacted a statute annulling three French treaties without providing for any notice by the president. It does not mean that the president alone can make the decision to give that notice. Surely the president's implied power over foreign relations does not give him power to repeal the express provision of the Constitution that requires him to faithfully execute the laws. Nor does it override the system of balance of powers and accountability that the framers have so carefully embedded elsewhere in the Constitution. The people would lose the security of deliberation upon the subject of unmaking treaties, no less than they would lose that security in the making of treaties, if no check by Congress or the Senate were put upon the power of termination.

The general rule might be stated as follows: As the president alone cannot repeal a statute, so he alone cannot repeal a treaty. My colleagues in the Senate will find the truth of this expressed in a book that most of us keep on our desks, the *Rules and Manual of the Senate*. Our rules still include a precedent set forth by Thomas Jefferson, who compiled the first manual of rules and practices of the Senate when he was Vice President of the United States. Jefferson writes: "Treaties being declared equally with the laws of the United States to be the supreme law of the land, it is understood that an act of the legislature alone can declare them infringed and rescinded."[9]

This also was the belief held by James Madison, who wrote in 1791, less than four years after the Constitutional Convention, of "the same authority, precisely, being exercised in annulling, as in making, a treaty."[10]

Historical practice supports Madison and Jefferson. Far more often than not the Senate, or the whole Congress, has exercised power to approve the termination of treaties. As a matter of fact, presidents have usually come to Congress for its approval before giving notice of withdrawing from any treaty.

There are exceptions, but none supports a wide-open power of the president to annul any treaty he wishes. In particular, the United States has never repudiated a defense treaty with a friendly nation. Nor has any president terminated a treaty that was not breached by the other party, that was not in conflict with or supplanted by a later Act of Congress or another treaty, or that did not become inapplicable or impossible to perform due to circumstances not of our own making. And if the Constitution does not spell out how to repeal a treaty, nor does it say how to repeal a statute. Yet it is obvious the president cannot repeal an Act of Congress on his own. So he cannot repeal any other law, which the Constitution defines as including treaties. The same logic which denies the President a power to cancel a statute prevents him from independently terminating a treaty.

III

TERMINATING TREATIES: THE EARLY PRACTICE

It is a little known fact that the first treaties ever to be declared null and void by the United States were cancelled by Congress alone. These were the three French-American Treaties of 1778. Congress, acting through a public law, deemed them to be no longer binding on this country because they had "been repeatedly violated on the part of the French government."[11]

This step followed attacks by French warships on unarmed American merchant vessels and the infamous X Y Z Affair in which the French sought to extract bribes from American peace negotiators.

The Abrogating Act of July 7, 1798 was approved by President Adams, and it is true that to that extent there was presidential consent. However, the statute did not call upon the president to give notice of abrogation, and it appears from the legislative debates that Congress assumed no further act was necessary on his part.

In 1887, the U.S. Court of Claims upheld the statute as having terminated both the domestic and the international aspects of the Franco-American treaties. In *Hooper v. U.S.* the court said:

> We are of the opinion that the circumstances justified the United States in annulling the treaties of 1778; that the act was a valid one, not only as a municipal statute but as between nations; and that thereafter the compacts were ended.[12]

This early precedent represents the clear omission by President Adams of a legislative role in the abrogation of a treaty, since he signed the law. It also is a concession by the Senate that, in at least some circumstances, the power to void treaties belongs to Congress as a corporate body, and not exclusively to the president and Senate.

The first instance of terminating a treaty by presidential notice did not occur until 1846, fifty-seven years after the government started operations. The agreement rescinded was the convention allowing Great Britain to share joint occupation with America of the Oregon Territory. In response to strong pressure from the House of Representatives, President Polk recommended to Congress that he be given authority by law to give notice of the convention's annulment. The issue was heatedly debated in 1846, with the majority position being that the abrogation of a treaty is clearly a legislative duty that cannot be performed constitutionally by any other power than the joint power of both Houses of Congress. And so a joint resolution was enacted granting the requested power.

The third time we withdrew from a treaty was by the will of the president and Senate acting together as the treaty-making power. In the Resolution of March 3, 1855, two-thirds of the senators present advised and consented to remove our commerce from what we believed were burdensome and oppressive duties under a commercial treaty with Denmark. The resolution authorized President Pierce to give Denmark notice, as required in the treaty for its termination, and it was in response to the expressed wish of the President for such power. President Pierce later publicly acknowledged he had given the notice "in pursuance of the authority conferred" by the Senate resolution.

Curiously, our government used three different methods the first three times it withdrew from or denounced treaties as void. While the measures differed, the significant thing is that each approach required some form of legislative participation in the decision to cancel a treaty. And, of particular relevance to the 1954 Taiwan treaty, two of the first treaties terminated contained notice provisions, yet those provisions were not exercised until new legislative authority was given.

In practice, an Act of Congress would never again be used without anticipating presidential notice as the means of communicating our intention to annul a treaty to the foreign government concerned, and a Senate resolution would be used only once more. As we shall see, the joint resolution, followed by presidential notice to the other country, would become the general vehicle for removing our nation from treaties that we no longer could or wished to enforce. On rare occasions, Congress would also consent to adopt and ratify presidential decisions after they had been proclaimed.

Senate Committee Claims Joint Power

Publicity of the method used in abrogating the treaty with Denmark aroused a storm in Congress. Doubt was even raised in the Senate itself. But the controversy was not over whether the Senate had invaded a presidential prerogative. Rather, the issue was whether the treaty should properly have been annulled by the full Congress.

In response to this debate, the Foreign Relations Committee issued a report on April 7, 1856, strongly claiming for the Senate, acting together with the president, competence to terminate a treaty "without the aid or intervention of legislation" by both houses of Congress. Pertinent to the Taiwan treaties, which allow termination after notice by either party, the committee asserted that "where the right to terminate a treaty at discretion is reserved in the treaty itself, such discretion resides in the president *and* Senate."[13]

The committee reasoned as follows:

The whole power to bind the government by treaty is vested in the president and Senate, two-thirds of the senators present concurring. The treaty in question was created by the will of the treaty-making power, and it contained a reservation by which that will should be revoked or its exercise cease on a stipulated notice. It is thus the will of the treaty-making power which is the subject of revocation, and it follows that the revocation is incident to the will.[14]

The committee conceded that in certain cases it would be wise to have the concurrence of the House of Representatives in order to make the decision to annul a treaty appear more impressive upon the other government. Thus, the committee took the position:

Although it be true, as an exercise of constitutional power, that the advice of the Senate alone is sufficient to enable the president to give the notice, it does not follow that the joint assent of the Senate and House of Representatives involves a denial of the separate power of the Senate.[15]

In May 1858, the Foreign Relations Committee boldly reaffirmed its position by changing a proposed joint resolution, authorizing the president to give Denmark the notice required for the termination of a treaty, to a mere Senate resolution.

Congress Rebukes Lincoln

The first time a president openly attempted to terminate a treaty without any prior legislative approval was late in 1864, when President Lincoln notified Great Britain of our withdrawal from the Rush-Baggot Convention regulating naval forces upon the Great Lakes. This episode does not serve as a precedent for unilateral presidential action because Congress rushed to defend its prerogative by passing a joint resolution deeming Lincoln's conduct invalid until ratified and confirmed by Congress. The Executive Branch itself argues the Rush-Baggot accord was an executive agreement, not a treaty, since it originated in an exchange of notes between Canada and the United States. This would further deprive the incident of any value it may have as a precedent.

Senate debate was dominated by senators who argued that the act of the president was wholly invalid until adopted by Congress. The prevailing view was expressed by Senator Garrett Davis of Kentucky, who said: "It is indispensably incumbent and necessary, in order to secure the termination of this treaty, that it shall be terminated, not by the action of the president, but by the action of Congress."[16]

Senator Charles Sumner of Massachusetts, then Chairman of the Foreign Relations Committee, agreed that "the intervention of Congress is necessary to the termination of this treaty." He explained that the legislation embodied the conclusion that since a treaty is a part of the law of the land, it is "to be repealed or set aside only as other law is repealed or set aside: that is, by act of Congress."[17]

Congress did not wait long to reaffirm its position. The joint resolution of January 8, 1865 charged President Lincoln with the duty of communication notice of termination of the Reciprocity Treaty of 1854 with Great Britain. The same legislative formula was used in June 1874, when Congress enacted a law authorizing President Grant to give notice of termination of our Treaty of Commerce and Navigation of 1857 with Belgium.

Two years later, the same president sent a curious message to Congress appearing to acknowledge the need for a legislative role in the termination of treaties while asserting power to decline enforcement of a treaty he thought has been abrogated by the other party.

Grant's message of June 10, 1876, regarding the extradition article of the Treaty of 1842 with Great Britain, said:

It is for the wisdom of Congress to determine whether the article of the treaty relating to extradition is to be any longer regarded obligatory on the government of the United States or as forming part of the supreme law of the land.[18]

286

He added, however:

> Should the attitude of the British government remain unchanged, I shall
> not, without an expression of the wish of Congress that I should do so,
> take any action either in making or granting requisitions for the sur-
> render of fugitive criminals under the treaty of 1842.[19]

At most, this is a precedent for presidential authority to consider a
breach of a treaty as having suspended it by making enforcement impossible, *subject to* the correction of the President's judgment by Congress.

Hayes Vetoes Law, But Concedes Legislative Role

In 1879, President Hayes recognized the joint power of Congress in terminating treaties, although it was in the process of vetoing an Act of Congress. The legislature had passed a statute seeking to require him to abrogate two articles of the Burlingame Treaty of 1868 with China. His veto
rested on the ground that the legislation amended an existing treaty by striking out selected provisions of it. The power to amend treaties, he said, is
"not lodged by the Constitution in Congress, but in the President, by and
with the consent of the Senate."[20]

Hayes also conceded that the "authority of Congress to terminate a
treaty with a foreign power by expressing the will of the nation no longer to
adhere to it is . . . free from controversy under our Constitution."[21] Thus, he
made no claim of power for the executive to annul a treaty without legislative
approval, but rather upheld the traditional joint role of the president and
Senate together to make or modify treaties.

In 1883, Congress passed another joint resolution reaffirming a legislative role in the termination of treaties. This law, the Act of February 26,
1883, flatly directed President Arthur to give notice of the termination of
several articles of an 1871 treaty with Great Britain.

Presidential Interpretation of Congressional Intent

Occasionally, presidents have given notice of our nation's withdrawal
from a treaty on the basis of their interpretation of congressional intent.
This occurs when Congress passes legislation in conflict with a prior
treaty, but does not specifically direct our withdrawal from the treaty.

Since the president cannot enforce two equally valid laws which are in
conflict, he is compelled to select the one which reflects the current will of
Congress. While the president may seem to be using his own power, he
actually is fulfilling his duty to faithfully execute the laws by enforcing the
latest expression of Congress on the subject.

An interesting example of this principle in practice is found in the events leading up to denunciation of certain parts of the 1850 Commercial Convention with Switzerland. Following enactment of the Tariff Act of July 24, 1897, the United States entered into a reciprocity agreement with France under authority specifically granted to the president by that law. The Swiss government promptly claimed a right under the most-favored nation clause of the convention to enjoy the same concessions for Swiss imports as we had given to French products.

We responded that it was our long-continuing policy not to construe the most-favored nation clause as entitling a third government to demand benefits of a special trade agreement purchased by another party with equivalent concessions. In other words, we told the Swiss that they could not receive something for nothing. If we made an exception in their case, it would embarrass us in relations with all other trading partners.

Moreover, the 1897 Tariff Act had reaffirmed this historic policy. Section 3 specifically provided that the president is to negotiate commercial agreements "in which reciprocal and equivalent concessions may be secured in favor of the products and manufactures of the United States." The president lacked authority to conclude agreements in which the other country made no concessions, and if he had yielded to the Swiss demand it would have been out of line with the clear policy of the law.

Thus, in the face of Switzerland's refusal to renegotiate the contested articles of the agreement, the State Department notified her that the provisions were arrested. Although the State Department would later claim that this action served as a precedent for independent presidential power, it would have been inconsistent with the trade policy set by Congress in 1897 law if Switzerland had been granted privileged treatment without making any compensating concessions. In any event, President McKinley did not act in the total absence of any pertinent supporting statute as proponents of abrogating the defense treaty with Taiwan are urging President Carter to do.

Taft Seeks Ratification

Another action mistakenly asserted in support of executive treaty-breaking is the effort of President Taft to head off passage by Congress of what he considered an inflammatory resolution calling for abrogation of the Commercial Treaty of 1832 between the United States and Russia. Disputes had arisen with Russia as early as then over the treatment of Americans of the Jewish faith, and on December 13, 1911, the House of Representatives passed a strongly-worded joint resolution demanding termination of the treaty. In order to beat action by the Senate, President Taft informed Russia on December 15 of our intention to terminate the treaty.

On December 18, the president dutifully gave notice of his action to the Senate "as a part of the treaty-making power of this government, with a view to its ratification and approval."[22] He openly recognized the need for the Senate and the president to act together in order to end an existing treaty and made no claim that his diplomatic notice would have any validity without legislative approval.

Both houses of Congress passed a joint resolution, which the president signed on December 21, just three days after his message to the Senate. The House vote was 301 to 1, and the Senate vote was unanimous, proving that the president's advance notice to Russia was a concession to recognized congressional power, rather than a sign of independent authority of the president.

Wilson Challenges Congress, But Concedes Joint Role

Congress again asserted its power in the Seamen's Act of March 5, 1915. This law ordered President Wilson to notify several countries of the termination of all articles in treaties and conventions of the United States "in conflict with this act." The notices were duly given and the authority of Congress to impose this obligation on the president was upheld by the Supreme Court in a case discussed below. Twenty-five treaties were affected.

Then, in the Merchant Marine Act of 1920, Congress directed President Wilson to give blanket notice of the termination of all provisions in treaties which imposed any restriction on the right of the United States to vary its duties on imports, depending upon whether the carrier vessels were domestic or foreign. This time President Wilson rebuffed the legislature by announcing that he must distinguish between the power of Congress to enact a substantive law inconsistent with entire treaties and the power to call piecemeal for the violation of parts of treaties. This law was not an effort to terminate treaties, he contended, but to modify them, which Congress could not do.[23]

A memorandum prepared by Secretary of State Hughes for President Harding in October 1921 also conceded the power of Congress to terminate entire treaties if it so provided in clear and unambiguous language. While Congress had called only for a partial termination in the Merchant Marine Act, the law would have the practical effect of a total termination. If Congress actually intended to abrogate entire treaties, Hughes reasoned, it must say so in plain language.[24]

The positions taken by Presidents Wilson and Harding were a refusal to interpret a law as conveying an intention by Congress to violate numerous treaties outright. There was no presidential denial of the power of Congress to direct the abrogation of treaties when "its intention is unequivocally expressed," and especially absent was any claim for the president of a power to terminate treaties without the shared responsibility of the Congress.[25]

Evidence of President Wilson's recognition of the essential role of Congress in the treaty annulment process is found in the fact that he first sought the advice and consent of the Senate before attempting to withdraw from the International Sanitary Convention of 1903. Only after two-thirds of the Senate present resolved to "advise and consent to the denunciation of the said convention" on May 26, 1921, by which time Harding had become president, did the United States give notice of its intention to withdraw.

IV
TERMINATING TREATIES: THE MODERN PRACTICE

This brings us up to more recent practice, some of which at first impression may appear to break with the almost universal prior practice of terminating treaties, and giving notice of intent to terminate, only following legislative approval or ratification. Starting in 1927, there are nine instances in which presidents have given notice of the termination of treaties without receiving accompanying congressional authority or seeking ratification.

Upon close examination, however, the recent record does not support an untrammeled power of the president to annul any treaty he wishes. In two instances the notice of termination was withdrawn and the United States did not denounce the treaties. Two other treaties were abrogated because they were inconsistent with more recent legislation of Congress, and one was plainly superseded by our obligations under a later treaty. The remaining four appear to have been annulled or suspended due to a fundamental change in conditions or after it became impossible to effectively carry them out. In addition, there are five recent instances where notice has been given pursuant to Acts of Congress.

The following treaties are involved:

In 1927, President Coolidge gave notice that the 1925 Convention for Prevention of Smuggling with Mexico was terminated. At the time, United States relations with Mexico were the subject of emotional debate in Congress regarding alleged religious persecution against American Catholics and the confiscation of American-owned agricultural and oil lands in Mexico. In fact, President Coolidge accused Mexico of smuggling arms and munitions to revolutionists in Nicaragua and warned publicly of the lack of order in Mexico. In the disruptive situation of the period, it appears to have been impossible to implement the convention.

In 1933, President Franklin Roosevelt gave notice of termination of an extradition treaty with Greece. But the notice was withdrawn and the treaty was not abrogated. The incident was triggered because Greece had refused to extradite an individual accused of fraud. Thus, the president's proposed action was based on the fact that the treaty had already been voided by breach of the other party.

Also in 1933, President Roosevelt terminated the 1927 Tariff Convention as having a restrictive effect on the National Industrial Recovery Act of 1933. Then, in 1936, he terminated the 1871 Treaty of Commerce with Italy because its provisions would limit the president's ability to carry out the

Trade Agreements Act of June 1934. In both these cases the treaties were inconsistent with prevailing legislation.

In 1939, President Roosevelt notified Japan of our nation's intent to terminate the Commercial Treaty of 1911. Although the Department of State argued broadly that "the power to denounce a treaty inheres in the President of the United States in his capacity as chief executive of a sovereign state," President Roosevelt's authority clearly stemmed out of acts of war by Japan toward allied nations.[26] Our cancellation of the Commercial Treaty was an integral part of American policy to "quarantine" Japanese aggression against China by cutting off shipments of needed commodities, such as planes, parts and gasoline. In fact, it was persuasively argued in the Senate that the president was *compelled* to denounce the 1911 Treaty with Japan because of our obligations under a later treaty, the Nine Power Agreement, committing the United States to respect the territorial integrity of China. After the invasion of China by Japan, we would have aided in the violation of that obligation by adhering to the Japanese treaty.[27]

On October 3, 1939, the State Department gave notice of our intention to suspend operation of the London Naval Treaty of 1936. Our stated reason was the changed circumstances resulting from the earlier suspension by several other parties to the treaty. In view of the state of war then existing in Europe it was impossible to carry out a treaty that was supposed to limit naval armaments and promote the exchange of information concerning naval construction.

The next precedent occurred in August 1941 when the International Load Line Convention governing ocean shipping was suspended by President Roosevelt. He relied on the opinion of acting Attorney General Biddle that, as in the case of the Naval Treaty, fundamental changes in the circumstances created an impossibility of performance. Accordingly, Roosevelt suspended the convention for the duration of the war emergency because of aggression then being waged by Germany, Italy, Japan and the Soviet Union.

It is interesting that the opinion of the acting Attorney General declared: "It is not proposed that the United States denounce the convention . . . nor that it be otherwise abrogated. Consequently, action by the Senate or by the Congress is not required."[28]

From this, it is obvious that the incident cannot be considered as support for independent presidential action. To the contrary, it appears to be an admission by the acting Attorney General that some legislative approval is normal for the abrogation of a treaty, even where the treaty itself provides for notice of termination, as the Load Line Convention did. Biddle said legislative action was required if Roosevelt chose to act under the notice provision, as President Carter has done.

A recent, but not the latest, assertion of the abrogation power by Congress occurred in 1951. In that year, Congress enacted the Trade Agreements Extension Act instructing President Truman to terminate trade concessions to communist countries. Most of them were granted by executive agreements, but two, those with Poland and Hungary, involved formal treaties. The required notices were promptly given by President Truman.

A fundamental change in circumstances resulting in basic change of conditions, if not an actual impossibility of performance was again invoked by the United States in announcing our withdrawal in 1955 from the 1923 Convention on Uniformity of Nomenclature for the Classification of Merchandise. The U.S. notice specifically observed that the convention had been "rendered inapplicable" since a fundamental component, the Brussels nomenclature of 1913, had itself "become outdated."

An aborted incident occurred in November 1965 when the United States announced its planned withdrawal from the Warsaw Convention relating to recovery of damages by international air passengers who suffer death or personal injury. One day before the effective date of the withdrawal, the United States withdrew its notice. At least two legal commentators reacted with publication of articles condemning the power grab by President Johnson as unconstitutional.[29]

Next, we furnished notice of terminating the 1902 commercial convention with Cuba. This step was an integral part of the U.S. economic embargo of Castro's Cuba, declared on February 2, 1962, in which we were joined by the Organization of American States. The notice, given August 21, 1962, preceded President Kennedy's naval blockade of Cuba by only eight weeks.

The president acted under provisions of the Foreign Assistance Act of 1961 and the Export Control Act of 1948. Also, he had ample authority to impose a trade embargo under the Trading with the Enemy Act and Mutual Assistance Act of 1954, known as the Battle Act. Notice of terminating the commercial convention was a mere formality mandated by a national policy authorized and sanctioned by Congress.

Termination of the convention also was in accordance with the Punta del Este Agreement of January 1962 by which the Ministers of Foreign Affairs of most American nations resolved, by application of the Inter-American Treaty of Reciprocal Assistance of 1947, to embargo trade with Cuba in arms and implements of war of every kind and to study extending the embargo to other items. Article 8 of the 1947 treaty specifically contemplated such a "partial or complete interruption of economic relations."

Finally, Congress may be said to have ratified the decision in September 1962, if any ratification were needed, by enacting the joint resolution known as the Cuban Resolution. This legislation recognized broad authority in the president to take whatever means may be necessary to prevent Cuba from "exporting its aggressive purposes" in the hemisphere and to prevent establishment of a Soviet military base. Thus, the termination was at one and the same time ratified and authorized by legislation and in accordance with a treaty later in time.

In the Byrd Amendment of 1971, Congress repealed our government's obligation under the United Nations Charter to carry out a U.N. Security

Council resolution putting an embargo on imports of Rhodesian chrome. But in 1977 Congress authorized President Carter to restore the ban.

The most recent incidents of treaty termination followed enactment of the Fishery Conservation and Management Act of 1976. This law establishes a two hundred mile-limit fishery conservation zone within which we shall exercise exclusive management authority over nearly all fish and extends our exclusive authority even beyond the zone.

Section 202(b) of the law directs the Secretary of State to initiate the renegotiation of any treaty which pertains to fishing within these management areas and is "in any manner inconsistent with the purposes, policy, or provisions of this act, in order to conform such treaty to such purposes, policy, and provisions." This section also declares such treaty, in accordance with its provisions, if such treaty is not so renegotiated within a reasonable period of time after such date of enactment."

Pursuant to this express statement of national policy by Congress, the Department of State has given notice of our withdrawal from the 1949 International Convention for the Northwest Atlantic Fisheries and the 1952 International Convention for the High Seas Fisheries of the North Pacific Ocean. Notice regarding the former convention was given on June 22, 1976, and notice regarding the latter agreement was made on February 10, 1977. These two annulments, the latest on record, may fairly be classified as having occurred pursuant to specific congressional authorization and direction.

A number of other treaties have been terminated by ratification of new treaties on the same subject. This form of treaty abrogation does not have bearing on purported executive independence, except that it obviously follows affirmative action by the Senate.

None of this type of treaties, usually covering technical subjects, have been included in the above listing, and they are mentioned here only to prevent confusion arising from a failure to identify them. In these cases, the Senate in effect advises and consents to the termination of one treaty and its substitution by another in the very act of agreeing to ratification of the new treaty, it being a well-settled diplomatic practice that a later treaty supersedes or revises an earlier one on the same subject.[30]

Historical Usage Demands Legislative Participation
in the Abrogation of Treaties

The historical usage described above upholds the general position asserted by the late Professor Edward Corwin, one of this century's foremost authorities on the Constitution, who wrote:

All in all, it appears that legislative precedent, which moreover is generally supported by the attitude of the executive, sanctions the proposition that the power of terminating the international compacts to which the United States is party belongs, as a prerogative of sovereignty, to Congress alone.[31]

The only clarification I would add to Professor Corwin's statement is that the abrogation of a treaty also can be made by the exercise of the treaty-making power itself, meaning the president together with two-thirds of the Senate, or possibly, if Congress goes along, by prompt congressional ratification of a presidential initiative.

Also, it may be conceded for purposes of the situation at hand, our treaty relations with the Republic of China, that history indicates the president may, if Congress raises no objection, determine whether or not a treaty (1) has been superseded by a later law or treaty inconsistent with or clearly intended to revise an earlier one, (2) has already been abrogated because of its violation by the other party, or (3) cannot be carried out because conditions essential to its continued effectiveness no longer exist and the change is not the result of our own action.

Exceptions Are Not Applicable to the Republic of China

It is important to note that none of the exceptions recorded above applies to the Republic of China. She has faithfully adhered to all our treaties with her and has not given us any cause to consider them void.

Nor could impossibility of performance be raised as an excuse, because we would be the party at fault. As proposed by the sympathizers of Communist China, our break in treaty relations with Taiwan would follow recognition of the mainland regime. The basis for our annulment of the treaty would be our own voluntary action in breaking diplomatic ties with Taiwan.

It is clear that international law forbids a nation from raising a change in circumstances as the ground for terminating a treaty where that change results from an action of the party invoking it. This is spelled out in the 1969 Vienna Convention on the Law of Treaties, which the United States has signed, but not yet ratified.

Article 61 of that Convention reads:

Impossibility of performance may not be invoked by a party as a ground for terminating, withdrawing from or suspending the operation of a treaty if the impossibility is the result of a breach by that party either of an obligation under the treaty or of any other international obligation owed to any other party to the treaty.

Article 62 of the same Convention also provides that a "fundamental change of circumstances may not be invoked as a ground for terminating or withdrawing from a treaty . . . if the fundamental change is the result of a breach by the party invoking it."

Thus, it would not only be a dishonor to the United States and a violation of the Constitution if the president should unilaterally break our treaties with Taiwan, but it would be a violation of international law as well.

In the words of the Department of State itself at an earlier time in our history: "Such a course would be wholly irreconcilable with the historical respect which the United States has shown for its international engagements, and would falsify every profession of all belief in the binding force and the reciprocal obligation of treaties in general."[32]

V

TERMINATING TREATIES: THE NATURE OF UNITED STATES-REPUBLIC OF CHINA RELATIONS

This leaves the question of whether a treaty can be entered into with a government that we do not recognize. If, for the sake of argument, the United States should break relations with Taiwan, can we still have treaties with her?

Yes, we can. Although we have never before withdrawn recognition from any friendly country, we have had dealings in the past with powers whom we have not recognized so long as they have exercised practical control over a particular area. Mainland China is a case in point.

The past international experience of our own and other governments bears out the validity of this practice. For example, the Netherlands at one and the same time recognized the official government of Spain while entering into formal treaty relations with the government of the Franco regime in 1938. And, in the 1950s, Egypt concluded several treaties with East Germany and Communist China without recognizing those countries.

As to the United States, we not only currently have a liaison office in Communist China, but we dealt with the communist regime once to negotiate the armistice in Korea and again during the 1954 Geneva Conference on reunification of Korea. Also, in 1962, the United States concluded an international agreement on Laos to which Communist China was an official party.

Other precedents involving the United States included the Postal Conventions of 1924 and 1929 to which both we and the Soviet Union became parties, even though the United States did not then recognize the USSR. Then there is a well-known political treaty, the Kellogg-Briand Pact of 1929 for the renunciation of war. The United States, which did not recognize the Soviet Union, nevertheless agreed to invite her to become a party. We even went so far as to send Russia a diplomatic note reminding her of Russian obligations under the pact, again prior to having diplomatic relations with her.

Another example is the Nuclear Weapons Test Ban Treaty of 1963, which appoints three depositories for new members in order to enable both Communist China and Taiwan, and East Germany, to become parties along with nations that do not recognize them. The United States, which does not recognize Communist China, extended an invitation to it to come into the agreement.

The question of having dealings with a non-recognized power was examined in the context of our China policy by Stanford University law professor Victor Li in a 1977 study sponsored by the Carnegie Endowment for International Peace. Professor Li concluded that there are no legal impediments to considering Communist China as the *de jure* government of China, while the Taiwan authorities are regarded as being in *de facto* administrative control of the territory and population of Taiwan.

If the Taiwan authorities were regarded as having practical power over a territorial entity, whether or not it is called a state, Professor Li writes that international law contemplates the possibility "that treaties applying to territory actually controlled by Taiwan would remain in force even after withdrawal of *de jure* recognition."[33]

Professor Li concludes his paper by specifically declaring:

> International law does not *require* that treaties affecting only the territories controlled by the Taiwan authorities must lapse. On the contrary, there is strong support for protecting on-going relations, especially those involving commercial affairs and private rights.[34]

In his authoritative book, *Non-Recognition and Treaty Relations,* Dr. Bernard R. Bot agrees that derecognition of a government does not automatically suspend or terminate treaties previously entered into by that government. To the contrary, he argues:

> A non-recognized state can be a party to international agreements provided that its *de facto* authorities carry on, even if only as agents, the external relations and can avail themselves of the resources of the territory and control the population if necessary, for the purpose of observing treaty obligations assumed.[35]

Moreover, Dr. Bot finds "that non-recognition of states and governments does not necessarily impede the latter's capacity to conclude bilateral treaties."[36] He adds, "It becomes increasingly clear that the criterion for participation in multilateral treaties is no longer the recognition status, but the issue of political desirability."[37]

Thus no impediments exist in international law which would prevent the United States from dealing both with the People's Republic of China as the legally recognized government in China and with the Republic of China on Taiwan as the separate authorities in control of a portion of the Chinese state.

The Recognition Power Differs from Treaty Abrogation

Another matter to be resolved is whether the recognition power itself gives the president the power to terminate treaties. The one power does not follow from the other, although Alexander Hamilton once argued that in special circumstances they do.

In the course of his famous debates with James Madison over the constitutionality of President Washington's Proclamation of Neutrality among warring France and Britain in 1793, Hamilton, writing as Pacificus, claimed:

The right of the executive to receive ambassadors and other public ministers . . . includes that of judging, the case of a revolution of government in a foreign country, whether the new rulers are competent organs of the national will, and ought to be recognized, or not; which, where a treaty antecedently exists between the United States and such nation, involves the power of continuing or suspending its operation. For until the new government is *acknowledged,* the treaties between the nations, so far at least as regards *public* rights, are of course suspended.[38]

Hamilton was writing of a situation where only one government, that of the rebels, survived a revolution. He was not considering the situation where there are two competing powers demanding recognition, one representing the former legitimate authorities and the other the insurrectionists. In particular, Hamilton made no reference to a setting in which the United States had continued recognition of the original authorities following a revolution and had even entered into a treaty with that same government after the revolution, as is true in the case of the Republic of China.

Far from this being an instance where all treaties between the nations were suspended, as in Hamilton's supposition, here the mutual defense treaty was concluded years after the revolution. For us to renounce that treaty by switching recognition after a quarter of a century's adherence to it would be a new development of our own making, not an immediate and unavoidable result of a revolution. Thus, Hamilton's argument is inapplicable to present Sino-American relations.

It would be sheer legal gimmickry for anyone to argue that the recognition power carries with it the power to abrogate our treaties with the Republic of China. It might as well be claimed that recognition includes the power to make formal treaties independently of the Senate.

As discussed above, should the United States now decide to drop relations with the Republic of China, the question of whether treaties and other international agreements with her would continue in effect would be left up to mutual agreement between the United States and the still *de facto* government of Taiwan.

Thus, it is clear that should we switch embassies from Taipei to Peking, no rule or tradition of domestic or international law would require the president to consider treaties with the authorities on Taiwan as having lapsed. Rather this would become a political decision to be determined by political reasons, not by legal theory or grounds. And since, as we have seen, the Constitution demands a legislative role in such a political decision, a presidential act of derecognition could not annul those treaties absent the separate, concurring decision of Congress or the Senate.

The Removal Power Cannot Be Equated with the Treaty Termination Power

At a recent Washington, D.C. seminar on China, the main speaker, one of the leading proponents of immediate recognition of the mainland China regime, attempted to justify his opinion that the president may terminate a treaty without the consent of the Senate or Congress by drawing a curious analogue to the removal power. Since it is well settled that the president can remove cabinet members and other high officials of the executive branch, who have been appointed "by and with the advice and consent of the Senate," without returning to the Senate for its further consent, so it is claimed that the president can remove treaties which have been made "by and with the advice and consent of the Senate."

This line of argument is totally unsatisfactory for the following reasons. First, it is nonsense to equate the president's relationship to subordinate officials of his own administration with the relationship of this country to other sovereign nations. Allowing the president to dismiss officers whom the Constitution has plainly put under him is one thing. But allowing the president to discard a formal treaty entered into between our government and our legal peer under international law, another sovereignty, is quite a different matter. There is simply no factual ground on which to make a parallel between the two powers.

Second, unlike the case of the removal power, there is a specific constitutional provision which conflicts with any inference of the power to terminate treaties. As we have seen, the president is directed by the Constitution to faithfully execute the laws. Another provision of the Constitution tells us that a treaty is a law. Thus, the president would run afoul of express provisions of the Constitution if he should attempt to unilaterally terminate a treaty. The novel doctrine that a power to annul a treaty can be implied where it runs squarely into express provisions of the Constitution on the basis that a power to remove officers has been implied where there are no conflicting express provisions of the Constitution cannot be sustained.

Third, the need for application of the checks and balances feature of the Constitution is still acute in the case of the proposed termination of treaties, but is not felt in the case of removing executive officers. The presidential power of removing officials who are placed under his direction is not surprising. The power aids in the smooth performance of his conduct of the government without the potential sabotage or disruption of his program caused by inferior officers who disagree with his policy or are discovered to be incompetent.

In contrast, his decision to annul a treaty or allow a treaty to lapse is a decision of the highest national importance. Instead of aiding in carrying out the laws, it does just the opposite. It has the effect of breaking or negating a

298

law. Such a decision is surely the kind of public action which the framers did not want taken until it had received great deliberation. The termination of a formal compact with another sovereign nation is exactly the type of situation where the checks and balances doctrine has its fullest force and effect. The added deliberation called for, if the decision must be sent to the Senate for its advice and consent before its completion, offers security to the people that an action of major consequences will not be taken lightly or without an opportunity for adequate consideration. Thus, the removal power is not comparable to the treaty termination power.

Lack of Judicial Precedents

To this point I have emphasized the clear logic of the Constitution itself and the lessons to be drawn from historical usage. Judicial precedents have not been cited because there simply are no court holdings squarely deciding a conflict between the president and the Senate or Congress over the treaty abrogation power.

What few related cases exist can be discussed briefly. First, there is a 1913 Supreme Court decision, *Charlton v. Kelly*,[39] which some commentators argue supports a discretion for the president to interpret whether a treaty is void in circumstances where the other party violates it. But the case has no application to the situation where the president, without legislative approval, seeks to declare a treaty void when no breach has occurred. Moreover, *Charlton* involved an extradition treaty with Italy which neither the executive nor Congress wanted to void. Since the treaty was not denounced, the case is not even a decisive ruling for the single situation where a breach occurs.

A second case is *Van der Weyde v. Ocean Transport Company* in 1936.[40] Here, the Supreme Court decided that since Congress had directed the president by the Seamen's Act of 1915 to give notice of the termination of treaty provisions in conflict with that act, "it was incumbent" upon him to determine the inconsistency between the law and a treaty with Norway.

The Court expressly avoided any question "as to the authority of the executive in the absence of congressional action, or of action by the treaty-making power, to denounce a treaty."[41] But it did appear to recognize the power of Congress to require the president to interpret whether a treaty is inconsistent with a statute.

A third case involving treaty abrogation is *Clark v. Allen*,[42] where the Supreme Court examined the question of whether the outbreak of war necessarily suspends or abrogates treaties. On its face, this 1947 case involved a construction of national policy expressed in an act of Congress, the Trading with the Enemy Act.

Although it is *dicta,* the pertinent part of the opinion for our analysis comes from the favorable use by the Court of a statement made by then New York State Court Judge Cardozo: "[The] president and Senate may denounce the treaty, and thus terminate its life. Congress may enact an inconsistent rule, which will control the action of the courts."[43]

By favorably quoting this interpretation of the treaty abrogation power, the Supreme Court seems to have approved the proposition that either the Senate or Congress must participate in the annulment of a treaty.

Two other voices from the bench add weight to the power of Congress in this field. In an opinion he published with the case of *Ware v. Hylton* in 1796, Supreme Court Justice Iredell twice emphasized his belief that Congress alone has "authority under our government" of declaring a treaty vacated by reason of the breach by the other party.[44] Although his statements were *dicta* to the Court's decision, they are significant as an eighteenth-century understanding of the annulment power by one of the original members of the first Supreme Court.

In his *Commentaries on the Constitution,* Justice Story declared that the treaty power "will be found to partake more of the legislative than of the executive character."[45] He also explained it is essential that treaties "should have the obligation and force of a law, that they may be executed by the judicial power and be obeyed like other laws. This will not prevent them from being cancelled or abrogated by the nation upon grave and suitable occasions; for it will not be disputed that *they are subject to the legislative power, and may be repealed, like other laws, at its pleasure."*[46] (Emphasis added.)

From what few judicial pronouncements exist, there is no basis for executive power over treaty abrogation and some, but not definitive, authority for congressional power. Although the issue is ultimately a legal one, the answer lies in history and the Constitution, not in earlier cases.

Breach of Treaties with the Republic of China Would Affect Private Rights

Not only the mutual defense treaty is involved in the scheme to allow our treaties with the Republic of China to lapse. The 1977 Department of State publication *Treaties in Force* lists at least fifty-nine treaties and other agreements now in effect between the two nations. If the United States were to adopt the approach put forward on behalf of the Communist Chinese, every one of these agreements would fall, not just the formal treaties.

It should be observed that this group of international agreements concerns such important subjects as shoe and textile quotas, aviation landing rights, tariffs on imports and exports, guarantees of American investments of private capital in Taiwan, safeguard of nuclear materials, and protection of rights of American citizens located in Taiwan.

It is irresponsible to propose that all these agreements shall be simultanously extinguished upon recognition of Communist China, yet this is the logical extension of the policy being urged upon President Carter. As indicated, many of these agreements establish rights for private individuals and businesses. Considering them as having lapsed would create serious political and economic consequences and open a flood of litigation by private parties whose interests are adversely affected by such a government policy.

Impact Upon Other Treaties

Another potential implication of presidential discretion to void treaties which has not been considered, publicly at least, by proponents of the concept is its effect upon the basic meaning of the rule of law to a free people.

If a president can violate any treaty he wants, what becomes of the order and stability in which law is supposed to operate?

If a president, independently of Congress, can withdraw from the Universal Copyright Convention, for example, what happens to private rights that were protected by this convention?

If a president chooses to violate the Outer Space Treaty, which prohibits our nation from placing in orbit around the earth any objects carrying nuclear weapons, what effect would this have upon world stability?

The fact that the defense treaty with Taiwan includes a provision regarding duration in no way adds to presidential power. A moment's reflection will confirm that judgment. Remember, the defense treaty with Taiwan does not stand alone. Nearly every treaty this nation has with other countries contains a provision similar to the one in our treaty with Taiwan.

It is true that section X of the 1954 treaty states: "Either party may terminate it one year after notice has been given to the other party." It is also true that this provision is repeated in similar terms in nearly all our bilateral or multilateral treaties. For example, NATO, the Test Ban Treaty, the Statute of the International Atomic Energy Agency, the Nuclear Non-Proliferation Treaty, the Biological Weapons Convention, the Universal Copyright Convention, and the Outer Space Treaty all contain provisions expressly laying down agreed ways the parties can terminate them with one year's or less notice having been given to the other parties. If the Taiwan defense treaty were interpreted as allowing the president alone to provide such notice, each of the above treaties would be hostage to the sole discretion of the executive. This news would undoubtedly come as a surprise to the Senate which has advised and consented to each of these documents without being informed of any such design.

Without fear of contradiction, I can predict an uproar among my colleagues, for example, should any president assert power to unilaterally, without giving an opportunity for prior deliberation in the Senate or Congress, violate the Non-Proliferation Treaty by transferring nuclear warheads to South Africa.

The truth is that, were the shoe reversed, many Americans who are falling all over themselves to give in to every demand by Communist China would be the first to condemn unilateral presidential action of a kind they do not like. They have not thought through the possible implications of the legal theory they are asking President Carter to adopt, and if they would, the fallacy in their proposal would be obvious.

Moreover, an examination of each of the formal treaties described above which have been denounced or terminated by the United States in the past reveals that nearly all included provisions allowing withdrawal upon notice.[47] The fact that presidents have generally interpreted provisions regarding duration as still requiring them to seek congressional or at least senatorial approval before giving notice to the other party proves that inclusion of such a provision in a treaty does not change the domestic constitutional arrangement of powers between the executive and Congress.

As shown above, Congress has heretofore collaborated in the termination of over forty treaties by enacting a joint resolution, by agreeing to a Senate resolution, or by act of Congress. Congress obviously believed it retained a role in the treaty abrogation process in each of these instances, all but three of which involved the annulment of treaties having duration provisions. There is no record to the contrary showing that the existence of such provisions in treaties has any relation to the powers of the president and Congress.

It may belabor the subject to point out the obvious, but treaties never say they can be terminated after notice given by "the president" or "head of state" of any government. Rather, the customary phrase specifies that when notice is made it shall be given by one of the "parties" to the treaty.

The term "party" means the government of the state or international personality involved, which compels a reference to the constitutional processes of the government in order to determine the manner in which the decision to give notice shall be made. In our case, this brings us back to the fact that under the Constitution the power is a joint one shared by the president and Senate or Congress.

VI
CONCLUSION

In conclusion, no president acting alone can abrogate, or give notice of the intention to abrogate, our existing treaties with the government on Taiwan. Of course, neither the Senate, nor the Congress, will agree to dropping those treaties.

It is the clear instruction of history that the president cannot give valid notice of an intention to withdraw from a treaty, let alone void a treaty in violation of the formalities required by any provision it may contain regarding duration, without the approval or ratification of two-thirds of the Senate or a majority of both houses of Congress. Any president who would seek to thwart this constitutional mandate runs the risk of impeachment.

This is not a threat. It is a simple statement of fact which those who are unwisely urging this course of action upon the president should understand. They apparently do not know the consequence of what they are asking the president to do.

For it must be clearly understood that the check of impeachment is one of the safeguards provided by the Founding Fathers against political offenses, such as an irresponsible abuse by a president of a constitutional discretion.[48] In fact, a study made by the Library of Congress in 1974 on the abrogation of treaties concludes by observing that where a conflict arises between the president and the Senate or Congress over the question of abrogation of a treaty, and the president acts contrary to the wishes of the Senate or Congress, the president "might be impeached."[49]

This answers the too clever reasoning of the legal advisor of the Department of State which surfaced in a 1936 memorandum to President Roosevelt. His argument contended that the failure of the Congress or the Senate to approve the action of the president in giving notice of intention to terminate a treaty would be of no avail because once the notice is given, the foreign government concerned may decline to accept a withdrawal of such a notice.[50] What the argument failed to note is that even if the foreign government is entitled and wants to rely on such a notice without inquiring into the constitutional authority of the president, this does not change the domestic constitutional situation of the president in relation to the Senate or Congress.[51] The president is still answerable to the Constitution and accountable to the Congress and people.

NOTES

1. The *Washington Post* of August 17, 1977 reported that officials of the State Department had assisted in the preparation of Senator Kennedy's speech.

2. U.S. Bureau of the Census, *Highlights of U.S. Export and Import Trade* (December 1977). Imports based on FAS value.

3. For a broader analysis of the significance of relations between the U.S. and the Republic of China see Edwin J. Feulner, Jr., ed., *China—the Turning Point* (Washington, D.C.: Council on American Affairs, 1976).

4. Louis Henkin, *Foreign Affairs and the Constitution* (Mineola, N.Y.: Foundation Press, 1972), p. 169.

5. For example, C. C. Pinckney, a member of the Federal Convention, explained before the South Carolina legislature during the ratification process that South Carolina, "considering the valuable produce it has to export, is particularly interested in maintaining the sacredness of treaties"—J. Elliott, *Debates in the Several State Conventions on the Adoption of the Federal Constitution* (5 vols., Philadelphia: J. B. Lippincott, 1861), IV, p. 279. [Hereinafter cited as Elliot's *Debates*.]

6. Robert G. McCloskey, ed., *The Works of James Wilson* (2 vols., Cambridge: Belknap Press of Harvard University Press, 1967), I, pp. 166-167.

7. Joseph Story, *Commentaries on the Constitution* (3 vols., Boston: Hilliard, Gray & Co., 1833), I, p. 359.

8. *Ibid.*, p. 360.

9. *Senate Manual*, S. Doc. No. 93-1 (1973), p. 560.

10. Philip R. Fendall, ed., *Letters and Other Writings of James Madison* (4 vols., Philadelphia: J. B. Lippincott, 1865). I, p. 524.

11. Act of July 7, 1798; 1 Stat. 578.

12. 22 Ct. Cl. 404 (1887).

13. S. Rep. No. 97, 34th Congress, 1st Session (1856). Reprinted in S. Doc. No. 231, pp. 107-108; emphasis added.

14. *Ibid.*, p. 111.

15. *Ibid.*

16. *The Congressional Globe*, Vol. 35, p. 313 (1865).

17. *Ibid.*, p. 312.

18. James D. Richardson, *A Compilation of the Messages and Papers of the Presidents* (20 vols., New York: Bureau of National Literature) IX, p. 4327 (1897).

19. *Ibid.*

20. *Ibid.*, pp. 4466-4472.

21. *Ibid.*, p. 4470.

22. Reprinted in G. Hackworth, *Digest of International Law* (8 vols., Washington, D.C.: U.S. Government Printing Office, 1940-1944). V, p. 320.

23. *Ibid.*, pp. 323-324.

24. *Ibid.*, pp. 324-326.

25. *Ibid.*, p. 325.

26. *Ibid.*, p. 331.

27. See remarks by Senator Schwellenback, *Congressional Record* (84th Congress, 1939), pp. 10750-10787.

28. Reprinted in Hackworth, *op. cit.*, pp. 338-339.

29. J. Riggs, "Termination of Treaties by the Executive Without Congressional Approval: The Case of the Warsaw Convention," *Journal of Air Law and Commerce*, Vol. 32, p. 526 (1966) and "Presidential Amendment and Termination of Treaties: The Case of the Warsaw Convention," *Univesity of Chicago Law Review*, Vol. 34, p. 580 (1967).

30. On December 15, 1978, the State Department issued a memorandum claiming 12 precedents for presidential treaty termination. The memo is obviously a desperate attempt to justify President Carter's announcement the same day that he will terminate the 1954 defense treaty by 1980. The memo does not cite a single defense treaty as ever having been cancelled by notice, nor do any of the incidents listed bear any resemblance to the present case.

31. Edward S. Corwin, *The President's Control of Foreign Relations* (Princeton: Princeton University Press, 1917), p. 115.

32. See Department of State press release of September 24, 1920, reprinted in Hackworth, *op. cit.*, p. 323.

33. Victor H. Li, *De-Recognizing Taiwan: The Legal Problems* (Washington, D.C.: Carnegie Endowment for International Peace, 1977), p. 33.

34. *Ibid.*, p. 34.

35. Bernard R. Bot, *Non-Recognition and Treaty Relations* (Leyden, A. W. Sijthoff; Dobbs Ferry, New York, Oceana Publications, 1968), p. 208.

36. *Ibid.*, p. 104.

37. *Ibid.*, p. 123.

38. Reprinted in W. M. McClure, *International Executive Agreements* (New York: Columbia University Press, 1941), pp. 305-306.

39. 229 U.S., p. 447 (1913).

40. 297 U.S. p. 114 (1936).

41. *Ibid.*, p. 118.

42. 331 U.S., p. 503.

43. *Ibid.*, p. 509.

44. 3 U.S., pp. 199, 260, 261 (1796).

45. Story, *op. cit.*, p. 366.

46. *Ibid.*, p. 695. *United States v. Pink*, 315 U.S., p. 203 (1941), upholding presidential power to enter into an executive agreement assigning certain Soviet claims to the United States incident to recognition of Russia, contains sweeping *dicta* regarding the recognition power, but the case in no way relates to presidential voiding of formal treaties and has been omitted from the above discussion. *Pink* involved the president's power to conclude an international agreement without the consent of the Senate, exactly the opposite of the present situation where it is proposed he break a treaty which has been ratified after he has received the advice and consent of the Senate. In brief, the Court held that the United States was entitled by the assignment to the New York assets of an insurance company nationalized by the Soviets, thereby protecting claims of American citizens against foreign creditors of the company. Unlike *Pink*, where Justice Douglas said the "power to remove such obstacles to full recognition as settlement of claims of our nationals . . . is a modest implied power of the president," here it would be a major action of the gravest international consequences if the president should consider a treaty void where a friendly ally has given no cause and conditions do not render it impossible to perform. Douglas specifically tied his opinion to evidence that it was common practice for presidents to conclude executive agreements, and he also relied on a prior case by the Court which specifically determined that the Soviet assignment was valid. Here, on the other hand, there is no historical record showing that presidents have routinely abrogated treaties by their own power, and there is no prior case recognizing such a power in the president. Also, unlike *Pink*, here a specific provision of the Constitution directs the president to faithfully execute the laws, of which treaties are a part. Surely the president's implied power incident to recognition does not give him the power to repeal an express provision of the Constitution to the contrary.

47. Only the three eighteenth-century treaties with France entirely lacked any duration provision. One other agreement, the International Sanitary Convention of 1903, did not include such a provision in the text, but the process-verbal of the deposit of ratification conferred a right of denunciation.

48. Several of the delegates to state conventions on adopting the Constitution argued that the president was to be subject to impeachment and conviction if he abused his treaty or diplomatic power. Elliot's *Debates*, III, p. 240 (Nicholas); III, p. 516 (Madison); IV, p. 124 (Spaight); IV, p. 276 (E. Rutledge); IV, p. 281 (C. C. Pinckney).

49. V. Bite, "Precedent For U.S. Abrogation of Treaties" (Congressional Research Service, Library of Congress, February 25, 1974), p. 107.

50. Reprinted in Hackworth, *op. cit.*, p. 328.

51. Of course, in the case of the Republic of China, it may be presumed that the authorities would not consider the defense treaty as void, but rather would continue to hold the United States responsible under international law for adhering to its treaty obligations and thereby preserve the opportunity for restoring the treaty to its full effectiveness at any time.

Realities of the
China Trade

Jeremiah Novak*

I
THE LONG VIEW

For the past several months the world has marveled at the opening of China to Western firms as part of the modernization policy that Vice Premier Teng has implemented. Every day we read of new orders for hotels, plants, equipment and joint ventures by China from Western sources. Enthusiasm for the opening of China sometimes runs beyond good sense however, but such enthusiasm is understandable given the change taking place in China.

Nevertheless, while not wishing to take the role of Cassandra and predict that the enthusiasm is misplaced, in these remarks I would like to raise the longer view of the Chinese economy and political scene within the international economy. By taking this longer view my hope is to lay the basis for an honest skepticism about the China trade in the hopes of bringing the subject back down to earth. Hopefully such a longer view will lead to a better program of trade that aids China and the industrialized world over a period of time. Moreover, by doing so I hope to predict some of the news that will appear about China in the next several years.

In this longer view I would like to discuss the effects of the new China trade on China and Taiwan, the effect on other developing countries, the long-term interests of the industrialized countries, the finance of this trade, and some geopolitical-geoeconomic aspects of the trade. With luck, I may be able to integrate these diverse subjects into one theme that says that China is a very poor country that needs modernization, but that the price of this modernization on China and the world may be higher than we all wish to pay unless we can stretch out the time payments over a long enough period. Instant actions and too hasty modernization may lead to chaos and reaction.

Let me begin by saying that China is not the first country that has been

---

*Jeremiah Novak is the Economics columnist of *The Asia Mail*.

opened after being closed for a long period. Asia is full of countries that have gone through relative periods of withdrawal followed by relative periods of openness. Indeed, the whole tidal pattern of history in Asia has seen this phenomenon over and over again, not only in the past two centuries, but in the post-World War II era as well.

Between the seventeenth century, when the Portuguese controlled trade in Macao, and the 1850s, China remained closed to outside penetration. Indeed, the period prior to the British Opium Wars is very similar to the 1949-1976 period when foreigners were ruthlessly excluded. Having lived in Hong Kong in the early 1970s, before Nixon's trip to Peking, I came to admire Father Matteo Ricci, the first modern Westerner who was able to reach the Great Emperor at Peking. His effort reminded me of my attempts to get to the Canton Fair in 1971-1973.

From 1850 to 1949 China remained "open," despite the Taiping and Boxer Rebellions. This was followed by a "closed period" from 1949 to 1976.

Similar "openings" and "closings" characterized Western dealings with Japan. Perry, in 1866, opened Japan. Between 1866 and 1929 Japan remained open. Then Japan closed from 1929 until 1945 when once again it was forced open.

In the post-war era Indonesia and India and Iran have gone through phases of being open and closed. In 1968 Indonesia opened, after sixteen years of Sukarno. India opened up in 1957-1960 and again from 1966-1967, only to close up again in 1968-1974. But in 1977 India began to force out multinational companies, including Coca Cola and IBM. Iran closed itself under Mossadegh and reopened under the Shah in 1952. In 1978 we have seen an uprising that in large part is not opposed as much to modernization as to Westernization. Whether the current revolution in Iran will lead to hostility and closing to the West is unclear.

What these examples show, I think, is that China's current opening must be taken in a relatively long-range context and seen as moving between ying and yang where, in a given cycle, we often see both extremes as well as a happy medium position. We now seem to be at an extreme of openness that may well be, over the medium term, moved to a more central position. And we can expect to see perhaps a period of reaction set in over a longer period. Therefore, although we shall touch on this below, I would like to caution all observers of China, including the breathless reporters of the networks and wire services, to keep in mind that what opens up can close.

Secondly, there is an unconscious tendency in the West to confuse modernization with "Westernization." The former term relates to science, technology and technique, which, depending on how it is used or for what ends it is used, can be either Eastern or Western. The latter term refers to seeing in Asians a Western way of thinking and acting. In dealing with China, the Japanese are more conscious with this distinction than we in the U.S. are.

Hopefully, although I doubt such a caution will be heeded, our policy toward China should end in modernizing China, not Westernizing it. By stressing the former and eschewing the latter, the forces in favor of modernization will not set off a reaction by Chinese nationalists who see the forces indigenous in modernization as tools or lackeys of the West. Our goal should not be to make China a replica of the West, but rather to allow China to modernize in a Chinese way that often may not please Westerners.

This is no minor point. One can almost form an aphorism that we can call Novak's Rule which states: If China's elite Westernize themselves instead of modernize, a period of intense reaction will follow and once again close up China.

Let me give two examples of this.

In Iran the rebel Muslim leaders have stated that they do not oppose modernization at all. Unveiled women participate as equals in riots alongside veiled ones. Many students in the United States also oppose the Shah. The rebels do oppose the Shah's courting of Western leaders, his Western-based approach to government and his articulation of Western ideals. The Shah is much like the congressman who needs votes from blacks to win elections but publicly courts the leaders of the Ku Klux Klan.

In Japan, in 1970, one of that country's most intelligent novelists committed ritual suicide in an effort to rekindle Japanese values, as opposed to Western ones. His last novel, indeed, contrasted the Asian and Japanese ideals with Western ones. In October, *Atlas Magazine* wrote how, since 1970, a new mood of pro-Japanese values and anti-Western values has grown up in Japan.

These two examples—and there are countless others—suggest that modernization and Westernization are not the same thing and that we Westerners, for our own good, should avoid any cultural chauvinism in our description of China. Matteo Ricci counseled the Christian West not to westernize China but to Sinicize Christianity. No one listened to him, and Christianity gave way to a Sinicized communism instead.

II

THE EFFECTS ON CHINA

Let us turn now to some of the effects of the China trade on China.

As noted above, China is a very poor country. Secretary of Energy Schlesinger praised the Chinese recently for admitting the primitive nature of science and education in China. In some ways China is poorer than India because China's closed society protected the Chinese from the gales of modernity more effectively than India's open society. But India has had thirty years of openness and a population hardened to modernity—indeed, educated for modernity.

As new plants, new techniques and new elites emerge in China's modernized sectors, severe dislocations will take place in China's traditional industries. New steel plants will cause unemployment in old ones. Workers who rate high today will tomorrow be unable to keep up. Military officers today will be replaced with more technically trained experts. And plants once considered modern will be closed down as new ones open. Each new plant, each new technique, will cause dislocations.

Even putting aside the immense social and political effects of these changes, the economic effects will be monumental. Bottlenecks will occur as traditional industries try to supply high production modern sectors. Energy will be scarce, causing blackouts as now occur in most developing countries.

Second, Chinese industry will be put under severe pressure to meet export standards so that China can sell enough overseas to meet its debt payments. This will require speedups and intense quality control procedures that in themselves will cause bottlenecks and economic chaos.

Third, China will have to follow macro-economic policies that account for its balance of payments position. Until now, China, economically, has lived a relatively autarchic and isolated economic life, always balancing exports with imports. Within the past year China has signed over sixty billion dollars of contracts, far in excess of its nine billion dollars of exports. And no matter how these contracts are being financed—through barter, or sellbacks, or joint profits—at some point the Chinese are going to have to sell sixty billion dollars more in exports to raise the foreign exchange to pay for the imports.

If all goes as it has in other countries, like India or Indonesia, China will face periodic foreign exchange crisis which will result in economic slowdowns and more bottlenecks. Anyone who has lived and worked in industry in Asia has seen every country from Korea to Israel endure stop-and-go periods of foreign exchange crises. To expect China to be different is absurd.

These stop-and-go crises, however, will have a profound effect on China's economy. The crises will always occur in midstride, so to speak. A plant will be half complete when foreign exchange becomes scarce, stopping the project. Resources that were scheduled for domestic use will be diverted and dumped on foreign markets to earn foreign exchange. Wage rates will be frozen and incentives reduced. And when as the crisis is overcome, the stride forward will start again.

Modernization will lead then to dislocations, a new export-oriented economy, and periodic foreign exchange crises. Each of these phenomona will be new, even terrifying to both the planners and workers and peasants. And in a country like China, so protected for so long, the effects will lead to political unrest and often to instability.

Still another effect will have to be a reshaping of the centrally planned economy to a more market-oriented system. Yugoslavia, when it opened itself up, faced this task and successfully turned its economy to a more market-oriented approach. So did Rumania. China has sent delegations to both Rumania and Yugoslavia to learn the technique.

But such a "market-oriented" development approach neither eliminates communism nor brings about capitalism, while it does create problems of its own because plans go awry and the market in these economies often results in decisions taken at cross-purposes. In an economy of the size of China's, the market-oriented system may lead to inter-regional conflicts as well as production snafus of enormous proportions. Indonesia's oil industry, for example, although not half the scale of China's, recently went bankrupt after corrupt and inexperienced leadership operated the industry as if it were a private fiefdom. China will have similar problems.

Still another problem will be "absorption." China can only absorb so much modernization at a time and truly digest it. One of the fears often expressed by businessmen in Hong Kong and Tokyo is that China is trying to do too much at once. There is a good chance that plants and machinery ordered from abroad will remain on the docks or stashed near construction sites for months or years because of an inability to digest them. This will lead to a crisis of confidence in the planning elites and the political situation.

Thus the problems of loosening up the economy toward market models and the problems of absorption will also, no doubt, occur in China.

Another fear held by many is the age of the current leadership. China is being opened up today by Teng and others, most of whom are over seventy. Only Hua Kuo-fung and Wang Tung-hsing are younger. And the latter are not ardent modernists, but traditional Maoist-communists. Consequently, as the aging leadership dies, new direction will no doubt take over, often with the effect of wasting progress in some areas as priorities change.

And this leads to another fear. The China trade today depends on credit and faith.

Credit is essential because China does not have the exports or the foreign exchange reserves to pay for the goods she is importing. Because of this, Western banks and firms are lending China money to pay Western suppliers.

The faith is essential because we assume that China will invest the money wisely in productive investments and absorb it and use it effectively, not frittering it away on arms or high living among the elites or prestige projects. China, while it has no debt and is so far scrupulous in paying debts, nevertheless has a lot to learn, and much of the faith in the current aged leadership is based on the track record of Mao's China. The scale of the current modernization may be unabsorbable when added on to the Maoist past.

III
THE EFFECTS ON TAIWAN

Now let us turn to the effects of China's modernization on Taiwan.

During my recent journey there I was surprised to find a Taiwan that has huge foreign exchange reserves—twice the level of China's—and a currency so strong that it will be revalued by at least twenty percent in the next few months. Taipei is a modern city, and the country has moved into the twentieth century well on its way to the twenty-first.

Assuming that Taiwan will not be and cannot be invaded by the mainland, Taiwan's economic progress is threatened by the U.S. moves to normalize relations with China.

To survive and continue to progress, Taiwan needs "access" to markets, access to resources, access to oil, access to weapons, access to technology and access to credit. Without such access, Taiwan's economy would wither on the vine. Nevertheless, this "access" is threatened by U.S. derecognition.

For example, Taiwan now gets its oil from Saudi Arabia. If the U.S. derecognizes Taiwan, will Saudi Arabia follow? Also, the U.S. has yielded to the mainland the oil deposits in the Strait of Taiwan by refusing to protect U.S. exploration teams working on Taiwan originated leases.

Secondly, Taiwan depends on the U.S. for markets through generous quotas of TV's, shoes, plastics, textiles, etc. Will the U.S. give Taiwan's quotas to China? Will U.S. industry permit China to get a separate quota?

Moreover, will U.S. banks provide credit to Taiwan if the mainland makes not granting such credit a condition of loans to Peking?

Will the U.S. sell competing technologies to Taiwan and Peking? And weapons?

Will the U.S., in recognizing the mainland, submit if China demands that all exports and imports of Taiwan have to pass through a mainland port?

One development in recent days is the remark by Vice Premier Teng that China would permit Taiwan to have its own economic independence. However, as noted above, Teng is an old man who may be sincere. Whether his successors feel the same way cannot be predicted.

All of these economic questions are up in the air. Kang Ning-hsing, the rebel Taiwanese independence member of the legislative Yuan of Taiwan, is as concerned about these questions as the most diehard, return-to-the-mainland, Kuomintang party member. Yet there are simply no answers forthcoming, especially in the U.S.

IV

THE EFFECTS ON DEVELOPING COUNTRIES

Beyond Taiwan is the problem of the effects of China's modernization on the third world.

China's emergence affects the third world two ways: one immediate short-term way and one long-term way. The short-term effect is the credit effect. The long-term is the trade effect.

The short-term credit effect directly affects the third world by attracting capital, both private and public, from the third world in general to China.

China's capital needs range anywhere from sixty to three hundred billion dollars over the next five to ten years. At present the total borrowing annually of the whole non-OPEC third world is thirty billion dollars annually. Thus China threatens to absorb not only new loans but also credit that now goes to the third world.

At present, China does not belong to the World Bank, the Asian Development Bank, or the IMF. Should China join these institutions, a major shake-up in world public flows of aid would have to occur.

India, for example, absorbs forty percent of World Bank consortia loans and soft loans and forty percent of ADB financing. Is the world prepared to shift extra funds into the World Bank consortia-ADB channels so that China gets a paltry two billion dollars just as India gets? China will either have to live with two billion dollars or a major overhaul of these institutions will have to take place.

Similarly, Brazil, with thirty billion dollars of debt, mostly to private banks, is one of the biggest borrowers in the third world. Are private capital markets capable of giving the same amount to China?

I raise these questions because there are very real limits to the amount of credit now available in the world, and China will have to live within those limits. Even then it may draw credit from Thailand, Bangladesh, India or Pakistan or other desperately poor countries.

The long-term effects of China's modernization on the third world are even more devastating. China will have to export manufactured goods to Western markets in order to pay for the loans it has incurred. China will, because of its low wages and the exigencies of its foreign exchange crises, have to sell cheaply to muscle out current third world production. By lending China money we force China into the export markets and face, as a result, the possibility of a ruthless competitor supported by private bankers who have to get their payments from China.

Few people look ahead to the days when China starts exporting Red Flag autos, Peking TV's, and Shanghai chemicals into world markets already flooded by cheap manufactures from third world nations.

Brooks Adams, the eccentric but prescient brother of Henry Adams, foresaw in 1900 that to modernize China would pose an economic threat not only to the third world but to the industrialized West as well. The irony is that if China does not export, China cannot pay its creditors.

The other side of our opening the China market is that China is, in effect, opening ours as well.

V

THE EFFECTS ON INDUSTRIALIZED COUNTRIES

This leads to the fourth effect—the effect on the industrialized countries. At present the hope is that China, like all developing countries, will import more than it exports, thus providing the slowly growing and weak industrialized economies with new and desperately needed markets for their excess capital goods.

As noted above, the reciprocal effect of this deficit in China's trade will be the need to open U.S. and other industrialized markets to China's industries if only to make possible the payment of the loans China has incurred. The question is, as time goes on, whether the industrialized world is ready to face what this means. China now exports nine billion dollars a year, the same as Taiwan. Last year we lowered Taiwan's quotas of exports of shoes and TV's to the U.S. If China, which exports about five hundred million to the U.S. now, were to increase its exports to two billion like Taiwan, could we absorb the goods without either major dislocations or a retreat into protectionism? The question cannot be avoided any longer. Can we lead with even another Taiwan, much less a China?

The consequence of opening the China trade is opening the U.S. to Chinese goods. I am not sure that the U.S. or the industrial world could tolerate too many more Taiwans or Brazils or even another tiny Hong Kong.

What has to be seen is that China now exports oil, some textiles, and other raw resources. In the future she has to export manufactures. When the future arrives, will we be able to absorb them ourselves?

VI
FINANCIAL EFFECTS

Lastly, the opening of our China market needs a very well-tuned financial system to see that China does not borrow more than she can absorb and repay and to ensure that China does not draw too much credit from developing countries, especially in south Asia.

Consequently, there is a need for a public and private institution in Hong Kong, Singapore or Tokyo that regulates credit flows to China and allocates these flows based on China's performance and the needs of others. Without such a device I am certain that China's entry into the modern world will be filled with shocks and bumps when speculators and shysters prey on this large but grossly inexperienced country.

Indonesia, despite some of the best thinkers in Asia, nearly went bankrupt in 1976. Italy, Turkey, Zaire, Peru and Portugal also have teetered at the edge of bankruptcy in 1977. Even Great Britain had to beg for credit in 1977. And in 1978 the U.S. was forced to borrow currencies from other countries and impose an austerity program through wage and price controls and higher interest rates on November 1.

Therefore, in looking at the China trade I urge all thoughtful writers to see the need to impose regulation on this trade—especially on credit—

313

before China overextends itself and either cannot pay or decides once again to withdraw from the world. China did withdraw in 1949 because of unpayable debts. She could do so again in 1985.

VII
THE CHINA CARD

China is such a large market with so many poor people that nothing so turns my stomach as talk of the China card, wherein China is seen as a military threat to the USSR. It is my belief that such a policy not only looks at China as a means and not an end in itself, but also raises false hopes in America that China will be a military ally when China is a very weak, backward country. Pakistan is on the Soviet border, but no one speaks of a Pakistani card because Pakistan is too poor to be anyone's card.

It seems to me that the only way to perceive China rationally is to keep in mind that the task ahead is to help China modernize its economy in such a way that modernization takes place gradually and effectively so that both the Chinese people and the American and Western peoples can adjust to this new reality.

In a sense, modernization means concentration on the economic development of China, providing capital in such a way as to not destabilize its government and social order. The task involves one-quarter of mankind and is so much larger than anything else we have attempted since World War II that we should have a little humility that we have been given this chance. To take off helter-skelter, playing military Chinese cards that do not exist, is, to my mind, insane. The job in China is long-term, one of developing her economy and integrating her economy into a very fragile world economic system. Failure to achieve this will lead to an economic and political disaster.

VIII
CONFLICT WITH OUR ALLIES

There is another issue that worries me, and that is the effects that the China trade will have on our outlook relative to our allies. For the United States, to enter the China trade, will have to compete with both Japan and Western Europe. This competition with our allies may be friendly or it may be fierce. In the latter case, unless we make serious efforts to draw up rules of behavior with our allies, the China trade may be used by Peking as a way of exacerbating conflicts among the allies.

I see four areas of conflict: conflict over resources, conflict over terms of sales and prices, conflict over finance, and competition on the opening of home markets.

1. In regard to resources, according to Seling Harrison's brilliant book *China and Oil: Asian Conflict Ahead?* (Columbia University Press, 1977), estimates are that by 1990 China will pump oil equivalent to Saudi Arabia's output in 1974. While much of this oil will be used internally, the most natural market for this oil is Japan.

At present, Japan secures ninety percent of its needs from the Middle East through the American multinationals. This dependence on a shaky Middle East and supply lines in the now unstable Persian Gulf and Indian Ocean and through the Straits of Malacca puts Japan not at the end of a very long supply line, but, through the role of the American oil companies, at the mercy of American policy. The oil lever is one of the most potent tools of leverage for the American government, relative to Japan.

To counter these concerns Japan has decided to diversify her supplies—and suppliers—through the establishment of the Japan National Oil Company which will negotiate directly with China and refine the oil in Japanese-owned refineries. This transition is of itself of major geopolitical importance and of major geopolitical concern.

Secondly, relative to the offshore oil, there are inherent conflicts between the Chinese and Japanese and between the Chinese and the Koreans as to ownership of the seabeds, especially near the Senkakku Islands. The U.S., through the Trilateral Commission, already yielded these claims to China—a sore point in U.S.-Japanese relations.

2. Relative to sales terms and prices, as we all know, Western Europe and Japan, as well as other nations, often subsidize exports. In the China trade where China needs favorable terms, subsidized trade by these blocs will be a factor that will cause friction between the U.S. and its allies, since, at least up to now, the U.S. does very little to subsidize exports. A trade war between allies in the China trade could be fearful. As there is no trade treaty or rules of trade with China, this is a real fear.

3. On credit the same applies. If bankers from different countries get greedy—as they did in Indonesia—credit lines could be extended beyond reason as European, American and Japanese banks raced to corner the market. Aside from the fear of overextension of credit, there is a real chance of setting off a "credit war" between the allies that could end in disaster. Pressures to boost exports from the home markets could set the credit war on its course.

4. As stated above, the opening of the China market reciprocally means the opening of the home markets. Both Western Europe and Japan are known to be more protectionist than the U.S. If the U.S. must absorb the burden of China's exports, a real crisis in relations among the allies will ensue.

The China trade therefore may have some terrifying effects on the free world—effects that all of us will be writing about in the near future.

IX

The Wider View of Northeast Asia

Let us make one last point. We have, in looking at the China trade, ignored the bigger picture: first of northeast Asia as a whole, which includes Siberia, and then of southeast and south Asia.

1. Relative to northeast Asia, one of the striking changes of the past several years has been the gradual opening up of Siberia and its resources. The USSR is in the throes of completing its Siberian rail route and has offered Japan and others the chance of developing the timber, copper and other resources in Irkutsk and Yakutsk. Japan is already in joint oil development and resource development projects there, and U.S. companies are ready to export oil equipment for development when the Jackson-Vanik Amendment is finally over-ridden.

I foresee a great trade and development in the Siberian area—a sort of triangular trade where, say, Japan imports raw materials from Siberia, transforms these materials into capital goods for sale to China, where China turns them into consumer goods and exports them to the world. That such a trade is in the cards is reflected in the arrival in Japan last October of a Soviet delegation to expand Japan-Soviet trade. Northeast Asia, including Siberia, is well worth watching.

2. As to the rest of Asia, already the resources-to-capital-goods-to-China cycle is underway. However, we should keep in mind that the five nations of southeast Asia (Thailand, Malaysia, Singapore, Indonesia and the Philippines) have formed a new common market, ASEAN, which will no doubt play a pivotal role in the china trade. Although that role is yet unclear, the chance of a "special relationship" between ASEAN and Japan is most probable, and Japan will no doubt offer privileged prices and tariff privileges to these nations.

3. The great question mark in the effects of the China trade is India—a country already exporting more manufactured goods than raw materials and a country whose openness over the past thirty years has produced an educated professional elite, wise to the ways of the world. Already Indian multinationals and trading companies are major factors in the export markets of Asia, and no doubt the Indians are gearing up to meet Chinese competition. My bet is that the China trade will be the ultimate spur to India's long delayed takeoff. My visit there last year and talks with major cabinet officials convinced me that India is well aware of the threat China poses over the medium term of India's export position. My guess is that India, in the next ten years, will emerge in Asia as a major trading rival to China.

This then is the long view of the China trade. I hope it has made you ask questions beyond tomorrow's deadline and provides leads for the future.

Myths of the
China Trade*

*Thomas G. Corcoran***

In these pages I wish to examine two questions.

1. What may the mainland China commercial market mean in profitable business for U.S. exporters and shipping companies if the U.S. government grants the People's Republic of China on the mainland everything mainland China wants under the guide of "normalizing relations"?

2. What may such action cost in profit for U.S. business interests if specifically such "normalization" requires the derecognition of the Republic of China on Taiwan and the abrogation between the United States and Taiwan of the defense treaty which now guarantees Taiwan security like that of Japan?

This will *not* argue that under *any* circumstances full diplomatic recognition should not be given to the People's Republic of China on the mainland. But it will argue that dreams of commercial profit to U.S. entrepreneurs and U.S. employment do not stand up as reasons why such diplomatic recognition and "normalization" of relations should be accorded only on mainland China's dictated terms—as in the Canadian Olympic case. Such terms demanding the derecognition of the Republic of China on Taiwan are to the commercial and economic advantage of the U.S. both in the short run and the long run.

Compared to larger issues of international affairs involved in the U.S. choices, such an inquiry about commercial expectations may seem narrow. But in terms of U.S. politics it is important—important because the hope of money profit is the ceaseless political driving power behind other supposedly idealistic and romantic interests rationalizing at any cost an agreement with mainland China. That commercial driving power is the ever hopeful receptivity by profit-eager U.S. business of mainland China's encouragement of dreams that mainland China is a virgin market of continental proportions for U.S. business whose benefits to the U.S. economy

*Copyright 1976, Council on American Affairs, Washington, D.C. Reprinted by permission.

**Thomas G. Corcoran is the former Special Assistant to the Attorney General of the United States in Franklin Delano Roosevelt's administration. He is currently the senior partner in the law firm of Corcoran, Youngman and Rowe of Washington, D.C.

in profits and jobs outweighs any disadvantages of other kinds in acceding to mainland China's demands. "Men believe what they want to believe," and the storied dream of "oil for the lamps of China" is being romantically expanded—assuming of course that U.S. government banking and the entire taxable citizenry subsidize the commerce by taking the risk in government export credits.

Even in the United States, of course, "figures can lie but liars can figure," but what we really *know* about the economy of mainland China is only what the mainland government *wants* us to *know*. The overriding fact which we *do know* is that like totalitarian Russia the economy of mainland China is a government instrument.

As with all totalitarian nations all trade with mainland China will be politically, not competitively, motivated. At bottom all such trade will be barter of advantages in political warfare. Totalitarian trade in commercial negotiations will pit competing and divided U.S. entrepreneurs against a monolithic totalitarian buyer and seller. In such confrontation the private enterprise nation will naturally be over-reached as in the recent Russian purchase of U.S. wheat.

However, assume (a) as a planned economy the mainland economy is doing what mainland China public relations say it is doing, and (b) that economy desperately needs foreign technology and the risk of foreign capital which the U.S. has for export.

It still does not follow that in the foreseeable future there is an opportunity for substantial U.S. private business profits in meeting mainland China's needs. Again the dominating fact is one in comparison with which all statistical projections are unimportant. The governmental direction of the economy of the People's Republic of China on the mainland is completely unlike the economy of the Republic of China on Taiwan where there has been an outstanding opportunity for private U.S. commerce. By comparison the economy on mainland China is, like the economy of Russia, an instrument of government international policy—in Bismarckian words an instrument of "diplomacy that is war by another means."

That policy as presently conceived and executed by mainland China can not favor the interests of U.S. commercial entrepreneurs either in goods or in transportation. The situation parallels our experience with the Russian use of its domestic market since the commercially disappointing recognition of totalitarian Russia in 1933. Totalitarian China like Russia plans ultimate total internal production, buying nothing important abroad.

Only after forty years, when increasingly its European satellites and ultimately Russia itself find themselves necessitous, *buyers*, is there a glimmer of profit for U.S. suppliers—so long as European totalitarianism remains a necessitous buyer.

Leaving aside therefore any abstract calculation of economics on paper, the true indicators of what will be the application of totalitarian economics to U.S. free enterprise economics is clear in two concrete leading

318

cases. The first is the Olympic situation in Canada. The second is the forty-year experience with totalitarian Russia. Each illustrates the near impossibility of free enterprise dealing on a profitable basis with nationalistic economic pressure for political purposes.

There is no doubt—even among the Canadian spokesmen themselves—that the action of the Canadian government in the Olympic case has violated all rules and precedents of supposedly non-political Olympic games. The story is told in detail in July 26, 1976 issue of *Time* magazine that when a large trading arrangement for wheat and other items was being negotiated Peking made it clear to Ottawa that the price of the $300,000,000 trade—and of the involved profit to individual Canadian farmers—was the humiliation and loss of face of the Republic of China's entry in the Olympics.

The Canadian government situation is pathetically understandable. In a precarious situation the present Canadian government apparently had no choice but to yield to these demands—it was a necessitous seller. Unlike the Canadian economy and the Canadian political situation the U.S. and its government is not now a necessitous seller.

What is interesting as a matter of degree is the cold ruthlessness of mainland China's demand on Canada and its risking of the future of the whole international Olympics concept. Thoughtful Canadians are admittedly aghast at Canada's "paper tiger" loss of face. This loss of face for Canada may be particularly relevant to the United States. Mainland China, mindful for domestic politics of one-time British economic "exploitation" and still vilifying "U.S. imperialism," may see psychological advantage in breaking the face of the Anglo-Saxon beaten out of Asia.

By comparison, the Republic of China and Taiwan already gives the U.S. economy a market ten times that of mainland China and is developed with U.S. private investment of over half a billion dollars. In 1978, U.S. trade with Taiwan reached $7.3 billion, more than eight times the difficult and erratic trade with Communist China. Taiwan, like Japan, with no important raw materials of its own, has proved, along with the Chinese emigrees from the mainland in the rest of eastern Asia, that the precious cultural and human values of the most ancient civilization of the earth can be preserved to benefit all classes of Chinese society in combination with the economic values of modern technology.

What economic benefits are the mainland Chinese after in this demand for U.S. abandonment of the protection of Taiwan soft-soaped with non-believable communist promises to disclaim physical conquest?

Transparent to an informed observer is the hope of the government on mainland China that withdrawal of the defense association with the United States will discourage the supporters of the Republic of China government on Taiwan about its long-term prospects against the mainland's "wave of the future." So discouraged, without physical assault and capital destruction Taiwan will at some future date be open for subversion from within.

319

Then Taiwan's U.S. technological development can be added intact to the mainland economic base without a struggle.

Somewhere for the long future both mainland China and Siberian Russia are thinking the same way. Among all offshore islands of the Asian continent, that is, Japan and Taiwan, the Philippines, Indonesia and Singapore, and the peninsula of South Korea, there is brooding ultimate apprehension. That apprehension is that the ambition of both continental Russia and continental China to annex technology without paying for it clearly forecasts that in their long range projections these two powerful totalitarian states see the Russian-German-Czechoslovakian route their ultimate economic solution. The totalitarian seizure of the U.S. investment of half a billion on Taiwan with U.S. State Department assistance could be the accelerator of further depredations and confiscations and nationalizations of Western capital over all offshore Asia and the whole world.

Thus contrary to hopes of U.S. business to "do business" with an indefinite mainland market, the takeover of Taiwan could directly to the contrary solve many of mainland China's economic problems without the cost of any of the imports from the Western world from which American exporters and transporters could make a commercial profit. This assumes that within the competitors of the Western world the mainland Chinese would choose to favor the U.S. businessman. All indications now are that they see more political advantage in buying technology through Europe where, as in Canada, there are more necessitous sellers.

By existing treaty terms a portion of the Hong Kong economy in the new territories will within a definite time fall intact into mainland China hands. Hong Kong is extremely valuable to the mainland economy as a buyer, a source of foreign exchange, port facilities and light manufacturing. But by comparison Taiwan with its heavy technology produced by U.S. investment and aid is a prize exceeded only by Japan. Japan, defenseless, is protected by a defense treaty no one considers the U.S. abandoning.

In submitting to the "Japanese plans" for relations with Taiwan, as the commercial price of relations with mainland China, Japan is protected by the same kind of a defense treaty mainland China proposes to strip from Taiwan. No nation is more concerned than Japan that stripping Taiwan of U.S. protection may be the precedent for next Korea and next Japan.

The Russian inexpensive acquisition of German, Czechoslovakian and Manchurian plant technology and skilled labor is an irrefutable warning. So is the U.S. individual commercial experience with totalitarian Russia. The Russians held out as bait for their diplomatic recognition, i.e., the international "respectability" which they most wanted, token payment of some part of the debt of the previous government to foreigners. But immediately after U.S. Ambassador William Bullitt took residence in Moscow and gave them the international position they wanted, the Russian government repudiated that agreement. No part of the Russian tsarist debt has ever been paid as contemplated in the agreements for diplomatic recognition. Further the

World War II Lend Lease debt has lately been repudiated when the present Russian government was not able to obtain the additional credits they expected to get from the Export-Import Bank as the price for meeting their obligations.

With relation to prospective private commercial transactions, Ambassador William Bullitt, later well known in Asia, in 1933 urged President Roosevelt to recognize Russia as a way of opening the way to get the United States out of a then recession by supplying an "inexhaustible" market in Russia for U.S. goods. To pay for such imports to get the U.S. economy out of the depression the U.S. suppliers were to depend, at the ultimate risk of the U.S. government, on Export-Import Bank credits. Judging that only a few loss-leader transactions would ever be effected on easy terms which U.S. exporters could take—bait to get follow-ups on harder terms—the Secretary of State as titular chairman of the Bank and Mr. Jesse Jones, Chairman of the Reconstruction Finance Corporation, which supplied the capital were unenthusiastic. They were both right.

Secretary Hull protected his position in the Bank hierarchy on the ground that "the State Department knows nothing and never will know anything about money and should be kept out of it."

Within a year after the repudiation by the Russians of their commercial understandings, after his ambassadorial presence in Moscow had gotten Russia the international "respectability" they wanted about everything, the ambassador returned to Washington a disillusioned and bitter man and the most adamant opponent of Communist Russia we have ever had. Thereafter he wrote his book *The Great Globe Itself* illustrating what he saw as totalitarian ambitions on the whole world utilizing an inextricable tie-up of their commercial transactions with their political designs.

Ambassador Bullitt once speculated that one unsolvable commercial problem was that in the Russian ruling class there were few native Russians experienced in commercial transactions with foreign countries. "Business" was considered beneath the Russian upper class just as for a time the English landowning aristocracy had a prejudice against "people in trade." Russian business with the outside world had always been done by German and Armenian entrepreneurs. Because of this lack of respect for or interest in private entrepreneuring there were few Russian native commerciants trained to do business with foreigners. To this lack Ambassador Bullitt attributed some part of the failure of his hopes to take the United States out of "depression" by selling to the underdeveloped market of Russia.

That lack persists today forty years after recognition in hopes of substantial private commercial opportunities in the undeveloped economy of totalitarian Russia. Necessitous buying and the political extension of credit by U.S. government banks risking U.S. tax revenues have loosened up the odds considerably in Russian satellites and slightly in Russia itself. But recognizing the degree of their dependence is to the advantage of the United

States in superpower competition with Soviet Russia. Even on a necessitous buyer basis, détente is hardly perceptible in Russian-American commercial operations. And the interest rates demanded for such commercial purchase at U.S. government risks by the U.S. Export-Import Bank are for easier credit than is domestically available to U.S. borrowers.

The U.S. oil and gas interests who have been in Moscow or Vienna trying to deal with the Russians found them most extortionate in their harsh terms and have begun to give up. Without an infusion of offshore "overseas Chinese" commercial expertise and attitude in trading, the same unbridgable gap will make impractical hopes for ultimate trade with continental China.

Fortunately exactly the oppposite of the Russian situation can ultimately exist in the China case as it does exist today on Taiwan. If, by not changing the present status of the Republic of China, the U.S. does not interfere with the historical capacity of the Chinese to find their own ways of adjustment, with the death of Mao and of Chiang as Chinese contra non-Chinese, Taiwan and the mainland will surely find their own method of adjustment. Possibly after the disappearance of Mao as well as Chiang, all Chinese with their historic ability to find solutions will work out their relationships in one China—a work-out that will come in a traditional Chinese time frame that understands the long uses of time to heal wounds.

Thus while the U.S. cannot "ignore the fact" of a mainland China, neither in the long-term interest of a better united China can it refuse to sustain those we can *now* be sure of, i.e., the twenty million overseas Chinese who look to Taiwan as their intellectual and cultural preservation, and who are our permanent friends for the best of political reasons—because individually they need us as much as collectively we need them.

The success of U.S.-Taiwan business is certainly related to the kind of Chinese on Taiwan. They are the American-educated private enterprise minded Chinese who after the mainland takeover emigrated not only to Taiwan but also to southeast Asia.

These U.S.-oriented Chinese are the cumulative result of:

(a) the nearly fifty years of scholarships in U.S. colleges and the U.S. missionary schools in China;

(b) the pre-war cooperation with U.S. banks and business;

(c) the long experience of World War II Chinese-U.S. cooperation in, among others, the Flying Tigers, the Fourteenth Air Force, the CAT Airline and post-war free east Asia investment.

Over such an available bridge of mutual understanding U.S. commerce might truly find a market in China developme: '. For as in the case of U.S. good will toward China, an enormous reservoir of good will still exists for the U.S. in the Chinese common people irrespective of temporary leadership because in the war Britain failed them and the United States helped. The attempted British head start in the headlong recognition of Communist China by Hong Kong-directed Britain immediately after the mainland revolution could quickly be reserved, and the Chinese have never forgotten the German annexation of Shantung or the French domination of Indochina.

There is now no comparison between the paucity of Russians who can deal comfortably in commerce in English and the significant number of Chinese educated in English with U.S. attitudes in the U.S. due to pre-war scholarship aid and post-war education aid and the generations of missionary colleges such as Yale in China and the Rockefeller Foundation. The results in half a century have provided a truly English-speaking Chinese population in the millions which has been demonstrably successful in U.S. ways of doing business in the overseas Chinese private enterprise operations in Hong Kong, Taiwan and beyond. For important purposes all business in Taiwan as well as Hong Kong is transacted in English. And Taiwan is particulary important because U.S. investment headquarters are moving rapidly from Hong Kong into Taiwan because of the extraordinary inflation and cost of doing business in Hong Kong and the fear of ultimate totalitarian takeover of Hong Kong.

Derecognition of Taiwan will destroy the value to U.S. business opportunity of this asset-of-understanding of U.S.-educated U.S.-oriented Chinese in the overseas Chinese communities, and in the loss of this potential asset-in-understanding it would create a loss to the U.S. trade of the first magnitude. Leaving the Chinese to their own devices, i.e., changing nothing now, is therefore prudent for any long-term eventual U.S. possibility of a market for private U.S. business on the Asiatic mainland.

To reiterate, for the purpose of business profits of the United States the American-educated Chinese and the overseas Chinese they lead are the largest potential U.S. asset in non-Japanese Asia. They are nearly twenty million of non-third world second and third generation U.S.-educated, U.S.-minded and consequently private-enterprise-oriented "overseas" Chinese. In addition to those on Taiwan, these "overseas" Chinese are important economically, commercially and politically in Hong Kong, the Philippines, Malaya, Thailand, Indonesia, Guam, Hawaii, and even in the continental United States, where they number 500,000.

Other than U.S. citizens, all such "overseas" Chinese wherever located look to Taiwan as their intellectual and cultural capital and to its exceptional U.S.-educated diplomatic corps as their indispensable diplomatic representative in their dealings with the host countries in which they are aliens. And as representatives of the U.S. tradition of free economic enterprise and free government in the emerging nations on the rim of the Pacific basin— groping out of centuries-old traditions of government and economics of another style—always in the forefront of change, the "overseas" Chinese always are in need of sympathetic and effective feeling for a homeland which only a free Taiwan can give.

These twenty million of "our kind" looking to Taiwan as their intellectual and cultural capital preserved and protected by the U.S. defense treaty now can be a unique bridge between the technological needs of an ultimate United China and the U.S. investor, exporter and importer.

The re-education of Taiwan to totalitarian economics would certainly mean for the ablest a probable new dispersion beyond totalitarian influence and U.S. usefulness. The usefulness of the entire overseas Chinese colony to the long-run development by U.S. private enterprise-minded business of the market of continental Asia is therefore tied up with keeping the overseas Chinese related to a Taiwan free of communist domination. Deprived of this freedom these twenty million free and free-enterprise Chinese will have no utility to U.S. commerce to avoid U.S. entrepreneurs having to "do business" with a monopolistic communist state concentrating in itself all buying and selling, manipulating its labor costs to dump at will, and for political reasons making commercial decisions and pricings.

For these commercial reasons among more important military and political reasons, the problem of Taiwan and mainland China should be left in status quo for all the Chinese to settle whenever they get around it. This is the suggestion of Senator Fong who, understanding the Chinese mind from an ethnic Chinese background, has visited both Chinas.

There is a story in Aesop about a dog who had a very satisfactory bone in his mouth. Going by a still pond he saw in the water a reflection of that bone bigger in the water than it was in his mouth. He dropped the bone in his mouth to get the bone in the water and he found himself with no bone at all.

The U.S. businessman knows what he is doing in Taiwan because he is dealing with the same kind of mentality and culture as his own and he is dealing very profitably. Commercially Taiwan is the bone in our mouth. Commercially the mirage of mainland China is a bone in the water. In common sense we should stick with the bone in our mouth until we know whether there really can be a bone in the water.

Part IV
Analysis of the Decision
To Betray Taiwan

Carter as Negotiator:
The Taiwan Issue

R. Sean Randolph*

President Carter's December 15 annoucement of the "normalization" of U.S. relations with the People's Republic of China hardly came, on its own merits, as a surprise. Few, including many conservative friends of Taiwan, questioned the desirability or inevitability of broadening Washington's ties with Peking. This appeared sound from both the short-term tactical and the long-term diplomatic standpoints. The broader question remained, however, "At what price?" The price the Carter administration was prepared to pay and the price that a majority of the Congress and the American public believed should be paid varied considerably. A July 29, 1978 congressional poll taken by the Washington-based American Conservative Union found that of 437 members of Congress, 211 opposed normalization of United States-People's Republic of China relations if this meant the severance of diplomatic relations with the Republic of China and abrogation of the mutual defense treaty. Only five expressed support for those terms, while thirty-four were found to be "leaning against," and only one was "leaning in favor," while one hundred and eighty were either undecided or gave no response. In another poll, published on September 12, 1978 by the Harris Survey, the American public was found to favor full U.S. diplomatic recognition of the People's Republic by a margin of 66 to 25 percent. At the same time, however, by a majority of 66 to 19 percent the public opposed withdrawal of U.S. recognition from Taiwan, and by 64 to 19 percent favored the continuation of the mutual defense treaty.

Thus, on the eve of normalization a substantial majority of both the public and the Congress favored a "two Chinas" policy, recognizing the reality of continuing American interests in both Chinese states. This fact makes it all the more important to analyze the Carter administration's diplomatic approach to the Taiwan question, since the American experience in this instance may well shed light on what might be expected from the United States in future negotiating scenarios.

To begin with, a distinction ought to be made between President

*R. Sean Randolph is a Research Associate for the National Security Research Group of the U.S. House of Representatives.

Carter's handling of the normalization issue domestically as opposed to internationally. On the domestic side it was in 1978 a well-known fact, reflected in the above polls, that both the Congress and the American people favored the normalization of U.S. relations with Peking, though not at the expense of existing ties with Taiwan. This fact had prevented normalization from occurring in the six years since the signing of the 1972 Shanghai Communiqué, for it was clearly understood by both the White House and the State Department that any denigration of U.S. relations with Taiwan would no doubt raise a storm of congressional protests, making it a costly political move for any administration.

Since the effective mobilization of both public and congressional opinion promised to draw political blood and to possibly scuttle any well-publicized normalization moves, one avenue open to the White House lay in using the element of surprise. By presenting the Congress with a *fait accompli,* the organization of an effective congressional or public opposition movement could be precluded. This possiblity was, in fact, foreseen by many in the Congress. This led to an amendment to the International Security Assistance Act in July 1978, introduced by Senator Dole (R.-Kan.) and Stone (D.-Ga.), which called on the president to consult with the Senate before making any policy changes affecting the continuation of the U.S.-Republic of China Security Treaty. The amendment was adopted unanimously, 94-0, and was later approved in a House-Senate Conference Committee, making it a resolution of the full Congress. Resolutions of this type do not have the force of law, being only statements of congressional intent. As expressions of principle, however, they do carry significant moral weight, and can be ignored by a sitting president only at his political peril. Passage of the Stone-Dole amendment was, in the summer of 1978, seen as necessary not only to ensure the continuity of U.S. defense interests in Taiwan, but also to assure the right of Congress to full participation in future foreign policy decisions of this magnitude.

In practice, however, Congress was never consulted. "Consultation" amounted to a handful of informational telephone calls to congressional leaders some hours prior to the president's formal normalization announcement. Presidential advisor Morris Oskenberg even went so far as to claim that "consultations" had taken place because administration intentions regarding China had already been made clear as a matter of record. The fact remains that, on the Taiwan question, the Congress was "scooped"—that the announcement of normalization was timed by the administration to occur at a moment when the Congress would least be able to react. While it has been often said that the announcement was made at the time it was in order to give President Carter a major foreign policy "victory," an equally important consideration may have been the fact that on December 15 Congress was in the midst of a three-month recess and was not scheduled to return into session until January 15. Members of Congress and Senators were, in that week before Christmas, scattered throughout the United States and in many countries of the world. This effectively precluded the organization of a coherent, timely opposition. (This tactic had been used previously when, in July 1977, President Carter announced the cancellation of the B-1 Bomber program during a congressional July 4 recess.) By the time the Congress was scheduled to return, America's new relationship with both Chinas would be a *fait accompli.*

It is also worth noting, in passing, that at the time of the president's announcement the Democratic Party had just emerged from the November 1978 elections. With House members safe for two more years, the congressional Christmas recess was a tailor-made time for such a controversial announcement. Delay of the announcement into 1979 might well have overlapped the China issue with the pending SALT II debate, leaving the president in the politically difficult position of fighting a two-front battle in Congress and having to call in political IOU's on both. Any further delay into 1980, however, would have brought the president and his party perilously close to the 1980 elections—obviously an inexpedient time to raise such a potentially volatile issue.

It thus appears that, when considering the China issue, the Carter administration calculated that the political costs of an irritated but disorganized Congress, which had not been consulted, were less than those of an inflamed and fully participant Congress, which might have successfully interposed itself between the president and his foreign policy goal. While earlier Carter promises of an "open" and "responsive" administration were thus allowed to lapse into the shadows, the political soundness of the president's domestic calculations may well prove correct.

A different case presents itself when one analyzes the bases of the administration's dealings not with the Congress but with the Peking Chinese themselves. How hard a bargain did Carter, the negotiator, drive? Did his position ensure the continuity, to the maximum extent possible, of the whole range of American interests in both Chinas. From this writer's perspective, the answer must be "no."

The best framework for approaching this question is provided by the administration's own statements. These suggest both the gains and losses of the Chinese negotiations, as well as some of the underlying rationale.

It should be recalled, to begin with, that Peking had earlier articulated a set of three major principles which were to be its price for the opening of full diplomatic relations. These were (1) abrogation of the 1954 U.S.-Republic of China Mutual Defense Treaty, (2) withdrawal of all remaining U.S. troops from Taiwan, and (3) complete severance of U.S. diplomatic relations with Taiwan. From the American perspective, on the other hand, U.S. interests lay in the opening of closer relations with Peking, and also in the effective assurance of the continued security and viability of Taiwan. Could these two be reconciled?

In its official statement announcing normalization, the United States stated:

As of January 1, 1979, the United States of America recognizes the People's Republic of China as the sole legal government of China. On the same date, the People's Republic of China accords similar recognition to the United States of America. The United States thereby establishes diplomatic relations with the People's Republic of China.

On that same date, January 1, 1979, the United States of America will notify Taiwan that it is terminating diplomatic relations and that the Mutual Defense Treaty between the United States and the Republic of China is being terminated in accordance with the provisions of the Treaty. The United States also states that it will be withdrawing its remaining military personnel from Taiwan within four months.

In the future, the American people and the people of Taiwan will maintain commercial, cultural, and other relations without official government representation and without diplomatic relations.

Thus, with no visible modification, all three of Peking's primary terms for normalization were met by the United States.

It is interesting to see what was gained in return. Administration spokesmen point to four major "concessions" achieved in negotiations with Peking. These were claimed particularly by Secretary of State Cyrus Vance on NBC's "Meet the Press" on December 17, 1978. First, Mr. Vance asserted that the change in U.S. policy would be "very positive" for all involved, because "we insisted that, as far as the people of Taiwan were concerned, that [sic] normal relationships on an unofficial basis, culturally, trade and other matters, will be maintained." Second, he pointed out that "we have expressed very clearly our deep concern that the welfare of the people of Taiwan be protected, and that the transition be a peaceful transition, that the Taiwan solution should be a peaceful solution. This has not been contradicted by the People's Republic of China." Third: "In addition, we made it clear that we would continue in the period of post-normalization to supply a limited number of defensive weapons to the people of Taiwan, and we will continue to do so." Fourth: "And of great importance is the fact that we insisted that the treaty be terminated in accordance with its terms, and not terminated immediately, as the People's Republic of China would have liked." Put differently, the Carter administration claims to have wrung from Peking the right to continue unofficial relations with Taiwan, a Chinese agreement not to use force against Taiwan, the right to continue to sell defensive arms to Taiwan, and the right to terminate the United States-Republic of China Mutual Defense Treaty after one year rather than immediately. What in fact do these "concessions" amount to?

The answer, unfortunately is: "Very little." On the matter of continued unofficial relations with Taipei, this cannot be counted as a gain, since it has always been assumed by all concerned that such relations would continue.

This is the "Japanese formula" which had been the vehicle for Peking's normalization with Japan and other nations. Given the magnitude of American interests in Taiwan and the precedents already established, Peking certainly could concede, and the U.S. could demand, nothing less.

What of Peking's agreement not to use force against Taiwan? In point of fact, there was no "agreement." In this case the United States merely stated its understanding of the situation, and this view was "not contradicted" by Peking. Neither, however, was it affirmed. Subsequent assurances of peaceful intentions to the contrary, such assurances from Peking are not part of any formal agreement and so carry no legal weight. Changed Chinese attitudes or policies in the future may make Carter's "understanding" of Chinese intent as valid and lasting as Chamberlain's "understanding" of Hitler's. This "concession" thus appears to be a creative product of the administration's wishful (or hopeful) thinking. Even at that, administration spokesmen appear to have been stretching the truth. In a statement read in Peking by party chairman Hua Kuo-feng, the Chinese did in fact contradict the Americans. There, Peking's leadership expressed its position that "as for the way of bringing Taiwan back to the embrace of the motherland and reunifying the country, it is entirely China's internal affair." Peking, in other words, conceded nothing.

One finds a similar problem with continued American rights to sell defensive arms to the Republic of China. Again, the United States has stated its own reading of the situation and its intention to continue the sale of such arms. The People's Republic has not "agreed" to such sales, however. Instead it has "agreed to disagree" for the time being. Thus this is another case of Peking not "contradicting" the American view, but still refraining from making any actual concession. Since America's right to sell arms to the Republic of China has not been positively affirmed in the normalization agreement, it could at any time in the future be challenged by the People's Republic. At that time, if the United States continues its arms supply program, it will be technically guilty of unilateral intervention in internal Chinese affairs, since the United States has since January 1, 1979 acknowledged Peking's legal sovereignty over the whole of China, including Taiwan.

Finally there is the matter of the termination date for the United States-Republic of China Security Treaty. Very clearly this is a concession that is of only ephemeral value, and is little more than a cosmetic device. The bottom line on this question is that Taiwan has been completely stripped of its defensive relationship with the United States. From Taipei's perspective, it makes little difference whether the Mutual Defense Treaty remains on the books for one more day or one more year. The ultimate military isolation of the Republic of China has now been achieved, and the United States has won for itself no more than the right to produce that result in accordance with the existing legal procedures established by the treaty, that is, termination on one year's notice.

The underlying rationale of the Carter administration's China initiative was suggested by the president himself in his December 15 announcement. There, the President said: "In recognizing that government of the People's Republic of China is the single government of China, we are recognizing simple reality." What is the true reality, though? The reality of the China situation, and what has brought about the dilemma of U.S.-China policy in the last six years, is the fact that there are in truth two Chinas: two viable, functioning governments, two working economic and social systems, two well-armed military forces, and two populations presumably loyal to their respective governments. Both systems have been tried and proven by thirty years of experience. Indeed, just as it is a distortion of reality to assert, as the United States has for thirty years, that Taipei is the sole government of China, it is no less a distortion to insist that Peking alone holds that distinction.

So, regardless of the merits of the normalization of U.S. relations with the People's Republic of China, it appears that from a negotiating standpoint the administration's achievement has not been distinguished. This becomes all the more apparent when one considers that normalization will for the foreseeable future benefit the People's Republic of China far more than the United States. Not only will European arms sale to Peking now be expedited and the prospect of eventual U.S. sales increased, but the People's Republic will also be able to shift a number of its best divisions from the military regions facing Taiwan to China's critical northern border with the Soviet Union. (As of December 1978, approximately forty key divisions were tied down in the immediate Taiwan area.) The economic advantages to the People's Republic of better relations with the United States also appear substantial.

These advantages accruing to Peking, plus the fact that it was essentially at Peking's initiative that the China deal was closed so rapidly (for a number of reasons the month of December was an advantageous time for Peking's leaders as well), raise the question of what can be expected from the administration on other international negotiations either pending or in progress. Given the superior leverage of the United States and the absence of meaningful concessions from the People's Republic, the Carter administration's handling of the Taiwan question must give pause for the future. At the least, the United States should have insisted on, and might well have obtained, the right to maintain continued government-to-government relations with Tapei, presumably through a liaison office similar to the one the United States had previously maintained in Peking. Having failed to achieve even that minimal concession, however, the "reality" of a Chinese state of seventeen million people and America's eighth largest trading partner is now officially ignored by U.S. policy.

The China Decision
and the Future of Taiwan*

*Jeffrey Gayner***

Ever since the 1972 Shanghai Communiqué, the People's Republic of China (PRC) has demanded three pre-conditions before establishing full diplomatic relations with the United States: (1) the United States must recognize the PRC as the only legitimate government of all of China, including Taiwan; (2) the United States must withdraw all military forces from Taiwan; (3) the United States must terminate its mutual defense treaty with the Republic of China (ROC).

For nearly six years, the PRC stubbornly insisted on fulfillment of these three demands as the United Sttes sought to modify them and secure some firm assurance from Peking that it would not attack Taiwan if the United States withdrew formal support from the ROC. The United States constantly moved in the direction of the fulfillment of these terms by incrementally withdrawing forces from Taiwan and steadily upgrading its mission in Peking and downgrading the one in Taipei. Thus, the PRC liaison office in Washington became a virtual embassy in Washington as did the American liaison office in Peking.

Finally, on December 15, 1978, President Carter agreed to the three demands by Peking in order to complete the process of normalization begun by Richard Nixon in 1972. While important details of this decision are examined below, the most basic question raised, particularly by critics of the action, is: What specific benefits did the United States receive in exchange for accepting Peking's conditions for diplomatic recognition? Presumably prior to taking any action with the gravity of breaking diplomatic relations with a nation and unilaterally terminating a defense treaty with an ally who has not violated the terms of the treaty, the United States should have had compelling reasons for making such a change.

The Nature and Timing of the Announcement

The announcement by President Carter that he would establish diplo-

---

**Jeffrey Gayner is Director of Foreign Policy Studies, *The Heritage Foundation.*

matic relations with the People's Republic of China came quite unexpectedly in his national television address. Only seven hours before the announcement did the United States inform the Republic of China of the action, awaking President Chiang Ching-kuo in the middle of the night, Taiwan time. Similarly, only hours before the speech, the president informed key congressional leaders of the impending action.

Although early in the Carter administration a definite decision was made to establish full diplomatic relations with Peking, only in early December did it have what they felt was a breakthrough in negotiations with Peking, and then it moved quickly toward a Joint Communiqué and prepared for a visit of Chinese Vice Premier Teng Hsiao-ping to Washington in late January. The administration provided no compelling reasons for the hasty decision which coincided with, and diverted attention from, the failure to achieve the December 17 deadline on completing a Middle East treaty between Israel and Egypt. Some members of Congress particularly resented the president's taking the action at a time when they were out of session and, therefore, apparently avoiding deliberately their consultation and advice.

The Congress and the China Decision

The actions by the president undoubtedly will lead to some confrontation with the Congress—both because of his failure to consult with them and for assuming the authority to unilaterally terminate the 1954 Mutual Defense Treaty with the Republic of China. In a resolution passed by a unanimous 94-0 Senate roll call vote, and subsequently adopted by the House, the Congress last summer instructed the president to consult with the Congress before taking action to terminate the treaty with Taipei. The most relevant clauses of the amendment stated the following after acceptance by both the Senate and then a joint conference committee on the bill: "It is the responsibility of the Senate to give its advice and consent to treaties entered into by the United States. It is the sense of the Congress that there should be prior consultation between the Congress and the executive branch on any proposed policy changes affecting the continuation in force of the Mutual Defense Treaty of 1954." Senator John Glenn, Chairman of the Far East Subcommittee of the Senate Foreign Relations Committee, somewhat bitterly stated: "Calling a few of us in one hour before he goes on television doesn't seem like much consultation."

Serious legal questions have been raised over the authority of the president to act under Article X of the Mutual Defense Treaty without approval of the Congress. Article X provides for termination by stating: "Either party may terminate it [the treaty] one year after notice has been given to the other party." Senator Goldwater argues that just as the president cannot make treaties without a two-thirds approval vote of the Senate, he cannot terminate them without its consent. He notes that, historically, the definition of "party" to a treaty means not simply the president, but the president and the Congress.[1] Otherwise, it is argued, all defense treaties of the United States, such as those with NATO, Japan, Korea and the Philippines, could be canceled by a unilateral presidential action.

Other senators, beyond those who questioned the wisdom of terminating the treaty with the Republic of China, have raised this serious constitutional question that ultimately may have to be resolved in litigation before the Supreme Court. Senator Goldwater bluntly warned that if the president "attempts to circumvent the Congress in abrogating our defense treaty with Taiwan, I plan to take him to court and show the action to be both illegal and unconstitutional." By challenging the legal authority of the Congress to participate in the China decision, the Carter administration has further complicated its efforts to proceed with an orderly process of normalization.

By failing to even consult with the Congress in the initial stages of changing U.S.-China policy, the president has risked serious confrontation with Congress as he attempts to legislatively carry out the policy. He must secure congressional approval of his new ambassador to Peking as well as extensive legislation ostensibly designed to preserve the enormous range of treaties and other agreements currently in force with the Republic of China. By setting January 1, 1979, as the date for breaking relations with the Republic of China, the president precluded the possibility of Congress enacting new legislation to protect American interests in the Republic of China and thus cast many present relationships into a very ambiguous legal situation.

The Reality of Two Chinas

At the center of President Carter's address to the nation is the fundamental point that has promoted the entire normalization process for the past six years: "In recognizing that the government of the People's Republic is the single government of China, we are recognizing simple reality." In an interview that same day, White House national security advisor Dr. Brzezinski emphasized that point: "We are simply ending a fiction, namely that the government on the island of Taiwan governs one billion Chinese who live on the mainland and who in fact are governed by somebody else. Once this becomes clear, I think most people will realize that we have not only recognized reality, but we have taken a step which is good for international peace and very much in the American national security interest." Thus, the U.S. government formally ended recognition of the government of the Republic of China in Taipei as the government of China.

However, the administration has substituted a new fiction by now ignoring the reality of the existence of the Republic of China. The communiqué states that the U.S. "recognizes the government of the People's Republic of China as the sole legal government of China" and that the U.S. "acknowledges the Chinese position that there is but one China and Taiwan is part of China." In reality, the communist government in Peking has never controlled or governed the territory of Taiwan, whereas the Republican government in Taipei once governed all of China with the last freely elected government. Senator Richard Stone, a member of the Foreign Relations Committee, emphasized in a "Face the Nation" interview that "where the opposition is, in the country and the Congress, is to stating that the sole legal government of Taiwan is the mainland government when it isn't." The government in Peking does govern and control mainland China, but Taipei certainly governs and controls Taiwan and the offshore islands of Kinmen and Matsu. Recognizing Peking's claim as the legal government of Taiwan thus creates an even greater fiction than the claim that Taipei continues to govern all of China.

A policy of conforming to reality would thus have recognized the existence of two separate governments controlling different portions of one country, such as the United States currently does formally with East and West Germany and tacitly with North and South Korea. In 1971, the United States previously advanced this two-China position before the United Nations, so a precedent existed for such action in negotiating with Peking. But rather than advance this position, the United States simply capitulated to the PRC terms for formal recognition.

Many analysts of China believe that the United States had the capacity to resolve the Taiwan question by demanding recognition of the reality of two Chinas. Administration spokesmen, on the other hand, insisted that this would constitute interference in the internal affairs of another country and also that no other nation has been able to have formal government relations with both Taipei and Peking. However, the United States, as the most important nation in the free world, undoubtedly has the capacity to make rather than simply imitate policy and possibly could have, and maybe still can, insisted upon ending the fiction that either Chinese government controls the territory of the other. By withdrawing from Taiwan, the United States merely postpones rather than resolves the disposition of Taiwan when the attempt may be made (as indicated below) to reunite China. The mediation role of the United States (as in the Middle East) could be crucial, but will be less likely with Washington apparently aligning itself with Peking on the question of the legal status of Taiwan.

Public Opinion and U.S.-China Policy

The president's decision to establish formal diplomatic relations with Peking undoubtedly has the support of the overwhelming majority of the American people. but an even larger majority dissents from the conditions he accepted by securing an American embassy in Peking at the expense of the American embassy in Taipei and the termination of the Mutual Defense Treaty.

An extensive survey of American opinion on China published by the Gallup Organization in August 1977 found that while fifty-six percent of the

336

American people favored establishing diplomatic relations with Peking, an even larger majority of sixty-four percent favored continuing relations with Taipei. And a slightly larger majority of sixty-five percent felt that the U.S. should not withdraw recognition from the Republic of China in order to establish relations with the People's Republic of China.

Similarly, a survey by Daniel Yankelovich early this year found that Americans both favored recognition of Peking by a 62-17 percent margin, but at the same time did not want to abandon Taiwan by a slightly larger 62-11 margin and wanted to preserve the Mutual Defense Treaty by a 57-12 margin.

Finally, a Harris Survey released in early September 1978 uncovered similarly lopsided sentiment, as Americans favored recognition of Peking by 66-25 margin, but again opposed withdrawing recognition of Taipei as a condition for it by a 66-19 margin and continuing the defense treaty by a 64-19 margin.

In the initial polls following the decision, opinion remained divided about the same way. A CBS News poll following the December 15 announcement found that Americans opposed closer ties with China at the expense of relations with Taiwan by a forty-five percent to twenty-seven percent margin. The poll also showed that most Americans felt that Peking had benefited more from the agreement than had the United States. A Gallup Poll in early January 1979 showed that forty-seven percent of the people surveyed believed that the decision of Carter was wrong, while only thirty-five percent supported the president. Both polls demonstrated initial confusion, as large segments of the population felt that diplomatic relations would continue with Taiwan. As people become more aware of precisely what has transpired, dissent from the action quite likely will increase and China could become a major divisive issue on the American political scene.

The Shanghai Communiqué

At the keystone of the structure of American relations with the People's Republic of China stands the Shanghai Communiqué. This agreement formally initiated the normalization process and invariably is cited as the most important document in U.S.-China relations. The PRC has consistently called for the fulfillment of the Shanghai Communiqué, and in the joint communiqué issued on December 15, 1978, President Carter "reaffirmed the principles agreed on by the two sides in the Shanghai Communiqué" and reiterated them with some slight modifications.

Given the importance of the agreement, an enormous amount of ignorance surrounds both the meaning and implications of the actual text. For the purposes of arriving at the nature of the American commitment embodied in this agreement, one must examine the precise wording of the document issued in the form of a joint communiqué on February 27, 1972. The American side simply declared the following:

337

The United States acknowledges that all Chinese on either side of the Taiwan Strait maintain there is but one China and that Taiwan is a part of China. The United States government does not challenge that position. It reaffirms its interest in a peaceful settlement of the Taiwan question by the Chinese themselves. With this prospect in mind, it affirms the ultimate objective of the withdrawal of all U.S. forces and military installations from Taiwan. In the meantime, it will progressively reduce its forces and military installations on Taiwan as the tension in the area diminishes.

Quite significantly, the declaration did not state what the American position on Taiwan was, only that the U.S. government does not challenge the position that both Chinese governments agree on the unity of all of China. The December 15 communiqué similarly stated that the U.S. "acknowledges the Chinese position that there is but one China and Taiwan is a part of China." Once again, no clear American position appeared.

In the Shanghai Communiqué, the United States only agreed to the removal of military forces from Taiwan "as the tensions in the area diminish." President Carter did not mention this in his communiqué. But it would seem that unless the PRC were willing to proclaim peaceful intentions in the area, then the United States should not withdraw its remaining forces, which have now diminished to about seven hundred men. However, the PRC has still refused to foreswear the use of force in settling its dispute with Taiwan. Therefore, it is difficult to contend that "tensions in the area" have diminished to the point that a complete American military withdrawal is in order and that the treaty should terminate.

While it is now contended that carrying out the terms of the Shanghai Communiqué required an American withdrawal from Taiwan and abrogation of the Mutual Defense Treaty, Dr. Kissinger denied such implications in a press conference following the signing of the agreement in 1972:

Let me state in response to this and any related question. Let me do it once and not repeat it. Let me state our position with respect to this issue, that is, the treaty commitment to Taiwan, in the President's world report, in which we say this treaty will be maintained. Nothing has changed in that position.

The agreement later acquired a somewhat ambiguous place in American diplomacy. Neither of the two principals who signed the Communiqué— Richard Nixon and Chou En-lai—is any longer in office, and many of their policies have been repudiated. The agreement was never submitted for approval to the United States Congress and thus simply enjoys the status of an executive declaration of policy.

In contrast to the Shanghai Communiqué, the United States still has a formal Mutual Defense Treaty with the Republic of China, adopted in 1954, which President Carter intends to terminate in one year. In this treaty, Article II pledges both governments to "maintain and develop their individual and collective capacity to resist armed attack and communist subversive activities directly from without against their territorial integrity and political stability." Thus, Article V goes on to provide:

An armed attack in the west Pacific area directed against the territories of either of the parties would be dangerous to its own peace and safety, and each declares that it would act to meet the common danger in accordance with its constitutional processes.

Quite clearly the language of a formal treaty ratified by the United States Senate takes legal precedence over a somewhat ambiguously worded executive agreement signed by two former office-holders. Nonetheless, the recent actions taken by President Carter allegedly have been mandated by the Shanghai Communiqué as though that agreement contained a clarity and authority that is entirely unjustified.

The Japanese Model of Chinese Relations

In announcing that the United States would break formal diplomatic relations with the Republic of China, President Carter emphasized:

The people of the United States will maintain our current commercial, cultural and other relations with Taiwan through non-governmental means. Many other countries are already successfully doing so.

Many analysts point to the example of Japan in the breaking of diplomatic relations. The president thus alluded to what has come to be called the Japanese model of relations with the Republic of China. Under this formula, the United States allegedly would largely continue its present relations with Taiwan but simply conduct them from non-governmental offices. The underlying assumption behind this proposal is that because the Japanese pursued such a course of action when they broke diplomatic relations with the ROC, no adverse consequences would follow for either the United States or the ROC if this policy were imitated by Washington. Unfortunately, this simple formula of "changing the nameplates" is largely irrelevant to the present circumstances.

First, it is not often mentioned that Japan never enjoyed the long and close relationship with the Republic of China that the United States has had. In fact, the island of Taiwan was a colony of Japan for the first half of this century. This has historical ramifications but also leads to a different basis for the relationship that exists between Japan and the ROC than exists between the United States and the ROC.

Japan never had a mutual defense treaty with the Republic of China, nor did she have military bases located on Taiwan at the request of the ruling government. For three decades Japan's relations since her occupation were essentially commercial. Similarly, while Japan has no military forces outside her own territory, the United States maintains bases in the Philippines, Korea, Japan, and Guam. Thus, Taiwan constitutes an important element in a defense designed for the entire Pacific region, as was the case during the Vietnam War. As tensions may again rise in Korea with the withdrawal of American ground forces, the use of facilities on Taiwan could again be important to the United States.

The Japanese formula is also inadequate because it was largely designed as a reaction to the Kissinger secret trip to the PRC in 1971 and subsequent secret diplomacy with Peking. Because the Japanese felt isolated after these events in 1971-72, they opted for a dramatic move to bolster their own diplomatic position in the region and established full relations with the PRC.

Members of the Japanese Diet, and former Foreign Minister Kiichi Miyazawa, have pointed out differences which indicated that the Japanese model is not relevant for U.S.-Chinese relations. In fact, they contend that the Japanese action was only feasible because the United States continued to maintain full diplomatic relations with the Republic of China as the necessary back-up support for Japan. Only in this manner could Japan and other nations lessen their own diplomatic relations but retain economic relations. Thus, the Japanese formula only worked because the fall-back position of the United States still sustained the *de facto* "full diplomatic" status of the Republic of China for all other countries. At this time, the Repubilc of Korea is the next largest country that maintains full diplomatic relations with the Republic of China. Therefore, with the United States breaking relations with the Republic of China and attempting to follow the Japanese formula, no other country could act in a similar supportive position for the United States.

Given the differences in their relations with Taiwan, the Japanese could much more easily acquiesce to the demands of Peking than could the United States. Quite simply, Japan only had to terminate its formal relations with Taipei in order to establish an embassy in Peking. However, the PRC demanded that the United States not only terminate diplomatic relations with the ROC but also end the Mutual Defense Treaty of 1954 and remove all military personnel from the island.

The Security of Taiwan

In a press conference on May 12, 1977, President Carter indicated that his principal concern with normalizing relations with Peking centered on the future security of Taiwan: "We don't want to see the Taiwanese people punished or attacked and if we can resolve that major difficulty, I would move expeditiously to normalize relations with China."

The president implied that if only the Chinese would forswear the use of force in settling the "Taiwan problem," then a satisfactory resolution of the great China dilemma could be found. As indicated below, other probably more serious questions must also be answered, but even this minimal request posed to the PRC has been sternly rejected. The Chinese Vice Premier promptly responded to Carter's views three days later. Chi Teng-kuei simply stated that China would accept no such conditions. He declared that "to liberate Taiwan in a peaceful way or by armed force—this is China's domestic affair and not a U.S. affair." In the following nineteen months, the Chinese have not changed their adamant position.

According to the December 15, 1978 statement, "the United States continues to have an interest in the peaceful resolution of the Taiwan issue and expects that the Taiwan issue will be settled peacefully by the Chinese themselves." However, the statement by the PRC on the same day remains inflexible on the issue by proclaiming again: "As for the way of bringing Taiwan back to the embrace of the motherland and reunifying the country, it is entirely China's internal affair." When pressed on this issue, Secretary of State Vance indicated that the PRC would make no public declaration on this point but he simply expected a peaceful resolution of the conflict between the two Chinese governments.

The administration insists that Peking made a major concession in negotiations by both allowing the Mutual Security Treaty to continue for one year beyond the establishment of diplomatic relations and in that the PRC also will continue to allow U.S. arms sale to Taiwan even after the completion of the normalization process and termination of the security treaty in 1980. Largely on the basis of these two concessions from Peking, the Carter administration contends that the continued security of Taiwan can be guaranteed at least for the next five years.

As indicated earlier, the Mutual Security Treaty contained a provision for a termination with a one-year notification. Thus, rather than a concession by Peking, it would seem that the administration had little choice but to obey the terms of the treaty both for legal reasons and to prevent panic in Taiwan and diminished credibility of U.S. security treaty guarantees everywhere in the world.

The question of the sale of arms has led to the greatest initial disagreement with Peking over the meaning of normalization and implications for future U.S. relations with Taiwan. Secretary of State Vance insisted that the United States would not only continue to fulfill orders for weapons already in process for Taiwan, but also would continue to sell additional equipment even after the termination of the Mutual Defense Treaty at the beginning of 1980. But in his first open press conference taking questions from Western reporters, Chinese Communist Party Chairman Hua Kuo-feng warned that "after the normalization, the continued sale of arms to Taiwan by the United States does not conform to the principles of the normalization. So our two sides have differences on this point; nevertheless we reached agreement on the joint communiqué." The administration insisted that this protest was simply *pro forma* and that Peking would not challenge the continued sale of arms to Taiwan, but their public disagreements do not auger well for the future.

Very few analysts expect Peking to attack Taiwan in order to reunify China anytime in the near future. Although it is very curious that many supporters of normalization of relations with Peking emphasize the value of the PRC to offset Soviet military power, at the same time they insist that the PRC does not even have the military capability to attack Taiwan. Either a strange inconsistency exists or Taiwan must represent such an awesome military power that the United States should seriously question moving away from its side.

When asked by reporters whether he feared a military attack by the PRC, the ROC ambassador to Washington responded to the question as follows: "Not at the moment. We know that they have the intention, but the question is whether they have the capacity to mount an amphibious assault attack across the ninety miles of water or whether they find themselves free to do something like that without inviting trouble on their own borders on both the north and south." The ROC currently has a better air force than does the PRC and a well-equipped and trained army of 500,000 men—one of the largest standing armies in the non-communist world.

A military threat to Taiwan would arise only over a period of years if the United States refused to sell it new equipment or provide spare parts for existing material. Even before the December 15 communiqué, the United States has refused to sell numerous military items to Taiwan, and thus the ROC has not been able to upgrade its forces to keep pace with the advances in offensive capabilities of the PRC.

In 1974, the ROC began producing its own F-5E fighters under a contract with the Northrop Corporation. It also manufactures its own helicopters, machine guns, rifles, military vehicles and trainer aircraft. However, the ROC has thus far been refused other, more sophisticated equipment by the United States. The ROC has sought F-4 Phantoms, F-16 and F-18 fighters, and Harpoon anti-ship missiles. Several months ago, the U.S. refused to allow Taiwan to purchase even the much less sophisticated F-5G fighter plane. But while willing to sell 160 F-16s to Iran, the Defense Department refuses to make them or other advanced fighters available to Taiwan. Similarly, delays in the sale of Harpoons led Taiwan to attempt to buy Israeli-produced Gabriel missiles, having previously purchased Rafael Shafrir air-to-air missiles from Israel in 1973. Taiwan is willing to purchase military equipment and thereby redress part of its balance of trade surplus with the United States, but the Carter administration has refused to permit such sales. Such sales would now seem much more necessary to insure that the ROC can maintain both the military balance in the area and the confidence of the people in Taiwan that the United States will reliably replace equipment as the American military forces withdraw from the island. In

Korea the American military withdrawal is being accompanied by a large-scale upgrading of Korean forces even as the Mutual Security Treaty and U.S. air bases remain intact in the country.

Lastly, without adequate U.S. conventional weapons, Taiwan may have no choice but to develop nuclear weapons to preserve its independence. And technically, as a nation now considered legally part of the PRC, it should no longer be bound as far as the U.S. is concerned by the Nuclear Proliferation Treaty which Peking refused to sign.[2]

Economic Problems of Breaking Relations with the Republic of China

While most of the discussion of U.S.-ROC-PRC relations revolve around politics, alliances, balances of power and potential formulas for reconciling differences, very little consideration has been given to exactly what the American relationship with the ROC currently entails. If there is a change of relations, as indicated by something like the Japanese formula discussed above, then just what will this mean for the Republic of China? Since no real precedent exists for the situation, one can only ponder what will happen to the vast web of economic and other relations that the ROC currently enjoys. Enumerated below are some of the problems that have not been even mentioned in much of the discussion, let alone resolved in any satisfactory manner.

1. What will become of the status of the Republic of China in the various financial institutions that facilitate its tremendous trade? In the past year, the PRC has signed contracts for over $60 billion, yet now only exports about $9 billion in goods and services, so she must borrow enormous sums. Thus, she will undoubtedly try to displace the borrowing status of the ROC in such places as the Export-Import Bank. Would the Export-Import Bank call in all loans to the ROC at the demand of the PRC? As of December 1978, the ROC had outstanding loans of $2.2 billion, making her the second largest customer in the bank after Brazil.

2. What will happen to the seat of the ROC in the International Monetary Fund and the International Bank for Reconstruction and Development? Will the PRC be able to force out the then unrecognized government of the ROC? How would this affect the vital trade relations of the ROC? What happens if the PRC demands to join the World Bank as the successor to the seat held by the ROC? If Peking joins the bank, could it request a share of loans comparable to India and therefore force the bank to increase its capital by an estimated two billion dollars simply for loans to China? Would the U.S. have to contribute a part of such an amount if requested? In the past, Peking has demanded the ouster of Taipei but never agreed to actually join herself. American efforts have kept the ROC in the bank over the years. Would this be compromised with the change in diplomatic relations?

3. What will happen to the eight American banks in the ROC? What will happen to their status? Who will legally control their funds? Could they

continue to operate in an ordinary way? U.S. private banks estimate total loans amounting to $2.8 billion have been advanced to the ROC.

4. What will happen to the over one-half billion dollars ($516 million) of U.S. investments in the ROC? The ROC currently has one of the most advantageous climates for American investment in the world. Will this be able to continue, or will the ROC lose some legal authority to the PRC? In contrast, Japanese investment only amounted to $7.7 million. At present American commercial relations with the ROC are governed by the Taiwan Treaty of Friendship, Commerce and Navigation. A total of forty-nine treaties govern U.S.-ROC commercial and other relations. But as of January 1, 1979, apparently all of these treaties were cast into legal limbo as the U.S. ceased to recognize the legitimacy of the government which negotiated them.

5. If the PRC, through whatever circumstances, actually comes to power in the ROC and expropriates American properties, would compensation for losses occur? If so, how would a determination of value be made? Or if future political chaos ushers in uncertainty that causes a business collapse in Taiwan, would resulting losses be covered? What about the drastic ripple effect on the American economy of the total disruption of over $6 billion in trade with the ROC? For example, the U.S. exported $612 million of agricultural goods to Taiwan in 1978. Could a substitute market be readily found?

6. What will happen to all standard commercial agreements, such as long-term contracts now in effect? Can they be honored or extended? This would include a range of items from nuclear fuel to textile quotas. Would these agreements revert to the PRC as the only legitimate government in China or as the successor government of the ROC?

7. As a result of the recognition of the PRC as the only legitimate government of all of China, could it intervene in commercial and other affairs of Taiwan? Could the PRC call for an embargo of all goods coming from Taiwan, or demand that all commercial relations with Taiwan be first approved in Peking? Could it act in a manner similar to the British and the Sugar Act of 1764, and demand that all shipping to Taiwan must first touch port with the mainland and pay taxes? Could the PRC demand a special levy on any goods being exported from Taiwan?

8. Could the PRC propose economic sanctions at the United Nations against the allegedly rebellious province of Taiwan? Could sanctions similar to those imposed on Rhodesia be implemented and any American trade be condemned by the U.N.? As the only recognized legitimate sovereign government of all of China, could not Peking declare a general blockade of Taiwan similar to the Union's blockade of the South during the American Civil War? Could they close the Straits of Taiwan to international shipping destined for ROC ports?

9. Similarly, would the PRC eventually demand an end to any "covert" support of the ROC through trade or bank loans by the United States and

contend that the United States is interfering in its internal affairs and thus violating the spirit of the normalization process?

10. What will happen to the flow of people between the ROC, the U.S., and other countries? Could the PRC as the legitimate government of China impose restrictions upon the issuance of visas and thereby intervene in tourism, cultural or educational exchanges of the ROC? Who would control the air space over the ROC and what would become of international air traffic agreements with the ROC and their flag carrier, China Air Lines? Can Taiwanese declare themselves political refugees from communism?

The questions posed above deal with the enormous web of relations of the ROC that only indirectly relate to the security of the country. Yet the questions indicate quite clearly that even without the use of actual military force, Peking has an enormous range of options available to pursue a policy of economic strangulation of the ROC. The complete political isolation of the ROC can easily lead to economic isolation and the destruction of the country because of its dependence on international commercial and other relations. This is a much more likely course of action for the PRC to take against the ROC than any precipitous military assault and could easily be defined as a "peaceful" resolution of the so-called Taiwan problem. Thus, very serious problems inevitably arise in the proposed formula involving the termination of diplomatic relations with the ROC and discounting all governmantal relations with the ROC.

The China Market Myth

President Carter implied a definite connection between trade and normalization in his December 15 speech, stating: "Normalization—and the expanded commercial and cultural relations it will bring with it—will contribute to the well-being of our own nation, and will enhance stability in Asia." Similarly, Christopher Phillips, president of the National Council for U.S.-China trade, expected "to see a substantial increase in our trade with China as a result of this announcement." An initial boom in trade with the PRC did follow quickly in the wake of the Nixon visit to China in 1972. However, this initial rise in trade precariously depended upon the purchase of several Boeing aircraft and some food supplies needed to satisfy a short-term shortage. Thus, the level of trade precipitously fell after only two years. In 1977 trade rose only slightly, and in 1978 it is expected to finally surpass the earlier 1974 level. Still, total U.S.-PRC trade amounts to less than one-seventh of U.S.-ROC trade.

The trade figures reveal quite conspicuously the great myth of the China market. Even with full diplomatic relations the initial projections for trade indicate a widening gap between the U.S.-ROC trade and U.S.-PRC trade. Barring any interference, U.S.-ROC trade expects to rise to a total of $12 billion by 1981. In contrast, U.S.-PRC trade will only rise to about $3 billion, or one-fourth of U.S.-ROC trade. Thus the current $6 billion difference will grow to $9 billion in the next three years.

Unlike the ROC, the PRC has no significant consumer market and produces few products in demand by Americans. Although China expects to become a major exporter of oil and has concluded substantial economic deals with Japan based on this, it cannot contribute to American energy problems. Alaskan oil already overwhelms west coast ports, and Chinese oil has a high sulphur content not suited for U.S. refineries. The oil revenues may be able to promote some purchases, however.

Formal diplomatic relations may help promote some trade, but it cannot change the basic structural problems in the PRC that mitigate against such basic things as foreign investment. Curiously, the same people who assert that full diplomatic relations with Peking are necessary to create a trade boom insist at the same time that even without benefit of a liaison office the Republic of China can continue her enormous trade with the U.S. If political stability continues in Taiwan, this may be true, but it has more to do with the economic systems existing in the two parts of China than to the diplomatic status of businessmen. Eugene A. Theroux, former vice president of the National Council for U.S.-China (PRC) Trade, has concluded that "there is no prospect of trade with the Chinese sufficient to warrant proceeding with normalization."

Beyond marketing problems, the PRC also suffers from existing congressional restrictions on any future trade. Even with full recognition, the PRC could not qualify for most favored nation status or major credit guarantees, because under the Jackson/Vanik Amendment to the Trade Act the PRC violates the freedom of emigration requirements. At present, virtually no restrictions exist on the sales of U.S. goods to China; nonetheless, PRC purchases have never risen substantially because of a lack of sufficient foreign reserves for overseas purchases. The United States could only sell a large volume of goods to the PRC if American banks loaned the funds necessary for purchasing such goods.

Possibly only through the influx of enormous amounts of foreign goods and technology may the PRC be able to overcome some of the disastrous effects of Mao's economic policies over the past two decades. But the core of its economic problem remains its communist system, and hence it will never be able to achieve the levels of growth reached by its neighbors in Japan, Korea, and the ROC. Given the increased Soviet threats to Peking and the public acknowledgment by Teng of China's backwardness, China has begun to borrow money for some foreign purchases.

The Future of Taiwan

As indicated in the discussion above, the fundamental question initially surrounding the decision of December 15 must focus on the future of Taiwan. The president, in his speech, felt compelled to state the following:

[I wish to] convey a special message to the people of Taiwan, with whom the American people have had and will have extensive close and friendly relations. As the United States asserted in the Shanghai Communiqué of 1972, we continue to have an interest in the peaceful resolution of the Taiwan issue. I have paid special attention to ensuring that normalization of relations between the United States and the People's Republic of China will not jeopardize the well-being of the people of Taiwan.

Unfortunately, the nature of the rhetoric used to convey this message as well as the failure to consult with Taiwan substantially undermines the credibility of the Carter administration. In his entire speech, the president never once referred to the Republic of China nor to the government of the Republic of China; instead references only allude to the "people of Taiwan" as though they constituted an entity separate from the government. In effect, such language can only serve to undermine the authority of the government of the Republic of China.

Moreover, the emphasis on a "peaceful resolution of the Taiwan issue" implies that the Republic of China should attempt to negotiate a reintegration into mainland China or face perpetual isolation in the world. Without continued support from the United States, the Republic of China will be in a much more vulnerable position to eventually succumb to pressure from the PRC and sacrifice independence and with it an alternative way of life for the Chinese people. At present, the Republic of China remains the custodian of ancient Chinese civilization as the mainland continues, even if in a more pragmatic way, to refashion China in the crucible of Marxism.

If the concern of the United States is only on a "peaceful" way of reuniting China, then presumably no objection will arise if Peking uses the economic pressures indicated above and thereby destroys a society whose values the United States should particularly appreciate. This is an especially peculiar position for an administration to adhere to after it has placed such an emphasis on human rights. Instead, it appears that American pragmatism somehow requires a viable nation of eighteen million people to become expendable in quest of better relations with its more populous and powerful neighbor.[3]

In order to survive, the Republic of China may now be forced to consider unpleasant alternatives that quite possibly would cause far greater difficulties for the United States in east Asia than continuing the kinds of relations that have existed for the past six years with the two Chinas. The ROC may, as indicated above, be forced to develop nuclear weapons if it no longer has a defense commitment from the United States or some other alternative alliance framework.

The ROC may also have to opt, in its war for survival, with some kind of tacit alliance relationship with the Soviet Union. Precisely the same kind

347

of logic that dictated American normalization of relations with Peking to off-set growing Soviet power in east Asia could compel President Chiang, who grew up in Russia, to turn again to Moscow in order to deal with the common threat they both face from an ostensible American-Peking axis.

Others have suggested that the Republic of China simply should formally declare its independence as the Republic of Taiwan and renounce its claims to mainland China. But even this drastic action would quite likely fail to enlist any more support for the reality of two Chinas than does the current situation, as Peking seemingly maintains a veto power over such an option. Such action would also invalidate all the existing ROC agreements on trade and other matters.

Aside from taking some kind of dramatic action, the Republic of China can attempt to survive its diplomatic isolation as it survived its ouster from the United Nations and derecognition of so many other governments over the past seven years. But survival this time must be much more precarious because Taiwan's relation with the United States consisted of far more than did its relations with any other nation. Moreover, by ostensibly aligning itself with Peking and recognizing the communist government as the legitimate government of all of China, including Taiwan, the United States becomes a legal adversary even while claiming not to "jeopardize the well-being of the people of Taiwan."

The future of Taiwan then remains, even with a break in recognition, substantially in the hands of the United States as the American people and the Congress react to the actions of the president and attempt to alter the terms of the new China policy to provide more likelihood of the survival of the Republic of China.

Conclusion

Without some fundamental changes or successful court or congressional challenges, the normalization of relations with Peking will quite likely lead to very abnormal relations with Taiwan and eventually the destruction of the Republic of China as an independent nation. Rather than attempting to resolve the conflict between Peking and Taipei and recognize the reality of two Chinas, the Carter administration chose to, in effect, change sides in the conflict.

This precipitous action, without prior consultation with Taipei after years of benign neglect, can do little to engender the kind of confidence among the Chinese in Taiwan that the United States will remain a reliable ally in the years ahead. Only continued governmental contact can provide such confidence.

Although no military conflict appears imminent, the breaking of the Mutual Defense Treaty can only eventually encourage Peking adventurism at an opportune time. The PRC will undoubtedly attempt to move Taiwan from complete diplomatic isolation to complete economic isolation.

Through pursuit of this "peaceful" manner of resolving the Peking-Taipei conflict, the PRC may be able to avoid a war and thereby seize the industrial infrastructure of the island intact.

Far from creating either peace or stability, the decision to break relations with the Republic of China in favor of relations with the People's Republic can only create new tension in east Asia and leave to an uncertain fate both the eighteen million people on Taiwan and, prospectively, other nations such as Korea and Israel who rely upon American commitments for their continued independence.

NOTES

1. The question of the Congress and the Mutual Defense Treaty is examined at length by Senator Goldwater in *China and the Abrogation of Treaties* earlier in this book.

2. On this point see George H. Quester, "Taiwan and Nuclear Proliferation," *Orbis,* Spring 1974.

3. On the human rights question, see the author's "The Status of Liberty in China," in Edwin J. Feulner, Jr., *China—The Turning Point,* Council on American Affairs, 1976.

The China Decision:
The Moral Dimension

Allan C. Brownfeld*

For a variety of reasons, President Carter and his foreign policy advisors believed that their decision to "normalize" relations with Peking, even by accepting all of Peking's pre-conditions, was a wise political decision. It would boost the president's popularity, they argued, and would also serve as a counter-weight in the world to growing Soviet strength. American business, both they and many businessmen themselves stated, would benefit from the decision.

There were other, perhaps more important, dimensions involved in the dramatic abandonment of a long-time friend and ally than were considered by those who decided to do so. Bismarck once said that a country has no "permanent friends" or "permanent enemies" but only "interests." President Carter, however, has repeatedly argued that one of America's major "interests" in the world is the advancement of "human rights." In the pursuit of this "interest" he has not hesitated to put pressure upon such allies of the United States as Iran, Nicaragua, South Africa, Argentina, Brazil, the Philippines—the list goes on and on. Yet the president, who has prided himself upon not being a traditional politician but, instead, a man with a moral vision, has ignored his own criteria for decision-making when the China issue was to be resolved.

In *Pere Goriot,* Honoré de Balzac puts words in the mouths of one of his characters which were probably on the lips of Mr. Carter's advisors as they planned what they believed would be a popular political action: "A man who prides himself on going in a straight line through life is an idiot who believes in infallibility. There are no such things as principles, there are only events, and there are no laws but those of expediency. A man of talent accepts events and the circumstances in which he finds himself, and turns everything to his owns ends. If laws and principles were fixed and invariable, nations would not change them as readily as we change our shirts. . . . Do you believe that there is any absolute standard in this world? Despise mankind and find out the meshes that you can slip through in the net of the Code. The secret of a great success for which you are at a loss to account is

*Allan C. Brownfeld is a Washington-based journalist.

a crime that has never been found out, because it was done properly."

In announcing his policy, President Carter submitted to the demands of the totalitarian rulers in Peking. They said that recognition depended upon the abandonment of Taiwan and the abrogation of the U.S. treaty. These, they said, were pre-conditions. The U.S. accepted these terms. In return, the president tells us, he received vague "assurances" from Peking that Taiwan would not be physically attacked. George Bush, former head of the U.S. liaison office in Peking, declared: "We gave all and got nothing." Mr. Bush, who favors improved relations with Peking, said that he feared that "in acquiescing to China's three demands, with no apparent guarantee to a Taiwan solution, we are simply diminishing U.S. credibility around the world."

President Carter showed no concern at all for either the status of human rights in Communist China or the future of human rights for the seventeen million citizens of Taiwan. In this sense, there was no moral dimension to this decision on the part of a president who lectures our friends repeatedly about morality.

It is interesting to note that only weeks before the president's declaration, Amnesty International published a 176-page report detailing the real status of human rights in Communist China. Among the findings are these:

• Loosely worded laws have permitted large-scale imprisonment on political grounds, while categories of persons described as "class enemies" have been deprived of their political and civil rights on the basis of "class origin" or political background.

• Trials either in secret or in the form of mass public meetings too often have permitted no real defense. They have not begun until a defendant has confessed, and their main purpose is to announce a sentence.

• Once an arrest warrant has been issued, pre-trial detention has too often been unlimited. Certain political offenders could be punished by compulsory labor without judicial investigation. Wide scope for pre-trial detention has allowed authorities to pressure defendants into confessing before being brought to trial.

• Detention conditions often fall below standards set by the United Nations and Chinese law itself. Psychological abuse, isolation, shortages of food and medicine, and use of handcuffs and chains have been reported.

Amnesty International declared that for thirty years the Chinese Communist regime has systematically repressed political dissent, jailing and executing large numbers of people for their political views. The report stated: "The government of the People's Republic of China is, today, one of those governments which, in the last year, has executed persons convicted of political offenses."

Among the specific cases reported:

• Teacher Ho Chun-su was immediately executed in February 1978, after a death sentence was imposed for writing and distributing a "counter-revolutionary" leaflet.

- Farmer Teng Ching-san was sentenced to fifteen years in prison after his 1970 arrest on charges of slandering Chairman Mao.
- Tibetan monk Chamba Lobsang received a life term in prison after a public meeting in 1960 accused him of "exploiting the masses in the name of religion."

Unfortunately, most of what Western journalists and travelers have told us about life in Communist China differs significantly from reality. In a recent book, *Chinese Shadows* (Penguin Books, 1978), Simon Leys (a pseudonym for Belgian Sinologist Pierre Ryckmans, which enabled him to continue visiting China) tells us a story which all who are concerned about human rights and human dignity will find depressing indeed.

Leys has a Chinese wife and a deep abiding love for both the Chinese people and Chinese culture. He is, in addition, fluent in Chinese. He laments: "Most of the praise bestowed on Mao and his bureaucrats by Westerners comes from people who feel only contempt for Chinese people and who are ignorant of Chinese culture. Is it not time, then, for someone who owes China all that he treasures most in life to stand up and criticize Maoism on behalf of those who taught him so much?"

This is the task which Pierre Ryckmans set for himself. Around the world, he has been hailed for his analysis of life in Communist China. Writing in the *New York Times,* John K. Fairbank said that Ryckmans has provided "one of the most caustic exposés by a Sinologist of the Cultural Revolution's basically anti-intellectual attack on China's cultural heritage." Stanley Karnow, the author of *Mao and China,* declared that Ryckmans has "finally demystified China."

The author has much to say about the manner in which efforts to keep to the ever-changing Communist Party line have eliminated virtually all rational discourse in China. "Thus," he writes, "the most furious foes of Liu Shao-chi are those who described his China of the early 1960s as a kind of paradise: they suddenly discover now that China then suffered from famine and bureaucratic oppression, which of course were due to the sabotages of the all-powerful and ever-present Liu. But anybody who might have been bold enough at the time to see the evidence of famine and oppression—and it was certainly obvious enough—would have been nothing but a lying detractor in the pay of the Americans."

The situation which has become all too familiar under Maoism is similar, Ryckmans points out, to what occurred during the time of the scheming prime minister of the second Chin emperor (third century B.C.) who, trying to determine who among the courtiers were his followers, pretended that a deer presented in court was actually a horse. All those who insisted that it was a deer were later eradicated.

It was not, however, only those living in China under the grip of Maoism who denied the truth. Western observers of Mao's China during the Cultural Revolution also kept closely to the party line. Ryckmans writes: "Even its most delirious manifestations did not shake the faithful: on the contrary, they became indignant when they saw the smirk of unbelief on the faces of those who observed their delirium. Only when new instructions were issued in 1971-72 did these enthusiasts begin to suspect 'formalist deviations' or even 'Lin Piaoist plots' in the madness they had supported so happily for four years. The bloody violence of the Cultural Revolution was known to all: one would have thought that confronted with the stark evidence our Maoists would have at least kept quiet. But no. Once again, they accused all witnesses of lying—until—until Mao himself exonerated the witnesses, confiding to Edgar Snow: 'Foreign journalists have written about the excesses of the Cultural Revolution, but in fact they understated them.'"

While the Chinese Communists and their sympathizers in the West have spoken of the "egalitarianism" of life in China, the fact remains that they have created a system of hierarchical privilege which is even more pronounced than that of other Chinese dynasties.

The author notes: "In the sixth century B.C., at the time the Tso Chuan refers to, China's social hierarchy had only ten degrees. We have progressed since then: the Maoist bureaucracy today has thirty hierarchical classes, each with specific privileges and prerogatives. Its scrupulous care, nay obsession, for protocol is a permanent cause for wonderment among Western diplomats in Peking. . . . In old China, the mandarins were called, in a very telling phrase, 'Those who eat meat.' . . . Various gastronomical privileges still distinguish officials of a certain level from mere mortals. . . . But if a new phrase must be found to qualify modern mandarins, 'those-who-ride-in-cars' would probably be most appropriate. In China, there are no cars but mandarinal cars."

The Cultural Revolution did not in any way change this hierarchy of privilege; it only masked it. The author reports that in trains, for example, "first, second and third classes have disappeared 'in name' but are now referred to as 'sitting hard' (ying tso), 'sleeping hard' (ying wo), and 'sleeping soft' (ying wo)." These, he writes, "are exactly the same classes as before, ranging from single to triple prices."

The Communist Chinese destruction of ancient Chinese culture and civilization is described in detail. Professor Ryckmans believes that the infatuation of many Western intellectuals with Maoism is not based, in any sense, upon either an understanding of its real nature or a sympathy with China and the Chinese. He argues: "The Maoist fashions that prevail in the West today in some intellectual circles are remarkably similar in their dynamic to the passion for all chinoiserie in the eighteenth century. It is a new exoticism based, like the earlier ones, on ignorance and imagination. With the best intention in the world it shows, unconsciously, an immense contempt for the Chinese, for their humanity, their real life, their language, their culture, their past and their present. As in the eighteenth century, China is far away; this very distance, which allowed Boucher to paint fancy mandarins for the adornment of Paris drawing rooms, now allows philosophers to give Maoism whatever shape they fancy."

There is much more involved in President Carter's decision, of course, than simply overlooking the fact that the People's Republic of China is one of the world's most serious violators of human rights, or even overlooking the fact that it is a friend and ally of the government of Cambodia, which is even more extreme in its policies.

The President seems also to have overlooked that the United States has repeatedly assured the government on Taiwan of its own honorable intentions. In February 1977, for example, Senator John Sparkman (D-Ala.), chairman of the Senate Foreign Relations Committee, asserted in Taipei that the United States would "not alter its relations with the Republic of China" while seeking normalization of relations with Peking. Senator Sparkman said: "It seems to me that it would be both unwise and unnecessary" to accept Peking's terms to establish normal relations. These terms, he said, call for an end to the U.S.-Republic of China treaty.

When President Carter decided to abandon Taiwan, he did it through the very method of secret diplomacy he had repeatedly said he deplored. He did not consult with either the U.S. Congress or the government of the Republic of China. Beyond this, his approach to the people of Taiwan can properly be characterized as shabby indeed. In Taipei, U.S. Ambassador Leonard Unger called President Chiang Ching-kuo "in the middle of the night, at 2 A.M. Taipei time, eight hours before the announcement, and asked to see him," according to Ambassador James C. Shen, the representative of the Republic of China in Washington.

In Washington, until the very day of the president's announcement, Ambassador Shen was not informed of the impending statement. "We figured that the time to watch for was about six or eight months after the mid-term elections," Shen said. "It came as a complete surprise. Even a week before, in routine contacts with the State Department, there had been no indications." He further declared: "It's a great blow, a shattering experience to think the United States would do it the way they have done it. . . . All along they promised they would consult us."

While the president and his advisors repeatedly spoke of "playing the China card," they overlooked completely both the good faith and honor of the United States and the deplorable record of the Chinese Communist regime. In his study, *The Human Cost of Communism in China,* Professor Richard Walker, director of the Institute of International Studies at the University of South Carolina, states: "It is my considered judgment, after following Communist China for more than two decades, that the cost of progress achieved under communist rule is too high for the conscience of the world to absolve its perpetrators. In terms of human life and human suffering and in terms of destruction of moral and cultural values, this cost cannot be condoned by any rationalization."

That human cost is almost unbelievable—according to Dr. Walker's report, between thirty-four and sixty-four million human beings put to death since Mao Tse-tung's rise to power. While many in the Carter administration and the American business community speak of increased commercial relations with Communist China, they ignore the fact that Peking has constructed a society upon slave labor. Dr. Walker notes: "It is an interesting commentary on Western wishful thinking about . . . China that although forced labor is an organic and essential element of the communist economy, it has received practically no attention in more than a decade." He writes that the very lowest estimate of the slaves in the forced labor camps is ten million, and declares: "It is probable that the Chinese forced labor camps have exacted a higher toll in human life than the mass executions. . . . The Chinese Communists have resorted to numerous campaigns which have separated members of families or arbitrarily sent individuals off either to the countryside or out to frontier areas."

In July 1977, Fan Yuan-yen, a Chinese Communist pilot, defected with his MIG 19 to Taiwan. He reported: "Life on the Chinese mainland is too miserable. I have to seek freedom because I can stand no more communist persecution. There are no freedoms, no human rights on the Chinese mainland. People there are hankering after freedom." Then he added: "The eight hundred million people on the Chinese mainland are leading a miserable life which is beyond the imagination of foreign visitors. Peasants in many places lack food and clothes. Even such 'better-conditioned' cities as Chengchow, Hangchow and Shanghai are filled with beggars. They all came from the countryside. Local authorities are unable to do anything to prevent the hungry rural people from flocking to the cities. There are too many of them to be arrested or fed. Many people in rural areas are starving. They even try to sell their children. . . . According to the 'constitution,' the mainland people seem to enjoy freedom of speech, correspondence, press and assembly. . . . Actually no such freedoms exist."

Unfortunately, while the United States continues to proclaim its concern for "human rights" and "morality," its policy has led the world to an opposite conclusion—that the U.S. cares little for those who have depended upon it and will do whatever appears expedient. Discussing the Vietnamese "boat people," for example, Rutgers Professor Peter Berger writes: "These boats bear a message. It is a simple and ugly message: *Here is what happens to those who put their faith and trust in the United States of America.* . . . All of this is terrible in itself. But it now appears that the abandonment of those who trust us is becoming a habit. *We are getting ready to do it again—this time in Taiwan.* . . . If there is one universal, indeed primeval, principle of morality, it is that one must not deliver one's friends to their enemies. And if there is one maxim in which morality coincides with politics, it is that a nation that breaks its solemn word twice will never be trusted again."

Reassessments for Taiwan, Japan, and South Korea: U.S. Reliability in Asia

Donald J. Senese*

I

President Jimmy Carter's announcement on December 15, 1978 of the "normalization" of relations with the People's Republic of China (Communist China) and the abandonment of the United States' long-time ally the Republic of China on Taiwan by announcing the abrogation of the Mutual Defense Treaty of 1954 hit the American public by surprise—and sent shock-waves of uncertainty and concern to American allies in Asia as well as other world trouble spots. The credibility of the United States took a nose dive due to both the method and the timing of the announcement as the U.S. allies constituting the cornerstone of an alliance of peace and stability in free Asia—Taiwan, Japan, and South Korea—were thrown into a tailspin with new doubts arising and fresh reassessments being made of future developments in the Asian powder keg situation.

In his December 15 broadcast, Carter justified the action as one which would be of "long-term benefit to the people of both the United States and China . . . and to all the peoples of the world; it will also enhance stability in Asia and promote the advancement of peace."[1] The president's national security advisor, Zbigniew Brzezinski, in a speech to the Foreign Policy Association a few days later, stressed that a strong and secure China could contribute to international stability and would allow the United States to "expand our bilateral ties and to consult more closely on matters of common strategic concern."[2]

Besides breaking a three-decade post-World War II alliance with the Republic of China on Taiwan and putting aside the 1954 Mutual Defense Treaty, the Carter action had extended recognition by caving into the three terms laid down by the government of Peking: complete United States withdrawal of its troops from Taiwan, cancellation of existing treaties with Taiwan, and the severing of diplomatic relations with Taiwan. Carter an-

*Donald J. Senese is a Research Associate for the Republican Study Committee of the U.S. House of Representatives.

nounced the one-year notification for ending the Mutual Defense Treaty and stated that all United States troops would be withdrawn within four months, by April 1979. Formal diplomatic relations were established between the United States and the People's Republic of China on January 1, 1979.

In the official text released, the United States agreed to recognize "the People's Republic as the sole legal government of China," though pledging, within that context, to "maintain cultural, commercial, and other unofficial relations with the people of Taiwan." Emphasizing a reaffirmation of the principles agreed upon in the Shanghai Communiqué of 1972, it stated the desire of both powers to reduce "the danger of international military conflict." Neither power would seek hegemony in Asia or any other part of the world or seek to negotiate on behalf of any third party or enter into agreements against other nations. The United States "acknowledges the Chinese position that there is but one China and Taiwan is part of China." And finally the agreement announced that "normalization of Sino-American relations is not only in the interest of the Chinese and American peoples but also contributes to the cause of peace in Asia and the world."[3]

Critics of the Carter move questioned the precedent of the United States openly abandoning a long-time ally in order to embrace a communist power which has been a longtime enemy of the United States and the people of the free nations of Asia. While proponents such a Senator Edward M. Kennedy of Massachusetts praised the action,[4] others, both in and out of Congress, criticized the action and especially the long-range significance of such a move. Senator Barry M. Goldwater of Arizona, joined by other members of Congress, filed suit in the U.S. District Court to have the court declare the president's action in terminating the Mutual Defense Treaty to be unconstitutional and block any further action. The suit maintains that since the Senate is a partner with the president in treaty-making because of the constitutional provision that the Senate must "advise and consent" to agreements with foreign powers, the president cannot terminate a treaty without the participation of the Senate. Goldwater maintains that such action, if unchallenged, would set a dangerous precedent enabling a president to end any defense treaty at will.[5]

Senator Robert Dole of Kansas noted that the United States Senate had clearly expressed itself on the issue by the passage of the Dole-Stone amendment to the Foreign Assistance Authorization Act, stating that "there should be prior consultation between Congress and the executive branch on any proposed policy changes affecting the continuation in force of the Mutual Defense Treaty" between the United States and the Republic of China.[6] The measure passed the Senate on July 25, 1978 by a vote of 94-0.[7] Congress approved this provision, noted Senator Dole, because "it wanted to ensure a substantive role for itself in policy changes affecting the China issue."[8] The co-author of the amendment, Senator Richard Stone of Florida, a member of the Senate Foreign Relations Committee, noted that despite the passage of the amendment for consultation, there was no consultation with Congress when the president took his action on China.[9]

Representative Lester L. Wolff of New York, Chairman of the subcommittee on Asian and Pacific Affairs of the House Committee on International Relations, criticized President Carter for a return to secret negotiations in foreign policy by failure to consult with Congress. He cited the recommendations of the subcommittee which made clear that "the issue of consultation with Congress is seen as being an essential part of the normalization process," since normalization as a process "includes a package of legislation by Congress which is needed to facilitate the security and economic apsects of a normal relationship between Washington and Peking."[10] The magazine *National Review* editorialized:

> The Republic of China on Taiwan, properous and relatively free as the nations of the world go these days, is a long time U.S. ally. We possessed a solemn treaty obligation to that nation of seventeen million people—an obligation now treated as a scrap of paper.[11]

Members of Congress and other informed observers, aside from unhappiness about the abrogation of a treaty and a failure to consult with Congress, expressed concern about the future on the rest of Asia (especially the failure to get a non-aggression pledge from mainland China regarding the solution of the Taiwan question). Senator Stone stated that Congress, in its passage of the Dole-Stone amendment, "found that that security treaty with the Republic of China on Taiwan aided the stability of east Asia."[12] Senator Dole viewed the presidential action as carrying "serious consequences for the safety of seventeen million people in Taiwan, for the security of the north Pacific region, and for the preservation of American security interests in that area."[13] The acceptance of the Communist Chinese "pre-conditions" also raised the question over the U.S. future security strategy for the Asian-Pacific region.[14]

George Meany, president of the AFL-CIO, charged that President Carter had "undermined the credibility of the United States in its relations with other countries" by unilaterally abrogating the U.S. treaty with Taiwan and that other nations "may well now wonder whether the United States can be relied upon to fulfill its treaty obligations and for how long."[15]

Representative Phil Crane of Illinois, a declared Republican presidential candidate, stated that Carter had "shown himself before the world to be a weak and unreliable ally as well as an ineffective leader of free nations" and that the decision "will be harmful to both the interests of the United States and the interests of our allies, and to stability in Asia and the world as a whole."[16]

And George Bush, former United States ambassador to the United Nations and former U.S. representative to Peking, has written that in the period following World War II, American credibility, combined with American military strength, served as the glue that held together the non-communist world, and that, as a result of the China action, "both friend and foe alike are now asking, however, whether the United States can still be counted on to keep its word." After citing examples of the U.S. taking a position and then changing its position (e.g., Rhodesia, negotiations in the Middle East, the neutron bomb), he noted that the abandonment of Taiwan comes at a particularly inopportune time. Mainland China, concerned over the growing power of the Soviet Union, realized that there was a deadlock on the terms of normalization but, because of the importance of the Russian threat, had decided not to let the Taiwan question be a major barrier to progress on commercial and strategic issues. The United States had not only capitulated to Peking's demands but had also failed to get any guarantee whatsoever on protection for Taiwan. The United States had renounced a treaty with an ally without cause or benefit:

> The ultimate irony, then, of this "normalization" is that China, whose primary interest lies in a strong, steadfast American presence in the world, has now seen just how easily we can be pushed around. The Chinese realize that we have given all and gained nothing, and while they engage in self-congratulations, they know in their hearts that by our actions, we have also made the world a more dangerous place than it was only a few weeks ago.[17]

The blow to our ally, the Republic of China on Taiwan, came through in statements from the leadership—and in demonstrations by Chinese and American students in front of the White House and in cities throughout the United States. When United States negotiators (headed by Deputy Secretary of State Warren Christopher) went to Taiwan during the last week of December 1978 to work out terms for negotiating continued commercial relations, they were met by hostile demonstrations in Taipei. A Taipei taxi driver set himself afire in protest of the United States decision and was hospitalized in critical condition. Dr. Soong Chu-yui, a spokesman for the government of Taiwan, stated that President Chiang Ching-kuo had requested that the United States give assurances of a legal nature that it would continue to supply defense weapons as well as adopt appropriate legislative measures to assure continued cultural, trade, and other relations.[18] President Chiang stated that, despite repeated assurances to maintain diplomatic relations with the Republic of China on Taiwan, the United States had broken its word, broken diplomatic relations, and abrogated a treaty. Further, he maintained that the "United States government cannot be expected to have the confidence of any free nations in the future" and that the United States road to normalization of relations with Communist China "did not protect the security of free Asian nations."[19] The National Assembly of the Republic of China in criticizing the Carter policy emphasized that the betrayal of Taiwan would "make the U.S. government lose its credibility among the free countries of the world."[20] Ambassador James C. H. Shen, the Republic of China's last ambassador to the United States, criticized the United States for yielding to Communist China's demands without consulting or sufficiently notifying Taiwan; the message to the free Chinese everywhere was that "they can no longer rely on the United States of America."[21] He requested urgent action to assure the Chinese Communists that the United States would come to the aid of Taiwan if it should be attacked by mainland China.[22]

The Carter action was not the only alternative open in handling the China issue. Other options were available. It did seem likely that the United States would move toward better relations with Communist China since the announcement of the Shanghai Communiqué of February 28, 1972, a statement of broad and rather vague principles. One proposal was to continue the deadlock on normalization while commercial and other cultural agreements proceeded with mainland China.[23] Another possibility was the "German model"—in which the United States established full diplomatic relations with Communist East Germany while maintaining full diplomatic recognition and treaty commitments to West Germany. Thus the United States would have extended diplomatic recognition to the People's Republic of China while keeping diplomatic relations with Taiwan and our defense treaty with Taiwan. It would view the Republic of China on Taiwan as an independent state, a political entity with full sovereignty; it would be a recognition of one Chinese civilization but two Chinese states.[24]

The "Japanese formula"—recognition of the People's Republic of China as the legitimate government of China with Taiwan a province of the PRC under its control and maintaining commercial and economic relations with Taiwan at an unofficial level—may have been beneficial to Japan but the same benefits could not be expected to come to the United States by adopting the same formula. The reason this "solution" has worked for Japan and countries like Thailand and Australia—allowing them to continue their trade and investment in Taiwan without interference by Peking—has been because of the U.S. shield of protection extended through various treaties. As predicted, the United States acceptance of a Japanese-type formula has eliminated the U.S. commitment by treaty to Taiwan, has brought U.S. credibility into question elsewhere in the world, and may have made any understanding or implication that Peking would not use force to bring Taiwan under its control useless and ineffective. Dr. Richard L. Walker, citing the pressures used by Communist China against the Republic of China on Taiwan in connection with the Olympic Games in Canada in 1976, observes that "the Chinese Communist leaders will not hesitate to apply a full range of economic and political pressures to bring the government on Taiwan to heel once the U.S. guarantee has been disposed of." Such a development, he adds, "could prove a disruption of a vital and complex web of economic, commercial and political interdependencies which are part of the American contribution to development in the western Pacific."[25] And as Dr. Ramon H.

Myers, curator-scholar and research coordinator in the East Asian Collection at the Hoover Institution on War, Revolution and Peace, predicted in a perceptive essay published before the Carter China action: "The question of America's willingness to fulfill its commitments to the Republic of China on Taiwan actually raises doubts about U.S. credibility in many regions."[26]

II

When the Portuguese came upon Taiwan, an island off the coast of mainland China, they called it Formosa, the "beautiful" island. The Dutch established fortified posts in it and used it as a trading connection between 1624 and 1661. The Ching Dynasty, which ruled China from 1644 to 1911, took control of Taiwan in 1683 and made it part of Fukien province, located in southern China. When China suffered defeat in the Sino-Japanese War of 1894-1895, Japan took over Taiwan as well as the adjacent Pescadores Islands. (Japan acquired Taiwan from China in the same decade that the United States gained a foothold in Asia by acquisition of the Philippines.) Taiwan was freed from Japanese control with the defeat of Japan and the end of World War II in 1945; it reverted to China. China, under the leadership of Chiang Kai-shek, had been hampered during its World War II defense against Japan by a strong and growing Communist Party. The struggle intensified in the period between 1945-1949 when the Chinese Communists took control of the mainland and Mao Tse-tung came to power October 1, 1949. Chiang Kai-shek and his forces escaped to Taiwan where the Republic of China was established.[27]

The United States recognized the Republic of China (ROC) as the legitimate government of China and extended aid; it sought to protect the free Chinese from aggression through the Mutual Defense Treaty of 1954. As part of an effort to keep Asia safe from communist expansion, the United States concluded defense treaties with South Korea (1953) and Japan (1954), and the Southeast Asia Treaty Organization (SEATO) was formed as a defensive alliance in 1954.[28] The Republic of China on Taiwan, strongly backed by the United States, survived Communist China's challenge to the Chinese Nationalist-held island off the shore of mainland China in 1955 and 1958 (Quemoy or Kinmen). With the adoption of a successful land reform program, productive agricultural techniques increasing land productivity, the starting of significant export industries, and the building of a powerful defense force, Taiwan became so successful economically that the United States was able to terminate its economic aid program in the 1960s. While the United States continued its diplomatic recognition of the Republic of China, nations like Britain and France succumbed to the lure of Communist China and extended diplomatic recognition. The ROC suffered a diplomatic setback when the United Nations in 1971 voted to admit Communist China to the United Nations and expelled the ROC. More than two dozen nations still recognize the ROC as the government of the Chinese people, while many more have extensive trade and commercial relations with it.

The Republic of China on Taiwan has a strong and booming economy, and, next to Japan, its people enjoy one of the highest living standards in Asia. Since 1952 the economy of the ROC has been experiencing rapid and sustained economic growth, and during the mid-1970s Taiwan became the seventh largest source of U.S. exports, with the United States remaining Taiwan's largest market. The United States in 1977 absorbed about forty percent of Taiwan's exports at a time when per capita income in Taiwan reached nine hundred dollars. The United States has made direct investments in Taiwan totaling about $500 million, and Taiwan has become the United States' thirteenth-ranked trading partner. U.S. manufacturing subsidiaries benefit from among the highest rates of profitability and sales growth in the world, while the United States has been increasing purchases of Taiwan products (especially textiles and electrical supplies) because of low price and high quality. Bilateral trade between the United States and Taiwan totals seven billion dollars. The economic benefits from direct investments and United States trade can be expected to continue as long as stability can be maintained in the area.[29]

For the year 1979 fixed investment is expected to top eight billion dollars accounting for about 28.3 percent of the gross domestic product; growth during 1979 is expected to reach 21.6 percent in real terms. The government and public investment is expected to increase by 21.3 percent in real terms (four billion dollars), with investments scheduled to carry out at least twelve new major economic development projects, implement rural reconstruction projects, and develop sophisticated technology-intensive industries.[30]

The resolve of the leadership on Taiwan remains strong to resist any move toward absorption into the mainland. President Chiang Ching-kuo put the armed forces on alert for any attempts by the Chinese Communists to use force or conspiratorial tactics to infiltrate the divided Taiwan.[31] He also rejected an offer by Peking to send representatives to begin "reunification" talks which would lead to a surrender of Taiwan, and he pledged that his government would still maintain the national policy of recovery of the mainland. The armed forces of Taiwan include about 500,000 regular armed troops, with about 2.5 million well-trained reservists. Increases are now scheduled for the defense budget.[32]

The Republic of China leadership is concerned about the failure of the United States to secure from Peking even a public statement that the Taiwan issue will not be settled by force. While continued United States arms sales to Taiwan would be "permitted" by Peking, the United States stated that such sales would be "restrained." While Peking has been steadily building up its military forces, Lieutenant General Daniel Graham, retired former head of the Defense Intelligence Agency, has stressed that Taiwan needs air capability over the straits between Taiwan and mainland China which would give the Republic of China the capacity to strike airfields on the mainland if such an assault came from Communist China. General Graham noted that such aircraft (e.g., fighter bombers) seem to be excluded from the wording of the Carter agreement with mainland China; Peking, if it launched a military attack on Taiwan, could gain superiority through attrition.[33]

Taiwan is cognizant of the threat. Communist China could exercise the military option, or it could bring economic pressure on Taiwan—subtle and overt—by insisting that all trade be routed through Peking, thus executing an economic strangulation of Taiwan. Certainly this is more likely at a time when Peking increases its trade and wishes to eliminate a viable economic rival.[34]

Besides the build-up of defenses at home and strengthening commercial relations, two other possible options remain open for Taiwan—the Russian option and the nuclear option. The former would require Taiwan seeking an accommodation with Russia as a counterweight to Peking's influence in Asia. The military aspect of such relations could include stationing Soviet naval or air units on Taiwan or the Pescadores, arms sales, and military aid programs; it could also include open political, economic, and cultural ties. Peking thus would risk Soviet opposition if it decided to attack Taiwan; the Soviets might prove a greater deterrent to the Chinese Communists than the United States, already viewed as a "paper tiger" in some quarters. Taiwan would also realize that such a tie to Soviet Russia would have serious dangers as well—disruptions of commerce, increased chances of armed conflict, and the possibility of total control by the Soviets (or a Soviet sell-out to Peking for some concession by Peking). This option gains some discussion because of Chiang Ching-kuo's study in Russia.[35]

The nuclear option is a more realistic one. It is clear that Taiwan has already assembled the necessary facilities to reprocess spent nuclear fuel from plant powers in order to produce plutonium to develop nuclear arms. The United States brought earlier pressure against Taiwan, stressing that Taiwan could better serve its security needs by maintaining its relationship with the United States rather than by trying to develop nuclear weapons. This argument has lost some of its appeal with the United States action regarding Communist China. An opinion has been expressed that if Taiwan launched a major effort to acquire nuclear weapons, it could produce its first atomic device in less than two years.[36]

Republic of China officials on a number of occasions have said that the ROC would play neither the Russian nor the nuclear option.[37] Yet, a nation like Taiwan may be willing to use any option for survival when pressed to the wall. In the United States, the friends of free China, the Republic of China on Taiwan, will seek to reinstate a guarantee, most likely through the United States Congress, that the United States would resist any military action take by Communist China against Taiwan. Taiwan will be working to keep its strength so that nothing encourages the Communists that Taiwan can be conquered militarily, pressured politically, or intimidated economically.

III

Japan stands in a precarious role under the terms of the new United States China policy. Japan made its own accommodation with Peking when the prime ministers of both nations, Kakuei Tanaka for Japan and Chou En-lai for China, agreed on September 29, 1972 for the establishment of diplomatic relations and the exchange of ambassadors. Japan accepted Peking's three terms of recognition: recognition of the People's Republic of China as the sole legitimate government of China, acceptance of the Communist Chinese position that Taiwan is a part of China, and the abrogation of the treaty between Japan and Taiwan. Japan was able to maintain a precarious balance by establishing official diplomatic and commercial relations with mainland China while continuing an active trade with Taiwan through unofficial (and non-governmental) channels. Despite some initial problems involving conflicting claims between mainland China and the Republic of China on Taiwan on fishery and aviation agreements, Japan secured a satisfactory arrangement with both Chinas.[38] On August 12, 1978, Japan and Communist China signed a Treaty of Perpetual Peace and Friendship which promised to open up additional opportunities for expanded trade between the two nations. The Soviets appeared reluctant to see the treaty concluded—especially on Peking's terms. One of the major results was the announcement of the biggest trade deal ever between Japan and Communist China—Nippon Steel Corporation of Japan agreed to provide the government of China $2.03 billion worth of equipment to build a giant steel mill near Shanghai.[39]

Although Japanese officials publicly welcomed the United States-China diplomatic relations, doubts remained below the surface regarding the future effects of the action in Japan. As a condition of the post-World War II settlement, Japan adopted Article IX in it Constitution—a renunciation of war and a denial of armed forces as an instrument of national policy.[40] The United States and Japan have a defense treaty. Although Japan could maintain a limited self-defense force, the protection of the United States "nuclear umbrella" enabled Japan to devote a great share of its resources to become the most economically prosperous nation in Asia and the major trading partner of the United States in that part of the world. Yet, an abrogation of the treaty with Taiwan (with the withdrawal of all United States troops) and the continued withdrawal of United States troops from South Korea (scheduled to be completed by 1982) will raise legitimate concerns in Japanese political circles over the continuing reliability of United States military promises to Japan. Unless Japan feels assured, it

364

might be necessary to rethink its role in the Asian defense system with the possibility of acquiring nuclear weapons.[41]

The reassessment of Japan's defense position had already begun in earnest before the China move of the United States. Even during 1977, Japanese leaders believed that they could no longer take military presence of the United States in South Korea as a fact of international politics or request that the Americans stay because it was essential for Japan's security. President Carter's call for a total ban on commercial reprocessing of spent nuclear fuel and on the development of fast-breeder reactors proved unpopular at a time when resource-poor Japan was getting ready to start operations of its first reprocessing plant. Japan viewed the development of nuclear energy as an economic imperative.[42]

Osamu Miyoshi, professor of political science at Kyoto Sangyo University, has noted that Japan will reach a superpower status only second to the United States in the 1980s but will emerge as "a colossus with clay feet in military terms."[43] American ambivalence has tended to divide Japanese society on defense posture, thus complicating Japan's search for a new and more active role in the world.[44] Hitoshi Hanai, also of Kyoto Sangyo University and advisor to the Japan Liberal Democratic Party, observed that the 1978 Japan White Paper on Defense contended that basic trends in the military situations as they influence Japan have not drastically changed. Yet, Professor Hanai notes that the growth of the Soviet presence in the Far East, the conclusion of the peace treaty between Japan and China, and the American withdrawal from Asia have brought major changes and placed the Japanese domestic situation in a new light. The proponents of a stronger defense policy in Japan within the ruling Liberal Democratic Party have been gaining a greater voice because of these international developments; this development has also weakened the Socialist and Communist parties in influencing Japan's defense policy. Even discussion in the legislative assembly, the Diet, is focusing on a more realistic approach to defense (e.g., what to do if Japan is attacked).[45] The predecessor to Prime Minister Masayoshi Ohira, Takeo Fukuda, became the first Japanese prime minister since World War II to include a discussion of defense policy in his annual address to the opening of the national legislature. Michael Pillsbury, a defense consultant at the System Planning Corporation, made the following observation after a month-long trip to Asia, including Japan, as part of the Senate Budget Committee staff:

No longer does parliamentary debate in Tokyo focus on whether or not to have a mutual security treaty and self-defense forces. Rather, questions are being raised by Japanese defense specialists about how much military spending is needed, what kinds of major new weapons systems are required, and what degree of consultation should be undertaken with the U.S. Although no definitive answers to these questions have yet emerged, the striking development is that they are being seriously reviewed. . . . For the first time in thirty years, the Japanese are not being shy about defense.[46]

Public opnion also shows signs of change: while in 1951 fifty-three percent of the Japanese accepted the existence of Japan's self-defense forces, this acceptance had increased to eighty-three percent in a 1978 public opinion poll. This eighty-three percent support included seventy-eight percent of the Socialists and fifty-five percent of the Communists polled.[47]

Shortly after assuming the presidency in January 1977, President Carter sent Vice President Walter Mondale to Japan to notify its leaders of the decision to withdraw American troops from South Korea over a five-year period; the schedule of withdrawal was revealed in mid-year when Secretary of Defense Harold Brown visited Seoul. The Japanese considered it a one-sided decision without the "full consultation" promised by President Carter.[48] The sensitivity of this change and the coming to power of a new prime minister toward the end of 1978, Masayoshi Ohira, will likely keep the defense issue a major consideration in Japan's domestic policies.[49]

The political atmosphere existed in Japan—even before the United States played its "China card"—to move toward a stronger defense capability and to view with less realibility the protection of the U.S. "nuclear umbrella."

IV

The Republic of South Korea may have suffered the most in terms of the method of United States-China rapprochement. If any nation must base its survival on the credibility of the United States commitment, it is South Korea which faces a hostile, aggressive enemy, North Korea, on its borders. Only a short time ago South Korea witnessed the United States recall of General John Singlaub for expressing doubts on the United States Korean withdrawal plan. In addition, South Korea has experienced the reality of the North Korean "tunnels" under the demilitarized zone (DMZ), observed growing evidence of the strengthening of North Korea forces, suffered the embarrassment of the congressional investigation of "Koreagate," felt threats from the United States Congress over aid restrictions on the "human rights" issue, and experienced the implementation of the United States Korean troop withdrawal plan (with the last battalions of the United States 2nd Infantry Division scheduled to go in 1982), a decision made without adequate consultation or a meeting of the minds with South Korean governmental leaders. A report by newspaper columnists from the DMZ near South Korea at the end of November 1978 concluded that despite all the public reassurances coming from Washington, D.C., these statements have not been able to "dispel the foreboding among U.S. and South Korean generals that President Carter's planned withdrawal of U.S. infantrymen from Korea will bring communist legions down across this most heavily fortified border in the world."[50] This dismal assessment appeared in print three weeks before the China decision and the United States credibility question surfaced again.

Additional concern surfaced with the news account in January 1979 of a new United States Army intelligence study which substantially increased the estimate of North Korean ground combat power—from a previously estimated twenty-five divisions to the equivalent of forty-one divisions as well as a major increase in tanks and other weapons. The report led to a request by the chairman and the ranking minority member of the investigations subcommittee of the House Armed Services Committee, Representative Samuel S. Stratton of New York and Representative Robin L. Beard of Tennessee, that further information be furnished to Congress and the United States Korean troop pullout be halted until the House Armed Services Committee can make a full evaluation.[51]

During the last decade of the nineteenth century, Korea became entangled in the growing rivalry between China and Japan. Korea officially lost its independent status in August 1910 when Japan announced the annexation of Korea; the Korean people remained under Japanese control until the defeat of Japan in 1945. Korea had received a promise of independence in the Cairo Declaration of 1943. The immediate post-World War II period left Korea a divided nation at the 38th parallel, a division by military occupation of United States and Soviet troops. The Soviets began strengthening their control in the northern half of the Korean peninsula. The United Nations declared the Republic of Korea on December 12, 1946 as the only legitimate government of Korea. Ten days later the communists in the northern part established the "Democratic People's Republic of Korea" and sought to bring all of Korea under its control with the launching of the Korean War on June 25, 1950. The United Nations branded the attack aggression and responded by sending in troops, largely American, to help the Republic of Korea's army regain control of the country. The Chinese Communists entered the war to assist the North Koreans. The tide was turned and the communist forces which had invaded South Korea were driven back. A ceasefire was proposed, and on July 27, 1953, the Korean armistice was signed at Panmunjom. On August 16, 1953, the Republic of Korea-United States Mutual Defense Treaty was signed. Attempts to unify Korea met with failure as North Korea's leaders insisted on communist control of all the Korean people. The DMZ was set up at Panmunjom to prevent further aggression. The United States launched a program to provide the Republic of Korea with billions of dollars in economic and military aid to build up its strength.[52]

With assistance from the United States, South Korea made rapid strides in building its economy. Park Chung Hee, who came to power in December 1963, has presided over this period of prosperity. During his first five years in office the Korean economy grew at an average annual rate of 8.3

percent, and during the next five years it grew at the increased rate of 11.8 percent.[53] The nation is in its fourth five-year plan for economic development, a plan which seeks an average annual growth of 9.2 percent. Despite the oil related recession experienced by South Korea and the rest of the world in the 1970s, South Korea managed a full recovery from it, and per capita income has been on a steady increase (from $532 in 1976 to $700 in 1977). The nation opened its first atomic power plant at the end of 1977, one of almost twenty planned projects going through the turn of the century. Fortunately for its people and its own security, South Korea rebounded from great difficulties and has been able to maintain a sustained and stable growth.[54] But South Korea remains a ripe target for its aggressive neighbor to the north.

During the last few weeks of 1978, President Park Chung Hee replaced eleven out of twenty cabinet ministers (including the head of economic planning) and granted a political amnesty for thousands of prisoners on December 27, 1978, the day he took the oath of office for another six-year term.[55]

Besides the concern over the communist strength on its borders and the removal of United States troops, South Korea's government has been concerned over criticism from United States officials for alleged "human rights" violations—while the totalitarian system in North Korea goes uncriticized.[56] One scholarly observer noted that South Korea's participation in assisting the United States in the Vietnam War helped to alter the "client-state" relationship between the two since South Korea "became acutely aware of America's limitations to her power and determination." Even examining the United States action in the Pueblo affair in 1968 and the Panmunjom incident in 1976, in both of which North Korea openly challenged the United States authority, the South Koreans felt that the U.S. failure to act more forcefully "raised questions in the minds of the South Korean leaders about the determination of the United States to repel aggression in Korea if it ever became necessary."[57] While South Korean leaders have gone along with the Carter administration desire that South Korea not develop a plutonium reprocessing plant (a facility which would produce material suitable for use in nuclear weapons), it has been a reluctant acquiescence.[58]

The China incident and the new U.S. Army intelligence study increasing the estimate of North Korean military strength have raised the questions about American reliability again, encouraging the South Koreans to take a more careful look at resources in case of a North Korean attack—and no American military aid or aid which might come too late. The capital city of South Korea, Seoul, is less than forty miles from the North Korean border, and it is likely that the forces of Kim Il Sung of North Korea would seek to capture Seoul even quicker than the three days it took them in the 1950 invasion.

South Korea may now earnestly approach mainland China with the possibility of establishing diplomatic relations, an approach signaled almost five years ago when President Park stated that South Korea was willing to have diplomatic relations with any nation regardless of ideological differences.[59] The South Koreans realize the close ties between Communist China and North Korea and the influence Communist China has over the North Korean leaders. The North Koreans praised the United States-China relationship, seeking to apply lessons to their own situation. One publication noted that in normalizing its relationship with China the United States recognized the Taiwan issue as an internal matter for China and agreed to withdraw United States troops from Taiwan. It then queried: "Then what is the ground for American refusal to leave the solution of the Korean question to the Korean people and withdraw GI's from South Korea? [60] Another article noted that it has "become a trendy act to reach accommodation with communism" and that the time had come for South Korea "to learn to live with communism" and agree to "reunification."[61] The message is clear to Seoul: North Korea recognizes the weakness of the U.S. commitment and may be waiting for the opportune moment to launch a major attack.

The China action by the United States is likely to make the South Koreans less willing to trust the American nuclear guarantee. They may seek to improve their relations with both Soviet Russia and Communist China but only as a means to guarantee their own protection and survival. At the very time South Korea has abandoned nuclear weapons development at the urging of the United States, the United States-China decision may push South Korea into resuming the technology to produce nuclear weapons for its own protection. There is great validity to the observation that South Korea's desire to postpone the 1982 troop pullout is an issue which transcends "Koreagate, human rights and trade problems as the focus of U.S.-Korean relations."[62]

V

The ramifications of the United States action in recognizing the People's Republic of China extends to other Asian states beyond Taiwan, Japan, and South Korea. Although public reactions from other Asian powers was polite, all the nations of the area will undergo their own individual reassessments. Aside from the treaties with the Republic of China on Taiwan (which the United States abrogated), the Republic of Korea, and Japan, the United States has concluded mutual defense treaties in the Pacific region with the Philippines, Australia and New Zealand. Certainly, any of these three latter powers will be carefully watching developments in the Taiwan Straits and contemplating future United States credibility. All these treaties were concluded about the same period (1951-1954) and contain generally similar provisions.[63] After almost a decade of negotiations, the United States and the Philippines concluded, in a three-hour negotiation session finishing up on New Year's Eve (December 31, 1978), a five hundred million dollar aid package and new arrangements involving bases in the Philippines, running to 1991. The agreements include retention of the largest United States military bases in Asia—Clark Air Base, Subic Naval Base, and several smaller United States facilities. The U.S. State Department spokesman, Thomas Reston, noted that the Philippine bases were important for the ability of the United States to project its military strength throughout the Pacific in order to preserve peace and stability in the region.[64] The contradictory signals sent out by United States policy in Asia will be closely watched by Singapore, Indonesia, Malaysia, Thailand, and other Asian nations.[65]

United States credibility must have been questioned in other parts of the world as well. At the very time of the China announcement, the Carter administration was seeking to convince Israel to make new concessions to seek an agreement in the Middle East. Although United States interests differ somewhat in both cases, the question of the military reliability of the United States and the ability to maintain an arrangement and treaty commitment is an issue of concern for Israel as well as Taiwan. In other areas of foreign policy where the United States has had difficulties—in Iran, in Nicaragua, in the SALT II negotiations—the United States stands on less reliable ground because of the China decision. Reverberations are likely to be seen in other areas of the world as future international trouble spots develop and the communist nations test the resolve of the United States.[66]

Communist China and the Soviet Union represent major military powers, and no free Asian nation could successfully challenge each one alone. The military potential and desire for control are evident to the observer as the warfare continues between Cambodia and Vietnam. And the fate of any free Asian nation willing to accept Peking-style "liberation" is clear from the unfolding story in Cambodia, and even Vietnam.[67] The flood of refugees from Indochina serves as a reminder to Hong Kong, Malaysia, New Zealand, Australia, and the Philippines of people willing to risk life-style, possessions, and even death rather than live under a communist regime in their homeland. The desperation was evidenced as 2,700 Vietnam refugees stranded on a Taiwan-owned freighter off Hong Kong reached such despair that they considered mass suicide.[68] The tide of refugees in Asia have been flowing out of communist-controlled countries, and not the reverse. This exodus is a reality to all Asian nations and a sobering thought to the people of Asia if their own homeland loses its status as a free Asian nation to communist control.

Overall, the United States decision to recognize the People's Republic of China—on terms laid down by Peking—was a risky action with little benefit for the United States. Peking's view of the United States as a "paper tiger" has been confirmed, while the Soviets have serious doubts about the U.S. willingness to adhere to its stated policy. The United States has set a reliable ally (the Republic of China on Taiwan) adrift, and put two other allies (Japan and South Korea) in a precarious position. The action by President Carter was a violation of three promises made on a number of occasions—to the Republic of China of securing its protection militarily, closer consultation with allies on key decisions of foreign and military decisions, and the avoidance of secret negotiations. The Carter administration upset a three-decade United States policy which brought relative peace, economic prosperity, and political stability to east Asia; it exchanged this proven policy of performance for a situation where all is in flux and two major communist powers—the People's Republic of China and Soviet Russia—gained renewed manueverability and advantageous power positions on the Asian front. There is renewed evidence of a United States withdrawal from Asia and a lessening United States commitment to allies in case of a military threat or economic pressures applied to them. Taiwan, Japan, and South Korea will have to look more to their own defenses, and the very program which President Carter has worked to prevent (e.g., nuclear proliferation) may be put in operation by the results of the Carter China decision as these three powers realize that only an independent nuclear force can provide adequate protection.

The China decision has sent a message to the free world that the United States once again has failed to understand the techniques and strategies of the communist nations. The post-World War II alliance of free Asian nations was put together to secure the positions of Asian nations against the aggressive actions of Communist China and Soviet Russia; these two communist powers have not changed their objectives in the intervening years but have only grown stronger and more determined to bring additional free people under their control. Those concerned Americans with a sense of history may turn their minds back to the warning issued almost three decades ago, spoken at the beginning of this chain of alliances by General of the Army Douglas MacArthur in his famous address before a joint session of Congress on April 19, 1951:

> The communist threat is a global one. Its successful advance in one sector threatens the destruction of every other sector. You cannot appease or otherwise surrender to communism in Asia without simultaneously undermining our efforts to halt its advance in Europe. . . .

> The holding of this littoral defense line in the western Pacific is entirely dependent upon holding all segments thereof, for any major breach of that line by an unfriendly power would render vulnerable to determined attack every other major segment. This is a military estimate as to which I have yet to find a military leader who will take exception. . . .

> For that reason I have strongly recommended in the past as a matter of military urgency that under no circumstances must Formosa [Taiwan] fall under communist control. . . . Such an eventuality would at once

threaten the freedom of the Philippines and the loss of Japan, and might well force our western frontier back to the coasts of California, Oregon, and Washington.[69]

The credibility of the United States and the security of key Asian allies in the struggle for the free world—the Republic of China on Taiwan, Japan, and the Republic of Korea—have suffered a setback by the Carter decision to recognize Communist China on the terms dictated by the communist leadership in Peking. Overall, the United States decision to extend recognition to the People's Republic of China has guaranteed neither peace nor stability but only has assured more tension in east Asia presently and in future years.

NOTES

1. Fred Barnes, "U.S., Peking to Establish Ties Jan. 1," *Washington Star,* December 16, 1978.

2. Vernon A. Guidry, Jr. and Fred Barnes, "U.S. Not Seeking Short-Term Gains in China Move, Brzezinski Asserts," *Washington Star,* December 20, 1978.

3. Joint Communiqué on the Establishment of Diplomatic Relations Between the United States of America and the People's Republic of China, January 1, 1979.

4. "This historic agreement marks the beginning of a new era of cooperation between two great nations whose peoples have been isolated from one another for so many years. This will assure the establishment of normal and enduring relations with nine hundred million Chinese people on the mainland while assuring the peace and prosperity of the people on Taiwan. . . . This agreement shows that great nations can accept differences and still work together for a more peaceful world"—statement of Senator Edward M. Kennedy, "On Ties Between the United States and the People's Republic of China," December 16, 1978.

5. "Goldwater Sues Carter To Protect Taiwan Treaty," *Chicago Tribune,* December 23, 1978; Kenneth Bredemeier, "Goldwater, Other Lawmakers File Suit Over Repeal of Taiwan Defense Pact," *Washington Post,* December 23, 1978. Senator Goldwater set forth his view on the treaty question in a booklet published during 1978, *China and the Abrogation of Treaties* (Washington, D.C.: The Heritage Foundation, 1978). Senator Goldwater states: "In conclusion, no president acting alone can abrogate, or give notice of the intention to abrogate, our existing treaties with the government of Taiwan. . . . It is the clear instruction of history that the president cannot give valid notice of an intention to withdraw from a treaty, let alone void a treaty in violation of the formalities required by any provision it may contain regarding duration, without the approval or ratification of two-thirds of the Senate or a majority of both houses of Congress" (p. 39). The U.S. State Department, in a memo prepared by its legal advisor Herbert J. Hansell, maintains that executive and performance of the terms of a treaty (including duration and termination) are delegated by the Constitution to the Chief Executive and thus the president has the right acting alone to terminate the United States defense treaty with Taiwan. "Carter Has Right To Terminate Taiwan Pact, U.S. Memo Argues," *Washington Post,* December 28, 1978. See Senator Barry M. Goldwater, *et al.,* Plaintiffs v. James Earl Carter, *et al.,* Defendants, United States District Court for the District of Columbia, Civil Action, No. 78-2412.

6. Statement of Senator Robert Dole, December 20, 1978.

7. See *Congressional Record,* July 25, 1978, S11713-S11728. The word "Congress" was included in the conference report, replacing "Senate." The conference report was approved by the Senate on voice vote on September 11 and the House of Representatives by a vote of 225-126 on September 12, 1978.

8. Statement of Senator Robert Dole, December 20, 1978.

9. "Face the Nation" Transcript, Guest: Senator Richard Stone, December 17, 1978, p. 5.

10. Statement of the Hon. Lester L. Wolff, December 20, 1978.

11. "The China Card," *National Review,* XXXI (January 5, 1979), p. 13.

12. "Face the Nation" broadcast, December 17, 1978.

13. Statement of Senator Robert Dole, December 20, 1978.

14. *Ibid.* Columnist John P. Roche wrote that the acceptance of the Peking terms for normalization was an unconditional surrender to Peking and would give strong evidence for the position that the U.S. is a "paper tiger"—"The Habit of Dumping Allies," *Washington Star,* December 22, 1978. He added: "In short, my view is that the mutual defense treaty with Taipei is fundamentally an anachronism. But whatever its status, the Republic of China was by treaty an American ally and— as I somberly noted in 1975 as Saigon went down the tubes—dumping allies is habit-forming."

15. News from the AFL-CIO, Department of Public Relations, December 20, 1978. Referring to President Carter's human rights policy, Meany expressed a lack of understanding of how President Carter "could so suddenly and callously reject the human rights concerns of both those enslaved on mainland China and those on Taiwan who feared such enslavement." The final paragraph of the statement was a strong indictment of the Carter administration foreign policy: "Nor can we be silent in the face of an inconstant foreign policy which makes this nation's word suspect in the world community. Without consultation with the American people, without open public debate so essential in a democratic society, President Carter has dealt away America's commitment and support for the independence and freedom of the Chinese on Taiwan. And he has received nothing in return—not even a pledge of non-aggression."

16. Statement by Philip Crane, December 16, 1978.

17. George Bush, "Our Deal With Peking: All Cost, No Benefit," *Washington Post,* December 24, 1978. Mr. Bush makes an effective indictment of the Carter approach which deserves quoting:

By the administration's own admission, it never received—or even asked for— specific assurances from Peking about a peaceful solution to the Taiwanese question. In Peking's eyes, the Taiwanese matter continues to be strictly an internal issue, and in its constitution the "liberation" of Taiwan remains an unchallenged goal.

In response, the administration argues that the mainland will wink at future U.S. arms sales to the Taiwanese. But in the same breath, administration officials say *sotto voce* that those sales will be "restrained."

The administration also argues that Peking has neither the capability nor the incentive to conquer Taiwan. But any student of Chinese history—remembering that during the Cultural Revolution, only ten years ago, some of today's Chinese leaders were driven down Peking streets with sticks—can properly ask: Who knows with certainty what lies ahead? It is true that armed conquest by the mainland does not seem imminent, but because of unilateral action by the United States, the seventeen million people on Taiwan are now hostage to the changing whims of the Peking leadership.

The terms that the Carter administration has accepted, and even trumpeted, are the same terms that have been available for the past seven years. But they were always refused before because we knew—just as the Chinese knew—that in the absence of sufficient guarantees, they were but a figleaf for an abject American retreat.

The terrible truth is that the United States now stands exposed to the world as a nation willing to betray a friend—even when there is no apparent gain.

18. "Taiwan Leader Voices Outrage at U.S. Action," *Washington Star,* December 29, 1978.
19. "Chiang: We Will Never Give Up Tasks," *The China Post* (Taipei, Taiwan), December 18, 1978.
20. "Carter Brings Tragedy to Mankind: Assemblymen," *The China Post,* December 26, 1978.
21. "Next for Taiwan: Interview with James C. H. Shen, Republic of China's Last Ambassador to U.S.," *U.S. News and World Report,* January 8, 1979.
22. *Ibid.*
23. *The Wall Street Journal* noted in an editorial of June 15, 1976 entitled "Normalizing Relations With China": "If Peking really does insist that it will not normalize relations unless the U.S. abandons Taiwan, Washington should tender its regrets and allow Peking to live with that decision."
24. The proposal is explained by Dr. Ray S. Cline, "Future U.S. Policy with Regard to China," pp. 132-136, in Edwin J. Feulner Jr. (ed.), *China: The Turning Point* (Washington, D.C.: Council on American Affairs, 1976). Dr. Cline notes: "If the Chinese Communists are so rigid in their politics and ideology as to spurn this compromise solution, it is their loss. This model is the only one that promises stability and order in east Asia and hence the only one compatible with U.S. strategic interests. This middle-of-the-road policy puts us on the tenable ground of willingness to do business with both Chinese governments on the basis of reciprocal interests. This model gives our nation an equitable way out of an evolving trend toward a disastrous one-sided, pro-Peking policy. It removes U.S. policy on China from the anguishing either-or choice posed by proponents of recognition of Peking's claims at any price" (p. 136).
25. Richard L. Walker, *The Normalization Process: More at Stake Than Meets the Eye* (Washington, D.C.: The Heritage Foundation, 1976), pp. 9-10.
26. Ramon H. Myers in "Introduction" in Ramon H. Myers (ed.), *Two Chinese States: U.S. Foreign Policy and Interests* (Stanford, California: Hoover Institution Press, 1978), p. 10.
27. John K. Fairbank, Edwin O. Reischauer, and Albert M. Craig, *East Asia: The Modern Transformation* (Boston: Houghton Mifflin Company, 1965), pp. 28-29, 303, 409; Paul H. Clyde and Burton F. Beers, *The Far East: A History of the Western Impact and the Eastern Response (1830-1970)* (Englewood Cliffs, New Jersey: Prentice-Hall Inc., 1971), pp. 428-439; Claude A. Buss, *The People's Republic of China* (Princeton, New Jersey: D. Van Nostrand Company, Inc., 1962).
28. Fairbank, Reischauer, and Craig, *East Asia,* pp. 879-880. The parties to SEATO included the United States, Britain, France, Australia, New Zealand, the Philippines, Thailand, and Pakistan.
29. Norma Schroder, "Economic Costs and Benefits," in Myers (ed.), *Two Chinese States,* pp. 25-27, 35. An informative report on the development in Taiwan could be found by James C. Roberts in "Taiwan: The Ally We Are Abandoning," *Human Events,* December 30, 1978, pp. 10-15. While in earlier years the United

States sought to limit the number of Japanese color television sets coming into the United States, recent concern has focused on the new technological developments which has brought large numbers of color television sets from Taiwan and South Korea. Taiwan, for example, in a short time was able to almost double the amount of completed color television sets (about 600,000); this number does not include the "incomplete" television sets which are about ninety percent assembled coming into the United States. See "Korea, Taiwan TVs Flood U.S.," *Chicago Tribune*, December 6, 1978.

30. "Government To Push Economic Growth and New Investment," *Free China Weekly*, December 24, 1978. An interesting discussion of considerations for the foreign investor in Taiwan is an article by W. Klatt, "Taiwan and the Foreign Investor," *Pacific Affairs, 50* (Winter 1977-78), pp. 644-659. There is a total of seven billion dollars worth of bilateral trade between the United States and Taiwan for 1978; U.S. trade with Communist China for 1978 will be about one billion dollars. See "U.S. Trade Options With Peking Assessed," *New York Times*, December 17, 1978.

31. "President Orders Combat Ready," *The China Post*, December 18, 1978.

32. "Taiwan Rejects Talks with Peking," *Chicago Tribune*, December 19, 1978; "President: ROC Will Never Negotiate with Peiping, Other Red Nations," and "Sun: Defense Budget To Be Boosted," *The China Post*, December 19, 1978.

33. "Carter Policy Leaves Taiwan on Edge of Forced Surrender," *Human Events*, December 30, 1978, p. 17.

34. Nick Thimmesch discusses these possibilities in two perceptive columns: "A Peking 'Scenario': Sign U.S. Pact, Then Grab Taiwan," *Chicago Tribune*, December 29, 1978; "Economic Oppression Threatens Taiwan," *Human Events*, January 6, 1979. See also Jeffrey B. Gayner, "The China Decision and the Future of Taiwan," *Backgrounder* (Washington, D.C.: The Heritage Foundation, December 20, 1978) on "The Security of Taiwan," pp. 11-16.

35. This whole problem is thoroughly discussed by John W. Garver in "Taiwan's Russian Option: Image and Reality," *Asian Survey*, 18 (July, 1978), pp. 751-766.

36. Milton R. Benjamin, "Taiwan's Nuclear Plans Concern U.S. Officials," *Washington Post*, December 20, 1978.

37. I-Cheng Loh, Minister of Information for the embassy of the Republic of China (before the derecognition), wrote a week after the Carter announcement: "We [the Republic of China] will never 'play the Russian card,' which some of our friends, driven by the cynicism of the recent U.S. move in the power game, urged us to threaten to do. Our reasons are simple. We must remain true to our beliefs, our moral standards, regardless of what others have done. Neither will we 'go nuclear,' even if the technology is there. The only nuclear programs Taiwan will engage in are power-generation plants which by 1984 will provide almost half of the country's needs for electricity"—"Taiwan: 'We'll Fight, We'll Die for Freedom,' " *Daily News* (New York), December 26, 1978.

38. Joachim Glaubitz, "Balancing Between Adversaries: Sino-Japanese Relations and Soviet Interference," *Pacific Community*, 9 (October, 1977), pp. 31-32.

39. "Japanese Firm, China Sign $2.03 Billion Pact to Build Steel Plant," *Washington Star*, December 6, 1978.

40. See Wolf Mendl, "The Japanese Constitution and Japan's Security Policy," *Millennium: Journal of International Studies*, 7 (Spring, 1978), pp. 36-51. Japan has a self-defense force numbering about 180,000.

41. The question is discussed by U.S. Army Major James V. Young in "Japan's Continuing Nuclear Dilemma," *Military Review*, 58 (July, 1978), pp. 19-25—although he concludes, after discussing the pro and con of nuclear weapons, that a continuation of the present overall international development would make it

unlikely that Japan would develop nuclear weapons. The article, of course, was written before the surprise U.S.-China decision. Michael Pillsbury discusses some of the possible factors which could lead Japan to undertake "real rearmament": a breakdown in U.S.-Japanese security arrangements, a serious conflict between the United States and the Soviet Union, a Sino-Soviet rapprochement, a deterioration in U.S.-Chinese relations, or a major change in the military balance in Korea. He notes: "In the future, those, including the Soviet Union and the United States, who do not desire Japan to rearm, as that word is defined in Tokyo, would do well to avoid pulling these triggers"—"A Japanese Card?" *Foreign Policy*, 33 (Winter, 1978-79), p. 30.

42. *The Asia Yearbook (1978)* Hong Kong: Far Eastern Economic Review, 1977), p. 206.

43. Osamu Miyoshi, "Japan, A Changing Nation," Outline of a paper presented at a meeting in Washington, D.C. on Capitol Hill on November 2, 1978.

44. *Ibid.*

45. Hitoshi Hanai, "Japan's Defense Policy: Views from the Domestic Environment," Outline of a paper presented at a meeting in Washington, D.C. on Capitol Hill on November 2, 1978.

46. Pillsbury, "A Japanese Card?" p. 5. He notes: "Japan's decision to upgrade its defense forces is based on a realistic assessment of the changing political and military balance" (p. 30). The Japanese National Defense Study Group Report for 1977 reported that with the Soviet threat and changing United States military posture in Asia, Japan should improve its defense both quantitatively and qualitatively. See Tsunoda Jun, "Is Japan's Defense Posture Adequate?" *Asian Affairs*, 5 (March-April, 1978), pp. 199-215.

47. Hanai, "Japan's Defense Policy"; Pillsbury, "A Japanese Card?" p. 4.

48. Tsuneari Fukuda, *Future of Japan and the Korean Peninsula* (Elizabeth, New Jersey: Holly International Corporation, 1978), pp. 7-8.

49. Reporter William Chapman offers an early assessment of the prime minister and some major issues he will face in "Japan's Ohira: Keeping Tradition," *Washington Post*, November 29, 1978.

50. Rowland Evans and Robert Novak, "Foreboding on Korea's DMZ," *Washington Post*, November 24, 1978.

51. Don Oberdorfer, "Estimate of North Korean Army Raised," *Washington Post*, January 4, 1979. The U.S. has withdrawn 3,600 of its 40,000 ground troops in Korea, with about 2,400 scheduled to go in 1979. South Korea's army numbers about 560,000, with North Korea's armed forces previously estimated at about 440,000. An excellent analysis of the whole problem of withdrawal of U.S. troops from Korea can be found by Jeffrey B. Gayner, "Withdrawal of U.S. Ground Forces From South Korea," *Backgrounder*, Washington, D.C.: The Heritage Foundation, June 15, 1977, pp. 1-19.

52. Korea: Past and Present (Seoul, Korea: Kwangmyong Publishing Company, 1972), pp. 69-81. For additional information on the period, see Kim Chum-Kon, *The Korean War* (Seoul, Korea: Kwangmyong Publishing Company, 1973); Franz Michael and George Taylor, *The Far East in the Modern World* (New York: Holt, Rinehart and Winston, Inc., 1964).

53. Michael Keon, *Korean Phoenix: A Nation from the Ashes* (Englewood Cliffs, New Jersey: Prentice Hall International, 1977), p. 2. An official South Korean version of the growth of the country can be found by Park Chung Hee in *To Build a Nation* (Washington, D.C.: Acropolis Books, 1971).

54. *The Asia Yearbook (1978)* (Hong Kong: Far Eastern Economic Review, 1977), pp. 227-229.

55. "Shuffle in South Korea Follows Amnesty Rule," *Washington Post*, December 23, 1978.

56. Ernest W. Lefever, Director of the Ethics and Public Policy Center affiliated

376

with Georgetown University of Washington, D.C., notes: "On the human rights issue, South Korea and Taiwan get far more critical attention than North Korea and Communist China. Once again, it is a classic case of straining out a gnat and swallowing a camel"—Ernest W. Lefever, "Carter, Korea, and the Decline of the West," *Korea and World Affairs*, 1 (Fall, 1977), p. 257.

57. Sungjoo Han, "The Republic of Korea and the United States: The Changing Alliance," *Korea and World Affairs*, 1 (Summer, 1977), pp. 133, 137.

58. Milton R. Benjamin, "Quest for Independence: The Spread of Nuclear Technology," *Washington Post*, December 7, 1978.

59. William Chapman, "Seoul Signals Eagerness To Establish China Ties," *Washington Post*, December 30, 1978. When General Ock Man Ho, ambassador-designate of the Republic of Korea to the Republic of China, arrived in Taipei on December 19, 1978, he said that the relations between the Republic of Korea and the Republic of China would not be affected by the U.S. effort to sever formal ties with the ROC. Ambassador Ock, who served as military attaché of the South Korean embassy in Taipei between 1960 and 1963, criticized the United States decision as one which hurt America's world leadership—"ROK Ambassador Designate Arrives," *The China Post*, December 20, 1978.

60. "Korea Focus: China-U.S. Normalization and Korea," *The People's Korea* (Tokyo, Japan).

61. "Time for Seoul To Live with Communism," *The People's Korea*, December 27, 1978.

62. Evans and Novak, "Foreboding on Korea's DMZ." See also Joseph M. Ha, "U.S. Withdrawal from Korea: A Means, Not an End," *Orbis*, 21 (Fall, 1977), pp. 607-622; Richard G. Stillwell, "The Need for U.S. Ground Forces in Korea," *Korea and World Affairs*, 1 (Summer, 1977), pp. 140-160 (reprinted from the *AEI Defense Review*); John F. Tarpey, "Korea: 25 Years Later," *United States Naval Institute Proceedings*, 104 (August, 1978), pp. 51-57; and Rowland Evans and Robert Novak, "The Faltering Korean Alliance," *Washington Post*, December 22, 1978.

63. A discussion of the United States role in Asia is contained in Tsai Wei-ping, "Washington-Peiping Relations After Mao," *Issues and Studies*, 14 (June, 1978), pp. 1-12.

64. Don Oberdorfer, "Accord Reached on Two U.S. Bases, Aid to Philippines," *Washington Post*, January 1, 1979. Philippine President Ferdinand Marcos earlier had reached an agreement with Hanoi that he would not allow the Philippine bases to be used for intervention against Vietnam or other countries in the region. Marcos stressed in a statement issued after the agreement was reached with the United States that the U.S. bases are only for "defensive purposes."

65. A pre-China decision assessment of balance of power in Asia can be viewed in the following articles: Alejandro Melchor Jr., "Assessing ASEAN's Viability in a Changing World," *Asian Survey*, 18 (April, 1978), pp. 422-434; U. Alexis Johnson, "The Present and Future Role of the United States in Asia," *Issues and Studies*, 14 (June, 1978), pp. 13-19; Russell Spurr, "Carter's Front Line Fighters," *Far Eastern Economic Review*, 100 (June 2, 1978), pp. 24-30; Sheldon W. Simon, "The ASEAN States: Obstacles to Security Cooperation," *Orbis*, 22 (Summer, 1978), pp. 415-434.

66. A pre-China decision critique of Carter administration policy in Asia can be found in Donald Brandon, "Carter and Asia: The Wages of Inexperience," *Asian Affairs*, 5 (May-June, 1978), pp. 265-274.

67. The Cambodian situation is described by John Barron and Anthony Paul in *Murder of a Gentle Land: The Untold Story of Communist Genocide in Cambodia*. Also Christopher Dickey, "Former Vietnamese Captive Describes Life—and Death—in Saigon Prison," *Washington Post*, December 28, 1978, reveals the situation in Vietnam. See also Richard Dudman, "Fear Gives Cambodia Faceless Leaders," *Chicago Tribune*, December 30, 1978.

68. "Boat People May Commit 'Mass Suicide,' Refugee Says," *Chicago Tribune,* December 28, 1978; William Chapman, "Vietnam Accused of Promoting Latest Exodus of Refugees," *Washington Post,* December 15, 1978; Peter Costigan, "Refugees Bring Bit of Asia to Australia," *Washington Post,* December 16, 1978; Jay Mathews, "Tide of Vietnamese Refugees Reach Hong Kong," *Washington Post,* December 28, 1978; "Refugees' Plight Continues off Hong Kong, Philippines," *Washington Post,* December 29, 1978.

69. *Congressional Record,* April 19, 1951, pp. 4123-4124.

China's Military Power

William Schneider*

China is emerging from a period of more than a decade of neglect of its armed forces. Since the Great Proletarian Cultural Revolution (GPCR) of 1967, virtually every element of the People's Liberation Army (PLA) has experienced the consequences of decay that persisted until Mao Tse-tung's death in 1976.[1] The conspicuous absence of mobility equipment for the infantry-heavy PLA, the lack of modern all-weather terminal (surface-to-air missiles and tube-fired anti-aircraft artillery) and area (manned interceptors) air defense, the dearth of medium and heavy artillery, tanks and anti-tank weapons, and a deep water naval capability merely begin a long list of deficiencies of the PLA as the new Chinese leadership must have seen it in 1976-77.[2] As a result, China could not conduct effective defensive operations along its periphery, much less project its power beyond its borders, save for the special case of the Korean penninsula.[3] The death of Mao, and, perhaps with it, important aspects of Maoist military doctrine, may be a watershed in Chinese military history. It is premature to forecast the configuration of the PLA a decade hence, but post-Mao initiatives have been undertaken which may transform the PLA into a genuine regional and possibly global power over the course of the next two decades if the announced course of action is effectively pursued.

Prediction is a particularly hazardous occupation for a Western observer of the PLA due to the opaque character of Chinese institutions, their unique (and impenetrable) political "style," and the *sui generous* nature of the Chinese decision-making process. Moreover, modern Chinese history (not only the communist period since 1949) has been marked by abrupt changes in direction—changes whose origins and objectives remain obscure to foreign observers. This essay will make an effort to evaluate a plausible path for the evolution of Chinese military power, particularly as it pertains to the projection of that power beyond the continental limits of China's territory.

The People's War Doctrine[4]

The concept of "People's War" dominated China's military strategy, particularly for territorial defense since the ascendency of communist

*William Schneider is a Staff Associate on the Committee on Appropriations, U.S. House of Representatives, and a consultant with the Hudson Institute.

forces to power in China in 1949. Simply stated, "People's War" is an effort to exploit the military potential of China's vast population. The PLA, which has maintained a very extensive force structure (in part owing to its comprehensive civil as well as military responsibilities) since the establishment of the present regime is normally composed of two to three million troops. The PLA is supported by a vast militia which may number two hundred million or more.[5] The purposes of the militia are to provide a modest training base for the PLA (analogous in this sense to the Soviet's paramilitary DOSAAF organization), to provide a local defense for China's rural population (comprising eighty-five percent of the total), and to act as a supporting element for guerrilla operations by the PLA if the nation were overrun by an invading army. The PLA is to retreat inland from forward positions, causing the adversary to extend his lines of communication (LOC) in pursuit of the withdrawing PLA. The extended LOCs would then become vulnerable to the PLA's guerrila operations which would be supported by local militia elements. Thus, a poorly trained population, unacceptable for normal military functions within the PLA, could become a useful adjunct to regular forces *in extremis*. In Mao's words, the militia's function in a "People's War" is to "drown" the enemy in a "sea of humanity."

Although the concept of "People's War" for territorial defense is not without merit in the Chinese context, its implementation was a failure. The militia as such was not a military organization. No more than fifteen percent of the participants normally received any training pertinent to military operations or their support. Nor was the militia ever fully equipped—even with small arms and other light infantry paraphernalia. The utter disorganization of Chinese industry and agriculture resulting from the failure of the "Great Leap" (known to Western economic observers as the "Great Depression of 1959-61")[6] was not offset by the economic growth achieved prior to the GPCR in 1967. The political shockwaves of the GPCR and the subsequent immersion of the PLA into the regional administrative apparatus of government caused the PLA to fall further behind in its ability to meet its military objectives.[7] Under such circumstances, there was little likelihood that the PLA could improve the military potential of the militia.

Maoist doctrine significantly influenced the Chinese assimilation of the military consequences of the introduction of nuclear weapons to modern warfare. In a famous post-war interview with Anna Louise Strong, Mao denigrated the significance of nuclear weapons, emphasizing instead the temporary and partial military effects of nuclear weapons, and the primacy of man rather than weapons in modern war—a precursor of the "red versus expert" debate of the GPCR two decades later.[8] Nevertheless, the Chinese have made a diligent effort to acquire nuclear weapons and their means of delivery, and have conducted nearly two dozen nuclear detonations since their test program began in 1964 (the nuclear weapon program apparently began circa 1958). One source states that an inventory of two to three hundred fission and thermonuclear weapons have been accumulated.[10]

Chinese production facilities for weapon-grade fissile material include both a plutonium production capability and a gaseous diffusion plant, assuring a substantial nuclear weapon production base for high-efficiency nuclear weapon design, a feature particularly desirable for weight- and volume-constrained ballistic missile delivery.

Strategic delivery systems include sixty-five Tu-16 Badger medium bombers of Soviet design (with a combat radius of 2,000 n.m.), fifty to one hundred medium and intermediate range ballistic missiles, and a Chinese space booster, apparently an uprated version of the Soviet SS-4 storable liquid fueled missile (used as an ICBM with a range of 3,000-3,500 n.m.). The latter will probably be replaced by a longer range system of 7,000-8,000 n.m. Chinese tactical aircraft will also be usable nuclear delivery systems if high-efficiency nuclear weapon designs are found and modifications to the aircraft such as external fuel tanks are made.

China's Military Power Today

China's military forces currently deployed reflect Mao's doctrinal legacy accumulated over nearly three decades in the form of tactics, organization, and equipment. China is divided into eleven military regions which in turn are sub-divided into two or three military districts. The major military districts are Shenyang, Peking, Lanchow, Sinkiang, Tsinan, Nanking, Foochow, Canton, Wuhan, Chengtu, and Kunming.[11]

The PLA is organized along the traditional triangular basis in forty field armies normally consisting of three infantry and three artillery divisions, and, in a few cases, three armored divisions as well. The PLA ground forces are organized into two classes of forces, main force and local force divisions. Although main force divisions are administred by the local military region commander, they are under central command from Peking. The divisional substructure is triangular as well, organized into three regiments per division with each regiment containing three battalions. The PLA's force structure provides for a large number of independent regiments which can be attached and/or integrated into the operations of a division as the need arises. The order of battle for the PLA's ground forces is:

Main Force	Local Force
121 Infantry Divisions	65 Infantry Divisions
10 Armored Divisions	110 Independent Regiments
3 Cavalry Divisions	
4 Airborne Divisions	*Naval Infantry*
40 Artillery Divisions (incl. organic division anti-aircraft artillery)	28,000 Marines
41 Railway and Construction Engr. Div.	

Not surprisingly, the primary deployments of PLA ground forces are along the Sino-Soviet frontier, particularly in the Shenyang, Peking, Lanchow, and Sinkiang military regions. Forces deployed in these four military regions are seventy-five main force and thirty-two local force divisions as well as thirty-six independent infantry regiments. These deployments are, of course, almost entirely composed of infantry divisions with little organic mobility. Hence, large numbers are required for the defense of static positions, and are ill-matched to the mechanized threat the Soviets can deploy in the region through the "filling out" of their Category II and III divisions (with reserves) deployed in the region in addition to Category I (maximum readiness). Chinese forces are deployed athwart the primary invasion route from the Soviet Union via Manchuria. As the loss of Manchuria would strip China of its most heavily industrialized region, it is reasonable that the area be the beneficiary of the most vigorous defense effort.

Second in the allocation of PLA assets is the Fukien Province area opposite Taiwan (Republic of China). Here more than thirty main force and fifteen local force divisions as well as twenty-eight independent regiments have been tied down for nearly three decades. Taiwan's troops have demonstrated a capability to conduct Dieppe-like strikes along the Chinese coastal area. Once again, due to the lack of mobility of the PLA, large forces must be committed to the defense of fixed positions.

The recent emergence of the Sino-Vietnamese conflict has lent new interest to Chinese deployments in the southern part of the country. It is unlikely that China will substantially increase the deployment of PLA ground forces above their current level in the region, but it is likely that additional tactical aircraft deployments (and perhaps the construction of new bases) will be made in Yunnan Province and the Kwangsi Chuang Autonomous Region north of the Vietnam/Laos border to enhance the ability of Chinese forces to react to border "incidents."

China's naval forces are deployed among three fleets: the Northern Fleet (one hundred and fifty vessels of all types) from the Yalu River to Lienyunkang (including major naval installations at Tsingtao, Lushun, and Luta), the East Sea Fleet (four hundred vessels) from Lienyunkang to Chaoan Wan (with facilities at Shanghai, Chou Shan, and Ta Hsiehtao), and the South Sea Fleet (one hundred and fifty vessels) from Chaoan Wau to the Vietnamese border (including major deployments at Huangpu, Chanchiang, and Yulin). Although the navy has large numbers of small coastal craft (accounting in part for the high manpower level of the Chinese navy—217,000 excluding Marines and Naval Air Force personnel), it is almost totally devoid of a significant deep water navy. Conspicuous weaknesses in the Chinese navy are the lack of deep water operational experience, the lack of modern submarines, and the absence of a viable amphibious force and a suitable doctrine to direct the deployment of such a force. China's amphibious capability according to public sources is concentrated in fifty-four elderly ex-American World War II amphibious vessels, presumably left over from the Chinese Civil War in 1949. These vessel types and the inventory holdings are known to include 16 LSTs, 13 LSMs, 15 LSTLs, and 10 LSUs.

The lack of either submarines or surface escorts to facilitate the deployment of even the minimal amphibious assault capability now in Chinese hands and the absence of tactical aircraft with sufficient range/ endurance to support overwater power projection make all but the most modest amphibious assault operations unfeasible.[12]

Like the Soviet Union, the Chinese maintain a separate naval air force. This force is integrated into the nationwide air defense network, but concentrates on the protection of coastal airspace. Its force of seven hundred aircraft is dominated by five hundred MIG-17s and MIG-19s, as well as Chinese-manufactured F-6 and F-9 aircraft. They are day-fighters with short range and limited endurance. As a result, most of the bases are located adjacent to coastal areas and are therefore vulnerable to pre-emptive attack and early destruction in a conflict. Because of the dependence of China on the limited capability of the naval air force for the protection of coastal airspace, the coastal infrastructure, particularly the railroad network, is insufficiently guarded, further (potentially) weakening China's internal lines of communication.[13]

The Chinese air force has suffered from the same lack of modernization that has affected Chinese naval forces. The Chinese strategic bomber force, composed of sixty-five TU-16 Badger bombers of Soviet design, but of Chinese manufacture, and several TR-4 Bull aircraft, a copy of the U.S. World War II B-29, is twenty or more years behind their Soviet and American counterparts. Although Chinese nuclear forces appeared to be immune from the effects of the GPCR, few of the benefits have accrued to the advantage of the aircraft-delivered nuclear weapon force of the Chinese air force. It remains saddled with antiquated aircraft.

The balance of the Chinese attack force is limited to a theater role due to the very limited range/payload characteristics of the small number of Soviet-made IL-28 Beagle aircraft, and a few ancient World War II-vintage TU-2 piston aircraft. Most of the 4,250 aircraft in the Chinese air force inventory are 1950s-era day fighters. These include two thousand MIG-19s and fifteen hundred MIG-17s, as well as two hundred obsolete MIG-15 aircraft.

Air transport is similarly limited to providing short-range deployment of airborne troops and limited cargo missions. Only four hundred limited-payload fix wing aircraft are available as well as three hundred light helicopters. The organic airlift of the Chinese air force can be augmented by four hundred (mainly Soviet) civil transport aircraft. The air transport capability of the Chinese air force can do little to offset the lack of ground-based mobility assets of the PLA for its numerous ground force units.

Unlike the U.S. air force, the Chinese air force has the entire strategic air defense mission. For this purpose, it has several thousand anti-aircraft artillery (AAA) batteries employing a variety of radar slewed and optically-guided tube-fired gun systems. These systems are useful only for low-altitude air defense over a very limited area ("footprint"). High altitude coverage over limited portions of Chinese air space is provided by several hundred CSA-1 surface-to-air missile batteries. The CSA-1, an improved version of the Soviet-designed SA-2, could be effectively employed for many years. The area interceptor mission is carried out by MIG-17/19/21s as well as F-6/9s of the Chinese air force.

The strategic nuclear missile mission is assigned to a special unit of the Chinese army, the 2nd Artillery. The Chinese have made impressive progress in their strategic nuclear forces which appear to have suffered least from the GPCR and the turmoil following the death of Mao. Moreover, the Chinese have made effective use of topographic features to reduce the vulnerability of their forces from attack. The expected effort to develop Chinese strategic nuclear forces makes it likely that the strategic missile program will be the early focus of the R&D and production program.

Few recent visitors to China have come away unimpressed with Chinese passive defense measures, particularly those designed to protect the urban population. The civil defense system in China is more advanced than its Soviet counterpart from the perspective of protecting the non-critical urban worker. The civil defense effort is of a scale that almost certainly has psychological effects on the civilian population as well, placing them in a state of readiness that will reduce their vulnerability to nuclear attack, should such an attack come with little warning. It is not clear, however, whether or not the Chinese civil defense system is integrated into the strategic and tactical warning systems available to the PLA and the national leadership.

The Evolution of Chinese Military Power

As mentioned at the outset of this essay, the passing of Mao and perhaps much of his influence on Chinese military thought is certain to have a profound influence on the manner in which the PLA evolves. The defense sector is likely to be the most important benefactor of the new-found emphasis on Chou-En-lai's 1964 dictum on the "Four Modernizations"—namely, industry, agriculture, science and technology, and defense.[14] The renewed emphasis on defense has touched off a vigorous debate concerning the manner in which the defense posture is improved. The debate has three basic elements: (1) the role of foreign technology imports, (2) the view that defense investment should be emphasized as a means of accelerating related industrial and scientific innovation, or (3) that defense investment should follow the acceleration in the growth of basic industries.

China has encountered no ideological difficulty in shedding the Maoist dictum of self-reliance in its quest to accelerate the pace of modernization of foreign imports. Foreign technology imports have now been subsumed under the general rubric of "making foreign things serve China."[15]

This quick acceptance of foreign technology imports has extended to intense interest on the part of the PLA in foreign weapons procurement. The largest orders appear to be directed toward Britain for seventy vertical/ short take-off and landing AV-8 Harrier aircraft worth between two and two and a half billion dollars. Similarly, up to 15,000 anti-tank missiles, the HOT, Milan, and Crotale, will be purchased from French producers over the next several years at a cost of four to seven hundred million dollars. In March 1978, a Chinese military delegation visited West Germany in pursuit of the celebrated (and costly) Leopard. A subsequent decision of the West German government precludes the sale of weapon systems to China, but it reflects the broad scope of Chinese interest in the procurement of foreign weapon systems as opposed to acquiring only military-related technology. Similar interest has been expressed in the French Roland mobile low-altitude air defense system (being built in the U.S. under a French license) as well. China has also initiated procurement of the British Spey engine for use in its tactical aircraft modernization program, probably for an improved-performance version of the MIG-21.

A school of thought that can be discerned in the recent Chinese literature that comes to the Western observer, mainly through the medium of local and international radio broadcasts, suggests that all possible haste should be taken to accelerate the modernization of the Chinese defense posture, a step which will accelerate the development of the industrial and scientific infrastructure due to the extensive employment of advanced technology in defense-related industry.[16]

The alternative point of view, and the perspective subsequently approved by the Chinese leadership, holds that defense modernization should build on the modernization of the civilian economy, particularly the basic industries. This decision, announced by Hua Kuo-feng at the Fifth National People's Congress in February 1978, emphasized basic industrial and agricultural development as the road leading to defense modernization.[17]

The most logical consequence of this evidence is that China will continue to seek to purchase complete foreign weapon systems with sufficient operational inventories and spare parts to assure their successful integration into the PLA while basic industry and agricultural development is accelerated. What cannot be deduced from the evidence yet available concerning Chinese plans is how conflicts between these objectives will be addressed, inasmuch as Chinese industrial development can only be accelerated if there is sufficient foreign investment to augment the limited indigenous resources currently available in China.

A crucial element that has emerged from the post-Mao turmoil over future defense policy has been the absence of evidence of a crash program or a "quick fix" to meet some early contingency. Rather, the development of China's defense capability appears to be evolutionary without a pronounced emphasis on any dimension of its defense posture. Indeed, it is difficult to deduce a cost-effective mission for the Harrier for any Sino-Soviet conflict due to the short range/payload characteristics of the aircraft. Rather, the aircraft would be most useful in a direct assault on Taiwan due to its utility in support of amphibious operations, but there is little evidence that the naval forces associated with amphibious operations are scheduled for early improvement.

Similarly, the large-scale procurement of anti-tank missiles will be of little utility without procurement of survivable delivery systems and an improvement in the combined-arms forces of the PLA (infantry-armor-artillery-tactical aircraft). Soviet tactics employ suppressive terrain tube and missile artillery fire that would sharply diminish the number of the HOT, Milan, and Crotale missiles which could be brought to bear against Soviet tanks.

The fragmentary character of what is known of China's foreign weapons procurement activities implies that there may be a more complex rationale animating Chinese plans than is currently apparent. The reluctance of China to renounce the use of force in the case of Taiwan establishes a clear motive for the emphasis on selected elements of the PLA (i.e., tactical airpower and amphibious forces), while the fear of the Soviet Union establishes a second and more demanding motive for military modernization, but as yet the foreign procurement undertaken by China offers few clues as to what foreign policy objective China is seeking to support with its modernization program.

Perhaps the realm of Chinese effort for which the fewest details are available is the modernization of their strategic nuclear sector. China has long had a "no first use" policy with respect to nuclear weapons. However it is not clear whether or not this applies to what China regards as an "internal" matter, namely, the question of Taiwan. Taiwan is highly vulnerable to nuclear attack due to the limited coastal plain on which virtually all of the ROC's economic capability is situated. However, the mountainous inland terrain provides a sanctuary which could make the government extremely difficult to dislodge, even under nuclear bombardment from land-based missile strikes and aircraft-delivered weapons. Mounting a full-scale invasion may be the only feasible tactic for China to pursue, an objective that is perhaps several decades away if Taiwan's defense posture is strengthened, if indeed it can be done at all.

China's nuclear forces may be much more effectively employed against Soviet targets for several reasons. First, most hardened Soviet missile sites are relatively close to the Sino-Soviet border areas (primarily in the Soviet's Turkestan, Siberian, and Far Eastern military districts near the Trans-Siberian railway), while the numerous Soviet urban-industrial centers are "soft" with respect to nuclear attack. Most of these targets will be vulnerable to the next generation of Chinese delivery systems. Second, a combination of Chinese population dispersal due to the nation's rural character and the absence of a large industrial infrastructure as well as a large civil defense effort very significantly reduces Chinese vulnerability to reciprocal Soviet nuclear attack. Hence, China may not have to engage in a restrained, measured attack should nuclear war break out in order to encourage a restrained and measured Soviet retaliatory strike. China's potential diplomatic dominance of circumstances where military (nuclear) escalation is likely can only encourage greater investment in their nuclear forces.

As noted earlier, it is premature to forecast the contours of the PLA a decade hence, since the major investment decisions have yet to be made. Based upon what we know today, however, it seems likely to expect that the PLA will have a much augmented capability in selected areas of military power. These will include tactical airpower (particularly theater air defense and ground attack aircraft), anti-tank defense organic to infantry companies and battalions, low-altitude divisional air defense (including tube AAA and SAMs), and nuclear delivery systems. Also likely are improvements in fast patrol boats and nuclear-powered attack submarines, and nuclear weapon delivery systems, particularly intermediate and intercontinental ballistic missile systems. The demonstrated capability of China to deploy large-scale phased array radars may allow them to develop a modest ABM capability by the end of the next decade as well which would require a major alteration of the existing Soviet-American ABM Treaty.

Less likely developments include the deployment of a large modern tank force (because of its competition with civilian motor transport) and the development of a large-scale amphibious assault capability (due to their lack of experience with such operations). Such expectations are, however, made within the framework of current Chinese declaratory policy—a foundation upon which scores of failed forecasts have been built in the past.

NOTES

1. This essay employs the common (comprehensive) definition of the PLA including the army, navy and air force as well as reserve elements, but excludes the militia. Informative reviews of PLA history and organization are contained in Edgar O'Ballance, *The Red Army of China* (London: Faber and Faber, 1962); Samuel B. Griffith II, *The Chinese People's Liberation Army* (New York: McGraw-Hill, 1967); A. M. Fraser, *The PLA: Communist China's Armed Forces* (New York: Crane, Russak, 1973); H. W. Nelsen, *The Chinese Military System: An Organizational Study of the Chinese People's Liberation Army* (London: Thornton Cox, 1977).

2. The weaknesses of the PLA in training, equipment, and readiness were well understood through the mid-1960s due to the compromise of twenty-nine issues of secret and top secret versions of an irregularly published organ of the PLA, the *Bulletin of Activities (Kung-tso Tung-hsun)*. This publication distributed (respectively) to regimental and division commanders of the PLA were recovered by Khamba tribesmen in Tibet who overran a PLA regimental headquarters in Sep-

tember 1961. The documents were made available to the U.S. government, and subsequently released publicly by the Department of State in 1963.

3. Korea is adjacent to the primary industrial and transportation infrastructure of China, namely Manchuria. A high-quality Japanese-built railway exists there that is crucial to the movement of combat consumables. As an infantry division will consume six to eight hundred tons of combat consumables (fuel and ammunition) per day, and eight hundred to one thousand or more tons per day for an armored division in a fire-fight, an adequate rail infrastructure is essential to sustain combat for an extended period. No other area of the Chinese littoral is endowed with an adequate infrastructure to support offensive overland operations. For a discussion of the Chinese reliance on their Manchurian infrastructure for support of the Korean War operations, see J. Miller, et al, Korea, 1951-53, Office of the Chief of Military History, Department of the Army (Washington: GPO, 1956), and Robert Futrell, The U.S. Air Force in Korea, 1950-53 (New York: Duell, Sloan, and Pearce, 1961).

4. The notion of "People's War" was firmly established in Maoist doctrine in the 1930s, but it received its modern authoritative presentation by Lin Piao in "Long Live the Victory of the People's War," New China News Agency, September 2, 1965.

5. See John Gittings, "China's Militia," The China Quarterly, No. 18, April-June, 1964. For an incisive evaluation of the weaknesses of the PLA under Mao's military doctrine by a former U.S. Air Force intelligence officer (one of the very few intelligence analysts to predict the failure of the "Great Leap Forward" in the 1950s), Cf. F. E. Armbruster, "China's Conventional Military Capability," in Tang Tsou, China In Crisis: China's Policy in Asia and America's Alternatives, Vol. 2 (Chicago: University of Chicago Press, 1968), pp. 161-96. For a European view of the militia concept, see Adam Roberts, Nations in Arms: The Theory and Practice of Territorial Defense, Studies in International Security, International Institute for Strategic Studies (London: Macmillan Press). The armed militia is currently approximately five million troops, organized into seventy-five divisions. Other elements of the militia include the urban militia, the Civilian Production and Construction Corps, and the ordinary and basic militia who are unarmed but receive rudimentary military training.

6. See, for example, Christopher Howe, China's Economy: A Basic Guide (London: Paul Elek, 1978).

7. At the end of the GPCR, PLA officers held twenty-one of the twenty-nine provincial party secretariats. By 1976, the year of Mao's death, this figure fell to thirteen, and reached nine by the end of 1978. See Ellis Joffe and Gerald Segal, "The Chinese Army and Professionalism," Problems of Communism, Vol. XXVII, No. 6 (November-December, 1978), p. 8. The PLA remains powerful in the Politburo—twelve of twenty-three posts, although this figure is fifteen percent below its 1969 level.

8. See Alice Langley Hsieh, Communist China's Strategy in the Nuclear Era (Englewood Cliffs: Prentice-Hall, 1962), and Morton Halperin, Sino-Soviet Relations and Arms Control (Cambridge: MIT Press, 1967).

9. On the occasion of China's first thermonuclear detonation, Mao was quoted in a June 1958 statement: "I think it is entirely possible for some atomic and hydrogen bombs to be made in ten years' time"—NCNA, June 17, 1967.

10. International Institute for Strategic Studies, The Military Balance, 1977-78 (London: IISS, 1977), p. 48.

11. Formerly there were thirteen military regions, but the Tibet military region has been absorbed into the Chengtu military region, and the Inner Mongolian military region has been abolished, with its territory being assigned in part to the Shenyang, Peking, and Lanchow military regions. For a relatively up-to-date source of information on China's topography and administrative organization, cf. the Central Intelligence Agency, People's Republic of China Atlas, November 1971.

12. A large body of water is a very formidable obstacle to the projection of military power. German armed forces, at the zenith of their military power in 1940-41 were unable to wrest air superiority over the twenty-mile wide English Channel to permit their ground forces to make a safe crossing. It is not surprising then that China encountered so much difficulty in 1958 in taking control of the air over Quemoy Island—virtually in Amoy Harbor—as a prelude to launching an invasion of the island. A description of China's difficulties is contained in Tibor Mende, *China and Her Shadow* (New York: Coward McCann, 1962).

13. China's rail network consists primarily of standard gauge (4-ft. 8.5-inch) single track railroads. With the exception of the rail network in Manchuria and the Peking-Chang-Sha railroad which are double tracked, all railroads are limited-capacity single track railroads. See *People's Republic of China Atlas, op. cit.,* pp. 46-47.

14. From a statement by Chou En-lai to the Third National People's Conference, December 1964, in Peking, cited in Howe, *op. cit.*

15. This new dogma was announced at the dedication of a 300,000-ton ethylene plant, built in part with foreign technology. See "300,000 Ton Ethylene Plant," *Peking Review,* 1977, No. 5.

16. Illustrative of this point of view are statements recorded in *Kuang-ming Jih-pao* (Peking), January 20, 1977, *FBIS-CHI,* January 31, 1977, and *Peking Home Service,* January 20, 1977, Summaries of World Broadcasts, FE 5721.

17. *Peking Review,* March 10, 1978, p. 22.

Another Day
To Live in Infamy:
The Carter Betrayal
of December 15, 1978*

*David Nelson Rowe***

It was in clear disregard of all the facts in the case, and in equally clear disregard of the will of Congress and of the American people, that on the evening of December 15, 1978, just a week after Pearl Harbor Day, President Carter staged from the White House his own version of political betrayal and moral abdication that, for pure opportunism and ruthless disregard of international decencies, has to rival the infamous Japanese sneak attack on Pearl Harbor of just over thirty-seven years ago. With, at times, a flickering, sickly smile over his face, President Carter astonished and astounded his listeners with the barefaced announcement that the United States and Communist China would enter into full diplomatic relations as of January 1, 1979. This meant, he said, that "the United States recognizes the government of the People's Republic of China as the sole legal government of China." Within this context, he went on, "the people of the United States will maintain cultural, commercial and other unofficial relations with the people of Taiwan." Further, he said that "the government of the United States of America acknowledges the Chinese position that there is but one China and Taiwan is part of China," and he announced that the U.S. and the PRC would exchange ambassadors and establish embassies on March 1, 1979.

These were the main features of a joint communiqué being issued at the same time in both Peking and Washington. In addition, the president stated, the United States would continue to sell defensive weapons to Taiwan. But it is notable that this was his own unilateral statement of intent, and was not in any way consented to by Peking. Since the U.S. recognized that hereafter Taiwan was Chinese territory and had, perforce, to be considered under international law as under the legal jurisdiction of Communist China, such sales there could be prevented at any time by Peking by the simple issuance of a prohibitory mandate.

Here, in fact, is the most pure and pristine embodiment of the Carter administration's proclivity for wishful thinking and for trying to "have your cake and eat it at the same time." For the obvious truth is that the ultimate aim of Peking is to destroy, by whatever means possible and necessary, the government of the Republic of China on Taiwan and to substitute its own rule there. This basic aim it has announced repeatedly, so many times and so consistently as to convince all but the most woolly-minded that it means what it says. Many people made the mistake of not believing what Hitler said in *Mein Kampf* about his ultimate goals and aims, and they lived to regret it. Quite evidently we have in the Carter administration today a preponderance of just such wishful thinkers as existed in respect to the aims of German fascism some fifty years ago. They will, similarly, lead the American people into disaster again.

It is illuminating to recall just how the Chinese Communists have proceeded in such and similar cases in the past. For example, even after the British government recognized Peking in 1950 it attempted to carry on its business with and in respect to Taiwan by the expedient of a consulate accredited, not to the government of the Republic of China, with which it no longer had diplomatic relations, but to the provincial government of Taiwan instead. But just as soon as the Peking regime had a request from London for something the British government very badly wanted, it made permission conditional upon British withdrawal of its consulate from Taiwan, and the British could do nothing but give in. Can anyone doubt that, since now President Carter states that "Taiwan is part of China" and a China that is now Peking-operated and nothing else, Hua Kuo-feng or his successors will crack down on what will now have become an illegal arms traffic between the U.S. and the government of Chiang Ching-kuo on Taiwan? An ignominious retreat will then be forced upon President Carter or *his* successor.

The "line" in the Carter administration seems to be that President Chiang Ching-kuo on Taiwan will now see the error of his ways and move rather promptly to accommodation with the Chinese Communists. Those who at least say they believe this clearly do not believe what President Chiang says or stands for. On the morning of December 16, 1978, Taipei time, he came out with his statement in light of the Carter action.

In the last few years the United States government has repeatedly reaffirmed its assurance to maintain diplomatic relations with the Republic of China and to honor its treaty commitments. Now that it has broken the assurances and abrogated the treaty the United States government cannot be expected to have the confidence of any free nations in the future.

He further asserted:

The United States in extending diplomatic recognition to the Chinese Communist regime which owes its very existence to terror and sup-

391

pression is not in conformity with her professed position of safeguarding human rights and strengthening the capabilities of democratic nations so as to resist the totalitarian dictatorships. Such a move is tantamount to denying the hundreds of millions of enslaved people on the Chinese mainland of their hope to an early restoration of freedom.

Most important, however, was President Chiang Ching-kuo's statement:

Under whatever circumstances, the Republic of China shall neither negotiate with the Chinese Communist regime nor compromise with communism. And she shall never give up her sacred task of recovering the mainland and delivering the compatriots there. This firm position shall remain unchanged.

In announcing diplomatic recognition of Peking by Washington, President Carter at the same time announced the full capitulation of his administration to the three conditions for such diplomatic relations that had been laid down by Peking over and over again through time in the past. These are:

1. Simultaneous withdrawal of U.S. diplomatic recognition of the Republic of China on Taiwan.
2. Total withdrawal of all U.S. military personnel from Taiwan.
3. Abrogation of the Treaty of Mutual Security between the United States and the Republic of China.

We are at least entitled to wonder whether the Carter administration quite realizes all the consequences of all these actions. For example, the total withdrawal of all U.S. military personnel from Taiwan means the absolute and complete destruction of all *joint* measures between Washington and Taiwan regarding the military security in the general region. The most important element here has always been the Taiwan Defense Command, and organization jointly staffed by American and Chinese military personnel on Taiwan, with direct and immediate reponsibility, under the supreme command of the President of the Republic of China as Commander-in-Chief, for *all* military actions and measures in the general region of Taiwan. This, it must be understood clearly, was and always has been, from the American point of view, a means whereby the United States could act effectively, in terms of the now abrogated Mutual Security Treaty between the two countries, to dampen down and even to completely inhibit any and all tendencies toward heating up the continuing civil war between Taipei and Peking into overt military hostilities in the Taiwan area. By destroying this force for peace in the area, President Carter has at one stroke accentuated critically the likelihood that, lacking any American moderating control, the Republic of China would develop policies of military activity in the area so that the civil war would again erupt, to the point where the security of the whole east Asian area would be jeopardized.

What would be the bearing of this on President Carter's announced policy of continuing to supply so-called "defensive" weapons to Taiwan? What, indeed, are "defensive" weapons? Any weapons supply from the United States might be terminated, indeed, if the Carter administration believed that Republic of China was embarking on a policy of military "aggression" against the Chinese mainland. But what is to prevent President Chiang Ching-kuo from obtaining from any number of other sources any and all weapons he wants? He has the money to buy them, and if, as President Carter announces, the U.S. intends to keep on with its business relations with Taiwan, Taiwan's funds from this trade surplus in its favor are likely to increase. Furthermore, by U.S. abandonment of the ROC, that government now has absolutely no inducement to abjure the use of force in the Taiwan area, including the mainland of China itself. Would there be another reason, here, for possible cooperation between the ROC and the USSR? It is far from impossible. Now that President Carter has unilaterally, and without the advice and consent of the Congress, and contrary to the clearly expressed will of the American people, abandoned the U.S. military position in and with regard to Taiwan, it must result in a vacuum of great-power power in the area. This vacuum, it can confidently be predicted, will not remain for very long. The whole history of Taiwan for the past hundred years is a history of contending great-power aspirations with respect to it. In the nineteenth century one after another of the then major powers expressed their interests in the area from a military-economic-political point of view. In the weakness of the Chinese imperial government of those days, the final result was the takeover of Taiwan by an imperialistic expansionist Japan, which held it for fifty years, ending in its defeat in World War II. Thereafter the island with its surrounding islands has been held by the Republic of China, to which it was returned under the terms of the various post-war settlements.

The geopolitical reality, however, was that to hold this island possession the Republic of China needed, and secured, the support of one of the two "superpowers" that emerged from the war. If that now sadly declining power, the United States, sees fit to abdicate its geopolitical role and responsibilities there, it cannot object if another one takes them over instead. This prospect is not just another imaginary "specter" arising from the fevered imagination of just another ivory tower intellectual. It is one of the most pressing realities of our time.

One of the most astounding features of this Carter misadventure in diplomacy is the fact that in return for surrendering completely to the conditions laid down by Peking for diplomatic relations between the U.S. and Communist China, Carter and his diplomatic troupe secured for our own country no concessions of any kind. It has been officially announced in the State Department, for example, that no effort was even made, at all, to get

Peking to state, either formally or informally, that it would not try to take Taiwan by force. This right is therefore specifically reserved to itself by Peking. The consequences have yet to be seen. They could be disastrous.

There are very numerous other areas of critical importance to the future welfare not only of the United States and its people that are also left completely undealt with. Included are Peking's adamant refusal to join in any agreement as to nuclear non-proliferation or even as to non-testing of nuclear bombs in the atmosphere. (Our anti-pollution enthusiasts are yet to be heard from on this, evidently.) And there is, quite obviously, the whole vaunted Carter emphasis upon human rights. Here, Peking's guilt is such as to cause Hitler Germany's holocaust against the Jews to pale into insignificance. The facts of Chinese Communist crimes against its own people have been documented for decades in the past. If President Carter does not believe in these revelations as proven by academic specialists, he might be able to believe the facts on Chinese Communist massive murders of the Chinese people as presented in the past by the AFL-CIO. Does President Carter believe that merely by strong criticism of denials of human rights in the USSR he can redeem himself from his sins of omission in respect to Communist China? Surely he cannot plead ignorance.

This is not to deny the possibility that this most recent disastrous essay by Carter into diplomacy might include a congeries of secret agreements and understandings with Peking. But in view of the abject surrender to Peking's terms that is embodied in the open agreement between Peking and Washington, one can be highly apprehensive about their possible agreements thus far kept secret and hidden from public knowledge and scrutiny. As to this we can only hope that the worst is not yet to come.

It will no doubt be pleaded by the Carter administration and its supporters that, after all, with Teng Hsiao-ping in central control in Peking, the Chinese Communists are now intent upon thoroughgoing "modernization" above all else, and would never do anything to jeopardize the support that could come from the United States by adventurism of any kind.

Here again we must try our best to learn from history. In the early stages of the Russian Communist revolution, American technical assistance was an important factor in Russian modernization, as it has indeed remained ever since, and is today more so than ever. But surely the lesson of history is that all this has achieved is to help the constant and never-ending course of Russian imperialist aggrandizement around the world, before which the United States is today more defenseless and impotent than ever before.

If, indeed, finally and for the first time since they took over mainland China, the Chinese Communists with Hua and Teng at their head are truly intent upon what they call "modernization," it will not be the first time such aims have been announced and promoted by Peking. The fundamental problem remains: *Chinese Communism is inherently incapable of modernizing*

China. What this really means is that if Hua and Teng really mean it, instead of taking over Taiwan, they should remodel their entire socio-economic-political system along the lines of the Republic of China's successful model of modernization. But to do this essentially requires the abandonment of whatever the Chinese Communist model is of Marxism-Leninism-Maoism, and a return to the realities of China as have so clearly been seen in the ideas and embodied in the practices of the Kuomintang, the Chinese Nationalist Party on Taiwan. It is this political entity that, assured of international and internal security by the great-power geopolitical involvement of the United States in the past nearly twenty-five years, and by its own mobilization of resources, has demonstrated to the whole world what the Chinese revolution of our time really is and really can achieve.

Starting with the only agrarian reform in Asia that was truly bloodless, non-confiscatory and aimed immediately and directly at the accentuation of peasant welfare, the Republic of China has moved steadily into light and consumer industries and more recently into technology-intensive and heavy industrial production. The result has been the exact opposite from that on the Chinese Communist mainland, i.e., instead of mass deprivation, technical poverty and primitivism and a focus on purely political-dominated economics, the Chinese on Taiwan now enjoy the second-best standard of living per unit population in all Asia, after Japan, and have an annual trade with the United States well over eight times that of the whole Chinese mainland with its some nine hundred million people against the some nineteen million of Republic of China.

Also, as is well known, all this has been achieved at the same time as the gap in income between the best-off and the worst-off in Taiwan has been steadily and very substantially decreased. For perhaps the greatest achievement of the Republic of China is just here, namely, in the care with which the fruits of hard work and disciplined endeavor have been distributed equitably to the common man. All this is well known to those specialists, even in the Carter administration, who deal with problems of development in the so-called "developing" countries.

It is safe to predict, however, that as in the past, Communist China's desires, for whatever reasons, for what they now term "modernization" will again run into the built-in obstacles of political ideology and will again be termed "revisionism" a la Russe. For the fact is that Maoist romanticist revolutionary mentality is so deeply ingrained into the many, many millions of his followers who are securely embedded in the Chinese Communist apparatus and society that it will take at least a whole political generation to dig them out. The basic insecurity of Teng Hsiao-ping's position in the Peking situation is thus quite clear. His previous political liquidations by the opposition, and his consequent restorations, constitute a type of danse macabre which is quite typical of Chinese Communism.

It is precisely into this type of unstable, earthquake-prone milieu complexity that our all-too-ingenuous President Carter seems intent upon thrusting us. This is what Teng Hsiao-ping's visit to Washington must portend.

Finally, let us remind ourselves again of one of the most important basic facts of international life today, that is, that whatever their temporary shifts of policy may be, the Chinese and Russian Communists share one common trait, namely, their fundamental hostility to us and to everything we stand for and can hope for. Here again I will quote Dr. Ray S. Cline of Georgetown University:

> We must recognize that the rulers of the USSR and the PRC are thinking in adversary terms in every kind of interaction with the United States. That does not mean we may not have some agreements or some common spheres of activity, but no amount of charm and diplomacy, or any number of generous concessions, in my view will change this Soviet and Chinese viewpoint over the next decade or two—"A New Grand Strategy for the United States: An Essay," *Asian Outlook,* Vol. 13, No. 10, Oct. 1978, p. 14.

This is the sober outlook to which we must unswervingly hold, as the Carter administration's diplomacy as to Chinese matters plunges us again into the maelstrom of Chinese Communism and of Chinese Communist intrigue.

Part V
Epilogue:
Reactions to the China Decision

Reflections on the China Decision

Edwin J. Feulner, Jr.*

When we examine major public policy like "The China Question," the primary point among U.S. policy-makers should be: "What is best for the interests for the United States?" In economic, strategic, and moral issues, a continuation of a close relationship with the Republic of China, in my own view, is clearly in the best national interest of the United States.

Our economic relations with the Republic of China are covered elsewhere in this book, but as the foreign trade between the U.S. and Taiwan is eight times that which exists between the U.S. and mainland China, there clearly is a need to maintain a close relationship with our island ally.

Some commentators have pointed out the prospects for future trade with the mainland. These prospects may be promising, however exaggerated they have been made, but the prospect of massive U.S. credits being granted to another communist country, particularly when world credit markets are already stretched thin, is not necessary in our own best interests.

The strategic issue has already been raised by such notables as Secretary of Energy James Schlesinger. When Schlesinger visited mainland China in 1976, he commented that the PRC was a *de facto* member of NATO due to its long and guarded frontier with the USSR. Yet, the case can be made that a closer relationship between mainland China and the United States could conceivably unleash reactions which neither the White House nor the State Department seems to have foreseen. For example, Professor Edward Luttwak in an insightful article in *Commentary* recently noted that a destabilizing move such as full recognition of mainland China by the United States could create such problem for the Soviets that they might well consider an invasion of the lightly populated Singaing province of China. Alternatively, an enhanced PRC-U.S. relationship could be destabilizing in Korea or other flash points throughout Asia.

As I have written elsewhere (*Asia Mail,* May 15, 1978), the Soviet Union must look on the Republic of China as a potential ally in the western Pacific. This alliance would give the Soviets their long-sought-after access to warm water ports in the Pacific. In view of their enmity with the PRC, such an

*Edwin J. Feulner, Jr. is President of *The Heritage Foundation*, Washington, D.C.

alliance could go a long way toward encircling the mainland in combination with the Soviet's recent successes in Vietnam, Afghanistan, and elsewhere around the rim of China. An examination of these geopolitical realities reveals the strategic importance of the location of the Republic of China on the western littoral of the Pacific chain of command. Taiwan has always formed an integral part of our western Pacific defenses ranging from Japan to Korea, south through Taiwan to Subic Bay and Clark Air Force Base in the Philippines. It is certainly not in the strategic interests of the United States to lose such a base at a time when U.S. power is widely perceived in retreat elsewhere around the world.

One of the most disturbing aspects of the China decision by the president and the State Department was the fact that there are other options available than the derecognition of China.

As early as 1971 with the expulsion of Taiwan from the United Nations, the then U.S. ambassador to the United Nations, George Bush, spoke of a possible two-China policy. This policy has been advocated by notable China experts such as Dr. Ray Cline and Dr. Richard Walker (*China—The Turning Point,* Washington, D.C., 1976, and elsewhere). With this arrangement, the United States could maintain full diplomatic relations with the People's Republic of China in Peking, while also maintaining relations at the ambassadorial level with the Republic of China in Taipei. The obvious prototype for this is the German model which currently has two German governments and one German state being recognized. These two governments with their respective ambassadors in Washington, and Ambassadors in East Berlin and Bonn, have managed to accept a real political situation despite the fact that some might consider it only a temporary solution to the problem.

This is a realistic basis of diplomatic relations, and it should be compatible with American moral and political principles. If the current administration is unwilling to do it, it can be assumed that a future administration with a different perspective on world affairs will be willing to establish full relations with Taipei.

Now let us take a long look at the practical implications of the president's action in recognizing Peking and his decision to unilaterally abrogate the Mutual Defense Treaty with Taiwan. There are a number of problems which this action has created—problems which most of the president's supporters tend to overlook.

The first is the credibility of the United States. On an interview program, one of the president's congressional supporters described the treaties as merely "scraps of paper." While that may be the cavalier way some view it, most Americans realize that a treaty involves a solemn obligation of our government jointly arrived at by the executive branch and two-thirds of the Senate. If our nation's word is merely a "scrap of paper," we can expect still more difficulties in various spots around the world.

For example, suppose you were a member of the Israeli parliament—

the Knesset—faced with a vote on a peace treaty of historic dimensions with Egypt. What would your reaction be when the president of the United States took action by himself to abrogate a twenty-five year commitment with an ally without even advising the Senate in advance?

It is not hard to imagine what the reaction of our allies will be. It won't be immediate or dramatic, but over the next several years as the balance of power gradually shifts away from the United States, one of the nails in the coffin of America's foreign policy will have to be that on December 15, 1978, for the first time in its history, the United States unilaterally abrogated a treaty with an ally.

We not only recognized Peking in haste; it appears that we have not considered the ramifications of our action. The easy words of the State Department that we will follow the "Japanese formula" and maintain people-to-people relations with Taiwan, instead of government-to-government relations, overlooks the most basic difference. The reason Japan was able to implement its policy was because it had formal U.S.-ROC relations to fall back on. The conventional wisdom states that no serious adverse consequences would follow from the pursual by the United States of the Japanese formula. Yet, it is often overlooked that Japan never had the long and close relationship with the United States that the Republic of China has experienced. Our alliance with free China is long-standing and close. And, moreover, Taiwan was a colony of Japan for the first half of the twentieth century; this fact has historical ramifications which lead to a different basis for a relationship between Taiwan and Japan than could evolve between Taiwan and the United States. Japan never had a mutual defense treaty with the Republic of China, nor did she have military bases located in Taiwan. Japan's relations were essentially commercial. Similarly, while Japan has no military forces outside her own territory, the United States maintains bases in the Philippines, Korea, Japan and Guam. Additionally, Taiwan has formed an important element in the defense design for the entire Pacific region, as we should have learned during the Vietnam War. Furthermore, the Japanese knew that Peking would not take any hostile action toward Taiwan as long as the United States had formal relations with her. Now that we no longer do, the formal diplomatic relations of the Republic of China are down to twenty-one countries, the largest of which are the Republic of Korea, Saudi Arabia, and South Africa.

What may be evolving over the longer run as we look at the shambles of the U.S. foreign policy around the world is an alliance of nations which formerly counted on the United States for assistance, but which now will have to go it alone and start to look directly to each other without U.S. participation—"a fourth world" alliance.

Thus, one can foresee evolving relationships among Taiwan and Israel and South Africa and various Latin American countries which have been squeezed and pressured by the administration on their so-called "human rights" stands.

At least one newspaper columnist, Nick Timmesch, pointed out that now "the big powers are in economic, not military, combat. Thus, the question becomes not so much one of the military invasion, but rather one of economic strangulation."

In fact, the attention focused on the military invulnerability of Taiwan is little more than the elementary debating technique of the straw man. That is, you come up with the worst possible case, set it up, and let your opponents waste a lot of time and energy knocking it down. The real issue is not military invasion, but rather economic strangulation of the Republic of China by the mainland.

The economic strangulation can take any one of a number of forms. For example, assume a China Air Lines Boeing 747 (owned by the private company in Taiwan) lands in a country that doesn't have diplomatic relations with Taiwan but does have them with the mainland. The mainland's local ambassador could direct that the plane be impounded as properly belonging to the regime in Peking. Some argue that this could have happened before we derecognized free China. Perhaps so, but until the United States abandoned its ally, there was not a country in the world which would have dared to confiscate the property of an ally of the United States.

Or, take another example: a ship sailing through the Formosa Straits into one of Taiwan's port cities is intercepted by a Communist Chinese naval gunboat and escorted into a communist port. Under international law, since we have now derecognized Taiwan, the mainland Chinese would be within their legal rights to demand recertification of the ship's cargo, or even possibly that it be off-loaded in a mainland port.

Or, suppose mainland China asks the U.N. to improve economic sanctions on the "rebellious province" of Taiwan, much as the U.S. has already done to Rhodesia.

Just one or two incidents like this would have what my attorney friends called a "chilling effect" on the whole economic viability of one of the world's most prosperous tradition nations, Taiwan.

There are countless other examples I could cite because there are still sixty treaties in force between the United States and free China. Most of these deal with economic and trade issues. Each one will have to be examined individually to determine how it can best be preserved.

These are the real problem issues that ought to be looked at and that haven't been answered by the State Department's legal experts or by the president. Yet, they could all be saved if we merely recognized some form of governmental contracts by the Republic of China with the United States.

For example, we can institute a liaison office for the Republic of China with the United States. This would give the ROC the same status which Peking formerly enjoyed with the United States. Thus, the precedent is clear and current.

It should be clear that the recognition of the mainland and the abandonment of our ally has created problems not just with the Republic of China, but also elsewhere throughout the world. For example, the Israeli government officially stated that "Israel must give thorough consideration to the U.S. decision about Taiwan and reconsider Washington's intention to maintain its obligation under its agreements and treaties with other countries."

The problem of third countries is not a false one. It is real and hard-hitting and one that we must be willing to face up to. Indeed, the point has been made that even the People's Republic of China cannot be entirely happy with the "paper tiger"—the United States—abandoning a twenty-five year military treaty because a third government demanded it. This entirely does not show the kind of fortitude and will which the PRC should be looking for from a new ally.

Another subject which requires comment is "human rights" as the cornerstone of the administration's foreign policy. The president has repeatedly reiterated his position that human rights is the basis of his foreign policy. Yet he has extended recognition to a government which is universally recognized as having disregarded the human rights of its own citizens and having murdered between thirty-five and fifty million of them to gain power. This must be viewed as a double standard of human rights: apply it strictly to small, weaker countries and ignore it in our dealings with the other superpowers.

Similarly, one has to look at the process by which China policy was altered. In a March 15, 1976, speech to the prestigious Council on Foreign Relations, candidate Carter established the ground rules for the conduct of foreign policy under his administration: "Our policies should be open and honest, and decent and compassionate as the American people themselves are. Our policies should be shaped with the participation of Congress. . . . And they should emerge from broad and well-informed public debate and participation. . . . Our policies should treat the people of other nations as individuals, with the same dignity and respect we demand for ourselves." Every time we have made a serious foreign policy mistake in recent years, he insisted, it was due to the fact that the American people had "been excluded from the process."

Now, let us ask: Was the decision to break diplomatic relations with the Republic of China on Taiwan and to cancel our mutual defense pact a "decent and compassionate" thing to do? Was the policy "shaped with the participation of Congress"? Have we treated the free Chinese "with the same dignity and respect" we demand for ourselves? Were the American people brought into the process?

The entire arrangement was worked out in absolute secrecy. Congress was not brought into the process, even though an amendment to the 1978 International Security Assistance Act, which was signed into law by the president—and approved by the Senate 94 to 0—specifically directed the administration to include Congress in regard to any proposed policy change affecting continuation of the Mutual Defense Treaty.

It also was, in more graphic terms, betrayal of a written promise made by Secretary of State Cyrus Vance to Senator John Sparkman (D-Ala.), former Chairman of the Senate Foreign Relations Committee, that the administration would consult with Congress before making any changes in our commitment to Taiwan.

As Senator Richard Stone (D-Fla.), Chairman of the Subcommittee on Mideast and South Asian Affairs, said, "The Congress found that the security treaty with the Republic of China on Taiwan aided the stability of east Asia and asked that there should be prior consultation between the Congress and executive branch on any proposed policy changes affecting the continuation of that treaty." There was no such consultation.

Obviously, there was no such "broad and well-informed public debate and participation" either. Rather, the American people were very clearly "excluded from the process." One must ask, then, whether the administration—in its haste and secretiveness—isn't guilty of the very sins it had accused its predecessors of committing.

Having said all this in regard to the triangular relationship with the United States and the People's Republic of China and the Republic of China on Taiwan, the ultimate question must be: "Where do we go from here?" The United States has formally recognized the People's Republic of China as the sole legitimate government of China. However, in doing this, the United States need not have withdrawn all governmental recognition from the Republic of China in Taiwan.

Having done it, however, certain actions can be taken to repair the damage. A lawsuit has already been instigated by Senator Goldwater and a number of other plaintiffs questioning the constitutionality of the abrogation of the Mutual Defense Treaty by the president acting alone. The Mutual Defense Treaty was signed into law by the president after being ratified by two-thirds of the Senate. Goldwater and his co-plaintiffs contend that the abrogation of such a treaty can only be done by similar joint executive/legislative action. They point to a long series of mutual defense treaties which have similar abrogation clauses and wonder aloud if this president or a future president might not come along and unilaterally abrogate the NATO treaty, for example. As a sidelight, it should be noted that some members of the Senate who favored full recognition of the People's Republic of China also support Goldwater's effort. In the past, strange coalitions of conservatives and liberals have united on subjects such as the War Powers Bill in the early 1970s to curb the rights of the president to unilaterally become involved in foreign policy. This could become a similar issue in 1979 and beyond.

Secondly, it is moral, realistic, and in the best interests of the United States that we should continue to maintain governmental relations with the Republic of China in Taiwan. If, as suggested earlier in this essay, the two-China policy is impractical, at the very least we should insist that a liaison office for the Republic of China be established. This not only has a clear role in international law, but it also is directly applicable here, because it is the legal status which the People's Republic of China enjoyed prior to the announcement of the switch of the nameplates on December 15, 1978 by President Carter.

One of the unanswered questions which will have to remain concerns the relationship of the ROC's military capabilities to the U.S. willingness to provide spare parts and other accessories through the pipeline. The Republic of China's military needs go beyond spare parts for existing weapon systems. The question has to be answered in such a way that the administration will keep the pipeline open into the indefinite future.

Similarly as the legal details are worked out regarding the sixty economic, technical, and scientific treaties which are bilaterally in effect between the United States and the Republic of China, we must be certain that our own commercial interests as well as those of our trading partners are protected. This will require considerable finesse and care. However, none of these problems are insurmountable. Rather, they must be faced squarely, and realistic answers which are in the best interest of the United States must be worked out. By definition, the best interests of the United States can never involve abandoning a long-time loyal ally for some potential transient gain, especially with a country whose declared strategic and ideological objectives are implacably hostile to our own.

Our Deal with Peking:
All Cost, No Benefit*

*George Bush****

The airwaves are filled now with glad tidings from the White House, proclaiming that President Carter's China initiative has brought us much closer to peace on earth, good will to man.

How joyous it would be if that were true, but, unfortunately, nearly every Christmas story has its grinch—and this one is no exception.

The tragic fact is that the price our government has paid in recognizing the People's Republic of China has not only diminished American credibility in the world but has also darkened the prospects for peace. And I would venture that in the privacy of the Great Hall, the Chinese are acutely aware of that.

Let me explain by first introducing a bit of history. When I arrived in Peking in 1974 as the U.S. representative there, the Nixon and Kissinger trips and the Shanghai Communiqué were already on record. The United States was committed to eventual recognition of the People's Republic.

Moreover, ordinary Chinese citizens were intensely emotional in their desire for reunification with Taiwan. I remember in the early days how Chinese workmen refused to hang a map of Asia on my office wall because it showed Taiwan in a different color from the mainland. Not long thereafter, at sporting games that drew provincial teams from all over the mainland, the stands exploded with cheers when the announcer identified one squad as "our brothers from Taiwan." Government propaganda reflected much the same sentiment.

Yet, in private conversations the rulers of the People's Republic took a very different view. They were committed, of course, to the "liberation" of Taiwan, but that was always a distinctly secondary issue. "You have time; there is no hurry," they said over and over again.

When President Ford, Secretary Kissinger and I met with Chairman Mao Tse-tung in October 1975, he repeated that settlement of the Taiwan

---

*Copyright 1978, *Washington Post*. Reprinted by permission.

**George Bush, former Chairman of the Republican National Committee, has also held the posts of U.S. ambassador to the United Nations, director of the Central Intelligence Agency, and U.S. representative to Peking.

question might take the United States and China "one year, ten years, or even a hundred years" to achieve. He clearly expected to die before it happened, and he was equally clear that if the United States wanted more time to modify opinion at home, that was readily acceptable.

What concerned Mao far more than the Taiwan question—and has since preoccupied his successors—was the gathering strength of the Soviet Union. The leaders in Peking are terrified that one day they may be encircled by a Soviet empire, eager to gobble them up. Forty-five Russian divisions are already poised on their northern border, and in recent months their security has deteriorated along their southern rim as well.

To the Chinese, the key to peace is for the United States and its Western allies to act as a firm, reliable counterweight to Soviet pressures. Only if the United States remains a credible world power—one that honors its commitments and lives up to its responsibilities—are they themselves secure.

Breaking a Treaty Without Cause

Here then, is the situation that Jimmy Carter found when he entered the Oval Office:

On one hand, Peking was transfixed with the idea that the Soviet Union sought "hegemony" in many parts of the globe and was already convinced that the West was growing "soft."

On the other hand, while continuing to pay lip service to "normalization" of relations with the United States, the Chinese quietly accepted the fact that the two sides were deadlocked on that issue. For several years, Peking had insisted on three pre-conditions before there could be "normalization": the United States had to abrogate its Mutual Defense Treaty with Taiwan, had to withdraw troops from there, and had to withdraw recognition from Taiwan, acknowledging Peking as the sole, legitimate government of China. The United States had consistently balked at those terms, insisting that it would not formally recognize Peking until there was a firm, explicit commitment to settle the Taiwanese issue peacefully. And there the negotiations were stuck.

Because of the importance of the Russian threat, however, the questions of full "normalization" and of Taiwan were never a major barrier to progress on commercial and strategic issues. China and the United States had entered a *de facto* political relationship that had two great virtues: it permitted both sides to begin working harmoniously together, and it also allowed the United States to maintain the integrity of its commitment to Taiwan. In an imperfect world, that was a major accomplishment.

It was in this context that President Carter's December 15 announcement was such a bombshell.

The immediate question was not whether we should recognize Peking. Many Americans now agree that a close working relationship between Washington and Peking should advance the cause of peace and world trade.

Personally, I have long felt that in spite of the totalitarian nature of the Chinese government, it was in our own national interest to improve relations with Peking.

But the critical question was the terms on which the recognition was negotiated. Incredibly, it turns out that the United States has now accepted all three of Peking's original demands—and has capitulated on its own demand for a guarantee on Taiwan, abandoning a faithful friend in the process. For the first time in our history, a peacetime American government has renounced a treaty with an ally without cause or benefit.

A Figleaf for Retreat

By the administration's own admission, it never received—or even asked for—specific assurances from Peking about a peaceful solution to the Taiwanese question. In Peking's eyes, the Taiwanese matter continues to be strictly an internal issue, and in its constitution the "liberation" of Taiwan remains an unchallenged goal.

In response, the administration argues that the mainland will wink at future U.S. arms sales to the Taiwanese. But in the same breath, administration officials say *sotto voce* that those sales will be "restrained."

The administration also argues that Peking has neither the capability nor the incentive to conquer Taiwan. But any student of Chinese history—remembering that during the Cultural Revolution, only ten years ago, some of today's Chinese leaders were driven down Peking streets with sticks—can properly ask: Who knows with certainty what lies ahead? It is true that armed conquest by the mainland does not seem imminent, but because of unilateral action by the United States, the seventeen million people on Taiwan are now hostage to the changing whims of the Peking leadership.

The terms that the Carter administration has accepted, and even trumpeted, are the same terms that have been available for the past seven years. But they were always refused before because we knew—just as the Chinese knew—that in the absence of sufficient guarantees they were but a figleaf for an abject American retreat.

The terrible truth is that the United States now stands exposed to the world as a nation willing to betray a friend—even when there is no apparent gain.

There is, of course, room for reasonable men to disagree about the benefits that might now accrue to China and the United States in trade and investment. Contrary to administration claims, however, I believe the gains that are likely to occur undoubtedly would have occurred anyway under our existing relationship.

Over the past year and a half, before these negotiations had even begun, the Chinese were ardently seeking Western technology and our sales to China were rising dramatically. Over the past four months the commercial pace has accelerated, and many American companies have begun making serious plans for trading with the mainland and investing there. But it has always been apparent in the commercial field that China needs us more than we need them. Indeed, it was precisely China's growing eagerness for trade that gave the United States greater leverage in our diplomatic bargaining than we had ever had before—leverage that we carelessly tossed aside.

Morality and Strategy

At its heart, however, the China question is not one of trade and technology but of fundamental morality and international strategy.

As sociologist Peter Berger wrote earlier this year, "If there is one universal, indeed primeval principal of morality, it is that one must not deliver one's friends to their enemies." Berger was writing of refugees fleeing from Vietnam in their small, makeshift dinghies. "These boats," he said, "bear a message. It is a simple and ugly message: *Here is what happens to those who put their trust in the United States of America.*"

For President Carter, who professes a strong belief in Christian ethics, it should be a tormenting thought that by his hand the United States has put an entire people adrift in a cruel, hostile sea—and for scarcely any purpose.

The moral question is closely linked to the strategic issue that is causing perhaps even greater consternation in many chanceries of the world.

Throughout the post-war period, America's credibility—joined with America's military might—has been the glue that has held together the noncommunist world. Justifiably, both friend and foe alike are now asking, however, whether the United States can still be counted on to keep its word. Increasingly in recent years the United States has staked out a clear, unequivocal position, has invited others to join us, and then, as counterpressures have built up, has suddenly, inexplicably buckled.

In Africa, we committed ourselves to support the forces of moderation. But when black moderates in Rhodesia arranged with Prime Minister Ian Smith for the transfer of power and free elections, we threw in our lot with Marxist radicals.

In recent negotiations in the Middle East, the Israelis announced that they were prepared to accept a final plan drafted with American help. But when Egypt raised the ante, we modified our position to accept the new Egyptian proposals, and when the Israelis refused to go along, we publicly kicked them in the shins.

In Europe, President Carter convinced our German and French allies that we would build a neutron bomb, and Helmut Schmidt courageously supported him. But then, in the face of a Soviet propaganda campaign, the administration knuckled under and shelved the project. Even now, as contradictory signals emanate from Washington, our NATO allies wonder whether the United States will honor its pledge to raise defense expenditures by about three percent a year.

In Iran, the Carter administration placed considerable pressure on the

Shah to accelerate his liberalization program—sometimes, according to reports, against his better judgment. But when trouble broke out, our government disappeared over the hill. The world recognizes, even if we do not, that the United States could have been demonstrative in its support for the Shah, issuing firmer statements, engaging in naval deployments, and responding with something more than timidity when the Russians warned us to stay out of it.

To friends of the United States who have been chilled by these recent events and by our posture on SALT, the mindless abandonment of Taiwan thus comes at a particularly inopportune time. Why now? And why would the president act so unilaterally, without consulting with the Congress, especially after the Senate had insisted by a unanimous 94-0 vote upon such consultations? Unfortunately, there are no easy answers.

Understandably, Peking has been prominent among those worried about America's deteriorating position in the world. It has been particularly dismayed about Cuban intervention in Ethiopia, the major Soviet role in Afghanistan (a neighbor to both China and Iran), and the pro-Soviet coup in South Yemen, as well as the hesitant U.S. response to Soviet claims with regard to a role in Iran. Indeed, this area of the world—including southern Asia, the Persian Gulf and the Indian Ocean—is just as important strategically to the Chinese as to the United States.

The ultimate irony, then, of this "normalization" is that China, whose primary interest lies in a strong, steadfast American presence in the world, has now seen just how easily we can be pushed around. The Chinese realize that we have given all and gained nothing, and while they engage in self-congratulations, they know in their hearts that by our actions we have also made the world a more dangerous place than it was only a few weeks ago.

The "Taiwan Question":
A Final Solution*

*James D. Hessman***

"Massive applause . . . throughout the nation."

The president obviously didn't realize the mike to the White House press room was still "live." But his own assessment of the probable public reaction to his December 15 announcement that the United States would recognize mainland China and abrogate the Mutual Defense Treaty with Taiwan was heard loud and clear by the reporters present—and, even though it received scant media attention afterward, it may turn out in retrospect to have been the most inadvertently revealing part of the president's relatively brief address to the nation.

Because, rather than "massive applause," which Mr. Carter was seeking and apparently expecting, the initial public reaction ran about 4 to 1 against the president. The Associated Press quoted associate White House press secretary Claudia Townsend as saying on December 19 that the telegrams, phone calls, and letters of opposition outnumbered the expressions of support 4,630 to 1,158.

Those figures would probably not in themselves be too worrisome to the administration, however. People opposed to any departure from previous policies are generally more outspoken than those in favor. Moreover, media and congressional reaction was relatively favorable. Besides, the timetable agreed to between Peking and Washington called for formal establishment of relations on January 1, 1979, which meant that the new Congress convening in mid-January would be presented with a *fait accompli*. With still overwhelming Democratic majorities in both House and Senate, with public attention distracted by other issues such as Iran, inflation, and SALT II, and with China's deputy premier Teng Hsiao-ping, *Time's* Man of the Year, charming the American press and visiting legislators like a public relations virtuoso, there seemed virtually no chance that what was done could ever be undone.

*Copyright 1979, *Seapower*. Reprinted by permission.
**James D. Hessman is editor-in-chief of *Seapower* magazine, the official publication of The Navy League of the United States.

But there was nevertheless a growing hope among Taiwan supporters that Congress could, and perhaps would, force the president to agree to some form of tangible guarantee of Taiwan's continued independence that would be considerably stronger in scope and longer in duration than the one-year's notice (of abrogation of the Mutual Defense Treaty) which the administration had given Taiwan only seven hours before the president's announcement (waking up President Chiang at 2 A.M. Taipei time to give him the news). And there was in some quarters a belief, ranging in strength from uneasy suspicion to absolute conviction, that the the president had not only done the wrong thing, he had done it the wrong way and for the wrong reasons, and might soon see it backfire—to his, the nation's, and the world's detriment.

A Dawning Realization

There was also a dawning realization that the president had been much less than candid in several important particulars related to the recognition announcement and the probable international consequences thereof.

On the December 19 "CBS Evening News," for example, Mr. Carter told Walter Cronkite that "a personal message delivered to me this afternoon from President Brezhnev" had been "very positive in tone" about the new relationship between the United States and the PRC.

"I can say, without any doubt," the president continued, "that our new relationship with China will not put any additional obstacles in the way of a successful SALT agreement and also will not endanger our good relationships with the Soviet Union."

Carter's optimistic reading of the Brezhnev letter was almost immediately contradicted by the Soviet Union, which—"in an unusual step," reported David K. Shipler in the December 22 New York Times—made public details of the message from Brezhnev to Carter "in an apparent effort to show that the Soviet leader did have questions about the new Chinese-American relationship and would watch it closely." Details of the message released through Tass, the Soviet press agency, "expressed concern" about use in the U.S./PRC recognition communiqué of the word "hegemony," a favorite PRC codeword for Soviet expansionism. The Tass release, Shipler said, "was reported as a response to what Moscow evidently regarded as a misinterpretation of the Soviet leader's views by President Carter."

A 1979 Moratorium

Another clarification, of a much more practical nature, and exceedingly important to Taiwan, was in the offing. On January 12 it was disclosed that, as part of the "normalization" agreement with mainland China, the United States had agreed to impose a one-year moratorium "on new U.S. weapons sales to Taiwan." Some members of Congress "expressed surprise and

412

concern upon learning belatedly of the U.S. commitment," Don Oberdorfer reported in that day's *Washington Post*. Carter administration officials, he added, "said that the failure to make the moratorium public was inadvertent, and some officials said they assumed it had been made known at the time of the normalization announcement."

Such relatively "minor" misjudgments, miscalculations, and—to be candid—misstatements by the president might be easily dismissed and soon forgotten were they atypical and/or if they were not symptomatic of more serious miscalculations. Unfortunately, a strong case can be made that (1) similar inconsistencies and confusions have occurred with distressing regularity since the Carter administration first took office, and (2) far from enhancing "the cause of peace in Asia and the world," as the December 15 U.S./PRC communiqué hopefully suggests, the new realignment in the western Pacific could bring the region and the world closer to war, could enlarge the size of the so-called "nuclear club" to a critical mass, could give impetus to the world's arms race in other ways, could enhance the power of the USSR at the same time it antagonizes that now encircled superpower, and could mark the beginning of the end of the U.S. role as a force for peace in the Pacific. It might also, just incidentally, eventually mean that "the people of Taiwan" will have to choose between death, or life under communism.

(In switching U.S. recognition from the Republic of China on Taiwan to the People's Republic of China on the mainland the administration that "we are recognizing simple reality"—then immediately proceeded to depart from simple reality by consistently referring thereafter not to the government of Taiwan but to "the people of Taiwan." Shifting from one fiction—that Taiwan ruled all of China, including the mainland—to another—that the mainland rules all of China, including Taiwan—may be defensible in diplomatic terms, but it is not "simple reality." Some would say, in fact, that the first fiction had greater validity: the ROC did at one time control the mainland; the PRC has never controlled Taiwan.)

Returning to the charge of "inconsistencies and confusions," it should be sufficient to mention, without elaboration, the Lance affair, the Polish translator, the frequent State Department "clarifications" (and eventually repudiations) of Andrew Young's pronouncements, the president's embarrassing vacillation on the neutron bomb, the gas deregulation flap, the repeated misreading of the economic situation, the premature announcement of plans to withdraw U.S. ground forces from South Korea, and, most recently, the belated sacking of Bella Abzug. Except for the problem of the Polish translator, the common denominator of each of the incidents mentioned was an administration reversal of policy.

A Nuclear ROC—Aligned with Soviets

Regarding the "more serious miscalculations" mentioned, the following points are relevant:

1. The Republic of China (ROC) on Taiwan has, even the administration concedes, the capability of making nuclear weapons. It has until now forsworn development, deployment, and use of such weapons and is, in fact, a signatory of the Nuclear Non-Proliferation Treaty (which Peking refused to sign). However: (a) Almost a year and a half ago Ranan R. Lurie reported, in the October 26, 1977 *Chicago Sun Times,* that the ROC already had developed "tactical nuclear bombs designed to annihilate an invading armada or prevent a Chinese sea blockade." The report was denied both by ROC officials and, with less certainty, by U.S. officials. (b) Mainland China already possesses a modest inventory of nuclear weapons, and is building more; it would be difficult to blame Taiwan for arming itself in kind—but secretly. (c) The United States has now made Taiwan a non-nation, no longer bound by the Nuclear Non-Proliferation Treaty.

2. There is a more serious danger: that other countries throughout the world previously dependent on the U.S. nuclear umbrella will lose faith in the credibility of the American commitment. Countries such as South Korea, Israel, and South Africa all have the ability to build nuclear weapons; all are threatened in varying degrees by enemies on their immediate borders; and all believe, rightly or wrongly, that the United States is a less reliable ally now than previously. (To cite but one example of the domino effect of misgivings caused by the Carter announcement: Henry S. Bradsher reported in the December 18 *Washington Star* that "the establishment of diplomatic relations between Washington and Peking has shaken officials here [in Jerusalem]. If the United States can so abruptly switch friends in the Far East, embracing China while abandoning Taiwan and abrogating the defense treaty with it, then Israelis fear it can also do so in the Middle East.")

3. The ROC government has another option of last resort—one admittedly odious to Taiwan itself, but a viable option nonetheless: Alliance with the USSR. Again, Taiwan's leaders have said they will "never" make common cause with Russia. But never is a sometime thing in today's world; U.S. presidents used to say the United States would never abandon Taiwan. So the question becomes this: Would a drowning man take refuge in a lifeboat full of lepers? If that is the only option available, he would. And for Russia an alliance with Taiwan would be a coup of unprecedented magnitude, giving it a strategically located island base ninety miles from the mainland which—with 1.5 million Soviet troops already on the Sino-Soviet border and with Vietnam, a Kremlin ally, pushing from the south—would complete the Kremlin's encirclement of mainland China.

4. Finally, the least quantifiable but, in the long term, most important result: U.S. credibility throughout the world has suffered perhaps irreparable damage. George Bush, former CIA director, former U.S. ambassador to the United Nations, and former U.S. representative to Peking, said in the December 24 *Washington Post:* "The tragic fact is that the price our government has paid in recognizing the People's Republic of China has not only

diminished American credibility in the world but has also darkened the prospects of peace . . . The terrible truth is that the United States now stands exposed to the world as a nation willing to betray a friend—even when there is no apparent gain." Bush also quoted from a column by sociologist Peter Berger, a Rutgers professor, in the February 24 *New York Times:* "If there is one universal, indeed primeval, principle of morality, it is that one must not deliver one's friends to their enemies." Berger was writing, Bush noted, of the "boat people" fleeing Vietnam "in their small, makeshift dinghies. 'These boats,' he said, 'bear a message. It is a simple and ugly message: *Here is what happens to those who put their trust in the United States of America* [Berger's emphasis].' " (Bush might also have noted another chillingly prescient Berger comment in the same column: "It now appears that the abandonment of those who trust us is becoming a habit. *We are getting ready to do it again—this time to Taiwan* [again, Berger's emphasis]." Berger's final dictum is also worth remembering: "If there is one maxim in which morality coincides with politics, it is that a nation that breaks its solemn word twice will never be trusted again.")

Silence on Human Rights

So far, no mention has been made of President Carter's widely publicized "human rights" policy—and with good reason: There is much to be silent about. Again, the testimony of others:

• Columnist George Will, in the December 21 *Washington Post:* "In his broadcast announcement on China, Carter did not see fit to mention to Americans that what he was doing involved disavowing a treaty obligation. He left that troubling detail to television commentators. Why? Having recently made a speech reminding Americans that, at last, they have a president virtuous enough to care about human rights, perhaps he did not want to dwell on the fact that he was doing more to jeopardize the rights of the Taiwanese than he has done to enhance the rights of any other people."

• AFL-CIO President George Meany, quoted by John M. Goshko (also in the December 21 *Washington Post*): "What we cannot understand . . . is how this president, who made human rights a world issue, could so suddenly and callously reject the human rights concerns of both those enslaved on mainland China and those on Taiwan who fear such enslavement."

It hasn't received too much publicity lately, but a report issued in 1971 by the Senate Internal Security Subcommittee estimated that the PRC regime had slaughtered anywhere from thirty-two million to sixty-one million people during its then less than a quarter century in power. The subcommittee noted that its estimates were necessarily, within the limits indicated, extremely imprecise because of the difficulty in gathering statistically valid data from the mainland. By way of comparison, the Nazis killed an estimated six million Jews in World War II.

415

More recently (in late November), Amnesty International issued a 176-page report indicating that, although the scale of slaughter has probably diminished, PRC authorities are still executing "large numbers" of their countrymen. "Since the purge of the 'gang of four' in October 1976," the respected human rights organization was quoted as saying, "many notices have disclosed that a number of executions have been carried out not only for crimes such as murder, rape, robbery, and other common-law offenses, but also for political offenses."

Comments and Observations

Following are a few additional comments and observations which would seem relevant:

• Few of those who oppose the president's action in breaking relations with Taiwan want to "ignore nine hundred million Chinese on the mainland," as the administration and its supporters try to imply. Most rational opponents say they *do* favor improved relations with the mainland, but they believe improved U.S./PRC relations are achievable without abrogation of the Mutual Defense Treaty with Taiwan. They oppose breaking that treaty, therefore,—and their opposition is supported by the American people, who, in a Harris survey in early September 1978, favored (62-25) recognition of the PRC as well as (66-19) continued recognition of the ROC and (64-19) continuation of the Mutual Defense Treaty.

• Improved trade with the mainland, supposedly one of the major benefits which will result from the U.S. recognition, could be an agonizingly long time in developing. Mainland China has a large population, but a per capita gross national product of only $410, and consumer spending is both minimal and tightly controlled. In 1978, the two-way U.S./PRC trade amounted to about one billion dollars. The two-way U.S./ROC trade totaled an estimated seven and a half billion. With less than one-fiftieth the PRC population (seventeen million compared to about nine hundred million), in other words, Taiwan conducted more than seven times as much trade with the United States. Despite some well-publicized agreements—the PRC's Coca-Cola license, for example—Taiwan is likely to retain a large trading edge for the foreseeable future. The reasons are simple. Mainland China, which under the Jackson/Vanik Amendment is ineligible for most-favored-nation status because it does not allow freedom of emigration, has little to export in any case; it does need, and is apparently now willing to accept, imports of all types—but has no money to pay for them. But it's willing to accept loans. The situation was well summarized by John Roche in his syndicated column of December 20: "The People's Republic of China will not normalize relations unless we dump Taiwan. What a heartbreaker! Unless we renege on a treaty, Teng will not allow us to set up an embassy in Peking, will speak wickedly of us, and worst of all will not let us loan him billions of dollars with which to modernize China."

416

- U.S. officials say they do not "expect" the PRC to attack Taiwan, but they concede there are no "secret deals" guaranteeing Taiwan's safety. Meanwhile, PRC Deputy Premier Teng, while outwardly amiable toward Taiwan in other respects, has steadfastly refused to forswear an armed takeover. "That is China's business," he and other PRC officials insist without exception. The comparisons are unpleasant, but also unavoidable: Neville Chamberlain did not expect war in Europe after Munich; U.S. leaders did not, in 1941, expect the Japanese to attack Pearl Harbor; and present U.S. leaders did not, until the last few weeks, perhaps, expect the Shah of Iran to fall from power. The lesson of history: an ounce of guarantee is worth a ton of expectations.

- As previously indicated, President Carter said, and undoubtedly believes, U.S. recognition of mainland China will contribute to "the cause of peace." But there are others who believe the reverse: that recognition could be destabilizing. *New York Times* military analyst Drew Middleton reported, in the December 18 *Times,* that U.S. government officials "expect that some of the [PRC] crack divisions in the military regions facing Taiwan will be switched to the north at the earliest possible moment to balance the Soviet buildup." The same officials "predicted" that PRC imports "of advanced aircraft and anti-aircraft and anti-tank missile systems from Britain and France will be expedited," Middleton reported. Earlier, Hans J. Morgenthau had suggested—in the July 25 *Times*—that "what frightens the Russians is not today's China . . . but the China of tomorrow and the day after. There are Russians who are not willing to wait until China, perhaps armed and modernized by the United States, has become a mega-super-power. In their thinking, war with China—a pre-emptive war initiated by the Soviet Union—is inevitable." Is a Soviet/PRC war inevitable? Perhaps, and perhaps not. But it is worth noting that many of those who do not "expect" such a war defend the recognition of mainland China on the grounds that such recognition, given the disparate PRC and ROC populations, was historically inevitable. Given the comparative populations of the combined Arab states and Israel, it might be that Israel's fall also is inevitable. But nobody in Israel believes it.

- It is probably true, as the administration claims, that the PRC lacks the necessary naval/military capabilities, particularly amphibious lift, to successfully invade Taiwan. But it has enough ships and air power, as well as, now, the political status, to carry out a successful sea blockade. Even if Teng, to retain U.S. good will, were to refrain from such overt action, there is no guarantee his successors would be as restrained. Teng is 74; he was twice purged in the past; his duration in power could be extremely short-lived, and the succession on the mainland is too precarious to predict. If a blockade were imposed, in the near or distant future—after what might be termed a "decent interval"—there would be few if any nations willing or able to break it.

- In September 1977 the Senate passed, 94-0, a "sense of the

Congress" resolution that "there should be prior consultation between the Congress and the executive branch on any proposed policy changes affecting the continuation in force of the Mutual Defense Treaty of 1954." The fact that Mr. Carter did not consult with Congress before the December 15 announcement has angered many legislators—enough so that some who were neutral on SALT II now may vote against it. The SALT II treaty, let it be understood, perhaps should be defeated—but on its merits (or defects.) Its defeat for any lesser reasons could be both politically and militarily disastrous.

- It is sometimes alleged that recognition of the mainland merely continues an evolutionary process begun in 1972, when President Nixon signed the Shanghai Communiqué. That is not so. Nixon went just so far, then stopped. President Ford continued the friendly overtures begun by Mr. Nixon, but informally. President Carter's recognition announcement was a new and abrupt movement forward from a clearly defined line which Presidents Nixon and Ford had approached, but never crossed. The difference is analogous to the difference between skirting the law and breaking the law.

- What has been almost completely ignored is the fact that, for whatever intangible benefits which might eventually result, the United States has given up a major tangible asset: a forward base in the Western Pacific which could serve as a major naval/military staging area. Under the Mutual Defense Treaty, the United States could base literally millions of men, hundreds of ships, and thousands of aircraft in and around a friendly Taiwan. Now it cannnot. And it cannot put one soldier with a sidearm on the mainland without PRC permission. The fact that the United States neither expects nor wants to fight another war in Asia is irrelevant. It didn't expect or want to fight the last three. Mr. Carter has reduced the number of naval and military options available to future presidents.

The Battle Continues

Supporters of Taiwan can take moderate comfort from the fact that a number of (mostly Republican) Senators and Representatives led by Senator Barry Goldwater (R.-Ariz.) are taking the matter to court on the grounds that—as Goldwater had earlier asserted in a 1978 Heritage Foundation study *(China and the Abrogation of Treaties)*—the president does not have the constitutional right to abrogate treaties without Senate consent. Meanwhile, Senator Harry Byrd (Ind.-Va.) was among those introducing legislation at the beginning of the new Congress to insure the Mutual Defense Treaty would be kept in force or, at worst, replaced with more adequate guarantees for Taiwan.

The battle, in other words, is still far from over. But considerable damage already has been done—much of it to the United States. Many Americans who want desperately to support their president doubtless would agree, as much in sorrow as in anger, with the following summation in the December 29 *New York Times* by John B. Oakes, that publication's former senior editor:

> It is not inconceivable that Taiwan, now bereft of any effective American support beyond the expression of pious hopes, might well start buying arms from an all-too-willing Soviet Union, which—given the state of Soviet-Chinese relations—would probably relish Taiwan's becoming an Asian "Cuba."

The ultimate results of American deference to Communist China on Taiwan as the price of normalization may thus not be quite so beneficial for the United States as some of the best and brightest minds in the administration (and outside of it, too) seem to think. That question is certainly arguable; but what is hardly arguable is that, by taking the action he has now taken in the way he has taken it, President Carter has seriously undermined American pretensions to be the moral leader of the world and an exemplar of constancy and steadfastness to our friends.

Twenty Questions
on the China Decisions

Dr. Walter Judd

---

1. Why did the president choose a holiday period, when the old Congress was out of session and the new Congress not yet in session, to announce his decision to terminate unilaterally, without cause, our diplomatic relations and Mutual Defense Treaty with the Republic of China on Taiwan?

2. Why did the president ignore the provision in a bill enacted by both houses of the Congress and signed by himself on September 26, 1978 that "there should be prior consultation between the Congress and the executive branch on any proposed policy changes affecting the continuation in force of the Mutual Defense Treaty of 1954"?

3. Has the president forgotten his own statement on June 16, 1976 before the Democratic Platform Committee that "our policies should be open and honest, shaped with the participation of Congress from the outset"?

4. If the president without the consent of the Congress, or even consultation, can abruptly announce withdrawal from one mutual defense treaty, what is to keep him or any president from withdrawing unilaterally from any other treaty, such as with NATO, Israel, Japan, South Korea, or Panama?

5. When the president states that "the government of the United States of America acknowledges the Chinese position that there is but one China and Taiwan is part of China," is he saying that the president *is* the government of the United States of America?

6. Does the president not recognize that Taiwan has never been part of *Communist* China?

7. What gives a president of the United States authority to consign the seventeen million human beings on Taiwan to a communist control they do not want?

8. When the president says, "In recognizing that the government of the People's Republic is the single government of China, we are recognizing simple reality," does he deny the "simple reality" that since 1950 there have

been, and there are today, *two* Chinese governments, one controlling Taiwan and the other controlling the Chinese mainland? How does the president explain normalization of relations with one "simple reality" and simultaneous *de*normalization of relations with another "simple reality"? Why did not the president follow the German precedent of diplomatic relations with two governments, controlling different parts of the same country"?

9. Why does the president consent to having *no* governmental relations with the ROC, not even a liaison office as we had in Peking for almost seven years? How can our "current commercial, cultural and other relations with Taiwan" (including "access to carefully chosen defensive military equipment") be maintained, as promised by the president, without some form of government-to-government relations?

10. Why does the president dishonor the commitments made openly by our leaders in our 1954 Mutual Defense Treaty, in violation of his public statement to the American Chamber of Commerce in Tokyo on May 28, 1975, "The U.S. will always honor those commitments which have been made openly by our leaders with the full knowledge and involvement of the people of our country"?

11. In developing the policy announced on December 15, 1978, why has the president followed the same course for which on June 23, 1976 he condemned previous administrations, saying they "have made highly publicized efforts to woo the major communist powers while neglecting our natural friends and allies"? Is not the PRC a major communist power? And is not the ROC a natural friend and ally?

12. Why has the president followed the very pattern of "secrecy and exclusion" he described and denounced in his October 6, 1976 debate with President Ford, saying, "We've ignored or excluded the American people and the Congress from participation in the shaping of our foreign policy; it's been one of secrecy and exclusion"?

13. How does the president expect to deal with a government whose chairman, Hua Kuo-feng, said on December 16, 1978, right after the joint announcement, "We made it clear that we absolutely would not agree to U.S. arms sales to Taiwan" and whose vice-premier, Teng Hsiao-ping, assured U.S. senators on January 9, 1979 that "Taiwan would not have to disarm"? Which, if either, should the president believe?

14. Why was it not revealed until January 11, 1979 that the president had also agreed to a one-year moratorium on new sales of U.S. weapons to the ROC on Taiwan? How can we be sure there are not other parts of the agreement still being withheld from the Congress and the American people? If the failure to disclose an arrangement so important to the "well-being of the people of Taiwan" was "inadvertent," are we to conclude that the administration officials responsible are imcompetent? Lying? Giving us the facts about the whole deal in divided doses?

15. If the United States raises productivity in the PRC by sales of our industrial technology, how long can American products compete successfully with commodities produced by what is virtually slave labor? Is it good business to increase the productivity of such labor which we know will drastically undercut the wages and living standards of American working men and women?

16. After many such statements as Chairman Hua Kuo-feng's to the Communist Party Congress in 1977: "The two hegemonic powers, the Soviet Union and the United States, are the biggest international exploiters and oppressors of today and the common enemies of the peoples of the world," and Foreign Minister Huang Hua's statement in Iran on June 17, 1978: "America is an imperialist country. . . . But *at the moment* the United States is in a defensive position while the Soviet Union is in an aggressive position and therefore *at this stage* the attention of the third world must be drawn to the "domineering attitude of the Soviet Union," is it not plain that PRC leaders see closer relations with the United States as a temporary tactical alliance with one "common enemy," the United States, against the other "common enemy," the Soviet Union, only because Russia is considered the more dangerous "at this stage"?

17. If the president's "commitment to human rights is absolute," as he has proclaimed, and "human rights is the soul of our foreign policy," how can he justify embracing officially one of the worst violators of human rights in all history?

18. If the president refuses to recognize Rhodesia because the people there do not have full civil rights, how can he accept Communist China on its terms when the people there do not have any civil rights?

19. In order to "normalize" relations with a regime that for years has called the United States an enemy, why is it necessary, and how can it be right, to break relations with a loyal ally?

20. Is the policy of sacrificing a friend to please an enemy wise, or worthy of America? Is it a decent thing to do?

The China Card*

The New Republic

The defense of small countries and threatened peoples has never counted much for Jimmy Carter. Already during his campaign for the presidency he signaled the Russians that he would not be a serious obstacle to any mischief they might undertake in Yugoslavia. In what he clearly takes to be a major coup—amidst the chimney ash of the Middle East negotiations, the stalled SALT talks, the shambles of the regime of our pal the Shah, and the transparent failure of Carter's Saudi diplomacy over both oil prices and peace—the administration has now just about told the Chinese government in Peking that Taiwan is theirs for the taking. Of course, we expect that they won't return Taiwan, in Communist Party Chairman Hua Kuo-feng's chilling phrase, to "the embrace of the motherland" too quickly, at least not in the coming twelve months. Moreover, we'd certainly prefer that they not take the prosperous island and its seventeen million people by force. But, as we've been hearing from the State Department pulpits, we don't even have private assurances on these matters. So much for the Taiwanese. Let those who count on us be warned.

There is no question that the U.S. and the People's Republic should have diplomatic relations, and good relations too. We should have had them, or tried to, for over a generation. Certainly we should never have maintained the fiction that the semi-retired warlords in forced exile on Formosa constituted the rightful government of China. In one of those painful ironies of history, it was Richard Nixon (doubtless persuaded by Henry Kissinger) who liberated us from our emotional commitment to the notion of one China run by Chiang Kai-shek's Kuomintang and its heirs.

Carter and his supporters seemed to assume that the most recent arrangements would bring the administration nearly unanimous plaudits. But once again they have underestimated the idealism of the American people, and our sense of moral obligation to nations and peoples trying to elude the grasp of tyranny. For, despite the much-heralded thaw in the latest version of the new China, a tyranny is exactly what China still is and is likely to remain. Its people are still in intellectual political and moral chains, not to mention economic chains, even if the chains are a bit looser for the moment.

Confronted by opposition they did not expect (that is, opposition across the political spectrum), White House supporters are now rather more defensively trying to depict Carter as an instrument of historical inevitability. Whatever he and Zbigniew Brzezinski have negotiated with Peking follows irresistibly, we've been told, from the Shanghai Communiqué of 1972. But nothing is irresistible, a wise man once said, except that which is not resisted.

The terms of the new Sino-American deal are the terms set down long ago by the Chinese. And why should they have won in bargaining now what they could not win six years ago? Would they have refused our technical assistance or investments if we declined to break our ties with Taiwan? Indeed, if the current regime is so much more flexible and conciliatory than the one chaired by Chairman Mao, why did they insist upon—and why do we accept—the harshest conditions for normalization of relations? Yes, the Chinese did want a symbolic acceptance of their dominion over Taiwan. But that did not mean that we had to provide it. Surely Peking would not for sheerly symbolic reasons sabotage a liaison with the U.S. that is of enormous strategic importance to China. And if they would, what does that say for them as partners or for us as bargainers at the green table?

One suspects, of course, that it is not merely symbolic recognition of the People's Republic's sovereignty over Taiwan that was at stake. This is why the minimal concessions we obtained from Peking seem no more than a fig leaf covering our betrayal, not so much of the government of Taiwan as of its people. Neither a few defensive weapons sold to Taiwan nor continued trade with it will stop the erosion of will for an independent life among the island's population. Skilled diplomacy, with a bit of backbone, should have been able to provide a way to recognize the reality on the mainland without ignoring the reality of a thriving, independent, pro-Western society on Taiwan.

And what have we gotten for changing the reality we choose to ignore? Not much, it appears. It is unlikely that the Soviets will be tamed or tempered by this diplomatic development. Instead we may find them more belligerent rather than less, a situation which President Carter's scandalously deceptive rendering of Leonid Brezhnev's message to him on the subject could not obscure. The China card, once played against Russia, is played for good. It may have made sense as graduate-seminar geopolitics, but it will not work in the real world. Part of the problem is that both Carter and Brzezinski are impatient and impulsive men. They have an idea and they try it. There'll always be other ideas to come. But the larger part of the problem is that they do not know how to bargain. Always seeking an opportunity to demonstrate deftness in negotiation, the president comes out looking, at best, half deft.

In negotiating with the Chinese, for example, we did not try to get them to trade off their very concrete and critical needs against their ideological desires. We did not even try to get them to curb their murderous clients in

Phnom Penh. Indeed, one finds at State and among Brzezinski's partisans a barely repressed sympathy for the Cambodians who are, after all, anti-Vietnamese who are, after all, in turn pro-Soviet. The enemy of my enemy is my friend.

In this country, the most exuberant enthusiasts for Carter's card tricks are American corporations. Not chastened by what should have been the sobering experience of post-détente commerce with the Soviets, the American multinationals now see eight hundred million new customers for everything from Coca Cola to computers—a new market for our entire flotilla of technology and junk. *The Wall Street Journal,* clear-eyed as usual about the illusions that may grip the capitalist class, tried on December 28 to put up some cautionary signs, though they probably won't help. China most likely will not pay us with gold or hard currency, as they will in great measure pay the harder-nosed Japanese. They will pay us with our own credits, deflated dollar after deflated dollar, which will have the side-effect of intensifying the capital crunch at home.

All of this amounts to a pathetic performance for a great power, and yet another blot on the presidency of its current steward, Jimmy Carter.

China and the
Twentieth Century

Steven Symms (R-Idaho)

It is impossible to distinguish the People's Republic from other nations without attempting to understand the politics and culture of the Chinese people. Far too often Occidentals, especially Americans, are wont to conceive of the Communist Chinese as either "Communists" or "Chinese," as if each were a separate entity. Such attempts at isolation are dangerous and have helped to further the state of non-knowledge regarding the current Communist government in Peking. The vast country of China is populated by about one billion people and is governed by the Marxist-Leninist-Maoist political concept of democratic centralism.

At the turn of the last century, China was still ruled by various landlords and had a feudal economy. The significant breakthrough came with Dr. Sun Yat-sen who published *The Principles of National Reconstruction* in 1911. This milestone gave a unifying political structure that allowed the uniting of a distinct Oriental mind set with an Occidental political theory. The religion and philosophy of Confucius was intertwined with the democratic concept of federalism as envisioned by various American politicans. Dr. Sun set out a timetable for the realization of central government that could unite all of China and culminate in democracy. These stages were: military operations to unify the nation, political tutelage to train the people in representative government, and finally democracy.

Unfortunately, the Western powers considered China a land fit for plunder and did nothing to help Dr. Sun realize the potential for a relatively democratic government. Instead short-term economic considerations continued to be the basis of Western relations with China, and the continued economic rape of the country was only halted by the facts that Sun turned to the Soviet Union for council and the country was invaded by Japan. The Soviets replied by sending Dr. Sun a master Soviet agent, Michael Borodin, who managed to help create a Communist Party and to open Sun's Nationalist Party for infiltration by the communists. A process of open recruitment led finally to a split in the Nationalist Party and a civil war situation. The Nationalists (or Kuomintang) under the leadership of Chiang Kai-shek, who took over the Kuomintang following Sun's death, was pitted against the

Communist Party led by Mao Tse-tung.

Civil war spread throughout China as the Communists attempted to overthrow the duly recognized government. The Japanese imperialists had already brutally invaded China and taken over Manchuria. As the Japanese sought to control all of mainland China, the Kuomintang found itself involved in two wars: one against the internal subversive armies of Mao and the other against Japanese fascists. The Kuomintang almost defeated the Communists in a battle near Shanghai, but Mao's forces fled in the Long March, arriving in Yenan where they developed an Eastern version of guerrilla warfare.

The World War II period stands as a beacon for China in the twentieth century. It was during this time that Chiang defeated the Japanese with the help of American aid. The Communists gained a "united front" operation with the Kuomintang wherein they helped fight the Japanese while still attacking Nationalist positions behind the lines. With the end of World War II, the Kuomintang was left with a ravaged nation and was immediately subjected to a civil war with the Communists. I shall not attempt to restate the duplicity engaged in by various identified Communists within the U.S. State Department at that time, but the role of such individuals as Alger Hiss figured prominently. This action on the part of known Communists within the Roosevelt administration helped to create a policy within our State Department claiming that the Maoists were only "agrarian reformers" and that the Kuomintang was corrupt. Such political duplicity allowed the Communists to militarily defeat the Nationalists and politically neutralized the friends of a free China in the United States.

The civil war in China ended in a Communist victory under the leadership of Mao Tse-tung. From 1949 until Mao's death in 1976 this Chinese century would be centered around the political model of Mao Tse-tung. As if a risen phoenix, Mao governed China like an old mandarin. His word was *the* word, and all of Chinese political life depended upon his various dictums. With the ascension of Mao as the "great helmsman" of China the nation was thrust into a new Orwellian political collectivism.

Even the Soviet Union, under the tutelage of Joseph Stalin, did not attempt the type of sociological and psychological Pavlovian rethink and character modification as practiced by Mao's minions. All land was nationalized, national terror was undertaken, people starved, and millions died as the West watched and did nothing. Students in the United States are often taught the horrors of the Nazi holocaust, and most know that Hitler was responsible for the murder of six million Jews. These same students know literally nothing of the slaughter of Stalin who murdered at least fifteen million persons or the genocide of Mao Tse-tung numbering somewhere around fifty million. Such human sacrifice to the edicts of Chinese Communism is documented in the testimony of Professor Richard Walker before the Senate Subcommittee on Internal Security.

These brutal facts make a mockery of Jimmy Carter's "human rights" song and dance act. The Red Chinese hold the world's record for genocide (with the possible qualitative advantage going to their political ally Cambodia). It can be argued, as Communists are wont to do, that a few eggs have to be broken to make an omelet (a few lives in the revolution), but it is difficult to countenance the continued human rights violations in Red China under the new dual leadership of Hua Kuo-feng and Teng Hsiao-ping as listed by Amnesty International.

I realize that I have simplified Chinese history in this all too short synopsis of China and the twentieth century. The essential point, however, is that the Chinese Communists have historically shown the ability for a type of roller-coaster political outlook. At one juncture Mao proclaimed "Let a hundred flowers bloom" and many Chinese began to write and speak out against the Maoist regime. Upon seeing the flowers bloom Mao sent in the lawn mower, in the form of the police, and killed the movement. The "Cultural Revolution" with its emphasis on ultra-left sectarian purity is followed by a branding of the "gang of four," including Mao's widow. What will come next?

Even in the Marxist dialect it is not difficult to note that the twentieth century has seen a clear policy of the Communist Chinese to utilize short-term gains and ignore what Occidentals consider long-term. The Western view has perceived China in quick grasps while the Oriental perception is one of long perspectives. The Chinese Communists are now happy to have the United States as a new ally against the imperialistic probes of the Soviet Union. Equally they were happy to have a "united front" with the Kuomintang against the Japanese. The history of Communist Chinese political theory has shown that they have tactical and strategic aims. Tactically, they will now apparently deal with their second enemy (the United States) in order to try some great leap into the era of twentieth-century technology. It must never be forgotten, however, that the strategic plan is always operational. Strategically, the Communist Chinese believe that history is on their side and that the capitalist countries will be destroyed and communism will triumph. Those who refuse, either through ignorance or deceit, to admit that the Chinese Communists (and their Russian counterparts) seek world domination are leading the United States into another world war. That war will most likely be lost by the Western nations, considering the sycophantic political trend in this nation to "recognize" our enemies and violate treaties with our friends.

Fortunately there is another alternative, God willing, that states that we are not in a Carter-type mind-set that is a self-fulfilling prophecy of kowtowing to the current communist leaders because things always get worse. A positive attitude of knowing your enemy and preparing a self-defense strategy against the imperialist aims of Communist China and Russia will save Western civilization. To do otherwise is to court disaster.

Will Israel Suffer
Taiwan's Fate?*

Norman F. Lent (R-New York)

Mr. Speaker, President Carter's unsettling decision to abandon our staunch ally of thirty years—Taiwan—to get the People's Republic of China to agree to diplomatic relations with the United States raises a most disturbing question: Will Israel be abandoned just as casually?

A liberal columnist John Roche pointed out after the startling move: "Dumping allies is habit-forming. Our friends in the world must be wondering who's next."

Especially is that true of Israel, which already has experienced some bitter disappointments and setbacks at the hands of President Carter and his advisors.

In fact, after the White House announced the abandonment of Taiwan, the Israeli Government declared publicly: "Israel must give thorough consideration to the U.S. decision about Taiwan and reconsider Washington's ability to maintain its obligations under its agreements and treaties with other nations."

Those are grim words indeed. But the Israeli's foreboding view of the effects of the Carter administration action can be appreciated by anyone reviewing the uncertain course of Israeli-United States relations in the past two years. Unfortunately the Carter policies in the Middle East have been so erratic and inconsistent that they have thwarted the brightest hopes for a workable peace agreement between Israel and the unfriendly Arab nations which surround her.

Beginning in 1977 with President Carter's unfortunate proclamation of his support for a Palestinian homeland, and continuing right up to this month, with the president's brother embracing representatives of the Libyan regime which has strongly backed Palestinian terrorists, Mr. Carter time and again has sabotaged his own best efforts to achieve peace. Furthermore, the president and his advisors have, in the pst two years, abandoned the traditional American role of mediator in the Middle East—a policy supported by six presidents—three Republican and three Democratic. Instead,

*From *Congressional Record,* January 18, 1979.

429

under Carter guidance, the United States has leaned more and more toward open advocacy of Arab views at the expense of Israel, America's strongest, staunchest and most reliable friend in the Middle East. In recent weeks, the Carter administration has increased its pro-Arab role in becoming a strong advocate for Egypt's new peace treaty demands, while upbraiding Israel for its refusal to accept drastic changes in a draft treaty already agreed to by Israel.

Now, the abandonment of Taiwan represents a harsh blow from a new direction for Israel. It is further cause for Israeli concern—a concern shared by many thoughtful persons in the United States. Among them is one of the foremost experts on the People's Republic of China, George Bush, former head of the U.S. Liaison Office in Peking, and former director of the Central Intelligence Agency. Says Bush: "For the first time in history a peacetime American government has renounced a treaty with an ally without cause or benefit. . . . We gave all and got nothing. . . . We are simply diminishing U.S. credibility around the world."

Equally concerned is the chairman of the Senate Foreign Relations Subcommittee on Near Eastern and South Asian Affairs, Senator Richard Stone. He calls on the Congress "to repair the damage done to our credibility as an ally."

Yes, indeed, Mr. Speaker, we in the Congress must move—on a reasoned but determined manner—to take positive bi-partisan action to assure Israel and our other allies throughout the world that they will not be sold down the river through some new presidential move made in hope of improving the President's political image. I call upon my colleagues in the Congress to require that any presidential decision to terminate mutual defense treaties be approved by the Congress before such a treaty cancellation can become effective. Without such reassuring action, Israel and all of our friends in the world will continue to feel the chill winds of doubt and uncertainty.

China Relations*

L. H. Fountain (D-North Carolina)

Mr. Speaker, like most of us in this House and around the nation, I was taken by surprise by the President's sudden and dramatic China announcement on December 15.

At the same time, I was left sincerely troubled, not so much by the decision itself to extend diplomatic recognition to the People's Republic of China as by the timing and the manner in which the decision was made—at the expense of Taiwan, a valuable and trusted friend and ally, and without meaningful "prior consultation" with the Congress called for in section 26 of the International Security Assistance Act of 1978.

Few of us, I believe, could have entertained reasonable doubts prior to December 15 that diplomatic recognition of the PRC was eventually going to take place, especially in the light of President Nixon's 1972 visit to the mainland, the Shanghai Communiqué, the establishment of official liaison offices, and several other overtures and official exchanges during the Ford and Carter administrations—all of which indicated probable diplomatic recognition at some point.

However, I was hopeful all along—as were many of my colleagues and most of my constituents in North Carolina—that an improved relationship with the PRC, or complete diplomatic recognition, could have been accomplished without abrogating or otherwise impairing our historical friendship with the Republic of China. Regrettably, the president's untimely and premature decision dashed those hopes.

In fact, I have always been a strong supporter not only of maintaining full diplomatic relations with the ROC, but also of not altering or diluting in any way the Mutual Defense Treaty of 1954—unless and until a responsible, equitable, and workable solution to the so-called "two-Chinas" problem could have been reached.

All of us knew that many negotiating sessions and much additional hard work would have been needed to arrive at an appropriate accord on the matter. In international affairs especially, difficult challenges require forthright and measured responses without a "rush to judgment" type of atmosphere.

*From *Congressional Record,* January 15, 1979.

Taken as a whole, however, the December 15 announcement was neither in the paramount interests of the United States nor in the overall interests of peace and security in east Asia and the western Pacific. Since its establishment thirty years ago, the ROC has preserved the traditional culture of the Chinese people, upheld basic human rights, done its part in shoring up our alliance, supported in every way the free enterprise system, and served as a major trading partner of ours. To have extended diplomatic recognition to the PRC, while concurrently ending unilaterally our diplomatic relations with the ROC and giving notice of terminating the 1954 treaty, was unwise and ill-advised.

Within a recent two-year period, I participated in two fact-finding missions to China and the Far East under the auspices of the House International Relations Committee of which I am ranking majority member. The first, in November 1976, included three days in the Republic of China, and the second, in July 1978, consisted of a ten-day conference in the People's Republic of China. Our 1976 report to the Committee, "Outlook on the Far East," discussed the normalization, economic, defense, and human rights issues which were then current and are familiar to most of us.

The report on the 1978 mission, entitled "A New Realism" and issued by the International Relations Subcommittee on Asia and Pacific Affairs just prior to the president's December 15 announcement, included five principal recommendations by our delegation. The recommendations follow:

(1) The possible implication of China's "new realism" as it affects establishing full diplomatic relations with the United States should be pursued by the administration in a timely manner. It has been nearly seven years since the signing of the Shanghai Communiqué. The question of timing, therefore, is important in order that U.S. inaction—or the appearance of inaction—not help induce a return to the more inflexible attitudes of recent years in China.

(2) An active search for the "grey area" between the fixed positions of both sides on the Taiwan question should be pursued in light of the presently favorable atmosphere perceived by the delegation. The 1955-56 offer to negotiate a treaty with the United States, combined with informal suggestions to the delegation of willingness to consider negotiations with the Kuomintang, would seem to constitute the boundaries of a "grey area" which could produce favorable results, so long as a positive attitude continues to exist between Washington and Peking.

(3) To foster a continued positive attitude on both sides, the United States and the People's Republic of China should encourage and develop increased exchanges of people and views on official, private, and corporate-business levels. Such exchanges, particularly when they are designed to increase trade, are both a stimulus to, and an actual com-

ponent of, the normalization process. The delegation feels that a growing trade and cultural relationship between China and the United States can lead to a genuine bond between our two countries. Specifically, the delegation now formally recommends what it has already informally suggested: that the administration send the president's special negotiator on trade at the head of an official trade mission to China to follow up and seek to expand on the initiatives being pursued by private corporations and organizations. The delegation urges a realistic and systematic approach to expanding United States-China relations, particularly in the areas of industrial and scientific exchange, coupled with a careful analysis of the estimated returns to the United States and its interests, particularly in the security area.

(4) The question of normalization should be based on the common bilateral interests and concerns of the United States and the People's Republic of China. The delegation notes that, despite their harsh statements concerning Soviet intentions, PRC leaders stressed that normalization should not be pursued purely as an anti-Soviet measure. The delegation feels that opposition to the Soviet Union is inadequate to serve as the foundation for a solid relationship between the United States and the People's Republic of China.

(5) The delegation urges upon the administration the necessity of full cooperation with the Congress regarding its normalization plans and policies. The work of the subcommittee and its predecessor (the Future Foreign Policy Subcommittee) since 1975, including the fact-finding mission of July 1978, has been designed to minimize the possibility of divisive debate (as occurred on the Panama Canal Treaty) because the Congress and the American people are unfamiliar with the history and issues involved in normalization, including progress, or lack of it. In order to avoid unwarranted fears or misunderstandings, the component parts or packages of the normalization process must be recognized and spelled out, particularly those regarding trade, security, and related questions which will require congressional approval, and which in many cases will require congressional initiative. The delegation recognizes that normalization is a process which may either begin with, or culminate in, an actual exchange of ambassadors, and that the decision regarding this exchange rests with the executive, but that its implications must be a shared process with the Congress.

Mr. Speaker, I ask that my own supplement statement in the report be included at this point:

While I am in general agreement with the recommendations of the delegation, I want to take this opportunity also to reaffirm my long-standing interest in maintaining cordial relations with our historic friend and ally, the Republic of China. As I have stated on past occasions, I favor continued diplomatic recognition of the Republic of China and preservation of the Mutual Defense Treaty. I oppose sacrificing Taiwan as the price of achieving normalization with Peking, and hope that it will be possible to move toward full diplomatic relations with the PRC without impairing our historical friendship with the ROC.

Also troublesome, Mr. Speaker, is the language of section 26 of last year's international security assistance legislation, Public Law 95-384, which reads as follows:

SEC. 226. (a) The Congress finds that—

(1) the continued security and stability of East Asia is a matter of major strategic interest to the United States;

(2) the United States and the Republic of China have for a period of twenty-four years been linked together by the Mutual Defense Treaty of 1954;

(3) the Republic of China has during that twenty-four-year period faithfully and continually carried out its duties and obligations under the treaty; and

(4) it is the responsibility of the Senate to give its advice and consent to treaties entered into by the United States.

(b) It is the sense of the Congress that there should be prior consultation between the Congress and the executive branch on any proposed policy changes affecting the continuation in force of the Mutual Defense Treaty of 1954.

Let me note also that the conference report on this bill, House Report 95-1546, said the legislative intent of this section was "to make clear that the House of Representatives is to be included in this consultation process."

Whatever consultation there may have been, Mr. Speaker, was inadequate in the sense contemplated by the statute. I do not believe that a few vague references to the negotiations from time to time plus telephone calls to a few congressional leaders a couple of hours before the President's announcement satisfied the letter and the spirit of section 26. At any rate, at no point before the President went on the air was I consulted by him or by any of his representatives.

In fact, within days of the announcement, I co-signed, along with several colleagues on the International Relations Committee, a letter to the president registering "our concern, displeasure and dismay over the cavalier way in which this decision was conveyed to the Congress."

Mr. Speaker, as a result of the China decision, I fear that some of our allies around the world might for a while simply not believe what our country says. Regrettably, we probably have lost for the time being a good deal of trust, faith, confidence, and credibility placed in us by many of our friends.

Despite my objections and reservations concerning the president's action, however, I stand ready to work with the International Relations Committee, the House, and the executive branch in fashioning responsible legislation to maintain and improve commercial, cultural, educational, and other ties and relations—however unofficial—with the people and leaders of Taiwan. Examples of such legislation would include bills to continue several dozen executive agreements and other treaties between the United States and Taiwan, to continue arms sales to Taiwan, and to grant most favored trade status to Taiwan.

Taking a Long Look
at the China Question*

Floyd J. Fithian (D-Indiana)

Mr. Speaker, the recent announcement by the Carter administration of the normalization of relations between our country and the People's Republic of China (PRC) is to be greeted by us with mixed feelings. On the one hand, the United States welcomes the opportunity to finally seal a pact of friendship with mainland China. The reduction of tensions between our two great nations will prove to be of benefit, not only to ourselves, but to the whole world as well. On the other hand, I am deeply concerned that this agreement not endanger our friends, the Taiwanese, nor our relations with them.

On one side, the administration's decision to extend *de facto* recognition to the PRC and establish diplomatic relations is the result of cumulative bi-partisan efforts of American presidents dating back to Eisenhower, which were intensified by Nixon's trip to Peking in 1972 and the signing of the Shanghai Communiqué. These diplomatic efforts recognize that the existing governmment in Peking is the government of China, that China needs to be brought into a discussion of world affairs, and that any nation with almost a billion inhabitants or one-fourth of the world's population cannot continue to be ignored.

The establishment of Sino-American relations will allow each an opportunity to strengthen the cooperation between our two nations, and to enhance our consultative relations on matters of common international concern. It would thus contribute to the stability of Asia, where the United States has important security and economic interests, and to the peace of the world.

China represents a substantial market for American manufactured goods as well as agricultural products. The recently declared four modernizations of the PRC—an effort to simultaneously develop industry, agriculture, science and technology, and defense—could prove economically advantageous to the United States. China's eagerness to develop its industry is presently hampered by its inadequate supply of foreign mone-

*From *Congressional Record*, January 22, 1979.

tary reserves. But this deficiency can be fairly easily remedied by the exploitation of what is believed to be a vast supply of oil. The sale of petroleum products abroad should provide it with capital sufficient to purchase the sophisticated machinery necessary to develop its industry and infrastructure. This solution could reduce the present Western dependence upon Arabian oil.

While the present modest per capita income of the PRC does not immediately open a large consumer market for American goods and services, the potential for industrialization holds great promise. The Chinese economic experience may parallel the tempo and success of post-war Japan.

American agricultural products and advanced technology can also have an impact on China's modernization. The PRC is still faced with a problem going back to antiquity: that forty percent of its land mass is inhospitable to cultivation or human habitation. Consequently, the fertile southeastern portion is densely populated, but its crop yield is much lower than the average in the United States or Europe. On a short-term basis, these conditions could be eased by the importation of American footstuffs and agricultural machinery. And in the long run, the introduction of modern techniques—irrigation, pesticides and fertilization—might allow the vast reaches of desert to blossom the way the Mideast has in recent years. Lastly, it should be remarked that eighty-five percent of the Chinese population is still rural. The adoption of sophisticated agricultural technology would free millions in manpower for industrial development.

The most troubling issue for years has been Taiwan. For the foreseeable future, mainland China has compelling reasons not to seek a settlement of the Taiwan issue by military force. The PRC faces a serious threat both to the North and South. China is fearful of a confrontation with the Soviet Union along its common 4,500 mile border, where the Russians have amassed forty-four divisions plus air and other support units. Additionally, hundreds of missiles armed with nuclear warheads stand aimed at the heart of China. The PRC is also faced with an impressive array of might in the form of Taiwan. Its well-equipped, American-trained armed forces number nearly one-half million or one of the largest in the non-communist world. These are backed by the latest air defense systems, Peking does not have the amphibious offensive capability to launch an attack on Taiwan, nor are there any signs that the PRC is trying to develop one. China is attempting to modernize its country at a rapid rate, and therefore is placing first priority on domestic development. Any armed conflict between the PRC and Taiwan would jeopardize the mainland's industrialization and retard modernization. China is attempting to build constructive relations with the United States, Japan, and other nations and has a major stake in avoiding actions that would put those relationships at grave risk, particularly during its modernization stage.

In a world of ever changing influences and dramatically shifting alliances, it is imperative that the United States face international realities.

It is in our national interest that we establish a good working relationship with so vital a nation as China while it is still at an early stage of development.

On the other side, some disturbing problems have arisen because of the president's decisions. Many believe, and I concur, that the United States could have held tougher on the Taiwan question. The logic of the wording in the agreement contains an implicit acknowledgement that Peking is now governing Taiwan. Although this may now seem a harmless point in semantics—merely reversing our previous recognition that Taipei ruled the mainland—the PRC may exploit it. Indeed, their intransigence over the issue of future arms sales to Taiwan would seem to indicate that from the outset they wish to isolate Taiwan as much as possible.

By effectively demoting Taiwan to the status of a rebellious province, Peking now has a number of available options which, if used, could lead to the eventual economic strangulation of our former ally. It is not inconceivable that Peking would seek to enforce restrictive sanctions similar to those now levied against Rhodesia and South Africa, or even employ a naval blockade. Less direct pressure could be exerted in the form of trade agreements in which other nations would cease their exchange with Taiwan in favor of a more lucrative trade with Peking.

The ending of the Mutual Defense Treaty with Taiwan may create doubts about the reliability of the United States to defend its friends and allies around the world. The heart of the numerous defense treaties and alliances, like NATO, is the willingness of the United States to go to war, if necessary, to protect her allies. Some friends may now question the will and capability of the United States.

The possibility of nuclear proliferation is alarming. With such a large threat looming so close to its borders, Taiwan may feel it necessary to insure its safety by tapping its advanced technology to develop nuclear defense capabilities.

The United States received neither public nor private assurances that Peking would not use military force against Taiwan, even if this seems unlikely in the foreseeable future. It is disappointing that additional Chinese concessions were not achieved during these negotiations. It is unfortunate that the negotiations for recognition did not include a resolution of the China claim issues—a settlement of claims of the U.S. citizens and companies against China for property that was expropriated or frozen by the present regime after Chinese assets in the United States were frozen in 1950.

I am disturbed at the method by which the president made this important decision. Despite the congressional consultation amendment to the International Security Assistance Act (Public Law 95-384), the president did not consult with the Congress except to inform some members a few hours in advance of the public announcement. I understand consultation to mean an opportunity to influence policy. In the case of the recognition of the PRC, this consultation clearly did not take place.

Although the United States will continue to honor almost sixty economic and cultural treaties and continue to supply Taiwan with sufficient defensive weapons, the decision to end our defensive treaty with Taiwan raises grave questions about its future. It is my personal hope that the normalization of relations with the PRC not jeopardize the well-being of the people of Taiwan. The United States should continue to have an interest in the peaceful resolution of the Taiwan issue and should expect that it will be settled peacefully by the Chinese themselves. The United States should continue to promote the economic development of Taiwan, to stimulate trade between our countries and to recognize that we as a nation have an important economic stake in the continued development of an independent Taiwan.

I will monitor closely the ensuing international events in China, Taiwan, and the rest of Asia. The opening of China cannot be allowed to result in tragedy for Taiwan. We as a nation must remain ever vigilant that the Taiwan issue is resolved peacefully and that Taiwan has adequate supplies of weapons to defend itself against aggression.

Religious Freedom and the China Decision

Richard B. Dingman*

Early settlers came to America because they were seeking religious freedom. They were determined to escape religious repression and dictation, and to find a land where they could worship as they chose.

Our Founding Fathers placed heavy dependence upon their religious faith. The early educational institutions of this nation were religious in nature. Harvard was a school that required religion classes and required the students to memorize Scripture.

Early American settlers were not only determined to find religious freedom, but they were willing to fight to preserve it.

Our religious heritage has been clearly evident in the development of this nation and in the sacred documents which are the foundation of our form of government. We still see on our coins, "In God We Trust." We still include in our pledge of allegiance to the flag the phrase, "One Nation Under God." We still open our House of Representatives and Senate sessions with the prayer of the chaplain. Belief in God is still a primary influence in the lives of millions of Americans. But whether one chooses to be a Christian, a Jew, a Buddhist, or even an atheist, he enjoys the right of religious freedom to do so. The government neither pushes people toward nor away from *any* religion. There are many churches, many faiths, many denominations, many cults, and yet all are allowed to operate freely.

As we attempt to assess the potential impact of President Carter's recognition of the People's Republic of China and the derecognition of Taiwan, we must assess the impact on religious freedom. How do these two countries compare? Do they both allow religious freedom as we know it in the United States? I believe we will find the comparisons to be rather startling.

Communist China—History of Repression

During the nineteenth and the early part of the twentieth centuries, the

*Richard B. Dingman is Executive Director of the Republic Study Committee, U.S. House of Representatives.

mainland of China was the beneficiary of one of the greatest outpourings of benevolence that mankind has ever seen. Many countries, particularly the United States, were extremely generous in sending missionaries to China, not only to teach religious faith, but also to establish educational and medical institutions. At one point in the early 1900s there were some ten thousand foreign missionaries in mainland China. Approximately two-thirds of all schools, hospitals and clinics were a direct result of foreign missionary efforts. The sacrificial effort of these thousands of foreigners gave a great boost to the development of mainland China.

Since the communist takeover, most of the achievements of these years of missionary work have been wiped out.

All of the missionaries were expelled from mainland China.

Four thousand church-affiliated institutions were closed.

Virtually, all churches were closed and the buildings were converted into warehouses, museums, garages and other public facilities.

In Peking only one Catholic cathedral and one non-denominational Protestant church have been allowed to continue functioning, and these only for the benefit of foreigners.

The Red Chinese government now prohibits missionary work and religious teaching in churches, homes or schools.

The Catholic Church has been almost completely annihilated by the communists. The Bishop of Shanghai was imprisoned for his faith. Religious groups willing to cooperate with the Communists in the 1950s maintained a few temples and churches and held services for the benefit of the foreign visitors, but with the advent of the Cultural Revolution in 1966 even this limited religious activity was brought to a virtual standstill.

When a tourist in 1965 asked a commune leader to show him a church, the leader proudly responded, "In the communes, sir, you will find no churches. You see, religion is for the helpless. Here in China we are not helpless anymore."

The official Communist Chinese policy and slogan is "Destroy Theism; Establish Atheism." The communists say that God arises from fear and that the Chinese have gotten rid of their fears.

Chinese society after liberation in 1949 left very little room for any religious authority. The most telling reform was the land reform, leaving monasteries only enough land for the monks themselves to till. Without income from rents, monasteries could not afford to operate as they had in the past. Most monks and nuns were obliged to return to lay life, now that the economic base for their practice had been removed.

Though freedom of religious belief is said to be tolerated, a mixture of encouragement, education and coercion has been used to wean people from religious practices and beliefs. The goal of a secular and atheistic society has been based on Mao's view that religion would collapse as a natural consequence of political and economic struggle.

Another gauge of religious freedom and tolerance is the availability of

441

religious literature. Most reports from the mainland indicate that Bibles and other religious literature are very scarce. Bibles are distributed primarily through underground organizations. There are now available a few writings for the Chinese to study in the area of Christianity, but these are mostly negative, stressing the evils of Western imperialism and how their religion weakened China before the communist takeover.

One slightly varying report indicates that in 1965 there were some occasions when Bibles were permitted to be imported, printed and sold in China. However, the government had so conditioned the people against religion that they either had no interest in Bibles or were afraid to purchase them.

One visiting missionary said he couldn't even give Bibles away. People would look at the Bibles and then hand them back. They would not take them.

Republic of China—History of Freedom

There is abundant evidence in Taiwan of the constitutional guarantee of religious freedom. Individuals regularly and frequently attend religious ceremonies and services at temples and churches. Thousands of students attend church-sponsored schools. Church-related clinics and hospitals render great medical services to the people of Taiwan.

Almost everywhere one goes in Taiwan, it is apparent that religion plays a major role in the daily lives of the people. As in the United States, the government remains neutral on religious matters but it is also very clear that the government does nothing to impede free exercise of religious choice. In fact, it appears that the government recognizes a positive influence from individual religious involvement, and thus encourages a wide spectrum of religious activities.

Buddhism, Taoism and Christianity have had great influence on Chinese life and culture. Over half of Taiwan's seventeen million people attend the more than five thousand Buddhist and Taoist temples, five hundred of which have been built in the last four years.

Protestant and Catholic churches have had a long and active history in Taiwan. Together, they have over six hundred thousand members, two thousand churches, one hundred and eighty-five hospitals and clinics, eight hundred primary and kindergarten schools, thirty-five high schools, eighteen seminaries, twenty-two Bible Schools, nine technical schools, three universities and six colleges. Protestants, alone, have six hundred missionaries in Taiwan. The Methodist affiliated Soo-Chow University has nine thousand students.

To American religious leaders, Taiwan is an absolutely open mission field. In addition to the indigenous churches, there are sixty-five different church denominations. The only known restriction on missionary activities is directed toward the Korean evangelist, Reverend Sung Myung Moon, and

442

his followers in the Unification Church. "Moonies" are not welcome in Taiwan because of their efforts to separate children from their families. The free Chinese place a very high value on the integrity of the family unit. (Quite to the contrary, the Communist Chinese deliberately take young children away from their parents.)

In 1975, American evangelist Billy Graham held a one-week series of meetings in Taipei. At every meeting, the 60,000-capacity stadium was filled to overflowing—even though it rained hard *every* night. The Republic of China's president, Chang Ching-kuo, even attended one service. Extra police were made available to assist in handling the large traffic jams caused by the crowds. The people of Taiwan had absolute freedom to participate in the major religious events.

Church and building permits are readily obtained. Church property and an equal amount of other property is tax-exempt. To aid the recent surge of construction of five hundred new Buddhist temples, twenty percent of the land required was donated by the government.

Religious book stores flourish in Taiwan. Bibles and other religious literature are freely printed, imported, sold and given away without government interference.Taiwanese eagerly seek such materials.

Following the 1975 Billy Graham crusade in Taipei, there was such a demand for Bibles that all book stores in the Taipei area sold out. Fresh supplies had to be printed and imported.

Impact of Carter's Actions

Historical patterns are very clear. The Communist Chinese want no religious influence in their society. The free Chinese grant absolute religious freedom and welcome religious influence in their society.

What changes, if any, can we expect in governmental attitudes toward religion in Taiwan and the PRC resulting from the changes in U.S. foreign policies.

Since freedom is an essential ingredient of life in Taiwan, it is not likely that there will be any change in policy toward indigenous religious activities. It is possible that missionary programs may experience a variety of new problems, but if such problems occur, I would expect them to result from U.S. actions, not Taiwanese. For example, it is conceivable that there could be new problems in processing visas, but I would expect such difficulties, if any, to be a product of protocol impediments created by U.S. policy rather than deliberate interference by the Republic of China.

Many American evangelical Christian leaders fear a negative backlash on the effectiveness of their ministries in Taiwan as a direct result of President Carter's actions. They fear that many Chinese, knowing of Jimmy Carter's frequent public professions as a "born-again Christian," will decide that they want no part of Christianity if it produces the poor character qualities they see in Jimmy Carter. They expect Christianity to produce such qualities as fairness, human concern, and integrity.

While President Carter's foreign policies regarding China will probably have no effect on religious freedom in Taiwan, they may have a lasting negative impact on the effectiveness of U.S. missionary programs.

On the Communist side of the Taiwan Strait, policies will probably continue to be as repressive as ever. Communists are dedicated and aggressive atheists. They can be expected to give the appearance of greater religious tolerance while making sure that nothing more than tokenism is ever achieved.

The Chinese Communist Party has never accepted church members as party members, and churches (when they were permitted) never accepted communists as church members. These two areas of thought are so antithetical that they can never be reconciled.

Even American church leaders who long favored normalization with the PRC do not see much hope for increased religious activity on the mainland. Immediately following President Carter's announcement, the Reverend Dr. Tracey K. Jones said, "I don't believe that there will be any time in many years that there will be an opening for foreigners to go in as missionaries." Dr. Jones is head of the United Methodist Church's Board of Global Ministries and the World Division of the National Council of Churches.

In summary, President Carter's recognition of the PRC and derecognition of Taiwan could well mean that an active member of one of the world's largest mission-oriented churches has been the key to the religious deprivation and enslavement of the free Chinese on the island of Taiwan.